Paris Eating & Drinking

timeout.com/paris

Penguin Books

PENGUIN BOOKS

Published by the Penguin Group
Penguin Books Ltd, 80 Strand, London WC2R ORL, England
Penguin Books USA Inc., 375 Hudson Street, New York, New York 10014, USA
Penguin Books Australia Ltd, 250 Camberwell Road, Camberwell, Victoria 3124, Australia
Penguin Books Canada Ltd, 10 Alcorn Avenue, Toronto, Ontario, Canada M4V 3B2
Penguin Books (NZ) Ltd, cnr Rosedale and Airborne Rds, Albany, Auckland, New Zealand

Penguin Books Ltd, Registered Offices: Harmondsworth, Middlesex, England

Editions 1-5 published by Time Out Guides Ltd.

First published 1996
Second edition 1997
Third edition 1999
Fourth edition 2000
Fifth edition 2002
Sixth edition 2003

10 9 8 7 6 5 4 3 2 1

Copyright © Time Out Group Ltd, 1996, 1997, 1999, 2000, 2002, 2003.
All rights reserved

Reprographics by Quebecor Numeric, 56 bd Davout, 75020 Paris
Cover reprographics by Icon, Crowne House, 56-58 Southwark Street, London SE1 1UN
Printed and bound by Cayfosa-Quebecor, Ctra. de Caldes, Km 3 08 130 Sta Perpètua de Mogoda, Barcelona, Spain

Except in the United States of America, this book is sold subject to the condition that it shall not, by way of trade or otherwise, be lent, re-sold, hired out, or otherwise circulated without the publisher's prior consent in any form of binding or cover other than that in which it is published and without a similar condition including this condition being imposed on the subsequent purchaser.

The spice is right

Young chefs are reinventing French cooking, writes Alexander Lobrano.

If the French have long been suspicious of fusion food, the most innovative young chefs in Paris today can't resist bringing a touch of spice to time-tested French techniques.

Pascal Barbot bowled over Parisians when, after a stint in Australia, he developed a style all his own at **L'Astrance**. From his trademark toasted breadcrumb soup to mysterious basil ice cream, a meal in this stone-grey dining room is a voyage for the tastebuds.

Similarly adventurous is William Ledeuil, who was chef at the Guy Savoy offshoot Les Bouquinistes before opening **Ze Kitchen Galerie** last year. Fascinated by Asian food and an assiduous shopper at Tang Frères (the huge Asian supermarket in the 13th arrondissement) and ethnic markets around town, Ledeuil makes nervy use of Asian herbs and spices. His menu comes in four eminently bobo (bohemian-bourgeois) declensions: soup, pasta, raw (as in sushi), and a la plancha (grilled).

Philippe Delacourcelle, at the newly opened **Le Pré Verre** in the Latin Quarter, also loves 'exotic' seasonings and uses them with tremendous originality. Typical of his creations are a lentil and squid 'terrine' on salad leaves, garnished with sautéed baby squid and dressed in sesame vinaigrette, and veal steak with a hauntingly good purée of celeriac, potato and almonds.

Another chef inspired by faraway lands is Jérôme Bodereau, formerly of L'Arpège, who offers a winsome riff on the flavours of Mauritius at **Chamarré**. What makes this hybrid work is the meeting of extraordinary French precision with the motley seasonings of this multicultural Indian Ocean island, as seen, for example, in a 'Mauritian pesto' sauce (Thai basil, ginger and various other seasonings).

Flora Mikula, at her handsome new restaurant **Flora**, works in a similar vein, finding delicious inspiration in a variety of foreign cuisines. Best known as a Provençal chef (she once ran the bistro Les Olivades), she now borrows flavours from all over the Mediterranean and Asia to produce dishes such as lacquered prawns with aubergine.

The most promising young bistro chef at the moment is Philippe Tredgeu, who cooked at the excellent Chez Casimir before opening his own, almost woefully popular **Restaurant L'Entredgeu**. Tredgeu shrewdly understands that hordes of Parisians crave home cooking, but in a cleverly modernised version. Think deboned pig's trotters in a crispy pastry leaf with céleri rémoulade as a starter, lamb stuffed with foie gras as a main, and caramelised bananas for dessert.

Flora Mikula puts a cosmopolitan gloss on the south.

Finally, if there's a single chef who's irrevocably destined for fame (his bashfulness notwithstanding), it's Alain Solivérès, who has made a brilliantly successful move from Les Elysées du Vernet to **Taillevent**. A native of Montpellier, Solivérès trained with several of the top chefs in France before becoming a star at Les Elysées, thanks to his ability to reinvent southern French cooking. Now, though, his creativity is in full luxuriance, as seen in an edible masterpiece such as his ventrèche de thon aux épices – immaculately cooked tuna belly, garnished with a tangle of Espelette peppers, lemon, capers and serrano ham. His cooking is sublime, and we suspect that the best is yet to come.

Cuisine by quartier

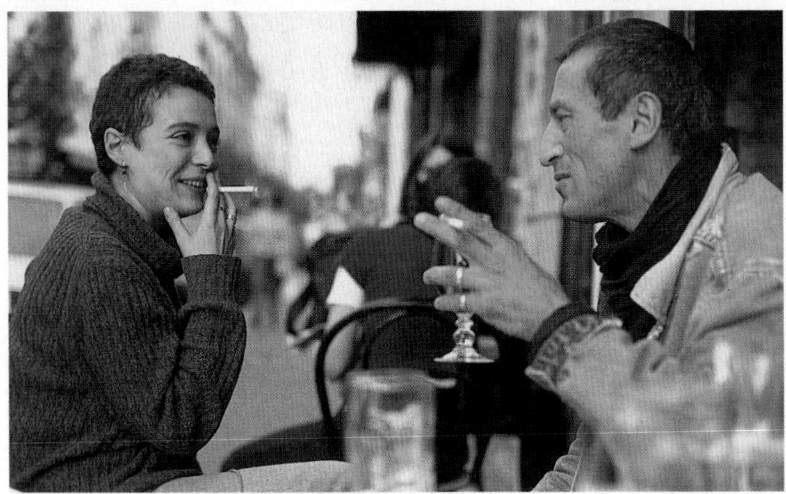

Artists, intellectuals and immigrants have left their mark on the menus of Paris' distinctly individual arrondissements. Tom Coveney offers a local's guide.

A melting pot for the best cuisine from all over France and the world, Paris is a proud metropolitan embodiment of the French passion for food. The 20 arrondissements are packed with bars, brasseries and bistros that pump the city's social lifeblood, the personality of each neighbourhood reflected in its local establishments. As a result, deciding which area of the city to eat in can be as important as choosing the restaurant itself. Here, we take you on a stroll around the city's dining scene.

It was just to the north of the Louvre that the word 'restaurant' was first used during the 1760s. Referring initially to a medicinal soup sold by a local baker, the word became synonymous with the salons that sprung up to sell the broth; and so the modern style of sociable eating began. Today, the grandiose restaurants in the arcades of the Palais-Royal (**Le Grand Véfour** and the **Restaurant du Palais-Royal**) still offer a sense of 18th-century dining at its most luxuriant. To rub shoulders with the area's influential players, **Willi's Wine Bar** is popular with fashion and media types, whereas bankers pack out the old-fashioned dining room at **Chez Georges**. Adding a cosmopolitan angle, Paris' Japanese community around the nearby rue Ste-Anne has brought with it the best in sushi, sashimi and cheap but delicious noodles.

When a crop of fashion-conscious restaurants opened in the late 1990s, it was the area around the Champs-Élysées that profited the most. Hip young things flocked to rue Marbeuf and rue de Marignan as top chefs and film stars laid down the challenge to the area's haute cuisine establishments. Recently guest lists have turned from mega-star to Star Academy, but you'll still find restaurants run by cutting-edge chefs such as Alain Ducasse (**Spoon, Food & Wine**), Jean-Georges Vongerichten (**Market**) and the Pourcel twins (**La Maison Blanche**).

In Montmartre, the restaurants around the Sacré-Coeur and the Moulin Rouge serve up over-priced meals to crowds of sightseers. Richer pickings are to be found at the northern and southern extremes of the area. **La Table de Lucullus** is one of a string of up-and-coming bistros to be found in the increasingly trendy Batignolles district. Head south into the 9th's St-Georges and you'll find a host of foodie havens such as boho bistro **Velly**. If you've left your polo-neck at home you could always head to rue Lamartine to wolf down some good-value Korean food instead at **Restaurant Euro**.

Centred around the rue des Francs-Bourgeois (or 'the street of the outspoken middle-classes' as Jack Kerouac put it), the café culture of the Marais provides a focus for Paris' arty media types. Home also to the city's gay and Jewish

communities, the Marais offers vibrant nightlife alongside an abundance of chopped liver. A summer's evening stroll through the pretty streets could wind up either with a trendy cocktail in the **Bliss Café** or a fistful of felafal in **L'As du Fallafel** depending on your mood.

To the north and east of the Marais, Paris' traditionally working class areas continue to be gentrified at an astounding rate. Popular bars and good-value bistros have galloped from place de la Bastille, up rue de Charonne (**Pause Café**), and towards Canal St-Martin (**Chez Prune**) and rue Oberkampf (**Café Charbon**). In multicultural Belleville, Arab, Jewish and Chinese restaurants rub shoulders with trendy, bric-a-brac bars.

'The Marais offers vibrant nightlife alongside an abundance of chopped liver.'

On the Left Bank, it was the literary café society of St-Germain des Prés that stole the limelight for many years. Overpriced restaurants have followed crowds of tourists to the area's narrow streets, but find the right spot for whiling away an evening (**Au Vieux Colombier**, for example), and you'll marvel at the neighbourhood's charm. In the nearby 5th the neon lights of rues de la Huchette and de la Harpe advertise fast food from around the globe and Greek kebabs reign supreme. Escape from the madding crowd can be found in classy bistros such as **Le Reminet**, and good regional restaurants such as the Corsican **Vivario**.

Heading south from the city centre, the Montparnasse brasseries **La Coupole** and **Le Dôme** put up a spirited resistance to the monolithic onslaught of the lumbering Tour Montparnasse. As the sun sets and the office workers board trains for the suburbs, the restaurants and bars that line the main drag come alive for the night. Over the years, immigrants from Brittany have come into town at the Gare Montparnasse, making rue du Montparnasse the place to head for whenever you fancy that great Breton favourite, the crêpe.

The stretch from the shadow of the Eiffel Tower in the 7th down to the south-western tip of the 15th is prime pearls and poodles territory. All those wealthy locals have brought lots of good restaurants to the area. Highlights include **L'Os à Moelle**, **Le Troquet** and **Les Frères Gaudet**. For something a little spicier you might seek out the local Iranian community's cooking in the 15th's Beaugrenelle district.

At the funky end of Left Bank eating and drinking, the 13th is an excellent area for a cheap night out. Twinkling amongst the tower blocks to the south of rue de Tolbiac, Chinatown's glowing lights offer any combination of Thai, Cambodian, Laotian, Vietnamese and of course Chinese food. Further north the lively bistros and loud bars of the Butte-aux-Cailles attract students seeking a villagey atmosphere and cheap beer.

Cheap lunch challenge

Armed with €15 and our insiders' advice, you can dodge the tourist traps to lunch like a local, writes Anna Brooke.

Despite Paris' reputation as a world capital of good eating, it's fairly rare for tourists to find the best-value restaurants through sheer luck. Bombarded by quadrilingual menus and inflated prices, visitors often don't have the time or knowledge of the city to quash hunger pangs cheaply. Even as residents, eating out can be hit or miss, but if we were tourists where would we go and how would we choose? We decided to compile some insiders' tips for visitors by embarking on a five-day mission to find and test lunch menus priced at up to €15 in the main tourist hot spots: the Champs-Elysées, Montmartre, Opéra, St-Michel and Les Halles.

Not surprisingly our hungry eyes scoured the Champs-Elysées for half an hour before finding a €15 set menu. Le Jet Set was on a side street off the main drag and turned out to be a brand-new Iranian restaurant. Filled with a lively business crowd it offered Eastern delights in Oriental surroundings. We munched on light homemade mint yoghurt and creamy garlic houmous starters. Turkey brochette, served with paprika cream on a bed of rice with raisins and almonds, melted on the tongue. The duck in pomegranate and walnut sauce was tender and dessert was also pleasant: refreshing rose and pistachio ice cream. It was a good find and we were thankful to have headed off the Champs-Elysées and its tourist-fleecing cafés.

Day Two took us to Montmartre's teeming Place du Tertre, near Sacré-Coeur. Swamped by cafés and restaurants, we couldn't find a tempting menu until we got past the square where we spotted a quaint place covered in shrubbery and named after the children's artist Poulbot. We chose Le Poulbot because the menu was in French only and ventured away from the overpriced omelettes and chips of its competitors. The decor was fantastic with adorable 1940s chintzy fabrics and floral wallpaper. We enjoyed juicy snails and piping-hot onion soup for starters. This was followed by a slightly overcooked salmon fillet in dill sauce, but the tasty cassoulet with duck and sausage made up for any shortcomings.

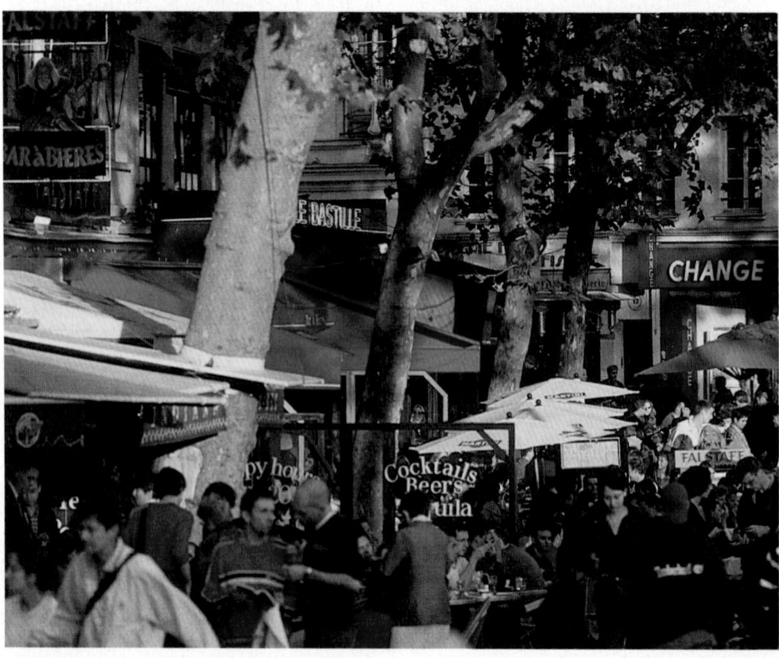

Pudding was a sticky homemade apple tart and a sweet crème caramel. Tasteful classical music added to the experience and made this a welcome escape from the tourist-crammed streets outside.

Opéra was the next day's adventure, where it took us 20 minutes to find anywhere that came close to a €15 menu. We did have to wait, but chose Le Chanterler because it was full, the cheapest in the area (coming in at €17 for three courses) and located next to the attractively modernised Marché St-Honoré. We began with a deliciously smooth chicken-liver mousse on a bed of crunchy lettuce and an ample smoked salmon platter. The appetising salmon main course came with al dente pasta in a warm tomato relish. The lamb chops were succulent and pink, served with a tangy sauce and chunky chips. An excellent poached pear in chocolate sauce finished everything off, making this place stand out from the plethora of expensive restaurants nearby.

'Our hungry eyes scoured the Champs-Elysées for half an hour before finding a €15 set menu.'

Day Four was not such a success. Set on a touristy lane in St-Michel, La Ferme St-Sévérin tempted us with an outside table dressed with colourful cheeses and meats. The reality inside, however, was one of barnyard extremes with a cheesy odour, stuffed animals and real flies buzzing round. The setting could have been excused had the food not been equally disappointing. The snail starter was still frozen (we sent it back) and the sautéed potatoes accompanying the main courses were swimming in grease. The only redemption came with a passable steak in roquefort sauce and decent veau à la normande. Dessert was less menacing, with a palatable caramelised apple tart and chocolate mousse, but all in all the experience was harrowing. (See Budget, p144 for better bets in the Latin Quarter).

Having recovered from the previous day, our final mission took us to Les Halles. Had a large number of people not been packed onto the terrace, La Fresque on rue Rambuteau might not have caught our eye. As it was, the staff seemed friendly and the clientele French, so we ventured in. Original tiles and frescoes covered parts of the walls, while tightly packed wooden tables created a cosy atmosphere for the arty types who were eating there. The food, like the service, was excellent. For starters we devoured thick slices of turkey sausage served on a bed of rocket leaves. Main course veal kidneys were tender and served in a mouth-watering Madeira sauce, while an unusual ostrich fillet came with crunchy potatoes roasted with bacon and mushrooms. Pudding was equally scrumptious: tangy, fruit pannacotta and cherry tiramisu. This was by far the best find of the week – our whole meal was wonderful.

So what can be deduced from our culinary adventure?

Well here, after much cogitation, deliberation and digestion, are our tips to make your fork-out as flavoursome as possible.

1) It's a good idea to wander away from the main road.

2) Menus without English translations are often a good bet.

3) It is usually worth waiting for a table in a place that is full (especially in an expensive area).

4) Don't be fooled by tempting food platters on display.

And finally…

5) Look out for crowds of happy locals, and order what most of them are having.

The lunch **bunch**

Jet Set *14 rue Washington, 8th (01.45.61.00.70). Mº George V.* **Open** Mon-Fri 9am-1am, Sat, Sun 9am-6am. **Lunch menu** €15. **Credit** AmEx, MC, V.

La Fresque *100 rue Rambuteau, 1st. (01.42.33.17.56). Mº Châtelet or Les Halles.* **Open** daily noon-3pm, 7pm-midnight. **Lunch menu** €11.50, €12.50. **Credit** MC, V.

La Ferme St Sévérin – Bistro St-Emilion *43 rue de la Harpe, 5th (01.44.07.07.28). Mº St Michel.* **Open** daily noon-3pm, 6pm-midnight. **Lunch menu** €8.90, €11.75. **Credit** MC, V.

Le Chanterler *42 pl du Marché St-Honoré, 1st (01.42.61.68.48). Mº Opéra or Tuileries.* **Open** Mon-Sat noon-2.30pm, 7-10.30pm. **Lunch menu** €17. **Credit** AmEx, MC, V.

Le Poulbot *3 rue Poulbot, 18th (01.42.23.32.07). Mº Abbesses or Anvers.* **Open** Mon-Fri noon-3pm, 7-10.30pm; Sat, Sun noon-11.30pm. **Lunch menu** €15. **Credit** MC, V.

Day-trip dining

Châteaux and Impressionists' haunts offer a feast for the eyes, but there's no reason to neglect your stomach at these popular tourist destinations.

Auvers-sur-Oise

Van Gogh fans can relive the fevered last few months of the artist's life in Auvers-sur-Oise, where crazed Vincent painted a canvas a day for three months before shooting himself in a wheatfield. The meandering village with its four museums, delightful château gardens and the still-recognisable sites of many of Van Gogh's most famous works is an enjoyable place to walk around, working up an appetite for the main event: dinner at the **Auberge Ravoux** (pl de la Mairie/01.30.36.60.60).
In the actual inn where Vincent lodged for 3.50F a day in 1890, this restaurant has considerable charm and not a hint of the tourist trap about it – set menus cost a very reasonable €26 or €32. Absinthe-coloured walls and lace curtains set the provincial mood and terrines are lined up along the zinc bar. Country-style stews such as duck gigondas with black cherries and a slow-cooked gigot d'agneau are served in their cast-iron pots and the grandma-ish desserts such as tarte Tatin, poached pears in wine and all-you-can-eat chocolate mousse are wonderful. Wines are good value and staff are utterly charming – if Vincent had been alive today he might have thought twice about ending it all. Most of Auvers' other restaurants are pizzerias; try to book a table here.

Barbizon

It's hard to believe now how isolated Barbizon felt to the artists who lived there in the 1830s (Corot, Théodore Rousseau, Daubigny and Millet), painting landscapes and scenes of peasant life that paved the way for Impressionism. Today, tour buses bring groups of Japanese and American sightseers to the art galleries that line the Grande Rue. These are frankly not the best reason to come to Barbizon, which is remarkable today for the beauty of its houses and the forest that surrounds it. The Maison-atelier Jean-François Millet is worth a visit, then it's time to think about food. If money is no object, treat yourself to a meal at the **Hôtellerie du Bas-Bréau** (22 Grande Rue/01.60.66.40.05) – once the inn where Robert Louis Stevenson wrote *Forest Notes*, now a luxury hotel where you can tuck into veal with asparagus meunière, turbot cooked on the bone and apple tart with honey. Otherwise, you'll find worthy bistro food and plenty of atmosphere, with good wines from small producers, at **L'Hermitage St-Antoine** (51 Grande Rue/01.64.81.96.96). Particularly delicious are the lentil salad with bacon, the confit de canard and the Fontainebleau, a fluffy mix of fromage frais and whipped cream.

Chartres

Chartres Cathedral, both the biggest cathedral in Europe and a perfectly preserved example of Gothic architecture, rises out of the agricultural plains south-west of Paris like a phoenix out of the ashes. And indeed at one time it did just that, having been built in the 13th century to replace its fire-ravaged Romanesque predecessor. Though the cathedral is the highlight of any Chartres itinerary, don't leave without wandering down to the River Eure via the steep cobbled back streets. Half-timbered buildings, humpback bridges, mills, tanneries and wash-houses line the river, invoking the town's medieval past.
Today, there are still plenty of places to feed hungry pilgrims.We opted to eat on the picturesque riverside terrasse of **L'Estocade** (1 rue de la Porte Guillaume/02.37.34.27.17) and, martyrs to our cause, religiously worked

How to **get there**

Auvers-sur-Oise By car 35km north of Paris by A15 exit 7, then N185 exit Méry-sur-Oise for Auvers. By train Gare du Nord or Gare St-Lazare, change at Persan-Beaumont.

Barbizon By car 57km south of Paris by A6, then N7 and D64. By train Gare de Lyon to Melun, then taxi (12km).

Chartres By car 88km from Paris by A11. By train Gare Montparnasse to Chartres.

Fontainebleau By car 60km from Paris by A6, then N7. By train Gare de Lyon to Fontainebleau-Avon.

Giverny By car 76km north-west of paris by A13 to Bonnières, then D201. By train Gare St-Lazare to Vernon, then bus or bike hire for 7km to Giverny.

Versailles By car 20km from Paris by A13 or D10 (direction Rouen). By train RER C Versailles-Rive Gauche. SNCF from Montparnasse direction Versailles-Chantiers or St-Lazare direction Versailles-Rive-Droite.

At the **Auberge Ravoux**, little has changed on the menu since 1890.

our way through the four-course menu (€22.50) of terrine de foie gras, pavé de boeuf with béarnaise, toasted goat's cheese on gingerbread and crème brûlée.

Fontainebleau

Fontainebleau's château – a former hunting lodge transformed in 1528 by François I – is the finest Italian Mannerist palace in France and a low-key alternative to the tourist madness of Versailles. The town itself is not quite as bourgeois and sedate as it looks, thanks to the student population of the INSEAD business school, and the pedestrian streets make for a pleasant stroll. When hunger strikes, avoid the tourist-fleecing cafés around the château and head instead to the tiny **Ty-Koz** (18 rue Cloche/01.64.22.00.55) for a crêpe, surprisingly Fontainebleau's best eating option (there are a few stuffy traditional restaurants, none of them great). You tick off your choice from a seemingly endless list, or invent your own. The fillings are fresh and the owners true eccentrics. Pastry-lovers should make a pilgrimage to **Cassel** (71 rue Grande/01.64.22.29.59), which rivals the best pâtisseries in Paris.

Giverny

A visit to Giverny, Claude Monet's home for 43 years, inevitably includes a visual assault by lily-covered umbrellas, T-shirts and mouse pads. But persevere beyond the tourists and the tat and this delightful Seine valley village makes a perfect day-trip destination.
Finding somewhere to eat in Giverny is not a problem. Finding somewhere atmospheric and authentic can prove harder. But the **Ancien Hôtel Baudy** (81 rue Claude Monet/ 02.32.21.10.03), once the hang-out of the artists whose works hang in the Musée d'Art Américain, offers both character and simple, reasonably priced French cuisine. Under the lime trees and canvas parasols, the generous bowls of salad (€10.50) were the perfect choice for a sultry summer's day. A stroll through the hotel's fragrant, rambling rose garden left us in no doubt as to why the Impressionist master and his admirers chose Giverny as their home.

Versailles

The reign of Sun King Louis XIV saw a new dawn for Versailles as it rose from humble hunting lodge to become both the epicentre of the French court and government and the biggest, costliest château in Europe. Its powers of attraction endure, with over three million visitors gravitating towards the palace yearly. Armies, be they soldiers or sightseers, march on their stomachs and the restaurateurs of Versailles are well-practised and well-prepared. Rue de Satory and rue du Maréchal Joffre have a good selection of touristy but good-value eateries offering fare from all corners of the globe. We ventured off the beaten track for a taste of the south-west at **La Terrasse** (11 rue St-Honoré/01.39.50.76.00). Out of the glare of the palace and under the shade of St-Louis' Cathedral we tucked into a fit-for-a-king gourmet salad topped with exquisitely prepared pieces of foie gras, an only slightly less decadent seafood salad, and a wickedly rich chocolate-Calvados creation, before taking the less-than-majestic RER back to Paris.

Whirlwind wine tour

Baffled by French wine lists? Fear not: Sophie Lyne's wine Tour de France will help you schmooze with the sommelier and sniff out the best bottles.

France offers a greater array of different wine-styles than any other country in the world. From the clean, aromatic, mineral rieslings of Alsace in the north-east to the powerful, chunky reds of the south-west, you'll find a wine to suit every mood, food and palate. However, the visiting wine buff needs a quick Tour de France to navigate complicated wine lists.

The big difference between a bottle from the New World and from France is that the grape variety that you know and love (chardonnay, merlot or sauvignon blanc for example) is seldom seen on a French wine label. The reason being that in France wine isn't just made from grapes – it's made from 'terroir'. This doesn't just mean the soil in which the vine is planted, it means all of the ways in which the place it comes from can influence the flavour of a wine.

So, let's climb aboard our trusty vélos and have a quick spin around the main wine producing regions, starting in the north-east with an apéritif. **Alsace** produces mainly white wine (the red is usually more like rosé) and is unique in France in describing the wines by grape variety. We have the clean but rather bland sylvaner, the classic lime- and mineral-infused rieslings, the spicy pinot gris (or tokay), the rich and grapey muscat and the oily and exotic gewürztraminers. They are very reasonably priced and popular in wine bars and restaurants.

Surprisingly close to Paris itself is **Champagne**, the undisputed king of sparkling wines. If you can afford it, step up to the mature complexity of a vintage, or 'millésime'.

Heading south into the heart of the country, the **Loire Valley** gives us clean, fresh, inexpensive muscadet, a traditional match for oysters. Also look for more serious flinty, steely sauvignon blancs of Sancerre and Pouilly-Fumé, sweet (yet rarely heavy) wines from Vouvray and Coteaux du Layon and some light reds from Chinon and Bourgeuil. More potent is the ruddy Saumur-Champigny.

The first chardonnay vineyards we hit south of Paris are those of Chablis, in **Burgundy**. Traditionally unoaked with good acidity these are the sharpest, most mineral expressions of chardonnay, a world away from the big, fat, buttery wines of Australia or California. Further south, Burgundy has hundreds of appellations but really only two wine styles – classic barrel-matured chardonnays and seductive, raspberry- and cherry-fruited pinot noir reds. St-Véran and Mâcon usually offer good deals, the more famous Pouilly-Fuissé less so. Just south of here is **Beaujolais** – juicy, purple-coloured, lip-smacking, quaffing reds best drunk leaning against the zinc bar of a Parisian bistro. Look for the Villages appellations, such as Morgon and Brouilly.

Moving ever closer to the Mediterranean we hit the **Rhône Valley**. In the north there are some wonderful syrah-based reds with aromas of blackcurrants, plums and olives (Côte Rôtie and Hermitage are the great names) and around Avignon and Orange the sun-baked, powerful red Côtes du Rhônes of which Châteauneuf du Pape is the best. White Rhônes are usually thick and heavy, but the peachy and flowery viognier grape reaches its zenith in Condrieu.

Further south into **Provence**, we move into rosé country, where vast quantities are produced for popular summer drinking by locals and tourists. There is a small production of generous whites, from more obscure varieties such as rolle, ugni blanc and clairette. In Bandol, powerful tannic reds made from mourvèdre provide wonderful food wines.

The biggest revolutions are taking place in the **Languedoc-Roussillon**. An area originally known for the enormous quantities of very mediocre wine produced by cooperatives has been re-thinking, re-planting and challenging the old ways, with enormous success. Sommeliers will be happy to recommend producers.

Moving north up the Atlantic coast we come to **Bordeaux**. The area is dominated by its reds: slow-maturing, classic cabernet sauvignons from the Médoc and the Graves and plumper, less structured merlot-based wines from St-Emilion and Pomerol. Look out for Fronsac, Côtes de Francs and Côtes de Castillon, which are far cheaper than their more illustrious neighbours. You won't find Pomerol's Château Pétrus at under €1,000 per bottle but less than a kilometre away lie the vineyards of Lalande de Pomerol, whose smooth and supple wines are still reasonably priced. Bordeaux is also home to magnificent sweet wines such as Barsac and Sauternes.

France also has hundreds of country wines, Vin de Pays and Vins de Table that can often surprise and delight at low prices. Remember, though, that the appellation gives an indication of the style of wine, but most important is the work of the individual winemaker.

A la carte

Where to start when you're spoilt for choice? Our guide will point you to just the right restaurant or watering hole for every imaginable Parisian moment.

Where to go ....

...to eat After Midnight

Chez Papa, Budget
A la Cloche d'Or, Bistros
Georges, Trendy
Joe Allen, The Americas
Les Philosophes, Cafés
Le Tambour, Bars & Pubs
Taninna, North African
La Tour de Montlhéry (Chez Denise), Bistros
Viaduc Café, Cafés
See also p90, Brasseries

...to drink After 2am

Le Bréguet, Bars & Pubs
Cabaret, Bars & Pubs
La Chope des Artistes, Cafés
Le Crocodile, Bars & Pubs
Flann O'Brien's, Bars & Pubs
Harry's Bar, Bars & Pubs
Mathis, Bars & Pubs
La Taverne de Nesle, Bars & Pubs
Aux Troix Mailletz, Bars & Pubs
Viaduc Café, Cafés

...to eat Al Fresco

L'Absinthe, Bistros
Apollo, Trendy
La Cagouille, Fish & Seafood
Café Marly, Cafés
Café Noir, Bistros
Contre-Allée, Bistros
Le Châlet des Iles, Classics
L'Espadon, Haute Cuisine
La Fontaine de Mars, Bistros
Georges, Trendy
La Girondine, Bistros
Le Grizzli, Cafés
Il Cortile, Italian
Laurent, Haute Cuisine
Pavillon Montsouris, Classics
Pavillon Puebla, Regional
Pitchi Poï, Jewish
Le Pré Catelan, Haute Cuisine
Restaurant du Palais-Royal, Contemporary
La Terrasse du Parc, Contemporary

...for Ancient Walls

Allard, Bistros
L'Ami Louis, Classics
Anahi, The Americas
Auberge Nicolas Flamel, Bistros
Chez Marianne, Jewish
L'Ecurie, Budget
La Fontaine Gourmande, Bistros

...for the Artworks

Le Carré des Feuillants, Haute Cuisine
La Coupole, Brasseries
Guy Savoy, Haute Cuisine
Le Méditerranée, Fish & Seafood
Le Stresa, Italian
Wadja, Bistros
Ze Kitchen Galerie, Contemporary

...for unusual Beers

La Fabrique, Bars & Pubs
Le Frog & Rosbif, Bars & Pubs
Le Général Lafayette, Bars & Pubs
Graindorge, Regional
La Gueuze, Bars & Pubs
La Taverne de Nesle, Bars & Pubs

...for a Business Lunch

Aki, Japanese
L'Astor, Contemporary
Bath's, Regional
Benoît, Bistros
La Butte Chaillot, Bistros
Chez Georges, Bistros
Chez la Vieille, Bistros
Chiberta, Contemporary
D'Chez Eux, Regional
Les Elysées du Vernet, Haute Cuisine
L'Estaminet Gaya, Fish & Seafood
Flora, Contemporary
Le Graindorge, Regional
Le Grand Colbert, Brasseries
Le Moulin à Vent, Bistros
Les Ormes, Bistros
Le Pamphlet, Bistros
Savy, Bistros
Taillevent, Haute Cuisine

...for a Carnivorous Feast

Au Boeuf Couronné, Brasseries
Le Bouclard, Bistros
Chez Omar, North African
L'Ecurie, Budget
Le Gavroche, Bistros
Georget, Bistros
La Maison de l'Aubrac, Brasseries
Le Nemrod, Cafés
Le Père Claude, Bistros

A la carte

Au Petit Marguery, Bistros
Le Pied de Cochon, Brasseries
Savy, Bistros
Sébillon, Bistros
La Tour de Montlhéry (Chez Denise), Bistros

...to Celebrity Spot

404, North African
Les Ambassadeurs, Haute Cuisine
L'Ami Louis, Bistros
Anahi, The Americas
L'Atelier de Joël Robuchon, Contemporary
Brasserie Lipp, Brasseries
Café de Flore, Cafés
Le V, Haute Cuisine
Chez Arthur, Bistros
L'Espadon, Haute Cuisine
Market, Contemporary
Mathis, Bars & Pubs
Le Père Claude, Bistros
Le Square Trousseau, Bistros
Le Stresa, Italian
Le Voltaire, Bistros
See also p106, Trendy

...for the Cheese Course

Astier, Bistros
Le Bistro de Gala, Bistros
Chez Michel, Bistros
Chez René, Bistros
Les Fernandises, Regional
Le Graindorge, Regional
Montparnasse 25, Classics
Restaurant Au Pressoir, Classics
See also p79, Haute Cuisine

...with Children

Altitude 95, Bistros
Brasserie Flo, Brasseries
La Coupole, Brasseries
Fogòn St-Julien, Spanish
New Nioullaville, Far East
Pizza Milano, Italian
Le Président, Far East
Quai Ouest, Contemporary
Thoumieux, Bistros
Le Troquet, Bistros
Wadja, Bistros

...for Cocktails

AbracadaBar, Bars & Pubs
Andy Wahloo, Bars & Pubs
Boteco, Bars & Pubs
Calle 24, Americas
Chez Richard, Bars & Pubs
China Club, Bars & Pubs
Le Crocodile, Bars & Pubs
Favela Chic, Trendy
F.B.I Paris, Bars & Pubs
Harry's Bar, Bars & Pubs
Hemingway Bar at the Ritz, Bars & Pubs
Impala Lounge, Bars & Pubs
The Lizard Lounge, Bars & Pubs
Le Plaza Athénée, Bars & Pubs
Le Rosebud, Bars & Pubs
Le Train Bleu, Brasseries
Zéro Zéro, Bars & Pubs

...in Designer Style

Aki, Japanese
Alcazar, Brasseries
Antoine et Lili, La Cantine, Tea Rooms
Atelier Renault, Cafés
Barrio Latino, Bars & Pubs
Café des Initiés, Cafés
Café Marly, Cafés
Hiramatsu, Haute Cuisine
Maison Blanche, Contemporary
Le Martel, Trendy
Le Salon d'Hélène, Contemporary
Senso, Bars & Pubs
Le Trésor, Bars
Wok, Far East
See also p106, Trendy.

...for unusual Desserts

Alain Ducasse au Plaza Athénée, Haute Cuisine
L'Astrance, Contemporary
Les Bombis Bistrot, Bistros
Café des Délices, Cafés
Chiberta, Contemporary
L'Epi Dupin, Bistros
O'à la Bouche, Bistros
Petrossian, Contemporary
Pierre Gagnaire, Haute Cuisine
La Régalade, Bistros
Ze Kitchen Galerie, Contemporary

...on a Diet

Alcazar, Brasseries
L'Avenue, Trendy
Blue Elephant, Far East
Khun Akorn, Far East
Hôtel Costes, Contemporary
Le Salon d'Hélène, Contemporary
Tanjia, Trendy
See also p203, Japanese, p161, Vegetarian.

...with your Dog

Café Beaubourg, Cafés
Le Clown Bar, Wine Bars
La Galère des Rois, Bistros
Khun Akorn, Far East
Le Safran, Bistros
Le Suffren, Brasseries

...before/after a Film

Così, Budget (Filling Stations)

La Coupole, Brasseries
Les Editeurs, Cafés
Korean Barbecue, Far East
La Maison de l'Aubrac, Brasseries
Nils, Budget (Filling Stations)
Le Reflet, Cafés
Le Rendez-vous des Quais, Cafés
Le Wepler, Brasseries

...with a serious Foodie

L'Arpège, Haute Cuisine
L'Astrance, Contemporary
L'Atelier de Joël Robuchon, Contemporary
Le Chavignol, Bistros
Hiramatsu, Haute Cuisine
Kinugawa, Japanese
Pierre Gagnaire, Haute Cuisine
Le Pré Verre, Bistros
La Régalade, Bistros
Le Salon d'Hélène, Contemporary
Le Soleil, Bistros
Stella Maris, Haute Cuisine
La Table de Lucullus, Fish

...on a First Date

404, North African
Les Bombis Bistrot, Bistros
Café Marly, Cafés
Chez Dom, Caribbean
China Club, Bars & Pubs
Le Clown Bar, Wine Bars
Julien, Brasseries
Le Reminet, Bistros
Les Zygomates, Bistros
La Terrasse du Parc, Contemporary

...for Game

Auberge le Quincy, Bistros
La Biche au Bois, Bistros
Chez Casimir, Budget
Chez Michel, Bistros
Chez Toinette, Budget
L'Intermède, Bistros
Michel Rostang, Haute Cuisine
Au Petit Marguery, Bistros
Le Repaire de Cartouche, Bistros

...with Grandma

Angelina, Tea Rooms
Le Dôme, Fish & Seafood
Josephine 'Chez Dumonet', Bistros
Ladurée, Tea Rooms
Le Soufflé, Classic
Le Train Bleu, Brasseries
La Truffière, Classics

...with a Group of Friends

Alcazar, Brasseries
Ave Maria, Bars & Pubs
Le Café du Commerce, Budget
La Catalogne, Spanish
Chez Gégène, Eating & Entertainment
Chez Janou, BIstros
L'Escapade, Budget
L'Espadon, Haute Cuisine
Fajitas, The Americas
New Nioullaville, Far East
Les Petits Marseillais, Bistros
La Table d'Aude, Regional
Thiou, Trendy

...for the Kitsch

Atlas, North African
La Charlotte en l'Ile, Tea Rooms
La Chine Masséna, Far East
Le Dénicheur, Cafés
Le Kitch, Cafés
La Madonnina, Italian
Au Pied de Cochon, Brasseries

...for a Late Lunch

L'Atelier de Joël Robuchon, Contemporary
Brasserie Zimmer, Brasseries
L'As du Fallafel, Jewish
La Bocca, Italian
Café Marly, Cafés
Café du Commerce, Budget
Café Ruc, Brasseries
Camille, Bistros
L'Entracte, Cafés
Georges, Trendy
La Grande Armée, Brasseries
L'Interlude, Budget
Juvéniles, Wine Bars
Polichinelle Café, Cafés
Restaurant Pho, Far East
Soufflot Café, Cafés

...for unusual Loos

Abazu, Japanese
Le Bar Dix, Bars & Pubs
Chai 33, Bars
L'Etoile Manquante, Cafés
La Folie en Tête, Bars & Pubs
Le Lèche-Vin, Bars & Pubs
The Lizard Lounge, Bars & Pubs
Le Pantalon, Bars & Pubs
Les Philosophes, Cafés
La Tour d'Argent, Haute Cuisine
Le Trésor, Bars & Pubs

...for Live Music

Batofar, Clubs
Chez Jean, Budget
Cithéa, Clubs
Connolly's Corner, Bars & Pubs
L'Entrepôt, Bars & Pubs
La Flèche d'Or, Bars & Pubs
Hard Rock Café, The Americas

A la carte

Le Mazet, Bars & Pubs
Le Piston Pelican, Bars & Pubs
Ti-Jos, Regional
Aux Trois Mailletz, Bars & Pubs
See also p279, Eating & Entertainment

...to eat Organic

Le Safran, Bistros
Le Potager du Marais, Vegetarian
Il Baccello, Italian

...to Play Pool or Billiards

Blue Bayou, The Americas
Flann O'Brien's, Bars & Pubs
Lou Pascalou, Bars & Pubs
Les Triolets, Bars & Pubs

...for a Romantic Meal

L'Angle du Faubourg, Contemporary
L'Astrance, Contemporary
Le Châlet des Iles, Classics
Le V, Haute Cuisine
L'Enoteca, Wine Bars
L'Espadon, Haute Cuisine
Flora, Contemporary
Gallopin, Brasseries
Le Grand Véfour, Haute Cuisine
Lapérouse, Classics
Lucas Carton, Haute Cuisine
Le Pamphlet, Bistros
Le Pavillon Montsouris, Classics
Le Pré Catelan, Haute Cuisine
Restaurant du Palais-Royal, Contemporary
Sardegna a Tavola, Italian
La Tour d'Argent, Haute Cuisine
Le Train Bleu, Brasseries

..to talk about the Rugby

La Maison de l'Aubrac, Brasseries
The Bowler, Pubs
Brasserie de l'Isle St-Louis, Brasseries
The Frog & Rosbif, Bars & Pubs
Kitty O'Shea's, Bars & Pubs
Au Métro, Budget
La Régalade, Bistros

...for Interesting Salads

Apparemment Café, Cafés
Bistro du Peintre, Bistros
Blue Elephant, Far East
Café Beaubourg, Cafés
Chez Papa, Budget
L'Entracte, Cafés
Le Grizzli, Bistros
Khun Akorn, Far East
Polichinelle Café, Cafés
Le Relais Gascon, Budget

...for rare Spirits

L'Alsaco, Regional
La Cagouille, Fish & Seafood
Dominique, Other International
Les Fernandises, Regional
Mazurka, Other International
Pitchi Poï, Jewish
Pravda, Bars & Pubs
Au Trou Gascon, Classics
See also p79, Haute Cuisine.

...for dinner on Sunday

Au 35, Bistros
Alexandre, Regional
L'Alivi, Regional
Altitude 95, Bistros
L'Ambassade d'Auvergne, Regional
L'Ardoise, Bistros
L'Atelier de Joël Robuchon, Contemporary
Le Bistro d'à Côté Flaubert, Bistros
Le Bistro d'Hubert, Bistros
La Butte Chaillot, Bistros
Café Burq, Bistros
Café Noir, Bistros
Camille, Bistros
Caves Saint Gilles, Spanish
Chardenoux, Bistros
Cheminée Royale, Eastern Mediterranean
Chez Dom, Caribbean
Chez Janou, Bistros
Chez Maître Paul, Regional
Chez Paul (11th), Bistros
Chez Paul (13th), Bistros
Chez Ramulaud, Bistros
A la Cloche d'Or, Bistros
Contre-Allée, Bistros
La Créole, Caribbean
Fogòn Saint Julien, Spanish
La Fontaine Gourmande, Bistros
La Fontaine de Mars, Bistros
Gli Angeli, Italian
La Grande Cascade, Classics
Le Jardin d'Hiver, Contemporary
Kazaphani, Eastern Mediterranean
Le Mâchon d'Henri, Bistros
Maison Blanche, Contemporary
Market, Contemporary
Mavrommatis, Eastern Mediterranean
Le Mono, Africa & Indian Ocean
Le Pamphlet, Bistros

Le Pavillon Montsouris, Classics
Le Père Claude, Bistros
Le Petit Dakar, African & Indian Ocean
Le Petit Marché, Bistros
Les Petits Marseillais, Bistros
Le Reminet, Bistros
Restaurant Ethiopia, Africa & Indian Ocean
Sébillon, Bistros
Thoumieux, Bistros
Le Vieux Bistro, Bistros
See also p169, The Americas; p144, Budget; p181, Far East; p139, Fish; p203, Japanese; p208, Jewish; p210, North African; p106, Trendy.

...for a Sunny Café Terrace

Café Beaubourg, Cafés
Café de Flore, Cafés
Café de la Musique, Cafés
Café du Marché, Cafés
La Chope Daguerre, Cafés
Les Deux Magots, Cafés
La Palette, Cafés
Pause Café, Cafés
Le Rendez-vous des Quais, Cafés
Le Rostand, Cafés
Le Soleil, Cafés
Tabac de la Sorbonne, Cafés
Vavin Café, Cafés

...for a Timewarp

Allard, Bistros
Chardenoux, Bistros
Chartier, Budget
Chez Georges, Bistros
Chez René, Bistros
Aux Crus de Bourgogne, Bistros
La Fermette Marbeuf, Brasseries
Julien, Brasseries
Perraudin, Bistros
Le Petit Rétro, Bistros
Savy, Bistros
Le Train Bleu, Brasseries
Vagenende, Brasseries

...with a Vegetarian Friend

Alexandre, Regional
L'Arpège, Haute Cuisine
La Bastide Odéon, Regional
Chez Marianne, Jewish
Au Coco de Mer, African
Kastoori, Indian
Macéo, Contemporary
Pause Café, Cafés
Le Safran, Bistros
Le Souk, North African
Spoon, Food & Wine, Trendy
La Voie Lactée, Eastern Mediterranean
Willi's Wine Bar, Wine Bars

...for the View

Altitude 95, Bistros
Georges, Trendy
Le Jules Verne, Haute Cuisine
Maison Blanche, Contemporary
R, Trendy
Le Totem, Cafés
La Tour d'Argent, Classics

...for Weekend Brunch

Amnesia, Gay & Lesbian
Blue Bayou, The Americas
Breakfast in America, The Americas
Café Charbon, Bars & Pubs
Le Chalet des Iles, Classics
Le Dénicheur, Cafés
The Lizard Lounge, Bars & Pubs
Pitchi Poï, Jewish
A Priori Thé, Tea Rooms
Quai Ouest, Contemporary
Le Safran, Bistros
Zebra Square, Brasseries
404, North African

...For the Wine List

Astier, Bistros
Chai 33, Bars & Pubs
Chez Georges, Bistros
A la Grange Batelière, Bistros
Le Passage des Carmagnoles, Bistros
Le Récamier, Classics
Spoon, Food & Wine, Trendy
Taillevent, Haute Cuisine
La Tour d'Argent, Haute Cuisine
La Truffière, Classics
Wadja, Bistros
Willi's Wine Bar, Bistros
Yugaraj, Indian
See also p129, Wine Bars

...with a Writer

La Belle Hortense, Wine Bars
Café des Lettres, Cafés
Café de Flore, Cafés
Le Couvent, Bars & Pubs
Les Editeurs, Cafés
Le Fumoir, Bars & Pubs
Le Perron, Italian

...on Your Own

L'Atelier de Joël Robuchon, Contemporary
L'As du Fallafel, Jewish
Le Bar à Huîtres, Fish & Seafood
Fish, Wine Bars
Garnier, Brasseries
Higuma, Japanese
Lô Sushi 2, Trendy

Gastronomie Vietnamienne

Savour authentic Vietnamese cuisine
from Saigon, Hanoi and Hué.

Chef-proprietor NGUYEN-LEE and her team are pleased to welcome you to the "Le Santal" restaurants, recommended by Gault et Millau and other European and North American restaurant guides.

A warm welcome and quality service.

Le Santal - Opéra
8 rue Halévy, 9th
M° Opéra
Tel: 01.47.42.24.69
www.le-santal.com
Paris, France

Le Santal - Côté Mer
6 rue de Poissy, 5th
M° Maubert-Mutualité
Tel: 01.43.26.30.56
Fax: 01.42.71.51.82
Paris, France

Escale a Saigon
Le Santal des neiges
107 av Laurier (ouest)
Montréal - Québec
Tel: 001.514.272.3456
Fax: 001.514.272.7304
as found on: www.restaurant.ca
Canada

French Cuisine

Bistros

From matronly kitchens serving beef on the bone to bijou addresses where young chefs spring surprises, the bistro is the pulsating heart of French cuisine.

No single category of restaurants is more indelibly associated with Paris than the bistro, that proverbial neighbourhood hole-in-the-wall with red-checked tablecloths, a chatty owner, wines that foster conviviality, and a mouth-watering run of long-simmered dishes we all wish we had the time and knowledge to make at home. Today, however, bistros offer a brilliantly idiosyncratic class of French eating that runs from resolutely traditional dishes, such as boeuf bourguignon, blanquette de veau and coq au vin in splendid stalwarts such as **Chez René** and **Benoît**, to edgier versions that playfully provoke by using decidedly non-Gallic ingredients in familiar French dishes. The ravioli stuffed with snails in a green aniseed-spiked cream sauce that chef Philippe Delacourcelle serves at the new **Le Pré Verre** in the Latin Quarter come to mind, as do some of chef Arnaud Pitrois' inventions at **Le Clos des Gourmets**. If there's any theme that links all Parisian bistros, though, it's a total devotion to food and wine and the pleasure they induce.

Be warned, though, that since the advent of the euro, bistro prices have risen dramatically; a bistro meal with wine for two can now easily hit €100, making dinner out more of an occasional treat than a regular event for the average Parisian. The 35-hour working week has also had a negative impact for diners – many restaurants close entirely at weekends.

1st Arrondissement

L'Absinthe

24 pl du Marché-St-Honoré, 1st (01.49.26.90.04). M° Tuileries. **Open** Mon-Fri 12.15-3pm, 7.45-10.30pm; Sat 7.45-10.30pm. Closed one week in Aug. **Average** €32. **Prix fixe** €26, €32. **Credit** AmEx, MC, V. **Map** G4.

Long before the Catalan architect Ricardo Bofill built a glass-walled building in the middle of this square, there was a little bar on the edge of it called L'Absinthe. Now the little bar has expanded into a biggish, and successful, bistro conveniently near to the Louvre, the Palais-Royal, the Tuileries gardens and the Opera. In summer, book a table on the spacious, fume-free terrace. This is one of the (fainter) stars in the galaxy of chef Michel Rostang, so the menu is not without invention (on a good day) and pretention (on a bad). Our chestnut véloute starter, for example, was original and delicious but its three floating discs of wild boar terrine were a pointless complication. For our main, we could just about taste the rosemary with which our scallop brochette was grilled, but the crushed potatoes it came with were greasy. For pudding, a pear Tatin with walnut sauce, caramel and salted butter was good but not as good as it sounds. The house red from the Ventoux and white from the Luberon were only OK but, for those who require something finer, the wines are helpfully grouped by price.

L'Ardoise ★

28 rue du Mont-Thabor, 1st (01.42.96.28.18). M° Concorde or Tuileries. **Open** Wed-Sun noon-2.15pm, 6.30-11pm. Closed 25 Dec-3 Jan, first week in May, three weeks in Aug. **Prix fixe** €30. **Credit** MC, V. **Map** G5.

Aside from a table of happily sozzled French bankers who dissolved into giggles when they decided to have another Cognac, everyone in this butter-yellow, decor-free bistro was either Japanese or American. Clearly, this crowd had found their way here through guidebooks or hotel concierges, but they approached young chef Pierre Jay's blackboard menu with almost touching seriousness. Jay, who trained at La Tour d'Argent, is a very good cook, but his hearty food, often echoing his Mâcon origins, inspires as much admiration for being good value as it does for its finesse. We were impressed that six plump langoustines with mayonnaise and eight oysters with chipolata sausages (a heavenly combination popular in Bordeaux) were offered as part of the €30 menu-carte. The steak with pommes Anna was outstanding – a generous fillet, expertly cooked and full of flavour, with a perfect galette of golden, crunchy sliced potatoes. A venison civet on a bed of potato purée was generously served and deeply satisfying. Since the meal, accompanied by a fine Morgon vieille vignes, had been such a success, our disappointment with mediocre desserts – a croustillant of apples in caramel sauce and a crème brûlée with blackcurrants – was tempered. The waitresses are friendly, efficient and English-speaking, and overall this remains an excellent address for a good, casual, reasonably priced meal.

Chez La Vieille

1 rue Bailleul/37 rue de l'Arbre-Sec, 1st (01.42.60.15.78). M° Louvre-Rivoli. **Open** Mon-Wed, Fri noon-2pm; Thur noon-2pm, 7.30-9.30pm.. Closed Aug. **Average** €40. **Prix fixe** €32. **Lunch menu** €26. **Credit** AmEx, MC, V. **Map** J6.

The brief was simple, to have lunch Chez La Vieille and be sufficiently alert to confront a business meeting in the afternoon. We ate on the first floor, a plain, bright room in sharp contrast to the rustic charm of the ground floor, which was already bursting with well-rounded regulars. From the wondrous ad-lib selection of starters including a hot chou farci, we decided to try the homemade terrine de foie gras. The smiling waitress, from the all-female team headed by the Corsican patronne, quickly arrived with a whole terrine which we could gorge on at liberty; the liver was of outstanding quality, and decidedly moreish. The tripe lover between us pronounced his cast-iron casserole of the stuff the finest he had eaten in Paris. The foie de veau was equally impressive, coated in a pungent reduction of shallots and vinegar – only the tepid potato purée disappointed. We dodged the puddings, which follow the same cornucopian principle as the starters, and with a classy half-bottle of Bordeaux from a list that includes a fine selection of Corsican wines, we emerged light of heart and fleet of foot. Opening hours are limited, booking is essential, and the prix fixe is a bargain for the quantity and quality of the fare.

Le Dauphin

167 rue St-Honoré, 1st (01.42.60.40.11).
M° Pyramides. **Open** daily noon-2.30pm, 7.30-10.30pm. **Prix fixe** €34. **Lunch menu** €23. **Credit** AmEx, DC, MC, V. **Map** H5.

Don't be put off by the uninspiring demeanour of this bistro – chefs Edgar Duhr and Didier Oudill trained with star chef Michel Guérard, before wowing the critics at the Café de Paris in Biarritz. Here they present a pared-down version of their exciting, south-western food, combining influences from the Basque country and the Landes. Diners are encouraged to share starters such as tuna confit, rustic terrines and goose rillettes, all served from Kilner jars and accompanied by toasted country bread. The grill menu offers various combinations of seafood, meat and vegetables. And for more conventional tastes there's a classical carte, with three courses for €34. From the latter, a tasty cep soup came with a plump foie gras ravioli in the centre, while anchovies and piquillo peppers marinated in olive oil were bursting with vibrancy. Well-roasted, if smallish, coquilles St-Jacques topped a rich mixture of crushed potatoes and black olives (€4 supplement), but the star dish was the meltingly tender pig's cheek, cooked for seven hours in aged Armagnac. Desserts are a strong point – we shared a fabulous tartelette à l'orange, with crisp sablé pastry, a drizzle of sticky orange confit and a refreshing, pink-tinted, orange sorbet. The wine list is mostly regional French, with a few prestigious bottles for good measure.

Le Safran

29 rue d'Argenteuil, 1st (01.42.61.25.30).
M° Pyramides. **Open** Mon-Fri noon-2.30pm, 7-11pm; Sat 7-11pm. **Average** €38. **Prix fixe** €24, €38. **Lunch menu** €14.50. **Credit** AmEx, MC, V. **Wheelchair access. Non-smoking room. Map** G5.

All-you-can-eat as you've never seen it before, **Chez La Vieille**.

Some readers have complained of small portions and stuck-up service at Le Safran; whether it's as a reaction to criticism or not, we found nothing of the kind on our recent visit. The saffron-coloured dining room feels immediately welcoming, while the maître d' was charming. He even spoke English to a table of Americans and accommodated one woman's request for a salad. The menu is unchanging, except for two seasonal starters and three main courses (which incur a price supplement). Sautéed girolles had a flavoursome sauce and the saffron-tinted velouté de fruits de mer was a fulsome soup tasting strongly of garlicky rouille with chunks of coley, king prawns and squid. Mains of scarcely-cooked tuna topped with foie gras, and lamb cooked for 'seven hours', were both served with the same crisp round of courgettes and carrots, mushrooms and a small potato cake. The tuna combination was surprisingly successful, and the lamb rich and tender. Our Mercurey 2000 carried us through to desserts of an admirably bitter fondant au chocolate and a nutty apple crumble in a caramel sauce. Chef Caroll Sinclair emerged from the kitchen in her pork pie hat, declaring pointedly that customers who appreciate good food are what makes her job worthwhile. We certainly did, and will be back.

La Tour de Montlhéry (Chez Denise)

5 rue des Prouvaires, 1st (01.42.36.21.82). RER Châtelet-Les Halles. **Open** 24 hours Mon 7am-Sat 7am. Closed 14 July-15 Aug. **Average** €45. **Credit** MC, V. **Map** J5.

If ever a bistro lives up to institution status it is the open-all-hours Chez Denise, also known by its posher name of La Tour de Montlhéry. Despite it being an international guidebook favourite, we were surprised to find that the lunchtime crowd was principally French, including our one-eyed pensioner neighbour with a seemingly bottomless appetite for blanquette de veau and flaky millefeuille. Portion size is the selling point of the place, and the cliché of 'groaning platters' applies here in spades. We began with two slabs of the fatty terrine du chef and a comforting chicken liver dish, which set us up nicely for our main courses. Our veal kidneys came in an oval dish sufficient to feed a family and were tasty in their light mustard sauce, while the copious foie de veau was perfectly seared and accompanied, à l'anglaise, by some crispy bacon. Two other friendly locals were quickly seated at our reserved table and if you are not prepared to enjoy the intimate company of your fellow diners or to find the Turkish-style loos amusing, then this is probably not your sort of place. We finished the meal with a good platter of cheese and some more of the drinkable house Brouilly, all served with a typically brusque Parisian bonhomie. Anybody seeking out the ultimate gingham-tablecloth-and-Gauloises experience in the heart of Les Halles need look no further.

Willi's Wine Bar ★

13 rue des Petits-Champs, 1st. (01.42.61.05.09/ williswinebar.com). M° Pyramides. **Open** Mon-Sat noon-2.30pm, 7pm-11pm. Closed two weeks in Aug. **Average** €35. **Prix fixe** €25 (lunch), €32 (dinner). **Credit** MC, V. **Map** H5.

Opened near the Palais-Royal in 1980, Willi's oak-beamed bar and dining-room is a modest legend, with its own collection of specially commissioned

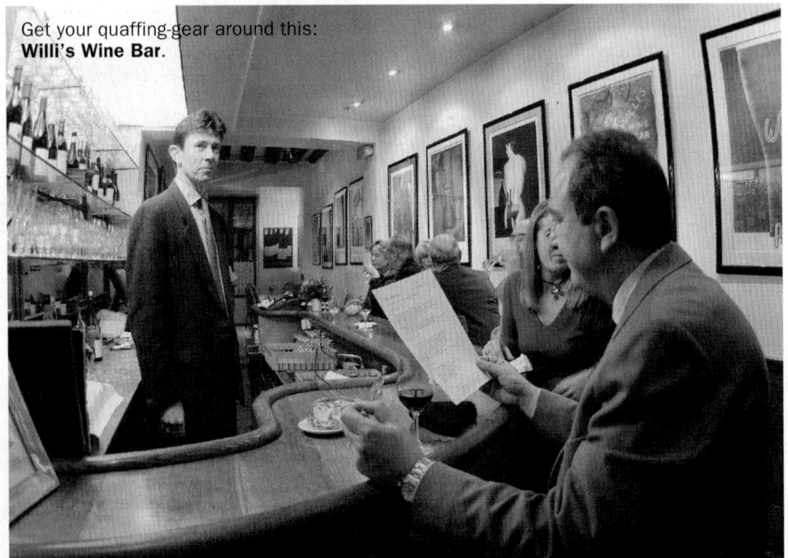
Get your quaffing-gear around this: **Willi's Wine Bar.**

wine posters. The simply presented menu is a mouthwatering read, so indulge in a generous glass from the fabulous selection of sherries while agonising over the relative merits of lightly sautéed scallops with a leek and sherry sauce or fillet of wild duck with red onion marmalade – and that's just for starters. For the main course, grilled sea bream fillet with a delicate buttery crust was set off to perfection by a ginger and lemon zest confit, while medallions of wild boar were oddly tasteless, grey and chewy (rather than pink, as requested). The wine list is huge, impressive and pricey, but there's a smaller selection available by the glass or carafe. The wine buff among us found some of these surprisingly young for drinking, but unexpected treats included sweet Hungarian Tokays from 1998 and 1993. Willi's is a smart choice for an informal business lunch, or a tasty alternative to a night of Molière's centuries-old jokes at the Comédie Française, and the prix fixe meals are excellent value.

2nd Arrondissement

Chez Georges

1 rue du Mail, 2nd, (01.42.60.07.11). M° Bourse. **Open** Mon-Sat noon-2pm, 7-9.30pm. Closed three weeks in Aug. **Average** €45. **Credit** AmEx, MC, V. **Map** H5.

The good, solid food and conviviality at Chez Georges are confirmation that the Parisian bistro of old is alive and well. Every table in this classic long, mirrored room is taken – every night. And people come as much for the food and atmosphere as for the motherly waitresses who glide about dishing out plates and advice. The starters are paragons of simplicity – a bowl of warm Puy lentils in a vinaigrette with grated onion; frisée tossed with warm bacon chunks and topped with a poached egg. Main courses are cooked with care; juicy, rose-coloured steak de canard with meaty ceps, and text-book sole meunière, which was considerately suggested by the waitress when she sensed us hesitating over the sole baked with wine and crème fraîche on the menu. Desserts include tried-and-tested profiteroles filled with ice cream and inundated by a warm, dark chocolate sauce, and a slice of pear Charlotte with a meringue centre in a custard lake. A small selection of wines on the stencilled menu, all around €22-€24, appeals to all pockets but, if you've got money to spare and spend, peruse the longer, printed list.

Aux Crus de Bourgogne

3 rue Bachaumont, 2nd (01.42.33.48.24). M° Sentier or Les Halles. **Open** Mon-Fri noon-3pm, 7.45-11pm. **Average** €34. **Prix fixe** €23.50 (dinner only). **Credit** AmEx, MC, V. **Wheelchair access. Non-smoking room. Map** J5.

In the heart of pedestrian Montorgueil, this check-clothed, polished wood bistro wins out on authentic, old-fashioned Parisian atmosphere. The other principal reason for eating here is the bargain price the chef offers on lobster in all its forms: hot on Thursdays, but available week-long with mayonnaise or in a salad for only a few more euros than the more mundane bistro offerings. We chose to begin our meals with the luxury crustacean and were not disappointed. Our main courses were in comparison penny-plain, the salmon steak and tagliatelle lacked interest and quenelles de brochet with the same pasta was more of a solid dumpling than this classic dish should be. The simple whole Dover sole or the entrecôte that our neighbours were enjoying would no doubt have been a wiser choice. Things got back on track with an excellent crème brûlée and a generous plate of cheese, accompanied by an outstanding white Burgundy chosen from a wine list with few affordable bottles. The place was humming with locals by the time we left, and in summer the terrace is well-placed for a relatively traffic-free al fresco meal, which makes booking advisable.

Le Gavroche ★

19 rue St-Marc, 2nd (01.42.96.89.70). M° Bourse or Richelieu-Drouot. **Open** Mon-Sat 7am-2am. Closed Aug. **Average** €29. **Lunch menu** €13. **Credit** MC, V. **Map** H4.

This wine bistro near the Bourse continues to pack in the regulars and delight passers-by. Slabs of roast lamb, plates of black pudding, platters of thick beef, extra, extra rare, all destined to be consumed with one or more bottles of Beaujolais, are carried past in a whirl of activity. The menu would be a cliché if it weren't so very good, from the fresh radishes served plain with salt and butter to the ham lunch special (carved from the massive ham bone by the bar). If you have a hankering for the classic steak-frites, come with a friend and share the special beef plate for two. It was a lunch worthy of the two serious heavyweight businessmen who impressed us featherweights by working their way through three courses including this platter. Order a bottle of excellent Beaujolais (€19), or take a cue from the media types at the next table and drink Brouilly. The wine is superior and well-priced, bottled for the restaurant by reliable Burgundy producers. Try to find room for the lovely crème caramel. We were smitten by the smiling waitress, who even while run off her feet managed to joke with lone diners. Booking is recommended for lunch, but you also can drop by La Gavroche after the theatre for a late dinner.

3rd Arrondissement

L'Ami Louis

32 rue du Vertbois, 3rd (01.48.87.77.48). M° Arts et Métiers. **Open** Wed-Sun 12.15-2pm, 7.30-11pm. Closed mid-July. **Average** €100. **Credit** AmEx, DC, MC, V. **Non-smoking room. Map** K4.

A strange place, this bistro that time forgot, where wealthy clients – bankers, artists and intellectuals, according to the owner, but on the basis of our visit, mostly tourists – tuck in to over-priced, mediocre dishes like poulet-frites or côte de boeuf. Bill Clinton may have squeezed down the narrow staircase to use the gents, and the carefully preserved pre-war

OPEN DAILY - EVEN ON SUNDAYS!
Lunch noon-2.30pm and dinner 7.30pm-midnight
Reservations recommended. Tel: 01.45.89.22.11

22 RUE DE LA BUTTE AUX CAILLES, 13th. Mº PLACE D'ITALIE

LES DÉCORS *Regional Franco-Swiss cuisine*

A small place to call home just like Switzerland... Just like Switzerland, you'll enjoy a simple and considerate

welcome... Just like Switzerland, the menu is varied, with dishes that are typical but cross many borders.

Open Tue-Sat noon-2.30pm, 7.30pm-10.30pm • Set-menus €13.80 / €18.40 / €24.50 - A la carte: €35
18 rue vulpian, 13th. Mº Glacière - Tel: 01.45.87.37.00 - Reservation recommended

interior, resplendent with stovepipe and red gingham curtains, could have been the inspiration for the sit-com *Allô, Allô*, but the food is outrageously priced for the quality. A large plate (enough for two) of decent, if too thickly cut, ham from the Ardennes and a côte de boeuf (again for two), nicely grilled on the outside, but grey, stringy and flavourless on the inside, notched up a whopping €117. Of course, there are some redeeming factors. The service is professional, unobtrusive and genuinely warm (perhaps with the exception of the rather self-important proprietor), and although the wine list features plenty of grand bottles at grand prices, producers are well chosen – we drank a juicy St-Joseph 2000 from Bernard Gripa at €52. If money is no object and you don't mind dull food, you could probably do worse.

L'Auberge Nicolas Flamel

51 rue de Montmorency, 3rd (01.42.71.77.78/ www.nicolasflamel.parisbistro.net). M° Rambuteau. **Open** Mon-Fri noon-2.30pm, 8-11pm; Sat 8-11.30pm. **Average** €35. **Credit** MC, V. **Non-smoking room. Map** K5.

The Auberge was built in the 15th century by Nicolas Flamel, a wealthy alchemist who, it was believed, had discovered the secret of turning lead into gold. The spectacular beamed room with its dusty chandeliers and haphazard modern art looks the part. Our apéritif made with wild strawberry liqueur was charmingly served, but first courses chosen from the blackboard were disappointing. A foie gras Tatin was drowned in a glutinous sweet sauce with a vague spice note. An assiette de legumes sétoise was a decent plate of cooked vegetables drizzled with vinaigrette, but these were to return in almost identical form as an accompaniment for our main courses, both of which were poor. The rack of lamb came without the promised beans; the meat itself was poorly trimmed and the meat not pink as ordered but a dull grey. Scallops with saffron butter tasted bland and lacked that plump, freshly shelled quality. We bypassed the rather dull-sounding desserts and opted for a plate of cheese which, coupled with the excellent red wine served by the carafe, perked up our spirits. At more than €100 for two the Auberge has obviously found its own alchemy for creating gold; the original Nicolas Flamel's powers are badly needed.

Camille

24 rue des Francs-Bourgeois, 3rd (01.42.72.20.50). M° St-Paul. **Open** daily noon-midnight. Closed Christmas and New Year. **Average** €33. **Lunch menu** €17 Mon-Fri, €19 Sat, Sun (two courses). **Credit** AmEx, DC, MC, V. **Map** L6.

Camille might look like a traditional bistro, but this is one place where you don't have to linger over lunch unless you want to. Pressed for time, we managed to have a meal here in little over an hour without feeling rushed – and when we said 'vite' the puddings arrived as it by magic, along with the bill. The €16 two-course menu was well-presented and substantial and our pitcher of house red very acceptable. A salade landaise was a simple but nicely dressed combination of gizzards on crisp lettuce, while the vegetable terrine in a tomato coulis was a beautiful red and green concoction featuring very fresh peppers, carrot and spinach. For mains, the pike-perch fillet, a symphony in green, came in a basil-flavoured sauce with a mound of very potatoey broccoli purée. The pot-au-feu comprised a huge chunk of beef cooked to melting point and served on a flat plate rather than in its juices. It outweighed the meagre vegetables with it (one morsel of carrot, turnip and leek) and more liquid would have been welcome, but you couldn't complain that they skimped on the expensive part of the dish. We followed up with €6 desserts, a superb pear flan and a superior millefeuille.

Chez Janou

2 rue Roger-Verlomme, 3rd (01.42.72.28.41). M° Chemin Vert. **Open** daily noon-2am. **Average** €23. **Lunch menu** €13 (Mon-Fri). **No credit cards. Map** L6.

There's something about Chez Janou. It's hard to put your finger on exactly what – the staff are friendly if somewhat frenetic, the decor is charming but unremarkable, and the food is reliable rather than great – but from where you're sitting, indoors or on the tiny terrace, the world somehow looks like a better place. Double-billed as a bistro and a Provençal restaurant, Chez Janou treads a rather zig-zag line between the two. We found the grapefruit, avocado

How to Eat **Snails**

Terrestrial gastropod molluscs may be a typically French delicacy, but heaps of shells found in prehistoric sites show that cavemen enjoyed them too. In France, the types of fresh snails you're most likely to encounter are the petit gris (about 2cm long) and the escargot de Bourgogne, about twice as long and the gourmet's choice. Snails are said to be tastier in summer and in winter, when they have been fasting, than in spring and autumn, when they are known as 'coureurs' (runners). The only problem is knowing whether yours came out of a tin and if they are French or imported. Snails are most often cooked in garlic, butter and parsley and brought to you with a gadget straight out of a Cronenberg film. Use the tongs to hold the shell and the two-pronged fork to fish out the snail. Whatever you do, don't forget to mop up the delicious garlic butter with your bread.

Look sharp at **Camille**. *See p27.*

and prawn salad and the tuna tartare served with an onion marmalade excellent; while for main courses the fish pie was disappointing and the lamb cutlets passable, while the duck proved delicious. Sweet tooths should not miss the chocolate mousse: how often in Paris – or anywhere – do you get to help yourself to as much as you want? But the real draw is the atmosphere. The waiters may be rushing around, but for those lucky enough to be dining here there's a prevailing feeling of convivial calm, despite being a stone's throw from posh place des Vosges. It's real, too – on several occasions we have been allowed to move to a different table with our wine while they cleared up around us.

La Fontaine Gourmande

11 rue Charlot, 3rd (01.42.78.72.40). M° Filles du Calvaire. **Open** daily noon-2.30pm, 7.30-10.30pm. Closed Sun in Aug. **Average** €28. **Credit** MC, V. **Map** L5.

This unassuming little bistro remains a real-people bolt hole as the rue Charlot continues to morph into one of the hippest streets on the continent. The place is, well, very motherly, with framed 20s adverts, stucco and stone walls, a barking poodle and a clique of happy ladies, who all seem to know each other, sipping wine. On a warm early-summer day, most of the miscellaneous crew here had ordered the cold roast beef with salad, and interleaved slices of tomato and mozzarella. We started with a nice salad liberally garnished with tiny boudin antillais (spicy, olive-sized black pudding on mixed leaves), and a better chiffonade of country ham and smoked duck breast, also on salad. Main courses were uneven. Swordfish steak was drab despite a silly little garnish that promised a whiff of pesto but didn't come through, while lamb en brochette with pommes dauphines was generously served and good. Advice: ignore the fish, stick with grills, and skip dessert, since an 'exotic' fruit crumble hardly warranted the billing. The wine list needs work, too – our St-Nicolas de Bourgeuil was thin and acidic – but, all told, if you're stalking the northern flank of the Marais and want a decent feed with no bells or whistles, you could do worse than this odd little spot.

Georget

64 rue Vieille-du-Temple, 3rd (01.42.78.55.89). M° St-Paul. **Open** Mon-Fri noon-2pm, 7.30-10pm; Sat 7.30-10pm. Closed Aug. **Average** €31. **No credit cards. Map** L6.

The first evidence of non-image-conscious, anachronistic dining: no sign of 'Georget' over the door. Look for 'Restaurant Robert et Louise', and enter the draughty, wood-smoke-filled chamber whose beamed interior is like a massive country kitchen. Openness is Georget's principal charm: you watch as a cleaver is taken first to a hunk of scrap wood to splinter kindling, then to a Renault-sized side of beef sitting at one end of a long table (we sat at the other), where your côte de boeuf or contre-filet is hand-selected, hacked and thrown sizzling onto the wood-fired griddle. As your meal sizzles away (be it lamb chops, black pudding or a mushroom-garnished omelette forestière), octogenarian matrons fry potatoes and spoon rillettes, a boy arrives from the courtyard to deliver lilacs and bisous, a poodle whines for its bowl of water. We found the food rib-sticking in the most pleasing sense possible: buttery grilled prawns, snails served in their shells, crisp confit de canard. Although not quite as rare as we'd ordered, the juicy beef, served on a wooden board, still melted effortlessly down our throats. A bottle of decent Cahors (€13.72), and the fluffy Charlotte au chocolat are respectable sidekicks to the main show – just beware the tap water which tasted of chlorine. Georget produces a timeless tableau – it could be 1910 or even 1620 were it not for the rotary dial phone and the location one block from one of the Marais' most popular café corners.

Le Hangar

12 impasse Berthaud, 3rd (01.42.74.55.44). M° Rambuteau. **Open** Tue-Sat noon-3pm, 6.30pm-midnight. Closed Aug. **Average** €30. **No credit cards. Map** K5.

With solicitious, good-humoured service and above-average food, this inventive little bistro with white-washed walls and a spacious terrace is worth seeking out, despite not being the bargain it once was. The cooking adheres to a mostly traditional line, but occasionally veers off towards something more creative, such as 'Tahitian' avocado stuffed with creamy, slightly peppery fish, or sea bass in a girolle mushroom cream sauce. We started with generous and impeccably fresh salads – green beans topped with fine slices of hearty foie gras and fresh mushroom salad in a light, lemony vinaigrette. The beef stroganoff was more shallot and mushroom than meat, but had a lovely flavour, while the linguine with sautéed prawns proved slightly under seasoned but perfectly cooked and generously served. Four well-ripened cheeses with a small salad comprised the cheese plate, and we were very impressed by a wine list that offered a large choice of good bottles for less than €15. The only real disappointment of the evening was a pear clafoutis whose scalding-hot temperature and curdled, grainy consistency suggested it had been brutally reheated – though other tables seemed to be enjoying their chocolate soufflé and runny chocolate cake.

Le Pamphlet ★

38 rue Debelleyme, 3rd (01.42.72.39.24). M° Filles du Calvaire. **Open** daily noon-2.30pm, 7.30-11pm. Closed 1-15 Jan, 5-21 Aug. **Prix fixe** €27, €45. **Credit** MC, V. **Non-smoking room. Map** L5.

The beamed room with its elegantly dressed and spaciously placed tables, combined with cooking that is modern and sophisticated without being insubstantial or over-elaborate, makes Le Pamphlet's €27 prix fixe menu one of the best deals in town. After chewing on some fragrant saucisson sec with our apéritifs, we were offered a good-sized ladle of creamy lentil soup as a pre-starter accompanied by some crusty warm bread rolls. Our first course kept up the high standard of presentation with an outstanding combination of escargots and rabbit rillettes, which seemed to capture all the flavours of rabbit, while a mini-brandade was enlivened by the addition of some tasty haddock. Main courses included a well-prepared Parmentier de canard, duck version of cottage pie, and glazed suckling pig, served French-style astride some roasted root vegetables. A biscuit tiède au chocolat was delicious,

one really loves is the [illegible] midnight, serving generous salads such as spinach topped with Parma ham, hearty main dishes including duck breast with ginger, steak tartare and calf's liver, and soothing desserts such as rice pudding. There is also a pleasant little terrace, but to be sure of snagging a table you'll need to avoid peak times. Service is friendly and prices are fair; now if only they would rev up the wine list a bit, the whole thing would be a perfect bull's eye.

Les Petits Marseillais ★

72 rue Vieille-du-Temple, 3rd (01.42.78.91.59). M° Rambuteau. **Open** daily noon-2.30pm, 8-11.30pm. **Average** €34. **Lunch menu** €10.60, €12. **Credit** AmEx, DC, MC, V. **Map** L6.

We peered through the window aghast: it was 10.30pm and Georget (*see left*), was already sipping his cup of cocoa. Where were we going to find a decent meal on a busy Saturday night in the Marais without a reservation? Lucikly, four doors down the funky Les Petits Marseillais is just cranking up around this time. One of the great things about this restaurant is that you can't book, meaning that if you are prepared to perch on the gymnastics 'horse' at the bar and have a pastis you will eventually get fed. The two Marseille boys of the title are amazingly friendly, to the extent of offering their motorbike as a mooring for our bikes. The mixed gay and straight crowd is also full of bonhomie and once seated, tightly squeezed at the black lacquer tables, we were immediately in conversation with our neighbours who exhorted us to try the oeufs en meurette (eggs poached in red wine). This naughty take on a nursery dish was sublime, and the goat's cheese starter with lamb's lettuce was also good. On to huge, chunky sautéed gambas with pastis, which were finger-licking delicious, and, presented on a planche of wood, a spicy house entrecôte, which the steak-lover in our party declared the best he'd ever had this side of the Atlantic. Puddings don't quite come up to the standard of the main courses, but a tarte Tatin and crème brûlée sustained us through a second bottle of wine so we could revel in the fun, frenetic atmosphere of the place, which buzzes late into the night.

…09.60). …en Mon-Sat noon- … noon-4pm. Closed one …27. **Lunch menu** €12, €15. …

…hush at this north Marais restau- … feel that you are entering some- … The decor is rather Buddha Bar-ish …ls, candles, a wacky chandelier, an oil … an Indian prince and ethnic bits and pieces …our lovely waitress was wearing a purple-and- … sari. Groups of well-dressed, well-behaved men … their 30s suggested that Le Réconfort is firmly established on the pink dining itinerary. Everything here is skilfully stage-managed, from the gently piped, ethnic lounge music that progressed seamlessly to clubby but not in-your-face house, to the menu, pasted into little hardback novels (useful for lone diners). From a selection of palate-cleansing starters, we chose the pungent, basil-marinated sardines and an excellent ceviche of meaty swordfish chunks with a dab of wasabi (a pleasant, though startling, surprise, hidden under a chunk of cucumber). The honey and cinnamon-flavoured chicken breast was too sweet for one of us, the magret de canard in blood orange sauce too well-cooked for the other – so we swapped plates, and only the rather soggy julienne of carrot and courgettes with the chicken disappointed. Desserts are superb: a thick, rich fondant au chocolat and the delicious crème renversée on its raspberry and biscuit base in a citrus caramel sauce. Sunday brunch is also served.

Taxi Jaune

13 rue Chapon, 3rd (01.42.76.00.40). M° Arts et Métiers. **Open** Mon-Fri noon-2.30pm, 8-10.30pm (bar open 9am-1am). Closed three weeks in Aug. **Average** €26. **Lunch menu** €12.81. **Credit** MC, V. **Map** K5.

Under new ownership, this reliable little bistro serves breakfast, lunch and dinner throughout the week. It's especially crowded at lunch, when people in the know rush over here as a break from the office. The name is a bit inexplicable (there's no taxi paraphernalia to be seen any more), but the food is a great deal, with an ever-varying selection of creative dishes. Recently, we started with a tiny triangular chèvre pie flavoured with mint, which added a lovely zing. Osso bucco tasted like the one nonna might have made. We were slightly less convinced by the rabbit, which came in too much sauce. But the fabulous homemade frozen nougat restored our good mood. The waiter happily told us the secret of the dessert's delicious blackberry-scented topping: a reduced red wine sauce with just a touch of sugar. Perfect to send you back to the office suffused with goodwill towards your colleagues. Of course, you can also come here for dinner, when you'll have a little more time to enjoy these original interpretations of traditional dishes. In the evenings, the little restaurant seems to glow with good cheer on the narrow street. Service is unstintingly friendly.

4th Arrondissement

Baracane

38 rue des Tournelles, 4th (01.42.71.43.33/ www.l-oulette.com). M° Chemin Vert. **Open** Mon-Fri noon-2.30pm, 7pm-midnight; Sat 7pm-midnight. **Average** €25. **Prix fixe** €20, €35. **Lunch menu** €9.50, €14. **Credit** DC, MC,V. **Map** L6.

The Baracane was quiet on the day we visited, lacking the authentic buzz of a French bistro, but we were warmly welcomed in English by the team, who also run the restaurant L'Oulette (*see p117*) in Bercy. The menu is very reasonably priced with various mix-and-match options including two courses for €14 at lunch, though each dish seemed to have a small flaw. A mackerel tartare was served so generously that the oily raw fish became a struggle to finish. Marrowbone toasts were overwhelmed by a thick red wine sauce; we pined for the traditional accompaniment of coarse salt. A slightly overcooked fried plaice was fine, but the accompanying rice lacked pizzazz, and the plat du jour chicken fricassée with tarragon was nicely browned but served with slightly incongruous plain pasta. Things picked up at pudding time with excellent rhubarb compote served with a squidgy lemon muffin and a dollop of crème fraîche, chosen from a tempting list. The wine list has many unusual choices from the south-west, and our white Pacherenc was an excellent and original choice at €17.10. The formula seemed to have grown a bit stale on this occasion, but this could still prove a useful address for a good-value meal near the place des Vosges.

Benoît

20 rue St-Martin, 4th (01.42.72.25.76) M° Châtelet or Hôtel-de-Ville. **Open** daily noon-2pm, 8-10pm. Closed Aug. **Average** €90. **Credit** AmEx. **Map** J6.

Granted, the victory of getting a good table in a restaurant with a seating caste system is paltry and petty, but this didn't stop us from feeling a sense of satisfaction when we were whisked into the back of this monument to French bistro cooking and culture and seated in the intimate corral created by wood-panelling-and-etched-glass panels. We ordered an apéritif, and the young waiter returned with a bottle of lovely white Mâcon, opened it, served us, and left it in a wine cooler. Throughout the meal, he was pure charm, particularly when dealing with an uncommonly rude Swede who insisted on smoking a stinking stogie, but also in his careful explanation of the entire menu. Dense, rich, coarse terrine laced with chicken livers and served with celeriac rémoulade was superb, as was a delicate, almost-mousse-like mushroom terrine generously topped with fresh morels. Main courses of monkfish in red wine and veal shank à la provençale – a casserole of tender meat in a light and perfectly seasoned tomato sauce with rice – were excellent. Since portions are so generous, few opt for cheese, but when we ordered a nougat glacé to split, the waiter served big portions on two different plates, a classy gesture.

Boyz and the food:
Les Petits Marseillais.
See p29.

"Tucked away amidst the chic boutiques of the 16th, this mock refuge (Chamonix posters, Wooden skis, cow bells crowd the walls) and its genuinely warm welcome will transport you to more Alpine altitudes."
–Time Out Paris Eating & Drinking Guide 2002

Enjoy specialities from the Savoie region, such as fondue savoyarde, raclette valesanne or the famous tartiflette au roblochon accompanied by fine wines from the region (Crépy, Gamay)

Free house apéritif for Time Out readers

19 rue Gustave Courbet, 16th. Mº Victor Hugo or Trocadéro
Tel: 01.47.27.09.84 - Reservation recommended

Benoît has a massive wine list with all sorts of gorgeous bottles, but the house-bottled wines are affordable, with a decent Fleurie going for €30. All told, it's great fun – especially when someone else is picking up the bill, which is a real stinker.

Le Dôme du Marais ★

53bis rue des Francs-Bourgeois, 4th (01.42.74.54.17). M° Rambuteau. **Open** Tue-Sat noon-2.30pm, 7.30-11pm. Closed three weeks in Aug. **Average** €30. **Lunch menu** €15, €23. **Credit** AmEx, MC, V. **Non-smoking room. Map** K6.

On a good day, this is one of the most enjoyable restaurants in Paris. The setting is unique – a remarkable octagonal dining room, lavishly decorated with marble cherubs and gilt walls, crowned by a striking dome (the building predates the Revolution; in the 1920s it served as the auction room for the French state-owned pawnbrokers). The interior courtyard now boasts its own glass roof, but, certainly for a first visit, it's worth asking for a table under the dome. Owner-chef Pierre Lecoutre's cooking seems more confident than ever, featuring robust ingredients such as tête de veau, andouille and lots of game (hare, pigeon and venison on one winter menu). However, recent meals have also included a delicate blanquette de veau, a top-notch sauté of free-range chicken with smoked garlic, saffron milk mushrooms and baby vegetables, and a thick fillet of sea bream with a spiced crust, served on a cauliflower purée. Crêpes of one sort or another are a regular feature – as a starter with pig's trotter and snails, or as a dessert with rhubarb compote and sorbet, while Lecoutre's taste for the exotic manifests itself in the likes of roast figs with lavender honey and star anise ice cream. It's exceptional value for the quality, and portions are generous.

Ma Bourgogne

19 pl des Vosges, 4th (01.42.78.44.64). M° St-Paul or Bastille. **Open** daily noon-1am. Closed Feb. **Average** €33. **Prix fixe** €32. **No credit cards. Map** L6.

On an early summer afternoon the terrace of Ma Bourgogne, under the arcades of place des Vosges, can hardly be bettered. The passing tourist trade dominates and our waiter was happy to provide a flourish of English to welcome us. We were less reassured when his mastery of the electronic ordering pad seemed rudimentary. Somehow the charm of ordering is lost when confronted with low muttering and much scrolling through the extensive menu. With such high-tech wizardry on display, it came as a body blow that the restaurant does not take credit cards. The food was acceptable if uninspiring; a plate of charcuterie was copious but lacked any star item, and the sarladaise salad was short on foie gras. The house speciality steak tartare was well seasoned and excellent, but the accompanying frites squidged rather than crunched. Hot Lyonnais sausage would have been better without the rather insipid gravy. Hankering after a few more sips of our Brouilly (€22.50), we ordered cheese, which had to be chosen individually. The goa[...] being earth-moving[...] said for the bright p[...] Probably best to st[...] wine and soak up [...]

Le Vieux Bis[...]

14 rue du Cloître-[...] M° Cité or St-Michel. **Open** [...] 10.15pm. **Average** €30. **Lunch menu** [...] **Credit** MC, V. **Map** J7.

With a corny name and a location just across the street from Notre-Dame, the odds would seem stacked against this long-running bistro serving even half-decent food. All of which makes it a great surprise to discover that the food here is often excellent, the dining room comfortable and well-run, and prices, given the quality, quite reasonable. Regulars quibble over which dining room is more desirable – the front one is more spacious, but the back room is cosy and its diners more likely to be French – but everyone agrees that the tiny terrace out front is a fine spot for a romantic meal in good weather, and also that the boeuf bourguignon is superb. Start with sliced pistachio-studded sausage and potatoes dressed in vinegar and oil or the sublime pâté de tête, chunks of head cheese in a dark amber-coloured beef aspic, and then sample the sole meunière, the bourguignon, a first-rate rib of beef for two, or maybe scallops sautéed in whisky. The house Bordeaux, a Château Layauga 1999, at a very reasonable €25, is excellent and goes down a treat with cheese, or choose from a short list of homely desserts including crème caramel.

5th Arrondissement

Le Buisson Ardent ★

25 rue Jussieu, 5th (01.43.54.93.02). M° Jussieu. **Open** Mon-Fri noon-2pm, 7.30-10.30pm. Closed Aug and one week at Christmas. **Prix fixe** €28. **Lunch menu** €15. **Credit** AmEx, DC, MC, V. **Map** K8.

The staple lunchtime trade of Jussieu academics at this old-world bistro generally gives way to a less highbrow clientele in the evening, so we were surprised to find ourselves seated for our evening meal next to a loud would-be intellectual holding forth, glass in hand, to a bored table of diners. Seeking solace in the food, we were impressed by the fine creamy tomato gazpacho topped with a basil sorbet, as well as a light prawn beignet, served with vegetables marinated in rich olive oil and scattered with chives. Main courses spanned some familiar territory with a hefty steak in pepper sauce, and the excellent juicy morsels of pork tenderloin in a cep sauce, soaked up by fluffy polenta. The tuna had been seared – a delicate operation – but was not overcooked and magically retained optimum juiciness. We were a little disappointed by the desserts: a passable, syrupy poires au vin and tarte Tatin in a sad caramel sauce. On the whole, though, this was an enjoyable meal in congenial surroundings.

e ★

rmain, 5th (01.43.54.30.23). *rt-Mutualité.* **Open** Tue-Fri 12.15-2.15pm, pm; Sat 7.45-11pm. **Average** €46. **Prix fixe** inner only). **Lunch menu** €29. **Credit** MC, V. **-smoking room**. **Map** K7.

very ten years or so since René Cinquin opened this place in 1957, the staff have gathered for a photo that's framed and added to the others hanging by the door. As far as change is concerned, that is pretty much that. These days it's not René but his son Jean-Paul who chats with the diners but there's still the same heavy silver cutlery, thick starched linen, black-jacketed waiters and honest hard work in the kitchen. Our starters – slices of tangy black radish in a cream and chive sauce and a sizzling plate of oyster mushrooms – were simple in a winsome kind of way. But the coq au vin? This is the reason for coming here. The secret of the dark, succulent sauce is no stock, just a good 20 minutes constantly stirring flour and butter over the feeblest of flames before adding the wine – just as René's granny taught him to do. Similar skills go into the boeuf bourguignon. After all that, we were expecting something a bit more grandmotherly from the rice pudding. A portly fellow diner had the better idea of ordering the cheese, which impressively came in two courses: cow's milk and goat's milk.

Flair's flair in the kitchens of **L'Equitable**.

L'Equitable ★

1 rue des Fossés-St-Marcel, 5th (01.43.31.69.20) M° Censier Daubenton or St-Marcel. **Open** Tue-Sat noon-2.30pm, 7.30-11pm. **Prix fixe** €29. **Lunch menu** €20.50, €26. **Credit** MC, V. **Non-smoking room**. **Map** K9.

The talent of chef Yves Mutin makes this quiet but popular bistro well worth seeking out, especially since the prix fixe menu offers amazing value for money. Beyond the exposed stone walls that make this old auberge seem as if it should be in the French countryside, and Mutin's fascination with antique scales, there's not much decor, but the first-rate food and an interesting crowd compensate. During a recent dinner, we loved starters of asparagus with poached egg in mousseline sauce and a superb rabbit and pine-nut terrine, and the generous and attractive presentation continued through mains of veal steak with baby vegetables in pesto and a cod in sauce vierge with anchovy-spiked aubergine purée. Finish up with the roasted peach or the crêpes with fresh fruit and lemon cream.

Les Fontaines

9 rue Soufflot, 5th (01.43.26.42.80). RER Luxembourg. **Open** Mon-Sat noon-3pm, 7-11pm. Closed 1 May, 25 Dec, 1 Jan. **Average** €35. **Credit** DC, MC, V. **Map** J8.

Walk past Les Fontaines at breakfast time and it resembles any local Parisian café. Come mealtime, though, and there's not a place to spare, as the tables, transformed by white tablecloths, fill with local worthies from the mairie, hairdressers, publishers, foodies and knowing tourists. We've sometimes found the food unspectacular but our latest visit laid doubts to rest as, after oysters and the prettily presented chicory, walnut and blue cheese salad (any health benefits negated by the huge dollop of mayonnaise), the regular steaks and calf's liver were supplemented by autumn specials that show they know their game. We dug into pheasant with muscat and raisin sauce, and tender, roast noisettes de biche in a red wine and blood-based sauce with all the trimmings: roast apple, red-wine-soaked pear, lozenges of carrot and celeriac purée. This left us with room only to share a sundae glass of mousse aux deux chocolats and finish off our well-priced 1993 Givry (€28). Reserve, and come with time to spare – this is slow food territory.

L'Intermède

4 bd du Port-Royal, 5th (01.47.07.08.99). M° Gobelins. **Open** Tue-Sat noon-2.30pm, 7.30-10.30pm; Sun noon-2.30pm. Closed three weeks in Aug. **Average** €23. **Prix fixe** (dinner only) €20.60, €27.50. **Lunch menu** €12.50, €17. **Credit** AmEx, MC, V. **Map** J9.

L'Intermède takes its classical cooking seriously. When we visited in November, we found that an entire game section had been added to the carte. The hare terrine lacked a little savagery, but the pheasant was both elegant and delicious: succulent leg and breast joints in a golden vin de paille sauce, accompanied by neatly sculpted vegetables and a sautée of lightly tossed morsels of cep, chanterelle and tiny mousseron mushrooms. From the set menu, we chose six, sizzling, good-sized snails and a herby

roast rack of lamb and then shared an assiette gourmande of different desserts, comprising a mini flan, tiny apple tart, chocolate fondant and other nibbles. The wine list is short and a little on the pricey side but yielded us a worthwhile Maranges 1999 1er cru red Burgundy. The only problem here is the atmosphere. The cooking is some of the most proficient in the area and everything is present and correct, but there's something ineffably morose that wafts out from the coffered ceiling, dark panelling and near-silent service. Bring your own entertainment.

Le Moulin à Vent

20 rue des Fossés-St-Bernard, 5th (01.43.54.99.37). M° Jussieu. **Open** Tue-Fri noon-2pm, 7.30-11pm; Sat 7.30-11pm. Closed Aug, Christmas. **Average** €50. **Credit** MC, V. **Wheelchair access. Map** K8.

It was good to see that our ample figures were by far the thinnest seated on the leather banquettes of the welcoming old-world moulin otherwise known as Chez Henri. The quivering layers of the lunchtime business crowd were obviously happy to rediscover the classical menu of old favourites, with an emphasis on quality Salers beef. We plunged in with a dozen Burgundy escargots, and a salad topped with warm gizzards. We have eaten more pungent snails and fresher, more generously topped salads, but we tucked in with nostalgic indulgence. Main courses included a predictably fine, spoon-tender Chateaubriand, which was rare as ordered but not hot through to the centre and served with a creamy homemade béarnaise, and a slightly unmemorable slice of foie de veau, piquantly deglazed with vinegar. The accompanying golden, sautéed potatoes were nonetheless classy and outstanding. To finish our meal, an exemplary tarte Tatin and a cheese course of excellent roquefort or camembert encouraged us to order more of the fruity Brouilly. The welcome was comfortingly warm, and time has happily caught up with the previously hefty bill in this windmill of Left Bank tradition.

Le Pré Verre ★

8 rue Thénard, 5th (01.43.54.59.47). M° Maubert-Mutualité. **Open** Mon 7.30-10.30pm; Tue-Sat noon-2pm, 7.30-10.30pm. Closed first two weeks in Aug. **Prix fixe** €24 (dinner only). **Lunch menu** €12. **Credit** MC, V. **Non-smoking room. Map** J7.

As soon as you've tucked into a superb starter, such as the sautée of baby squid with a terrine of lentils and squid on salad leaves dressed in sesame vinaigrette, you'll understand why this newly opened bistro-à-vins has become a roaring hit. Spare though the setting might be, the place has been packed ever since talented chef Philippe Delacourcelle opened shop. The blackboard menu changes daily, but we were seduced by ravioli stuffed with snails in a green aniseed-spiked cream sauce, and delighted by the roast suckling pig and a succulent veal steak accompanied by a richly flavoured purée of celeriac, potato and almonds. Desserts were similarly inspired, lovely to behold and delicious, including strawberries marinated with flat-leaf parsley and a brilliant croustillant of pineapple with stem ginger. The weakest part of our splendid meal was the wines, neither of which – we tried a Saumur

Champigny and a Chinon – was very good. Service is often overwhelmed, too, but if you score better than we did with the wine list, odds are you won't mind. Book now.

Le Reminet

3 rue des Grands-Degrés, 5th (01.44.07.04.24). M° Maubert-Mutualité or St-Michel. **Open** Mon, Thur-Sun noon-2pm, 7.30-11pm. Closed two weeks in Aug, two weeks in Feb. **Average** €34. **Prix fixe** €17 (Mon, Thur dinner only), €50. **Lunch menu** €13 (Mon, Thur, Fri). **Credit** MC, V. **Map** J7.

A cut above your average bistro, this little gem on a quiet street near Shakespeare & Co has put its prices up since the advent of the euro, but frankly it's worth it. Behind the velvet curtain are eight tables (the largest seats six) with crisp white table-linen in a room lit by three small chandeliers. This restaurant really knows its wine: the Savigny-lès-Beaune recommended by our waitress to accompany a difficult threesome of smoked haddock, guinea fowl and whiting mains was the making of our meal, revealing intricate flavours that brought out qualities in all our dishes; it was also served correctly in balloon-like Burgundy glasses. For starters, the white asparagus with its 'curry' sauce was a revelation that proved that the current fad for this flavour can produce successful results. The red onion baked in its skin and stuffed with Burgundy snails, mushrooms and serrano ham was nuttier and drier than we'd expected but still enjoyable. The day's special of whiting was simply sublime, served on a moist bed of aubergine caviar with a razor-thin slice of crisp aubergine skin as a strongly flavoured

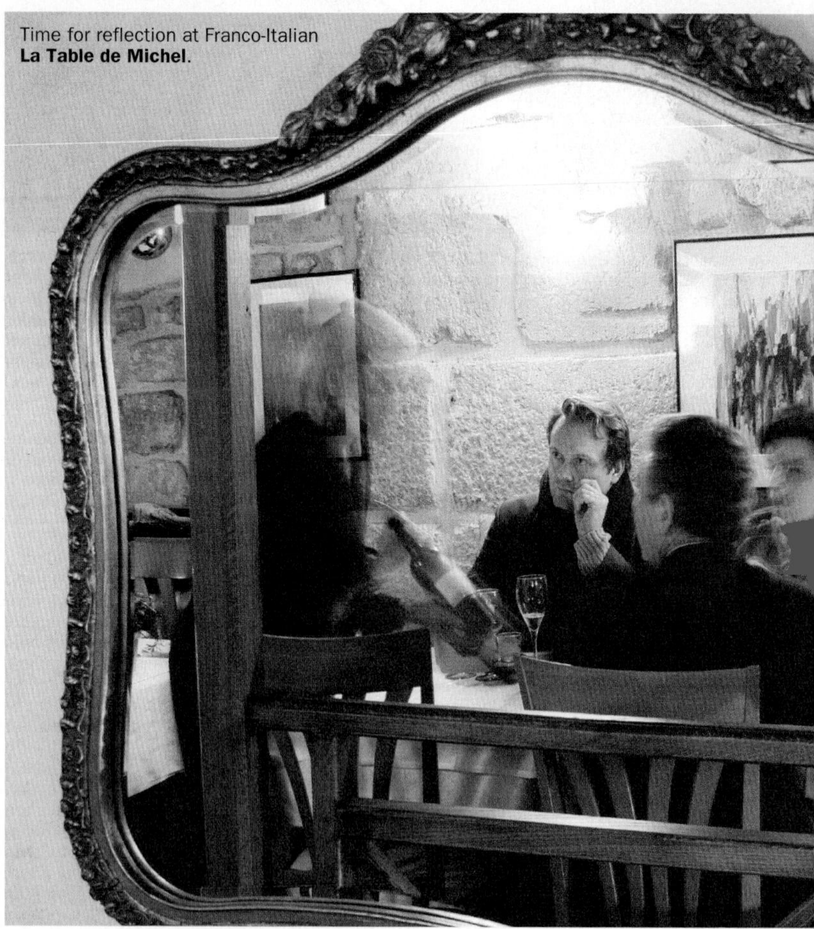

Time for reflection at Franco-Italian **La Table de Michel**.

adornment, the guinea fowl delicious in its cream sauce with carrots, turnips and parsley. Inventive desserts include a 'cake' of sponge fingers, chocolate ganache and coffee mascarpone cream layered with hints of cinnamon and liquorice, and a chestnut cake macerated with diced pears and grapes. Chef Hugues Gournay ended the evening serving coffee, taking credit cards, and politely ignoring the boorish Englishman at the neighbouring table who would have deserved a little Parisian disdain.

La Rôtisserie de Beaujolais

19 quai de la Tournelle, 5th (01.43.54.17.47). M° Jussieu. **Open** Tue-Sun noon-2.15pm, 7.30-10.15pm. **Average** €35. **Credit** MC, V. **Map** K7.

Traditional dishes such as onion soup, snails in garlic, coq au vin, Lyonnais sausage, confit de canard and grills are the order of the day in this jolly bistro overlooking the Seine. Although owner Claude Terrail also has the nearby, and much loftier, Tour d'Argent, this little sister is more country comfort than cut crystal, which means warm leeks in a creamy vinaigrette, oyster mushrooms with garlic and parsley as starters, and super mashed spuds partnering plump chicken legs hot from the rôtisserie for mains (the duckling and pigeon with garlic potatoes looked great, too). Lamb navarin en croûte has baby carrots, beans and mangetout and comes with a pastry béret and a gravy that just has to be mopped up with chunky wholemeal bread (basket at hand). Desserts run from tarte Tartin to titanic floating islands. Decor is cheery – yellow-checked cloths, walls adorned with autographs and photos of celebrities and staff – and the service is a perfect match. The Beaujolais goes down a treat, too.

La Table de Michel ★

13 quai de la Tournelle, 5th (01.44.07.17.57). M° Maubert-Mutualité. **Open** Mon 7-11pm; Tue-Sat noon-2.30pm, 7-10.30pm. Closed Aug. **Average** €35. **Prix fixe** €27. **Lunch menu** €19. **Credit** AmEx, MC, V. **Non-smoking room. Map** K7.

The Michel in question was previously the owner and chef of a popular trad French restaurant in the Butte-aux-Cailles. Now he has returned to his Italian origins and is doing his personal take on Franco-Italian fusion cuisine. Delicate crostini as an appetiser were followed by a tomato and mozzarella salad, in which the peeled tomatoes formed an artistic dome over the buffalo cheese, bathed in a rich basil and balsamic vinegar dressing. A luscious feuilleté d'escargots was equally successful. Our mains included a perfectly cooked, pungent cep risotto and a winning tagliatelle au foie gras, served in a filo pastry basket, the rich sauce enhanced by slices of foie gras. We were tempted by brie stuffed with roquefort and walnuts, a clever variant on the Italian mascarpone/gorgonzola version, but went for panna cotta, a classic preparation of the creamy vanilla dessert with a punchy bitter cherry coulis. With a bottle of exceptional Chianti and a bill of around €107 for two we will be back for more.

6th Arrondissement

Au 35

35 rue Jacob, 6th (01.42.60.23.24). M° St-Germain-des-Prés. **Open** daily noon-2.30pm, 7-11.30pm. **Average** €35. **Lunch menu** €16, €20 (Mon-Fri), €28 (Sat, Sun). **Credit** AmEx, DC, MC,V. **Map** H6.

You might expect St-Germain to be full of bistros such as this and yet they've become a surprisingly rare breed. An endearingly cramped interior (the kitchen is up a flight of perilous stairs), murals on the walls and Yves Saint Laurent's *Love* prints made as New Year wishes set the scene for the tweedy publishers and local ladies who pile in for the lunchtime set menu (apparently dinner is more international). If many customers are clearly regulars, the

Montmartre's Vegetarian Restaurant

24 rue de La Vieuville, 18th
Mº Abbesses Tel: 01.42.58.15.57
Open Mon-Sat noon-2.30pm,
evenings 7.30-11.30pm (Winter 7-10.30pm)
Sunday noon-10.30pm
Complimentary tea/coffee with this ad

"Probably the best vegetarian feast in Paris"
- Time Out Paris Eating & Drinking Guide 2002

La Victoire Suprême du cœur

VEGETARIAN RESTAURANT

CENTRAL PARIS
41 Rue des Bourdonnais, 1st
Mº Châtelet
Tel: 01.40.41.93.95

Monday to Saturday: Noon - 2.30pm & 7pm - 10pm

friendly patronne was genuinely welcoming to us first-timers, coming to check we were content. The food echoes the mood: simple, French home cooking with plenty of personalised touches. We began with a nicely crisp green bean salad with parmesan, then main courses of chicken in a tarragon cream sauce with basmati rice and a flaky, snowy-white steamed cod fillet with an interesting, if slightly dry, purée of potatoes and black olives. Finish with a moelleux au chocolat, pink grapefruit salad with honey or brie de meaux and a green salad. The house carafe of red cabernet sauvignon cost a satisfactory €9.

Allard ★

41 rue St-André-des-Arts, 6th (01.43.26.48.23). M° Odéon or RER St-Michel. **Open** Mon-Sat noon-2.30pm, 7-11pm. Closed three weeks in Aug. **Average** €50. **Prix fixe** €30.50. **Lunch menu** €22.90. **Credit** AmEx, DC, MC, V. **Map** H7.

If St-Germain seems to be turning into a suburb of Milan with the proliferation of Italian restaurants, it's reassuring to come across a truly excellent example of a traditional bistro. With its vanilla-coloured walls and a coat rack in the narrow hall connecting the two small dining rooms (the front one has more atmosphere), Allard has a delicious pre-war feel, a first impression that is confirmed by the kitchen itself. It sends out glorious Gallic grub that's exactly what everyone dreams of finding in Paris. Winter is the perfect time of the year for this place – start with sliced Lyonnais sausage studded with pistachios and served with potato salad in delicious vinaigrette, or maybe a sauté of wild mushrooms, and then chose between one of the three classics: roast shoulder of lamb, roast Bresse chicken with sautéed ceps or roast duck with olives. All three are superb, but be forewarned that portions are enormous. Finish up with the tarte fine de pommes and go with one of the good, if slightly pricey, Bordeaux.

Au Bon Saint-Pourçain

10bis rue Servandoni, 6th (01.43.54.93.63). M° St-Sulpice or Mabillon. **Open** Mon-Sat noon-2.30pm, 7.30-10.30pm. Closed Aug. **Average** €35. **No credit cards**. **Map** H7.

Heavy velvet curtains shield the entrance to this modest but charming little restaurant, where all the cooking is done in a broom-cupboard-sized kitchen. Once you've found a space on the rather broken-down old banquettes, wry boss François will welcome you with a small glass of white St-Pourçain wine while you study the blackboard menu, which changes daily. There are no surprises here, and this is what makes the large clique of locals so happy. They can also drink too much wine without spending a fortune, since the St-Pourçain is very cheap (for something better – not a bad idea – order the Irancy). So go in anticipation of better-than-average home cooking rather than a gastronomic feast, and you'll have a fine night out. A nicely made terrine and marinated leeks are among the better starters, while the regulars are keen on boeuf aux olives, chicken with tarragon or brandade de morue as main courses. Most seem happy to finish up their wine and have a smoke (and it is smoky here) instead of dessert, but the crème brûlée is fine.

Les Bouquinistes

53 quai des Grands-Augustins, 6th (01.43.25.45.94/ www.guysavoy.com). M° St-Michel. **Open** Mon-Fri noon-2.30pm, 7-11pm; Sat 7-11pm. **Average** €53. **Lunch menu** €24, €27. **Credit** AmEx, DC, MC, V. **Map** J6.

There are good and not-so-good things about this Guy Savoy offshoot. The food is smart and seasonally driven. The sunny-yellow walls studded with mirrors and multicoloured 'frames' make a fitting partner. It's the uneven service that jars; the wad of young waiters could do with some buffing up because they're a poor match for the food. Dishes might include avocado and prawns in radicchio leaves with a curried herring sauce; tuna tartare with soy bean and sunflower sprouts; grilled saddle of rabbit with carrots and pearl-like steamed radish; and roast John Dory with capers, olives, yellow pepper and olive-oil-mashed potato. Desserts are crowd-pleasers – lime macaroon filled with regal mango sorbet and served with coconut cream, or a blood-red 'cappuccino' of sour cherries and strawberries. Nice, too, is the offer of wine by the glass (starting at €4.60), or better still a bottle of chilled red Sancerre at €34. The word has long since spread: on our visit the bulk of the diners were English-speakers.

Bouillon Racine

3 rue Racine, 6th (01.44.32.15.60). M° Cluny-La Sorbonne. **Open** daily noon-2.30pm, 7-11pm. **Average** €35. **Prix fixe** €25. **Lunch menu** €15 (Mon-Fri). **Credit** AmEx, MC, V. **Wheelchair access**. **Map** J7.

A change of management for the Bouillon Racine has done away with the Belgian theme, with a return to classic French. The 1906 art nouveau decor is one of the most spectacular in Paris, and this former worker's soup kitchen caters for a guaranteed tourist trade who come to admire the magnificent interior. It is therefore a shame that, given such a head start, the kitchen cannot provide a more exciting offering. Our marinated salmon was the better of the first courses; a pig's trotter 'terrine' was in fact a fried croquette. Main courses of lamb shank and 'spiced' roast chicken were lacklustre, unless attractive presentation and excellent service can be said to save a meal. By now the loud and intrusive world music was beginning to pall. What a strange idea to try to create an alternative atmosphere in a building that provides its own so effectively. Downing our last sips of excellent Bandol rosé we left puddings to our fellow diners, and paid a bill which reflected the decor and location more than the cooking.

Brasserie Fernand

13 rue Guisarde, 6th (01.43.54.61.47). M° Mabillon. **Open** Mon-Sat noon-2.30pm, 7pm-midnight. Closed Aug. **Average** €30. **Credit** MC, V. **Wheelchair access**. **Map** H7.

In the throng of restaurants around the Marché St-Germain, Brasserie Fernand (more a bistro despite the name) is a friendly, relaxed place unlike some of its more cliquey neighbours, falling somewhere in the middle of those that cater to tourists, to style fiends, to expats and the wilfully shabby bistro that panders to hip St-Germain intellectuals. They were quite happy to let us chat well into the afternoon, as the owner behind the bar that divides the two dining rooms burst out with occasional peals of song. The blackboard reads like a round-up of bistro and regional standards: simple dishes prepared with care and some imagination. A Provençal-inspired 'tarte' consisted of warm goat's cheese and pistou over gently melted courgettes, onions and tomatoes atop filo pastry. Oxtail Parmentier was an elegant sandwich of succulent, shredded stewed meat between two layers of purée and its generously truffled gravy; the entrecôte came with a pile of bone marrow and excellent purée. Desserts focus on fruit and ice cream themes: vanilla ice and black cherries in kirsch, fromage frais and berry coulis.

Aux Charpentiers

10 rue Mabillon, 6th (01.43.26.30.05). Mº Mabillon or St-Germain-des-Prés. **Open** daily noon-2.30pm, 7-11.30pm. Closed 25 Dec. **Average** €32. **Prix fixe** €25 (dinner only). **Lunch menu** €19. **Credit** AmEx, DC, MC, V. **Map** H7.

It was 25 years since we had last eaten at Aux Charpentiers, when it was a cheap and cheerful student haunt overlooking the Marché St-Germain. Now, with unchanged, vintage decor, it has become a serious Parisian bistro, where simple hearty dishes are prepared with unusual care and served by a friendly team, which knows how to welcome tourists and regulars alike. We began our meal with a salad of crisply fried sweetbreads and a compote de lapereau – a highly seasoned rabbit terrine with an earthenware jar of crunchy gherkins on the side. We chose the plat du jour of stuffed cabbage (the ultimate comfort food) and a more elaborate duck with olives and port, which was well-cooked, but with just a touch of tourist blandness. Resisting the great-looking rum babas, we plumped for a slice of well-aged brie. Looking around at the splendid zinc bar and happy St-Germain crowd, we vowed not to wait another 25 years before returning, particularly as even à la carte prices remain surprisingly competitive.

Chez Marcel

7 rue Stanislas, 6th (01.45.48.29.94). Mº Notre-Dame-des-Champs. **Open** Mon-Fri noon-2pm, 7.30-10pm. Closed Aug. **Average** €27. **Lunch menu** €14. **Credit** MC, V. **Map** G8.

This tiny, turn-of-the-20th-century gem serves food in its own image – strong on tradition, taste and offbeat charm, savoured on our visit by an unhurried, regular lunchtime crowd. We half-expected a shot of absinthe to accompany the pungent old-style staples – pig's ear in jelly, beef brawn terrine and the rather fearsome house speciality, gras double – Lyonnais-style stewed tripe. Sounds offal? The faint-hearted will appreciate artichoke leaves with vinaigrette, tarragon chicken fricassée or steaks'n'sauce. A terrine of salt pork and lentils was sweetly seasoned with fresh dill and basil in creamy lemon dressing. Pink slices of duck magret were magically crisp on the outside, meltingly tender within, on a superb bitter orange sauce. Fish dishes are equally robust, including skate in roquefort sauce with tagliatelle-style courgettes. 'Seasonal cheese' (a generous slab of gorgonzola), and a frequently replenished basket of white and walnut bread were welcome touches. Torn between melt-in-the-mouth cherry or apple tarts (the latter with crumbly almond topping), we were served both, unprompted. The full-bodied wine of the week, a 2000 Moulin à Vent, held its own in such flavoursome company. Beef tripe all round next time.

L'Epi Dupin ★

11 rue Dupin, 6th (01.42.22.64.56). Mº Sèvres-Babylone. **Open** Mon 7-10.30pm; Tue-Fri noon-2.30pm, 7-10.30pm. Closed Aug. **Prix fixe** €29.80. **Lunch menu** €19.80. **Credit** MC, V. **Map** G8.

We were curious to see what had become of this sophisticated little bistro, one of the squadrons set up by owner-chefs in the early 90s. The answer seems to be that François Pasteau is still on form, combining terroir with invention and tangy mixes of sweet and savoury. Two neat bundles of green asparagus roast in just a whisper of filo pastry, on a lovely ginger cream with straggles of red cabbage, and a Charlotte of sardines (marinated fillets over aubergines and tomatoes with a clever herb emulsion) were two from a tempting list of starters. Bread

How to Eat **Artichokes**

Popularised in France by Catherine de Médicis, this flower-like member of the thistle family has been credited with aphrodisiac and antidepressant properties. This might explain its popularity in bistros, where the big round Breton artichoke or pointier-leaved Laon variety is most often cooked whole and served with a vinaigrette or mayonnaise. Start with the lower outside leaves, dipping the tender part into the sauce and sucking it off (sexily, if you can) before discarding the rest of the leaf. Continue until you reach the hairy centre, known as the choke. Use a small spoon to scrape off the choke and reveal the heart, which is the finest part of the artichoke. Eat this with a knife and fork, dipping the chunks into the sauce.

Laid-back in St-Germain: **Brasserie Fernand**. *See p39.*

is homemade and, unlike in many more traditional establishments, vegetables are plentiful. For mains, a 'millefeuille' of excellent-quality sea bream sandwiched with tangy black pudding on a bed of savoy cabbage worked remarkably well. Pigeon was neatly jointed and juicy if a little fatty, served on a pile of green broad beans with mild white onions. Desserts were satisfying, too: we adored the combination of orange ice cream and a gently caramelised pain perdu made with spice bread. True, the tables are a little too crammed-in, but staff are friendly (and try their best to translate for tables of English speakers) and the price is unbelievable for the quality.

Josephine 'Chez Dumonet'

117 rue du Cherche-Midi, 6th (01.45.48.52.40). M° Duroc. **Open** Mon-Fri 12.30-2.30pm, 7.30-11pm. **Closed** one week in Feb, all Aug. **Average** €50. **Credit** AmEx, MC,V. **Map** F8.

Behind crisp white curtains lies an interior with cracked-tile floor, frosted tulip lamps, huge mirrors and acres of warm wood ministered by a handful of courteous waiters. This trad terrain with atmosphere, not attitude, doesn't come cheaply, but the English-speaking tourists and incessantly chatty locals don't mind because Jean-Christian Dumonet's cooking seems almost worth it. Black truffles from Quercy starred in his line-up of winter dishes and the creamy omelette generously studded with this earthy tuber is a great, if extravagant, starter. Less expensive are a chicory and roquefort salad or slices of warm artichoke hearts in lime butter. For mains try plump scallops à la provençale, an ample duck confit or crowd-pleasing boeuf bourguignon. The gamey hare or pigeon millefeuille are, in season, hard to resist – and, if you find yourself dithering, half-portions are available. For a grand finale try the puffed-up Grand Marnier soufflé.

Le Mâchon d'Henri

8 rue Guisarde, 6th (01.43.29.08.70). M° Mabillon. **Open** daily noon-2.15pm, 7-11.15pm. **Average** €24. **Credit** MC, V. **Map** H7.

This bistro in the heart of St-Germain immediately put us in a good mood – firstly it was open for Sunday lunch, an increasingly rare phenomenon, and secondly we were given a plate of outstanding saucisson sec while we looked at the menu and enjoyed a chilled bottle of fruity Julienas (€20). In an area where tourist tat wins out over gastronomic excellence, this tiny bistro provides a reasonably priced selection of traditional rustic dishes. We began with a ramekin of escargots, doused in garlic butter and served with potatoes, and a Desperate Dan-style plate of marrow bones, accompanied by wholemeal toast and coarse salt. Main courses were equally authentic, with a generous, well-seasoned bowl of Caen-style tripe, and a superbly cooked magret de canard, served whole rather than fanned out on the plate in the modern fashion. The gratin dauphinois was wholesome rather than inspiring, but by then we were already on good terms with the charming waiter and the couple opposite, something which is inevitable in such intimate surroundings. Rather than attack a homely pudding we plumped for a serious vieille prune digestif, which was rightly recommended by a fellow diner.

HÔTEL
ARVOR
Saint-Georges
★★★

A charming, typically Parisian hotel between Montmartre and the shopping district around Opéra

8 rue Laferrière, 9th. M° St Georges

Tel: 01.48.78.60.92

Fax: 01.48.78.16.52

E-mail: info@arvor-hotel-paris.com

www.arvor-hotel-paris.com

SPECIAL RATES FOR TIME OUT READERS:

• Single: €80 • Double: €95 • Triple: €120

Le Parc Aux Cerfs

50 rue Vavin, 6th (01.43.54.87.83). M° Vavin or Notre-Dame-des-Champs. **Open** daily noon-2.30pm, 7.45-10.30pm. Closed Aug. **Average** €36. **Prix fixe** €26, €31 (dinner only). **Lunch menu** €19.50, €25. **Credit** MC, V. **Non-smoking room. Map** G8.

The most attractive aspect of this 'deer park' near Montparnasse is the tiny inner courtyard, which makes an ideal spot for al fresco dining. The €25 set menu is charmingly served and good value, carefully prepared with some imaginative touches. Our first courses were excellent examples of modern bistro cuisine – a slice of serrano ham wrapped around some tasty lentils and topped with a finely timed poached egg, and a salad combining different sorts of crunchy cabbage topped with prawns in a sweet, caramelised dressing. Main courses were more ordinary. The chunky magret de canard on its base of spring vegetables was slightly tough, while a fine piece of rump steak in port sauce was accompanied by a tower of gratin, which cunningly combined both apples and potatoes. Puddings included an excellent crème brûlée speckled with vanilla and a smooth nougat glacé surrounded by a perky orange coulis. With a bottle of well-chosen Petit Chablis, this was a meal that the local French crowd no doubt would describe as 'correct', and on a balmy summer's evening it definitely hit the spot.

Aux Saveurs de Claude

12 rue Stanislas, 6th (01.45.44.41.74). M° Vavin. **Open** Mon-Sat noon-2pm, 7.45-10.15pm. Closed two weeks Aug, one week Christmas, one week Easter. **Average** €30. **Prix fixe** (dinner only) €25, €30. **Lunch menu** €20, €26. **Credit** AmEx, MC, V. **Non-smoking room. Map** G8.

Run by a charming and talented young couple who sincerely want you to have a good meal (and you will), this sweet mini-bistro in Montparnasse is worth wending your way to the neighbourhood for. With parquet floors, soft lighting, vanilla-painted wainscotting and mirrors, the intimate room is a relaxing and pleasant place to dine. Recent starters on the blackboard have included a fine fricassée of ceps and other wild mushrooms, and ravioles de Royans (tiny ravioli stuffed with cheese) with yellow chanterelles. Typical main courses are the entrecôte with bordelaise sauce and puréed potato, veal kidneys sautéed with wild mushrooms and chestnuts, and salmon with an unusual 'gâteau' of rice mixed with fromage blanc. As part of the attentive care you will receive here, staff also let you in on the dish, dessert or even coffee 'du moment'. Desserts include a first-rate tarte Tatin or an equally delicious chocolate tart. Book ahead.

Le Timbre ★

3 rue Ste-Beuve, 6th (01.45.49.10.40). M° Vavin. **Open** Mon-Fri noon-2pm, 7.30-11pm; Sat 7.30-11pm. **Average** €30. **Lunch menu** €20. **Credit** MC, V. **Map** G8.

The name tells only half of the story here, since this place may well be as small as a stamp, but the kitchen cooks large and well, doing an excellent market menu that changes daily. Highlights of a recent meal included a delicious terrine de campagne and fresh tomato soup brightened with dill, coriander and basil as starters, followed by tuna steak with tomatoes and mousseron mushrooms in a light vinaigrette, pork cheeks braised in red wine with mash, and pan-fried salmon with mangetout. Cheeses come from British cheese shop Neal's Yard Dairy, and include stilton and a strong farmhouse cheddar. The charming Mancunian owner runs the tiny dining room and also suggests perfect seasonal tipples such as an Argentinian Pinot Grigio or a thoughtfully chilled Beaumes-de-Venise. With a Chet Baker soundtrack, soft lighting and a low-key, hip crowd, this place is a great night out.

Restaurant Wadja ★

10 rue de la Grande-Chaumière, 6th (01.46.33.02.02). M° Vavin. **Open** Mon 7.30-11pm; Tue-Sat noon-2pm, 7.30-11pm. **Average** €33. **Prix fixe** €13.57. **Credit** MC, V. **Map** G9.

Striking the right balance between simplicity and sophistication, this creamy yellow bistro has become one of our favourite destinations for Saturday lunch, when our fellow diners are likely to include families with young children, solitary artists from the studios next door, and foreign visitors. A la carte you might find foie gras sautéed with prunes, monkfish with bacon, seasonal game or a classic agneau de sept heures, but we usually opt for the daily-changing menu du jour. With a choice of two starters, two main courses (one meat, one fish) and two desserts for only €13.57 (which laudably didn't get rounded up with the euro), this surely has to be one of the greatest bargains in town. On our most recent visit tangy, brick-red fish soup, triangular parcels of mozzarella in crispy filo pastry with a salad of mixed young leaves, country sausages with purée, and a fillet of grenadier with tagliatelle and mushrooms; lozenges of creamy raspberry mousse and a tangy lemon meringue pie were typical of an offer that is always fresh and different. This is also a place for some interesting wine discoveries. There is a well-laid-out list but we usually trust Madame to produce something that will go with our meal: on one occasion a little-known white Burgundy, on another an unfiltered, non-chaptalised, organic red Bergerac.

7th Arrondissement

L'Affriolé ★

17 rue Malar, 7th (01.44.18.31.33). M° La Tour-Maubourg or Invalides. **Open** Tue-Sat noon-2.30pm, 7.30-10.30pm. **Prix fixe** €30. **Lunch menu** €20. **Credit** MC, V. **Map** D6.

Arriving here on a warm summer's night with rather wan appetites, we quickly found ourselves delighted anew by the first-rate cooking of chef Thierry Verola. The restaurant was completely booked with a crowd that ran from a table of four young men sporting new Prada shirts and a group of happy

Danes to decorous couples in freshly pressed linen. What everyone seems to appeciate is not only the remarkable value for money offered by the €30 prix fixe, but the underlying generosity of a meal here. As soon as you're seated, delicious country bread is offered with radishes and tapenade, and dessert is followed by a variation on mignardises – in our case, four tiny pots of milk chocolate, dark chocolate, vanilla and coffee cream, along with dried apricots and dates. A blackboard with market suggestions supplements the main menu, and starters such as house-smoked salmon with a salad of ratte potatoes in pepper oil with whipped cream, and gazpacho were both first-rate. A main course of red mullet with andouille was original, though the tripe sausage slightly overwhelmed the fish, while saddle of lamb was a succulent steak, perfectly cooked and served with an interesting garnish of mushrooms filled with sautéed fennel bulb. The brief wine list offers a variety of very fairly priced bottles that are well-suited to Verola's innovative modern bistro cooking, including an excellent white Côtes du Rhône for €19 and a fine Morgon.

Altitude 95

1st level, Tour Eiffel, Champ de Mars, 7th (01.45.55.20.04). M° Trocadéro or Bir Hakeim.
Open daily noon-2.45pm, 7-11.30pm. **Average** €50. **Lunch menu** (Mon-Sat) €19.50, €26.70. **Prix fixe** €50 (dinner and Sun lunch). **Credit** AmEx, DC, MC, V. **Wheelchair access**. **Map** C6.

Forgive us our childish glee, but we were pretty thrilled to eat on the first floor of the Eiffel Tower with a window seat overlooking the Pont d'Iéna and Trocadéro, and equally happy to dodge the queue for the lift. Like the haute cuisine restaurant a level up, Altitude 95 has a Jules Verne-themed decor involving lots of metal, nuts and bolts and barometers. A la carte is expensive but there are two lunch prix fixes with two choices on each. Both our soups were great – a crunchy vegetable version with peas, carrots, onions, leeks and croutons, and a creamy potage Parmentier, potato soup dribbled with basil-specked olive oil. Mains, however, were a bit disappointing – we suspected that both the chicken fricassée with green peppercorns and over-salted potato wedges and the shoulder of lamb in tomato sauce with far from al dente pasta had been cooked en masse. Things looked up again with the two-tone chocolate mousse with crème anglaise and a wonderfully moist, caramelly tarte Tatin chosen à la carte to supplement the 'formule duo'. We also thoroughly enjoyed our half-bottle of Brouilly for €16. By far the best thing about our meal here was the service. The two waiters and receptionist struck just the right balance of speaking English and French for our respective levels, cracked jokes that made us laugh and generally seemed in the ebullient mood that being 95m above Paris can induce.

L'Ami Jean ★

27 rue Malar, 7th (01.47.05.86.89). M° Invalides.
Open Tue-Sat noon-2pm, 7pm-midnight. Closed Aug. **Average** €35. **Prix fixe** €28. **Credit** MC, V. **Map** D6.

This long-running Basque address in one of the most alluring little streets in Paris has suddenly become a huge hit after the arrival of La Régalade's former sous-chef, Stéphane Jégo. The dark, crowded dining room is unlikely to win you over at first glance, but once seated and maybe sipping a glass of nice white wine from the Béarn, you'll start to sense the honest bonhomie of the place. Excellent bread from Poujauran, a street away, was perfect nibbling when slathered with a tangy, herby fromage blanc, and starters of sautéed baby squid on a bed of ratatouille, and little rolls of aubergine stuffed with perfectly seasoned braised lamb, were heavenly. Tender veal shank came de-boned with a lovely side of baby onions and broad beans with tiny cubes of ham, while house-salted cod was soaked, sautéed and doused with an elegant vinaigrette. The only off-note in this meal was the three dried-out slices of brebis that came without the black cherry jam noted on the menu (the waiter should have warned us), and rhubarb marmalade with pistachios was a tad bland, too. Still, there is a great wine list, including a great-value Cahors at €15, and some lovely Brana eau-de-vie should you decide to linger, which you very well might, since a party atmosphere sets in as the night grows long, completely with cigar-smoking young ladies on the arms of rugby players or well-worn playboys.

Au Bon Accueil ★

14 rue Monttessuy 7th (01.47.05.46.11). M° Alma-Marceau. **Open** Mon-Fri noon-2.15pm, 7.30-10.30pm. **Average** €40. **Prix fixe** €29. **Lunch menu** €25. **Credit** MC, V. **Map** D6.

Ever since Jacques Lacipière opened this bistro in 1990 it has been one of the good deals of the 7th arrondissement, and local residents' loyalty is still well-merited. The pleasantly redone dining room, with big windows, well-designed lighting and a stone satyr beaming down from a pilaster, provides the setting for excellent updating of French classics. We started with a chaud-froid combination of raw marinated sardines sandwiched between tiny, new spring leeks and a frazzle of deep-fried onion and chervil, and a tomato stuffed with petits gris snails, which was tasty, though the tomato was neither quite cooked nor quite raw. To follow, rosé veal kidneys were attractively presented pyramid-style on a bed of fresh spinach, while a rich braised beef cheek in deep red wine sauce, cleverly offset by the tart flavours of stewed rhubarb, showed how Lacipière injects tradition with a few surprising touches. A well-ripened assortment of cheeses from Marie-Anne Cantin and a chewy macaroon with raspberries and vanilla ice cream completed the €25 lunch menu, as we finished off an excellent 1998 Graves chosen from the good-value suggestions at the front of the wine list. A relaxed atmosphere and courteous, conscientious staff make this an address to cherish only a few metres from the Eiffel Tower.

The welcome is not the only plus-point **Au Bon Accueil**.

Café Max

7 av de la Motte Picquet, 7th (01.47.05.57.66). M° La Tour-Maubourg. **Open** Mon 7.30-11pm; Tue-Sat noon-2.30pm, 7.30-11pm. Closed Aug. **Prix fixe** €16, €20 (dinner only). **No credit cards. Wheelchair access. Map** E6.

In a part of town where loafers and button-downs link arms with pearls and curls, a man in his apron stands alone. Perhaps the only genuine resident of the area, Max, originally from the south-west, believes food should be served with gushing love. The warm, red interior (ignore the eclectic wall hangings) makes for the perfect hideaway in winter with stick-to-your-bones fare fit for hibernation. The solid €20 menu lands you a bucket salad full of foie gras, tuna, apples and tomatoes draped in a tangy curry dressing and an entire duck terrine from which you hack off your own portion. The grilled Lyonnais sausage with creamy, nutmeggy potatoes and perfectly stocky cassoulet, probably the way his mum used to make, were enough to feed a football team. Go for wife Lilli's apple tart if you find a second stomach. The small terrace with hanging vines is lovely in summer if you don't mind the passers-by.

La Cigale

11bis rue Chomel, 7th (01.45.48.87.87). M° Sèvres-Babylone. **Open** Mon-Fri noon-2.30pm, 7.30-11pm; Sat 7.30-11pm. **Average** €35. **Credit** MC, V. **Map** G7.

This restaurant's casual mood is perfectly suited to the clientele of local ladies relaxing after a morning of retail extravagance at the nearby Bon Marché. On the culinary front, things are similarly light and frothy, with soufflés as a speciality. Such is their reputation that many diners plump for a soufflé-only meal, combining savoury and sweet versions. If your diet requires something more varied than egg, milk and air, you'll be relieved to learn that chef Gérard Idoux also extends his talents to plat du jour blackboard offerings, as well as à la carte favourites such as moist chicken liver terrine with sweet onion chutney and salade frisée, and mains of well-prepared fish or simple grills. The main attraction, however, is to be found in white ramekins brimming over with fluffy soufflés, which include the basquade (cod, tomato and dill), Henri IV (époisses cheese) and cep. As for desserts, after opting for a chocolate version oozing with a frothy, milk-chocolate sauce and

Frites in the night...

American GIs thanked the French for their fries, but a good chip is hard to find.

In French-speaking lands, a plate of chips is known as frites. In the UK, just ask for chips. Only in America is (or was, before Jacques Chirac said 'no' to war against Saddam) the deep-fried potato associated with France.

But hold the ketchup: do chips even come from France? And can one still eat a decent plate of frites in Paris, or has their art been forgotten as fast food conquers the continent?

When 16th-century Spanish explorers first imported the potato from South America the European populace eyed it with suspicion. Some thought it caused leprosy, others considered it sacrilegious – after all, never once was it mentioned in the Bible. Potatoes finally arrived on the French dinner table thanks to Antoine Parmentier, a pharmacist who ate them while a prisoner in Germany. He presented potatoes to Louis XVI and Marie Antoinette, who made a fashion statement by decorating her hair with their blossoms.

The famed 'pommes Pont-Neuf' were commonplace by 1860, having been first cooked in horse fat near their namesake bridge. American GIs who'd gobbled up chips in Europe brought the craving home after WWI, and by the 1950s, they had became a fast-food staple.

The problem with finding full-flavoured, fresh chips in Paris, or virtually anywhere, is that

few restaurateurs think it is worth their while to prepare them from fresh, hand-cut potatoes. Thankfully, a few bistros do still serve the vraie chose. In Paris, the trick is to look on the menu for frites maison or frites au couteau. We defy you to find anywhere in Paris that makes real chips that you can chow down from a paper cone as you walk over the Pont-Neuf. Road trip to Belgium, anyone?
Ethan Gilsdorf.

Where to find frites maison:

La Girondine (*see p63*); **A La Biche au Bois** (*see p60*); **Chez Savy** (*see p49*); **Café de la Poste** (*see p147*); **Restaurant du Palais-Royal** (*see p120*); **Le Grand Colbert** (*see p93*).

swimming in melted dark chocolate, as well as a sugary soufflé drizzled with Grand Marnier served freely from the bottle, we were certainly inclined to agree with the waiter's laconic but pre-rehearsed comment that soufflés are more than just air.

Le Clos des Gourmets ★

16 av Rapp, 7th (01.45.51.75.61). M° Alma-Marceau/RER Pont de L'Alma. **Open** Tue-Sat 12.15-2pm, 7.15-11 pm. Closed Aug. **Average** €30. **Prix fixe** €30 (dinner only). **Lunch menu** €24, €27. **Credit** MC, V. **Map** D5.

As its name suggests, this small, elegant address three minutes from the Eiffel Tower takes its food very seriously. Pompous it's not, however. Arnaud and Christel Pitrois offer a genuinely warm welcome, happy to explain the ins and outs of a menu that's always inventive and, at €27 for a three-course lunch, excellent value. Roast mackerel, fresh market salad tossed in walnut oil, a lentil 'cappuccino', hare terrine – all sounded appetising as starters, and we opted for a superb cream of sweet chestnut soup, served with tiny chicken gnocchi and croutons. Main courses lived up to the same standard. Roast sea bass came on a bed of puréed potatoes and black truffles, set off by a delicate wild rocket sauce. Spring chicken came topped with pine nuts, mushrooms and crunchy roast potatoes, served in a rich jus. We deliberated long and hard over the mandarin soufflé, poached fennel and warm chocolate tart, before eventually opting for a sublime – and highly unusual – avocado millefeuille in a tangy orange sauce. A couple of glasses of Sancerre from a good list rounded things off nicely. Book in advance.

La Fontaine de Mars

129 rue St-Dominique, 7th (01.47.05.46.44). M° Ecole-Militaire or RER Pont de l'Alma. **Open** daily noon-3pm, 7.30-11pm. **Average** €45. **Lunch menu** €14 (Mon-Fri). **Credit** AmEx, MC, V. **Map** D6.

There are a lot of Americans at the Fontaine de Mars. What this signifies in this case is a scrupulous neatness, friendly waiters, red and white checked tablecloths and a brisk and proficient team in the kitchen. The food is traditional yet imaginative and is carefully prepared. We liked their list of 'unjustly forgotten apéritifs' from which we chose to sip a delicious fortified red wine, Lillet from Bordeaux, as we looked through the menu. A couple of interesting foie-gras affairs almost took our fancy but we were happy with our choice of a tart and invigorating 'ravigote' of fresh cod with black and red radishes, which we shared with no perceptible reduction of amiability from the waiter. The house speciality duck confit was a dull choice, and we regretted not having ordered the delicious looking (and smelling) John Dory with basil that we saw floating towards our neighbours. Tart, fresh puddings of peach soup and strawberries with a frothy sabayon sauce were perfect for a summer day. Book early for a table on the fine terrace next to the tinkling fountain and avoid if you can the slightly claustrophobic upstairs, though it is welcomingly air-conditioned.

Nabuchodonosor

6 av Bosquet, 7th (01.45.56.97.26/ www.nabuchodonosor.net). M° Alma Marceau. **Open** Mon-Fri noon-2.45pm, 7.30-11pm. Closed three weeks in Aug. **Average** €35. **Prix fixe** €29 (dinner only). **Lunch menu** €18.80. **Credit** AmEx, MC, V. **Wheelchair access**. **Map** D6.

The cigar-wielding Eric Rousseau makes his customers feel instantly at home in this elegant restaurant. Then again, anyone who names their place after a 15-litre bottle of Champagne has to be a natural bon vivant. Chef Thierry Garnier's carte is an inventive take on traditional French cuisine, with meticulously prepared dishes such as a rich, creamy chestnut soup with earthy-tasting snails, and a delicious mound of fresh goat's cheese served with peppers marinated in olive oil. Spotting daube provençale among the main courses, we were impressed: part of France's culinary heritage, this rich meat stew is an endangered dish, even in Provence. Preferring a lighter meal on the evening that we visited, we went sea-side. Roast langoustine tails were dawn-fresh, served with a delicate pepper sauce and perfectly cooked spinach. Roast sea bream was less successful, being slightly overcooked and served on a bundle of rigid vegetable sticks. From a choice of five desserts, we went for a refreshing lemon-balm-flavoured fruit soup and masterful bittersweet candied orange in a crispy batter with vanilla ice cream. As for the fascinating wine board, if our celestial Quincy Lavault Rouze 2000 was anything to go by, Rousseau – who jokingly offered to finish our wine – must be left with decidedly empty bottles when the lights go out.

Le Petit Troquet

28 rue de l'Exposition, 7th (01.47.05.80.39). M° Ecole-Militaire. **Open** Mon, Sat 7-10.30pm; Tue-Fri noon-2pm, 7-10.30pm. Closed three weeks in Aug. **Average** €28. **Credit** MC, V. **Map** D6.

Le Petit Troquet is the very definition of a good neighbourhood bistro. In an area abounding in substandard tourist traps, it offers unfailingly good value, generally excellent food and a warm, hospitable atmosphere: it feels like someone's cosy front parlour, the walls covered in a charming array of bric-a-brac. From an enticingly broad menu, we started with a crunchy filo parcel of melting pont l'évêque cheese served with warm apples, and a hearty country sausage with brown lentils. The grilled sea bream on a bed of spinach was excellent, the decoration of fresh herbs underlining the subtlety of the flavours. Unexpectedly, the guinea fowl in a creamy mushroom sauce disappointed slightly – the meat lukewarm, the puréed potatoes and carrots creating a rather doughy texture. All was redeemed, however, by a truly magnificent moelleux au chocolat and a velvety lemon soufflé with caramelised bananas. Portions are generous and the wine list good. Go later in the evening to avoid the tourist-dominated first wave and appreciate just why so many locals keep coming back.

Le Récamier

4 rue Récamier, 7th (01.45.48.86.58).
M° Sèvres-Babylone. **Open** Mon-Sat noon-2.30pm, 7.30-10.30pm. Closed 25 Dec, 1 Jan. **Average** €60. **Credit** AmEx, DC, MC, V. **Map** G7.

Serving buttoned-up classical cooking in fairly formal surroundings, Le Récamier has a loyal clientele of well-heeled locals and serious eaters in search of authentic Burgundian specialities. This is the place to measure the success of your own boeuf bourguignon. In summer the restaurant has one of the most pleasant terraces on the Left Bank, in a traffic-free cul-de-sac. We began an autumn lunch with a fricassée of firm girolles, and a slab of jambon persillé – here a tribute to the charcuterie tradition. To follow, the tête de veau, sauce gribiche was unusual in that it actually looked appetising, with the head meat skilfully displayed on the plate and the sharp-edged sauce served separately. We also chose the lobster, which was near enough in price (€37) to the other main courses not to be automatically discouraging. The classical sauce armoricaine was rich and pungent and the Breton lobster as tasty as this luxury should be. With still a few drops left of our excellent white Côtes du Rhône, we chose a plate of good but unspectacular cheese, and an exceptionally successful caramel mousse layered with ginger wafers.

Thoumieux

79 rue St-Dominique, 7th (01.47.05.49.75).
M° Invalides or La Tour-Maubourg. **Open** Mon-Sat noon-3.30pm, 6.45pm-midnight; Sun noon-midnight. **Average** €40. **Prix fixe** €31. **Lunch menu** €14 (Mon-Fri). **Credit** AmEx, MC, V. **Non-smoking room. Map** E6.

If you're upset by the way things have been going in the world over the past 70 years or so, a couple of hours with an earthenware pot of Thoumieux's cassoulet should put you right for an evening at least. This big and popular bistro opened in 1923 and has stayed in the same family ever since. The red velvet banquettes, starched white tablecloths and sturdy cutlery are a testament to tradition, as are the polite, black-jacketed waiters. Likewise, there's not much on the menu you won't have eaten before but plenty you'll want to eat again. Choosing à la carte, we ordered some excellent goat's cheese and the oxtail terrine. In our experience, oxtail terrine is even better when it's served warm, but we enjoyed it nevertheless. Ask the waiter nicely and you might get away with sharing the enormous cassoulet. Otherwise there are strong bistro standards such as grilled sole or côte de boeuf. Prices have climbed in the past couple of years but this remains the perfect address for a late and long Sunday lunch or winter supper.

Refined cooking accompanies – not surprisingly – gargantuan wines at **Nabuchodonosor**. *See p47.*

Le Voltaire

27 quai Voltaire, 7th (01.42.61.17.49). M° Rue du Bac. **Open** Tue-Sat 12.30-2.30pm, 7.30-10.30pm. Closed three weeks in Aug, one week at Christmas, in Feb, and in May. **Average** €50. **Credit** MC, V. **Map** G6.
The crème of tout Paris and their New York counterparts fill the lozenge-shaped banquettes of this 'Old Europe' hideaway. Bend your ear to the delicious scraps of conversation spicing the two intimate dining rooms and you are in Edith Wharton territory. 'I'm so impressed by the obituaries in the *Daily Telegraph*, I do hope they do mine, I must remember to tell Conrad.' This breed is inextinguishable, given the identical appearance of mothers and daughters in beige and black. A snobbish restaurant? Not a bit. The maître d'hôtel, Antoine Picot, is as respectful and discreetly helpful with dishevelled strangers as he is with slick habitués. Moreover, the large, entirely à la carte menu offers the simplest brasserie-style food (such as œufs mayonnaise at €0.90) to the most finicky traditional dish, including tête de veau, sauce gribiche (€27). We started with a beetroot and apple salad with walnut oil dressing, and poached eggs in a mousseline sorrel sauce, which restored our faith in France's sauce supremacy. To follow, saddle of rabbit roasted with thyme evoked the Haut Var countryside, and we quickly polished off the acccompanying matchstick frites. Our pike-perch quenelles were feather-light, with the delicate taste of the fish masterfully teasing the tastebuds. We finished with a bowl of gravity-defying homemade chocolate mousse for two and drank Couly-Duthell, one of the best Chinon wines and the cheapest red on the prohibitively expensive list, at €27. A meal here is costly, true, but we were entertained as well as impeccably well-fed.

8th Arrondissement

Le Rocher Gourmand

89 rue du Rocher, 8th (01.40.08.00.36). M° Villiers. **Open** Mon-Fri noon-2pm, 8-10pm; Sat 8-10pm. Closed Aug. **Prix-fixe** €30, €38. **Lunch menu** €25. **Credit** MC, V. **Map** F2.
It may not look it but this is a good place to sample original and often exquisite modern French cooking without breaking the bank. The decor, it's true, could do with a little ripping out and burning. The net curtains and general beigeness make it feel like a Calais bistro in the down season. But the welcome from young chef Sébastien Gilles was simple and friendly, and the lunch menu is very good value. We took a starter plus main and a main plus dessert and were, very kindly, served our half-starters and half-desserts on separate plates, which is important as this is food that looks every bit as good as it tastes. Our starter of cream of Jerusalem artichoke soup was particularly impressive. Here is a vegetable one would like to meet more often, served with nutmeg, cubes of roast salmon and whipped mascarpone with curry. Our sea bream main was also well worth brushing through the net curtains for, dashingly combined with onion chutney, a light aniseed sauce and a little grated spice bread. Sad to say, our other main, a Parmentier of pike-perch and green cabbage with a herb jus, was a masterclass in how to be dull – but the memorable ginger cream pudding made us reckon that the lacklustre Parmentier was an exception that proves the rule.

Savy ★

23 rue Bayard, 8th (01.47.23.46.98). M° Franklin D. Roosevelt. **Open** Mon-Fri noon-2.30pm, 7.30-11pm. Closed Aug. **Average** €30. **Lunch menu** €19.50-€26.50. **Credit** AmEx, MC, V. **Map** E4.
The night we visited chez Savy, controversial French interior minister Nicolas Sarkozy was appearing in the RTL radio studios opposite, so we made our way to the restaurant through an impressive security cordon, and were relieved to take refuge in this comfortable 1923 art deco bistro with its intimate rows of mirrored booths. In an area where fashion reigns, it is comforting that Savy continues to produce simple regional food based on the fine products of the Aveyron. We began with a generous plate of Cantal charcuterie, a creamy oeuf en cocotte with roquefort and the unusual farçou aveyronnais, which are fried herb and chard patties. For main courses, we enjoyed some light and delicate

Le Petit Pont

Brunches, lunch, dinner, cock-tails, cigars
Heated terrace with a splendid view of Notre Dame.

Sound session (house, garage and funk)
Thur, Fri & Sat nights

Open daily 5am-4am
1 rue du Petit Pont, 5th. Mº Saint Michel
Tel: 01.43.54.23.81

tripoux, highly seasoned tripe-and-trotter parcels to convert even a hardened offal-phobic diner, a generous slice of foie de veau, and a meaty if rather solid Auvergne sausage served with a wholesome purée of split peas. We greedily eyed the broad-cut frites, impressive-looking marrow bones and nobler cuts of Aubrac de Laguiole beef, for which we vowed to return. A fine hunk of st-nectaire cheese and a timeless chocolate mousse finished a wholly satisfactory meal, accompanied by some reasonably priced red Morgon. Service was charmingly old school but ground to a near standstill when challenged by a party of 20 senior French businessmen and their fidgety spouses.

Sébillon

66 rue Pierre-Charron, 8th (01.43.59.28.15). M° Franklin D. Roosevelt. **Open** daily noon-midnight. **Average** €40. **Prix fixe** €34. **Lunch menu** €26. **Credit** AmEx, DC, MC, V. **Map** D4.

There's something reassuring about this slumbering, old-fashioned spot, the in-town branch of a venerable bistro in cushy Neuilly. A honeycomb tile floor, waiters in long aprons and a rather anonymous decor of dark wood and small brass chandeliers create an appealing backdrop for a solid feed on the house specialities: oysters and roast lamb. We enjoyed a glass of the house white over a tray of impeccably fresh oysters, then went for the fabled lamb. Tender and cooked pink, it was carved tableside and served with white beans by a very friendly waiter, who later stopped by to see if we wanted more. The accompanying jus was thin and a bit lacking in flavour, but the meat was excellent and the atmosphere festive. Tourists, many of them French in from the provinces, grandparents and grandchildren, and businessmen lingering over a brandy, make up a heterogeneous mix. Having gone through our bottle of good Morgon like lightning, we decided we wanted a last glass with coffee, something the French themselves wouldn't do, but the waiter happily suggested a half-bottle, in no way making us feel we were holding him up as the last in at lunch.

9th Arrondissement

Le Bistro de Gala

45 rue du Fbg-Montmartre, 9th (01.40.22.90.50). M° Le Peletier or Grands Boulevards. **Open** Mon-Fri noon-2.30pm, 7-11pm; Sat 7-11pm. **Prix fixe** €26, €30. **Credit** AmEx, MC, V. **Map** J3.

With its framed photographs of actors and actresses, theatre posters alluding to the popularity of this place with a showbiz crowd, and brass lamps casting a soft light on every table, this bistro has an appealing cosiness, especially in a neighbourhood that's mostly given over to 'grecs' and other cheap ethnic restaurants. Not far from a flock of inexpensive hotels, it's also clearly a front-desk recommendation, since on a rainy spring night we were flanked by studious Swedes on one side and vivacious Spaniards on the other. The kitchen is serious, generously adding seasonal dishes, such as asparagus with a thick rasher of grilled bacon, to a moderately priced set menu. Lentil soup garnished with foie gras was another very good starter. We were delighted with mains of scallops in their shells served on a bed of buttered leeks, and a delicious pastry filled with apples, preserved duck and potatoes, served with green beans. Sadly the wonderful northern French cheeses once found here have vanished, to be replaced by a rather ordinary cheese plate, but desserts, including an apple croustillant and crème brûlée, are appealing. Eager service and a nice selection of inexpensive Loire valley wines make this place a good bet in an area without much choice.

Casa Olympe ★

48 rue St-Georges, 9th (01.42.85.26.01). M° St-Georges. **Open** Mon-Fri noon-2pm, 8-11pm. **Prix fixe** €34. **Credit** AmEx, MC, V. **Map** H3.

Once a star of the Paris night at her jet-setty restaurant Olympe in the 15th arrondissement, chef Dominique Versini has accomplished an admirable personal and professional transition at her superb bistro just off the place St-Georges. The attractive mustard-coloured room with pretty Murano chandeliers and wall sconces pulls a creative crowd, and well-paced, friendly service and a brief but very appealing wine list add to the experience. Excellent bread and a fine 1998 Bernard Gripa St-Joseph got the meal off to a fine start, and our pleasure grew with the excellent starters – a poached egg with spinach and salted butter on a chestnut-flour galette, and a casserole of autumn fruits and vegetables, including pears, celeriac, pumpkin, kale and cardoons, braised in an iron casserole in luscious veal stock. Main courses of guinea hen with a single, large, wild-mushroom-stuffed ravioli, and pork fillet with homemade sauerkraut in a sublime sauce of vinegar, sugar, spices and veal stock, were rustic but deeply satisfying. Desserts were exceptional, too, including the Paris-Brest (choux pastry filled with hazelnut cream) and a croustillant de pomme (apple baked in pastry) in salted caramel sauce.

Chez Jean

8 rue St-Lazare, 9th (01.48.78.62.73). M° Notre-Dame-de-Lorette. **Open** Mon-Fri noon-2.30pm, 7.30-10.30pm. Closed Aug. **Average** €45. **Lunch menu** €32. **Credit** MC, V. **Map** H3.

With a staff-diner ratio nearing the levels of haute cuisine establishments, a sumptuous high-ceilinged dining room replete with pine panelling and comfy banquettes, a long bar occupied by a glamorous barmaid, as well as a revolving wooden door through which to make an impressive entrance, it was only a matter of time before the prices at Chez Jean moved upwards. So we were unsurprised, though still disappointed, that the great-value €32 prix fixe has recently become a lunch-only affair, with an à la carte evening meal now a much more expensive outing. Food was still well-prepared and creative, while service by the plethora of waiters combined politeness and efficiency. Delicate yellow Chinese-style ravioli stuffed with crab were bursting with flavour and served with a light verbena sauce, while a ramekin of plump snails with quartered fresh artichokes were set off well by a tasty poultry gravy. Mains ranged from foie gras mi-cuit, scattered with toasted almonds and served with a rather bracing rhubarb sauce, to a delicious slow-cooked farmhouse pork with a chutney of apricots, preserved lemons and sage. For dessert, the amiable maître d' jokingly warned us against our taking the 'hot-cold' Morello cherries but our disobedience was rewarded with a pleasingly alcoholic dish of eau-de-vie marinated cherries scattered with pistachios.

A la Cloche d'Or

3 rue Mansart, 9th (01.48.74.48.88). M° Blanche. **Open** Mon-Fri noon-2.30pm, 7pm-4am; Sat 7pm-4am; Sun 7pm-1.30am. Closed Aug, Christmas. **Average** €35. **Prix fixe** €22 (dinner only), €25. **Lunch menu** €14, €20. **Credit** MC, V. **Map** G2.

This late-night Pigalle institution has always been a hit with showbiz folk playing in the area's many theatres, and thus with groupies and wannabes hoping some of the glitter will rub off. Actress Jeanne Moreau's parents opened the restaurant in 1928 and the boozy, smoky smell of decades of late-night revelry still hangs among the kitschy, faux-rustic decor, held in by the heavy curtain draping the doorway. That it was disco diva Claude François' favourite hangout makes perfect sense. Dozens of vintage celebrity snaps hang between the crossed beams on the walls. The homemade French fare is all reliable if unimaginative, just the thing at 2am after a long evening treading the boards – or waiting outside the stage door. Starters of snails, lamb's lettuce with warm chicken livers and the house chicken liver pâté were all well-executed, as was the soothing confit de canard on a bed of fried potatoes. The steak tartare stood out for its zesty seasoning and the plate of hefty golden chips. Prices are gentle, too, with a €25 three-course menu valid into the wee hours. Our bottle of very drinkable Haut Canteloup Médoc bore a label reminiscent of Toulouse-Lautrec, perfect for the neighbourhood and the mood.

A la Grange Batelière

16 rue de la Grange Batelière, 9th (01.47.70.85.15). M° Richelieu-Drouot. **Open** Mon-Fri 12.15-2.30pm, 7.15-10.15pm; Sat 7.15-10.15pm. Closed two weeks in Aug. **Prix fixe** €27. **Credit** AmEx, MC, V. **Map** H3.

This old-fashioned bistro has been spruced up with red-and-white-checked everything (even the friendly barman's waistcoat), but this still failed to jolly the rather staid, oddly seedy clientele, possibly celebrating a modest deal on an album in the dusty stamp shops nearby. From the €27 three-course 'panier du chef', we chose a sizeable salad of smoked boar, potatoes and walnuts, and crème de lentilles with langoustines: overly creamy, thin lentil soup containing three rather tired tails and chunks of parmesan. Our best main was the delicious, crisp-crusted roast bass with mushroom sauce and a fine ratatouille of tiny diced vegetables tucked underneath; but the coquilles St-Jacques were as tired (and few and far between) as the langoustines, albeit served with tangy beurre d'orange. To follow came crème brûlée overpowered with almond essence, and an overcooked chocolate fondant, lacking sweetness, tasting of omelette and oozing green 'pistachio' syrup. Our neighbours, gearing up to share a bottle of red, enjoyed lengthy consultations with the maîtresse de maison; but our own request for a glass each met with a summary 'blanc ou rouge?' of indeterminate origin. Good for game on a winter evening, perhaps (with an €8 supplement), but that's about as far as our recommendation goes.

La Table de la Fontaine

5 rue Henri-Monnier, 9th (01.45.26.26.30). M° St-Georges. **Open** Mon-Fri noon-2.30pm, 7.30-11.30pm. Closed two weeks in Aug. **Average** €30. **Prix fixe** €30. **Lunch menu** €25. **Credit** MC, V. **Map** H2.

The British, you may or may not be proud to know, are responsible for the sprinkler that gives this place its name. It is one of 50 fountains called Wallace bestowed on the city by the 19th-century Francophile Richard Wallace. The leafy little square around it is full of Parisian charm and the bistro isn't bad either. The decor is perhaps more tasteful than interesting (ditto for the suity, handbaggy clientele) but this is a good address for a business lunch or supper with a genteel relative. We started with prawns and celeriac in a rémoulade sauce (a posh prawn cocktail) and the ravioles de Royans, tiny ravioli stuffed with cheese. Both were utterly delicious. Then came a superbly fresh and juicy slab of red tuna, splendid amid bright-coloured vegetables from Provence and paprika sprinkled across the rim of the plate. Our other main course, a lamb navarin, was also a good-looker: the meat cooked with carrots, spring onions and crunchy mangetout arriving in a black, lidded casserole. Apple tart and ice cream posed no particular problems and coffee at the café terrace on the other side of the square completed an agreeable lunch.

Velly

52 rue Lamartine, 9th (01.48.78.60.05). M° Notre-Dame-de-Lorette. **Open** Mon-Fri noon-2.30pm, 7.45-10.30pm. Closed three weeks in Aug. **Prix fixe** €29. **Lunch menu** €22. **Credit** MC,V. **Map** H3.

Odds are you'll agree that the only problem with this cosy little bistro behind pretty old-fashioned windows is that it's not just downstairs from your flat. Friendly service and an interesting crowd create a nice buzz as you peruse the regularly changing €29 set menu, just as long as you don't get sent upstairs to the new dining room, which is a bit cold. Most of the stylish types who came in were greeted by name, always a good sign. The kitchen does homely, satisfying food, including starters such as pumpkin soup or a poached egg, on crunchy polenta in jus-spiked cream sauce with sichuan pepper and mains, such as stuffed cabbage, veal steak with new potatoes, red mullet on a bed of red cabbage and supions (small squid) on creamy, slightly overcooked rice with mushrooms. The food is generously and attractively presented, including a whole, perfectly ripened st-marcellin cheese, and desserts such as cocoa, pear and apricot sorbets. There's a nice wine list, too; we enjoyed a Château du Puy Bordeaux.

10th Arrondissement

Chez Arthur ★

25 rue du Fbg-St-Martin, 10th (01.42.08.34.33). M° Strasbourg St-Denis. **Open** Tue-Fri noon-2.30pm, 7-11.30pm; Sat 7-11.30pm. Closed Aug. **Prix fixe** €27, €22. **Credit** AmEx, MC, V. **Map** K4.

Ringing for a table at 11pm we said we could be there in 15 minutes. 'OK, but we lock the doors at 11.30pm,' warned the owner. Clearly Chez Arthur appreciates punctuality because when we turned up at 11.15 and the table wasn't ready we were plied at the bar with free kirs, olives, marinated vegetables and profuse apologies from the waiter who exuded an almost 18th-century gentlemanly charm. For three generations Chez Arthur has served the late-night crowd that swarms in from the Faubourg's independent theatres and its wood-lined interior filled with actors' portraits and starched white tablecloths has probably barely changed. The menu, on creamy parchment in copperplate, is easy to negotiate so as not to detract from the discussion in hand. Everything we ordered from the good-value prix fixe was just as it should be: a decent foie gras de canard served with hot toast, hot goat's cheese on a crisp, well-dressed salad, a fine steak with creamy potato gratin and flaky, firm cod with a crisp skin and garlicky tapenade, accompanied by a carafe of house red. Desserts such as crème brûlée and two-chocolate fondant with crème anglaise are also good, and though we were the last to leave we were not in any way hurried out by the charming Michael, grandson of the original Arthur.

Chez Casimir

6 rue de Belzunce, 10th (01.48.78.28.80). M° Gare du Nord or Poissonnière. **Open** Mon-Fri noon-2pm, 7-11pm; Sat 7-11pm. Closed three weeks in Aug. **Average** €27. **Credit** DC, MC, V. **Map** K2.

The kitchen at this Chez Michel offspring seems to be coping admirably following the departure of chef Philippe Tredgeu. There were plenty of enticing offerings, from pink slices of duck foie gras juxtaposed with slices of beetroot, to nuggets of salmon in a tart vinaigrette mixed with bitter chives. Despite its unappetising name, we opted for the croustillant de saucisson, which proved to be culinary light-years from the English sausage – slices of crisp pork served with Puy lentils soaked in a thick, meaty gravy. Another pleasurable dish was the lieu (pollack), perfectly cooked and served on a bed of black-olive couscous. Desserts are taken very seriously here; we enjoyed the Gallic grandma's favourite, pain perdu, well set-off by slow-baked apple seg-

A night on the tiles at **Chez Jean**. *See p51.*

RISTORANTE & TRATTORIA

Fuxia: three warm & welcoming restaurants. In an original and authentic setting, our menu brings the flavours of Italy to your table. Blackboard menu with daily specials and unmissable specialities.

FUXIA Ristorante
45 rue de Richelieu, 1st. Mº Pyramides
Tel: 01.42.60.19.16 / Fax: 01.42.60.13.55
Open Mon-Fri noon-3pm & 7pm-2am, Sat 7pm-2am

FUXIA Ristorante Trattoria
25 rue des Martyrs, 9th. Mº Notre Dame De Lorette
Tel: 01.48.78.93.25 / Fax: 01.48.78.91.64
Open daily 9am-2am

FUXIA Ristorante Trattoria
40 rue de Ponthieu, 8th. Mº Franklin D Roosevelt
Tel: 01.40.75.07.12 / Fax: 01.40.75.07.13
Open daily 9am-2am

ments, as well as the calorie-fest of bananas in salted-butter caramel sauce doused in praline mousse for good measure. Chez Casimir's dining room has a decidedly informal feel, service is efficient but at walking pace, and with the Gare du Nord only a stone's throw away, this is an ideal place for a final fix of authentic French bistro cuisine before departing by train for Albion.

Chez Michel ★

10 rue de Belzunce, 10th (01.44.53.06.20).
M° Gare du Nord. **Open** Mon 7pm-midnight; Tue-Fri noon-2pm, 7pm-midnight. Closed one week in Aug. **Average** €40. **Prix fixe** €30. **Credit** MC, V. **Map** K2.

Thierry Breton is now so well-established (reservations are essential) that he can afford to shut up shop for the weekend and pop home to Brittany. But success hasn't changed a thing. Homemade terrines and rillettes are our favourite starters (always moist, packed with flavour and accompanied by pickles, thick bread and coarse salt), but on a recent visit we were seduced by succulent slices of foie gras with a surprising beetroot millefeuille. A classic Breton main is the kig ha farz, a regional variation of pot-au-feu: following Breton père's recipe (culinary excellence runs in the family), this melt-in-your-mouth dish combines tender cuts of veal and pork, a buckwheat and raisin dumpling, cabbage, carrots and a hint of tarragon. Game-lovers are well served in autumn when hare, roast partridge and wood-pigeon as well as wild boar and venison are in season. A juicy slice of roe-deer, roasted with tangy grapes and elderberries, came with a silky celeriac purée. Try to leave room for dessert. Chocolate and mint quenelles were refined and delectable; farz forn aux pruneaux, a cakey custard tart stuffed with prunes, keeps up the Breton theme, but it's the rice pudding that's unbeatable. You get a sturdy bowl of creamy, unctuous rice, a jar of caramelised pineapple, and all you have to do is defend it from your salivating co-diners. There's a good wine list including decent house bottles for those on a budget; for a regional alternative try the farmhouse ciders at €7 and €8 a bottle. Our only reservation: with tables so close, smoke-phobes are ill-served.

Aux Deux Canards

8 rue du Fbg-Poissonnière, 10th (01.47.70.03.23).
M° Bonne Nouvelle. **Open** Mon, Sat 7.30-10.30pm; Tue-Fri noon-2.30pm, 7-10.30pm. Closed Aug. **Average** €38. **Lunch menu** €25. **Credit** AmEx, DC, MC, V. **Map** J4.

At first, you seem to be getting special treatment, hearing Gérard Faesch's cheery explanation of Aux Deux Canards' colourful history (a former clandestine HQ for a Résistance newspaper during the Nazi occupation) and the kitchen's ancient recipe for citrus rind sauces (you are implored to sniff the contents of jars which, bringing to mind specimens in a pathology lab, are in various states of decay). After about the sixth recital of his schtick this wears thin, but food comes to the rescue: a trustworthy menu of inventive takes on bistro cuisine, with lo[illegible] touches. A pan-fried foie gras with bilberry c[illegible] proved surprisingly complementary. Te[illegible] couteaux (razor clams) in garlic butter and parsle[illegible] brought to mind skinny snails. Two tuna fillets, served with beurre blanc, puréed carrots, and courgette and potato gratins, were grilled to perfection. Though we didn't order the duck à l'orange, the plate is magnificently adorned with a candle lighting up a hollowed-out orange. An archetypal crème brûlée arrives with branding-iron ('Look at the two ducks!' our waiter declared, pointing at the dessert's crispy emblem before backing away into a cloud smoke). It's all quite enjoyable while being a bit over-the-top. You're allowed one cigarette with your apéritif and one with coffee.

L'Hermitage

5 bd de Denain, 10th (01.48.78.77.09). M° Gare du Nord. **Open** Mon-Fri noon-2.30pm, 7-11pm, Sat 7-11pm. Closed two weeks in Aug. **Prix fixe** €23. **Credit** AmEx, DC, MC, V. **Non-smoking room**. **Map** K2.

At last, this bistro, hidden among the chains around Gare de Nord, has a decor to match the refined and surprisingly ambitious cooking of chef François Déage. The narrow booths and dated tapestry-backed chairs have been replaced by burnt oranges, modern lighting and well-spaced tables. The menu alone had us salivating, and when we bit into our first course – a pressé of rosy foie gras interleaved with tender figs – we were conquered. The house terrine of venison marinated in Muscadet with prunes and tarragon was equally delicious and generously served à volonté. Main courses are both imaginative and refined. There is a good selection of top-quality standards, such as côte de veau and magret de canard, as well as ideas to reward more adventurous palates. Scallops with a dash of Egyptian pepper melted in the mouth and the accompanying spinach and watercress, gently steamed, made a perfect match. Make sure you save room for one of the prettily presented desserts: a scoop of dense riz au lait, elegantly perched on a sablé biscuit, came crowned with thick slices of caramelised pineapple; despite appearances, it proved surprisingly light. Well-priced wine is available by the glass and bread comes in tasty rough chunks. But ultimately it's the tastebuds that count and L'Hermitage is an opportunity not to be missed.

11th Arrondissement

Les Amognes

243 rue du Fbg-St-Antoine, 11th (01.43.72.73.05).
M° Faidherbe-Chaligny. **Open** Tue-Sat noon-2pm, 8-11pm. Closed three weeks in Aug. **Average** €33. **Prix fixe** €33. **Credit** MC, V. **Map** N7.

It's easy to pass by Les Amognes with its cottage-style frontage on the upper reaches of the Fbg-St-Antoine, where grunge turns to grungier. Inside, despite some funky modern art and exposed stone

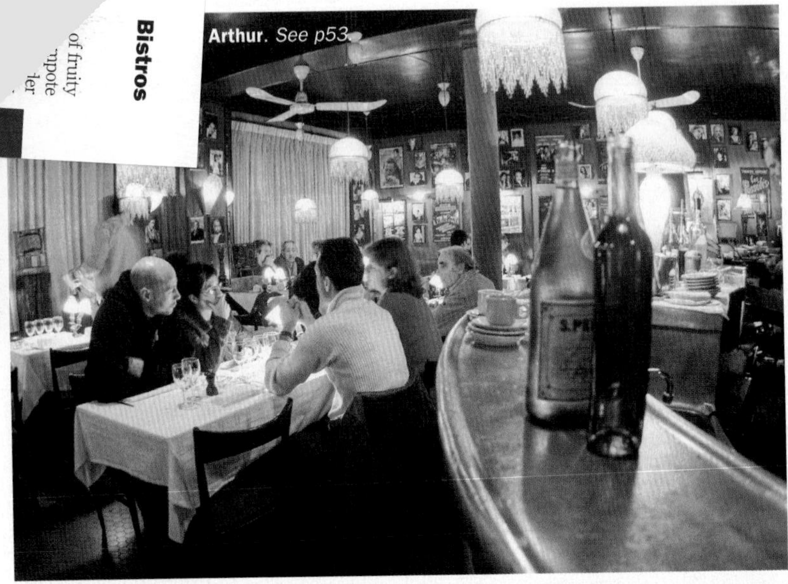

Arthur. See p53.

walls, the atmosphere can feel uncomfortably stilted. That said, on a rainy lunchtime Thierry Coué's €33 prix fixe was totally successful, if hardly a bargain. We began with a fresh sardine tart and a creamy slice of boudin noir served with blackcurrant-spiked onion chutney. The star of the meal was the suckling lamb. A mound of mini cutlets of delicate pale meat, lightly perfumed with rosemary, rested on a bed of de-skinned broad beans and mangetout. Pig's trotter came boned and wrapped in cabbage – a warming, hearty dish, but slightly at odds with the sophistication of the lamb. From the list of puddings we chose the chef's trademark crêpe stuffed with aubergines in a syrupy cardamom sauce, which worked surprisingly well, but a slightly solid poached pear with hot chocolate sauce was a more mundane proposition. The attentive waiter proposed a light red Bourgeuil at €24, which accompanied the meal perfectly. With its quiet atmosphere, this is a good place to get to know someone better.

Astier ★

44 rue Jean-Pierre-Timbaud, 11th (01.43.57.16.35). M° Parmentier. **Open** Mon-Fri noon-2pm, 8-10.15pm. Closed Easter, Aug, 25 Dec. **Prix fixe** €25. **Lunch menu** €20.50. **Credit** MC, V. **Wheelchair access** (ring in advance). **Map** M4.

On entering Astier all your senses tell you that this is a serious bastion of traditional food – the unmistakable smell of fine French cooking, the look of unbridled contentment on the crimson faces of the local businessmen, and the sound of frantic ordering across a crowded, unassumingly decorated room. The charming patronne squeezed us in to a corner table and gave us the handwritten menu. This is a place where homemade terrines lead the way and we went for the chicken liver and seafood versions. Both were highly flavoured and perfect fulfilments of expectation, particularly the seafood terrine, which is often bland yet here was a seaside holiday in itself and came with a beurre-blanc sauce. A generous dish of firm yet tender lamb sweetbreads with tiny mousseron mushrooms replaced controversial calf's sweetbreads with aplomb, and the accompanying gratin dauphinois was sinfully good. Monkfish was firm and fresh in a lake of unctuous, buttery sauce. The handsome baskets of cheese looked impressive, but we decided to take a chance on dessert. Astier came up trumps with a strawberry and rhubarb soup and a smooth nougat glacé enriched by chewy morsels of marrons glacés. The wine list is surprisingly sophisticated, with bottles ranging from the humble to the very grand. Amazingly this three-course feast cost a mere €20.50 at lunch, so it's wise to book ahead.

Le Bistrot Paul Bert ★

18 rue Paul-Bert, 11th (01.43.72.24.01). M° Charonne. **Open** Tue-Thur noon-2pm, 8-11pm; Fri, Sat noon-2pm, 8-11.45pm. **Average** €28. **Prix fixe** €24. **Lunch menu** €14. **Credit** MC, V. **Map** N7.

Few things are more exasperating than restaurant reviews that moan, 'it seems a shame to make such a delightful place known beyond its tight, happy circle of regulars'. When it comes to a bistro this wonderful, you absolutely deserve to be informed, since few tables in Paris offer such a good feed for such a fair price in a setting with such an amusing nostalgic edge. The service, from a lovely young Spanish woman and a Heathcliff-like American painter, is charming and the crowd is mixed, edgy and slightly louche. And as if all that weren't enough, the wine list, mostly organic bottles, is a dream. So snag a place on the moleskin banquette under the wonderfully kitsch glass chandelier and order from the daily-changing blackboard menu. Recent treats included a lovely lamb's lettuce salad with slices of fresh truffle and sautéed squid with risotto as starters, followed by a thick cod steak with girolle mushrooms and guinea hen with cabbage sautéed with bacon chunks. All were beautifully made and generously served, along with excellent bread, and we happily finished up our luscious Cairanne Domaine de l'Oratoire St-Martin by greedily serving ourselves from the left-behind-on-the-table cheese tray. A final round of contented sighs over a shared chocolate ganache cake in pistachio cream sauce and we shuffled into the night filled with determination to become regulars here. Oh, and by the way, don't tell your friends about this place.

C'Amelot

50 rue Amelot, 11th (01.43.55.54.04). M° Chemin Vert. **Open** Mon, Sat 7-10.30pm; Tue-Fri noon-2pm, 7-10.30pm. **Prix fixe** €33 (dinner only). **Lunch menu** €16, €23. **Credit** AmEx, MC, V. **Map** M6.

Didier Varnier is one of a group of young bistro chefs in Paris who relish the contrast of serving inventive and often refined food in low-key settings. C'Amelot's long, narrow dining room in the rather gloomy rue Amelot has a countrified, some might say dated, feel with its panelling and bare wood tables. Although only two other tables were occupied during our January lunch, the atmosphere was cheerful and we duly treated ourselves to a midwinter feast. There are only two options for each course. We started with a typically south-western lentil soup with foie gras – earthy, with morsels of oozy goodness – and unusual cured salmon with braised chicory in a sweet vinegar sauce that contrasted nicely with its bitterness. Lamb chops in poivrade (white wine) sauce with porridgy polenta were remarkable for the quality of the rosy meat. Against our better judgment we took the advice of the waitress and ordered the now ubiquitous gâteau mi-cuit au chocolat – there was nothing exceptional about Varnier's version. More interesting were prunes in spiced wine, a wintery end to this market-inspired meal.

Chardenoux

1 rue Jules-Vallès, 11th (01.43.71.49.52). M° Charonne. **Open** daily noon-2.30pm, 7-10.30pm. **Average** €38. **Lunch menu** €23 (Mon-Sat). **Credit** MC, V. **Map** N7.

A change of management at one of the capital's quaintest bistros was greeted with suspicion by die-hard traditionalists. Superficially the restaurant remains unchanged, but cleaner and smarter than in recent times, its romantic belle époque decor gleaming in the winter sunlight. The menu sticks to its classical repertoire, but the new chef has a more self-consciously modern approach. We began with a dozen well-selected snails, while a terrine de foie gras, enhanced by layers of onions and figs, was a total success. Fans of the restaurant's classic tête de veau may be alarmed at the chef's rehashing of the dish – gone was the head meat covered by a thick sauce gribiche, enter a bowl containing a savoury mix of meat, lentils and potatoes, accompanied by a small dish of over-pungent sauce. It must be admitted that the new version was tasty, but was nonetheless a surprise in a restaurant that was previously a bastion of classicism. Kidney fricassée was slightly the grey side of the requested pink, but moist and tender, accompanied by bacon and baby onions. We shared a rather sweet chocolate cake to finish off our excellent carafe of white Quincy. The new team is opening at weekends and is also offering a weekday lunch prix fixe , but a question mark now hangs over the enduring quality of this landmark bistro.

Le Chateaubriand

129 av Parmentier, 11th (01.43.57.45.95). M° Goncourt or Parmentier. **Open** Tue-Fri noon-2pm, 8-11pm; Sat 8-11pm. Closed Aug. **Average** €30. **Lunch menu** €11. **Credit** MC, V. **Map** M4.

Aside from the Anglo expat owner-hostess, there's something about this neighbourhood bistro that will have you expecting to step out the front door and find yourself on Clapham Common, and it's not just the fact that they charge a nervy €5 for a bottle of mineral water. Rather, it's a question of attitude, n'est-ce pas? One way or another, this is a hip little spot that pulls trend-meisters such as designer Christian Lacroix, plus a gaggle of photographers and other media types who have hauled this old working-class neighbourhood upmarket during the past few years. The spare decor, dominated by a big bar and a lovely fragment of fresco attesting to a previous incarnation as a grocer, makes a perfect backdrop for the head-to-toe-in-black crowd, and the food is no afterthought. The blackboard menu changes daily, but typical of the kitchen are starters such as couscous with roasted vegetables or serrano ham with kidney beans, and mains such as sea bream on a bed of courgettes. It's not all smooth sailing here – our lacquered poitrine de porc turned out to be dreary and fatty – but wines are well-chosen, prices are fair and the buzz is bona fide.

Chez Paul

13 rue de Charonne, 11th (01.47.00.34.57). M° Bastille. **Open** daily noon-2.30pm, 7pm-12.30am. Closed 24, 25 Dec. **Average** €25. **Credit** AmEx, DC, MC, V. **Map** M7.

You'll notice Chez Paul because it's the one that always seems to have a queue out the door – all year round. This is a fantasy French restaurant; both floors have a hue that looks as if it might owe more to tobacco pollution than paint, the walls are covered in Métro signs and indecipherable documents, and a maximum number of tables is packed into a minimum of space. The waiters and waitresses are frenetic and (mostly) friendly, although service is idiosyncratic rather than uniformly efficient. The menu groans with hearty traditional recipes and meat cuts to make the squeamish shudder. The old favourites are done well here. Chez Paul's steak is excellent, as is the foie gras with lentils. The servings are satisfying and reliably tasty. However, if you're thinking of something other than steak, choose with care – our perch with mushrooms was pretty drab, the taste of the fish all but drowned out by the sauce, and the puddings are average. Make sure you book, and even then be prepared to wait.

Chez Ramulaud ★

269 rue du Fbg-St-Antoine, 11th (01.43.72.23.29). M° Faidherbe-Chaligny. **Open** daily noon-3pm, 8-11pm. Closed one week at Christmas. **Average** €35. **Prix fixe** €26. **Lunch menu** €14. **Credit** MC, V. **Map** N7.

At the far end of the Faubourg, in an area formerly immune to fashion, a few interesting modern bistros are cropping up. Leading the bunch is Ramulaud, a relaxed neighbourhood place with wooden tables and a subtle retro decor. Our lunchtime visit found the room humming with a local crowd, who appreciate the care of the cooking and the reasonable prices. The blackboard offerings initially looked rather tame, but simplicity and clear, uncluttered tastes are always a winner. We began our meal with an olive and mushroom clafoutis – all the charm of a quiche with none of the crust. The main courses included perfectly cooked red mullet on a bed of aromatic fennel and other vegetables, and a chicken breast with pommes allumettes. Fearing industrial fried chicken, we were thrilled to find a magical golden parcel of moist, tasty meat, which was truly memorable. Turning our backs on the tempting dessert list, we opted for the à la carte cheese trolley, which we were left in charge of long enough to indulge in a tasty tour of well-aged specimens, washed down by the drinkable house red. Our joy was compounded when the whole meal came in at under €60. In the evenings the menu is slightly more sophisticated and on occasional Sundays there is a guinguette, an retro-style French dinner-dance, which according to the extremely charming staff is très sympa, like the bistro itself.

How to Eat **Mussels**

An Irish traveller, Patrick Walton, is credited with observing mussels' fondness for wooden posts and inventing a form of mussel culture in 1290, which is still used today on the West coast of France. Moules de bouchot, the result of this method, are the most prized French mussels – small, juicy and tasting of the sea. The French have a unique way of eating mussels that requires no man-made implements – they simply shell the first mussel, then use the empty shell to pinch out each of the remaining mussels, holding the full mussel in one hand and the shell in the other. Moules marinières, mussels cooked in white wine, are often served with frites, which can be used to mop up the sauce.

Les Jumeaux

73 rue Amelot, 11th (01.43.14.27.00). M° Chemin Vert. **Open** Tue-Sat noon-2.30pm, 7.30-10.30pm. Closed three weeks in Aug. **Prix fixe** €32 (dinner only). **Lunch menu** €24. **Credit** MC, V. **Map** M6.

Restaurateuring must exact its toll, if the evolution of the owners from the two winsome babies gurgling in the photo outside into today's doleful duo is any gauge. But it's a tough life, and at least the sacrifice of the twins' joie de vivre has produced fine food. Admiring the artworks that enliven the walls and are produced either by prodigiously talented children or cruelly impaired adults, we reflected that if the food were accompanied by even a smidgeon of the élan with which it's prepared, this place would merit fevered recommendation. Layers of smoked salmon and artichoke hearts refreshed with a swagger, while the pipérade bed for the moist red tuna left a stimulating labial tingle. The cod atop peas, broad beans and onion was expertly roasted, and the bread, which was replaced as quickly as we could wolf it down, almost stole the show. Bread indulgence explains why we were only strong enough to share the glorious, clinging chocolate mousse in pistachio sauce. But still the only flicker of emotion from the twins, despite our effusive congratulations, was the look of dignified horror when they realised that one of our number was wearing cut-down shorts.

Le Passage des Carmagnoles

18 passage de la Bonne-Graine, 11th (01.47.00.73.30). M° Ledru-Rollin. **Open** Mon-Sat noon-2.30pm, 7-11.30pm. Closed Aug, one week in spring. **Average** €25. **Credit** AmEx, DC, MC, V. **Wheelchair access. Non-smoking room. Map** N7.

Try to turn up at the Passage before your dining companion to have a chance to peruse the menu in peaceful solitude. It's a treat. And also very impressively long. There's an entire page for different types of Côte Rôtie wines and another for intestine, as the aptly named Passage boasts a dozen andouillettes (tripe sausages) created by numerous artisans of the stomach. The welcoming, woody decor is warm and pleasant and the place has a scrupulously salubrious feel. We chose to share a starter of deliciously creamy polenta and grilled vegetables before entering the wonderful world of digestive tracts: we went for a spicy Beaujolais andouillette and didn't regret

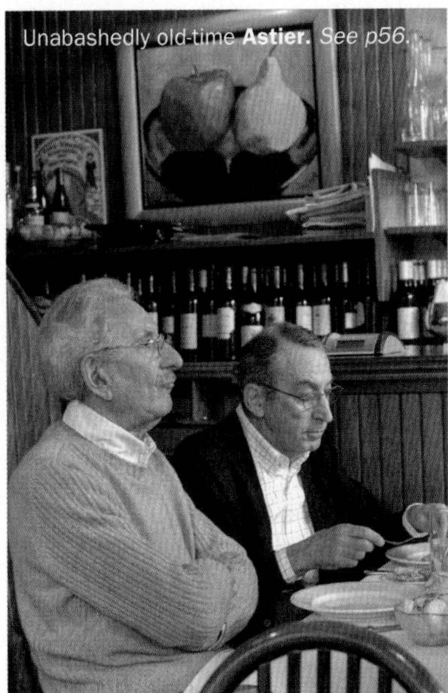
Unabashedly old-time **Astier.** See p56.

it for a minute. Did you know that one generally prefers white wine with andouillette? Neither did we but a bright, young Mâcon was a very convincing accompaniment. A perfect café liégeois and a cup of very good espresso confirmed our general impression of great care taken to get things right.

Le Repaire de Cartouche

99 rue Amelot/8 bd des Filles-du-Calvaire, 11th (01.47.00.25.86). M° St-Sébastien-Froissart. **Open** Tue-Sat noon-2pm, 7.30-11pm. Closed Aug. **Average** €30. **Lunch menu** €22. **Credit** MC, V. **Wheelchair access. Map** M5.

The rue Amelot has become a fashionable hub of youth activity, and the rather staid atmosphere of Cartouche's lair comes as something of surprise. The white tablecloths and wood-panelled room with its claustrophobic leaded windows create an atmosphere more akin to a Teutonic hunting lodge than a bustling brigand's haunt. However, for a late spring lunch the €22 menu du marché was excellent and the cooking showed attention to detail and careful product sourcing. After exemplary bread and rillettes, our first course of classic gésiers salad was enlivened by the presence of gelatinous cockscombs, and the foie gras au torchon was of excellent quality and generously served for a prix fixe. The Salers beef was exceptional, tender yet tasty, accompanied by a rich potato gratin which we learned owed its pungent cheesiness to the untraditional addition of camembert. Pied de veau was meltingly filling and a vibrant leek added a welcome green element, dressed in exemplary vinaigrette. Puddings were as carefully prepared as the rest, including thin, feather-light crêpes oozing raspberry jam, or, for those who prefer cheese, a selection of three well-chosen examples presented on a wooden board. Service was professional and the wine list contained a number of unusual regional bottles. We were particularly impressed by our Cap Corse white (€25), which brought a welcome whiff of sunshine to a restaurant that is most welcoming on a cold winter's evening.

12th Arrondissement

L'Auberge le Quincy ★

28 av Ledru-Rollin, 12th (01.46.28.46.76). M° Gare de Lyon. **Open** Tue-Fri noon-2.30pm, 7-10pm. Closed Aug. **Average** €70. **No credit cards. Map** M8.

We first tried to visit Le Quincy during Beaujolais nouveau celebrations and the country-style room, which combines gingham, model aeroplanes and gastronomic dictums, was bursting with good-humoured, well-rounded diners. Owner Bobosse, a character straight from central casting, turned us away with such charm that we determined to return as soon as possible. We were not disappointed, and anybody seeking a massive feast of trad French cooking will be in gastro-heaven. Our host proposed a cornucopian selection of starters, including fine foie gras, well aged, wafer-thin country ham, delicious warm caillettes (pork and chard patties) on a bed of mesclun salad, and a hunk of homemade terrine accompanied by a garlicky cabbage salad. The main courses kept up the quality with a creamy, succulent côte de veau aux morilles served in a copper pan and scallops which were untrimmed, quickly fried and served on a bed of pasta. Not sophisticated cuisine, but perfectly timed and irresistibly fresh. Our appetites were waning now and we resisted a serious-looking chocolate mousse, plumping instead for glasses of vieille prune served from a traditional wooden watering can, and flambéed at the table by Bobosse with well-rehearsed theatricality. The bill, which included a handsome quantity of fruity Brouilly, was substantial, but worth every penny. Remember that the cackling patronne does not have any truck with credit cards, so a wobbly totter to the cash machine is involved, which might just give you a thirst for that final nightcap.

A la Biche au Bois

45 av Ledru Rollin, 12th (01.43.43.34.38). M° Gare de Lyon. **Open** Mon-Fri noon-2.30pm, 7-11pm. Closed first three weeks in Aug. **Average** €23. **Prix fixe** €21.60. **Credit** AmEx, DC, MC, V. **Wheelchair access. Map** M8.

Among the big brasseries and tourist traps that surround the Gare de Lyon, it's a surprise to find this bistro buzzing with authenticity. We made an early reservation at 7.30pm to catch a train at 9.30pm, and the place was already hopping. The prix fixe is good value, not so much for the exceptional quality of the ingredients as for the hearty portions. A heap of white asparagus served with poached egg, and a feuilleté filled with goat cheese were fine though forgettable – the real event here is the stews, including game in season, served in enormous casserole dishes. The coq au vin was rustic rather than refined – big chunks of long-cooked meat bathing in a winey sauce with small whole potatoes and bacon – and the gibelotte de lapin was a white wine version of the same dish made with rabbit and served with a dish of potato purée, which our waiter kindly refilled. The cheese course nearly made us miss our train, but was worth it for the ripe specimens. We quickly downed a genuine crème caramel and mousse au chocolat bathed in Grand Marnier before hoofing it to the station five minutes away, in need of a rest to digest this rib-sticking meal.

Les Bombis Bistrot ★

22 rue de Chaligny, 12th (01.43.45.36.32). M° Reuilly-Diderot. **Open** Mon-Fri noon-2pm, 8-11pm. Closed two weeks in Dec. **Average** €32. **Lunch menu** €13. **Credit** MC, V. **Map** N8.

We don't know what bombis are but the aliterative name fits the bustling atmosphere at this popular bistro. On a Friday night boho couples and families were tightly wedged in to the tiny tables of the front room and diner-style banquettes of the back room which gives on to the tiled open kitchen. Prices are high for a place with no tablecloths (most mains are €18) but clearly a lot of care has gone into the persentation and flavour combinations. Some successful fusion was going on in a starter of sesame-coated scallops with Japanese pickled ginger and marinated black radish, and a main of filet mignon de porc in a red Thai curry sauce served with Mediterranean vegetables on a banana leaf. The rocket salad with Parma ham and parmesan had a melon sorbet which melted deliciously into the balsamic vinegar dressing, and the sea bass formed the centre of a star of radiating mangetout with an apple and passionfruit sauce. On no account turn down desserts: gianduja (a light type of chocolate and hazelnut mousse) with roast pineapple chunks and a peach and hibiscus nage with green tea ice cream were wonderfully refreshing and both served with crisp buttery crêpes dentelles. The wine list is strong on the Loire and Burgundy; the wine of the month, a 2000 Château Meillant Touraine for €17, was enjoyably light.

Le Saint Amarante

4 rue Biscornet, 12th (01.43.43.00.08). M° Bastille. **Open** Mon-Fri noon-3pm, 8-10.30pm; Sat 8-11pm. Closed two weeks in Aug. **Average** €40. **Prix fixe** €32. **Lunch menu** €28. **Credit** MC, V. **Map** M7.

This offbeat bistro has been through several chefs since Rodolphe Paquin first put it on the map (he's now cooking at Le Repaire de Cartouche), but with the arrival of Benoît Chemineau it has found its groove all over again. The bizarre decor of wood-panelling, 1950s-style floor tiles, and an attempt to be dressy with a few dissonant details – orchid sprays in silver-plated cups – notwithstanding, this is a relaxed place with aspirations. Glasses of white wine ordered as apéritifs came with warm, airy, little cheese puffs, and the meal itself was preceded by an amuse-bouche of frothy carrot soup. A first course of cauliflower soup with tempura oysters was fine and flavourful, and we were both delighted with our marine mains: cod steak on a bed of brandade (salt-cod purée) served with chard and spinach in a jus of baby clams, and small sole with mixed vegetables and a rich sauce of cream, butter and wine. Desserts were impressive, too, including a very original dish of fresh dates stuffed with marinated pineapple and a splendid frozen Grand Marnier soufflé. The owner's wife, assisted by a friendly young waitress, offers the type of proud, solicitous service you'll often find in the best restaurant in a smaller French provincial city, with wines to match.

Le Square Trousseau

1 rue Antoine-Vollon, 12th (01.43.43.06.00). M° Ledru-Rollin. **Open** Tue-Sat noon-2.30pm, 8-11.30pm. Closed Aug. **Average** €40. **Lunch menu** €20, €25. **Credit** MC, V. **Map** N7.

This restaurant would be worth visiting for its superb 1900s interior alone, but what makes the place a must is its joie de vivre. It's a favourite with a fashion and media crowd; the diners are uniformly elegant in urban nomad gear. Even the friendly waiters, relentlessly handsome in their long white aprons, appear celluloid-wrapped. The food, though, is for real. We started with a silky-textured smoked salmon and candied lemon timbale; a tomato, cucumber and avocado millefeuille with mozzarella, refreshing red, green and white layers of natural goodness showered with chives; and poached eggs in a fine, nutmeg-scented cheese sauce with Japanese herbs. Main courses were almost as satisfying: plump farm chicken served with a mini, creamy risotto, tender strips of duck in a delicious cherry sauce, and chicken in Moroccan-style pastry, which was a little dry. For dessert, the serving of chocolate quenelles in a saffron custard was on the frugal side, but a delight nonetheless. The relatively steep wine prices may come as a surprise, given the good-value food, but the selection shows expertise in unearthing the best from Touraine, Burgundy, Auvergne and the Vaucluse.

Les Zygomates

7 rue de Capri, 12th (01.40.19.93.04). M° Daumesnil. **Open** Mon, Sat 7.30-10.30pm, Tue-Fri noon-2pm, 7.30-10.30pm. Closed Aug. **Average** €27. **Prix fixe** €22, €27. **Lunch menu** €13. **Credit** MC, V. **Non-smoking room**. **Map** Q10.

Don't let the Radio Nostalgie pop music trickling from the kitchen or the boring amuse-bouche of wilted carrot sticks and creamy garlic dressing put you off, food at Les Zygomates is both solid and subtly inventive. Take the snail and mushroom ravioli, or the smoked salmon, red cabbage and galette appetisers – different takes on bistro staples. The turkey breast and mashed potatoes smothered in dark giblet gravy and lidded with a salted rosemary crust, or the monkfish in coriander sauce, with dollops of puréed leeks and root veggies, also ably met

No need to ask for the check at **Chez Ramulaud**. *See p58*.

the criteria of being both familiar and a bit daring. You'll find a lengthy wine list, and those interested in dining in a room with original fixtures will be pleased with the painted-tin ceiling and etched and frosted glass of this turn-of-the-20th-century former butcher's shop. In a funny way, it's at dessert time that the chef and proprietor Patrick Fray really shines. We'd never seen a dacquoise on a menu before: a macaroon-like cake with whipped cream (ours was banana-flavoured, topped with caramelised pineapple). The fondant au chocolat has a tantalising twist, too, combining bitter chocolate with orange zest and mango sorbet.

Game for anything **A la Biche au Bois**. *See p59.*

13th Arrondissement

L'Aimant du Sud

40 bd Arago, 13th (01.47.07.33.57). M° Les Gobelins or Glacière. **Open** Tue-Fri noon-2.30pm, 7.30-11pm; Sat 7.30-11pm. Closed first two weeks in Aug and one week at Christmas. **Average** €30. **Lunch menu** €13, €16. **Credit** AmEx, DC, MC, V. **Map** J10.

The name suggests an affection for the sun, a sentiment this modest bistro expresses with its golden-hued interior hung with nude-themed oil paintings, bar and table tops panelled in wine-crates and informal vibe from the waiters, who work against a background of Motown and 1980s hits. Most of chef David Sponga's menu is entrecôte and confit de canard territory, so look carefully for some innovation among the predictable if well-executed standards. We enjoyed our salmon carpaccio, bathed in a lemon marinade, and the chèvre croustillant, its cinnamon and nutmeg spicing pleasantly startling. A crisp and juicy saddle of lamb stuffed with fresh rosemary sprigs, and the filet mignon de porc infused with ginger were equally on target. Desserts are the expected classics, so we tried an exotic-sounding pistachio-flavoured clementine gratin, unfortunately soupy and ordinary, and the chocolate terrine, which scored high on the choco-meter. The wine selection is decent, though it's hard to find a bottle for under €20. The generous terrace would be a more pleasant oasis if the boulevard Arago wasn't so noisy, but interior tables are well-shielded from the traffic.

Anacréon

53 bd St-Marcel, 13th (01.43.31.71.18). M° Les Gobelins or St-Marcel. **Open** Tue, Thur-Sat noon-2.30pm, 7.30-11pm; Wed 7.30-11pm. Closed Aug. **Prix fixe** €32. **Lunch menu** €20. **Credit** AmEx, DC, MC, V. **Map** K9.

Anacréon has been reported as having a lacklustre decor and even glummer service, but we found the look and feel to be more than palatable. Youthful but energetic waiters efficiently attended to our needs while the interior design, a funky 1960s/70s-remnant mustard and green colour scheme, was still far from offensive. Chef André Le Letty wins you over and warms up your palate with a wee dish of cold leek velouté before the real show begins: escargots in a rosemary cream sauce set around a cornflour and egg soufflé, and a smoked pollack marinated in citrus juice and chopped raw veg. Next come some cleverly done fish and meats, many incorporating candied fruits and spices such as ginger. The chunk of cod roasted in a buckwheat beer sauce keeps the flesh rightly moist, a strategy used to equal effect in the fillet of capitaine (threadfin) in carrot milk. Tender duck breast slices topped with lemon zest arrive with complementary leeks and sweet potatoes. Desserts included nougat ice cream with seaweed confit and pineapple, and the stunning milk chocolate mousse, whose lighter flavours harmonise with the candied lemon and ginger.

L'Avant-Goût ★

26 rue Bobillot, 13th (01.53.80.24.00). M° Place d'Italie. **Open** Tue-Fri noon-2pm, 7.30-11pm. Closed one week in Jan, one week in May, three weeks in Aug/Sept. **Prix fixe** €26. **Lunch menu** €12. **Credit** MC, V.

Hugely popular with a following that hails from the 'hood – as well as Houston, Hull and Hamburg – this is one of the best and most generous modern bistros on the Left Bank. Chef Christophe Beaufront and his wife run the restaurant like a sort of all-comers party every night, but service is commendably professional and prompt. With a money-spinner on his hands, Beaufront might have been tempted to cut all sorts of corners – raise prices, lower quality, turn tables faster – but he hasn't for the simple reason that he insists on enjoying what he's doing. The blackboard menu doesn't change much, but who cares when it's a question of eating so well at this price? During a recent meal, everything was delicious. Starters of tuna tartare with roasted vegetables, herby cold spinach soup garnished with poppyseed-coated croutons, and a medley of spring vegetables in a light bouillon with a poached egg were all first-rate. Beaufront's signature dish is a pot-au-feu de cochon, and it was every bit as good as we remembered – a big, round, casserole brimming with off-cuts of pork, fennel and sweet potato, served with gherkins, horseradish sauce and ginger chips. Coley with broccoli purée and a drizzle of black olive cream was tasty, though the fish was a tad overcooked. We finished up our delicious €21 Cairanne with an intriguing terrine of roquefort, butter and preserved pear, and an unusual cocoa soup. Beaufront's takeaway address across the road would be reason enough to move to the area.

Chez Paul

22 rue de la Butte-aux-Cailles, 13th (01.45.89.22.11). M° Place d'Italie or Corvisart. **Open** daily noon-2.30pm, 7.30pm-midnight. Closed Christmas. **Average** €35. **Credit** MC, V. **Wheelchair access.**

Chez Paul is a beacon to professional types who lurk in the quirky 13th arrondissement, its white-cloth-and-wood approach offering a chic alternative to other offbeat spots along the strip. Tradition takes pride of plate (pot-au-feu, beef knuckle, bone marrow – in fact, bones galore) and you can eat your way from one end of a beast to the other, from beef tongue to tail or pig's ear to rear. Seafood makes an appearance on the blackboard menu with oysters, whelks, an excellent starter of pan-fried mullet fillets with olive tapenade and a main of monkfish nuggets in a creamy garlic sauce with gleaming green spinach. A classic saddle of lamb, with the house's famed mashed potatoes, was another good choice. Desserts such as réglisse (liquorice) ice cream and marquise au chocolat along with good-natured service and a carafe of chilled Brouilly also went down well. On a Monday night the joint was jumping, so if you want a bone to pick, book.

La Girondine

48 bd Arago, 13th (01.43.31.64.17). M° Glacière. **Open** Mon-Thur noon-2.30pm, 7.30-10.30pm; Fri noon-2.30pm, 7.30-11pm; Sat 7.30-11pm. **Average** €40. **Prix fixe** €16. **Credit** AmEx, DC, MC, V. **Map** J10.

On a busy boulevard, this superficially smart bistro was seemingly still in the throes of a post-Christmas hangover when we called on a sunny weekday in March – the food, setting and staff all showed signs of over-stretch. After being crammed next to a table of five dedicated smokers, we asked for the non-smoking area and were directed away from the terrace (weedy pots of white-painted Yuletide twigs, ripped plastic awnings fixed with gaffer tape) to a windowless pit between the back wall and a five-foot high wooden screen. From blackboards and à la carte menus screaming 'fish', we duly opted for a starter of crispy tempura-style scallops followed by scallops and red mullet 'en croûte' with pistou. The tempura were fresh and appetisingly presented with a salad featuring delicious crispy-fried shreds of leek, while the coquilles St-Jacques were few and far between, served with greasy vegetables and overpriced at €19. The mullet, coated with a dry herb crust on a pile of ordinary mashed potato, made for an unpleasantly textured and rather tasteless dish. By comparison, our neighbours' bistro staples – steak or half a baby chicken with fresh pasta – looked plain but ample and well-cooked. A dessert of chestnut cream sandwiched between home-made crispy wafers on a raspberry coulis was better, but overly heavy on the cream.

Au Petit Marguery ★

9 bd du Port-Royal, 13th (01.43.31.58.59). M° Gobelins. **Open** Tue-Sat noon-2.15pm, 7.30-10.15pm. Closed Aug, one week in Dec. **Average** €30. **Prix fixe** €33.60. **Lunch menu** €25.20. **Credit** AmEx, MC, V. **Map** J9.

'We really should go back in the game season,' is a comment often made about the attractively old-world Petit Marguery, formerly run by the Cousin brothers, and so it was with something of a sense of triumph that we entered the restaurant to have lunch in the first week of October. The three-course prix fixe (€33.60, plus rather too many supplements) is a game-lover's fantasy and we plunged straight in with a grouse purée and a pheasant and foie gras terrine. The purée was a real winner, a mousse-like

How to Eat **Bread**

Bread is to the French what rice is to Asians: the single most important staple. In bistros, a basket of sliced baguette is usually the first thing to land on your table; in classier establishments, the waiter will arrive with a basket of rolls and transfer them with tongs to your bread plate. When there is no bread plate, you're expected to place the bread on the tablecloth (or table), not on your plate. Instead of biting directly into the slice or roll, the French rip off bite-sized chunks. Butter is not usually provided in bistros, though salted Breton butter has become a fashionable addition. But the essential question is, 'To mop or not to mop?' At the restaurant L'Espadon in The Ritz, the maître d' assured us nearly all their customers give in to the urge to clean their plates with their bread, adding, 'I've never seen anyone use a fork to do this.'

paste with a rich game and juniper flavour. The terrine was well-made but there was disappointingly no perceptible taste of pheasant. Warming to our task we continued with that most classic of French game dishes, lièvre à la royale, a long-marinated wine- infused dish with a chocolate-brown sauce in which blood and foie gras play a part. This was a joyful autumn dish, as was the wonderfully moist partridge served plainly on liver-spread croutons with its thick bacon barding. Our strong Crozes Hermitage red (€24) held up well to the game assault, and to finish our meal we indulged in soufflés au Grand Marnier, which although spectacular in appearance and making, lacked enough punch to crown our hunter's feast. The only downside of the meal was the rather sullen service; perhaps our waiter hadn't bagged his bird.

Le Terroir

11 bd Arago, 13th (01.47.07.36.99). M° Gobelins.
Open Mon-Fri noon-3pm, 7.45-10.15pm. Closed Easter, three weeks in Aug, Christmas. **Average** €35. **Credit** MC, V. **Map** J10.

Such is the reputation of this temple of down-to-earth provincial cooking that our dinner invitation had our French friend salivating with anticipatory joy. When we arrived, locals and tourists were already wedged into the tightly packed tables tucking into hefty terrines of pâté de campagne. The ingredients that are the gastronomic pride of France are showcased here in a menu that includes classics such as chunky rumpsteak with mountains of chips or green beans, skate wing in butter and as much charcuterie as the beleaguered French pig can ever provide. Although helpings are on the whole generous (except for our minute poêlée of wild mushrooms), the service jokey and the general feeling one of the good old classic Paris bistro, there is something that is not quite right. Perhaps it was the toughish steak, the ratio of fat to meat in the terrine or the boring wine list? We thought the dishes lacked precision and, from the boss's sarcastic reaction to our neighbour's remark on soggy veg, we concluded that beneath the veneer of jokey patter, the cash register rings loud and clear. Indeed, the prices are not quite as convivial as the atmosphere: €119 for two starters, two mains and two bottles of extremely basic Beaujolais. Still, given the current vogue for rustic cuisine, Le Terroir is not likely to lose many customers in the immediate future.

14th Arrondissement

L'Assiette

181 rue du Château, 14th (01.43.22.64.86). M° Mouton-Duvernet. **Open** Wed-Sun noon-2.30pm, 8-10.30pm. Closed Aug. **Average** €65. **Lunch menu** €35. **Credit** AmEx, MC, V. **Map** G10.

Eccentric, hands-on chef Lulu, still sporting her characteristic beret, continues to pull celebrity crowds to her deluxe bistro. The stripped-wood floor and wipe-off laminated veneer tables make this an unusually relaxed and lively room for what is actually one of the capital's most expensive bistros. The exceptional freshness and quality of the products, coupled with the simple precision of the cooking, almost justify the price. Refreshingly free of frilly appetisers, our autumn meal began with a pheasant and foie gras terrine which retained a taste of game, and a mound of the plumpest imaginable cockles bathed in a frothy lemon butter. A simply roasted wild duck with a punchy jus was served with a preserved pear, which may have come from the tree that harboured our other dish of moist partridge. This was accompanied by gravy-infused cabbage, which had been cooked to melting point without sacrificing colour or texture. Lulu makes an apology on the menu for the nursery puddings such as crème caramel and marquise au chocolat, claiming disingenuously that these are the only ones she knows how to make. They looked the part but we opted for a pile of thinly shaved cheese from the Pyrenees, which brought the meal to a memorable close. The wine list features many regional choices, and our tannic red from the Roussillon region (€36) perfectly complemented the game. We will save up for a return visit to sample some fish, which looked tempting on our neighbour's assiette.

Contre-Allée ★

83 av Denfert-Rochereau, 14th (01.43.54.99.86/ www.contreallee.com). M° Denfert-Rochereau.
Open Mon-Fri, Sun noon-2pm, 7.30-10.30pm; Sat 8-10.30pm. Closed Christmas. **Average** €37. **Prix fixe** €37, €31. **Credit** AmEx, MC, V. **Wheelchair access. Non-smoking room. Map** H10.

One thing we've always liked about the Contre-Allée is its flexible formula. You can opt for two starters and a dessert, which allows you to eat lightly and creatively, or go the more conventional route. Fusion influences showed, on our latest visit, a marked Far Eastern shift. We followed the starters option, getting a panorama of cuisines and techniques. Asparagus served both warm (green and white with a creamy orange-flavoured mousseline sauce) and raw (thin slivers dressed with olive oil and red Espelette pepper) was well-judged and delicious. Crispy bonbons of prawns showed assorted Oriental influences at play, with crisp filo pastry bundles containing prawns and tiny bean sprouts, accompanied by peanut sauce and a tabouleh and lamb's lettuce salad. Mediterranean tendencies showed up in an artichoke stew served with thin slices of dry cured beef and bowl of meaty broth containing ricotta and parmesan ravioli and vegetables. Desserts mix some classic mainstays (a trio of strawberry preparations) and the distinctly peculiar: chocolate 'nems' with a pink rose jelly, frosted rose petals and apricot sorbet looked spectacular but were let down by the over-heavy combination of warm chocolate and Vietnamese rice crêpe. But, if some things work better than others, this remains a reliable place for an interesting meal, the setting is quietly stylish, service friendly and there's a great terrace in summer.

Natacha

17bis rue Campagne-Première, 14th (01.43.20.79.27). M° Raspail. **Open** Mon-Sat noon-2.30pm, 8-11.30pm; Sun 11am-4.30pm. Closed two weeks in Aug. **Average** €35. **Lunch menu** €19. **Credit** AmEx, MC, V. **Non-smoking room**. **Map** G9.

The celebrity-magnet Natacha is long gone – off travelling the world, visiting her glitterati mates it's rumoured. Welcome the new chef-owner, ex L'Ambroisie and Lasserre, to the stove and a new team to the dining room (a charmer and a scowler). Judging from a recent meal they're still finding their feet. The chef forgot the poached egg in the smoked salmon, potato and poached egg salad; although when this was pointed out a bullet-hard one was added to the scant slices of salmon and spuds. Gazpacho needed no additions; packed with fresh tomato, punchy onion flavour and crunchy croutons. A mediocre slice of lamb came with a hill of green beans while steamed cod was paired with halved artichokes, which were, according to the menu, supposed to be stuffed. Oh well, since when have menus told the truth? The runny chocolate moelleux with vanilla ice cream and homemade madeleines were nice, though. It's a pretty restaurant – rust-coloured walls and lots of modern artwork and silk cushions – and, when the food steps up to match the decor, it could be worth the detour.

L'O à la Bouche ★

124 bd du Montparnasse, 14th (01.56.54.01.55). M° Vavin. **Open** Tue-Thur noon-3pm, 7-11pm; Fri, Sat noon-3pm, 7pm-midnight. Closed three weeks in Aug. **Average** €50. **Prix fixe** (dinner only) €26-€31. **Lunch menu** €16, €19. **Credit** AmEx, MC, V. **Non-smoking room**. **Map** G9.

Guy Savoy-trained Franck Paquier was one of the pioneers of the modern bistro movement, launching this comfortable, slightly upmarket operation just over four years ago. Little appears to have changed – certainly not the vaguely Tuscan terracotta colour scheme, the reasonably priced menu-carte and the daily specials board, brought to each table in turn. And you still need to order dessert at the beginning of the meal. Of the original dishes, the salad of deep-fried tiger prawns with shredded root vegetables has stood the test of time, but elsewhere there's plenty of inspiration and creativity. Seasonality is at the heart of Paquier's cooking – winter brings the likes of a satisfying chestnut soup with lots of ceps and truffle oil, a homely lamb shank braised with rosemary, tomatoes, Tarbais and coco beans and an unusual pineapple cake with banana sorbet and rum-infused raisins. Fish is a mainstay, ranging from the fashionable (pan-fried scorpion fish fillet with piquillo peppers, crushed ratte potatoes and horseradish sauce) to the more classical (roast turbot with wilted greens and tarragon emulsion), while the tarte fine aux pommes caramélisées – light, buttery pastry, golden apples and smooth vanilla ice cream – is difficult to fault. Front-of-house, however, can sometimes lack the polish of the kitchen, and it would help if staff would smile a bit more.

Les Petites Sorcières

12 rue Liancourt, 14th (01.43.21.95.68). M° Denfert-Rochereau. **Open** Mon, Sat 8-10pm; Tue-Fri noon-2pm, 8-10pm. Closed mid-July to mid-Aug.

It's no half-measures at **Les Zygomates**. *See p60.*

Plates of style at **L'Assiette**. *See p64.*

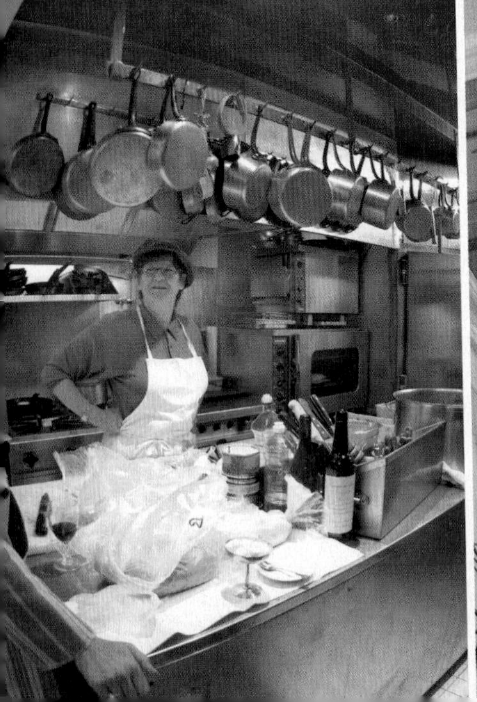

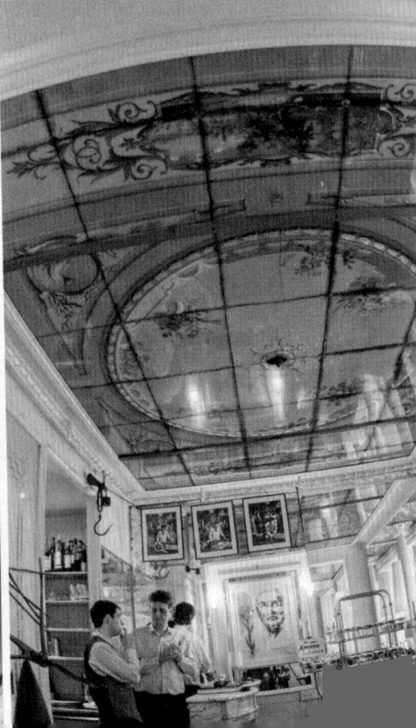

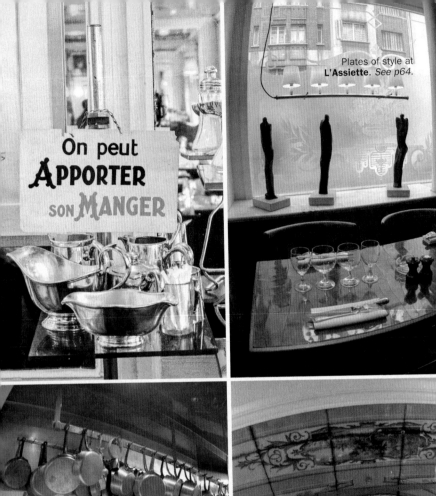

Average €30. **Prix fixe** €30. **Lunch menu** €22. **Credit** MC, V. **Map** G10.

Forget the hokey decor (red velvet entry curtains, Halloween theme lamps and a vast assembly of airborne witches), the real sorcery is in the kitchen. Christian Teule conjures up sophisticated French classics with a contemporary twist, spot-on every time. The rich lentil soup, cushioning a delicately earthy foie gras poêlé, was crowned with a drizzle of balsamic vinegar, while the splendid boudin noir tart, rings of grilled black pudding, caramelised onion 'jam' and a dense square of crisp pastry, was defiantly light. Main courses included a lemony blanquette de veau, a thick Aubrac steak, and a juicy hunk of pink canard rouennais with crisp, honey-pepper skin. Seamless service (once Mme Teule had dispensed her rather brusque welcome) ensured that desserts, most cooked to order, arrived just as we were wanting them. And the magic continued. The pear clafoutis was moist and almondy, and the warm chocolate tart – sablé pastry encasing an intense bittersweet soup – a chocoholic's fantasy. Wines are on the pricey side, although the low-end options are more than drinkable.

La Régalade ★

49 av Jean-Moulin, 14th (01.45.45.68.58).
M° Alésia. **Open** Mon-Thur 11am-2pm, 7-11pm; Fri, Sat 11am-2pm, 7pm-midnight. Closed Aug. **Prix fixe** €30. **Credit** MC, V.

It still takes a substantial effort to secure a booking at Yves Camdeborde's rustic, convivial and slightly out-of-the-way bistro, a great Parisian success story. We managed to squeeze in early before the dinner rush, and were rewarded with some of the best cooking to be had in the city. Camdeborde's approach is characterised by generosity (the trademark terrine with cornichons, served à volonté as an appetiser), and sheer exuberance. The choice of eight dishes for each course on the €30 prix fixe includes the likes of a black pudding gratin, a carpaccio of calf's head, and tiny squid cooked like piballes (elvers) with a squid ink risotto. For a few euros more you can have a ravioli of Breton lobster, a matelote of eel from the Loire or a whole roast duck liver from the Gers. Desserts are just as exciting, ranging from a refreshing guariguette strawberry soup with orange flower water and lemon confit to a rich, thoroughly indulgent Guanaja chocolate custard with langue de chat biscuits. Wines are well chosen and decently priced (it's worth asking for advice and trying some of the less-known appellations) and this is one place where apéritifs and dessert wines should not be missed.

15th Arrondissement

Bistro d'Hubert

41 bd Pasteur, 15th (01.47.34.15.50). M° Pasteur. **Open** Mon-Fri, Sun 12.30-2pm, 7.30-10.30pm; Sat 7.30-10.30pm. **Average** €39. **Prix fixe** €39. **Lunch menu** €19, €29.50. **Credit** AmEx, DC, MC, V. **Wheelchair access**. **Map** E9.

The sight of cooks at work in the open-plan kitchen immediately gave us an appetite, so we were grateful to sip the house apéritif, a potent cocktail of sweet white grape juice and Armagnac, and nibble on an appetiser of warm snails in a superbly flavourful and unctuous cream sauce. Turning to the menu, dishes were divided between 'Tradition' and the more exotic 'Discovery.' For starters, the salmon and prawn millefeuille was a grand name for a disappointingly plain dish – we preferred the more unusual offering of tuna sashimi with slivers of marinated fresh ginger in a sesame oil dressing. For mains, traditionalists can choose between chicken breast in an almond croûte, and black pudding with apple sautéed in duck fat, whereas the more audacious could try the lightly cooked, extremely fresh cod steak in a ratatouille sauce flavoured with aniseed, wild thyme, caraway seeds and blanc de chine. Desserts were similarly varied, and we particularly liked the two-tone chocolate and apple mousse with a light cream sprinkled with angels' hair.

Chez Les Frères Gaudet ★

19 rue Duranton, 15th (01.45.58.43.17).
M° Boucicaut. **Open** Mon, Sat 7.45-10pm; Tue-Fri noon-2pm, 7.45-10pm. **Prix fixe** €38. **Credit** AmEx, MC, V.

If this restaurant were anywhere but on a quiet street in an outlying part of the 15th arrondissement, it would surely have become a popular word-of-mouth address, since the food is excellent and a very good buy. For the time being, however, it remains an insider's address with an assiduous local following of professional couples in the evening and a television and UNESCO crowd at noon. The calm of the salmon-coloured dining room is part of its charm, since tables are well-spaced and service well-paced and friendly. The Gaudet brothers in the kitchen – Jean-Yves, the chef, who trained at Lucas Carton and L'Ambroisie, among other restaurants, and Hugues, the pastry chef – concoct truly delicious traditional French dishes with a stylish gloss of modernity. Start with the salad of skate, cabbage and walnuts, the marinated oysters or the homemade foie gras, and then try main courses such as the delicate dariole de homard, a sort of flan with a few discreet morsels of lobster, served with a baked apple, or the delicious bourride, a creamy, garlicky soup with monkfish. Desserts are first-rate, including orange-sauced crêpes, runny chocolate cake and a pear poached in Muscat wine with a slice of sugared brioche toast.

La Dînée

85 rue Leblanc, 15th (01.45.54.20.49). M° Balard. **Open** Mon-Fri noon-2.15pm, 7.30-11pm. Closed three weeks in Aug. **Prix fixe** €26.90, €29.90. **Credit** AmEx, DC, MC, V.

This classy address is well worth the trip to the end of Métro line 8. The eclectic mix of regulars and out-of-towners filling the place on a midweek evening underlined the point. There's a hint of something Japanese about the low-key atmosphere – it's simple yet elegant with prints of fruit and vegetables on the ochre walls, bamboo place-mats and attentive yet unobtrusive service. The prix fixe menus are an excellent way to sample Christophe Chabanel's inventive, often witty creations. From a tempting array of starters, we chose a light crab soufflé with mushrooms and raspberry coulis and the sautéed prawns in a tangy pepper and tomato gazpacho, set off – île flottante-style – by a peak of frothy egg white and chives. Haddock lasagne was tempting as a main, but we opted for a superb plate of mixed lamb cuts with fresh mint and tabouleh and a juicy suprême de pintade on a bed of chicory and mushrooms. The melting chocolate tart in a dark chocolate sauce was rich enough for the most decadent of palates; the flambéed banana in ginger coconut milk, accompanied by a delicate coconut-infused crème caramel, a lighter alternative. The Sancerre 2001 balanced things out nicely.

La Folletterie ★

34 rue Letellier, 15th (01.45.75.55.95). M° La Motte-Picquet-Grenelle. **Open** Tue-Fri noon-2pm, 7.30-10pm; Sat 7.30-10pm. Closed three weeks in Aug. **Prix fixe** €25 (dinner only). **Lunch menu** €21. **Credit** MC, V. **Non-smoking room**. Map C8.

For stylish, original fare at an affordable price, this modish little bistro behind the bustling rue du Commerce scores a real hit. Young chef Frédéric Breton changes his menu at least once a week according to what is market-fresh. Although that choice is limited to three options per course, the quality, inventiveness and presentation easily compensate. We started with a superb cream of Jerusalem artichoke soup topped off with thin slices of duck liver and a delightfully light filo parcel of melting ripe cheese, accompanied by leeks, red cabbage and a twist of chicory. The gigot d'agneau was succulent in its rich sauce and perfectly set off by the potato purée with a hint of hazelnut. Pork fillet, accompanied by shallots and roasted chicory, was also well-executed – although we found both dishes a little too salty. A puddingy moelleux au chocolat followed, and some perfectly judged honey and pine nut ice cream. A quiet spot well worth hunting down.

L'Os à Moëlle

3 rue Vasco-de-Gama, 15th (01.45.57.27.27). M° Lourmel. **Open** Tue-Thur 12.15-2pm, 7.30-11.30pm; Fri, Sat 12.15-2pm, 7.30pm-midnight. Closed two weeks in Aug. **Prix fixe** €32 (dinner only). **Lunch menu** €27. **Credit** MC, V. **Wheelchair access**.

The lace curtains and the sleepy location of this place do attract lunching 'dames d'un certain âge', but the evening we visited it was also populated by a crowd of young locals, attracted by the fine cuisine of chef Thierry Faucher and his team. The daily changing, six-course menu dégustation might sound dangerously close to gluttony, but we consumed the modest-sized portions of delicately prepared food without remorse. We started with a flavoursome pheasant broth sprinkled liberally with fresh coriander, which set the tone for the ensuing delicacies. The first fish course was a colourful creation of oven-cooked red mullet offset by slow-cooked sweet red peppers and lightly caramelised onions, all served with a beetroot coulis. This was followed by another great fish course of marked contrasts, with a choice between sea bream, roasted in rosemary and thyme and accompanied by leeks cooked in a buttery sauce, or perfectly cooked sea bass on a bed of trompette de la mort mushrooms married unusually with a pronounced lobster sauce. The meat course consisted of either gamey wild duck in a cep mushroom sauce studded with peppercorns, or succulent lamb delicately roasted with a head of garlic. This feast was rounded off by a slice of ewe's milk tomme, and a good selection of desserts including the chef's winning quenelle de chocolat in an unctuous saffron cream. Just opposite is the sister restaurant, La Cave de l'Os à Moëlle, which serves earthy dishes in an informal table d'hôte atmosphere.

Le Père Claude

51 av de la Motte-Picquet, 15th (01.47.34.03.05). M° La Motte-Picquet-Grenelle. **Open** daily noon-2pm, 7.30-10.30pm. **Average** €50. **Prix fixe** €24, €29. **Lunch menu** €20 (Mon-Fri). **Credit** AmEx, MC, V. **Non-smoking room. Map** D7.

Recent renovations have made this bistro as neat and unfussy as the lobby of a modern luxury hotel – beige carpeting, Scandinavian-style furniture, and pleasant, professional waiters. But the sleekness belies the basic if well-executed bistro food, some of it roasted right behind the zinc-and-marquetry bar. A chèvre croustillant with salad was just the right combination of creamy and crisp, while the cold fish terrine cleverly came with garlicky tomato salsa. For mains, we couldn't resist that sizzling rotisserie meat, ordering a mixed grill of chicken, beef, pork and boudin, and a poulet rôti moelleux, both accompanied by silky mashed potatoes which added to the home-cooked, comfort-food feeling. For dessert, we enjoyed an apple clafoutis and an assortment of sorbets, including green apple worthy of an Italian gelato. Surprisingly, the light-filled, glassed-in terrace jutting on to the pavement is reserved for non-smokers, a real plus. On the afternoon we visited, the crowd was mostly middle-aged couples and business bods (we were the sole English speakers) and, seeing the photo near the entryway of a smiling Chirac with Gregory Peck, we wondered how often heads of state and Hollywooders really eat here. Just then Lionel Jospin and his entourage arrived for lunch, proving that even ousted party leaders prefer a humble lunch in an executive setting.

Le Sept/Quinze

29 av Lowendal, 15th (01.43.06.23.06). M° Cambronne. **Open** Mon-Fri noon-2.30pm, 8-11pm; Sat 8-11pm. Closed three weeks in Aug. **Prix fixe** €26 (dinner only). **Lunch menu** €17, €23. **Credit** MC, V. **Map** D8.

There's a lot to love about the Sept/Quinze, from its obliging staff to the likeable food it dishes up. Admittedly, the area might not be renowned as a

Basqueing in its stylish surroundings: **Le Troquet**.

'fun' quartier but you could be persuaded otherwise perched at a table here. Despite a recent turnover of ownership and staff, the place is still pumping, packed with an effusive crowd who linger over juicy, red steaks with black olive crust and seared tuna with soy sauce, sesame seeds and long beans. Daily specials plump out the smallish menu: starters might include duck carpaccio with white truffle oil and pecorino cheese or creamy polenta with gorgonzola, while mains stretch from risotto with gambas, peas and fresh mint to lamb chops with creamy potato purée. Trad desserts are best, especially the crumbles; the more inventive efforts, such as aubergine wafers with basil ice cream, are best left for non-sugar-loving thrill-seekers. Friendly atmosphere, good, mod-Med food at a moderate price – is this really Paris?

Le Troquet ★

21 rue François-Bonvin, 15th (01.45.66.89.00). M° Sèvres-Lecourbe. **Open** Tue-Sat noon-2.30pm, 7.30-11pm. Closed three weeks in Aug, one week at Christmas. **Prix fixe** (dinner only) €28, €30. **Lunch menu** €23, €25. **Credit** MC, V. **Map** D8.

After polishing his technique in Christian Constant's famed kitchens, the burly Christian Etchebest took the reins of this bistro from his uncle a few years ago. Decorated with 1930s light fixtures and bawdy drawings alongside a proudly displayed Crillon certificate, the restaurant feels deceptively old-fashioned. If Etchebest's Basque-inspired cooking has occasional country touches, his style is far more modern than the surroundings suggest. Choosing from a limited but tempting lunch menu, we started with fresh goat's cheese on crisp pastry, sprinkled with Espelette pepper and served with just-cooked red cabbage. Vegetable soup sounded virtuous but, to our delight, turned out to be a creamy, cardamom-scented blend, which we ladled ourselves on to foie gras and a spoonful of crème fraîche. Both mains were stunning: a thick tuna steak wrapped in cured ham was served with a rich squash purée, while a plump farm chicken breast stuffed with tapenade was accompanied by deeply flavoured cabbage cooked with juniper, pork and olive oil. Desserts of soft meringue with roasted figs, and a crème renversée (upside-down custard) with raspberries, were less remarkable. But we could hardly complain, especially given the excellent service, with Etchebest bidding farewell to each diner.

16th Arrondissement

La Butte Chaillot

110bis av Kléber, 16th (01.47.27.88.88). M° Trocadéro. **Open** Mon-Fri, Sun noon-3pm, 7.30-11pm; Sat 7.30-11pm. **Average** €37. **Prix fixe** €30. **Credit** AmEx, DC, MC, V. **Wheelchair access. Map** B5.

This Guy Savoy satellite is an ideal place for a business meal, since the cool Jean-Michel Wilmotte decor has an odd aura of anonymity that allows one to concentrate on the business at hand. Otherwise, even though the food is good and the very young, and completely unsupervised, waiters friendly, it's in no way memorable. We started with a millefeuille of vegetables (tomato, aubergine and courgette, too cold and oversalted) with rocket salad and a 'carpaccio' of thinly sliced melon topped with diced serrano ham and rocket salad, and both were just fine. Seated by a busy waiters station we understood why the bread was stale—it was sorted and repeatedly re-served, but a pleasant if overpriced Colombo St-Joseph helped us to find a groove, even though our ears were filled with English from all corners of the globe. Steamed salmon on a bed of aubergine caviar with a citrus dressing was pleasant summer eating, while roast breast of guinea fowl in a cinammon-spiked reduction of its cooking juice came with sautéed spinach, to which the waiter agreeably added a little copper casserole of potato puree. The melted chocolate cake with vanilla ice cream was pleasant enough, too, but we left with no marked desire to return, except, perhaps, for a business meal.

Les Ormes ★

8 rue Chapu, 16th (01.46.47.83.98). M° Exelmans. **Open** Tue-Sat 12.15-2pm, 7.45-10pm. Closed Aug, first week in Jan. **Average** €45. **Prix fixe** €40.50 (dinner and Sat lunch). **Lunch menu** €26, €30. **Credit** AmEx, MC, V.

Although he's tucked away in a tiny, dressy dining room – yellow fabric walls and formally set tables – in a fairly remote part of town, it's worth the trip to discover the cooking of talented young chef Stéphane Molé. Molé trained with Joël Robuchon, and his pedigree shows in delicious cooking that's at once lusty and refined. The brief, good-value prix fixe – three courses plus cheese from the excellent fromagerie Alléosse – changes almost daily according to what Molé finds in the market, but typical dishes include quenelles de brochet (pike-perch dumplings) with sauce américaine, snails and wild mushrooms with a sorrel timbale, pumpkin soup garnished with sautéed lamb sweetbreads, and boneless veal knuckle with gnocchi. Desserts are excellent, too, from a runny moelleux au chocolat to an individual tarte Tatin, and the wine list offers many good buys, including a superb Cornas at €43. A favourite of sedate locals, the dining room draws its liveliness from a growing number of word-of-mouth diners from other parts of town.

Le Passiflore

33 rue de Longchamp, 16th (01.47.04.96.81). M° Trocadéro or Iéna. **Open** Mon-Fri noon-2pm, 7.30-10.30pm; Sat 8-10.30pm. Closed Aug. **Average** €65. **Prix fixe** €54 (dinner only). **Lunch menu** €33. **Credit** AmEx, MC, V. **Map** C5.

With their gracious and solicitous service, chef Roland Durand (formerly at the Pré Catalan) and his wife have made this intimate, elegant and surprisingly relaxed dining room a hit. Unfortunately, however, our most recent meal here was a decidedly mixed performance. Aside from inaccurate cooking and mixed-up orders, our main problem was the recurring sweetness in many dishes – we found a main course of oysters and langoustines with whipped sweet yams and lemongrass especially confused, since the lovely brinyness of the molluscs was lost to the purée and the dish lacked texture. If Durand enjoys visiting the flavour constellations of other cuisines – we once had a first-rate boudin antillais (spicy black pudding) here – the heavily perfumed and sugary notes in his cooking make many dishes seem like something you'd feed to children. When he cooks for a more adult palate, as seen in ceps sautéed with shallots and bacon or veal with lentils, the result is splendid. There are some good buys on the wine list, desserts are good, including a raspberry and lemon tart, and the young waiters mean well even though they sometimes lack skill.

Le Petit Rétro

5 rue Mesnil, 16th (01.44.05.06.05/ www.petitretro.fr). M° Victor-Hugo. **Open** Mon-Fri noon-2.30pm, 7-10.30pm. Closed Aug. **Average** €35. **Lunch menu** €18, €22. **Credit** AmEx, MC, V. **Non-smoking room. Map** B4.

Just around the corner from the fountains of place Victor-Hugo this art nouveau-tiled bistro serves hearty dishes that would make a butcher proud. There's lots of lovely offal and the dishes of the day chalked on a blackboard looked particularly enticing. To wit, we chose the oeufs pochés with foie gras, an indulgent combination of nannyish runny eggs and grown-up foie gras, while the regular menu yielded an impressive cassolette d'escargots with pleurottes. Like a magician at a children's party, the chef emerged from the kitchen to demonstrate how to cut the puffy crust of this dish and mash it in the wonderfully earthy snail- and mushroom-filled gravy. Utterly delicious. The croustillant de boudin was equally good: black pudding in a pastry crust with rich sauce, served with fried potatoes and apples, and the blackboard's canaillette grillée (duck andouillette) on a bed of potato purée was marred only by too much Dijon mustard in the sauce. Stuffed almost to the gills we had to request a respite before the ice-cream-filled profiteroles, lolling in their potent chocolate sauce, and a stickily good nougat glacée. Our only complaints are that the service is too swift for such lavish fare and that the waiter couldn't help much with our choice of wine. We struck out with a Beaumes-de-Venise, a bitter bottle that did not merit its €24 and rather marred our meal. The kir apéritifs, on the other hand, were perfect.

Le Scheffer

22 rue Scheffer, 16th (01.47.27.81.11). M° Trocadéro. **Open** Mon-Sat noon-2.30pm, 7.30-10.30pm. Closed Sat in July and Aug, 25 Dec-2 Jan. **Average** €24. **Credit** AmEx, MC, V. **Map** B5.

A stone's throw from busy Trocadéro, Le Scheffer is a tourist-free haven for French family-style dining. OK, so the BCBG couples (French Sloanes), some with immaculate enfants, aren't your average family, but their palates are reassuringly classical. Start with the os à moëlle, unctuous marrow bone which you slather on bread and top with coarse salt, or a hearty slice of duck terrine paired with onion jam: both guaranteed to take the edge off your appetite. Main courses include confit de canard maison, a crispy rendition of that bistro standard, and salmon grilled à l'unilatéral (a one-sided cooking

Roasting before your very eyes at **Le Père Claude**. *See p68*.

method that ensures moistness is retained) and topped with fresh herbs. We washed it all down with a tasty pichet of Chinon and braced ourselves for dessert. A mound of profiteroles, drenched in rich, dark chocolate, vied with the fluffy île flottante for top sweet and we were glad of both. There's no avant-garde gastronomy here, no unbeatable ambience, and your dinner will probably have lows as well as highs. But there's something inescapably 'authentic' about a night at Le Scheffer – checked tablecloths, vintage posters and a stern patronne not withstanding. Be sure to book ahead; even on Monday, it's a packed house.

17th Arrondissement

Le Bistrot d'à Côté Flaubert

10 rue Gustave-Flaubert, 17th (01.42.67.05.81/ www.michelrostang.com). **Open** daily 12.30-2.30pm, 7.30-11pm. Closed one week in Aug, 1 May, four days at Christmas. **Average** €46. **Lunch menu** €28. **Credit** AmEx, MC, V. **Map** D2.

Michel Rostang pioneered the star chef's bistro annexe when he took over the old épicerie next door in 1987, kept the pretty period interior and began serving up what he felt genuine bistro food should be. The great thing about this chef's bistro is that you get things you wouldn't normally expect in a bistro at all – starters, especially, have a degree of sophistication that surely reflect haute cuisine roots. We started with a wonderfully complex pressé of asparagus, sundried tomatoes and coppa ham accompanied by a raw artichoke and parmesan salad, and marinated lisette (small mackerel) with mushrooms, carrots and mesclun. Main courses are simpler but well prepared, with the emphasis on fine-quality meat (there's always a beef offering of the day), and in a democratic move you have a choice of accompaniments. We opted for lamb from the Pyrenees in a crumble crust with garlic shortbread biscuit and a bowl of smooth purée and dos de lieu (pollack) with spicebread crust and jus, served with Niçois vegetables. Then on to fruit salad with sprig of thyme and lemon and thyme ice cream, and the tiny pots of chocolate that have become a Rostang classic. Just what a bistro should be, only better.

Le Chavignol ★

135 av de Villiers, 17th (01.43.80.40.65). M° Porte de Champerret. **Open** Mon, Tue, Sat, Sun noon-3pm; Wed-Fri noon-3pm, 8-10.30pm. **Average** €50. **Credit** MC, V. **Map** D2.

The neon sign on the facade and the Formica-heavy interior might not immediately lead you to conclude that this is an address with serious gastronomic ambitions. After one meal, though, you'll easily be convinced, since owner Regis Le Bar generously practices the cult of the superior product (at a price), which means that the butter comes from Bordier in St-Malo, the bread from the organic Moisan bakery, the anchovies from Collioure, the andouillette from Duval in Drancy, etc. All of which is to say that everything you eat and drink here is first-rate. The only problem, besides the price, is getting a table and some attention, since this place has a clubby crowd of regulars who are prone to snubbing an unknown face. Persevere, however, and you will be rewarded with dishes such as black pudding with Espelette pepper, a Salers entrecôte studded with marrow, plus great cheeses and wines. No wonder this is the preferred Parisian haunt of famous chefs from the provinces when visiting the capital. Great desserts, too – don't miss the heavenly homemade ice cream.

Chez Léon

32 rue Legendre, 17th (01.42.27.06.82). M° Villiers. **Open** Mon-Fri noon-2pm, 7.30-10pm. Closed Aug. **Average** €40. **Prix fixe** €29. **Credit** AmEx, MC, V. **Map** E2.

Hidden away in a street that seems straight out of a French textbook, this old-fashioned spot is charming for its sincerity, fly-in-amber decor and carefully made, generously served selection of rare bistro classics. The €29 prix fixe offers stunning value for money since it includes a better-than-decent half bottle of wine. Seated on red, velvet-upholstered chairs under brass globe lamps, we were delighted with starters of homemade jambon persillé and a tomato and chèvre millefeuille. What a treat to find the Burgundian classic of ham in parsley aspic so rich with shredded meat and full of taste, while the whipped goat's cheese layered with tomatoes was beautifully accented by a lemony vinaigrette. Main courses of smoked herring with an aubergine timbale and rumpsteak with freshly made chips were both excellent, as was the cheese plate and a dessert of lime cream with raspberries. Entertainment came in the

How to Eat **Whole Fish**

If you're not prepared to look your fish in the eye, ask the waiter to bring it to you 'sans la tête'. He'll be either amused or grumpy, but chances are he'll cooperate (which will unfortunately prevent you from feasting on the prized fish cheeks). Whether or not the fish comes to you à la Marie Antoinette, the tidiest way to approach it is to lift the fillet by running your knife the length of the spine, then horizontally along the bones – if it's properly cooked, the fillet should come off easily. Then lift the backbone off the lower fillet and discard it. In classy joints the waiter will do this for you, but you'll pay. The reward for your efforts is tastier fish – flavour seeps in from the bones during cooking.

Dressed-up dining at **Les Ormes**. *See p70.*

form of our wry waiter – his shrug of the shoulders as he explained the apple jam served with the cheese (it's a Belgian and Dutch tradition) expressed an existential resignation worthy of a boulevard comedy. Not surprisingly, there's a real pro in the kitchen – chef Emmanuel Klein, formerly of Le Bistrot du Sommelier.

Le Clou

132 rue Cardinet, 17th (01.42.27.36.78).
M° Malesherbes. **Open** Mon-Fri noon-2.30pm, 7.30-10.30pm; Sat 7.30-10.30pm. Closed two weeks in Aug. **Average** €30. **Lunch menu** €19.40. **Credit** AmEx, DC, MC, V. **Map** E1.

This red-fronted former brasserie is somewhat off the beaten track, but its combination of honest cooking, smiling service and terrific value makes it well worth seeking out. Though keeping costs down means that tables are crammed together, the decor is classier than you'd expect, with white tablecloths, decent glassware and an abundance of dried flowers. Chef and owner Christian Leclou eschews gimmickry in favour of careful sourcing of ingredients, producing rustic dishes such a chunky terrine de volaille, or a more refined croustillant d'escargots, made with petits gris and filo pastry. Fish features strongly on the daily-changing menu, with, for example, a warm salad of coquilles St-Jacques and cod cheeks, or a huge fillet of pan-fried sea bass resting on chopped, roasted tomatoes. But the star (and one of the few permanent menu fixtures) must be the rosemary-scented, long-simmered, confit d'épaule d'agneau, meltingly tender and served with a smoky aubergine purée. Desserts maintain the high standard, with a homemade nougat glacé, studded with walnuts and candied angelica, and an excellent moelleux au chocolat. Wines are selected just as carefully as the food – Leclou tasting and buying directly from the vignerons in many instances – making for some truly remarkable prices.

Macis & Muscade

110 rue Legendre, 17th (01.42.26.62.26).
M° La Fourche. **Open** Tue-Thur noon-2pm, 8-10.15pm; Fri noon-2pm, 8-11pm; Sat 8-10.15pm; Sun noon-2pm. **Prix fixe** €23 (dinner only). **Lunch menu** €13, €16. **Credit** AmEx, DC, MC, V. **Map** F1.

Macis & Muscade? Well, muscade is nutmeg and macis is the husk that's used for its scent. Interesting? Or is all this sending you into a deep, possibly terminal sleep? If so, you'd best steer clear of Whodat & Wossisname because the subtleties don't end there. Some of the decor is muted orange, the rest is deep yellow; some of the customers are estate agents, the others are more like property brokers. But for those who have the patience and curiosity, this is a very original restaurant for the attention it brings to fragrance as well as taste and its use of essential oils as ingredients. We started with scallops lightly cooked then spiked with a point of neroli, the essential oil that comes from orange blossom. An aphrodisiac so we are told, although we're still waiting for the effects. Didn't taste too bad, though the fragrance was a little overpowering. For our main we took a fillet of red emperor, a fish better known in Asia than Europe, cooked with ginger and nicely accompanied by a dry, fruity Sancerre. For pudding, though, our faith in oriental stimulants rapidly fading, we went for the 'love wells', a sort of gingery crème brûlée, and sat around waiting for things to happen. The meal ended on an anticlimax: all that came was the bill.

Cooking with essential oils? Try it at **Macis & Muscade**. *See p73.*

Restaurant L'Entredgeu ★

83 rue Laugier, 17th (01.40.54.97.24). Mº Porte de Champerret. **Open** Tue-Sat noon-2pm, 8-10.15pm. **Prix fixe** €28. **Lunch menu** €20. **Credit** MC, V. **Map** C2.

This snug little bistro has been packed ever since it opened thanks to its excellent food at very reasonable prices. Young chef Philippe Tredgeu mastered this sure-fire formula while heading the kitchen at Chez Casimir. Since the food is so good, you almost can't complain about the squeeze-em-in seating, slow service or thick clouds of cigarette smoke, but we hope that the wine list will become more interesting in the future. The blackboard menu here changes daily, but scallops cooked in their shells with salted butter and crumbled cauliflower, and a croustillant of pig's trotter with celeriac rémoulade were fine starters, followed by delicious main courses of chewy, flavourful roast pork with braised chicory and lamb stuffed with foie gras. Homely desserts run to caramelised bananas and apple crumble, or go for a nice wedge of st-nectaire cheese. Try to book ahead and be on time, as late arrivals get sent to the cramped back dining room.

Tête de Goinfre

16 rue Jacquemont, 17th (01.42.29.89.80). Mº La Fourche. **Open** Mon-Sat noon-2pm, 8-10.30pm. **Average** €25. **Credit** MC V. **Map** F1.

Sensitive about your weight, or emotionally attached to pigs? Be warned: the name translates as 'greedy guts', and the interior designers' motif was clearly 'porky'. Dinky pig ornaments abound, their cute factor jarring abrasively against the reality of

the free platter of charcuterie you get while waiting for a seat in this popular (don't go in a rush) bistro. Having kicked off with honourable – if not inspirational – leeks in vinaigrette, and mackerel rillettes, we homed in on a black pudding that had a sensuously crumbly texture; the 'C'-word ('congealed') was uttered, approvingly. Things wobbled from the moment we realised that the poached salmon was in need of a holiday; the strawberries and the tart (of strawberry tart fame) seemed estranged; while the chocolate mousse headed straight for the roof of the mouth and clung there doggedly. So OK, we couldn't rave about the food. Maybe this was an off-day, because, as we've noted, it's busy enough. But we can recommend the Tête de Goinfre for its atmosphere. It's fun, it's friendly, and the overall experience is delightful.

18th Arrondissement

Le Bouclard

1 rue Cavalotti, 18th (01.45.22.60.01/ www.bouclard.com). M° Place de Clichy. **Open** Mon-Fri noon-2.30pm, 7.30-11.30pm. **Average** €45. **Lunch menu** €15, €22. **Credit** AmEx,DC, MC, V. **Map** G1.

The eclectic menu in this compact, traditional-style bistro, a short walk from the Moulin Rouge, highlights French rural cooking, with dishes such as cassoulet and prized regional meats including T-bone veal steak from Corrèze and saddle of lamb from Limousin. Owner Michel Bonnemort also offers European culinary landmarks: along with rabbit terrine and foie gras maison there are starters such as Spanish serrano ham (which we found too dry) and swordfish carpaccio, vegetarian dishes and the ever-so-British apple crumble. French gourmets of the old school are likely to pounce on the leeks with gribiche sauce (mayonnaise with chopped eggs and capers) – the bistro makes a particularly potent, mustardy variety. In contrast, our haddock Parmentier lacked flavour, while the accompanying huge green salad had a vinaigrette that tasted dangerously close to the bottled kind. The roast farmed pigeon, however, was tender and fragrant, served with a mini casserole of fresh garden peas. The apple crumble, although too sticky, had a redeeming, pleasant cinnamony flavour. The wine list is limited, given the pricey carte, but the Saumur Champigny turned out to be an excellent choice at around €22.

Café Burq

6 rue Burq, 18th (01.42.52.81.27). M° Abbesses. **Open** Tue-Sun 8pm-midnight. Closed Aug. **Average** €25. **Credit** MC, V. **Map** H1.

The rough-around-the-edges, rural-minded bistro Le Moulin à Vins has been reborn as the Café Burq, and its new proprietors Frédéric Peneau and Patrick Bouin have replaced the rustic decor with a minimalist theme of shiny black tables, translucent plastic lighting fixtures and a copper mirror behind the bar. A rather boisterous crowd grows louder and exhales more smoke as the evening progresses; due to some acoustical demon, noise seems to echo endlessly off the walls, which are weirdly adorned only with a framed puzzle of Castle Neuschwanstein. Our waiter was particularly enthusiastic and spirited – he has to be, to wade through the masses loitering at the bar and cross the cramped, dozen-table dining room to deliver your food. Dishes are competent, comfort-oriented meat-and-potatoes classics (the menu changes every two weeks). The supple magret de canard and poached salmon pleased us, but the moussaka-like lamb and potato hachis and the grilled slab of pork, while both generously sized, lacked any defining characteristic or dominant flavour. More impressive were appetisers such as a roasted camembert with honey and pine nuts, or a spiced chèvre ballotine wrapped in paper-thin aubergine slices. Like the mains, desserts take no big chances, but then the point here seems to be less about the food than the neighbourhoody, friendly, young and hip Montmartre to-be-seen scene.

French Cuisine

L'Entracte

44 rue d'Orsel, 18th (01.46.06.93.41). M° Abbesses or Anvers. **Open** Wed-Sat noon-2pm, 7-10.30pm; Sun noon-2pm. Closed Aug. **Average** €40. **Credit** MC, V. **Map** J2.

Stepping into this little bistro near the Sacré-Cœur, you can expect a locally charged atmosphere – a near impossible feat in this tourist-filled area. Start with a bowl of onion soup or a small salad and then move on the steak au poivre with a sauce so good it'll make your spine tingle. Soak that up with the homemade fries and move right on to the cheese – the oozing brie was a highlight. Then try the mousse au chocolat and a quick expresso and you should be on your way. Or, if Laurent, a fourth generation Montmartrois artist decides to step in, you might just want to listen to his stories over a nice glass of Cognac. Reserve or starve.

La Galère des Rois

8 rue Cavallotti 18th (01.42.93.34.58). M° Place de Clichy. **Open** Mon-Fri noon-2.30pm, 7.30-11pm; Sat 7.30-11pm. Closed Aug, one week at Christmas. **Average** €34. **Lunch menu**€12.20, €14.50. **Credit** MC, V. **Wheelchair access. Map** G1.

With its pitch-pine-panelled walls and oh-so-seventies fitted carpet, this is a nearly fly-in-amber example of that once common genus, the neighbourhood bistro. Such bistros were never meant to induce a gourmet swoon, but rather to offer a fair feed for a fair price in a convivial setting, and once this has been sorted, La Galère does a great job in its class. The male welcome is rather barking but, without being asked, the waiter brought a bowl of water for our dog, and, cued by our accents, patiently explained the daily specials in English. Starters of warm breaded goat's cheese on salad and green asparagus in mushroom juice with a poached egg were a notch better than average, and mains of braised lamb shank and steak were just fine, although the duck-fat-laced pommes de terre sarladaises were jarring with lamb and beef. Enjoying a superb Cahors at a knock-down bargain price of €14 we almost gave dessert a miss, but the chocolate mousse was a treat when we gave in. A useful address, since there's a lot of nightlife nearby.

Aux Négociants

27 rue Lambert, 18th (01.46.06.15.11). M° Château-Rouge. **Open** Mon noon-2.30pm, Tue-Fri noon-2.30pm, 8-10.30pm. Closed Aug. **Average** €23. **Credit** AmEx, MC, V. **Map** J1.

Don't be put off by the cramped tables or the prime view of the public toilets outside; this place belongs to a dying breed of rustic bistros. Locals stand at the bar debating furiously and there are photos on the wall to prove it. The best choice of apéritif is surely the Coteaux du Layon, a fortified white wine from the Loire valley. The attitude to the food here is generous: our traditional rabbit pâté starter was simply left on our table in its Pyrex dish with a large earthenware pot of cornichons for us to help ourselves. There's little choice and no frills, but the hearty portions and comforting homemade food make for a real treat. The approach to wine is equally down-to-earth – you order a bottle and return what you haven't drunk, paying according to how many markers have been revealed. The boeuf bourguignon was better than any we'd had in Burgundy and the strawberry tartlets and chocolate mousse were as good as grand-mère's. Not an ideal place for a first date but a brilliant choice for when you crave genuine French home cooking.

Le Petit Caboulot ★

6 pl Jacques-Froment, 18th (01.46.27.19.00). M° Guy-Moquet. **Open** Mon-Fri noon-2pm, 8-11pm; Sat noon-2:30pm, 8-11pm. Closed two weeks in Aug. **Average** €25. **Lunch menu** €10. **Credit** MC, V. **Wheelchair access.**

With all the trappings of a friendly neighbourhood bistro, and then some, you'll wish this were your local and, judging from the crowd on a Monday night, you're not the only one. Brik de chèvre aux pommes, a crisp pastry of apple and melting goat's cheese on a bed of salad, is the place to start. Tasty, very tasty, and not too filling. Foie gras maison is also well worth a try. The duck confit (ask for it bien grillé) – dark, succulent, and with a skin that crunched like heaven – was one of the best we've had in a restaurant and the haddock brandade, flakes of smoked fish blended with moist potato purée and oven-browned, was 100% comfort food. We weren't sure it could get better – until the tarte Tatin arrived. Ubiquitous in bistros but so rarely right, this one, caramelised to the core, had us booking our return. Mosaic pillars, a huge curved bar and a vast collection of old enamel adverts (look for the Arabic Kodak) evoke a bygone era. There's an extensive wine list to match all budgets; our Alsatian white, cool, fruity and a match for the foie gras, tasted like something more pricey.

19th Arrondissement

Le Bistro du 19e

45 rue des Alouettes, 19th (01.42.00.84.85). M° Buttes Chaumont or Botzaris. **Open** Mon, Sat 7.30-11pm; Tue-Fri, Sun noon-2.30pm, 7.30-11pm. Closed Aug. **Prix fixe** €12.05 (except Sat dinner), €29. **Credit** MC, V. **Map** D2.

Amid the mindless 80s French pop music, cooking diplomas, froofy curtains, ribbons, hearts and plug-in angel, serious attention is paid to each dining detail: goose rillettes to begin, the palate-blasting sorbet in Cognac between courses, and the throwback 'ladies' menu' sans prices. Dishes can be had à la carte, but you're far better off signing up for the prix fixe, which gives you a full choice of three courses, plus Champagne (in a chilled flute), wine and coffee. We started with a salmon, artichoke, walnut and radish salad and the grilled escargots with garlic nut oil, both inventive and fresh. The duck with roast peaches was equally pleasing, and a monkfish and fennel stew, chock-full of veggies, served as further evidence of the chef's skill. Desserts such as made-to-order profiteroles and tarte maison lived up to expectations set by earlier courses. The exceptional food and value will entice us back.

La Cave Gourmande ★

10 rue du Général-Brunet, 19th (01.40.40.03.30). M° Botzaris. **Open** Mon-Fri 12.15pm-2.30pm, 7.30-10.30pm. Closed one week in Feb., three weeks in Aug. **Prix fixe** €32 (dinner only). **Lunch menu** €25. **Credit** MC, V.

The day after moving into this quiet, Kosher neighbourhood we were ushered through the wonderful-smelling, welcoming front room of this restaurant and seated in a poky corner in the back, where a raucous family was playing jigsaws. The manageress was snappy, rushed us through our meal and we never saw the chef. Lured back a few weeks later by the fine food, the contrast was astonishing. American chef Mark Singer even brought to our table a live crayfish, which later appeared as an addition on one of the starter plates. Singer has an imaginative flair that makes each mouthful a discovery. The croustillant d'escargots was a Burgundy-influenced dish of fabulous, melt-in-your-mouth snails baked with onions, carrots, mushrooms and herbs, while the terrine d'artichauts with roast almonds and a zesty lemon sauce was a sensual marriage of flavours. The bon-bon d'agneau showed an eye for presentation – a sweet-wrapper of filo enclosing tender chunks of meat – while the pintade was lovingly wrapped in thin slices of aubergine with concentrated Provençal flavours in the red pepper and pesto garnish. Desserts – a light chocolate tart and delicious warm melon concoction – proved well chosen despite having to take your pick at the beginning of the meal, and on our happy second visit we were encouraged to linger over a bowl of walnuts. We'll give them the benefit of the doubt and attribute the first false note to frazzled nerves.

Restaurant L'Hermès

23 rue Mélingue, 19th (01.42.39.94.70). M° Pyrénées. **Open** Tue, Thur-Sat noon-2.30pm, 7.30-10pm; Wed 7.30-10pm. Closed Aug. **Average** €30. **Prix fixe** €24. **Lunch menu** €13. **Credit** MC, V. **Non-smoking room. Map** D3.

After an interior facelift L'Hermès is now all vivid yellows and floral, country-print tablecloths. The cheeriness extends beyond the decor: we were thoroughly welcomed and there is now a non-smoking room. We witnessed a genuine love of invention and playfulness, from the poetically phrased, weekly-changing menu to the south-western-inspired food. A langoustine, foie gras and veggie medley, stuffed into a crispy crêpe, kept pace with the other starter, a slice of silky-smooth aubergine flan with tomato. Confit de canard can be stringy, but our watchful waiter brought over a moist and tender thigh, served with a tart pickle relish, blinis, potato gratin and roasted tomatoes. A cod fillet in richly flavoured saffron sauce also made a splash. Try expertly crafted desserts such as prune, Armagnac and orange flower-water cake. Wines are on the pricey side.

A café called desire? The original **Café Noir**. *See p78.*

20th Arrondissement

Bistro des Capucins

27 av Gambetta, 20th (01.46.36.74.75). M° Père-Lachaise or Gambetta. **Open** Tue-Sat 12.15-1.45pm, 7.30-9.45pm. Closed three weeks in Aug, one week at Christmas. **Prix fixe** €20, €25. **Credit** AmEx, MC, V. **Map** D5.

Just across the street from Père Lachaise cemetery, this bistro has rapidly become one of the best in the area, thanks to the gentle prices and first-rate cooking of Gérard Fouché. The intriguing crowd – lots of young arty types, but also local stalwarts who appreciate a good deal – gives off a convivial buzz, a reflection of the friendly service and the communal pleasure of eating well. Fouché worked in top restaurants, including Jacques Cagna and Le Grand Véfour, before setting up shop in this former café, and if there's a certain south-western heartiness to his menu (he's from Bordeaux), a surprising precision and creativity elevate this place to a rank well beyond the average bistro. The menu changes daily, but runs to dishes such as duck terrine, rabbit compote, and an excellent gâteau of marinated sardines and aubergines to start, and then offers excellent Aubrac steaks in shallot sauce, liver deglazed with sherry vinegar, and grilled salmon. Delicious desserts such as the cannelé (a custardy, caramelised cake from Bordeaux) served with spiced melon compote, and very reasonably priced wines make this a great destination.

Café Noir ★

15 rue St-Blaise, 20th (01.40.09.75.80). M° Porte de Bagnolet. **Open** daily 7pm-midnight. Closed 1 May, Christmas and New Year. **Average** €30. **Credit** MC, V.

This film set of a cobbled street leading up to an abbey is the last thing you expect to find near Porte de Bagnolet, but only the first of many surprises at 'le resto pas pareil'. Behind an inviting terrace is a belle éqoque interior decorated with coffee pots, puppets and hats. The staff, all in dungarees and jeans, are the most genuinely friendly we have ever encountered. And then there is the menu, which is totally original, starting with a list of long-forgotten apéritifs. We couldn't resist trying the absinthe maison – not the hallucinogenic version but a bitter pastis – while la pousse rapière was an elegant combination of Champagne and Armagnac. On to the main attractions, and while the generous helping of fat white asparagus in a creamy, lemony mousseline was just what the menu said, the millefeuille d'artichaut au foie gras was a flight of fancy: a whole artichoke heart sandwiching an enormous hunk of meaty foie gras, surrounded by its leaves, gelée in a little pot and a garnish of cordifole and cape gooseberry. Why was it called millefeuille then? 'Because we liked the sound of the word,' explained the waitress. Mains of sea bream in a caramel d'épices and the Mauritian-influenced tandoori of foie de volaille were both rather dry but we'd hesitate to lay blame as we had lingered long over the artichoke. Finishing our very drinkable house chardonnay (€13), we could only manage to share the calorific coffee and walnut mousse. As we left, a napkin full of old-fashioned sweets was pressed into our hands.

Le Zéphyr

1 rue du Jourdain, 20th (01.46.36.65.81). M° Jourdain. **Open** Mon-Thur, Sun noon-3pm, 8-11.30pm; Fri, Sat noon-3pm, 8pm-midnight. Closed Aug. **Average** €40. **Prix fixe** €26. **Lunch menu** €12.50 (Mon-Fri). **Credit** AmEx, DC, MC, V. **Wheelchair access**.

At 10pm on a Monday night, the only seat left amid the buzz of the stunning art deco dining room was next to the coatrack. Even the newly renovated terrace was brimming with engaging arty-types, but after kitchen mix-ups, slow service and mediocre food we questioned its popularity. When the gleaming, healthy slab of foie gras on top of artichoke hearts did finally arrive, the artichoke was so wilted even the reduction sauce couldn't save it. The magret de canard with poached pear was appropriately peppery and went well with our €18 Clos de l'Echo Chinon, but red mullet fillets in a wonderfully tangy blood orange sauce were dry and stringy and the carrot purée overcooked. The lavender crème brûlée, however, was appropriately burned and it gently perfumed our mouths before the house offered us a plum digestif to end our evening more pleasantly than it began. Despite the culinary flaws, Belleville yuppies continue to crowd the dark-wood scene, though some simply opt for a drink at the bar.

Beyond the Périphérique

Le Soleil ★

109 av Michelet, 93400 St-Ouen (01.40.10.08.08). M° Porte de Clignancourt. **Open** Mon-Wed noon-2.30pm; Thur-Sat noon-2.30pm, 8-10pm; Sun noon-4pm. **Average** €35. **Credit** AmEx, MC, V.

Behind the windows of this former café near the flea market, the atmosphere feels light-years from the gritty, busy world outside, and at the centre of this little planet of conviviality is a deep devotion to good eating. So good is the food here, in fact, that this place is becoming something of a cult word-of-mouth address in Paris food circles, with the jovial waiter at a recent dinner confirming that both Alain Ducasse and Pierre Gagnaire had recently been customers. Once the food comes, you'll see why, since this place could give a real lesson to many other restaurants. Quite simply, everything is outstanding: the mound of yellow butter from the Cotentin region of Normandy, which comes with sourdough bread from a secret bakery in Neuilly, a salad of haricots verts with shavings of foie gras, the partridge with savoy cabbage, and a huge entrecôte in a deep, ruddy, delicious wine sauce. The wine list is excellent, too, as are desserts, including what must surely be the best baba au rhum in the Paris area. Reservations are essential.

Haute Cuisine

In the rarefied air of haute cuisine, chefs are more artists than cooks, and the price of their culinary canvases often reminiscent of old masters.

If haute cuisine is the pinnacle of the French food chain, this lofty little club of shockingly excellent and stunningly expensive restaurants might recently have been accused of having become a bit stale. Those that break the mould however, do so with reassuring success. The redeemers of the bunch are the sublime culinary imagination of **Pierre Gagnaire**, the Zen technique of **Hiramatsu** on the Ile St-Louis, the precision of the service at **Alain Ducasse au Plaza Athénée**, and the arrival of young chef Alain Solivérès at **Taillevent**. Finally, talented **Guy Savoy** is basking in much-deserved recognition and Philippe Legendre continues to produce an exquisite take on luxury fare at **Le V**. Our reviews vary between à la carte and prix fixe offerings. It is worth bearing in mind that splashing out €110-€250 (not including wine) à la carte will produce a meal that is significantly different from the lunch menu, as it allows the chef to give free reign to his creativity and use expensive ingredients. The lunch prix fixe, however, is a great way to experience the setting and service of an haute cuisine restaurant on a limited budget.

Le Carré des Feuillants

14 rue de Castiglione, 1st (01.42.86.82.82). M° Tuileries. **Open** Mon-Fri noon-2pm, 7.30-10pm. Closed Aug. **Average** €115. **Prix fixe** €138 (dinner only). **Lunch menu** €58. **Credit** AmEx, DC, MC, V. **Non-smoking room**. **Map** G5.

For one of the best-reputed restaurants in Paris, the Carré des Feuillants doesn't look like much. Despite its splendid address by place Vendôme, the entrance is at the back of what amounts to a shopping mall. Inside, the restaurant is full of arresting and beautiful details – the prints by Picasso, the splendid, Cocteau-esque candelabras – on a backdrop of granny-ish pastel colours. The service too, though technically proficient, fell a long way short of the complicit amiability that you hope for at a top restaurant. All of which would be forgivable if the food were truly outstanding. But our 'lunch of the season', though good, didn't rate much more than lunch of the week. It started well with a dazzling profusion of amuse-gueules and a couple of glasses of excellent Champagne. This made way for a tuna 'millefeuille' whose delicate stripes of tuna, aubergine, tomato and cheese were handsome on the plate and wonderful on the palate. But the move from all that almost-Japanese aestheticism to a house speciality from Alain Dutournier's native south-west France was a rather crunching gear change, even if our fillet of duck was accompanied by a Chinese-style spring roll. Our wine, well chosen by the sommelier, was a deliciously well-rounded red from the Languedoc-Roussillon which went nicely with the rustic roquefort-and-quince dessert.

L'Espadon

Hôtel Ritz, 15 pl Vendôme, 1st (01.43.16.30.80/ www.ritzparis.com). M° Madeleine or Concorde. **Open** daily noon-2.30pm, 7.30-10.30pm. **Average** €180. **Prix fixe** €160 (dinner only). **Lunch menu** €68. **Credit** AmEx, DC, MC, V. **Map** G4.

Perhaps no name is more synonymous with luxury than the Ritz, so it was with high expectations that we trod the plush carpet towards the dining room – never mind that one of us had arrived on a rickety old bicycle, determined not to be thwarted by a Métro strike. 'Bienvenue', said the maître d'hôtel with sincerity, and thus began an experience so charming it became hard to find flaw with anything. The gilded mirrors, silk swaggers and fluffy cloud ceiling motif are, well, Ritzy, and we sank happily into the velvet banquette and broad armchair, easily giving in to the temptation to have an apéritif. The €68 menu is not bad values as it includes cheese and coffee. After tasty but uneventful amuse-bouches, the meal began in earnest with oysters marinated with orange, pineapple and fennel (too crunchy and not entirely successful), a wonderfully smooth combination of poached chicken and foie gras garnished with the 'sot l'y laisse' (the part of the chicken also known as the 'oyster'), and silky green asparagus purée with beautifully cooked spiced langoustines. Domes were whisked off in unison to reveal our main courses, which were essentially bistro classics refined: meltingly tender duck breast with carved turnip and caramelised spring onions, sole in cockle-cream sauce with finely cut broad beans, green beans and peas, and a thick slice of flaky cod with chunks of lobster, grenaille potatoes and a meaty jus. We accompanied these with pricey wines by the glass (it might have been wiser to order one of the cheaper bottles at around €40). Then the hefty cheese trolley arrived, the waiter egging us on to try several kinds of chèvre, a delicious roquefort and nutty aged comté. By this time we had spotted none other than Mohammed Al-Fayed in the corner. A chilled hazelnut mousse, strawberries with hazelnut ice cream and a layered chocolate tart kept up the standard – everything about this meal was bright, fresh and eminently likeable.

French Cuisine

Le Grand Véfour

17 rue de Beaujolais, 1st (01.42.96.56.27/ www.relaischateaux.com). Mº Palais-Royal. **Open** Mon-Thur 12.30-1.30pm, 8-9.30pm; Fri 12.30-2pm. Closed Aug. **Average** €200. **Prix fixe** €225 (dinner only). **Lunch menu** €75. **Credit** AmEx, DC, MC, V. **Non-smoking room**. **Map** H5.

There is a luxury-theme-park side to the Grand Véfour, and we were duly impressed as we were led to 'Victor Hugo's table'. Follow-up questions revealed, however, that tables are randomly named after famous people who once ate in the former café. Its days as a hotbed of political intrigue are long past, and the lunch crowd contained an elegant mix of wealthy locals and tourists. The view of the Palais-Royal is spectacular and the decor – featuring exquisite painted panels and mirrors – is a glamorous historical gem, even if the size of the room means that tables are slightly too close for absolute comfort. We chose the lunch menu, which allows chef Guy Martin to show off his skills without the obligatory use of luxury ingredients. We began our meal with boned stuffed chicken, strewn with trompettes-de-la-mort mushrooms – attractively Asiatic but not gastronomically startling. A dish of Jerusalem artichokes was, however, stunning: creamy pallets of the vegetable were topped with fresh crab, an unctuous purée was studded with crispy wafers, and seafood and Jerusalem artichoke bisque completed this culinary tour de force. The main course was tête de veau, not perhaps the sort of dish you expect in these surroundings, but here it was prepared with a sauce verte and tarragon salad, and attained a level of sophistication which left other head meat standing – if such a thing is physically possible. Enjoying our meal as we did, we couldn't help spying the truffles-with-everything feast going on next door; the chicken was simply smothered in the black diamonds. The cheese trolley was outstanding, including a nutty, long-aged comté and some luscious end-of-season vacherin. The layered chocolate dessert was outstanding, with dark leaves floating over a pale creamy mousse, accompanied by a sublime praline ice cream. As Taittinger owns the restaurant we thought it only right to enjoy a glass of Champagne at this stage of the meal, having previously been lovingly guided towards quality half-bottles of Pouilly Fuissé and a vintage Margaux. More chocolates and petits fours accompanied our coffee, and the genuinely welcoming staff made us feel we had experienced something unforgettable. We even began to believe that Victor Hugo really had sat at our table.

How to Eat **Cheese**

A whole book could be devoted to the art of slicing different shapes of cheese (never, ever cut the tip off a wedge of brie). At a fine restaurant, the cheese waiter will take care of such delicate issues for you. What you need to know is that the cheeses will be placed on your plate in clockwise order, from mildest to strongest, allowing you fully to appreciate each specimen in this order. You can eat the cheese with a knife and fork (no bread shows you're a true cheese-lover), or slice off a chunk of cheese and perch it on a bite-sized piece of bread. Even cheese experts can't agree on whether you should eat the rinds of soft cheeses, so it's your call.

Le Meurice

Hôtel Meurice, 228 rue de Rivoli, 1st (01.44.58.10.10). Mº Tuileries. **Open** daily noon-2pm, 7-10.30pm. Closed Aug. **Average** €95. **Prix fixe** €95, €145 (dinner only). **Credit** AmEx, DC, MC, V. **Wheelchair access**. **Map** G5.

It's a delight to bask in the magnificence of this room overlooking the Tuileries. Excellent service and the comfortable intimacy created by generously spaced tables with hand-carved armchairs create an atmosphere that's the very definition of a Parisian palace hotel. The menu seeks to stun as well, with food that is calculated to be simultaneously luxurious, traditional and innovative. Following an amuse-gueule of tuna tartare with cornichons and capers, starters were excellent: lobster salad with summer vegetables, and poached eggs in a breadcrumb crust on a bed of girolle mushrooms with young salad leaves. Next, we sampled the langoustines with a caramelised garlic sauce and rack of lamb with small hazelnuts, watercress, and its own jus with fresh almonds. Both were excellent, though a guacamole-like salad with the langoustines gilded the lily. If the food here is generally beyond reproach, it tends to be over-elaborate. This baroque touch worked brilliantly with desserts, however, including a sublime nougat soufflé with a side dish of apricot marmalade, and roast figs with a raspberry and fig pastry, raspberry sauce and sorbet. Add flawless service and an exquisite wine list, and you find a dining room that's been restored to the front row of Parisian restaurants. Chef Yannick Aleno took over the kitchen just after this guide went to press.

L'Ambroisie

9 pl des Vosges, 4th (01.42.78.51.45). Mº Bastille or St-Paul. **Open** Tue-Sat noon-1.30pm, 8-9.30pm. Closed two weeks in Feb, three weeks in Aug. **Average** €200. **Credit** AmEx, MC, V. **Wheelchair access**. **Map** L6.

Perhaps it's a result of the current difficulties in the luxury tourism market and a subsequent reduction in the number of staff, but there's definitely a more casual feel at L'Ambroisie. On our prior visit to this discreet townhouse in the beautiful 17th-century place des Vosges, a three-strong welcoming com-

L'Ambroisie: a setting (and food) fit for the gods.

mittee greeted us at the entrance. This time, in contrast, we even had to open the door ourselves! (This might appear a somewhat churlish comment, but when you're paying upwards of €200 a head for dinner, you do have certain expectations.) The truth is, service has never been the strong point here. This is a restaurant that takes itself particularly seriously (the atmosphere is somewhat reverential), but the reputation is built on Bernard Pacaud's essentially honest, direct and approachable food. When it comes to ingredients, quality is everything and there's no doubt that much of the money goes into this. Precise technique serves simply to amplify flavour, and innovation is eschewed in favour of consistency. Seasonality, too, is a cause for celebration, so late spring, for instance, brings a profusion of morels (accompanying a starter of fine ravioli, chock-full of lobster), asparagus (with mustard-crusted turbot), and strawberries (an intense pre-dessert sorbet). Not everything is perfect though – an 'épigramme' of lamb from Lozère, the saddle done as a kind of pastilla (sandwiched with foie gras, wrapped in fine pastry and deep-fried), some little chunks of the fillet and two tiny chops, lacked balanced seasoning. There are, as you might expect, no bargains on the wine list, with only one lonely bottle under €50.

Hiramatsu ★

7 quai de Bourbon, 4th (01.56.81.08.80). M° Pont Marie. **Open** Tue-Sat noon-2pm, 8-10pm. Closed Aug. **Average** €120. **Prix fixe** €95, €130. **Credit** AmEx, DC, MC, V. **Map** K7.

If you love French cuisine at its most refined but dread the stuffiness of many haute cuisine establishments, Hiramatsu offers an alternative. The setting alone – a small, luminous modern dining room on the Ile St-Louis – tells you that this restaurant run by Hiroyuki Hiramatsu, hailed as a Japanese Alain Ducasse, is different. Hiramatsu is clearly in love with French produce: among the starters on his summer menu were foie gras with truffle sauce and cabbage, crème de grenouille (yes, frog cream) on a truffle feuilleté, and snail fricassée on a mushroom millefeuille; a typical main course is Bresse chicken breast served with its caramelised liver, pan-fried oysters and spinach. Ordering from a €50 lunch menu that has since been a casualty of restaurant inflation, we tasted pan-fried foie gras on a bed of stunning lemongrass-infused aubergine confit, and salmon in a delicate consommé flavoured with orange flower water, served with a tiny dice of Provençal vegetables and grapefruit. Citrus appeared again in dessert, a small orange-flavoured cake with coffee granita. Though apparently simple, all of these dishes showed chef Hajime Nakagawa's total mastery of technique; just as professional were the friendly staff, who were happy to explain Hiramatsu's approach to food. Carbohydrates are apparently not his thing, so for better or worse, you're unlikely to leave feeling stuffed.

La Tour d'Argent

15-17 quai de la Tournelle, 5th (01.43.54.23.31/ www.tourdargent.com). M° Pont Marie or Cardinal Lemoine. **Open** Tue 7.30-9pm; Wed-Sun noon-1.30pm, 7.30-9pm. **Average** €180. **Lunch menu**

Hiramatsu: a Zen take on haute cuisine. *See p81.*

€65. **Credit** AmEx, DC, MC, V. **Wheelchair access. Non-smoking room. Map** K7.

On 29 April 2003, La Tour d'Argent celebrated its millionth mallard served since 1890, which makes us curious about the numbering system: how exactly were they able to predict the big day months in advance? In any case, it's always a thrill to be handed a numbered postcard, which you can keep as a souvenir or give to the waiter to post. Our lunch got off to an inauspicious start, through no fault of the restaurant: told to arrive no later than 12.30pm, we then waited an hour for one member of our party to show up. Two of our group of five wore jeans and one (the only Parisian by birth) asked for a Coke; the teenage waiter stood as if waiting for the punch line, before scurrying off to find out whether such a thing exists at La Tour d'Argent (thankfully, it doesn't). Despite our rather eccentric behaviour, which included rejecting the young sommelier's suggestion of a Savigny-lès-Beaune for a less-suitable 1990 Fixin (€87), staff were delightful throughout. Ordering from the €65 lunch menu, which is really the way to go here, four of us had the signature quenelles de brochet (fluffy pike-perch dumplings, surely the best in Paris), and one rebel enjoyed the duck and foie gras terrine. None of us could resist the caneton rôti Pierre Elby, duck à l'orange served on apple compote, with a spinach-and-cream feuilleté on the side. The fabulous view of the Seine has a way of cancelling out flaws in the food, so we were able to overlook the fact that the duck was cooked through rather than rosé as requested. Desserts are a highlight here: a wine-red poached pear, caramelised apple millefeuille and intense chocolate tart delivered. Not the best food in Paris, but certainly one of the best experiences.

Restaurant Hélène Darroze

4 rue d'Assas, 6th (01.42.22.00.11). M° Sèvres-Babylone. **Open** Tue-Sat 12.30-2.30pm, 7.30-10.15pm. Closed for lunch 14 July-31Aug. **Average** €110. **Prix fixe** €110. **Lunch menu** €58. **Credit** AmEx, MC, V. **Wheelchair access. Map** G7.

Haute cuisine may still be a peculiarly male bastion, but a few women have managed to scale its dizzy heights. Ducasse-trained Hélène Darroze is one such, and the upstairs room (as opposed to the more casual 'Salon' below, *see p123*) is very much a serious restaurant. Well-spaced tables, dazzling glassware and sumptuous decor in shades of purple and orange (there's even a little stool for your handbag) provide the setting for a refined cuisine based on Basque and south-western traditions. As you'd expect, foie gras appears in various forms – confit with subtle spices, grilled over a wood fire, or perhaps in a rich flan with a chestnut 'cappuccino'. An element of wit is also a hallmark, as in a starter of cured ham, soft-boiled egg, black truffles and perfectly cooked leeks, with country toast soldiers for dipping. There's plenty of southern colour too, in the likes of perfectly timed red mullet with coco beans and green-tinged clam juice, or in a tremendous dessert of roast apricots, caramelised pain perdu and an intense, mouth puckering, apricot sorbet. It's certainly worth finishing with a tea or a coffee from a good selection, not least because they're served with wonderful warm madeleines and miniature pots of home-made jam – perhaps strawberry and rose, pear and vanilla, or fig. Of course, with fame and all the little touches that go with this kind of dining, prices inevitably creep upwards, and it's interesting to note that last year's set lunch with a half-bottle of wine for €60 has been replaced with this year's €58 *sans vin*.

L'Arpège

84 rue de Varenne, 7th (01.45.51.47.33/ www.alain-passard.com). M° Varenne. **Open** Mon-Fri 12.30-2pm, 8-10pm. **Average** €250. **Prix fixe** €300. **Credit** AmEx, DC, MC, V. **Map** F6.

L'Arpège is a serious restaurant for people who take their food very seriously indeed. Alain Passard's devotees are willing to overlook the surprisingly cramped conditions – waiters struggle to squeeze their trolleys between tables, and one of us narrowly averted three collisions on the way to the loo – for his unique way with food. Passard prefers pared-down simplicity to culinary acrobatics, but he is a genius (or at least ingenious). The problem is, you often feel you're paying more for his ideas than for the ingredients themselves. Take his now-famous beetroot, baked in a pyramid of coarse grey Guérande sea salt. You'll never taste a beetroot this good, that much is certain; but the technique, as explained to us by our chatty waiter, was something our six-year-old could learn. Is it worth €60 for two golf-ball-sized roots? That depends on how much €60 means to you – the Japanese businessmen, Americans and gauche caviar couples who filled the dining room seemed perfectly contented, and most of them ordered the €300 menu dégustation. We opted instead for one all-vegetable and one fish meal à la carte – Passard no longer cooks with red meat. An onion gratin with parmesan, helpfully split into two half-portions, was paper-thin but absolutely delicious, while aged balsamic vinegar elevated the aforementioned humble beetroot to luxury status. Another starter of mussels in two froths – one made with nasturtiums, the other with herbs – was the kind of silky delight you expect from haute cuisine. Turbot was cooked over low heat for two-and-a-half hours yet showed no hint of dryness in its cream sauce with fresh peas, while vegetables from Passard's own garden outside Paris were cooked to retain their crunchiness and served with a light sprinkling of couscous in Moroccan argania oil – a surprisingly filling dish. For dessert, we had to try his famous 12-flavour tomato filled with nuts, fruit and spices, and a gargantuan millefeuille, both split into two. The sommelier selected some intriguing white wines by the glass for us (€13-€20), but for €420 for two we would have liked to see more of an effort made on the extras, which were limited to Passard's signature soft-boiled egg with maple syrup and sherry vinegar, and mini madeleines.

Le Jules Verne

Second Level, Eiffel Tower, Champ de Mars, 7th (01.45.55.61.44). M° Bir-Hakeim/RER Champ de Mars. **Open** daily 12.15-1.30pm, 7.15-9.30pm. **Average** €100. **Prix fixe** €114. **Lunch menu** €51 (Mon-Fri). **Credit** AmEx, DC, MC, V. **Map** C6.

So wonderfully eccentric and winsomely old-fashioned is the Eiffel Tower that it seems slightly churlish to take a swipe at Le Jules Verne, internationally considered to be one of the most romantic restaurants in the world by dint of its setting on the second level. Unfortunately, however, lunch here was disappointing on all counts. The door man and lift operator couldn't be bothered with a greeting, and once seated at a splendid table next to the window, we were served stunningly dull hors d'oeuvres of soggy onion quiche and dried-out cheese puffs. The silly decor – all black, and rather disco-ey with halogen lamps on the tables – desperately needs a makeover. Ramekins of beef aspic, puréed sea bass and spinach, and new almonds as an amuse-bouche were an oversalted convalescent-home treat, while a first course of gaspacho garnished with tasteless crabmeat brought Heinz tomato soup to mind. Foie gras served in place of the sold-out goat-cheese-stuffed ravioli was mushy and had little taste. A tagine of pork cheeks came in a rich gravy with baby vegetables and was pleasant enough, as was hachis Parmentier (shepherd's pie) made with shredded preserved duck, but the problem with both of these dishes is that haute cuisine restaurants never do bistro cooking as well as bistros do. Though it was gracious of the restaurant to allow a switch to cheese instead of dessert (it was not one of the choices on the prix-fixe lunch menu), the quality was poor to middling. A dessert of rose ice cream with hibiscus sauce was refreshing and original, but the mignardises served with coffee were disappointingly standard issue. All told this meal was a very dated version of fancy French food for foreigners. So is the view worth a meal here? Only if you come for the poor-value €51 lunch menu with decidedly earthbound expectations.

Alain Ducasse au Plaza Athénée ★

Hôtel Plaza Athénée, 25 av Montaigne, 8th (01.53.67.65.00/www.alain-ducasse.com). M° Alma-Marceau. **Open** Mon-Wed 8-10.30pm; Thur, Fri 1-2.30pm, 8-10.30pm. Closed last two weeks in Dec, mid-July to mid-Aug. **Average** €220. **Prix fixe** €190, €280. **Credit** AmEx, DC, MC, V. **Map** D5.

Perhaps the best measure of an haute cuisine meal is the claim it makes on your attention span. In the case of a dinner at Alain Ducasse, two or three of the dishes we sampled were still on our minds a week later. We also came away in reverent admiration of the service, which is probably the most professional, engaging and precise of any restaurant in Paris. The decor by Patrick Jouin, however, is starting to seem a little gimmicky a few years on. This quibble aside, we had a spectacular meal, greedily devouring amuse-bouches of perfectly poached langoustines topped with caviar, and spider crab served in its orange shell beneath a bubbly foam of coral. Next, two brilliant first courses: French asparagus from Pertuis in Provence, poached and served under fine leaves of melted comté cheese with an exquisite sauce of black truffles and vin jaune from the Jura, and plump langoustines on a bed of first-of-season ceps – both sautéed and raw – red onion, and herbs. Sautéed Breton lobster with asparagus tips and morels in a light sauce of its own cooking juices was exquisite, while sea bass carpaccio in parsley juice with morels was perfectly executed but clearly aimed at more timid palates. Chef Jean-François Piège's real art is often almost undetectable, since the consistent goal is to enhance the natural flavours of the best French seasonal produce. After a superb plate of cheeses from Bernard Anthony, the famous Alsatian fromager, and Parisian Marie-Anne Cantin, desserts concluded the meal on a note of operatic triumph. Strawberries from Plougastel in Brittany were cut into matchsticks, carefully arranged on a pastry cream on a rectangle of puff pastry and topped with a caramelised stalk of poached rhubarb: brilliant.

Les Ambassadeurs

Hôtel de Crillon, 10 pl de la Concorde, 8th (01.44.71.16.17/www.crillon.com). M° Concorde. **Open** daily noon-2pm, 7.30-10pm. **Average** €155. **Prix fixe** €135. **Lunch menu** €62. **Credit** AmEx, DC, MC, V. **Map** F5.

If you hanker for gilt and crystal, polished marble and a velvet stool on which to perch your handbag, then this is your kind of place. The hotel is favoured by pop royalty and the other kind so you could pass them in the foyer, glimpse them at a table or just slip past the fans waiting outside and pretend. Chef Dominique Bouchet has a sure touch with produce and a flair for presentation: portly green and white asparagus crowned with a perfectly poached, yolk-oozing egg, a sliver of foie gras and truffle juice, or gem-coloured spring vegetables drizzled with olive oil then sprinkled with slices of cured ham and fresh coriander. The mains, too, extol simple excellence: langoustine ravioli floating in a broth of shellfish and verbena, and delicately sliced salmon arranged on tomato 'petals', dressed with thyme flowers, olive oil, lemon and balsamic vinegar. Cheese zealots will be sated by two heaving trolleys and chocophiles can't help but swoon shamelessly for the six chocolate 'grand cru' desserts on one plate. You'll pay (though the lunch prix fixe is quite a bargain for what you get), but what the hell – those flanks of doting waiters don't come cheap.

Le Bristol

Hôtel Bristol, 112 rue du Fbg-St-Honoré, 8th (01.53.43.43.00/www.lebristolparis.com). M° Miromesnil. **Open** daily noon-2.30pm, 7-10.30pm. **Average** €100. **Prix fixe** €130. **Lunch menu** €65. **Credit** AmEx, DC, MC, V. **Wheelchair access.** **Map** E4.

The summer dining room of this seriously swanky hotel is a slight disappointment. Spacious and light with huge windows looking onto a garden, it feels

A traditional setting for truffles and lobster: **Le V**.

more international than Parisian. The food, though, has some fine French flourishes. A very chic American couple next to us found themselves confronted with an enormous, steaming pig's bladder. As the truth sank in about what they'd actually ordered, the waiter punctured the bloated bag to reveal an exquisitely white fattened pullet from Bresse. In comparison, our (summer) seasonal menu was a little predictable, though not bad value. Perhaps our most memorable dish was one of the amuse-gueules: a fresh and invigorating cucumber mousse with tomato and horseradish. Our starter of duck foie gras was warm and deliciously tender as it should be, but the flavourings of spice bread, peach marmalade and almonds proved too sweet, especially with our Beaumes de Venise muscat. Our best main was the red mullet, the filleted fish arriving under a crust of breadcrumbs. This was served with puréed tomato, spiked with ginger. Not tremendous but better than the cod which, though perfectly cooked and deliciously buttery, came on a bed of watercress purée that tasted of nothing at all. The desserts were as elaborated constructed as always in this sort of restaurant but again the taste failed to dazzle. Next time we'll definitely go for the bladder.

Le V ★

Hôtel Four Seasons George V, 31 av George V, 8th (01.49.52.70.00/www.fourseasons.com). M° George V. **Open** daily noon-2.30pm, 6.30-11pm. **Average** €180. **Prix fixe** €90, €190. **Lunch menu** €70. **Credit** AmEx, DC, MC, V. **Wheelchair access. Map** D4.

We came out of here fully converted to the cult of the George V. A look at the menu replete with lobster, truffles, caviar, Bresse chicken, turbot and sea bass and you could believe it to be simply a roll-call of grandeur. Not so. Philippe Legendre does indeed produce luxury fare, but combined with precise execution, well-judged service and just a whiff of invention. A tiny artichoke and truffle tart on a delicate flaky pastry disc contained an almost indecent amount of pungent black truffle. A layer of morels and a dome of shredded spider crab meat were cleverly invigorated with fresh chopped sorrel. The undoubted highlight, though, was the lobster. Wood-smoked in its shell and surrounded by a delicate, frothy morel sauce, it was a revelation we won't forget. Potent rosy-red pigeon roast with hay and mead was less surprising but garnished with spring vegetables so full of flavour that they could have come out of the garden that morning. Then the cheese trolley full of well-aged specimens, among them the fabulous venaco de Corse, simply begged to be tried as well. Desserts – a rhubarb and strawberry concoction with a tangy lemon sorbet and the gourmandise de mangue, mango tubes filled with creamy chocolate, with a ginger-caramel ice cream – were fun but less exceptional. The dining room, redone a couple of years ago in neo-Louis XVI, could be ostentatious but somehow remains calmly discreet. Tables are simply miles apart and gilt flourishes are subtly offset by grey-green walls, all constrasting with towering assymmetrical flower arrangements. The service, for once in a grand establishment, got it just right.

Les Elysées du Vernet

Hôtel Vernet, 25 rue Vernet, 8th (01.44.31.98.98/www.hotelvernet.com). M° George V. **Open** Mon 7.30-9.30pm; Tue-Fri 12.30-2pm, 7.30-9.30pm. Closed 26 July-26 Aug, 25 Dec-1 Jan. **Average** €120. **Prix fixe**

€120 (dinner only). **Lunch menu** €45. **Credit** AmEx, DC, MC, V. **Wheelchair access. Map** D4.
This pretty, belle époque dining room, with its glass dome mounted in a sturdy iron framework designed by Gustave Eiffel, has always felt more like an Agatha Christie setting on the Riviera than Paris. Its old-fashioned look was the perfect foil for chef Alain Solivérès (see Taillevent, *p88*), a superb cook with a real talent for reinterpreting southern French food. Now that chef Eric Briffard is in the saddle, the room feels a bit wilted. Briffard is an excellent cook, but his classicism is, well, classic. Ravioli with herbs pressed into the pasta struck a rather ho-hum, 1980s note. A salad of seasonal baby vegetables from a small producer in Yvelines, however, was a delicious tumble, featuring crosnes (Chinese artichokes) and tiny onions with pot-au-feu aspic, scattered finely with matchstick-cut truffles and served with a horseradish canapé. A salad of scallops dotted with caviar was pleasant enough, but déjà vu. Given that Solivérès is a tough act to follow, Briffard is a chef very much worth watching, and the €45 lunch menu here is excellent value.

Laurent

41 av Gabriel, 8th (01.42.25.00.39/ www.le-laurent.com). M° Champs-Elysées-Clemenceau. **Open** Mon-Fri 12.30-2pm, 7.30-10.30pm; Sat 7.30-10.30pm. Closed public holidays. **Average** €150. **Prix fixe** €140. **Lunch menu** €65. **Credit** AmEx, DC, MC, V. **Wheelchair access**. **Map** F4.
With its combination of elegant setting, refined cuisine and relaxed atmosphere, Laurent has long been one of the unsung sleepers among Paris' top restaurants. The three-course lunch menu, allowing a reasonable choice of dishes that are also (much more expensively) on the carte, plus a visit from the mahogany cheese 'car', is a good sampling of Alain Péguret's style, which combines classicism with a partiality for sweet glazes and bitter accents. The soupe des maraîchers of a startling deep green had a delicious sorrel tang and came dotted with 'pickles' of girolle mushrooms. Violet artichokes sautéed with bacon and herbs were more rustic, topped by parmesan wafers and a perfectly mastered oeuf mollet with a golden butter and breadcrumb crust. Next, a generous, fleshy section of monkfish on the bone with an intense orange reduction, paired with tender fennel glazed with orange and coriander. Pigeon roast in a honey glaze was more classic, save for the thin sheets of peanut brittle posed on the meat, though it was the baby turnips with a speckled Bourbon vanilla glaze that pleased us most. Cheese, a light chewy macaroon with black cherries and a deep-red bitter cherry sauce and roast peaches in a frothy sabayon with verbena ice cream rounded off the meal. In summer, the action moves outside from the pretty Napoléon III pavilion to the lovely garden. The sight of Mick Jagger lunching with Charlie Watts and business magnates saluting each other somehow seemed a typically Parisian gourmet mix.

Ledoyen

1 av Dutuit, 8th (01.53.05.10.01). M° Champs-Elysées-Clémenceau. **Open** Mon 8-10pm; Tue-Fri 12.30-2pm, 8-10pm. Closed Aug, one week at Christmas. **Average** €150. **Prix fixe** €168, €244. **Lunch menu** €73. **Credit** AmEx, DC, MC, V. **Wheelchair access**. **Map** F5.
On an early summer evening, when this restaurant ought to have been at its most bewitching – it's a purely sensual pleasure to watch the light fade

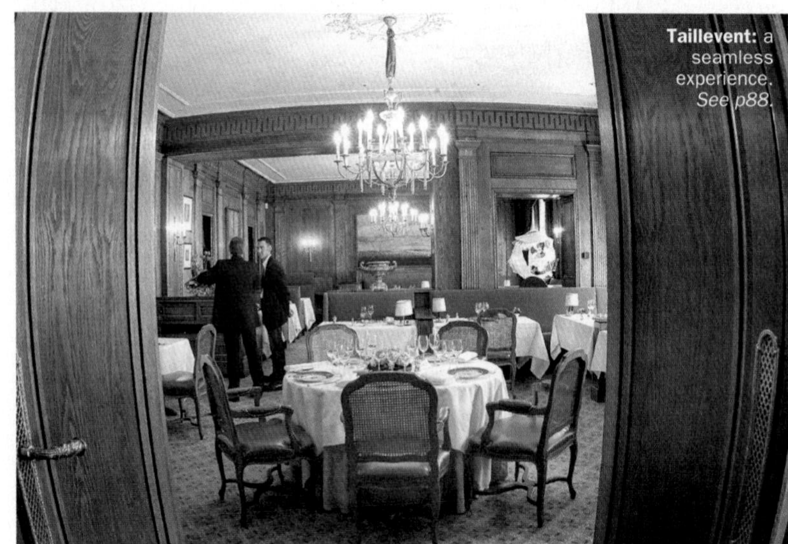

Taillevent: a seamless experience. *See p88.*

through the tree tops that surround the elegant second-floor Directoire dining room that is one of the loveliest settings in Paris – our dinner here was a maddening catastrophe. They had no record of our reservation, but somehow we were the ones labelled remiss. We were finally seated at a woeful table next to the busiest serving station in the dining room. A waitress managed to get us through a half-bottle of mineral water before our starters arrived, and then decided that we should have another one with no further consultation. The menu had changed little since the last time we came, but we remembered enjoying the langoustines, now priced at an absurd €72 for three, and hoped that 'cooked and raw' asparagus would be pleasant. The langoustines were certifiably flavour-free and mucked up in an insipid sauce, and the asparagus would have been all right were it not for a sauce that tasted as if waxed kitchen paper and butter were the main ingredients. Main courses were also a crashing disappointment: impeccably cooked turbot was ruined by a dreary sauce that had something to do with truffles, while dreadfully overcooked and almost tasteless sea bass came in yet another botched sauce with rubbery bits and pieces of shellfish. Though we didn't finish any of these dishes, none of the staff saw fit to ask if there was a reason why half of each plate had been left untouched. We skipped cheese and dessert, and concluded with coffee (€6), before being blasted by an absurd bill for a ghastly meal. Never again.

Lucas Carton ★

9 pl de la Madeleine, 8th (01.42.65.22.90/ www.lucascarton.com). M° Madeleine. **Open** Mon, Sat 8-10.30pm; Tue-Fri noon-2.30pm, 8-10.30pm. Closed Aug. **Average** €200. **Lunch menu** €76. **Credit** AmEx, DC, MC, V. **Map** F4.

We're not sure it gets any better than this. Cosseted in a merlot-coloured banquette, looking out through art nouveau carved wood partitions with glass encased dragonflies and butterflies, iris-embossed silver cutlery at hand, along with some genuinely accommodating young waiters and a glass of 1995 Dom Pérignon – it's lunchtime heaven on a plate. Opting for the 'déjeuner affaires', good value next to some eye-catching à la carte offerings such as €95 lobster and a €65 glass of wine, we didn't feel we were second-besting it. Tender green asparagus came surrounded by an emerald asparagus 'cappuccino' with almond milk and tiny chips of spicy pork sausage; plump little just-cooked scallops studded with shell-topped toothpicks threaded with pink pickled ginger and bright green courgette floated in a heady broth of coconut milk, lemongrass and coriander. Alain Senderens is passionate about marrying wine with food; thus each dish has a suggested tipple. A glass of Pouilly Fuissé Le Clos 1999 with the asparagus, and Condrieu Terrasses 2000 with the scallops, were inspired combinations. The standout main was a featherweight tempura of sole and peppery celery leaves, lightly flavoured with Madras curry, and ringed with a zingy cucumber emulsion. A marvellous layering of flavours, ably washed down with Condrieu Grandes Chaillées 2000 at €25 a glass. Dessert: a wickedly rich Tahitian vanilla millefeuille, crème brûlée and some exquisite petits-fours. Same time tomorrow? We wish!

Pierre Gagnaire

6 rue Balzac, 8th (01.58.36.12.50/ www.pierre-gagnaire.com). M° Charles de Gaulle-Etoile or George V. **Open** Mon-Fri noon-2pm, 7.30-10pm; Sun 7.30-10pm. Closed one week in Feb, last two weeks in July. **Average** €150. **Prix fixe** €195. **Lunch menu** €90. **Credit** AmEx, DC, MC, V. **Wheelchair access. Map** D3.

There is only one Pierre Gagnaire. The man is a creative genius, and a meal here is more of a breathtaking adventure than anything to do with satisfying a basic hunger. Dishes are made up of several elements, served separately, which attempt to tell the story of a particular ingredient: 'la langoustine', for instance, featuring a pan-fried version with a lime tuile, a mousseline with lemongrass, a tartare with apple and ginger, and grilled, with thyme nougatine. Others illustrate surprising complementarities (veal and frogs, for example). The prix fixe offers an ideal introduction, with some nine separate courses, including a stunning turnip soup with swede and black truffle, cuttlefish with cinnamon and creamy polenta, a pressé of leeks with crab and tuna loin, and pigeon with Malabar pepper and foie gras. Surprisingly, a few fine English ingredients – Maldon salt and Stilton – make it on to the menu (Gagnaire is consultant chef to the ultra-fashionable London restaurant Sketch). The pièce de résistance, for sweet tooths at any rate, is the Pierre Gagnaire grand dessert – seven delights including fruit-based concoctions, various chocolate creations, and a fabulous pistachio cream with roasted hazelnuts. The split-level dining room, with its gleaming wood and seductive lighting, has something of an art deco, ocean-liner feel, accentuated by choreographed staff in tailcoats.

Stella Maris

4 rue Arsène-Houssaye, 8th (01.42.89.16.22). M° Charles de Gaulle-Etoile. **Open** Mon, Sat 7.30-10.30pm; Tue-Fri noon-2.15pm, 7.45-10.30pm. Closed two weeks in Aug, 25 Dec. **Average** €100. **Prix fixe** €104, €71. **Lunch menu** €43. **Credit** AmEx, DC, MC, V. **Map** D3.

Two worlds meet with superb results at this intimate, two-storey restaurant, where Japanese chef Tateru Yoshino turns out astonishingly prepared food. Looking at the menu, which features fairly straightforward dishes such as foie gras, risotto and smoked salmon, it is immediately apparent that Yoshino has not fallen into the hackneyed trap of dishing out 'fusion' cuisine. Yet, East does indeed meet West here – in the discipline of the cooking. Yoshino has succeeded in creating dishes that are at once rich in flavour and clean in taste. The risotto with morels and asparagus was unctuously creamy, yet toothy, the richness edged with a sharp, parmesan tuile. The home-smoked, half-cooked salmon was equally excellent; the skin, separated and roasted to a dry crisp, betraying the chef's Japanese roots. Despite the restraint of the menu, Yoshino lets his creativity flow in the parade of amuse-bouche: a tiny spoonful of poached quail egg, studded with cracked pink peppercorns and chives and enlivened by a jus of bacon and balsamic vinegar; raw cuttlefish rolled in roasted Spanish red pepper and drizzled with squid ink and pesto; vichysoisse of nettle, served in an espresso cup – tantalising glimpses of the chef's experimental sensibilities before they are subdued in the perfectly grilled entrecôte steak with morels and turned potatoes. A veritable feast, made that much more poetic by service that was solicitous, knowledgeable and passionate.

Taillevent ★

15 rue Lamennais, 8th (01.44.95.15.01/ www.taillevent.com). M° Charles de Gaulle-Etoile or George V. **Open** Mon-Fri noon-2pm, 7.30-10pm. Closed Aug. **Average** €110. **Prix fixe** €130, €180. **Credit** AmEx,DC, MC, V. **Wheelchair access**. **Map** D3.

The ascension of chef Alain Solivérès, formerly of Les Elysées, to the kitchens of a restaurant widely considered to be among the top ten in the world is quite simply a brilliant success; it's been ages since we enjoyed a meal as much as we did our recent lunch at Taillevent. Even the company of blasé bankers and other lucky dogs who might be described as regulars couldn't numb our constant, quiet pleasure at the setting, service and most of all the food. Solivérès has a lusty style, but he always remains tantalisingly in control, with an astonishing ability to concentrate flavour. The amuse-bouche that began our meal – cauliflower cream with a buttery, faintly poultry-nuanced jus, was absolutely brilliant. Tipping his toque at his own past – he's a native of Montpellier and his reputation has so far been based on a stunning ability to reinvent the cooking of southern France – he produced three plump scallops topped with a miniature dice of Lucca olives, chorizo and parmesan and garnished with tender leaves of dandelion and rocket: a brilliant starter. His mastery of the more traditional dishes that are the bedrock of the menu here is impressive, too, as seen in a creamy soup of ratte potatoes from Noirmoutier ladled over a dainty sauté of shelled crayfish. A seasonal suggestion was a long strip of tuna belly, immaculately cooked so that the firm texture of the fish played off of its own almost buttery richness, served with an elegant tangle of Espelette peppers, lemon, capers and serrano ham. Sea bass in shellfish jus with a few tiny clams and raw and braised artichokes, from the à la carte menu, was pleasant, but a little underwhelming in comparison. Similarly, the dessert list will have to be thoroughly revised to play to Solivérès' style. Jean-Pierre Vrinat, one of the world's great restaurateurs, was a thoroughly charming host.

Jamin

32 rue de Longchamp, 16th (01.45.53.00.07). M° Trocadéro. **Open** Mon-Fri 12.30-2pm, 7.45-9.45pm. Closed Aug. **Average** €110. **Prix fixe** €88. **Lunch menu** €50. **Credit** AmEx, DC, MC, V. **Wheelchair access**. **Map** C5.

First impressions aren't great: stained-green wood walls like an Ile de Ré beach hut meet Regency stripe and ruched curtains in what can't even be described as a curious throwback (to what?). The fusty decor seems to be keeping away the French business clientele you'd expect to find here, judging from our lunchtime visit, populated only by two American couples and a party of Japanese clearly on the trail of Robuchon protégé Benoît Guichard in the master's old home. Fortunately, the setting is out of kilter with the food. While the carte has some luxury classics, such as lobster with morels, the overall emphasis is more modern and Mediterranean. At lunch, the menu du marché, a no-choice bargain which changes every two or three days, offers starter, fish course, meat course and the dessert trolley. Bite-size amuse-gueule of small mackerel on a pizza-like tomato base and an accra-style cod ball set the way. A pressée de légumes, courgette, tomato and aubergine surrounded by polka dots of red pepper coulis and black olive dressing, followed by fried cod with a vegetable 'bouillabaisse' – artichoke heart and fennel in a swirl of saffron-tinted sauce – then a mini-lamb chop, a dollop of tender stewed lamb with broad beans and peas, all showed Guichard's fondness for seasonal produce. From the dessert and ice cream trolleys, we indulged in an overly sweet wild strawberry tart, a rhubarb tart and – the definite winner – a cherry clafoutis with flaked almonds. This is not cooking that's going to change your life but our meal was well-prepared, elegantly (silver-handled carafe, silver water bottle holder, shiny silver domes) if mutely served and incredibly generous in these days of galloping restaurant inflation. If only they'd get rid of the frilly curtains, we'd feel much happier.

Le Pré Catelan

route de Suresnes, Bois de Boulogne, 16th (01.44.14.41.14/www.lenotre.fr). M° Porte-Maillot, then 244 bus. **Open** Tue-Sat noon-2pm, 7-9.30pm; Sun noon-2pm (May-Oct). Closed one week in Nov, three weeks in Feb. **Average** €100. **Prix fixe** €106, €140. **Lunch menu** €55. **Credit** AmEx, DC, MC, V.

What could be more civilised than a leisurely Sunday lunch in a grand French restaurant in the Bois de Boulogne? The Pré Catelan, a gleaming white wedding cake of a building, with its slightly kitsch interior (Caran d'Ache ceiling with chubby little cherubs) comes into its own from May to October, when they open the French windows and let the park into the dining room. But the setting isn't the only draw: although the clientele might appear to be more at home in a spa town (at Sunday lunch at any rate), Frédéric Anton's food is surprisingly modern. The spring menu kicked off with the thinnest discs of beetroot, paired with equally thin discs of aged comté, before proceeding to a beautifully smooth foie gras, rolled in coriander and fennel seeds, and served with a smear of bright orange pumpkin purée. A simply-cooked fillet of sea bass was drizzled with anchovy and lime-zest marmalade, followed by a main course of pigeon breast, poached in spices, with a broccoli couscous and spicy merguez made from the leg meat. Cheese is a particular pleasure here – an enormous trolley, with expert advice on hand, and plenty of great bread to go with it, leading up perhaps to a mini rum baba with a light vanilla cream. Staff were incredibly polite (nothing appears to be too much trouble, including substituting dishes on the fixed-price menus), and notably efficient, which, given the scale of the operation, is quite some feat.

Guy Savoy

18 rue Troyon, 17th (01.43.80.40.61/ www.guysavoy.com). M° Charles de Gaulle-Etoile.
Open Mon, Sat 7.30-10.30pm; Tue-Fri noon-2pm, 7.30-10.30pm. Closed mid-July to mid-Aug.
Average €230. **Prix fixe** €200, €245.
Credit AmEx, DC, MC, V. **Map** C3.

Guy Savoy inspires not just admiration but real affection from his fans. He's so likeable and his cooking, which emphasises the finest, freshest ingredients, textures and contrasts, is inventive but never overworked. Bite into his brilliant huîtres en nage glacée, oysters cooked in their own juice, made into a jelly and topped with a briny fresh oyster, and it's just like a dip in the ocean, while his now-legendary artichoke soup with black truffles and warm toasted brioche heaped with truffle butter is indecently soothing. For a one-night, gastronomic voyage, take the set menu. Sup on a cool tartare of meaty mackerel topped with Sevruga caviar and the same fish roasted and served on a potato slice; flinty lentils paired with earthy black truffles; plump langoustine steeped in citrus butter; and sweet, fleshy sea bass drifting on a vanilla sauce – a heavenly match. Then, milk-fed lamb 'dans tous ses états': grilled with fresh rosemary, rolled and stuffed with rocket, and souris, meltingly soft lamb shank, brightened with twice-peeled peas. For dessert, a festival of raspberries: sorbet layered with fresh fruit, granita, a biscuit crowned with upright berries and one deliciously caramelised fruit, followed by chocolate sorbet and deeply rich ganache dusted with bitter almond-tasting Tonka bean, then a sliver of warm apple tart. Oh, and mini madeleines fresh from the oven in between. The staff is generous, service is flawless and the surroundings – a grown-up scheme of warm wood, leather, African sculptures and Georges Autard canvases – candidly comfortable. Most of the diners are French, and you'll need to reserve at least a month in advance to join them and the ever-charming, ever-present Guy for dinner.

Michel Rostang

20 rue Rennequin, 17th (01.47.63.40.77/ www.michelrostang.com). M° Ternes or Pereire.
Open Mon, Sat 7.30-10.30pm; Tue-Fri 12.30-2.30pm, 7.30-10.30pm. Closed Aug. **Average** €160. **Prix fixe** €175, €230. **Lunch menu** €65. **Credit** AmEx, DC, MC, V. **Non-smoking room. Map** D2.

Michel Rostang proves there is nothing like the classic touch for building up a loyal following. We were shown into the cosy and beautifully appointed no-smoking section with wood panelling, Lalique glass insets, a magnificent Aubusson tapestry and a priceless collection of original drawings of Lalique jewellery. Although on the whole the cuisine lived up to the chef's reputation, there were a few expensive hiccups such as the measly portion of badly trimmed, pan-fried foie gras that launched the formidably priced €175 menu. Then there was the à la carte first course of spider crab and sea bass billed at €52: a small dome of raw fish with a few straggly strands of crab under a 'shell' of limp and tasteless artichoke and tomato petals. The head waiter showed his concern by offering to change it, but we declined as the mains were ready. The menu continued with a beautifully conceived dish of red mullet with a sauce made from its liver and an attractive tian of Provençal vegetables, followed by a plate of tasty but slightly too-salty lamb. The real masterpiece of the evening was the sublime casserole of Bresse chicken with plump, fresh morels bathing in the richest of rich cream sauces doused with a generous helping of vin jaune. We had opted for a bottle of Jacques Puffeney's fabulous rich, walnutty 1990 vin jaune to accompany the whole meal, super value at €64. The menu included a cheese course – the memory of our state-of-the-art munster will be with us for a long time to come. To finish, a captivating and unusual fennel and saffron soufflé with rhubarb compote and bouncy sponge cake. We thought that the evening menu was hugely overpriced; à la carte or the lunch prix fixe would be much better options.

How to Eat **Quail**

Wild quail has become something of a luxury in France as it's now quite scarce; this small but plump migratory bird has been largely replaced by a less-tasty, domestic breed. Wild quail is in season from April to October, and it is finest of all in the autumn. In a sophisticated restaurant it might be grilled, cooked in a casserole (en cocotte, often with grapes) or made into a pâté. If you're faced with fiddly little bones (and the same applies to pigeon), don't be shy about using your fingers. It's considered socially acceptable to hold the bone with your right hand (or left, if you're left-handed) while you gnaw, but avoid the caveman approach of using both hands.

Brasseries

Towering seafood platters, luminous period decor and clamouring waiters and clients ensure that Paris brasseries won't leave a bad taste in your mouth.

While brasseries have been in Paris since the 16th century, it wasn't until the 1870s that they morphed into the opulent dining rooms you see today. Originally, they were more humble establishments which brewed beer on the premises and served hearty Alsatian food.

In recent years, groups such as Flo and Les Frères Blanc have saved many a historic brasserie from extinction, sometimes to the detriment of the cuisine. At the other end of the spectrum lies the mod squad: **La Grande Armée**, **La Gare** and **Alcazar**, places that put a new spin on both food and decor. In between there's the independent **Le Suffren**, with its hip new look but the same sustaining food.

You can eat well in brasseries; just don't expect gastronomic highs. Stick to the classics and enjoy the spectacle of waiters screaming 'chaud devant' as they pilot a steaming plate of choucroute or a tower of shellfish.

Brasserie Zimmer

1 pl du Châtelet, 1st (01.42.36.74.03/ www.lezimmer.com). M° Châtelet. **Open** daily 9am-1am. Food served 11am-12.30am. **Average** €25. **Prix fixe** €18.60. **Credit** AmEx, MC, V. **Non-smoking room**. **Map** J6.

The Costes brothers now have so many lookalike restaurants with only vaguely different versions of Jacques Garcia's louche Napoléon III decor that it's easy to overlook one – which had previously been the case with this strategically located spot with, yes, leopard-print upholstery, etc. Though it's not exactly a destination restaurant, it's worth knowing about in August, when so many other places are closed, and the sort of dead simple food served here tastes best in summer. Try starters such as the green bean salad or the tomato with mozzarella, and move on to chicken brochette, a steak or pasta. The idea is not to have a screamingly good meal, but to eat just well enough in a pleasant setting with earnest young waiters and lounge-attitude buzz.

Au Pied de Cochon

6 rue Coquillière, 1st (01.40.13.77.00/ www.pieddecochon.com). M° Les Halles. **Open** daily 24 hours. **Average** €50. **Credit** AmEx, DC, MC, V. **Non-smoking room. Map** J5.

You enter this temple to the trotter through doors with handles cast in piggy-extremity-shaped bronze and eat off crockery decorated with the picture of a pig clutching a knife and fork. Once your crispy trotter arrives, accompanied by fries, watercress, sauce béarnaise and, in our case, a bottle of Chinon, it may not be immediately obvious what to do next; a pig's foot is a complicated anatomical construction containing 32 bones, so don't hesitate to ask for a bit of advice on how to go about eating one. Le Pied de Cochon has all the usual brasserie food for those who refuse to partake in the foot-fest and the onion soup and the oysters are rightly renowned. But that's all a bit like ordering an omelette in a curry house: this is a place to extend your gastronomic foothold.

Gallopin ★

40 rue Notre-Dame-des-Victoires, 2nd (01.42.36.45.38/www.brasseriegallopin.com). M° Bourse. **Open** Mon-Sat noon-midnight. Closed Sat in Aug. **Average** €45. **Prix fixe** €20.50-€30.50. **Credit** AmEx, DC, MC, V. **Wheelchair access. Non-smoking room. Map** J4.

Walking through the glass doors of Gallopin on an unusually warm spring night was a through-the-looking-glass experience. Inside, it feels as though nothing has changed since 1876. The polished mahogany panelling is dimly lit by pretty art nouveau wall lights, the handsome waiters in cut-away coats emanate pride in the their job and the customers (mainly French; incredibly none were smoking on the night we visited) are so self-assured that, bar the costume change, this could be a scene from Proust or Henry James. Our extremely tall waiter was a delight, happy to discuss at length the relative merits of dry and sweet wine with foie gras and the preparation of the food. Come early if you want the specials of the day – we arrived at 9.30pm and already the sea bream and the plum tart had gone. So, we started with the foie gras maison, which was superb, with a marmalade-like jelly in place of the usual yellow layer of grease; the half lobster à la Parisienne, however, was smothered in Russian salad and surrounded by lettuce leaf, tomato and all sorts of other unwanted accoutrements. Simplicity reigned for the main course of sea bass. Chargrilled with fennel seeds and stems inside, and served with an olive oil dressing and parsleyed new potatoes, it was a fish dish cooked to perfection and deliciously accompanied by the citrussy notes of the Petit Chablis Laroche (half bottle, €17). For puds, we enjoyed the spectacle of crêpes Alexandre being flambéed near our table, and appreciated the effort made to find a plum tart 'after all' – we suspect the chef had been saving the last one for himself, and with reason: it was inundated with tart, juicy plums.

Souped-up service at **Le Grand Colbert**. *See p93.*

Located in the heart of the Latin Quarter, the Bouillon Racine combines art nouveau charm and exceptionally tasty food.

Since 1906

Open daily noon-11pm

3 rue Racine, 6th.

M° Odéon.

Tel: 01.44.32.15.60

Fax: 01.44.32.15.61

www.bouillonracine.com

La Rose de France

Ideally located on the "Ile de la Cité," a central Paris' historic island

La Rose de France will win you over with its relaxed service, fine wines and delicious food. The terrace (weather permitting) is one of the most beautiful in Paris.

24 place Dauphine, 1st. M° Pont-neuf or Cité
Tel: 01.43.54.10.12 - www.la-rose-de-france.com

Le Grand Colbert

2-4 rue Vivienne, 2nd (01.42.86.87.88). M° Bourse. **Open** daily noon-1am. **Average** €37. **Lunch menu** €17.50. **Prix fixe** €26. **Credit** AmEx, DC, MC, V. **Wheelchair access. Map** H4.

A becapped and uniformed doorman ushers you in to the Grand Colbert with a smile, and this is typical of the friendly yet professional service in this laid-back brasserie. You still get the delicate painted friezes, palms and great brass globe lights, but the mirrors are covered with theatre posters and the menu laminated with plastic, reflecting a dressed-down clientele that included a large group of American teenagers and two birthday parties. Rather than plonking us down anywhere, the maître d' insisted we wait until a sweet corner table with right-angle banquettes was cleared. You can have fun here, with the limited-choice set menu at €26 leaving change for a decent wine (we splashed out on a nice half-bottle of St-Emilion for €16). Quantities are huge, but don't expect gastronomic flair. This meal got off to a fabulous start, however: the croustillant de chèvre served on a bed of mâche and beetroot was delightfully crisp, and the fat and juicy marinated herring were served in an enormous help-yourself dish, accompanied by another of freshly cooked waxy potatoes with shallots and chives. Things went downhill from there, with a mediocre faux-filet, and an enormous but soggy slice of calf's liver in a sweet sauce of tiny onions which was somewhat redeemed by perfectly cooked spinach. There were also breadcrumbed tomatoes, sautéed potatoes, plus a plate of thick-cut chips, so no nonsense here about ordering your veg separately, and we enjoyed the nursery desserts of a rich chocolate mousse and a superior île (or rather continent) flottante with caramel and toasted almonds.

Le Vaudeville ★

29 rue Vivienne, 2nd (01.40.20.04.62/ www.vaudevilleparis.com). M° Bourse. **Open** daily 7-11.30am (breakfast), noon-3pm, 7pm-1am. **Average** €40. **Prix fixe** €21.50, €30.50. **Lunch menu** €21.50. **Credit** AmEx, DC, MC, V. **Non-smoking room. Map** H4.

Yes, it's another Flo conquest (at last count, the chain had gobbled up nine brasseries in Paris), but Le Vaudeville has maintained its old-fashioned vibe, mainly through the stunning art deco interior and faultless service. The 1920s detailing – engraved glass, ironwork, warm-toned marble and inlaid wood – was designed by the Solvet brothers, whose only other remaining masterworks are La Coupole and La Closerie des Lilas. We sat at one of the long tables against the wall and marvelled at the waiters in their impeccable black and whites, constantly busy on our late Friday night visit seasoning dishes, delicately boning fish fillets on the sideboard or cheerily mixing up each steak tartare to order. The food, too, harkens back to days of yore – no nouveau anything. We first sampled a plain but satisfying cheese and cream ravioli dish and a well-executed salad with chèvre encrusted in toasted hazelnuts. Fine fish, such as a trio of charred salmon, red mullet and cod, or the chunky slab of grilled cod with truffle-infused mashed potatoes, make succulent main courses. Le Vaudeville's no-frills food is refreshingly confident about what it is and what it is not.

Bofinger

5-7 rue de la Bastille, 4th (01.42.72.87.82/ www.bofingerparis.com). M° Bastille. **Open** Mon-Fri noon-3pm, 6.30pm-1am; Sat, Sun noon-1am. **Average** €42. **Prix fixe** €30.50. **Lunch menu** €21.50 (Mon-Fri). **Credit** AmEx, DC, MC, V. **Non-smoking room. Map** M7.

Just opposite the Bastille opera house, Bofinger is a favourite post-opera haunt and draws big crowds at other times for its authentic art nouveau setting and buzzy brasserie atmosphere. Downstairs is the prettiest place to eat, but in the summer it's worth remembering that upstairs is air-conditioned. As in many restaurants owned by the Flo group, the food is never less than adequate but rarely aspires to great culinary heights. On a recent visit we enjoyed an à la carte meal of plump garlicky escargots, and a well-made langoustine terrine, followed by an intensely seasoned salmon tartare and a generous, if uneventful, cod steak. Calf's liver was pink and delicious but accompanied surprisingly by some cooked melon – melons were being featured that week. Not an idea which will send anyone rushing to the kitchen, but not aggressively unpleasant. By then we slightly regretted not having ordered our usual foolproof brasserie meal of oysters and fillet steak, so we got back on track with a rabidly pungent plate of munster cheese and its accompanying bowl of cumin, washed down by the fine raspberry-nosed Chinon at €35.50 a bottle.

Brasserie de l'Isle St Louis

55 quai de Bourbon, 4th (01.43.54.02.59). M° Pont Marie. **Open** Mon, Tue, Fri-Sun noon-1am; Thur 5pm-1am. Closed Aug. **Average** €40. **Credit** MC, V. **Map** K7.

Though this strategically located brasserie just over the footbridge linking the two islands of Paris maintains its popularity with Parisians and a herd of visiting foreigners, our most recent meal here was a let-down. The lovely dining room with heavy, dark-wood trencher tables, wrought iron light fixtures and the odd mounted animal head is so enchantingly Gallic that you might almost be tempted to forgive the shortcomings of the food, but this same tolerance has allowed some Parisian brasseries to soldier on in a slough of mediocrity. Here, the kitchen's performance was hampered by the middling-to-low quality produce. On a chilly early spring evening, the tarte à l'oignon tempted, and proved to be a mushy porridge-like mix of eggs and sloppily sliced onions with almost no seasoning or crust. A salad of lamb's lettuce with a poached egg and beetroot was the better choice – the egg was even lukewarm, but the beetroot was stingily served and the greens were gritty. Main courses of steak tartare and choucroute garnie were heartbreaking.

Soggy, tasteless sauerkraut came crowned with flabby sausages, a bit of decent bacon, a fishy-tasting slice of pork roast and a single boiled potato. The steak tartare had no texture and little taste. A slice of fruit tart was dull, and the only thing that rescued the meal was surprisingly good coffee, especially since the waiters took minimal interest in their clients throughout the evening.

Le Balzar

49 rue des Ecoles, 5th (01.43.54.13.67). M° Cluny-La Sorbonne. **Open** daily noon-11.45pm. **Average** €35. **Credit** AmEx, MC, V. **Map** J7.

This legendary brasserie has long been a favourite of precious Latin Quarter locals and well-behaved tourists, obviously attuned to its atmospheric 1930s decor and dependably plain food delivered by mature white-aproned messieurs. Le Balzar has been part of the Flo group (La Coupole, Bofinger, Julien, Flo, etc) for several years now and wisely they've elected not to tinker too much with its residue of Left Bank charm – a charm which owes much to its menu recalling 'la vieille France'. Starters, including goat's cheese salad, six fat snails in a buttery garlic sauce and pâté en croûte, were perfectly proper if not outstanding, and mains of a thick, bloody rump steak with a few crispy chips and slices of lamb with rather overcooked green beans followed the same customary track. Desserts such as crème brûlée, profiteroles and meringue with ice cream offer no suprises either.

Restaurant Marty ★

20 av des Gobelins, 5th (01.43.31.39.51/ www.marty-restaurant.com). M° Les Gobelins. **Open** daily noon-midnight. **Average** €40. **Prix fixe** €35. **Credit** AmEx, DC, MC, V. **Non-smoking room**. **Map** K10.

While most Parisian brasseries sport belle époque gilded and mirrored luxury, Marty is pure art deco. Sumptuous curves, leopard-print wooden chairs, and period chandeliers and murals adorn the spacious split-level dining areas. Were it not for the food and efficient staff (one monsieur wears a classic handlebar moustache) you might think this was a Prohibition-era jazz club. We found the starter of crabmeat and avocado purée rich and thoroughly rewarding with the tangy sourdough rolls. Likewise, an Asian-inspired starter of cold root veg and mangetout stuffed into a blossom-shaped crispy crêpe. Mains of salmon and cod brochette with corn cake, and a mixed grill of tuna, sea bream and salmon, were competently prepared. Our only complaint: chef Thierry Colas (or one of his assistants) seemed a tiny bit trigger-happy with the salt shaker. But a super fresh fruit-topped rice pudding, creamy and big enough to share, was beyond reproach. All in all, the €35 prix fixe is a steal, the covered terrace provides a fine refuge from foul weather, and the downstairs room would host a memorable reception. Afterwards, stroll up nearby rue Mouffetard to walk off this classy brasserie experience.

Pay **Lipp**-service to the cult of celebrity.

Alcazar

62 rue Mazarine, 6th (01.53.10.19.99/ www.alcazar.fr). M° Odéon. **Open** daily noon-3pm, 7pm-12.30am. Bar 7pm-2am **Average** €52. **Lunch menu** €23, €26. **Credit** AmEx, DC, MC, V. **Wheelchair access**. **Non-smoking room**. **Map** H7.

While Conran's Parisian gastrodome is still pulling in the punters, we suspect it's now got a lot more to do with its see-and-be-seen quota than the food. Tourists across on the Eurostar, expense-account Americans and sleek St-Germainites tuck in and try to out-snoot the staff. On our last visit we were disappointed by flabby foie gras and steak à la Joan of Arc. When we said rare we didn't mean burnt-at-the-stake. The seafood remains a safe bet and their lunchtime 'menu minceur' is a nice alternative to the naked-salad-and-Marlboros normally favoured by Parisian calorie counters. The space is impressive, light and airy and always replete with glorious flowers. The open kitchen, however, is more likely to inspire you to knock on the window and complain about your chips than swoon in admiration of the deft preparation happening before your eyes. As disappointing as dinner can be, Sir Tel and his minions can rustle up a good brunch. Perfect scrambled eggs, fluffy muffins and a diet-starts-on-Monday chocolate cake combine well with a wide-awake, upbeat crowd, a free massage chair and hangover-blitzing freshly squeezed orange juice.

L'Arbuci

25 rue de Buci, 6th (01.44.32.16.00/ www.arbuci.com). M° Odéon or Mabillon. **Open** daily noon-1am. Jazz club Thur-Sat midnight-5am.

Something's brewing at **Brasserie de l'Isle St Louis**. *See p93.*

Average €38. **Lunch menu** €14.80, €19.50. **Credit** AmEx, DC, MC, V. **Non-smoking room**. **Map** H7.
The hip new decor at this old warhorse of a brasserie has the same effect as Queen Elizabeth suddenly dressed in Azzedine Alaïa. In other words, the cool new look somehow seems out of place with the food on offer, despite an attempt to dress up the menu with chi-chi dishes such as scallops skewered on lemongrass with a bizarre accompaniment of salty chicken bouillon (not very good in all respects) or desserts such as 'roasted' pineapple (which seemed more like it had been poached or even microwaved) with rum-raisin ice cream. Service, though friendly, was frenzied, with the young dressed-in-black waiters racing back and forth. Clearly inspired by Conran, this is a story of the Emperor's new clothes. Happily, however, the all-you-can-eat oysters-and-rôtisserie formula – one of the best deals in town – survives, and this, along with good shellfish platters and roast chicken, makes L'Arbuci worthwhile.

Brasserie Lipp

151 bd St-Germain, 6th (01.45.48.53.91). M° St-Germain-des-Prés. **Open** daily noon-1am. **Average** €40. **Credit** AmEx, DC, MC, V. **Non-smoking room**. **Map** H7.
Once famously nasty, Lipp has been roused to a cautious and calculating bonhomie by the competition and the fact that a large portion of the clientele once willing to play its games – if you're seated upstairs, you're social cat food, etc. – has become extinct. We came for lunch expecting a long, happy slog involving good people-watching, lots of wine and maybe a blurry trot home just before the dinner service started, and went away with the fine surprise of having eaten well. Saunter in with boundless confidence, a whiff of metropolitan attitude and a sense of humour, and odds are you'll get a good table in the front portion of the downstairs dining room where everyone can see you and vice-versa. Then, go wildly traditional, as in pistachio-studded pâté en croûte or herring in white wine and herbs with juniper berries. Give the uninspired choucroute a miss and opt for a meaty feast instead, since the great steak tartare comes with some of the best frites in town, and the steaks are excellent (the roast chicken is also better than average), while fish here has its ups and downs. The wine list offers a nice treat or two, including a fine Chapoutier Crozes Hermitage, and the millefeuille is bliss.

Vagenende

142 bd St-Germain, 6th (01.43.26.68.18/ www.vagenende.com). M° Odéon. **Open** daily noon-1am. Closed three weeks in Aug. **Average** €32. **Prix fixe** €23. **Credit** AmEx, DC, MC, V. **Wheelchair access**. **Map** H7.
Thanks to the intervention of André Malraux, Minister of Culture in De Gaulle's government in the 1960s, plans to build a supermarket on this site were shelved. Instead, Vagenende's belle époque interior – elaborate carvings, sparkling mirrors, painted glass and faïence – was preserved for the nation, being listed as a historical monument in 1983. With its red velvet banquettes and white-clothed tables, no place could be more typically French. Discreet waiters in traditional uniform glide across the room, while diners of all ages tuck into classic brasserie dishes (it's amazing the fun children can have with a plate of seafood). The food, though, is the last reason to come. Tasty onion soup with a thick layer of melted cheese, a slightly dry chicken liver terrine

Le Grand Colbert

... a first rate, typically French Brasserie, open until late and affordable for all budgets. Meals vary from simple dishes to the most exquisite cuisine. Whatever takes your fancy, you can savour a relaxing moment in a lovely Parisian atmosphere.

New lunch menu (Monday-Friday): €17.50
Menu: €26 (including coffee)

Open daily from noon-1am
(with last orders taken up until 1am)

2 rue Vivienne, 2nd. Tel: 01.42.86.87.88
M° Bourse

with Armagnac and cornichons, a chicken suprême with rice, mushrooms and tarragon sauce, or boeuf bourguignon with fresh pasta neither thrill nor particularly disappoint. However, portions are generous, the bread is good, and wine (particularly the Saumur Champigny) is reasonable. Oh, and Jane Birkin is reputedly a regular.

L'Avenue

41 av Montaigne, 8th (01.40.70.14.91). M° Franklin D. Roosevelt. **Open** daily 8am-1am. **Average** €60. **Credit** AmEx, DC, MC, V. **Map** D4.

Of all the Costes brothers' restaurants, this is the one that probably works best in terms of what any Paris restaurant should do – serve good food with service that shows an understanding of the quartier. So here it's a real 'bingo', since the svelte young waitresses are fetching and chilly – a mirror image of the avenue Montaigne, one of the world's most famous fashion precincts. Oddly, they seat the French-speakers in the dark, smoky main dining room and banish foreigners to the terrace tables, which is where anyone would really want to be. So, settled at your too-small table, ease into the lounge music beat over a glass of decent chardonnay, and browse a menu that lets you lead off with a glass of fresh carrot juice if this is your want, or, more temptingly, macaroni with morel mushrooms, smoked salmon, an excellent salad of baby artichokes, rocket and parmesan, or another contemporary Parisian classic: green beans and mushrooms in a balsamic vinaigrette. Main courses of tuna steak with balsamic reduction – a pleasantly sticky syrup of the famous Italian vinegar – and a first-rate Chateaubriand with hollandaise sauce were offered with green beans, spinach, chips, mash or salad, another nice touch. Desserts aren't a forte here, and there are just two cheeses from fromager Marie-Anne Cantin – st-nectaire or rocamadour – but coffee is good and comes with a tiny bar of delicious Fouquet's chocolate.

Le Boeuf sur le Toit

34 rue du Colisée, 8th (01.53.93.65.55). M° St-Philippe du Roule. **Open** daily noon-3pm, 7pm-1am. **Average** €38. **Prix fixe** €31. **Credit** AmEx, DC, MC, V. **Non-smoking room**. **Map** E4.

Le Boeuf sur le Toit started out as a lively cabaret in the 1920s, taking its name from the comic ballet of the same era by Milhaud and Cocteau. Taken over by Groupe Flo in the mid-1980s, the brasserie was restored and enlarged, but echoes of 'les années folles' remain in the grandiose art deco surroundings with gilt mirrors, wood panelling and gigantic geometrical lights. On a weekday night it was bubbling, benefitting from the Champs-Elysées revival and a temptingly priced prix fixe. The huge bank of oysters is one of the highlights here, but there are also some satisfying Mediterranean-style dishes à la carte – a 'millefeuille' of feta cheese and grilled aubergine, and ravioli with ricotta and basil – alongside brasserie classics such as the andouillette de Troyes. The wine list offers a good choice, including carafes, and a range of prices.

Brasserie Lorraine

2-4 pl des Ternes, 8th (01.56.21.22.00). M° Ternes. **Open** daily noon-12.30am. **Average** €50. **Credit** AmEx, MC, V. **Non-smoking room**. **Map** D3.

Between the Arc de Triomphe and Parc Monceau, the Lorraine plays to stylish tourists and people-watching locals intent upon their platters of oysters, mounds of chilled seafood and bottles of Champagne. However, eating mid-afternoon can be perilous; we found the service rather shoddy, vacillating between ignoring our order at the start and, by the end, rushing us to decide on dessert and coffee. We assumed that the skeleton crew working the dead zone between lunch and dinner was to blame. Fortunately, the kitchen was on good form: our respectable meal began with a teensy melon ball amuse-bouche, then an upside-down warm tomato tart oozing with red juice and pine kernels, and a smoked salmon, artichoke and spring onion salad. Our big fish plates were winners: broiled cod dressed in aïoli and served, unusually, with Alsatian spatzle, and the daily special sea bass fillet in a seasonal cep cream sauce, topped with a nest of celery and onion greens and fried until crisp. With desserts at €8 to €10 – a lovely crêpe flambéed in Grand Marnier, and a less lovely profiterole with tepid chocolate sauce – the bill quickly added up. Still, if you're stuck in the neighbourhood and hungry, knowing that the Lorraine serves all day can be a comfort.

Fermette Marbeuf 1900

5 rue Marbeuf, 8th (01.53.23.08.00/ www.fermettemarbeuf.com). M° Alma-Marceau or Franklin D. Roosevelt. **Open** daily noon-3pm, 7-11.30pm. **Average** €50. **Prix fixe** €30. **Credit** AmEx, DC, MC, V. **Wheelchair access**. **Non-smoking room**. **Map** D4.

When Jean Laurent bought this restaurant in 1978, he had no idea of the treasure hidden under wood panelling since the 1950s. Fortunately a worker spotted the art nouveau masterwork which was fully restored by 1982 and declared a historic monument. Originally part of the Langham hotel, the belle époque conservatory was designed in 1898 by the architect Hurtré and painter Wielharski. Les Frères Blanc, the current owners, created more space by transporting and rebuilding a similarly styled winter garden from a park in Maisons-Laffitte. Unfortunately, La Fermette Marbeuf's strengths remain limited to its decor. Dissonant Cuban music and polyglot servers with a cool, professional manner welcome an international business crowd. More attention given to description than preparation on the set menu. Our starters of a chicken liver terrine and iced tomato soup with avocado were pleasant enough, but this food would have been more appropriate on a menu of half the price. The tender braised lamb shank was lost in an awkward jumble of harlequin pasta, while the grilled duck breast with a brochette of caramelised fruit was passable. Visit for the conservatory and order à la carte.

Fouquet's ★

99 av des Champs-Elysées, 8th (01.47.23.70.60/ www.lucienbarriere.com). M° George V. **Open** daily 8am-2am (last order 11.30pm). **Average** €75. **Prix fixe** €68 (dinner only). **Lunch menu** €54. **Credit** AmEx, DC, MC, V. **Wheelchair access. Non-smoking room. Map** D4.

With the arrival of chef Jean-Yves Leuranguer from the Martinez in Cannes, dining at Fouquet's, though still expensive, is now a real delight. We adored our five-course menu dégustation. A starter scallop salad with fresh mango and sautéed leeks – all light, modern and Habitat-y – was followed by a rich and rustic risotto of wild mushrooms and warm foie gras. This was definitely the high point of our dinner but the turbot with squid sauce, tomatoes, courgette flowers and aubergines was good too, with strong Mediterranean colours and flavours. With the Chablis going slightly to our heads, the desserts (yes, plural) went by in a flurry of sorbets, chocolate, praline and petits-fours. The service was impeccable… even after we asked to be moved away from a table of noisy trade union leaders. As for the decor, although the textured, red wallpaper is reminiscent of a British city pub more than a Parisian café, the overall effect is pleasantly old-style, a kind of 1950s-ish French charm.

Garnier

111 rue St-Lazare, 8th (01.43.87.50.40). M° St-Lazare. **Open** Tue-Sat noon-3pm, 7-11.30pm; Sun, Mon noon-3pm, 7-11pm. Closed Aug. **Average** €60. **Prix fixe** €38. **Credit** AmEx, DC, MC, V. **Non-smoking room. Map** G3.

Garnier underwent a revamp a few years ago, replacing its ode-to-the-60s decor with a quasi-elegant mix of glass partitions, candelabras with real candles, feather-shaped 50s glass lamps, pearwood chairs and Bernardaud china. As a result, it feels a little more reserved than most brasseries; a quiet contrast to the chains that now abound in Paris. Oysters seem an obvious starter given the classy little oyster bar just inside the door, and the small belons with their slightly salty, almost nutty taste are a good way to go. If you prefer something warm and spicy, there's excellent sautéed calamari with parsley and punchy Espelette pepper. Fish mains run from a simply grilled sea bass with carrots and cumin to classic sole meunière with a delicious purée of small ratte potatoes, plus seasonal specials. Desserts are above average, too, especially the crisp millefeuille oozing with Bourbon vanilla cream. Service is attentive but relaxed, with waiters negotiating tables of non-French speakers and pausing just long enough to spoil regulars.

La Maison de l'Aubrac ★

37 rue Marbeuf, 8th (01.43.59.05.14/www.maison-aubrac.fr). M° Franklin D. Roosevelt. **Open** daily 24 hours. Closed Sat, Sun in Aug. **Average** €34. **Credit** AmEx, MC, V. **Non-smoking room. Map** D4.

On a Thursday night, just off the chic Champs-Elysées, we found ourselves hemmed in by scrums of big, beefy men tucking into plates of saucisse aligot (pork sausages with a mix of mashed potatoes, garlic and cheese), giant ribs of beef and juicy steaks. This rustic little Auvergnat corner, complete with wooden booths, paper placemats and glossy photos of man and beast (bulls in particular), is a beacon for rugby lovers. We weighed in with a slab of fine foie gras then, deciding against the 'three meats platter' (tartare, sirloin steak and boeuf pressé), we went for slices of leg of lamb from the Lozère region (tender if a tad overcooked), roasted and served with green beans and crisply fried potato slices, and a perfectly grilled entrecôte. The excellent wine list is pricey with good choices from the Rhône and Languedoc-Roussillon. Service is friendly and efficient and the place, like a rugby line-out, is always jumping.

Charlot, Roi des Coquillages

81 bd de Clichy, 9th (01.53.20.48.00/ www.lesfreresblanc.com). M° Place de Clichy. **Open** Mon-Wed, Sun noon-3pm, 7pm-midnight; Thur-Sat noon-3pm, 7pm-1am. **Average** €53. **Lunch menu** €25, €30. **Credit** AmEx, DC, MC, V. **Non-smoking room. Map** G2.

Aside from its endearing, campy glamour – apricot velvet banquettes and peculiar laminated lithographs of shellfish – the main reason that this long-running fish-house is so popular is its flawless catch-of-the-day menu. A curious but buzzy mix of tourists, night people, arty locals, he-and-she executive couples and good-humoured folks in from the provinces patronise this place and, given such an eclectic clientele, staff are to be commended for their outstanding professional service. Depending on the season, the seafood platters are what the regulars opt for, and even in the middle of the summer – off-season for many shellfish – the prawns, sea urchins and lobster are impeccable. Otherwise, start with the excellent fish soup, followed by a classic such as grilled sea bass or superb aïoli (boiled salt cod with vegetables and lashings of garlic mayonnaise) and finish off with crêpes Suzette, or the delicious tarte Tatin with cinnamon.

Au Petit Riche

25 rue Le Peletier, 9th (01.47.70.68.68/ www.aupetitriche.com). M° Richelieu-Drouot. **Open** Mon-Sat noon-2.15pm, 7pm-12.15am. Closed Sat, Sun in July and Aug. **Average** €38. **Prix fixe** €28.50 (dinner only). **Lunch menu** €22, €25.50. **Credit** AmEx, DC, MC, V. **Non-smoking room. Map** H3.

With crisply dressed waiters and a striking decor of wood panelling, etched-glass windows and painted ceilings, Au Petit Riche could very well get by on its setting alone and, unfortunately, this is exactly what it tries to do. Our waiter sighed wearily when we opted for the prix fixe menu, and henceforth gave us minimal attention. The watery and flavourless fish soup was accompanied by a positively atrocious sweaty rouille. Lentil salad was better – a simple mixture of Puy lentils, diced carrots and onions, doused in a pleasant vinaigrette but strangely served in a mound which looked as if it had been dropped from a height into the square salad bowl. From a very limited choice of main courses, we chose the salmon, served with flat pasta so greasy it could have been deep-fried with the accompanying fish, itself fairly dripping in oil, and the rump steak, served with fat, greasy chips and mayonnaise. Ice cream was predictably plain but the prunes marinated in sweet Vouvray were very enjoyable, and ended the evening on a more positive culinary note. Au Petit Riche has an unfortunate policy of separating English-speaking tourists from locals, so Parisian atmosphere can be as elusive as good food here.

Brasserie Flo

7 cour des Petites-Ecuries, 10th (01.47.70.13.59/ www.floparis.com). M° Château d'Eau. **Open** daily noon-3pm, 7pm-1.30am. **Average** €45. **Prix fixe** €31.50. **Lunch menu** €30.50. **Credit** AmEx, DC, MC, V. **Wheelchair access. Non-smoking room. Map** K3.

On past experience, Flo, closest to an Alsatian tavern and first member of Jean-Paul Bucher's brasserie group, has always been a fun place to go after the theatre or for a family outing on a bank holiday. On our most recent visit, though, a blast of old age seemed to have hit not only the tobacco-stained murals of gutsy drinkers but also the kitchen, even if the service remains as good-humoured as ever. An emincé de boeuf proved to be a decidedly mediocre steak served with rocket salad and a greasy square of polenta. A small swordfish steak was better; though lacking flavour, it was redeemed by well-prepared fresh spinach and a beurre blanc sauce, suggesting that dishes here are a bit of a lottery. Desserts – a generous café liègeois and a surprisingly good tarte Tatin with well caramelised apple and very little pastry, accompanied by a pot of thick crème fraîche – were much the best part of the meal. Flo could do with a wake-up call, but if you're here for a late-night eat, then your best bet is probably to go for classic choucroute, oysters or the shellfish platters and avoid anything too complicated.

Julien ★

16 rue du Fbg-St-Denis, 10th (01.47.70.12.06/ www.julienparis.com). M° Strasbourg-St-Denis. **Open** daily noon-3pm, 7pm-1.30am. **Average** €30. **Prix fixe** €23, €31. **Credit** AmEx, DC, MC, V. **Wheelchair access. Map** K4.

Behind two doors and a red velvet curtain off the seedy Faubourg-St-Denis is a world of potted palms, stained glass peacocks and art nouveau maidens. The maitre d' clapped his hands and a waiter bustled to ready the table for a lone male diner who might have been Flo group chairman Jean-Paul Bucher himself, such was the flurry. Busy in the evenings, Julien is a peaceful refuge for Sunday lunch, a rarity in this city. There are no surprises on the menu but the food is dependable. To see how à la carte might compare with the prix fixe, we went for the set menu, which included half a bottle of a decent house white, and the 'ardoise du jour'. The menu's starter of passable foie gras was rather meagre, while the girolle mushrooms cooked à la Bourgogne with garlic, breadcrumbs and parsley arrived with ceremony sizzling in their copper dish but were distinctly flavourless. The mains were excellent. The prix fixe's suprême de flétan (halibut) was crispy on the outside and firm on the inside, nestling among red and yellow peppers with pistou. Sea bass fillet was brought whole to the table for inspection then

The richly adorned **Au Petit Riche.**

French Cuisine

(OPEN DAILY NOON > 2.30pm, 8pm > 11.30pm
SUNDAY BRUNCH 11am > 4.30pm)

17, BIS RUE CAMPAGNE PREMIÈRE 75014 PARIS - Ⓜ RASPAIL
T +33 (1) 4320 7927 - restaurantnatacha@wanadoo.fr

taken away and deboned, topped and tailed. When we expressed disappointment that we couldn't eat the cheeks the waiter smiled and brought back the head on a saucer. With this delectable fish came a side dish of buttery fennel that was its perfect accompaniment. Desserts were just as good – a dark chocolate tart topped with firm chocolate mousse and served with crème anglaise, and a divine charlotte aux framboises, moist with fresh and juicy fruit in a raspberry sauce. The chocolate truffles that come with coffee are fabulous.

Terminus Nord

23 rue de Dunkerque, 10th (01.42.85.05.15/ www.terminusnord.com). M° Gare du Nord. **Open** daily 11am-1am. **Average** €25. **Prix fixe** €30.50 (dinner only). **Lunch menu** €21.50. **Credit** AmEx, DC, MC, V. **Non-smoking room**. **Map** K2.

As it's the first place you hit on the way out of the Eurostar terminal at Gare du Nord, you might expect Terminus Nord to be a tourist trap. In fact, it's a perfect place to get re-acquainted with the joys of Paris. As you're guided to your table by the maître d'hôtel, up to a dozen white-uniformed waiters will wish you 'bonjour'. Boarding an ocean liner must feel something like this. And although this is not the most splendid Parisian brasserie, it is full of fin-de-siècle charm. If you've got the time and the money, this is a good place to order a towering platter of seafood. But there are also possibilities for those seeking to do a lifestyle-of-the-rich-and-famous on the cheap with good-value set menus, wine and coffee included, at lunch and after 10pm. Our tips: steer clear of the pig's trotters (a deboned poor relation of this stunning French delicacy) and the snails (stale and musty on our last visit). A good choice for starters is the fish soup or the onion soup. For mains, the day's fish dishes are often more elaborate, interesting and carefully prepared than standard brasserie fare. Try the superb (and spectacular) crêpes Suzette for dessert. And, don't be too proud to check your bill (here or anywhere else for that matter). Small rip-offs have been known to occur.

Les Grandes Marches

6 pl de la Bastille, 12th (01.43.42.90.32/ www.lesgrandesmarches.com). M° Bastille.
Open daily noon-midnight. Closed 1-21 Aug. **Average** €45. **Prix fixe** €33. **Lunch menu** €23. **Credit** AmEx, DC, MC, V. **Wheelchair access**. **Non-smoking room**. **Map** M7.

The Flo group, responsible for restoring La Coupole, Brasserie Flo and Julien in period style, employed Elisabeth and Christian de Portzamparc to redecorate this modern brasserie near the Bastille opera. It feels like an advertising agency lobby complete with colour-coordinated orange and grey chairs, menus and 'high concept' spiral staircase, while waiters in dark suits dash about like junior executives on deadline. The starter, served fresh from the fridge with a basket of stale bread, was pot-au-feu of foie gras Jurançon style, a rich pâté with apricot, prune and raisin topped with a mild gelatine. Then came the bland duck steak with too-salty, soggy beans and the salmon steak with linguine and pesto sauce. We had barely finished our last bite of undercooked pasta when the items were cleared a beat too fast. The chocolate tart with pear sorbet and raspberry mascarpone with honey sauce did hit the spot, but, neither the decor nor the food would bring us back.

Le Train Bleu ★

Gare de Lyon, pl Louis-Armand, 12th (01.43.43.09.06/www.le-train-bleu.com). M° Gare de Lyon. **Open** daily 11.30am-3pm, 7-11pm. **Average** €50. **Prix fixe** €42.50. **Credit** AmEx, DC, MC, V. **Wheelchair access**.

This listed dining room has long been one of the most romantic restaurants in Paris, with magnificent 1900 vintage frescoes of the alluring destinations once served by the Paris-Lyon-Marseille railway, big oak benches with shiny brass coat racks, and a pleasant air of wistfulness and expectation derived from arrivals and departures. Don't come expecting cutting-edge cooking, but rather fine renderings of French classics and first-rate produce. Lobster served on a bed of walnut-oil-dressed salad leaves was a generous, beautifully prepared starter – easily a luxurious supper on its own – while pistachio-studded saucisson de Lyon with a warm salad of small ratte potatoes was perfectly cooked and copious. Mains of veal chop topped with a cap of cheese and sandre (pike-perch) with a 'risotto' of crozettes (tiny squares of pasta from Savoie) were also pleasant, although given the size of the starters and the superb cheese tray, you could easily have a satisfying three-course meal here without a main. A large baba au rhum was split at the table, doused with good Martinique rum, and slathered with cream. Charming and efficient service adds to the pleasure of a meal here, and the only obvious improvement would be the addition of a few reasonably priced wines to the list.

La Coupole

102 bd du Montparnasse, 14th (01.43.20.14.20/ www.coupoleparis.com). M° Vavin.
Open Mon-Thur 8.30am-1am; Fri, Sat 8.30am-1.30am. **Average** €45. **Prix fixe** €31.50. **Credit** AmEx, DC, MC, V. **Map** G9.

Given the sheer size of this restaurant it's amazing that it should ever fill up completely. But fill up it does, with a seething, eclectic crowd of Parisians, suburbanites and tourists who come to live the Coupole experience. You can book at lunch, but evenings after 8.30pm (8pm on Fridays and Saturdays) are more complicated. After being issued with a ticket at the entrance, we joined the throng of some 30 or so wannabe diners at the bar and dutifully waited. Finally our number came up and we wedged into our table along with the dozens of others along the endless rows of banquettes. Service was good-natured with plenty of corny jokes from the wisecracking waiters. It all adds to the atmosphere. We couldn't resist the truffled scrambled eggs for a starter and, although they looked fluffy and appetis-

ing enough, they were, predictably, almost a truffle-free zone. La Coupole has plenty of seafood on offer: one of us spent a good hour tackling a plate-sized crab while another managed a beautifully cooked but pricey sole meunière. Don't miss the gargantuan coupes of ice cream for dessert, or the classic parfait glacé au café. Fun, rather than a gastronomic experience, a meal at La Coupole makes for great people-watching at a timeless venue.

Le Suffren ★

84 av de Suffren, 15th (01.45.66.97.86) M° La Motte-Picquet Grenelle. **Open** daily noon-midnight. **Average** €30. **Credit** AmEx, MC, V. **Map** D7.

Le Suffren, one of the few remaining independently-owned brasseries in Paris, has undergone an upmarket make-over. Out with the frowsy nautical miscellany, circa 1970, and in with gleaming orange, red and black, complete with clubby chairs and sleek lampshades. Not quite as flashy as a Costes café but avenues away from a vintage brasserie. And the well-behaved locals, including military folk from nearby Ecole Militaire, love it – bagging a table inside (or out in summer) often means a wait at the bar. The prix fixe menus have gone and the carte has undergone a little pruning, but most of the old favourites remain: confit de canard, rump steak, lamb chops, heaving seafood platters and a selection of choucroutes. The waiters are familiar, too, even in their new blazing-red shirts. Starters such as oysters, rillettes d'oie (potted goose) and warm goat's cheese salad were as good as usual on our last visit but the normally reliable duck foie gras was a tad too dry and crumbly. Mains of grilled salmon, rosy lamb chops, a tender ostrich steak and a rump steak with an avalanche of sautéed potatoes, however, all worked well. Desserts are reassuringly everyday, from wedges of apple and lemon tart to huge bowls of ice cream topped with shimmery tinsel sticks.

Brasserie de la Poste

54 rue de Longchamp, 16th (01.47.55.01.31/ www.brasserie-de-la-poste.com). M° Trocadéro. **Open** daily noon-10pm. **Average** €25. **Prix fixe** €32. **Lunch menu** €15. **Credit** AmEx, DC, MC, V. **Non-smoking room. Map** C5.

The setting of subdued yellow paint, dark wood, and mirrors sporting old black-and-white photographs is pleasant enough but lacks a certain spark, and, sadly, the same can be said for the food. A starter of aubergine and goat's cheese in a pepper sauce would have been helped by a stronger cheese, and while the comté-stuffed ravioli were good, their plain cream sauce made for a monotonous flavour. For mains, we tried an excellent andouillette and a sauté de veau – a cosy, creamy stew laced with golden raisins. Dessert, a slice of dense, creamy chocolate in crème anglaise, looked promising but left an aftertaste that seemed artificial. Service was impeccable, friendly and efficient but, overall, nothing seemed to justify the increase in prices since our last visit.

Table-bodied diners at **Le Suffren.**

La Gare

19 chaussée de la Muette, 16th (01.42.15.15.31/ www.restaurantlagare.com). M° La Muette. **Open** daily 12.30-3pm, 7.30-11.30pm. **Average** €29. **Prix fixe** €23, €29. **Credit** AmEx, MC, V. **Wheelchair access. Non-smoking room. Map** A6.

This was once a train station on the Petite Ceinture, the railway circling Paris built by Napoléon III. The ticket office is now the bar and the platforms downstairs have become a colossal dining area. After pushing the train theme hard, however, it seems the restaurant is now taking itself more seriously. The menu, while still dominated by the rôtisserie specialities, has been refined. We were seduced by the pince de tourteau (crab claw) with an avocado mousseline, and the black truffle risotto. Stuck awkwardly into the middle of the rice was a grilled wafer of comté: unexpected and delicious. The no-nonsense mains were excellent: the gigot d'agneau, accompanied with a jus so concentrated that it is served in a shot glass, was very tender and cooked exactly as we had requested. The portions seemed undersized until the giant bucket of accompanying purée was dropped off. Salty but divine. La Gare is in the heart of the posh 16th – if you ask for water, they will assume you want it from a bottle – but prices are varied and reasonable. Evenings are generally calm, but lunch is often packed with locals with coiffed pooches in tow and an international crowd from the OECD, just around the corner.

La Grande Armée

3 av de la Grande-Armée, 16th (01.45.00.24.77). M° Charles de Gaulle-Etoile. **Open** daily 7am-2am. **Average** €40. **Credit** AmEx, DC, MC, V. **Non-smoking room. Map** C3.

Admirers of Napoléon Bonaparte might appreciate a more robust tribute to the Corsican upstart than the too-cool-to-be-serious decor for the Grande Armée, jointly owned by the Costes brothers and Jacques Garcia. Perhaps a brace of canon, or a tricolore brought back from Austerlitz shot through with gunfire? What you actually get is a couple of cut-out hussars and a bit of synthetic leopard skin (a reference to the Egyptian campaign perhaps?). With its red and blue walls, there is a cosy gloom about La Grande Armée that makes for intimate conversation. You'd say it was almost like a pub, if that weren't sacrilegious in a place dedicated to history's greatest anglophobe. The menu is strong on prawns, oysters and langoustines, as you'd expect in a Parisian brasserie, but the parmesan soufflé starter is an excellent re-working of the old French peasant dish. On to the mains: we wrote off the offer of a cheeseburger as a sort of joke and went for the duck Parmentier, a delicious combination of duck confit and fluffy mashed potato topped with two sublimely tender slices of piping-hot duck's liver. For pudding: a combination of tiny apple crumble, tiny apple pie and scoop of fresh apple ice cream called a pom pom pomme… like the sound of a distant artillery barrage.

protect
AID
Le seul moyen d'arrêter le sida,

Zébra Square

3 pl Clément Ader, 16th (01.44.14.91.91/ www.zebrasquare.com). M° Passy/RER Kennedy-Radio France. **Open** daily noon-3pm, 7.30-11pm. **Average** €35. **Lunch menu** €22. **Brunch** €20, €26. **Credit** AmEx, DC, MC, V. **Wheelchair access. Map** A7.

Part of the Hôtel Square complex, Zebra Square may not be the celeb-thronged haunt it once was, but the 90s decor – pendulous lights hanging from the high ceilings, green leather chairs, enormous canvases with scrawled quotations and zebra-themed napkins, lamps and coffee cups – has stood the test of time remarkably well. Not so the sound track, which included Tina Turner and Madonna and rather jarred with the attempt at urban sophistication. Above all, this is a good choice for lunch – two courses and glass of red, white or rosé for €22, with the option to add a dessert for €6 – and the modern European cooking is more akin to what you might find in London than in a Paris brasserie. The relaxed crowd included a concentration of radio folk and journalists, but we were delighted to see, by 3.30pm, a couple of ladies of the 16th slurping piña coladas near the bar. A market-inspired plat du jour (one for each course) is offered as part of the prix fixe. Grilled aubergine carpaccio with a sesame vinaigrette successfully combined Mediterranean and Far Eastern flavours and was served with a superb salad of fresh dill, fennel, parsley, coriander and mint leaves, while the market-special tartare de tomate had cinnamon notes, a nicely dressed mixed salad and a tuile aux parmesan, a cheesy contrast to the tomato. The sesame coating on the pan-fried tuna made it filling though enjoyable, while the lieu jaune (pollack) proved to be rather ordinary, though crisply cooked. Thin strips of courgette and carrots with fresh coriander made tasty accompaniments. Both the Brouilly and the Touraine were very drinkable. The sole disappointment was the apple and ginger tart – too light on the ginger and with a nasty burnt crust taste. Go instead for the deliciously indulgent gâteau de crêpes au Grand Marnier with its filling of fragrant mousse and sticky alcoholic sauce.

Le Wepler

14 pl de Clichy, 18th (01.45.22.53.24/ www.wepler.com). M° Place de Clichy. **Open** daily noon-1am. **Average** €35. **Prix fixe** €25. **Credit** AmEx, DC, MC, V. **Map** G2.

There are lots of reasons to like this big brasserie overlooking the busy place de Clichy, but the food isn't one of them. Still, given its convenient location, great people watching, interesting crowd – lots of media and movie types, mixed with tourists and locals – and wonderfully ugly late-50s-early-60s decor, you can manage a decent meal here as long as you order very simply. Avoid anything that requires real cooking, especially dishes with sauces, since the kitchen really isn't up to anything even remotely ambitious. So, start with the oysters or maybe a salad, and then have a grill or the decent choucroute garnie, and finish up with ice cream or sorbet if you want dessert. Otherwise, the sandwiches served on the terrace at noon are perfectly fine.

Au Boeuf Couronné

188 av Jean-Jaurès, 19th (01.42.39.54.54/ www.au-boeuf-couronne.com). M° Porte de Pantin. **Open** daily noon-3pm, 7.30pm-midnight. **Average** €40. **Prix fixe** €32. **Credit** AmEx, DC, MC, V. **Wheelchair access. Map** inset.

Near the site of the original La Villette abattoirs, this old-fashioned brasserie has been serving up massive portions of quality, chargrilled meat since 1930. Its solid, unruffled atmosphere and out-of-the-way location make you feel as though you're dining somewhere *en province*. The large, cavernous room, fitted out with the typical banquettes, wood panelling, mirrors and white linen cloths, has a charming faded elegance – the high-tech till appears to be the only addition since circa 1962. The food is traditional French fare done impeccably, delivered by a team of unflappable waitresses in matching frilly white aprons. This time we decided to bypass the beef and explore less familiar portions of the menu. The enormous tournedos of salmon accompanied by steamed potatoes and mirepoix was of excellent quality and perfectly cooked. As was the juicy lamb chop with herbes de provence, served with watercress, grilled tomato and the famous pommes soufflées. The speciality here, though, is steak, and most of our fellow diners were enthusiastically tucking into some startling hunks of meat. Desserts were monumental: crêpes Suzette cooked dramatically at the table, profiteroles filled with ice cream and doused with chocolate sauce, etc. Dining at the Boeuf Couronné is a thoroughly enjoyable, nostalgic experience.

Café la Jatte

60 bd Vital Bouhot, Ile de la Jatte, 92200 Neuilly-sur-Seine (01.47.45.04.20). M° Pont de Levallois. **Open** daily noon-2pm, 7.30-11.30pm. **Average** €46. **Credit** AmEx, DC, MC, V. **Wheelchair access.**

When Paris gets too much, it's worth a trek out to this tiny island to shake off the city blues. Painter Seurat obviously thought so – thus his famous canvas *Un dimanche après-midi à l'Ile de la Grande Jatte*. The Café is housed in a vast red brick building that once served as Napoléon's riding school but nowadays a giant faux dinosaur skeleton spreads its wings across the dining room ceiling. A winner with the kids, as are the nearby park and tree-lined riverbank. Less captivating was the food on a recent visit: a starter of tiny spinach leaves with generous slices of chicken drizzled with a curry sauce looked pretty but tasted like nothing at all. The homemade duck foie gras with nut bread was much better. Grilled swordfish, slapped on a plate with a soggy baked aubergine and braised fennel, was decidedly average and chicken pan-fried with pickled ginger, lemongrass and carrots was just as unimpressive. And the staff, bar one very obliging waiter, seemed bored beyond measure. But the sun was shining so things could have been worse.

Trendy

Get out with the in-crowd and inspect the Parisian weapons of class construction. It's all a game of hide and chic.

It took a long time for the divorce to occur, but now, catastrophically, it has. Good food and fashion seem to have gone their own ways, as Paris has developed a large number of restaurants where the decor, concept and high-voltage clientele are more important than what you find in your plate. If the Costes brothers pioneered a whole empire of see-and-be-seen tables, many other local entrepreneurs, sensing quick money, have jumped on the boat. Fortunately, not all of the most stylish addresses are a culinary letdown, and some are actually excellent.

Hôtel Costes ★

239 rue St-Honoré, 1st (01.42.44.50.25). M° Concorde or Tuileries. **Open** daily 7am-1am. **Average** €60. **Credit** AmEx, DC, MC, V. **Wheelchair access. Map** G5.

By rights the of-a-certain-age Hôtel Costes should by now be ensconced in a corner with a bottle of Tio Pepe, muttering to itself about its glory days as the hottest place to push food around your plate. But while its trendy contemporaries have let themselves go and are all awaiting hip replacements, the Costes, with its permanent coterie of bright young things, a little discreet lifting and a calculated air of disdain, hasn't changed a bit. Same giggle-inducing prices, same stupid or stupidly named food ('an undressed lettuce heart and two weeping tigers, please'), same snooty but breathtakingly beautiful staff and, astoundingly, the same buzz. The Napoléon III bordello feel, the obligatory slinky soundtrack and the glorious courtyard conspire to bring out the outrageous hedonist in the most puritanical punter. Nooks and crannies are strategically placed to accommodate the rich and the reclusive, but if your accessories (shoes, date, AmEx Centurion) are up to it then push for a visible table and enjoy your Champagne, your Marlboro Medium, the conversation at the next table and, of course, the attention.

Lô Sushi Pont Neuf

1 rue du Pont-Neuf, 1st (01.42.33.09.09/ www.losushi.com). M° Pont-Neuf or Châtelet. **Open** daily 11am-midnight. Happy hour 6-8pm. **Average** €25. **Credit** AmEx, MC, V. **Map** J6.

Somehow Japan's high-tech image makes a sushi bar perfectly suited to the latest dating concept. A computer screen is installed at each of the 65 places around the sushi conveyer belt, allowing you to send messages to fellow diners with the Blind@lo internal communication system while keeping a beady eye on the goodies circulating on their different coloured saucers. Although it's also designed by Andrée Putman, the creamy-white plastic counter, dove-grey oak and leather stools with low backs give this Lô Sushi a softer, gentler feel than the original branch. The food is pretty competent, too: the selection of maki and rolls goes beyond the standard cucumber or tuna with some original variants, rolled in sesame seeds or gently spiced up; there are also crunchy Japanese green beans in their pods and a tasty seaweed salad. The only problem is not muddling up your chopsticks with the wooden mouse.
Branch: 8 rue de Berri, 8th (01.45.62.01.00).

Bon 2

2 rue du Quatre-Septembre, 2nd (01.44.55.51.55/ www.bon.fr). M° Bourse. **Open** daily 8.30am-12.30am. **Average** €35. **Prix fixe** €22 (dinner only). **Credit** AmEx, MC, V. **Wheelchair access. Map** H4.

Philippe Starck's Bon 2 proves that fashion food in Paris can indeed be 'bon' – the trick is to serve dressed-up bistro fare on rectangular plates. The menu, revised by the respected south-western chef Jean-Marie Amat, still takes a health-conscious approach, listing the benefits of each dish to nip potential guilt in the bud. A close look, though, reveals it to be fairly classic, with several welcome regional dishes. We splashed out on the crab salad – fresh-tasting crabmeat on a bed of cold rice flavoured with squid ink, and topped with mixed fresh herbs. Poulet-frites, the only item in the menu section titled 'maman', was popular with the stock exchange crowd. The two pieces of leg were moist and succulent, and had been partially deboned, a nice touch. We also loved the fat, symmetrically stacked frites. Desserts, supplied by Ladurée, tasted of little more than the fridge. Decor-wise, this Bon is actually quite sober, with only the occasional mismatched chair and three gigantic chandeliers, plus a boutique at the back, hinting that Starck is behind the venture. Service showed no hint of the attitude that you might expect in such a place.
Branch: 25 rue de la Pompe, 16th (01.40.72.70.00).

Georges

Centre Pompidou, 6th floor, rue Rambuteau, 4th (01.44.78.47.99). M° Rambuteau. **Open** Mon, Wed-Sun noon-2am. Closed 1 May. **Average** €55. **Credit** AmEx, DC, MC, V. **Wheelchair access. Map** K5.

This Costes restaurant, like any Costes restaurant, has precious little to do with eating well. Instead, the dining room perched atop the Centre Pompidou is run like some sort of sociological chess board whose power game revolves around a single question: who gets the view? It all comes down to the shoes, it seems – turning up in your favourite Clark's or even a pair of hip, rustic Campers will get you banished to the dreaded, brightly lit tables near the toilets. Among the many other things that might get up your nose here is the fact that such a fabulous space, which is part of a state-owned museum, should have been hijacked for such bald commercial advantage. Oh, and the food. Well, it's a range of inoffensive, forgettable, over-priced fuss-free dishes. Think lobster spring rolls, potato and (tasteless) truffle soup, aller-retour (aka a hamburger, with green salad), a few Asian-themed fish and poultry dishes and the inevitable moelleux au chocolat for dessert. It's a shame there's no bar here, since the view is sublime, but you can come for a mid-afternoon drink.

Le Bélier ★

13 rue des Beaux-Arts, 6th (01.44.41.99.01/www.l-hotel.com). M° St-Germain-des-Prés. **Open** Tue-Sun 12.30-2.15pm, 7.30-10.15pm. Closed Aug. **Average** €55. **Lunch menu** €24.50. **Credit** AmEx, DC, MC, V. **Map** H6.

In the lush Jacques Garcia decor of L'Hôtel, which preserves just a phantom whiff of the premises' former incarnation as the flop-house where Oscar Wilde so famously expired, this intimate restaurant is a clubby hit with surprisingly excellent food. The lavishly upholstered Napoléon III room with several love seats and strategic sight lines is populated by neighbourhood editors and art and antiques dealers at noon, and stylish well-heeled locals in the evening, plus the occasional star staying in the hotel. Expect well-executed, high-quality French comfort food, with the odd cosmopolitan touch – Iberian ham with fresh tomato-rubbed bread, or gazpacho, references to the young chef's Catalan origins. A starter of prawns with artichokes was excellent, as was foie gras with a fine layer of fig purée, and lacquered lamb shank was delicate, while a perfectly cooked steak on white beans was delicious. Cheese comes from Barthélémy, and desserts like melted chocolate cake with fromage blanc ice cream and trio of lemony treats – mousse, sorbet and tart – echoed Wilde's famous: 'I can resist everything but temptation'.

Thiou

49 quai d'Orsay, 7th (01.45.51.58.58). M° Invalides. **Open** Mon-Fri noon-2pm, 8-10.30pm; Sat 8-10.30pm. Closed Aug. **Average** €60. **Credit** AmEx, MC, V. **Map** E5.

Owner-chef Thiou subscribes to a simple mantra: super-fresh, high-quality ingredients prepared with care and flair. And it's proved a big hit. Thiou's previous stint at the restaurant of Les Bains Douches ensures that fashion puppies – and hounds – deco-

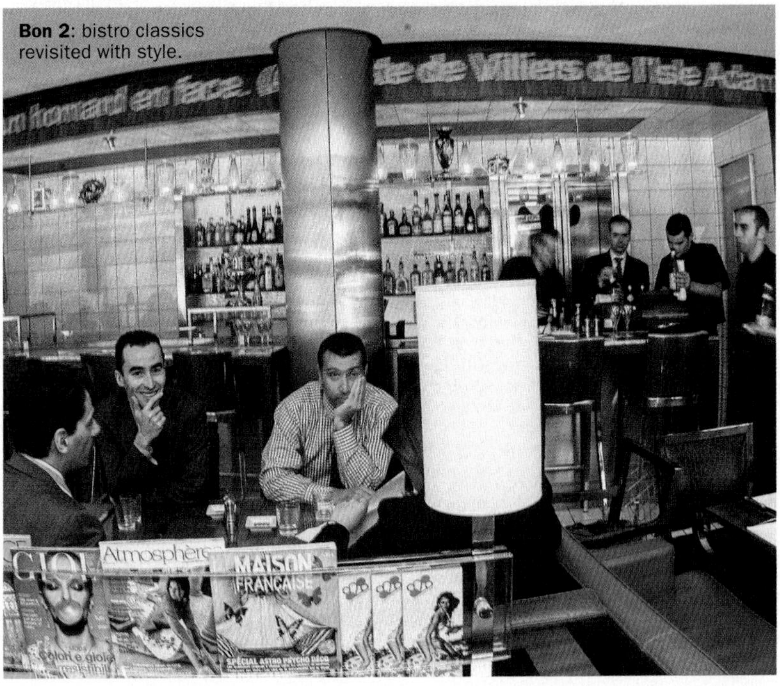

Bon 2: bistro classics revisited with style.

rate this place, along with stylish young and old money – in other words, the locals. Start with juicy, peanutty chicken satay, a prawn soup heavy with lemongrass, or cold, grilled aubergine topped with prawns and drizzled with a fish sauce vinaigrette (sounds awful, tastes great). Follow with impressive main courses such as kae phad prik wan, tender cubes of lamb sautéed with red and green pepper and served with fried rice, or grilled John Dory fillets with spinach, bean sprouts and soy sauce. Desserts are mainly fruit-based; mini bananas with syrup and vanilla ice cream makes a good finisher. The wine list is reasonably priced, the service is attentive and polite, and the setting is elegant and cosy. A nearby annexe specialises in fish.
Branch: Le Petit Thiou, 3 rue Surcouf (01.40.62.96.70).

Le Buddha Bar

8 rue Boissy d'Anglas, 8th (01.53.05.90.00/ www.buddhabar.com). M° Concorde. **Open** Mon-Fri noon-3pm, 6pm-2am; Sat, Sun 6pm-midnight. **Average** €60. **Prix fixe** €60. **Lunch menu** €32. **Credit** AmEx, MC, V. **Wheelchair access**. **Map** F4.

Meditate before you get here, as the Zen-ometer in this trendster temple of Asian hype, nowadays worshipped by businessmen and try-hard pilgrims from around the world, is so stressed it is pointing at 'nervous breakdown'. The staff army of infamously spiky ice-queens greets you with a militaristic walkie-talkie sparring-match, before marching you down the sweeping staircase and ignoring you for most of the night. Get Dutch courage at the balcony bar, where the near total darkness is booby-trapped with protruding pretty young limbs, and gyrating brokers' bellies. Meanwhile, the giant gold Buddha lords over the glamour, keeping his cool despite the thumping fusion soundtrack. You come for the grand-scale spectacle, and it is unfailingly magnificent. The food is also surprisingly good. Starters included an intriguing mix of deep-fried frogs' legs and squid, and fresh, pulpy sushi of yellowtail and salmon. Our main course of lacquered duck blended well with a chunky pear and apple confit, and 'maki' sole came in light, crisp slices with black bean sauce and Chinese cabbage. The taste pinnacle was dessert: an exotic fruit salad, bobbing with aniseed and basil-flecked stawberry sorbet, and a crême brûlée trio of chocolate, vanilla and coconut. Definitely worth being treated like scum.

L'Envue ★

39 rue Boissy d'Anglas, 8th (01.42.65.10.49) M° Madeleine or Concorde. **Open** Mon-Sat 8am-11pm. Closed Aug. **Average** €35. **Credit** AmEx, DC, MC, V. **Map** F4.

Even if you have an aversion to fashion restaurants, make an exception for this place, since the decor, food and service are really good in a part of Paris that desperately needed an option between the plastic corner café and haute cuisine. Here, against a backdrop of bird's eye maple panelling and soft lighting from contemporary chandeliers, carefully dressed tables in pink and grey are done up with tableware so tempting that it's all for sale. The menu is ideal for grazing, since you can order a tasting plate of seafood – sea bass sashimi, salmon tartare and rillettes, brandade and green beans – and a similar all-in veg plate, or go à la carte with a cheese-and-chive soufflé or tomatoes stuffed with chèvre, followed by steak tartare, chicken in lemon-saffron sauce, or langoustine risotto with mango. Wines are served by the glass, cheese comes with salad, and the dessert menu delivers treats such as baba au rhum with roasted pineapple.

Man Ray

34 rue Marbeuf, 8th (01.56.88.36.36/ www.manray.fr). M° Franklin D. Roosevelt. **Open** daily noon-3pm, 7pm-midnight. Bar daily noon-2am. Closed at lunch in Aug. **Average** €50. **Prix fixe** €29, €39 (Mon-Thur only). **Lunch menu** €20. **Credit** MC, V. **Wheelchair access**. **Map** D4.

Given that you book a table here to celeb-spot, as opposed to eat, you can't really complain if you leave hungry. Man Ray is a 'dining experience' in so far as your mealtime conversation involves whispering 'Don't look now, but at your four o'clock, Mick Jagger', punctuated by lengthy gaping at the extravagant (and now rather tired looking) pan-Asian decor. The food is an afterthought, and comically bland, though we've had good luck with the sashimi. Safe-bet fried spring rolls, labelled 'comme je les aime', aren't disappointing if you like bland and greasy, and the insipid foie gras with chutney was like a butter and fig jam breakfast. Dry tuna steak was beached on spinach leaves drowned in tangy ginger sauce, and turning blacker by the second as we waited 20 minutes for the salmon to arrive. Tiramisu came in a sundae glass, with coffee jelly lurking beneath, and the raspberry macaroon squeaked like ripping cling film when cut open to reveal a heart of lemon curd. Be warned. Better to taste the buzz from the mezzanine bar for the 'After Work' drink and free massage during the week, which swells into a club-night on Fridays and weekends.

Rue Balzac

3-5 rue Balzac, 8th (01.53.89.90.91). M° Charles de Gaulle. **Open** Mon-Fri 12.30-2.30pm, 7.30-11.30pm; Sat, Sun 7.30-11.30pm. Closed two weeks in Aug. **Average** €60. **Credit** AmEx, DC, MC, V. **Wheelchair access**. **Map** D3.

Rue Balzac is Johnny Hallyday's baby (aside from his wife Laeticia that is). And despite his dyed rocker roots, it's all soothing burgundy and beige with pastel geometric paintings and cute lamps. The menu is designed by consultant chef Michel Rostang, who runs his own haute cuisine restaurant and bistros in Paris. Starters such as 'Laeticia's' crispy, tempura-like prawns with seaweed tartare, spicy tomato sauce and mustard cream, a generous serving of delicious minced lobster plus a sweet shelled claw, were choice. Blanquette de veau and souris d'agneau lost out to a neat little package of scallop 'tournedos', six on a fat disc of mashed potato wrapped in a leek ribbon, and a rather sad grilled sea bass with artichokes – overcooked fish with two tiny charred artichoke leaves and a hill of raw bean sprouts. For dessert: chilly, barely edible gingerbread with diced baked apple. Like Johnny, this Rue runs hot and cold.

Senso

Hôtel Trémoille, 16 rue de la Trémoille, 8th (01.56.52.14.14) M° Alma-Marceau or Franklin D. Roosevelt. **Open** noon-3pm, 7pm-10.45pm. Bar 7am-2am. **Average** €55. **Lunch menu** €29, €36. **Credit** AmEx, DC, MC, V. **Wheelchair access. Map** D4.

Occupying an oblong dining room with dark stained parquet floors, dove-grey walls, and a red-decorated niche at the end of the room, Sir Terence Conran's second Paris restaurant in the recently renovated Hôtel Trémoille has an attitude problem – staff smirked their way all through the meal and raced everyone, even though the room was half-empty. At lunch, however, a good-value menu lets you get at some delicious food. We loved the foamy pumpkin soup with a little gâteau of white beans topped with grilled pancetta, and smoked Scottish salmon was also tasty, if carelessly sliced. Niçois-style tomatoes stuffed with veal, accompanied by a minuscule salad, were wonderful, too, if a bit scanty, while a chicken Caesar salad was woefully stingy – just a slice or two of the bird and a couple of strips of parmesan tossed with a few leaves. As is unfailingly true of Conran restaurants, the wine list is splendid, right down to a first-rate Côtes du Rhône by the glass. Desserts looked tempting, too.

Spoon, Food & Wine

14 rue de Marignan, 8th (01.40.76.34.44/ www.spoon.tm.fr). M° Franklin D. Roosevelt. **Open** Mon-Fri noon-2pm, 7-11pm. Closed 14 July, last week in July and first three weeks in Aug. **Average** €75. **Prix fixe** €37 (dinner only). **Lunch menu** €37, €43. **Credit** AmEx, DC, MC, V. **Map** E4.

While much has changed in the area since this restaurant's opening in 1998 – Nobu and Korova have come and gone, Lô Sushi and Market have found their niche – Spoon, with its mix-and-match menu, has stayed much the same. We decided to try the Speedy Spoon, a recently introduced 40-minute lunch menu that draws on a different continent every day. Monday's menu was (very) loosely inspired by Africa: the tray arrived bearing skewered prawns with peanut and garlic sauce on a chickpea salad; chicory and lettuce leaves topped with houmous and aubergine salad; chunks of 'spicy/snacked' chicken fillet; and samosas filled with dried fruits and spices. It was all pretty tasty as far as TV dinners go, but we had to send the undercooked chicken back to the kitchen and the samosas left grease on our fingers. We enjoyed the Spoon Top Five desserts, including great cheesecake and the original Toble-Spoon (nougat ice cream with a chocolate coating), but the cheeky prices explain why the room, which is starting to look a little frayed around the edges, was half-empty.

Tanjia

23 rue de Ponthieu, 8th (01.42.25.95.00). M° Franklin D. Roosevelt. **Open** Mon-Fri noon-3pm, 8pm-1am; Sat, Sun 8pm-1 am. **Average** €50. **Prix fixe** €58 (for groups only). **Lunch menu** €20. **Credit** AmEx, DC, MC, V. **Map** E4.

We were expecting high voltage air kisses and a side of couscous at Tanjia, the ex-Bains Douches team's (Cathy and David Guetta and Hubert Boukobza) Moroccan restaurant. After all, Bobby (de Niro) and Jack (Nicholson) and all manner of Hollywouldbes, models and moguls pop in when in Paris. Once past the phalanx of black-cling-wrap-clad, wired-for-sound staff at the door (we had a reservation), we downed a small, overpriced cocktail in the bar downstairs and then settled in to the super-sheikh restaurant upstairs. The food is better than you'd expect and the staff seem, believe it or not, attitude-free. The assorted starters for two – pricey but sufficient to feed a small army – included briouates (turnovers) of gambas, chicken and chèvre, aubergine caviar, and salads. Then it's on to pigeon pastilla and generous servings of mild lamb tagine (cooked ten hours with 25 spices) or couscous with organic veggies. Try the fig ice cream and order mint tea – just to see the waiters pour it deftly from a great height.

Le Martel ★

3 rue Martel, 10th (01.47.70.67.56) M° Château d'Eau. **Open** Mon-Fri noon-2.30pm, 8-11pm; Sat 8-11.30pm. **Average** €30. **Lunch menu** €17. **Credit** DC, MC, V. **Map** K3.

Anyone looking for proof that the formerly shabby 10th arrondissement is surfing a new wave of hip need go no further than this hybrid French-Algerian bistro, an insiders' address that has become one of the trendiest spots in town. And if this story sounds rather familiar – a forgotten old bistro becomes a hit with fashionistas by serving good grills and North African food – well, it is, since the proprietor, Mehdi, formerly worked as a waiter at Chez Omar (*see p210*). He learned his lessons well, too, since this place has a simmering cool with a décor of globe lamps, framed photos, soft lighting and bare wood tables and floors, and an über-hip crowd that runs to photographer Peter Beard, Vivienne Westwood and John Galliano, along with a throng of models, stylists. journalists and wannabes. Beyond the hot scene, what about the food? It's fine, but if you want a really first-rate couscous méchoui, Chez Omar wins hands-down.

Favela Chic

18 rue du Fbg-du-Temple, 11th (01.40.21.38.14/ www.favelachic.com). M° République. **Open** Mon-Sat 8pm-2am. **Average** €30. **Credit** MC, V. **Wheelchair access. Map** L4.

Be sure to get here early as Favela Chic don't take reservations and is permanently packed. If you're eating at the weekend then the earlier the better as

L'Envue: a mirror's eye view. *See p108.*

you really need a good table here, not for any snotty, social-Siberia reasons, but because you'll be dancing on your placemat later and so may as well pick your podium with care. The shabby chic interior full of foliage, flowers and kitsch artefacts is welcoming if a little overwhelming, while the buzz in the open-plan kitchen contributes to the frenetic atmosphere. Get to know your neighbours over decent, though limited, food: the menu has recently been scaled back to just three dishes (beans and rice, chicken and vegetarian lasagne). But the food isn't really the point; Favela Chic is more about shaking your booty and coming over a bit bling bling. To this end, the blinding mojitos, and caipirinhas are indispensable. You might want to aim to finish eating before 11pm if you don't want to be juggling condiments whilst others jiggle far more interesting things. And, choose your food wisely to avoid indigestion when the bump and grind starts.

Apollo ★

3 pl Denfert-Rochereau, 14th (01.45.38.76.77)
M° Denfert-Rochereau. **Open** daily noon-3pm, 8-11pm. Closed 24 Dec. **Average** €40. **Lunch menu** €16. **Credit** AmEx, DC, MC, V. **Wheelchair access. Map** H10.

From the same team that conceived Quai Ouest, this high-design-content new restaurant in the former RER offices of Denfert-Rochereau station brings a welcome breath of novelty into a pleasant but rather staid part of town. The decor takes a leaf from the once-seen-as-ghastly, now-cautiously-appreciated original 1970s design of the RER (high-speed rail system) itself with white leatherette banquettes, tomato-coloured chairs, oval convex mirrors and brown formica galore, but the menu is emphatically 21st centur, with modern takes on comfort food: herring caviar and potatoes, blanquette de coquilles St-Jacques, and braised beef with carrots. And if the kitchen has no great gastronomic aspirations, the food is generally good and generously served, including desserts such as delicious pineapple and bananas sautéed in vanilla-flavoured rum. Service was friendly and efficient.

Quinze

8 rue Nicolas-Charlet, 15th (01.42.19.08.59).
M° Pasteur. **Open** Mon-Thur noon-2.30pm, 7.30-10.30pm; Fri, Sat noon-2.30pm, 7.30-11.30pm. Closed ten days in Aug. **Average** €37. **Lunch menu** €26. **Credit** AmEx, MC, V. **Map** E9.

After stints at the Bristol, the Crillon, Caffe Armani and, most recently, Le Caffe in the 7th, Thierry Burlot has finally spread his wings and opened his own place in a restaurant that once housed the super-trendy Olympe, and later Philippe Detourbe, who had a more comet-like success. Burlot has given this intimate space a new look with linen-dressed tables,

graphic photos of food on cocoa-coloured walls, and comfortable dark wood chairs, and though the dance soundtrack is a bit too agitated for a relaxed meal, his menu is very appealing. An excellent pumpkin soup garnished with croutons, cubes of calf's foot, and chunks of chewy roast pork was a superb amuse bouche, followed by small artichokes braised with bacon and vegetables, and a superb 'pressée' of leeks and ceps. Scallops on a bed of cabbage in a sauce of 'smoked' milk, and John Dory cooked with calf's foot, both accompanied by a small bowl of mashed ratte potatoes,were first-rate. A vanilla millefeuille was a pleasant conclusion to the meal; our only quibble was the dull wine list.

R ★

8 rue de la Cavalerie, 15th (01.45.67.06.85) M° La Motte-Piquet-Grenelle. **Open** Mon-Sat noon-2.30pm, 8-11.30pm; Sun brunch 11am-4.30pm. **Average** €40. **Credit** AmEx, MC, V. **Map** D7.

The welcome at this hip new spot in a penthouse space is warm, and the service competent and friendly. The main feature of the dining room is the Eiffel Tower view, which adds some real drama to a very attractive setting by star designer Christophe Pillet. The outside terrace is entirely white, while the main dining room has rough stone walls, black floors, moulded pedestal chairs and white laminate tables. The real surprise here is the quality of the food; chef Eric Danel does a seasonal menu with dishes such as sautéed girolles or langoustine-garnished guacamole to start, a fine navarin of lamb with preserved lemons (though we longed for a side of couscous) or a tuna steak rolled in sesame seeds and served with mixed sautéed vegetables, and imaginative desserts – the 'cappuccino' of red fruits is first-rate. The best wine pick is the Drostdy Hof Cabernet Sauvignon from South Africa.

Quai Ouest

1200 quai Marcel Dassault, 92210 St-Cloud (01.46.02.35.54). M° Porte de St-Cloud (then 175 bus). **Open** Mon-Sat noon-3pm, 8pm-midnight; Sun noon-4pm. **Average** €40. **Lunch menu** €18 (Mon-Fri). **Credit** AmEx, DC, MC, V.

The world-weary floorboards had obviously seen a lot of use before this airy Seine-side warehouse was ever a restaurant, with gas heaters keeping things cosy in winter. Despite its privileged location (and customers – we had to squeeze between a Lotus and a Jaguar E-type to get to the door), prices are reasonable. We stopped by for the Sunday brunch, complete with clown and face-painting for the kids. Sitting in the adult-only annexe, we took advantage of the bottomless cups of coffee and all-you-can-eat pancakes – cunningly served as dessert, after the generous main brunch plates of salmon, chicken, chips, bacon and fresh fruit.

Classics

Puffy soufflées, heady truffles and flaming crêpes – these grandes dames of Parisian dining take you back to a more theatrical era.

In almost any other major city in the world, the term classic would be interpreted as a warning to expect stalwart cooking; in Paris, however, the label is often an invitation to sample French food at its most glorious and timeless best. Typical dishes in this category run to terrines, soufflés, impeccable roasts and grills, and spectacular desserts that no-one else has time to prepare any more. The settings are often remarkable from the ancient Seine-side townhouse **Lapérouse** to the art nouveau splendour of **Maxim's**. It's worth noting that most 'classic' restaurants in Paris these days are sagely pushing the limits, food-wise, with delicious results.

Le Jardin d'Hiver ★

Hôtel Meurice, 228 rue de Rivoli, 1st (01.44.58.10.15/www.meuricehotel.com). M° Tuileries. **Open** daily noon-2.30pm, 7-10pm. **Average** €40. **Lunch menu** €34, €42. **Credit** AmEx, DC, M, V. **Wheelchair access. Map** G5.

Offer yourself a mini-holiday with a slice of the lush life by dining at the very pleasant lobby restaurant of one of the city's grandest hotels. A whole coterie of Paris ice cream lovers has made a cult of its salted-caramel ice cream with caramel sauce, hazelnuts and almonds, whipped cream and maraschino cherries, but this grand finale is far from the only reason to indulge in a luxurious nibble under the potted palms and elegant verrière of the hotel lobby. Excellent live piano music sets the mood, and the clientele offers a bit of a show. John Travolta's polite and pretty daughter was dining with Mum, while across the way a trio of perfumed eccentrics, including a gent in jabot, large ruby ring and ostrich feather fan, did the hotel proud; it has a long and benign tradition of turning a blind eye. Go with starters such as tomato and mozzarella in pesto sauce or a Caesar salad, and then try a superb steak tartare or maybe duck breast with black cherries on a bed of cabbage. Nice wines are served by the glass, including an Austrian grüner veltliner and a Moroccan syrah, and the service is lovely.

Le Poquelin

17 rue Molière, 1st (01.42.96.22.19). M° Palais Royal. **Open** Mon, Sat 7-10pm; Tue-Fri noon-2pm, 7-10pm. Closed three weeks in Aug. **Average** €46. **Prix fixe** €33 (dinner only). **Lunch menu** €25. **Credit** AmEx, DC, MC, V. **Map** H5.

Given the name of the street and the close proximity to the Comédie Française, it's no surprise that Molière looms large in this diminutive restaurant. It's named after him (his real name rather than his nom de plume) and his face, along with trompe l'oeil bookshelves and theatre masks, decorates the walls. If you like chocolate-box pretty, you'll enjoy this. The kitchen serves up agreeable traditional food with a nod to today: roast rabbit with mustard and green peppercorns and new potatoes, rascasse (scorpion fish) with Provençal vegetables, or starters such as smoked duck slices atop a crispy green salad, and spinach and coriander ravioli dipped in a light curry cream. Oeufs à la neige topped with cracked sugared almonds, and a vanilla ice cream ball dusted with cocoa and served with raspberry coulis are fine finishers. A la carte prices are on the high side so stick with the prix fixe as many of the best dishes make an appearance. Lunch is the domain of locals while internationals rule at night.

Le Soufflé

36 rue du Mont-Thabor, 1st (01.42.60.27.19). M° Concorde. **Open** Mon-Sat noon-2.30pm, 7.30-10pm. Closed public holidays. **Average** €38. **Prix fixe** €29-€41. **Credit** AmEx. **Non-smoking room. Map** G5.

This matronly restaurant located in a chic hotel district attracts a fair amount of tourists and families with its sweet and salty versions of the 18th-century invention, the soufflé. Choices include savoury standards, such as cheese, ham, leek, mushroom and salmon, or sweet dessert ones such as lime, pear, chestnut and Grand Marnier. The waiters in crisp white jackets and blue ties are efficient, patient and ready to offer advice as well as take orders in fluent English. We started with a crowd-pleasing spinach soufflé and ended with rich chocolate and raspberry versions, puffed high with custardy centres. Sizeable portions came at an upbeat pace, served piping hot on quaint flowered dishes. We also enjoyed non-soufflé choices of fresh tomato stuffed with crab and chives, a buttery-soft rack of lamb and breaded sea bass with mashed sweet potatoes.

La Truffière

4 rue Blainville, 5th (01.46.33.29.82/ www.latruffiere.com). M° Place Monge. **Open** Tue-Sun noon-2pm, 7-10pm. **Average** €40. **Prix fixe** €79. **Lunch menu** €16 (Tue-Sat). **Credit** AmEx, DC, MC, V. **Non-smoking room. Map** J8.

There are some very good things about this place but, like truffle hunters, you have to sniff them out. Allow us to be your truffle pigs and, at the very least, you will avoid a trip to the Truffière becoming what we fear it may be for many: a financial misadventure. First, choose your season. There are few better places to sip an apéritif on a cold winter's day than beneath these medieval beams in front of an open fire. Come on a weekday lunch for the very reasonable prix fixe; the rest of the time the sky's the limit. Unless you feel like a Château Pétrus at €2,360, ask the sommelier to choose something within your means. And who cares if you don't get any truffles with the lunch special? Previous visits have produced ecstatic truffle experiences, but not this time. Slices of the elusive tuber were plainly visible in our black truffle salad, but we couldn't actually taste them. A foie gras mi-cuit with a tangy fruit confit was a much more accomplished starter, as were the snail and wild mushroom cannelloni. Mains – poached turbot with truffle butter, roast sea bass with marrow bone – were good, too, but never justified their price. So, stick to the prix fixe and spend some of your savings on a Cognac by the fire.

Lapérouse

51 quai des Grands-Augustins, 6th (01.43.26.68.04). M° St-Michel. **Open** Mon-Fri noon-2.30pm, 7.30-10.30pm; Sat 7.30-10.30pm. Closed mid-July to mid-Aug. **Average** €80. **Lunch menu** €30. **Credit** AmEx, DC, MC, V. **Non-smoking room. Map** J6.

One of the oldest restaurants in Europe – it has been in business for three centuries – Lapérouse is a place that one wants very much to like. And the sybaritic aura of the low-ceilinged dining rooms with lovely views of the Seine, or the famous private salons, furnished with plush sin-red divans should temptation get the better of you, have an emollient effect as a meal progresses. Chef Alain Hacquard has made an intelligent attempt to reinterpret what 'classic' French cooking means. He mostly succeeds, though the menthol-tasting Sichuan pepper in a dish of smoked John Dory cooked with bacon and served on a bed of braised artichokes and tomatoes was excessive punctuation, while the carrot-butter garnish on a nicely cooked steak was so mild as to be barely present. Warm pastry sticks filled with aniseed better showed of Hacquard's imagination, as did the dried-fig bread served with very good foie gras, and a rich, resonant cold crab soup, a first-rate summer dish. An individual soufflé with hot raspberry sauce was a treat, while a tian of apricots seemed targeted at false-teeth wearers. With an enchanting setting, friendly staff and a competent kitchen, the real problem here is the prices – the wine list is boldly marked up, while any option but the good-value lunch menu will have you spending more money than the overall experience warrants.

Le Violon d'Ingres

135 rue St-Dominique, 7th (01.45.55.15.05). M° Ecole-Militaire or RER Pont de l'Alma. **Open** Tue-Sat noon-3pm, 7-11pm. Closed last week July, two weeks in Aug. **Average** €80. **Prix fixe** €110 (dinner only). **Lunch menu** €39. **Credit** AmEx, MC, V. **Wheelchair access. Map** D6.

Though we very much admired Christian Constant when he was chef at the Hôtel Crillon, and are much in his debt for the superb tribe of young bistro chefs who passed through his kitchen, we've never been

Underground truffle-hunting at **La Truffière**.

"This gracious and friendly Turkish restaurant makes you feel your're dining at someone's home. A complimentary *raki* (an anise-flavoured aperitif) is served while you peruse the menu, and portions are generous. In fact, the assorted *mezze* are so substantial you can easily share a plate between two (though the home-made taramasalata, mushroom salad, houmous and aubergine fritters are so delicious you might not want to share them). Main courses, all-meat or vegetarian, are just as copious: try the succulent *kuzu sis* (leg of lamb kebab), *mantarli sis*, (lamb and mushroom kebab) or *bagdat sistu* (skewered lamb in aubergine purée and yogurt). Nice home-made desserts, good Turkish wines, including the *Yakut* at a bargain €11, plus warm, professional sevice, make this a very pleasant and good-value address."
–Time Out Paris with Pariscope 2002

47 rue St Georges, 9th - M° St. Georges. Closed Sun.
Tel: 01.44.63.02.28 - www.sizin-restaurant.com

"With an excellent catch-of-the-day blackboard menu offered at good prices in a hip neighbourhood setting, this seafooder not too far from Les Halles is an ongoing hit."
—Time Out Paris with Pariscope

Open Mon-Fri 12.30pm-3pm, 8.30pm-11.30pm & Sat 8.30pm-11.30pm

48 rue d'Argout, 2nd. M° Sentier.
Tel: 01.42.36.46.45.

able to make sense of this stuffy and overpriced restaurant with a mostly North American crowd. The frosty service we remembered has relaxed, and the decor has taken on a warmer look, with Chinese jars and framed prints. We were surprised, though, to see that the menu had barely changed in two years. Finding the starters too rich, we split an order of scallops with chicory in bitter orange sauce, a pleasant and well-balanced dish, and then continued with turbot and chestnut (one) on a bed of Jerusalem artichokes, and sole with shellfish. Both mains were served tepid, the turbot was dried out, and the portion of sole was scandalously small – four thin strips in a foamy cream with three small clams and some very stringy fried parsley. We dallied over plates of three very good Auvergnat cheeses and finished our wine, a superb Côtes de Provence Richaume Cuvée Columelle 1999. Sadly, Constant seems to have lost his passion for innovation.

L'Angle du Faubourg

195 rue du Fbg-St-Honoré, 8th (01.40.74.20.20/ www.taillevent.com). M° Ternes or George V.
Open Mon-Fri noon-2.30pm, 7-10.30pm. Closed 26 July-26 Aug. **Average** €48. **Prix fixe** €35, €60 (dinner only). **Credit** AmEx, DC, MC, V. **Map** D3.
Parchment-thin ravioli of potimarron (a type of pumpkin) in a tantalising foie gras emulsion augured well, as did a Provençal-style barigoule of artichokes with mesclun. Rather a long wait later, the roast pigeon was perfectly rosé with crisp-baked chicory. However, the braised shoulder of lamb with garlic was disappointingly greasy, its flavour dominated by an over-caramelised gravy; it cried out for green vegetables rather than the stodgy potato cylinder that accompanied it. From a limited dessert choice, the Reine Saba – Queen of Sheba – baked chocolate pudding took fashionably bitter to its extreme, thankfully saved by the small glass of coffee ice. Full marks, though, to the young female sommelier who suggested the cheapest, and very agreeable, red Burgundy from a list that goes from sane to sensational (not surprising when the Angle du Faubourg's parent is exalted Taillevent). The well-spaced tables, calm grey and terracotta decor and serious service all spell upmarket, but this felt closer to bistro cooking. The starters showed the sort of refined, rustic chic that young chef Stéphane Cosnier can produce, but this restaurant still seems to be in search of its true culinary identity.

Le Bistrot du Sommelier ★

97 bd Haussmann 8th (01.42.65.24.85/ www.bistrotdusommelier.com). M° St-Augustin.
Open Mon-Fri noon-2.30pm, 7.30-9.30pm. Closed 25 Dec-1 Jan, three weeks in Aug. **Average** €50. **Prix fixe** €60-€100 (dinner only). **Lunch menu** €39. **Credit** AmEx, MC, V. **Non-smoking room. Map** F3.
Something of an industry has sprung up around Philippe Faure-Brac, who won the world sommelier competition in 1992. So to his restaurant, with bated breath. We were promptly greeted and seated by the charming maître d'hôtel at the worst table in the house – directly behind a waiter's station and a very distracting office corner (with manic ever-changing screen saver). Otherwise the decor – twiddly lamps, wine photos, Dionysus frieze – was nothing to write home about. The carte looked confusing and pricey; it struck us as more interesting to try one of the blind formulas which includes a glass of wine with each course. The menu découverte at €60 kicked off nicely with a rabbit terrine with a chorizo and pepper marinade and what turned out to be not a Rhône wine but a glass of Fitou 2000 from Gérard Bertrand. Next up, a tiny piece of roast salmon with cider butter and a leek flan with a glass of Muscadet de Sèvre-et-Maine that we had down as Sancerre. Delicious, tender veal with a fine cauliflower purée and a carrot cream was served alongside a cunning red wine which also had us foxed (Château Hostens Picant). Of the cheeses, pungent livarot and murol worked well with the dirty-nosed Tempranillo, Condado de Haza; only the zingy ste-maure goat's cheese seemed to balk at the idea. Apple crème brûlée was served with a skinny Sauternes, Rayne-Vigneau 1997 which we felt was masquerading as a Coteaux du Layon. No prizes for us then, but lots of fun and plenty of patience from our lovely Japanese sommelier. We even had a 'good evening' from the man himself, who turned up and did the rounds.

Lasserre ★

17 av Franklin Roosevelt, 8th (01.43.59.53.43/ www.lasserre.com). M° Franklin D. Roosevelt.
Open Tue-Sat 12.30-2pm, 7.30-10pm. Closed Aug. **Average** €140. **Prix fixe** €165 (dinner only). **Lunch menu** €110. **Credit** AmEx, DC, MC, V. **Wheelchair access. Map** E4.
Sixties babies should be aware that Lasserre remains a bastion of traditional Parisian chic, where jacket and tie are compulsory. The dining room is reached by a padded lift controlled by uniformed staff, and the first impression takes you back to a 1950s dream of upmarket living. Quaintly old fashioned chandeliers and bourgeois comfort frame the famous opening roof, which even in relatively inclement weather will perform its magical open sky effect to please the child in all but the most hard-hearted diner. After some amuse-bouches of delicate foie gras toasts and a tasty parcel of fish we were impressed by our first courses. Seared foie gras accompanied by preserved fruits managed to be firm and free of any excess fat, while a timbale of black truffle and foie gras macaroni was intensely flavoured. Our main courses included one of the house specialities, pigeon André Malraux, which was exceptionally moist, plump and tender, accompanied by melting spears of salsify. Some pungent slivers of black truffle and a side dish of perfect pommes de terre soufflées crowned fork-tender fillet steak into which slivers of foie gras had been artfully introduced. It was hard to resist the pudding of the day, sensational crêpes Suzette, prepared at the table with all the swish professionalism that can

Lap up the luxury at **Lapérouse.**
See p113.

only be found at this sort of French establishment. We could have lived without the tinkling pianist's repertoire of muzak, but the unglamorous expense-account crowd seemed to be lapping it up. The wine list is short but expensive and our attempts at ordering a reasonably priced half-bottle of white were somewhat disastrous, but the slightly condescending sommelier dealt with our complaints with admirable sang froid and the ensuing Chassagne Montrachet red was expensively delicious. With a meal coming to around €200 a head, this is somewhere to take a pampered heiress.

Maxim's

3 rue Royale, 8th (01.42.65.27.94/www.maxims-de-paris.com). M° Concorde. **Open** Tue-Fri 12.30-2pm, 7.30-10.30pm, Sat 7.30-11.30pm. Closed 1 May, 1 Jan, 25 Dec. **Average** €90 (lunch), €150 (dinner). **Credit** AmEx, DC, MC, V. **Map** F4.

'I'm going to Maxim's...' sings Danilo in Léhar's operetta the Merry Widow, and as a Parisian landmark the restaurant is almost as famous as the Eiffel Tower. So, armed with a pretty young Parisian débutante, where better to go for a stylish lunch? The extravagant swirling belle époque decor lives up to its reputation, and the slight hint of shabbiness only adds to the charm. We were expecting a room crammed with international tourists and assorted glitterati, but, aside from our own glamorous presence, there were just four other diners, two mature French businessmen exploring the wrongs of the modern world, and a pair of stout English ladies straight out of Agatha Christie, who boomed in fruity tones their desire for 'pancakes'. Word had it that the cooking was no longer great, but despite the lack of modern fripperies such as appetising nibbles, a groaning plate of green asparagus with sauce mousseline impressed us, even if the terrine of duck with truffles and foie gras was only adequate. Our comforting main course was a plump Challans duck for two, perfectly roasted with accompanying baby turnips and salsify. The puddings were a classic millefeuille and a more elaborate construction of violet-scented wild strawberries with a rhubarb sorbet, which was pronounced as delicious by the débutante, who by now had me firmly marked as an old-timer. The naughty 90s of Maxim's are long past, but the staff were wonderfully old-school, and the bottle of Maxim's own Mercurey surprisingly delicious. A time-warp experience, which if your budget can bear it still has a unique, dusty magic.

Le Céladon

Hôtel Westminster, 13 rue de la Paix, 9th (01.47.03.40.42). M° Opéra. **Open** daily 12.30-2pm, 7.30-10pm. **Average** €80. **Prix fixe** €60 (dinner only). **Lunch menu** €45 (Sat, Sun only). **Credit** AmEx, DC, MC, V. **Map** G4.

The Hôtel Westminster's illustrious neighbour, Cartier, may be a draw for the Elizabeth Taylors of this world, but its pastel-decorated restaurant, Le Céladon, draws a more eclectic, low-key clientele. On a recent evening visit, we were placed at one of the well-spaced tables in the liveliest section next to the bar, where our neighbours were a big family complete with five-year-old, a whispering American courting couple and three straitlaced *vieille France* seniors. We began with a glass of Laurent Perrier rosé, which made a worthy partner for the daintily presented selection of amuse-bouches. From a tantalising selection of starters, we chose the delicious crab with caramelised spring onions encased in fried courgette flowers and flanked by a frothy shellfish sauce, and the scampi, which had received a too-liberal sprinkling of lemongrass, but was accompanied by a thoroughly delicious gelée of étrilles (tiny crabs). For mains, the John Dory had an original 'snail-butter' sauce and the sole was served with a garnish of ratatouille-style tomatoes and courgettes which proved an incongruous match for this cold-water fish. Desserts were excellent, particularly the delicate Williamine soufflé and the state-of-the-art, shiny palet de chocolat. The hotel's Austrian manager ensures that the wine list features his country's top bottles while sommelier Richard Rahard has unearthed some of the Rhône's rarest whites.

L'Oulette

15 pl Lachambeaudie, 12th (01.40.02.02.12/www.l-oulette.com). M° Cour St-Emilion. **Open** Mon-Fri noon-2.15pm, 8-10.15pm. **Average** €70. **Prix fixe** €46. **Lunch menu** €28. **Credit** AmEx, DC, MC, V. **Wheelchair access. Map** P10.

Marcel Baudis is a sincere, generous and talented chef, so it would be wonderful if the overall experience of this restaurant lived up to his cooking. Aside from a decor that feels like the lounge in a retirement home, the problem during a recent dinner was the very green if well-intentioned staff. After a long wait for mineral water, the meal advanced at such a lightning pace that the waiters had to carry our main courses back to the kitchen to keep them warm since we hadn't yet finished our starters, and then had us speeding by the cheese course that's included in the €46 menu. Despite this, we thoroughly enjoyed our food, beginning with an excellent duck pâté with a big velvety lump of foie gras in its centre and pods of apricot purée on the side, and courgette soup seasoned with saffron and spiked with anchovy cream. Confit de canard was impeccably cooked and splendidly accompanied by a tiny rocket salad and a generous potato-and-bacon galette, while scorpion fish was astutely served with braised fennel, Thai rice with star anise, and spring vegetables dressed with lush olive oil from Lucques. The cheeses were worth insisting on, and desserts were excellent including a berry compote with crumbly shortbread, and pink grapefruit sections with grapefruit ice and cocoa sorbet. There is a small, pleasant terrace overlooking the lovely church of Notre Dame de Bercy.

Au Pressoir ★

257 av Daumesnil, 12th (01.43.44.38.21). M° Michel Bizot. **Open** Mon-Fri noon-2.30pm, 7.30-10.30pm. Closed Aug, 25-31 Dec. **Average** €100. **Prix fixe** €70. **Credit** AmEx, MC, V. **Map** Q9.

Cô Ba

Saigon

Exotic French-Indochina and finest Vietnamese cuisine.

Taste wonderfully creative dishes in a classy and friendly atmosphere.

«In the heart of the moneyed and posh eighth arrondissement, this little vietnamese enclave is a rare pearl.»
–Gault Millau 2003

For prestige events or receptions, contact Cô Ba Traiteur
receptions@cobasaigon.com

181 rue du Faubourg Saint Honoré, 8th. Tel: 01.45.63.70.37
Open Mon-Sat noon-3pm, 7pm-10pm
M° Charles De Gaulle Etoile or Friedland

www.cobasaigon.com

Once in the wood-lined, clubby interior of Henri Séguin's temple to serious eating we were quickly led to a table by the smiling patronne. Lunchtime saw an exclusively male clientele, popping out of their business suits in all directions, sporting complexions which keep cardiologists in work. We knew we were in for some serious food; even the appetiser of cold lobster soup was sublime. The starters included a special of the day, foie gras terrine with the contrasting texture of artichokes; we also tried a salad of warm roseval potatoes topped with foie gras. Both portions were generous and the preparation of the liver exceptionally fine. The sommelier suggested an excellent Bordeaux from the cheaper end of the list. The tournedos aux cèpes surpassed all expectations; not only was the meat spoon-tender but it seemed to be permeated by the rich mushroom sauce. An escalope de foie gras chaud was a perfect version accompanied by some nicely tart quartered apples. We had greedily watched the cheese trolley from the beginning of the meal and found ourselves with groaning platefuls. A dessert of wild strawberries magically held in thrall by spun sugar, accompanied by homemade vanilla ice cream, was unmissable. Our eye had also been caught by a silver chalice of soupe au chocolat, which turned out to be possibly the richest pudding we have ever tasted; later the dish and its accompanying sponge cakes had to be pulled away from us.

Le Pavillon Montsouris

20 rue Gazan, 14th (01.43.13.29.00/www.pavillon-montsouris.fr). M° Glacière/RER Cité Universitaire. **Open** daily noon-2.30pm, 7.30-10.30pm. Closed Sun evening mid-Sept to Apr. **Prix fixe** €49. **Credit** AmEx, MC, V. **Wheelchair access. Non-smoking room.**

The only building inside the pleasant Parc Montsouris, the Pavillon was recently renovated in a style that can best described as belle époque colonial greenhouse. The glass walls provide unobstructed views of the park, red-faced joggers and envious amblers. Service is truly complete, with a different keen waiter to look after your wine, bread, and crumbs; their friendliness and professionalism certainly add to the pleasure of the meal. Nibbles arrive as you contemplate the many possibilities of the three-course prix fixe. Among the starters, we enjoyed the marinated salmon and crabmeat cannelloni, and, with a €4 supplement, the lightly poached duck foie gras served with toasted raisin brioche. Our main courses – roast duckling fillet with green olives and mushroom stuffing, and a coq au vin with parmesan and truffle risotto – were unusually copious. At a stretch, they could perhaps be faulted for being overly rich; but that is easily tempered with some of the incredible in-house bread, brought steaming to the table at regular intervals. When you order your dessert (at the start of the meal), you'd be wise to resist the chocolate and go with something light. There are a few reasonably priced bottles to be found in the wine book.

Le Chalet des Iles ★

Carrefour des Cascades, lac inférieur du Bois de Boulogne, 16th (01.42.88.04.69/ www.lechaletdesiles.net). M° La Muette or RER Henri Martin. **Open** Mon-Fri noon-2.30pm, 8-10pm; Sat noon-3.30pm, 8-10.30pm; Sun noon-3.30pm, 8-10pm. **Average** €40. **Lunch menu** €20, €28 (Mon-Fri). **Children's menu** €10, €16. **Credit** AmEx, MC, V.

After an early evening stroll in the Bois de Boulogne take the little launch across to the island and escape for a couple of hours into a fantasy world. Seated on the elevated terrace under huge burgundy umbrellas with a breathtaking view of the lake we felt as happy as the extremely fat cat that prowls beneath the tables, and asked the friendly waiter for glasses of the excellent brut Champagne. The atmosphere is festive, and when a peacock started crowing at the diners beside us, it raised a laugh from everyone around. The menu was ideal for the end of a hot summer's day, starting with very fresh goat's cheese surrounded by tiny morsels of lemon confit and fig, and a clafoutis of yellow tomatoes cooked in a terracotta dish with cumin and turmeric. Turmeric also coloured the delicious colombo of prawns, accompanied by wild rice from the Camargue, while the carré d'agneau, judiciously scattered with fleur de sel, was succulently rosé and served with a tian of aubergine, onion and courgette. Our wines by the glass, a 1999 St-Estèphe and a Pouilly-Fumé, were both enjoyable, but the icing on the cake was the moelleux au chocolat – five tiny cakes with a miniature scoop of ice cream and berry confit. As we left our waiter waved us a 'happy holiday' and we wished the ferryman could have circled the island just to prolong the moonlit moment.

La Grande Cascade

Pavillon de la Grande Cascade, Bois de Boulogne, 16th (01.45.27.33.51/www.lagrandecascade.fr). M° Porte Maillot, then taxi or 244 bus. **Open** daily 12.30-2pm, 7.30-9.15pm. **Average** €130. **Prix fixe** €165. **Lunch menu** €59 (Mon-Fri). **Credit** AmEx, DC, MC, V.

This intimate pavilion tucked away in the Bois de Boulogne was built in 1856 as a hunting lodge for Napoleon III. With its dramatic fan-like glass porte-cochère over the terrace, where meals are served in good weather, it makes a wonderful escape when you want to get out of town without going far. Though star chef Jean-Louis Nomicos has moved on to Lasserre, Richard Mebkhout is proving to be a talented and able successor, with a style that clearly shows the influence of Alain Ducasse. Start with the open tart of raw and cooked ceps with snails or the superb macaroni stuffed with black truffle, foie gras and celeriac, and then go with the luscious hare à la royale or maybe the sole with capers and croutons for two. The young sommelier ably manages an interesting list, and has a particularly original selection of Provençal and Languedoc-Roussillon bottles, so ask for a suggestion. Finish your meal with the citrus tart and heavenly mango-chocolate ice cream, or delightfully retro crêpes soufflées.

Contemporary

Just call it custom mode cuisine – inventive chefs making a meal out of traditional techniques and all the right modern ingredients.

To taste the future of French cuisine, look no further than this chapter. Probably the most exciting restaurant event of 2003 was the opening of the Left Bank tapas-meets-sushi venture, **L'Atelier de Joël Robuchon** – the superchef, after a seven-year 'retirement', has opted out of the haute cuisine world with all its bells, whistles and migraines. At **L'Astrance**, Pascal Barbot is keeping up a brilliant standard at accessible prices, a rare combination indeed. Flora Mikula, who once ran the Provençal bistro Les Olivades, has quietly gone global at her classy restaurant **Flora**, while Catherine Guerraz has also leapt to a more ambitious level at **Chez Catherine**. For London-style dining among chic Parisians, head to Jean-Georges Vongerichten's **Market**.

Macéo ★

15 rue des Petits-Champs, 1st (01.42.97.53.85). M° Bourse or Opéra. **Open** Mon-Fri 12.30-2.30pm, 7-11pm; Sat 7-11pm. **Average** €48. **Prix fixe** €35, €38 (dinner only). **Lunch menu** €29, €34. **Credit** MC, V. **Map** H5.

Macéo is one of the rare restaurants in Paris where you might actually be tempted to turn vegetarian, even offering a full vegetarian menu – no doubt the influence of its British ownership as a sibling of Willi's Wine Bar. Meat eaters, happily, are allowed to mix from both menus, as we did, choosing two veggie starters: a wonderful, smooth, pale orange pumpkin soup with morsels of chestnut, and a vegetable pastilla. Chef Jean-Paul Deyries gives south-west-tinged French cuisine (he trained with Michel Guérard at Eugénie-les-Bains and André Deguin at Auch) a contemporary, cosmopolitan lift, as seen in a succulent lamb and aubergine main course, and cod roasted on its skin, accompanied by a garam masala spice reduction and a solid dollop of split green pea purée with chunks of bacon. A crisp pistachio sablé with an unctuous Guanaja chocolate mousse and an arrangement of citrus fruit and sorbets provided a fine contrast to finish the meal. Spacious, high-ceilinged salons with large windows and Second Empire mouldings are given a clever update by sculptural bronze and twig light-fittings. We've heard complaints about the service in the past, but we found the waiters helpful and good-humoured, even jokey, while the female sommelier guided us to a pleasant Rioja. Note that people eat late here: the room was almost empty when we arrived at 8.30pm, almost full by the time we left.

Restaurant du Palais-Royal

110 galerie Valois, 1st (01.40.20.00.27). M° Palais Royal. **Open** May-Sept Mon-Sat 12.15-2.15pm, 7.15-10pm; Oct-Apr Mon-Fri 12.15-2.15pm, 7.15-11.30pm. Closed 20 Dec-20 Jan. **Average** €46. **Credit** AmEx, DC, MC, V. **Non-smoking room. Map** H5.

Stroll through the Palais-Royal gardens in the summer, and it's hard not to feel envious of those privileged enough to dine on the terrace here. The dining room – brick-red walls, silver and gold panelling, chairs upholstered in jewel tones – is also choice. We chose from the small, seasonal menu. Duck foie gras 'maison' turned out to be a thick, round slab, served with mango chutney and toasted brioche, while thinly sliced raw scallops came with a bright green salad of small broad beans, mangetout and green beans. Tagliatelle with clams, tomato and leek was deeply flavoured, if a little sticky; the juicy tenderloin steak, served with symmetrically stacked frites, remains a house classic. When we ordered a chestnut millefeuille for two, the waiters presented it on two plates, a mark of the thoughtful service.

Le Park

Park Hyatt Paris-Vendôme Hôtel, 3 rue de la Paix, 2nd (01.42.44.27.89). M° Opéra. **Open** Mon-Fri noon-3pm, 7-11pm; Sat 7-11pm. **Average** €80. **Prix fixe** €120 (dinner only). **Lunch menu** €48, €53. **Credit** AmEx, DC, MC, V. **Wheelchair access. Map** G4.

Offering a new idiom of luxury for Parisians, Le Park is a plush but minimalist space frequented by a sleek international crowd. Working in an open kitchen, chef Christophe David, who trained at Lucas Carton and Taillevent before beginning a world tour with stints in Australia, California and Argentina, has created a modern grill repertoire that reflects the influence of all three ports of call. Starters include artichoke soup, plump langoustines with kassoundi (Moroccan-style tomato chutney), and a delicious composition of tomatoes and goat's cheese with a small salad of fresh herbs. Mains run to pedigreed French meat – Charolais beef, Corrèze veal, Bresse chicken – and fish, all grilled and served with an amusing assortment of eight different mustards and chutneys, the most original of which are the green apple chutney and the violet mustard. All mains come with a choice of side dishes: potato purée with garlic chips, mixed sautéed mushrooms or wok-tossed vegetables. Desserts include a wonderful composition of liquorice ice cream, figs and walnut-bread pain perdu.

Aesthetic satisfaction guaranteed at **Macéo**.

Edible art

Modern Parisian chefs are treating the plate like a blank slate.

There was a time when design was almost a dirty word in Paris restaurants that took their food seriously. Ambitious chefs conformed to a fusty provincial look – floral chair covers, starched tablecloths, shiny silver domes and a plain monogrammed dinner service – and let the cooking speak for itself, with few flights of fancy.

Today, though a sober style still prevails in haute cuisine institutions, a number of rising contemporary chefs are approaching food with an artist's sensibility. Taste is still paramount, but shapes, colours and textures (not just of the food, but of the plates and cutlery) combine to turn a meal into a feast for the senses.

Many chefs will use extra-large circular plates for more traditional dishes, minimalist rectangular plates and glass for adventurous starters and colourful desserts, and shot glasses for all manner of amuse-gueule gazpachos, jellies and creams. Mini cast-iron casseroles for reborn hotpots evoke a deliberate nostalgia trip of serve-yourself tradition and long-simmering generosity.

How food looks also seems to go hand-in-hand with a linguistic mutation of culinary terms: 'millefeuille' without pastry, 'cannelloni' without pasta, 'cappuccino' without coffee, not to mention tartares, sushis and carpaccios (all variants on the trend for raw) that are as likely to be made of tomatoes or mushrooms as they are of beef or tuna. Thus, Pascal Barbot at **L'Astrance** makes a clever 'millefeuille' of crab, lifted by just the right dose of lime zest, sandwiched between two thin slices of avocado.

Today, the innovations of 1970s nouvelle cuisine – where sauces made of jus and reductions no longer swamped food or arrived in sauce boats, but were swirled around or arranged beneath – have become so well-accepted as to seem the norm. In the 1990s, vertical stacks brought out contrasting tastes and textures (as well as sometimes being phenomenally difficult to eat). If the worst excesses of vertical piling seem to be out in favour of more horizontal methods, layering still allows chefs to revisit tradition. At **Au Bon Accueil** (*see p44*), wine-imbued beef cheek rests on tangy lengths of stewed rhubarb.

Rectangular plates have been adopted as a way of showing off ingredients and techniques laid out in linear format. At **La Bastide Odéon**

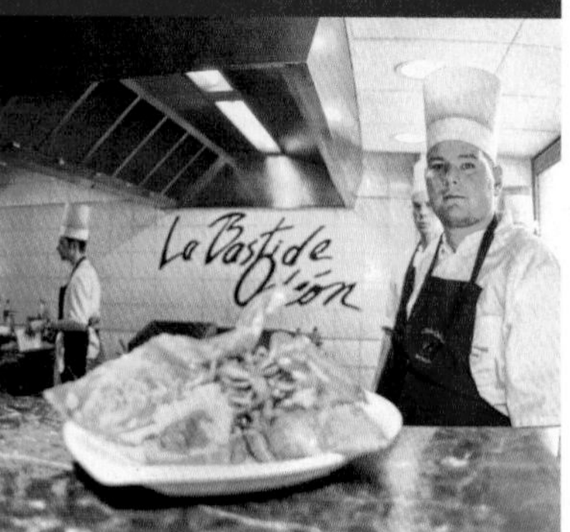

(*see p135*), Gilles Ajuelos serves a delicious lapin confit with whole new carrots and polenta, set off by tangy wild rocket, elegantly arranged on a long, glass plate. At **Ze Kitchen Galerie**, William Ledeuil combines classic French culinary technique with the use of Asian vegetables and spices and Spanish-style plancha grilling. Thus Ledeuil lines up raw tuna, a tangy condiment and a salad of thin slices of green and white radish.

At **Le Salon d'Hélène**, where you sit around low tables amid deep velvet cushions, a selection of four mini tapas, such as foie gras ice cream with Puy lentils, langoustine tempura with cucumber and mango risotto, and foie gras prepared three different ways, come on tiny square plates that fit together. And at the tapas-style **L'Atelier de Joël Robuchon**, the sensibility to ingredients extends as far as the plates, some of which are made of volcanic lava from Mount Fuji.

The nibbly approach draws out the contrasting elements of a dish – raw and cooked, soft and crunchy, frothy or crisp, green and white. It's probably Alain Ducasse at **Spoon, Food & Wine** (*see p109*) who has had most influence in introducing this trend to Paris. The eponymous spoon, however, probably remains the most radical way of serving: an appetiser on a Chinese-style china spoon that you down in one bite.

Has French cooking gained from this increasingly playful approach? Seen from a foreign perspective, it's not that revolutionary – chefs in London, New York and Sydney have been more daring for years. The strength of this group of Paris chefs lies in never losing sight of good taste. *Natasha Edwards.*

Café des Délices

87 rue d'Assas, 6th (01.43.54.70.00). M° Vavin or RER Port Royal. **Open** Mon-Fri noon-2.30pm, 7.30-11.30pm. Closed Aug. **Average** €33. **Prix fixe** €33. **Lunch menu** €14. **Credit** AmEx, DC, MC, V. **Map** H8.

The pretty art nouveau facade, the wooden blinds, the pale fabric walls and bright, quirky lamps of the Café des Délices are subtly seductive, but our recent meal was a let-down – lots of ideas, few of them successful. We tried carrot strips with an orange and cumin-flavoured chickpea purée crowned with a popadom – too much cumin left a bitter aftertaste. Fleshy langoustines in pistachio crumbs with a crisp rocket salad proved the pick of the starter bunch. Slow-cooked pork belly was a stewy affair with beans and a hint of lemon, while the duck leg, poached in spices, leeks and liquorice, was submerged in broth and underseasoned. Cuttlefish, simply pan-fried, had lots of flavour but why pair it with a sour-tasting confit of mushy macaroni, sun-dried tomatoes, chickpeas and olives? A chewy dessert 'sandwich' of sliced dried figs and banana with mint dressing and melted honey ice cream did not help. Service is cheery, although recommending a €40 bottle of wine in place of un unavailable €28 one and not mentioning the price hike was naughty.

Le Salon d'Hélène ★

4 rue d'Assas, 6th (01.42.22.00.11). M° Sèvres-Babylone. **Open** Tue-Sat 12.30-2.15pm, 7.30-10.15pm. Closed Aug. **Average** €55. **Prix fixe** €53 (dinner only). **Credit** AmEx, MC, V. **Wheelchair access**. **Map** G7.

Chef Hélène Darroze's (*see p82*) casual ground-floor salon is devoted to bright, beautiful tapas; a perfect counterpart to the zesty pink, plum, orange and dark chocolate surroundings. While there's a daily entrée-plat-dessert option (for sticklers for French culinary grammar), don't go beyond the tapas. Indeed, better to splurge on the set menu: nine glorious taste sensations served in pairs on pristine white china squares. Highlights included a tempura of plump langoustine on sweet-salty mango and cucumber risotto; a lone, large oyster with a scoop of foie gras ice cream; chicory soup mottled with sea urchin coral and citrus peel; a Lilliputian lamb chop anointed with sheep's cheese and powdered chorizo sauce; her celebrated grilled foie gras married with dried fruit chutney and delicious Banyuls wine. Sheep's cheese follows, then dessert: seriously addictive (and warm and runny) chocolate moelleux with a dollop of intensely chocolatey ice cream, and a baba saturated in blazing rum complete with a weenie baked apple half. Interesting, sophisticated and just plain mouthwatering.

Ze Kitchen Galerie

4 rue des Grands-Augustins, 6th (01.44.32.00.32). M° St-Michel. **Open** Mon-Fri noon-2pm, 7-11pm; Sat 7-11pm. **Average** €39. **Lunch menu** €21-€32. **Credit** AmEx, DC, MC, V. **Wheelchair access**. **Map** H6.

William Ledeuil was chef at Guy Savoy satellite Les Bouquinistes before opening his own contemporary restaurant just next door. The space feels a bit like a bachelor's loft with white walls, dark wood, a slightly baffling multicoloured pillar, bright contemporary paintings, and the compact yet tidy open kitchen behind glass. Not exactly warm, but a suitably spare background for his beautifully presented dishes, which subtly draw on ingredients from around the globe. The three-course €32 menu with a glass of wine and coffee is the way to go even at lunch, since small portions leave you feeling sprightly. We started with four rounds of crab-and-prawn-filled cucumber with green mango and papaya matchsticks and a rather meek 'tomato-curry' sauce, and the day's special of salmon marinated in rice vinegar with a passion fruit vinaigrette – both refreshing, but lacking a certain punch. A main of marinated chicken with galanga raised an uncomfortable question – why do a Thai curry halfway, when the real thing is so much more exciting? Scorpion fish a la plancha was perfectly cooked, served with new potatoes and whole roasted cherry tomatoes. Desserts were the most memorable part of our meal – a dense chocolate cream topped with cardamom-scented coconut milk, and little passion fruit crèmes brûlées. Service from smiley waiters couldn't have been better, and we admire Ledeuil for his desire to innovate (he now gives cooking classes, too).

L'Atelier de Joël Robuchon ★

5 rue de Montalembert, 7th (01.42.22.56.56). M° Rue du Bac. **Open** daily 11.30am-3pm, 6.30pm-midnight. **Average** €55. **Credit** MC, V. **Wheelchair access**. **Non smoking**. **Map** G6.

The retired chef who was once the best-known gastronaut in France is finally back – with a Parisian take on a New York coffee shop-cum-sushi-and-tapas bar. The black and Chinese red lacquer interior and the two U-shaped bars – there are no tables here, you sit on stools at a wenge wood counter by Pierre-Yves Rochon– has a sassy Left Bank chic, completed by spotlit glass jars of fruits and vegetables, dangling Spanish hams, and an on-view wine cellar in chrome racks. To his credit, Robuchon, chic in an all-black Chinese worker-style costume, was actually on hand on our visit, and he seemed to be having a ball, occasionally passing through the open kitchen to see what was going on and astutely surveying the counter to assure that his formula of 'la convivialité d'abord' (conviviality first and foremost) was working, which it mainly was. Re the food, it was just fine, with a bit of obvious inspiration from El Bulli in Spain, and Spoon and L'Astrance in Paris. The menu is divided into three different corrals, with the idea that you can eat as much or as little, as elaborately or as simply, as you choose. So start with caviar, Spanish ham, a large seasonal salad, or spaghetti carbonara, or maybe an assortment of the little tasting plates (the most inventive part of the menu, this French take on tapas), including veal sweetbreads skewered with a bay leaf twig and served with Swiss chard in cream, a tart of mackerel fillet, parmesan shavings and olives, or marinated anchovies with aubergine. Then, go classic (a steak), fanciful (vitello tonnato, veal in tuna and anchovy sauce) or lush (sublime 'cannelloni' of Bresse chicken and foie gras). Desserts are a bit less inspired, the passion fruit soufflé with pistachio ice cream being the star. Bravo for the friendly service, nice selection of wines by the glass, and overall cooking quality, thumbs down that they keep changing their reservation policy, causing great confusion, long queues and temper tantrums at the door.

Le Chamarré

13 bd de La Tour-Maubourg, 7th (01.47.05.50.18). M° Invalides or La Tour Maubourg. **Open** Mon-Fri noon-2pm, 7-10pm; Sat. 8-10pm. Closed Aug. **Average** €60. **Prix fixe** €70, €90 (dinner only). **Lunch menu** €35. **Credit** AmEx, MC, V. **Wheelchair access. Map** E6.

Working in tandem with friendly maître d'hôtel Antoine Heerah, a Mauritian who was a professional chef on his home island before coming to Paris, Jérome Bodereau, most recently sous-chef at L'Arpège, shows off his impressive skills at this original, if rather too formal, new restaurant. Though he's wielding seasonings that are not part of his indigenous palette, Bodereau does a respectable job of creating the curried nuances that dominate the cuisine of Mauritius. An appealing starter of spring vegetables – some European, some tropical – in a Mauritian pesto sauce (Thai basil, ginger, and various other seasonings) showed that the kitchen is serious here, while a take on a nem where marlin replaced the rice-paper wrapper was less successful for the timidity of the fish. Lobster with Chinese cabbage stuffed with crab, and an impeccable chicken roast with curry leaves under its skin were both pleasant. The final impression is that it's agreeable and off-beat enough to make it an occasional, rather than a regular, pleasure.

Restaurant Claude Colliot

15 rue de Babylone, 7th (01.45.49.14.40). M° Sévres-Babylone. **Open** Mon-Fri noon-2pm, 8-11pm. Closed 15-22 Aug. **Average** €55. **Prix fixe** €59 (dinner only). **Lunch menu** €35. **Credit** V. **Map** G7.

Thanks to owner-chef Claude Colliot, this little bistro offers some of the most inventive, seasonally based cooking on the Left Bank. Take his glace aux huîtres, a huge ice cream-like scoop of pure oysters whipped into a creamy mass, set atop a bed of lemon verbena sauce. Just like swallowing a wave. The pairing of grilled coquilles St-Jacques, albeit just two, with finely minced cauliflower and shreds of caramelised orange peel also works a treat. Pigeon breast comes deliciously roasted in beetroot juice and Sichuan pepper while wild duck is coated in gingerbread crumbs. Desserts impress, too: figs roasted with bay leaves and perhaps the city's best mille-feuille – caramelised pastry leaves bursting with vanilla cream, lemon and rosemary syrup. A petty gripe: the servings are sparse for the price and the decor of dreary browns and dusty pinks might be cheery surroundings for depressive personalities, but for the rest of us it feels somewhat soulless.

Restaurant Petrossian

18 bd de La Tour-Maubourg, 7th (01.44.11.32.32/ www.petrossian.fr). M° Invalides or La Tour Maubourg. **Open** Tue-Sat 12.30-2.30pm, 7.30-10.30pm. Closed Aug. **Average** €115. **Prix fixe** €48-€150 (dinner only). **Lunch menu** €38. **Credit** AmEx, DC, MC, V. **Map** E6.

Petrossian is famous for its glossy, premium Russian caviar and smoked fish but the dove-grey dining room above the boutique dishes up much more exciting, contemporary fare. Pastry virtuoso Philippe Conticini, who inaugurated an elegantly upmarket savoury and sweet menu in 2001, has departed but his predilection for playing with tastes and textures is evident in the cooking of Sébastien Faré. Langoustines coated in coconut, lightly fried and served on a disc of tomato chutney burnished with parmesan, were paired with angelic chocolate buttons filled with a Curaçao 'vinaigrette', while a main of scallops came on a crusty biscuit of inky black rice adorned with jewel-coloured miniature spring vegetables. Desserts are just as stylish. Le kyscielli featured a curl of avocado and coconut mousse, a square of sweet fried pastry with apple confit, and dainty layers of fruit coulis and tea-flavoured jelly. The €48 prix fixe (the average price of a main), however, pales in comparison. A good address if you're feeling worldly and grown-up.

Chez Catherine

3 rue Berryer, 8th (01.40.76.01.40) M° Ternes or St-Philippe du Roule. **Open** Mon-Fri noon-2pm, 8-10.15pm. Closed one week in May, Aug, one week in Dec, public holidays. **Average** €60. **Lunch menu** €40. **Credit** AmEx, DC, MC, V. **Non-smoking room**. **Map** D3.

For anyone who loved this restaurant in its former location, it's a bittersweet pleasure to rediscover the cooking of Catherine Guerraz, one of the best female chefs in town, since her ambitions are so clearly upmarket that you're forced to cast a slightly different eye on her cooking. Furthermore, while Paris has plenty of expense-account restaurants, what it lacks is bistros with soul, and so every time another one closes, it's saddening. Guerraz's lovely husband continues to supervise service and the excellent wine list, while she turns out some very nice food such as langoustine-stuffed ravioli with chicory compote or a really delicious, earthy salad of girolles, escarole and sot l'y laisse (a tasty chicken morsel), both fine starters. Main courses run to an exceptionally good cod steak with finely chopped peppers and courgette in an aromatic jus, or veal medallion with winter vegetables in horseradish sauce. Cheeses come from swanky Alléosse, and desserts include a nice fruit crumble or chocolate tart. Ultimately, there's a value gap between the cooking and the prices, and the service needs drilling, but we'll be back to see how Guerraz settles into her new setting.

Le Chiberta

3 rue Arsène-Houssaye, 8th (01.53.53.42.00/ www.lechiberta.com). M° Charles de Gaulle-Etoile. **Open** Mon-Fri noon-2.30pm, 7.30-10.30pm; Sat 7.30-10.30pm. Closed Aug. **Average** €75. **Credit** Am Ex, DC, MC, V. **Wheelchair access. Map** C3.

Chiberta means business at lunchtime. But in the evening the suit troop is joined by designer-decked, smooth-skinned locals. It's modern, even elegant in a black-lacquer 1980s way, staff are judiciously polite and efficient and prices are frightfully Champs Elysées. The food, inventive but conservative, reflects the seasons: foie gras with wild mushrooms, truffles in Champagne, cauliflower cream with fresh sardines, a snowy fillet of lightly salted, steamed cod paired with caramelised endives with ginger and thyme and a sauce of glazed shallots. Desserts go the adult route. The délice du Chiberta is a glass brimming with layers of sharp coffee, marscarpone and dark chocolate. Or try the ultimate choc therapy: tea-flavoured chocolate ganache, intense cocoa sorbet, an Araguani chocolate soufflé and a feuillantine of dark chocolate topped with a morsel of gold leaf (a favourite asset in this crowd). And then there are the trimmings throughout: black olive cupcakes and crudités, a pot of chocolate, banana and coconut cream, and trays of artistic petits fours.

Flora ★

36 av George V, 8th (01.40.70.10.49). M° George V. **Open** Mon-Fri noon-2pm, 8-10.30pm; Sat 8-10.30pm. Closed two weeks in Aug. **Average** €40. **Credit** AmEx, MC, V. **Wheelchair access. Map** D4.

Engaging chef Flora Mikula, founder of Les Olivades and former second to Alain Passard at L'Arpège, runs this stylish new restaurant. With floral-upon-floral wallpaper, 1940s-style glass wall sconces, mirrors, wedgwood-style mouldings and a grown-up colour scheme of tobacco, dove-grey and ivory, this place is gunning to be a stylish hit. Mikula, a native of Avignon and one of the best Provençal chefs in Europe, has broadened her horizons to include an international version of the south that visits Morocco, Turkey, India and Vietnam. The hospitality is southern in the broadest and best sense of the word, too, since a meal immediately begins with delicious complimentary amuse-bouches and generously concludes with mignardises, including chocolate caramels, Turkish delight and miniature cannelés. Starters such as a croustillant de crabe (crispy cigar-shaped pastries filled with dressed crab) in tomato soup and lacquered prawns and aubergine were excellent, as was a main of lobster with broad beans and tiny girolle mushrooms in a jus of its own coral. Desserts are wonderful, including a macaroon in rose syrup with lime sorbet, and the wine list is fair and friendly.

Maison Blanche

15 av Montaigne, 8th (01.47.23.55.99/ www.maison-blanche.fr). M° Alma-Marceau. **Open** daily noon-2.30pm, 8pm-midnight. **Average** €100. **Lunch menu** €75. **Credit** AmEx, MC, V. **Map** D5.

The Pourcel twins, the talented duo behind the top-rated Jardin des Sens in Montepellier, have done a brilliant job of reviving this perenially trendy restaurant on top of the Théâtre des Champs-Elysées. The decor is slick and the menu is superb. It's the starters that star, with dishes as visually interesting as they are appetising: sea urchins stuffed with dressed crab and garnished with caviar; raw and cooked vegetables with beetroot caramel; tarte Tatin of shallots with grilled red mullet; and foamy chestnut soup. The best of the mains are sea bass baked with preserved lemons; pasta with tiny clams, broad beans, parmesan and pesto; and roast duck fillet with a 'pastilla' of carrots and apricots in a spiced sauce. Desserts are brilliant, too, including a preserved pink grapefruit with almonds and lemongrass sorbet, vanilla sauce, and grilled-almond toffee.

Market

15 av Matignon, 8th (01.56.43.40.90/ www.jeangeorges.com). M° Champs-Elysées-Clemenceau or Franklin D. Roosevelt. **Open** Mon-Thur, Sun noon-3pm, 6.30-10.30pm; Fri noon-3pm, 6.30-11.30pm; Sat noon-3pm, 6.30pm-12.30am. **Average** €80. **Lunch menu** €32, €39. **Credit** AmEx, DC, MC, V. **Map** E4.

Sporting a disco-glamorous decor by designer Christian Liaigre, globe-trotting chef Jean-Georges Vongerichten's restaurant has become fashionable in spite of steep prices and occasionally nerve-racking service. Vongerichten's talent for creating new culinary hybrids (cep, onion, walnut and garlic oil pizza; scallops marinated in citrus juice with roasted peppers; and duck breast with sesame seeds and a confit with tamarind sauce, for example). The latest idea is breakfast (Mon-Fri, 8-11am), and this is welcome, since just about the only place to meet someone for this meal in Paris beyond a café is in stuffy and/or over-priced hotel dining rooms. Here the pastries, including killer kouglof and apple turnovers, are done by star pâtissier Pierre Hermé, and the tea selection is excellent.

Shozan

11 rue de la Trémoille, 8th (01.47.23.37.32). M° Alma-Marceau. **Open** Mon-Fri noon-2:30pm, 7.30-10.15pm. Closed 1 May, 25 Dec, 1 Jan. **Average** €85. **Lunch menu** €26, €30. **Prix fixe** (dinner only) €60.50, €75.50. **Credit** AmEx, DC, MC, V. **Map** D4.

Owned by sake-maker Katsuyama, Shozan is a calm haven for sake enthusiasts with a taste for fusion cuisine. Our amuse-bouches appeared as four shot glasses arranged on a tray: a yellow calla lily, a serving of old sweet sake, a tasty carrot-coriander soup, and an original mussel mousse. These were whisked away as we finished our glasses of the wonderfully-fruity daigingo sake. Tuna, cured like prosciutto, came with tiny balls of melon and parmesan 'ice cream'. Even with 20 years' chopstick experience, though, the foie gras sushi defeated us – foie gras is simply too slippery, and this seemed a not-very-successful fusion. Next, there was shabu lamb, sim-

Market: Plate accompli. *See p125.*

mered quickly in salt, sake, and water – tender but a little bland without its sauce, a foie gras reduction. More impressive was the lacquered rare beef with slivers of tuna sashimi.

Montparnasse 25

Le Méridien Montparnasse Hôtel, 19 rue du Commandant René Mouchotte, 14th (01.44.36.44.25). M° Montparnasse-Bienvenüe. **Open** Mon-Fri 12.15-2.30pm, 7.30-10.30pm. **Average** €90. **Prix fixe** €100 (dinner only). **Lunch menu** €48. **Credit** AmEx, DC, MC, V. **Wheelchair access. Non-smoking room. Map** F9.

This excellent restaurant with chef Christian Moine at the helm deserves better than being buried deep inside of the Méridien Montparnasse, a chain hotel with a wilting quantity of salmon walls and fabrics. The restaurant itself isn't unattractive, though, with artful lighting, a mostly black decor and an art deco theme. First courses of foie gras interleaved with dried fruit and drizzled with gooseberry coulis, and sea bass carpaccio with celery remoulade, mini artichoke hearts stuffed with brousse (a fresh Provençal cheese), and rocket salad with tomato oil showed off a chef with culinary nerve. Sole, perfectly deboned, gently swabbed with a paste of pistou sauce and breadcrumbs, was sublime (although the accompanying side of minestrone was puzzling), and pigeon was exquisite, perfectly cooked and garnished with tiny peas in lomo-spiked cream. Desserts may well be lovely, but Moine's excellent cooking aside, the great lure here is the cheese course, orchestrated by maître fromager Gérard Poulard. He brought his groaning trolley tableside and, astutely assessing his audience, set to work with his knives, generously serving up exquisite lozenges of the cheeses that he so carefully culls from farmyards all over France.

Le 16 au 16

16 av Bugeaud, 16th (01.56.28.16.16). M° Victor Hugo. **Open** Tue-Sat noon-2.30pm, 7.30-10.30pm. **Average** €80. **Lunch menu** €35. **Credit** AmEx, DC, MC, V. **Wheelchair access. Map** B4.

Ghislaine Arabian's former restaurant, rather flashily decored in gold leaf and Venetian glass, has been adroitly reinvented and even improved by the team she left behind. A meal here gets off to a nice start with appetisers that show off the sassy creativity of chef Frédéric Simonin – nibbles included red pepper and anchovy canapés, quails' eggs with tapenade, and tempura mussels and roasted tomatoes with garlic mayonnaise. First courses of very lightly poached lobster on guacamole and ceps on toast were pleasant, and the precision, in terms of seasoning and cooking times, of a fillet of beef in a rich shallot and red wine reduction with ratte potatoes, and sea bass with white beans and thyme, was very impressive, too. Dessert provided the biggest thrill, though – sublime figs poached in wine with pine nuts, a thatch of caramelised sugar and rosemary ice cream, and the assiette 16 sur 16, a spectacular study in chocolate and caramel. There's a brilliant wine list with an amazing selection of foreign bottles, and a buzzy crowd.

L'Astrance ★

4 rue Beethoven, 16th (01.40.50.84.40). M° Passy. **Open** Mon-Fri 12.30-1.30pm, 8-9.30pm. Closed Aug. **Average** €75. **Prix fixe** €75, €95. **Lunch menu** €35. **Credit** AmEx, DC, MC, V. **Map** B6.

There is no other young chef working in Paris today who has the pure talent and gastronomic imagination of Pascal Barbot. Everything about this restaurant is delightful, including the exquisitely graceful, cordial and impeccably timed service. L'Astrance is the quintessential modern French restaurant, brilliantly leading the way to the future of Gallic gastronomy. We sampled a magnificent millefeuille made with slices of button mushroom sprinkled with verjus (the juice of unripe grapes) and caramelised foie gras – bliss, and a fine example of Barbot's spectacular balancing of flavours and textures. Next up was a fascinating dish of langoustines in a featherweight batter of egg and beer served with a colourful salad of mini cos, begonia and garlic flowers, pansy petals and a garnish of pleasantly astringent begonia juice surrounded by peppery nasturtium oil – sweet, sour and bitter. Little courgette flowers stuffed with diced feta cheese, courgette, and tomato and accompanied by a bowl of mozzarella cream, black olive purée and yellow courgette purée offered a sophisticated exploration of the nuances of bitter. A round of perfectly poached monkfish on a bed of finely diced green mango with rounds of fresh and toasted coconut was Paris via Kerala. Grilled lamb in a citrus sauce with fresh dates, a roasted new potato and a medley of tiny broad beans and peas was fantastic, and a pepper sorbet proceeded a dessert of gariguette strawberries on green tea mousse between two transparent rice galettes. The wine list is superb. With a month's lead time for a dinner reservation, book now.

La Terrasse du Parc

Le Parc-Sofitel Hôtel, 55-57 av Raymond-Poincaré, 16th (01.44.05.66.10). M° Trocadéro or Victor Hugo. **Open** daily noon-2.30pm, 3-6.30pm (light meals only), 7-10.30pm. Closed 1 Oct-17 May. **Average** €60. **Credit** AmEx, DC, V. **Wheelchair access. Map** B5.

Open only in summer, this terrace restaurant has one of the prettiest and quietest outdoor settings in Paris, occupying a courtyard lavishly planted with trees and flowers. It has a decidedly St-Tropez tint since it's been given a once-over by Patrick Jouin, Ducasse's favourite decorator – dusty rose canvas, cobalt-blue glasses, orange faïence and other touches create a modish holiday atmosphere. The menu, conceived by Alain Ducasse and chef Alain Soulard, is a stylish roster of good seasonal eating, too, including an inventive Caesar salad of steamed prawns, giant capers, parmesan and cos lettuce; white gazpacho (made with almonds and vegetables and topped with pesto and roast langoustines), tuna steak with green tea noodles, and almond milk ice cream with apricot sorbet. Wine prices are a bit stiff, but overall it's a fun place.

Regional

A Métro pass is all you'll need to graze your way from the rugged Breton coast to the flashy Côte d'Azur, from the Bordeaux vineyards to the Jura mountains.

Thanks to its geography and its history, France has a more spectacular variety of regional cuisines than any other country in Europe. Almost every part of the country has contributed a dish or product to the gastronomic battery, ranging from the obvious – quiche lorraine from Lorraine in eastern France – to the quirky, such as the fiery Espelette pepper that's so much in vogue with Paris chefs (it comes from the tiny village of Espelette in the foothills of the Pyrenees). And if Alsatian (don't miss **L'Alsaco**), Provençal (**La Bastide Odéon** is a great modern take on this) and south-western (try the refined **Au Trou Gascon**) lead the regional hit parade in Paris, Corsican cooking has been coming on strong, as seen at fine new tables such as **Le Cosi** in the Latin Quarter.

Alsace

Alsace's schizo-identity (it was alternately French and German four times between 1870 and 1945) is abundantly apparent in its cuisine: a German hardiness coupled with a French elegance. Local ingredients star alongside items introduced by Jewish immigrants – such as certain spices, foie gras and chocolate. Alsace's signature dish is choucroute (sauerkraut), spiced, salt-pickled cabbage traditionally topped with sausage, ham and pork. Both beer and local wine are poured into the culinary equation in dishes such as beer-braised ham hock, wine-soaked truite au riesling and the meaty (and potatoey) bäckaofa. The region is also renowned for its charcuterie, freshwater fish, munster cheese, and fragrant white wines such as riesling, silvaner and gewürztraminer. Brasseries (*see p90*) originated in Alsace so you can be sure of finding (Alsatian) things that make you go 'woof' there, too.

Chez Jenny

39 bd du Temple, 3rd (01.44.54.39.00/ www.chez-jenny.com). M° République. **Open** Mon-Thur, Sun noon-midnight; Fri, Sat noon-1am. Closed 15 June-18 Aug. **Average** €35. **Prix fixe** €17, €19, €24. **Credit** AmEx, DC, MC, V. **Non-smoking room. Map** L5.

Be prepared to queue, particularly at weekends, at this hugely popular brasserie run by the Frères Blanc. By the time we were seated, we had taken in the magnificent marquetry by Alsatian Charles Spindler, the festive atmosphere and the gargantuan platters of seafood and choucroute ferried deftly around the dining room by waitresses in regional dress. Our crab – a formidable beast with pincers to be reckoned with – was ordered as a starter but could easily have made a main course. Then came what has to be some of the best choucroute this side of Alsace – a steaming mound dotted with crunchy juniper berries and topped with pork knuckle. Skip dessert – the iced kougelhopf was rather bland and the profiteroles reminiscent of cardboard – and splash out on an excellent bottle of Alsatian wine such as the 1995 riesling Les Murailles from Dopff et Irion or the grand cru Altenberg from Lorentz.

L'Alsaco ★

10 rue Condorcet, 9th (01.45.26.44.31). M° Poissonnière. **Open** Mon, Sat, 8-10.30pm; Tue-Fri noon-2pm, 8-10.30pm. **Average** €30. **Prix fixe** (dinner only) €20, €30. **Credit** DC, MC, V. **Map** J2.

With its convivial atmosphere, pretty painted wood-panelled walls and wooden chairs with heart-shaped backs recreating the cosy winstubs that dot Alsace, this place serves as a sort of de facto showcase for one of the country's best regional cuisines. Let friendly owner Claude Steger chose a wine for you – he knows his cellar by heart, and will pick something that suits your taste and budget – then sample some presskopf (head cheese) or delicious Black Forest ham. Next, go with the best choucroute garnie in Paris. Generous portions mean you might want to consider ordering one with sausages and one with the full works (grilled pork knuckle, smoked pork, bacon and sausages) to share. Unlike the sad steam-table versions of these dishes served at some Parisian brasseries, the meats here are grilled and the pickled cabbage is crunchy and full of flavour. In the unlikely event that you can manage a dessert, finish up with a slice of fruit tart, which could be quetsches (plum), mirabelle (yellow plum) or wild blueberry depending on the season.

Auvergne & Limousin

France's mountainous central region is famous not only for its folklore but also its foodlore: hale and hearty cooking that's perfect when winter winds are howling. Cured hams and sausages, sturdy soups and stews feature along with prime Salers and Limousin beef and aligot (a creamy mix of mashed potatoes, garlic and tomme cheese served in long strands straight from the

If you like your salad with goose fat, head to **L'Ambassade d'Auvergne**.

pan). Auvergnat chefs have stacks of 'insider knowledge' – skilfully stuffing cabbage with pork, veal with sausage meat, and ravioli with local cantal cheese. Other local cheeses include bleu d'auvergne, st-nectaire and fourme d'ambert, which team well with St-Pourçain, a fruity red wine. As Auvergnats own many Paris cafés, regional produce often features on café menus as well as in bistros such as **Chez Savy** and **Au Bon-St-Pourçain** (*see p22,* **Bistros**).

L'Ambassade d'Auvergne ★

22 rue du Grenier St-Lazare, 3rd (01.42.72.31.22/ www.ambassade-auvergne.com). M° Rambuteau. **Open** daily noon-2pm, 7.30-10.30pm. Closed Sun 14 July to 15 Aug. **Average** €40. **Prix fixe** €27. **Credit** MC, V. **Non-smoking room**. **Map** K5.

This rustic auberge is a fitting embassy indeed for the hearty, filling fare of central France. Go easy on the complimentary pâté and thick-sliced country bread left on the table while you look at the menu; we guarantee that it is impossible to feel hungry on leaving. Our choice of cured ham came as two hefty, plate-filling slices which we shared, as we did our salad bowl chock full of green lentils cooked in goose fat, studded with bacon bits and shallots. The noise coming from the table next to us abated as the group of boisterous businessmen discarded their ties, rolled up their sleeves and got down to the serious business of what they approvingly declared to be 'real' food. Our 'rôti d'agneau' arrived as a pot of melting chunks of lamb in a rich meaty sauce with a generous helping of tender white beans. Luscious Salers beef in red wine sauce was juicily cooked, unlike on a previous visit when we had found it rather dry. These dishes came with the Ambassade's flagship aligot served with great pomp as the waiter lifted great strands of the creamy, softly elastic mash and cheese concoction into the air and let it plop onto the plates with a dramatic flourish. There is a comprehensive selection of the region's gluggable wines with intriguing names such as Chanturgue, Boudes, Madargues, from which the richly fruity AOC Marcillac made a worthy partner for a very successful meal.

Bath's

9 rue de la Trémoille, 8th (01.40.70.01.09/ www.baths.fr). M° Alma-Marceau. **Open** Mon-Fri noon-2.30pm, 7-10.30pm. Closed Aug. **Average** €70. **Prix fixe** €30, €70. **Credit** AmEx, MC, V. **Wheelchair access**. **Map** D4.

Jean-Yves Bath was a bright star of the Clermont-Ferrand restaurant scene and Auvergne is never far from his culinary thoughts, but this is a serious, sophisticated restaurant where country dishes are reinterpreted with a light, modern touch. The dining room, where abstract art meets country house hotel, is not the happiest piece of interior design, but the welcome is genuinely warm and the staff exceptionally helpful and courteous. The lentil soup with pan-fried morsels of foie gras and slices of pungent black truffle was the sort of heady broth that nobody's granny ever served, while the ravioli stuffed with cantal cheese in a meat reduction were as light and melting as Chinese dim sum. Main courses were equally inventive, with a crispy and gelatinous pig's trotter Tatin and a quality fillet of Salers beef accompanied by virtuoso 'chips' of breaded cheese. It is unlikely that you will come across finer puddings in the capital; biscotin à la vanille with wild strawberries and a dollop of basil ice cream was sublime (the biscotin being a hot puff pastry parcel oozing fragrant warm vanilla custard). We were equally enchanted with an Irish-coffee-flavoured pavé glacé accompanied by whisky jelly. With a bottle of unusual chardonnay from the Auvergne (€27), we found the hefty bill competitive for the standard of cooking, something that the local gourmet business crowd seems to appreciate.

Brittany

Brittany's best-known staple is the ubiquitous crêpe and its buckwheat cousin, the galette, which serve as both main course and dessert, usually washed down with cider. Coastal Brittany also produces an abundance of top fish and shellfish – look for anguille (conger eel), Cancale oysters, mussels and Breton lobster (*see also p139*, **Fish**). Also highly regarded are artichokes, sea salt crystals from the Guérande peninsula, pork products such as andouille (tripe sausage), and salt-marsh lamb from Belle-Ile and the Mont St-Michel.

Ty Coz

35 rue St-Georges, 9th (01.48.78.42.95). M° St-Georges. **Open** Tue-Sat noon-2pm, 7-10pm. Closed two weeks in Aug. **Average** €45. **Prix fixe** €26 (dinner only). **Credit** AmEx, DC, MC, V.

The beamed ceiling, dark carved wood trim, grandfather clock and nautical lamps with tinted glass seem out of place in a Haussmann-era building in this business district. But this is no cheesy fish and chips shop. The seafaring theme is classily executed and you feel transported to some Atlantic coast tavern. Proprietor Marie-Françoise Lachaud has a cheery, chatty manner and is happy to explain the finer points of the menu, whose hallmark is exceptional-quality seafood. We declined a tempting smoked salmon galette in favour of two salads: warm lentils, prawns and langoustines, and the house salade Ty Coz with prawns, langoustines and tender cured salmon slices. A plate of seared scallops with spinach, mushrooms and a deglazed shallot sauce could not have been more pleasing, but the slab of steamed cod – itself a fine piece of fish – was dragged down by a dull Dijon mustard dressing, mushy broccoli and dried-out rice (especially shocking given the €21.35 price tag). Dessert won us back: a big block of far Breton, a flan of eggs, cornflour and prunes in a portion huge enough for two.

Crêperie Bretonne Fleurie

67 rue de Charonne, 11th (01.43.55.62.29). M° Ledru-Rollin or Charonne. **Open** Mon-Fri noon-3pm, 7pm-midnight; Sat 7pm-midnight. **Average** €10. **Credit** MC, V. **Map** M7.

Was it a stick-on beard? No, everything about this restaurant is authentic, including the crêpe chef's pointy chin thatch, wiggly pipe and striped sailor shirt. It has been amazingly quiet on our two lunch visits, giving us plenty of space at the long, dark-wood benches with hinged lids to conceal hidden treasures. The menu is reassuringly straightforward: to fill your savoury, freshly cooked buckwheat galette, you can choose a ham/cheese/egg combination (all three is a complète), andouille (tripe sausage) or the more inventive camembert with walnuts. The complète comes beautifully presented in a perfect square, topped off with a gleaming egg yolk, while the camembert variation stops short of overpowering. Old-fashioned manners prevailed: the sashaying waitress served the ladies first while the gents politely contemplated the Celtic flags, Breton Tin-Tin book, black-and-white photos and puzzling tribal mask. Dessert crêpes were perhaps a little too crisp around the edges, but the oozy pear-and-chocolate and banana-and-chocolate fillings made up for it. Dry cider would have been the logical accompaniment, but we couldn't resist the Breton Breizh cola in its nifty glass bottle.

Burgundy

Burgundy's long history, wealth and world-famous wines have given rise to one of France's most refined and renowned regional cuisines. Even if many of the foods traditionally associated with the region, including snails (dubbed the oysters of Burgundy), frogs' legs and mustard, are now imported and locally prepared, there is some produce, such as tangy époisses cheese, that remains distinctly local. Much of the cooking originated as farm food: jambon persillé, chunks of ham in a parsleyed aspic jelly, and oeufs en meurette, poached eggs in a red wine sauce with onions, mushrooms and bacon, as well as classics such as coq au vin and boeuf bourguignon. Dijon is also famous for its pain d'épices, a spice bread from the Middle Ages, and kir, the apéritif of blackcurrant liqueur and dry aligoté wine.

Au Bourguignon du Marais

52 rue François-Miron, 4th (01.48.87.15.40). M° St-Paul. **Open** Mon-Fri noon-3pm, 8-10.15pm; Sat noon-3pm. Closed mid-July to mid-Aug. **Average** €35. **Credit** AmEx, DC, MC, V. **Map** K6.

With its big bow windows overlooking a pretty, busy street in the Marais, this bistro à vins has become a fixture in the area over the past eight years. Antique dealers, shopkeepers, politicians, architects, and other working locals give it a worldly if industrious buzz at noon, while in the evening the crowd includes more foreigners and serious bons vivants. If the owner has long been a staunch defender of Burgundian wines, we found the offer by-the-glass at a recent lunch to be very disappointing; it's not that our 2001 white Joblot Givry or our 1998 Hautes Côtes de Nuit weren't good – they were delicious – but if the mission here is to promote Burgundies, a larger choice would be welcome, including, perhaps, the occasional more affordable

Shell out for top-quality shellfish at **Ty Coz**.

Irancy or Petit Chablis. Daily specials of plump oysters and asparagus in an anchovy vinaigrette were first rate, if again a bit pricey, while tuna 'mignons' swam in a pool of oil and saucisson chasseur and sabodet, two of the best known Lyonnais sausages, weren't worth €18 by a long stretch. There were only two cheeses on offer – sad in a wine bar – and desserts were dull, so we concluded with coffee. With two glasses of wine apiece, the bill here teetered on the brink of €100, and even if the cooking was better than decent, this seemed rather exorbitant for a neighbourhood wine bar. So would we come back? Perhaps, but only for a glass of that delicious Hautes Côtes de Nuit and a single course, which would be the grilled steak with potato purée that all the regulars seemed to be relishing.

Tante Jeanne

116 bd Pereire, 17th (01.43.80.88.68). M° Pereire. **Open** Mon-Fri noon-2.30pm; 7-10.30pm. Closed Aug and bank holidays. **Prix fixe** €43 (dinner only). **Lunch menu** €36. **Credit** AmEx, DC, MC, V. **Wheelchair access**.

Following the suicide of great Burgundian chef Bernard Loiseau, we took our lunch places on the sunny veranda of one of his three Paris bistros with a little trepidation. How does a restaurant cope when its creator has ended it all? Well, the reply in this case is 'rather well'. The service was exactly the right mix of friendliness and deference you should expect from a restaurant with a doorman, and our fixed lunch menu was memorable. Our artichoke velouté with foie gras toast was a fine balance of duck liver richness and artichokal severity. Great, too, was the stuffed rabbit's leg main. One of the things you should hope to find in an expensive French restaurant is cooking that, almost miraculously, unlocks the taste of the ingredients. Here was cooking of that standard. Our best pudding looked, rather fetchingly, like a scale-model space station; it was a tremendously light creation in meringue, pistachio and cream. Let us hope Monsieur Loiseau is enjoying food as good as this in the place he is now.
Branches: Tante Marguerite, 5 rue de Bourgogne, 7th (01.45.51.79.42); Tante Louise, 41 rue Boissy-d'Anglas, 8th (01.42.65.06.85).

Corsica

As distinctive as the Corsicans themselves, the robust food of this rocky Mediterranean island features aromatic herbs, soft white brocciu cheese (the Corsican version of ricotta, made with goat's milk in summer and ewe's milk in winter), cured meats, chestnuts, kid, lamb and wild boar (in season). The cooking reflects the island's two habitats, wild mountain and rugged coast, with a limited number of fish and shellfish dishes. As a result of the Genoese rule, there are Italian-inspired preparations, such as aubergine gratin or brocciu and tomato salad. Chestnut flour (courtesy of the chestnut forests) is used as a substitute for wheat flour in an earthy-looking polenta. Wine growing dates back to Phoenician times, producing zesty reds, whites and rosés.

L'Alivi

27 rue du Roi-de-Sicile, 4th (01.48.87.90.20/ www.restaurant-alivi.com). M° St-Paul. **Open** daily noon-2pm, 7-11.30pm. **Average** €40-€45. **Prix fixe** €20 (dinner only). **Credit** MC, V. **Map** K6.

L'Alivi (which mean's the olive tree) is a rather elegant Marais restaurant with stone walls, large glass windows, tapestry tablecloths and the a capella voices of A Filetta gently chorusing in the background. They don't go in for the chunky, mountain-style servings you get in some Corsican places, but you will enjoy a very civilised meal with exceptionally courteous service. We started with a good fish soup and sardines marinated with chunks and fronds of fennel which were delicously cut through by our dry white Domaine Leccia 2001. A main of veal cooked with green olives could have been enhanced by more fresh herbs but the aubergine gratin was delectable, the aubergine finely puréed for very satisfying bread dipping. They don't make a point of it, but this and some other dishes on the menu are entirely vegetarian, making l'Alivi an excellent choice for mixed veggie/carnivore diners. But the best was yet to come – fine desserts of ganache de chocolat, a light mousse with chunks of dried fruit, and a piquant apricot mousse. We finished with an acqua vita di morta (myrtle eau de vie) from an interesting list of digestifs.

Vivario

6 rue Cochin, 5th (01.43.25.08.19). M° Maubert-Mutualité. **Open** Mon, Sat 7.30pm-midnight; Tue-Fri noon-2pm, 7.30pm-midnight. **Average** €22. **Credit** AmEx, MC, V. **Map** K7.

There is something of a clubby feel to Vivario, which might have to do with its dark wood interior and the fact that regulars know the menu by heart and order without even looking (or mispronouncing). Brocciu, the soft white Corsican cheese, features in several starters including the spinach and herb tourte, tomato salad and an excellent, fluffy omelette oozing with the stuff. For main courses, the roast cabri (kid) was good enough to have every morsel stripped from its bones and the plate of salt cod doused with garlic disappeared almost as fast. We downed our last drops of rosé with some Corsican cheeses including an earthy brebis (ewe's milk cheese).

Le Cosi ★

9 rue Cujas, 5th (01.43.29.20.20). M° Cluny-La Sorbonne or RER Luxembourg. **Open** noon-2.30pm, 7.30-11pm. Closed Aug. **Average** €45. **Lunch menu** €14.50. **Credit** MC, V. **Map** J8.

This place was Chez Pento, one of the great Left Bank student bistros, for almost 40 years, went briefly up market as Bistro Jef, and now, once again, has found a vocation that makes sense to the locals – serving up delicious Corsican cooking in generous portions at moderate prices. High-ceilinged with big picture windows, Pompeian red walls and posters of Corsica, it's a pleasant space in which to have a meal day or night. The lightness, precision and even elegance of what the kitchen sends out here come as a surprise. Try the soupe corse on a cold winter day – a deep dish brimming with smoky broth, white beans, nuggets of pork and veal and root vegetables which could easily provide a satisfying meal on its own, followed by a plate of Corsican cheeses. The gâteau of aubergine and brocciu is full of flavour and served with a nicely dressed salad garnished with toasted pine nuts. The friendly waitress recommended the cabri (goat) ribs cooked rare, and she was right – slightly pink, they had a luscious, gently gamey taste that complemented a honey and herb sauce. Veal cooked with herbs, tomatoes, and olives in a cast-iron casserole was excellent and copious too. Ask for recommendations if you want to sample a Corsican wine – the red from near Calvi that our waitress suggested was excellent.

Paris Main d'Or

133 rue du Fbg-St-Antoine, 11th (01.44.68.04.68). M° Ledru-Rollin. **Open** Mon-Sat noon-3pm, 8pm-midnight. Closed Sun, Mon in Aug. **Average** €30.. **Lunch menu** €11. **Credit** MC, V. **Map** M7.
The attraction of dinner at this popular restaurant not far from the Bastille owes as much to the waiters' good-humoured, non-stop banter as to the cooking itself (it's Corsican only in the evenings). Any Corsican restaurant worthy of the name will offer several variations on the theme of brocciu, which resembles Italy's ricotta. Inevitably, then, one of our starters was plump cannelloni which arrived oozing with the stuff and bathing in a rich tomato sauce. The other was a plate of charcuterie, crowded with sausages, ham and coppa. For mains, we chose cabri (kid) served in the pot and a little too well-cooked for our liking, and a much more successful dish of airy but filling storzapretti, dumplings made from yet more brocciu and sprinkled with the Corsican herb nepita, which tastes like a cross between mint and marjoram. As usual with the capital's Corsican establishments, attractive vintages listed on the wine list are not necessarily always available. We ended up downing sizeable quantities of Pietra, the island's flagship chestnut beer.

How to Eat **Fish soups**

Outside Marseille, bouillabaisse is never going to be the real thing. But, authenticity aside, how do you cope with the fiddly bits? At the famous bouillabaisse specialist Chez Fonfon in Marseille, the cooking stock is served first. You spread the rouille (spicy garlic mayonnaise) and aïoli (garlic mayonnaise) on the croutons and float these in the stock. The fish are served as a second course with more stock, which is constantly replenished to keep the dish hot. Soupe de poisson, a smooth, orange-coloured broth, is usually served with croutons, rouille and gruyère. Spread the croutons with rouille, top them with gruyère and float them in the soup.

Lyon

Lyon, the traditional gateway dividing north and south, earned its reputation as a gastronomic capital during the second half of the 19th century with the development of the bouchon, a small bistro that served simple home cooking at any time of day. While few genuine bouchons remain, Lyon's culinary emissaries in Paris continue to serve up the kind of hearty, homely fare common in Lyonnais homes. Go armed with an insatiable appetite: typical dishes include warm potato salad with sausage slices, tripe in various forms (andouillette à la lyonnaise or tablier de sapeur), gratin dauphinois (potatoes cooked with cream) and poulet de Bresse.

Aux Lyonnais ★

32 rue St-Marc, 2nd (01.42.96.65.04). M° Bourse or Richelieu-Drouot. **Open** Tue-Fri noon-2pm, 7.30-11pm; Sat 7.30-11pm. **Average** €45. **Prix fixe** €28. **Credit** AmEx, MC, V. **Map** H4.
With a delicious Majorelle interior and gorgeous belle époque tiles, it's a surprise that this place isn't listed. Bistro-lovers should be relieved that it's now owned by Alain Ducasse and Thierry de la Brosse of L'Ami Louis, two wealthy and passionate defenders of French culinary tradition. With the exception of adding a big antique zinc bar in the back dining room and rather more comfortable dark wood furniture, nothing has changed here except the food. The menu of intelligently modernised Lyonnais, Bressane and Beaujolais classics is enough to warm anyone's heart. After pleasant glasses of Bugey sparkling wine, served with cheese and sausage nibbles, first courses of charcuterie from Sibilla (the best charcutier in Lyon), and luscious suckling pig meat confit with foie gras were excellent. The quenelle (perch dumpling) with crayfish 'as in Nantua' was more of a flan than a real quenelle, but was quite tasty, as was a steak served with sautéed shallots and a side of cheesy, garlicky mash . A sublime st-marcellin and the sight of a Cointreau soufflé at our neighbours' table have us itching to return here as soon as possible, especially since service is so friendly (if rather slow) and the wines so good.

Moissonnier

28 rue des Fossés-St-Bernard, 5th (01.43.29.87.65). M° Cardinal Lemoine. **Open** Tue-Sat noon-2pm, 7.30-

10pm. Closed Aug. **Average** €40. **Lunch menu** €22.90 (Tue-Fri). **Credit** MC, V. **Map** K8.
Moissonnier, with its red leather banquettes and bright interior, has for many years stylishly upheld the cooking of Lyon. At lunchtime a mixture of informed tourists and seriously greedy academics from the Jussieu university campus were sitting down to enjoy a gastronomic experience that leaves any afternoon activity seriously compromised. Begin your exploration of this region's cooking with the saladiers lyonnais. Twelve bowls will be wheeled towards you, but put aside any idea that salads are a low-calorie option, for this feast includes not only mushrooms, lentils and celeriac, but also tripe, pied de porc and various sausages, not to mention some meaty, well-seasoned rillettes and winning soused herrings. By this time your appetite should be well and truly open for a tablier de sapeur, a rare dish that is to tripe what wiener schnitzel is to veal, only here served with a rich sauce gribiche; or you could try the puffy expanse of quenelles de brochet floating in a torrid pool of seafood sauce. Bypassing Lyon you could also enjoy a simple grilled fish or steak, accompanied by the richest of potato gratins, weeping cream and garlic. By now, even buoyed by a carafe of light Coteaux du Lyonnais, your body should reject the idea of a traditional but carefully prepared pudding in favour of a long walk in the nearby Jardin des Plantes. Alternatively you could diet tomorrow, as the charming patronne suggested.

Normandy

Dairy produce and apples are the hallmarks of Normandy fare. While the famed creamy sauces of the region are frequently flavoured with refreshing local cider or Calvados (a potent apple brandy), the cheeses, including cow's milk cheeses camembert, livarot, neufchâtel and pont l'évêque, stand firmly alone. Despite the fields of cows – the dairy godmothers – pork is the favoured meat, and fruits, particularly apples and pears, act as a pleasantly sharp foil to the richness. Seafood also features in moules marinières, marmite dieppoise (fish stew) and sole normande.

Les Fernandises

19 rue de la Fontaine-au-Roi, 11th (01.48.06.16.96). Mº République. **Open** Tue-Sat noon-2.30pm, 7.30-10.30pm. Closed two weeks in May, Aug. **Average** €30. **Prix fixe** €21 (dinner only). **Credit** MC, V. **Map** M4.
Perfect camemberts are rare, but at Fernand Asseline's convivial bistro the selection of Normandy's finest – oozing, unctuous and ripened in-house – is virtually unbeatable. A large wooden platter was generously left at our table and no one grumbled when we carved a healthy slice of each of the eight varieties. Those doused in Calvados and lie de vin (wine sediment) were superb, the 'noix' (walnut) satisfyingly earthy, and the 'nature' a must for the purist, but the best surprise was 'foin' (delicately coated in hay). Pre-cheese treats included poultry-laden starters – a warm lentil salad laced with strips of tender duck and chicken livers – a nicely crisped duck breast paired with gratin dauphinois, and a tasty roast pigeon. For dessert there are scrumptious cider crêpes and a tarte aux pommes flambée that's well worth ordering for the spectacle of the two-minute flame dance. The wine list is reasonably priced and there is a good selection of Calvados.

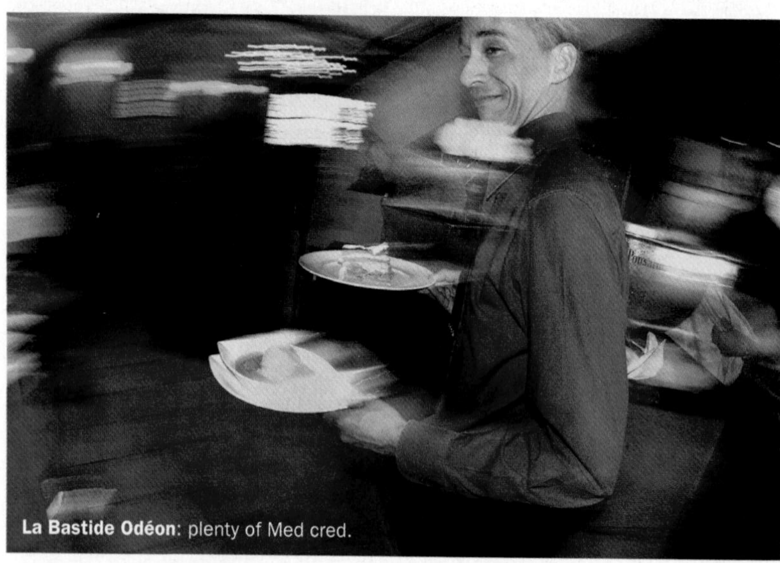
La Bastide Odéon: plenty of Med cred.

North

The hardy cooking of Picardy and Flanders is closely linked to that of neighbouring Belgium. Wine makes way for beer both at the table and in dishes such as carbonnade, a stew usually made with beef. The classic Belgian moules-frites (mussels with chips) pops up in northern French cities such as Lille along with another import, waterzooï, a stew of chicken or fish and vegetables. A favourite side dish is braised chicory, known as chicon. Also on offer are the pungent northern cheeses such as maroilles, deep-orange mimolette (known as 'hollande' in the north) and, for the truly brave, sharp and salty vieux lille. Sweets include spice breads and speculoos, crunchy spice biscuits served with coffee.

Graindorge

15 rue de l'Arc de Triomphe, 17th (01.47.54.00.28/ www.legraindorge.free.fr). M° Charles de Gaulle-Etoile. **Open** Mon-Fri noon-2pm, 7-11pm; Sat 7-11pm. Closed 1-25 Aug. **Average** €30. Prix fixe €32. **Lunch menu** €28. **Credit** AmEx, MC, V. **Wheelchair access. Map** C3.

The cooking of the north is probably one of the least known in France, yet chef Bernard Broux makes it well worth discovering in his comfortable, art deco-inspired restaurant. Broux is from Lille and he treats the area's Franco-Flemish ancestry with quality produce and a light touch. We started with a cep pâté, resembling an airy egg and mushroom mousse in a deep-green parsley emulsion, and a pink terrine of Challans duck around a lozenge of foie gras. Main courses took an elegant spin on Flemish classics. Our guinea fowl braised in Gueuze beer was served in two ways: an aumonière of shredded breast meat with pine kernels in a bundle of filo pastry and a roast leg with an appetising mound of fresh broad beans. The waterzooï de la mer, a bowl laden with prawns, two types of fish, julienned carrots, leeks and boiled potatoes in a soup-like pink sauce, was a marine version of the Flemish meal in a dish. Desserts include apple crumble, a chocolate fondant with speculoos, and café liégeois, as well as a selection of northern cheeses, while the drinks list includes beers as well as wine. Our fellow lunchtime diners consisted mainly of a chatty business crew, but this is the sort of place where they greet you with equanimity whether you are in a suit or not.

Provence & South

Mediterranean cuisine's rapid rise to fame has contributed to a variety of misconceptions about southern French cooking. While it's true that olive oil is almost always used in preference to butter, and that garlic, tomatoes, courgettes and aubergines appear in many recipes, the cuisine is varied and often more delicate than is popularly thought. Fish, vegetables and pasta figure in the cooking of the Riviera and Provence. Signature dishes include bouillabaisse (a once humble fishermen's soup, made from the lowliest part of the catch, which has become emblematic of Marseille), les petits farcis (baby vegetables stuffed with meat, vegetables and breadcrumbs) and aïoli, a garlic mayonnaise served with boiled cod and vegetables. From Montpellier to the Spanish border the Italian influence yields to Catalan dishes, reflecting the fact that Perpignan to the Pyrenees was once part of this Spanish province.

La Bastide Odéon ★

7 rue Corneille, 6th (01.43.26.03.65/www-bastide-odeon.com). M° Odéon. **Open** Tue-Sat 12.30-2pm, 7.30-10.30pm. Closed three weeks in Aug, 25 Dec-2 Jan. **Average** €38. **Credit** AmEx, MC, V. **Wheelchair access. Map** H7.

Owner-chef Gilles Azuelos' stylish and reliable modern cooking is not so much Provençal as a sort of contemporary evocation of all things southern, skimming along the Mediterranean seaboard from Spain to Italy using plentiful herbs that recall the perfumes of the maquis. It's a recipe that works, enticing senators, Parisians and tourists on a southern trip only metres from the Odéon and the Senate. We began with a refreshing gazpacho laced with ricotta cheese, and anchovy and avocado bruschetta. For the main courses there is plenty of fish and a pasta option that will keep non-meat eaters happy, but we went the meat route. Delicious lapin confit with new carrots and polenta was set off by tangy wild rocket and elegantly presented on a long, glass plate. Poulet fermier with baby potatoes in their skins was more traditional but full of flavour. Desserts are fruity and fashionable: a soup of strawberries and melon with sorbet and a lovely sablé biscuit with apricots and salt butter ice cream. Add very reasonable prices, friendly service, an attractive setting and relaxed atmosphere for an address worth hanging on to in this part of town.

Pataquès

40-42 bd de Bercy, 12th (01.43.07.37.75). M° Bercy. **Open** Mon-Sat noon-2.30pm, 7-11pm. **Prix fixe** €26. **Lunch menu** €12.80, €13.50. **Credit** AmEx, MC, V. **Map** N9.

With its sun-inspired yellow and orange walls, Pataquès does a good job imitating the breeziness of the south, abetted by its Provence-meets-Italy menu: aubergine parmigiana, salmon ravioli, pistou soup and salt cod lasagne. A starter of fresh sardines stuffed with raisins and caramelised onions, wrapped in pastry and deep-fried, served with green salad, was a good choice but the grilled langoustine tails were meagre, underdone, swamped by a pesto sauce and hidden beneath a hill of salad leaves. Not worth the price supplement. A swordfish main came crumbed and fried (and served again with green salad) and we couldn't help wonder why fry when grilling seems a more sympathetic end for this fleshy fish? No complaints about the rosy-pink honeyed duckling with beans, though. To finish off,

Hamming it up at **D'Chez Eux**.

patiences d'Aix (a biscuity house version of the almond-flavoured calissons d'Aix) served with creamy nougat ice cream and sweet raspberry sauce was summer on a plate.

La Table O & Co.

Oliviers & Co, 8 rue de Lévis, 17th (01.53.42.18.04/ www.oliviers-co.com). M° Villiers. **Open** Mon-Sat noon-2.30pm. **Average** €15. **Prix fixe** €15-€19. **Credit** AmEx, MC, V. **Wheelchair access**. **Map** E2.

This branch of the boutique chain devoted to olive oil and olive-oil-derived products is a pleasant place for a light, reasonably priced lunch. The menu changes daily and features dishes prepared with the various oils on sale here. Select two or three dishes from the five on offer, which are served in little terracotta dishes fitted into a wooden tray. We liked the brandade de morue with Greek olive oil, the stuffed aubergines with Croatian oil, the stuffed peppers with Tunisian oil and the cheese-filled ravioli sprinkled with lemon-spiked oil, all accompanied by socca, Niçois-style chickpea flour crêpes. Desserts – a blancmange with watermelon preserves, strawberry clafoutis, baked apple with olive jam and chocolate mousse – were inventive and tasty.

Pavillon Puebla

parc des Buttes-Chaumont, 19th (01.42.08.92.62). M° Buttes-Chaumont. **Open** Tue-Sat noon-2.30pm, 7.30-10.30pm. Closed three weeks in Aug. **Average** €50. **Prix fixe** €33-€65. **Credit** AmEx, MC, V. **Map** N2.

The setting of this restaurant in the park is perhaps more reminiscent of Surrey than the Mediterranean – an impression strengthened by a hedgehog shuffling around the periphery and a clientele in navy blazers and Hermès scarves – but it's not without charm. Seated far out on the terrace in near darkness, however, we were consistently ignored by the waiter; no apéritif or water was offered with our fine amuse-bouches, and things only got worse. From the three-course 'menu Catalan' we enjoyed the coco de gambas, a filo pastry rectangle topped with prawns, artichoke, peppers and tomatoes, and a main course of magret de canard in a sweet, tagine-like sauce with figs, turnip and carrots. The more refined menu du marché brought smoked salmon rolled round mixed salad greens, a pan-fried duck liver (undoubtedly the high point) with garlicky girolles and raisins, and half a pigeon, gamey but rather scrawny in its blood sauce with more girolles. The waiter had to be reminded about the cheese and produced a slice of cold fourme d'ambert. The Catalan dessert of bras de gitan, a Swiss roll filled with mousse, was enhanced by raisins soused in alcohol, and the strawberry sorbet with fruit would have been enjoyable, had we not been shivering after the interminable wait. There is clearly an extensive cellar lurking beneath the red brick house, but with a serious mark-up. The sole half-bottle, a 1998 Lalande de Pomerol, was rather disappointing for its €24.

Savoie & Franche-Comté

If Savoie is best known for its superb cheeses, including beaufort, reblochon, tomme de Savoie and the rare bleu de gex, there is much more to the region's menu than the fondue and raclette that have become its claim to culinary fame. Fishermen land crayfish and omble chevalier (the delicate, much-prized char lakefish). Crozettes, tiny squares of buckwheat pasta, are eaten buttered with – what else but? – grated cheese. Fine quality charcuterie includes viande des Grisons (air-dried beef) and smoked sausage. Gratin dauphinois and ravioles de Royans, tiny cheese-stuffed ravioli from the Vercors, denote the adjacent Dauphiné, while Mondeuse, a hearty red, is the best-known Savoyard wine. The Franche-Comté's rich pastures yield a variety of excellent cheeses. Smoked Morteau and Montbéliard sausages are served with warm potato salad, and excellent wines are produced around Arbois, including the sherry-like vin jaune.

Alexandre

24 rue de la Parcheminerie, 5th (01.43.26.49.66). M° St-Michel or Cluny-La Sorbonne. **Open** daily 6-11.30pm. **Average** €15. **Credit** MC, V. **Map** J7.

A tiny restaurant on a picturesque cobbled street, Alexandre has pared its menu down to three dishes: fondue bourguignonne, pierrade and fondue savoyarde. The first consists of 300 grams of sliced raw beef to be cooked on skewers in hot oil. The second adds mushrooms, peppers, tomatoes and onions to slices of beef, all to be barbecued on a hot stone slab sprinkled with rosemary. The third is the traditional cheese fondue. All three come with huge portions of golden-brown crispy roast potatoes, a salad of lettuce, cucumber, tomato and green pepper, and assorted sauces in plastic squirt bottles. Eating here is very convivial, as each table shares a single cooking pot or stone in the centre. This does of course mean that you have to agree on what to order. The walls of bare white stone are covered with large gallery posters in ornate frames, alongside kitsch gold stars and red sash curtains. Though this tiny restaurant only seats 28, big marble tables and comfortable red velvet banquettes mean you don't feel squashed in. No bookings are accepted.

Chez Maître Paul ★

12 rue Monsieur-le-Prince, 6th (01.43.54.74.59/ www.chezmaitrepaul.com). M° Odéon. **Open** daily 12.15-2.15pm, 7.15-10.30pm. Closed Sun, Mon in July and Aug. **Average** €40. **Prix fixe** €28, €32. **Credit** AmEx, DC, MC, V. **Map** H7.

The sweet maître d'hôtel of Chez Maître Paul creates a feeling of well-being, as do waiters whose attention to detail includes kindly removing the charred bits from your mountain of cassoulet. Though the walnut, comté and lettuce salad was ample, better ways to start were the warm dandelion and bacon salad, fried Jura sausage with potatoes, or a salmon and potato plate with a scrumptious corn galette (sadly, only one). A table of Americans could not resist taking matters into their own hands when it came to tackling the poulette fermière à la crème gratinée, a luscious hunk of chicken smothered in mushroom cheese sauce. Grilled scallops with minced cabbage and its tangy jus was a happy meeting of land and sea. For dessert, we took on on a poached pear with eggy sabayon, pineapple sorbet, regional macvin liqueur and toasted almonds.

How to Eat **Crevettes**

You've just sat down for a meal when a bowl of tiny grey shrimp, apparently more shell than flesh, lands on your table. Resist the urge to flee – crevettes grises, also known as crevettes des sables, are a northern French delicacy. The name comes from their colour once cooked – raw, they are pinkish brown. The good news is that there is no 'correct' way to tackle them, though you might look slightly ridiculous if you attempt to use cutlery. You can shell them entirely (a delicate operation); tear off the heads and chew up the rest; or simply follow the lead of crevette connoisseurs and pop the whole thing, head and all, into your mouth.

South-west

Combining Périgord (Dordogne), Bordeaux, Gascony and the Basque country, this part of France is known for its filling yet refined fare. Foie gras, the liver of fattened duck or goose, is a speciality of Gascony and the Dordogne. It is eaten in various guises; often very lightly cooked (mi-cuit) and served cold as a terrine (a 'pâté' is lower-quality, mixed with pork), or lightly pan-fried so that the inside still quivers. Duck also features heavily: magret is the breast, and confit de canard is duck preserved in its own fat. Another famed dish is cassoulet, a rib-sticking stew of white beans, duck or goose confit, lamb and sausage. Look out, too, for tasty lamb from the Pyrenees. Bordeaux's contributions, unsurprisingly, often contain wine: à la bordelaise implies a red wine sauce. Ceps and pricey truffles from the Périgord are also prized. Basque cuisine is often quite spicy thanks to the addition of Espelette peppers. Try pipérade (scrambled eggs with peppers, onions and ham), stuffed squid, tuna, delicate, raw-cured jambon de Bayonne, and the ewe's-milk iraty cheese of the Pyrenees.

D'Chez Eux

2 av de Lowendal, 7th (01.47.05.52.55/ www.chezeux.com). M° Ecole-Militaire. **Open** Mon-Sat noon-2.30pm, 7.30-10.30pm. Closed three weeks in Aug. **Average** €50. **Lunch menu** €30, €35. **Credit** AmEx, DC, MC, V. **Wheelchair access. Non-smoking room. Map** E7.

A warm welcome from the owner and long- serving staff are a prelude to a complimentary kir and a hunk of excellent saucisson. The cosseting, interlinked rooms feel comfortingly provincial and the menu is an essay in a certain type of traditional French cuisine. Begin with either the salad trolley, which includes plump fresh anchovies, delicious long-cooked pearl onions plus other delicacies, or the equally tempting range of charcuterie. Our mains included a guinea fowl grand-mère, served in a copper pan and carved at the table on its comfortable bed of potatoes, bacon and mushrooms. If the bird itself was slightly dry, the intensely flavoured jus compensated for this. An enormous slab of calf's liver was coated in a melting mixture of shallots and sharp vinegar. The meat itself was slightly less pink than ordered, the sort of imprecision which is the downside to this rustic, country approach to big eating, but warming to the experience we tucked into the dessert trolley with gusto: a winning chocolate mousse, creamy vanilla ice cream and an impressive collection of stewed fruits.

La Maison de la Lozère

4 rue Hautefeuille, 6th (01.43.54.26.64/ www.lozere-a-paris.com). M° St-Michel. **Open** Tue-Sat noon-2pm, 7.30-10pm. **Closed** first week in Jan, Easter, mid-Jul to mid Aug. **Average** €23. **Prix fixe** €21, €25. **Lunch menu** €15.50. **Credit** MC, V. **Map** J7.

Just behind the Fontaine St-Michel, this restaurant provides delicious cuisine in an area where it is increasingly difficult to find decent regional cooking. A lunch visit found the tiny, beamed room buzzing with a crowd of regulars. All the tables are laid with a welcoming quarter-loaf of country bread, ready for you to hack off a chunk to accompany your starters. These included a plate of good-quality regional charcuterie and tasty pâté caussenard flavoured with juniper berries; the homemade soup, from one of the set menus, also looked tempting. Our table's tripe man, something of an endangered species these days, was more than happy with two authentic tripoux parcels accompanied by oniony sautéed potatoes, while veal fillet with prunes was tender and homely. A chestnut Charlotte was the most interesting of the puddings, and with a bottle of excellent Domaine Hortus from the Languedoc and a house apéritif, the bill was a bargain. Added to which, the staff were attentive and welcoming. We'll be back on a chilly Thursday for their aligot (creamy potatoes, cheese and garlic) evening.

La Table d'Aude

8 rue de Vaugirard, 6th (01.43.26.36.36/ www.latabledaude.com). M° Odéon or RER Luxembourg. **Open** Mon noon-2pm, Tue-Fri noon-2pm; 7-9.30pm; Sat 7-9.30pm. Closed Aug. **Average** €30. **Prix fixe** €30 (dinner only). **Lunch menu** €20. **Credit** MC, V. **Map** H7.

This skinny and charmingly informal restaurant, set amid 17th-century beams, stone walls and tourist posters, serves food from the Aude region of the Languedoc-Roussillon, famed for its cassoulet and other dishes involving duck, goose, hen and their various internal organs. This cuisine is not for the faint of stomach: on La Table d'Aude's menu, quaintly translated into English, are such delicacies as 'neck surprise'. We found the €30 menu a good deal, as it lets you sample a traditional green salad with chèvre on toast, a standard cassoulet of beans, sausage and duck meat (a little mushy for our taste), spice bread topped with yoghurt and honey, and a pitcher of decent house red big enough for two. A la carte, we opted for the powerful purée of earth-toned rock fish soup, made from red mullet and served with rouille, and then the poule de l'Aric façon grand-mère, infused with olives and gamey undertones. Rosemary or thyme sorbet might be an adventurous way to end your meal. The host, Bernard Patou, is endlessly chatty and gracious, and he often makes the rounds towards coffee-time to pour smooth shots of marc, raising the temperature of your internal organs before your walk home. Wines and cassoulets are available to go.

Au Trou Gascon ★

40 rue Taine, 12th (01.43.44.34.26). M° Daumesnil. **Open** Mon-Fri noon-2pm, 7.30-10pm. Closed Aug, 25 Dec-5 Jan. **Average** €65. **Lunch menu** €36. **Credit** AmEx, DC, MC, V. **Wheelchair access**. **Map** P9.

This bastion of south-western cooking has become a rather elegant 'trou' with a sleek modern look and a serious crowd of locals, who can gaze up at the modern art with the nod of the would-be connoisseur. The food is a clever modern take on the heavier dishes of the region, and we began our €36 lunch menu with a cassolette d'escargots with artichokes, and a potato cake from the Landes. The snails were well-flavoured if a little short of distinct artichoke flavour, while the melting potatoes were enhanced by slivers of foie gras. Our main course was a moist and tender capon from the Chalosse region, presented as contemporary cylindrical constructions with sautéed potatoes forming the foundations. A la carte diners could choose a winningly crisp confit de canard or a traditional yet delicate cassoulet. We finished our meal with creamy discs of regional cheese and a russe, combining layers of soft meringue with pungent pistachio paste and served with smooth ice cream. The wine and digestif list is impressive; we asked for advice on the extensive list of earthy red Madirans and were guided towards a supple 1996 vintage (€38), which accompanied our meal admirably. The formal service was unhurried to the point of slow, but this may be an attempt to instil a leisurely Gascony lifestyle on the capital.

L'Auberge Etchegorry

41 rue de Croulebarbe, 13th (01.44.08.83.51). M° Place d'Italie or Les Gobelins. **Open** Tue-Sat noon-2.30pm, 7.30-10.30pm. Closed 11-25 Aug. **Average** €30. **Prix fixe** €24, €30, €36 (dinner only). **Credit** MC, V.

This area was once a rural Paris suburb, and the Auberge a watering hole for literary city slickers like Victor Hugo, Jean de Béranger and Chateaubriand, who'd come here to cut loose and sing a few songs. A century later, the tavern is dwarfed by apartment blocks. Still, owners Maïté and Henri Laborde (who also run the adjacent Le Vert Galant hotel) successfully create a Basque-countrified ambiance, from wreaths of garlic and piment d'Espelette (Basque red peppers) hanging from the beams to the three dark-red floral curtained dining rooms, plus a quiet outdoor street-side seating area. Look out for succulent confit de canard, tender roast duck breast (both with fantastic pan-fried potatoes and apples), beef fillet with morels, and foie gras, but also lesser-known fare such as the salade Etchegorry, a mixed plate of salmon, liver, bacon and melon, or pipérade, a scrambled egg, tomato, onion and smoked ham stew. Various chocolate desserts can end the night on a rich note, or try the flaky apple tart with Armagnac ice cream. The Cure and Black Sabbath tunes that impeded our conversation were just an unfortunate misstep in this otherwise enjoyable experience, perhaps due to the boss' absence that night.

Fish & Seafood

Granted, it's no water wonderland but that doesn't mean you can't coast along in Paris. That just-caught flavour is to dive for.

French Cuisine

Paris may be a brisk drive from the nearest littoral, but the wealth and sophistication of the French capital demand the very best of a catch of the day that extends in the most local terms to the North Sea, the Atlantic and the Mediterranean, as well as numerous lakes and rivers. Locals and visitors glory in the indulgence of shellfish platters at addresses such as **Garnier** (*see p90*, **Brasseries**) and **Le Bar à Huîtres**, and while a new minimalist idiom of fish cookery has evolved during the past decade or two, traditional addresses such as the **Le Divellec** and **Le Dôme** set the standard by which the others are judged.

L'Estaminet Gaya

17 rue Duphot, 1st (01.42.60.43.03). M° Madeleine or Concorde. **Open** Mon-Fri noon-2pm, 8-11pm. **Average** €50. **Prix fixe** €29. **Credit** AmEx, MC, V. **Map** G4.

With a handsome decor of vintage yellow, ivory and blue azuelos (hand-painted Portuguese tiles), this centrally located seafood house with notably cordial service is a fine bet if you're hankering after a quality maritime feed with an astute creative touch. A good indication of the intelligent modern approach here is the fact that seven different white wines are served by the glass and a large portion of bigorneaux (winkles) arrive as soon as you're seated. Good bread and delicious salted butter pleasantly framed superb first courses – a generous mound of prawns in chive-flecked vinaigrette on a bed of spaghetti squash and a creamy shellfish gratin (mussles, cockles, baby clams) with gnocchi. Main courses were similarly impressive. A thick tuna steak bounded in bacon came on a bed of freshly made ratatouille, while goujonnettes (grilled strips) of sole on rigatoni with oyster mushrooms turned out to be two perfectly deboned whole fillets rather than the usual dubious little fish fingers. A bowl of raspberries with a big dollop of crème fraîche, proved the perfect ending to a very good meal.

Iode ★

48 rue d'Argout, 2nd (01.42.36.46.45). M° Sentier. **Open** Mon-Fri noon-2.45pm, 8-11.30pm; Sat 6pm-11.30pm. Closed 10 days in Aug. **Lunch menu** €15. **Average** €35. **Credit** MC, V. **Map** J5.

We don't often describe a meal as flawless, but we found ourselves murmuring the word after eating at Iode, Steve Arcelin's smart little restaurant. Chefs Arnaud Cren and Christophe Ritzenthaler don't aim for over-complicated effects or fancy presentation, but their ingredients are perfectly matched and the cooking impeccably timed. We began with two exquisite appetisers: a rocket salad with shaved parmesan and lightly breaded and pan-fried langoustines, and an ample plate of marinated calamari with sweet onions and warm potatoes. Mains were no less spectacular: grilled sea bass fillet atop preserved lemon, courgette and aubergine, dressed with a verjus sauce (whose tangy flavour comes from unripe grapes), and a seared tuna steak with basil and parsley tempura. We dined during the height of fruit season, so opted for the cherry and mint soup (stupendous) and the fresh strawberries with basil sorbet (unusual and outstanding).

Le Bistrot Côté Mer

16 bd St-Germain, 5th (01.43.54.59.10/ www.michelrostang.com). M° Maubert-Mutualité. **Open** daily noon-2.30pm, 7.30-11pm. Closed 1 May, first week in Aug. **Average** €40. **Lunch menu** €17, €22. **Credit** AmEx, MC, V. **Map** K7.

Chef Michel Rostang's daughter, Caroline, runs this bistro with a contemporary Breton menu and oodles of crowd-winning charm (no doubt it's in her genes). On a recent visit, we crunched our way through the day's fry-up, a toothsome appetiser of tiny whitefish, prawns and squid, deep-fried so quickly that there was no greasiness, just delightful crispy seafood. The oysters are also a great way to start off your meal. An outstanding main course is the sea bass, served with olive tapenade, polenta and a delicate mushroom filo pastry. With our main course, we enjoyed the recommended Alsatian gewürztraminer at a reasonable €24 a bottle. To further explore wine and fish combinations, call to reserve for the monthly 'vigneron' evenings.

L'Huître et Demie

80 rue Mouffetard, 5th (01.43.37.98.21). M° Place Monge. **Open** daily noon-2pm, 7-11pm. **Average** €46. **Prix fixe** €17, €28. **Credit** AmEx, DC, MC, V. **Non-smoking room. Map** J8.

The €28 menu is no half-hearted effort here – it includes a choice of nine oysters, in keeping with the restaurant's name. One of us teased fresh oysters out of their shells, while the other tackled the seafood salad. It turned out to be a generous heaping of prawns arranged on greens, with an unusual and tasty kiwi sorbet. Just as satisfying were our main courses: scallops succulently roasted with garlic and olive oil, and salmon and monkfish cooked with lashings of butter and cream. We cooled our palates with iced nougat, homemade and fabulously sweet.

Falling for **Iode** hook, line and sinker. *See p139.*

La Méditérranée ★

2 pl de l'Odéon, 6th (01.43.26.02.30/ www.lamediterranee.com). M° Odéon. **Open** daily noon-2.30pm, 7.30-11pm. Closed 25 Dec, 1 Jan. **Average** €50. **Prix fixe** €25, €29. **Credit** AmEx, DC, MC, V. **Non-smoking room**. **Map** H7.

Opened in the 1940s by artist-loving Jean Subrenat, La Méditérranée has seen its share of glamour and art – Jackie Kennedy, Picasso and Cocteau (the dinner plates and menus sport his doodlings). Romantic murals by Vertès and Bérard decorate the walls, along with a Picasso and a Chagall or two, so you're dining in fine company. And the young team at the helm ensures that the food suits. From the prix fixe menu, a petit tian niçois de légumes (layers of aubergine caviar, caramelised onion, roasted courgette and tomatoes) accompanied by quenelles of black olive tapenade and a poached egg was simply delicious. Then came golden-crusted merlu (hake) with a crisp spinach salad and a caper and gherkin dressing. Gaspacho with a pod of red pepper sorbet, from the carte, was just so right on a sticky summer's day, and their bouillabaisse of red mullet, hake and cod with masses of cheese, croutons and rouille (spicy mayonnaise), a refined version of the famed fish soup of Marseille, is satisfying. So, too, the cooling nougat ice cream with mango sauce.

Le Divellec

107 rue de l'Université, 7th (01.45.51.91.96/www. le-divellec.com). M° Invalides. **Open** Mon-Fri noon-2pm, 7.30-9.30pm. Closed 25 Dec-1 Jan, 1 May, Aug. **Average** €110. **Lunch menu** €50, €65. **Credit** AmEx, DC, MC, V. **Non-smoking room**. **Map** E5.

Often in restaurants of this calibre, you get the proverbial fish eye when you opt for the cheapest prix fixe, but never once during our superb meal were we made to feel like poor relations. Delicious appetisers of tiny grey North Sea shrimp, fresh marinated sardine and accras (salt cod fritters) arrived immediately, and our very good, €30-plus Muscadet, one of the cheapest options, was expertly served. We were extremely impressed by the fish soup, served tableside and garnished with grated gruyère, garlicky croutons and a first-rate rouille, and a plate of Cancale oysters. Sautéed salmon on a bed of spinach in a lemony cream sauce spiked with herring roe was impeccably cooked, as was a thick cod steak in an excellent sauce of meat stock and red wine. Le Divellec also offers a superb dessert trolley, brimming with chocolate mousse, fresh raspberries and strawberries, fruit tarts, oeufs à la neige, poached blood oranges and other delicious choices.

Les Glénan

54 rue de Bourgogne, 7th (01.45.51.61.09/ http://lesglenan.free.fr). M° Varenne. **Open** Mon-Fri 12.30-2.30pm, 7.30-10.30pm. Closed Aug and 22nd-30th Dec. **Average** €55. **Prix fixe** €30-€80. **Lunch menu** €24. **Credit** AmEx, DC, MC, V. **Map** F6.

A shot-glass appetiser of watercress coulis, topped with tomato fondue, wisps of deep-fried carrot and tiny prawns, and starters of lentils dotted with prawns on a bed of lamb's lettuce gently drizzled with vinaigrette, and melting tuna carpaccio with squid ink, revealed an attention to produce and presentation finely honed by chef Emmanuel Jerz's stints at Lasserre, Guy Savoy and the Ritz. While a main of cockerel on a disc of fluffy couscous and the trio of pan-fried fish with tagliatelle drew praise, the zingy fresh fillet of daurade (sea bream) deserved a better prop than the almost-soggy mound of broccoli, beans and spinach. L'assiette Glénan – seven sweet treats – is the pick of the desserts.

T.M. Café

54 bd La Tour-Maubourg, 7th (01.47.05.89.86) M° La Tour-Maubourg. **Open** Tue-Sat noon-3pm, 7-11.30pm. **Average** €38. **Lunch menu** €22. **Credit** AmEx, DC, MC, V. **Non-smoking room**. **Map** E6.

In the place of the boldly and baldly expensive Paul Minchelli, this new seafood restaurant by everyone who previously worked for Minchelli is much more moderately priced. The new clientele, however, run to solidly wealthy, aristo-aspiring bourgeois penny-pinchers; not exactly the jolliest crowd around. Still, the charming Slavik decor of mustard walls and paintings with a maritime theme survives and the catch of the day is generally good-quality and well-cooked. Complimentary tapenade was served with apéritifs of overpriced Burgundian chardonnay, but a first course of thin squid rings lightly pan-fried and served with a thick homemade tartar sauce showed a kitchen on course. Scottish smoked salmon was generously served but rather fatty. A special of steamed sea bass at €29 was specifically des-cribed on the menu as line-caught (as opposed to farmed) and keenly promoted as such by the waiter, with the implication that the sea bass cooked with fennel, another possibility, was inferior. In any event, a sole meunière was excellent, as was the line-caught bass. This place has the potential to become a good restaurant if the farmed vs. wild question is resolved, the wine list improved, and staff lose a certain foppish gloss on the service.

Restaurant Cap Vernet

82 av Marceau, 8th (01.47.20.20.40/ www.guysavoy.com). M° Charles de Gaulle-Etoile. **Open** Mon-Fri noon-2.30pm, 7-11pm; Sat 7-11pm. Closed 1 July-31 Aug. **Average** €40. **Credit** AmEx, DC, MC, V. **Non-smoking room**. **Map** D4.

In the time since Guy Savoy took over this fish establishment, it has kept its excellent bank of shellfish and some of the animated informality while its cuisine has gained in assurance and aspirations. A speciality here is the assorted crus of oysters (available from approximately September to May), which can be ordered by six or nine, or as a tasting plate of 12 which gives you three each of oysters from Cancale, Prat Ar Coum (near Brest), Isigny and Marennes-Oléron for a briney tour of Brittany, Normandy and Charente-Maritime – just right with a crisp white Quincy wine. Although a couple of meat options are available, modern fish cooking dominates the rest of the carte. A thick slice of flaky cod had been marinated in soya sauce and honey, giving it a tangy sweetness that complemented a creamy celeriac mousseline. Other dishes hark south, such as tuna with ratatouille and sea bass with fennel. Desserts provide a sugar fix after the salt air: strawberries sautéed with Sichuan pepper served with fromage blanc ice cream; raspberries arranged on a shortbread sablé with pistachio ice cream and a sprinkling of hot roasted pistachios. Service has greatly improved, too.

Le Guilvinec

34 Cour St-Emilion, 12th (01.44.68.01.35). M° Cour St-Emilion. **Open** Mon-Fri noon-2.30pm, 7-10.30pm; Sat 7-10.30pm; Sun noon-2.30pm. **Average** €46. **Prix fixe** €25. **Credit** AmEx, DC, MC, V. **Wheelchair access. Non-smoking room. Map** P10.

The most gastronomically ambitious of the restaurants and cafés that now line the Cour St-Emilion has a name that pays tribute to the thriving Breton fishing port and a decor of vast barrel ends that speak old Bercy wine warehouse. But it's fish and seafood that are the name of the game. As the lunchtime market menu didn't inspire, we went for the carte and bravely opted for the hardcore Breton flavours of smoky andouille de Guémené (pig offal sausage) wrapping a terrine of red mullet and goat's cheese. Perhaps unsurprisingly, it was more curious than delicious, with any delicate fish flavour drowned out by pungent offal, though tempered by the creamy cheese. Home-marinated salmon was a safer if totally unadorned choice. For main courses, a big wedge of tuna came rather overpowered by a curry spice crust, while the steamed sandre on a bed of carrots, courgettes and salsify would have been prettily presented if only overheating had not soldered its dessicated red pepper coulis on to the scorching-hot plate. Perhaps the kitchen should revise its more complicated ideas, for the results – like the offhand service – are indifferent.

Le Bar à Huîtres

112 bd du Montparnasse, 14th (01.43.20.71.01/ www.lebarahuitres.fr). M° Vavin. **Open** Sun-Thur noon-midnight; Fri, Sat noon-1am. **Average** €42. **Prix fixe** €18-€34. **Credit** AmEx, DC, MC, V. **Non-smoking room. Map** G9.

Anyone after an oyster feast and some metropolitan bustle would be well advised to head for a branch of this little chain with its stylish Baroque shell-themed scheme by decorator Jacques Garcia. We made our way through a dozen superbly fresh and perfectly opened oysters and continued a first-rate meal with a tender, cooked-exactly-as-ordered tuna steak with green beans and roasted tomato and a similarly generous sauté of sliced encornets (squid) with garlic and olive oil, plus rice. Even dessert – a nicely made fruit crumble and good quality lemon sorbet – proved satisfying.

Branches: 33 bd Beaumarchais, 3rd (01.48.87.98.92); 33 rue St-Jacques, 5th (01.44.07.27.37).

Bistrot du Dôme

1 rue Delambre, 14th (01.43.35.32.00). M° Vavin. **Open** daily 12.15-2.30pm, 7.30-11pm. Closed Sun and Mon in Aug. **Average** €36. **Credit** AmEx, MC, V. **Non-smoking room. Map** G9.

The brasserie Le Dôme spun off two bistros a dozen years ago, one in Montparnasse and the other near the Bastille. This is the better of the two. The mood is serious but relaxed – staff, dressed in black and white, are thoroughly professional yet will even take

Sea the world

Calling all cockle cravers, oysters gulpers and lobster fanciers.

Plates (flat oysters, including the celebrated Belon from Brittany) and creuses (the common rough-shelled, cup-shaped oysters) are size-graded. Plates run from tiny no. 5 (about 25g of meat) to 0000, also known as pied de cheval or horse's hoof oysters, that contain about 75g of meat. Creuses follow a similar weight-based system beginning with petites (roughly 25g) and progressing to 'très grosses' (approximately 75g). Plates are rarer and prized for their distinctive taste – a hint of hazelnut. Among the creuses four other grades exist – huîtres de parc, fines de claires, claires and spéciales, which indicate the length of time the oysters have been allowed to fatten, and at what density of shellfish. (The idea being that lower numbers of oysters per 30cm allow them a richer diet of plankton).

The best langoustines (Dublin Bay prawns) land at market during the spring, ditto turbot and North Sea prawns. Lobster and freshwater delicacies such as écrevisses (crayfish) are summer arrivals while autumn is ideal for all things that swim and crawl in the briny, especially oysters and scallops.

Among the common shellfish delicacies worth sampling are amandes de mer (like clams, but smaller, firmer and nuttier tasting), bulots (whelks eaten with mayonnaise as an hors d'oeuvre), cigale de mer (rare, delicious and expensive, it's an odd-looking, square-nosed rock lobster with a fat, thick meaty tail), oursins (spiny sea urchins, which are sliced open and eaten raw), tellines and clovis (tiny baby clams), and violets (a powerfully briney barnacle-like crustacean from the Mediterranean). *Alexander Lobrano*

pity on budget diners by filling wines by the glass practically to the brim. Each fish was prepared conservatively but expertly, and infused with flavour. The grilled skewers of little squid were tender, while the rusty-coloured fish soup reminded us of other classic versions. Tiny soles meunières, drenched in flour and pan-fried in butter, and the monkfish in garlic cream were both respectably good. There's nothing innovative happening in the kitchen, but that doesn't mean you can't love it for its impeccable seafood standards and reasonable prices.
Branch: 2 rue de la Bastille, 4th (01.48.04.88.44).

La Cagouille

10-12 pl Constantin-Brancusi, 14th (01.43.22.09.01/ www.la-cagouille.fr). M° Gaîté. **Open** daily 12.30-2.30pm, 7.30-10.30pm. **Average** €45. **Prix fixe** €23, €38. **Credit** AmEx, MC, V. **Map** F9.

Even if you won't see the Med through the shrubbery around the terrace, this is a fine address for seafood lovers, since chef-owner Gérard Allemandou is one of the capital's great fish cooks, and it's one of the rare Paris fish houses to stay open all summer long. If griddle-cooked mussels are a classic starter, the small squid with onions, parsley and garlic was light and flavourful. Beyond delicious red mullet, main courses of eel stewed in red wine, tuna steak wrapped in bacon, and sole were all first-rate. The wine list offers some great summer drinking – try the delicious Morgon for a chilled red or the Guigal Côtes du Rhone for a white.

Le Dôme

108 bd Montparnasse, 14th (01.43.35.25.81). M° Vavin. **Open** daily noon-3pm, 7pm-12.30am. Closed Sun and Mon in Aug. **Average** €70. **Credit** AmEx, DC, MC, V. **Map** G9.

Le Dôme is all about squeaky fresh fish and seafood. Nothing edgy or experimental; in fact, the less fuss the better. A platter of briny oysters or clams served with cut lemons and lashings of rye bread, a cluster of tiny fried sole and tuna carpaccio are reliably good, unadorned starters while grilled langoustines, at €21.50 for just four tails, is palate-pleasing but pocket-punishing. Mains offer more sustenance: juicy John Dory, lightly pan-fried and balanced on a bed of roasted potatoes and tomatoes, and outstanding sole medallions topped with a slice of buttery foie gras, all washed down with crisp white Sancerre. Meaty monkfish cooked on the bone is a treat, too: neighbouring tables slathered juicy slices with béarnaise sauce, stopping only when the bones were bare. The Art Deco setting also shines.

L'Huîtrier

16 rue Saussier-Leroy, 17th (01.40.54.83.44). M° Ternes. **Open** Tue-Sun 7-11pm, noon-2.30pm, 7-11pm. Closed July, Aug; Sun in May, June and Sept. **Average** €45. **Credit** AmEx, DC, MC, V. **Map** C2.

An understated nautical theme graces this all-seafood restaurant. You manoeuvre through the cramped and skiff-thin dining room to your aluminium chairs that seem pinched from a 1920s luxury liner. The obvious choice here is the oysters from the Marennes-Oléron region, available in multiple combinations and types. But if you're not up for the raw ones, try the oversized oysters lightly baked in a shallot and cream sauce, voluptuous and positively naughty as they slither down. The prepared fish and crustacean dishes are also ocean-fresh, such as the platter of skinny, deep-fried smelt (winter only), which you eat in forkfuls like frites and dip into aïoli. Breaded and pan-fried squid or gambas fricassée in garlic and oil are also fine choices, though the selection changes continually.

La Table de Lucullus ★

129 rue Legendre, 17th (01.40.25.02.68). M° La Fourche or Guy Môquet. **Open** Tue-Fri 12.30-2pm, 8-11pm; Sat 8-11pm. Closed Aug, first week in May. **Average** €55. **Lunch menu** €20. **Credit** AmEx, DC, MC, V. **Wheelchair access. Non-smoking room. Map** F1.

One of the freshest and most inventive chefs in Paris today, self-taught Nicolas Vagnon brings a rare enthusiasm and inventiveness to French cuisine. Try an entire meal, for instance, themed around a particular fish. Eel, for example, is a Vagnon favourite. We chose what was a sort of anatomical and culinary tour of the sea bream: first a steaming cup of bouillon, then a very complex and fine dish of crusty bream belly. On our visit, Vagnon was excited about frying – an under-rated art, in his view. He advised us to eat the sea bream fins which were, as he promised, like crisps. The fried coriander with a touch of garlic was also extraordinary. After this elaborate beginning, our main was a lesson in simplicity: roast fish which might even have been considered ordinary had it not been for its bed of celeriac, carrot and lamb's lettuce and some sublime olive oil. In fact, the oil was so good that it appeared again for dessert in a creation that combined lemon peel, pear, almonds and curry. La Table de Lucullus isn't cheap, but it's nonetheless one of the best-value restaurants in Paris.

Taira

10 rue des Acacias, 17th (01.47.66.74.14). M° Argentine. **Open** Mon-Fri noon-2.15pm, 7.30-10pm; Sat 7.30-10pm. Closed 15-31 Aug. **Average** €50. **Prix fixe** €29, €32, €62. **Credit** AmEx, DC, MC, V. **Map** C3.

Taira Kurihara offers an intriguing Franco-Japanese take on seafood at this quiet dining room, just a five-minute walk from the Arc de Triomphe. If you opt for the €32 menu you'll enjoy one of the best bargains in Paris, since Kurihara works with exceptionally fresh fish and shellfish and seasons it gently and judiciously to enhance the natural tastes. Start off with his small squid sautéed in olive oil, basil and tomatoes, or maybe the salad of cod and green cabbage with a syrupy 'jam' of cabernet sauvignon, and then try main courses such as John Dory sautéed with Sichuan pepper and shitake mushrooms or salmon grilled with fleur de sel and spinach.

Budget

No *sous en poche*? Don't worry: you can still fill up on three courses and have change from €20 at a variety of bargain joints.

If Britons go to work on an egg (or used to) Paris is still a city that believes in a substantial three-course lunch to keep body and spirit going throughout the working day. Happily for the visitor, this means there is a proliferation of down-to-earth, hearty bistros serving good-value prix fixes at lunchtime and often in the evenings too. Starter, main course and dessert for €10-€12 is not a rarity, especially around the historically working class 11th and 12th arrondissements and studenty Latin Quarter. In the feature **Tourist trap dining** (*see p10*), we look at how to overcome the odds to eat cheaply and well in the most challenging quartiers. Don't expect many vegetarian options, although more places have been making an effort lately, particularly such health-conscious self-serve spots as **La Ferme Opéra** and **Cosi** (*see p150*, **Filling stations**).

In this chapter we have concentrated on restaurants where you can have an evening meal for €20 or less, but remember that many pricier bistros become accessible at lunch, when reservations are easier to come by (*see p22*, **Bistros**). Many cafés also serve decent food prepared with fresh ingredients (*see p220*, **Cafés**).

Ethnic food can be a bargain alternative. For affordable Chinese, Vietnamese and Thai food, head to Belleville or the 13th arrondissement (*see p181*, **Far East**). North African couscous restaurants (*see p210*) are another option, and there is a cluster of cheap Italian pizza and pasta joints around the Marché St-Germain (*see p197*).

1st Arrondissement

Flam's

62 rue des Lombards, 1st (01.42.21.10.30/ www.flams.fr). M° Châtelet. **Open** Mon-Fri noon-3pm, 7pm-midnight; Sat, Sun 12.30pm-midnight. **Average** €15. **Prix fixe** €11.90, €16.90. **Lunch menu** €7.90. **Credit** AmEx, MC, V. **Map** K6.

Restore your street cred with your kids by taking them to this teeming student haunt with its thumping Euro-pap soundtrack. Green wooden tables are lit by halogen lamps and yellow sponge-painted walls are covered with Bud posters and modern paintings. Downstairs is a huge cellar with high red-brick arches and long tables ideal for parties. This is also the perfect place for insatiable appetites as the 'à volonté' menu really is genuine: as many flammenküche as you can stomach with a starter or dessert for only €11.90. The flammenküche is an Alsatian cross between a thin pizza and a crispy pancake, with a pliable base covered in white cream cheese sauce and sprinkled with different combinations of onion, mushroom, bacon and grated cheese. Alternatively try the lighter vegetarian version: tomato, runner beans, cabbage and carrots drizzled with olive oil. They come on big wooden pallets; you fold them over and eat with your fingers, and wash them down with beer or Picon-bière, bitter-orange shandy. The starters and desserts are uninteresting – lazy salads and basic ice-creams – but the atmosphere is fun and you won't leave hungry.

Le Petit Flore

6 rue Croix des Petits Champs, 1st (01.42.60.25.53). M° Palais Royal. **Open** Mon-Sat 6am-8pm. Food served Mon-Sat noon-2.30pm. Closed Aug. **Prix fixe** €12. **Credit** DC, MC, V. **Wheelchair access. Map** H5.

Hiding its culinary pleasures behind an unobtrusive exterior, this little restaurant offers a slap-up French menu for a wondrous €12. The front café area sports plastic wicker chairs and small tables just waiting to be covered in crumbs, while at the back diners get the red banquette and thick linen treatment. A starter of herring fillet tasted good on first bite – fresh and firm – and then with the introduction of sliced, boiled potato and chopped onion and parsley got even better. A judicious amount of butter made this into a rather brilliant little dish, reminiscent of meals chez a talented grandma. Faded patterned crockery and meadowsweet napkins helped with the illusion. Swarthy charcoal tastes in the entrecôte made us think of smoked wildebeest (in a good way), but the exciting-sounding goose magret proved rather monotonous. Almost everything comes with chips, and that's no bad thing. Taking up an even half of each plate, they were the best thing a potato can ever become – fine, crisp golden sticks that remain firm in the middle. We assumed that pudding would excel in the same way, but a very sorry, tasteless crème caramel let us down. If the chips have done their duty, though, you shouldn't have much room left to complain.

2nd Arrondissement

The Kitchen

153 rue Montmartre, 2nd (01.42.33.33.97/ www.thekitchen.fr). M° Grands Boulevards or Bourse. **Open** Mon-Thur 9am-midnight; Fri 9am-1.30am; Sat 11.30am-1.30am; Sun noon-4pm.

Average €13 (lunch), €23 (dinner). **Lunch menu** €9.50, €10.50. **Credit** MC, V. **Non-smoking room** (lunch only). **Map** J4.
Recently opened by Irishman Bennet Holmes, The Kitchen is a refreshing and welcome addition to the area. It looks like a design-junkie's dream kitchen, straight out of *Wallpaper* magazine. The sleek tables, cool lighting and amazing floral displays set the lounging tone but it's the homemade cakes and quiches and delicious cooking smells that make this place somewhere special. The staff are laid-back and helpful if occasionally a bit vague and, taking the concept of a kitchen-supper to its logical conclusion, always offer seconds. Serious willpower was required to not indulge in thirds of the chunky terrine and organic bread starter. We were glad we resisted when the vast bowl of hearty vegetable soup arrived. Valiantly ploughing on we can say that the apple crumble was even better than Mum makes. The wine list is short but well-chosen with a decent Argentine red as tipple of the month and on-tap Guinness providing an interesting option for beer fans. Come with friends and grab one of the big kitchen tables for a fab brunch on weekends (€16.50): excellent tea, an impressive open sandwich full of top-quality ham and brie, followed by eggs, pancakes and lots of other goodies. The mi-casa-su-casa vibe works so well that it's an excellent place to come if eating alone is on the menu.

Mimosa ★

44 rue d'Argout, 2nd (01.40.28.15.75). M° Sentier. **Open** Mon-Fri noon-4pm (evenings for private parties by arrangement). **Lunch menu** €12, €14. **Credit** MC, V. **Map** J5.
Business is booming in this increasingly popular local canteen. The simple blackboard formula of daily-changing specials has cemented a solid crew of regulars, faithful to owner Thierry Soulat's good home cooking and the gentle warmth of his partner Xavier Trauet's welcome. Prices remain competitive: €12 for two courses and €14 for three. The proper daily specials (which are crossed off as they run out) included rump-steak with pepper sauce, grilled andouillette (tripe sausage), and black pudding with apples, with side dishes of leaf spinach, potato, tomato and olive gratin, mash, green beans and so on. These can be mixed and matched as desired. Good omelettes cost €8.50 with green salad and, in summer, there is a selection of salads. Save room for Thierry's desserts: chocolate mousse with orange flower water, vanilla cream (light and delicious) or castagnaccio, an airy Corsican cake made with chestnuts. Good-quality wines by the glass or carafe are supplied by nearby wine merchants Legrand filles et fils. Avoid the office hordes between noon-2pm and arrive later when things calm down.

3rd Arrondissement

Fontaines d'Elysabeth

1 rue Ste-Elisabeth, 3rd (01.42.74.36.41). M° Temple or Arts et Métiers. **Open** Mon-Fri noon-3pm, 8-11pm; Sat 8-11pm. Closed Aug. **Average** €20. **Prix fixe** €15. **Lunch menu** €12. **No credit cards. Map** L5.

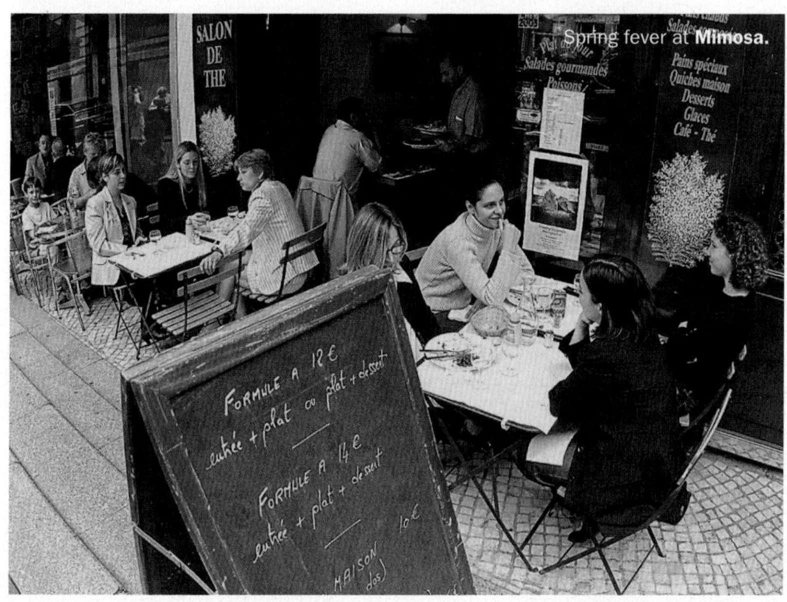

Spring fever at **Mimosa.**

La Canaille: a quirky Marais institution.

Once through the curtained door of this backstreet restaurant, you'll quickly forget the urban bustle of the surrounding area. In its place, a homely bric-a-brac decor and welcoming staff invite you to settle in and peruse the simple handwritten menus that are passed around. The kitchen specialises in French provincial favourites that warm stomachs and satisfy tastebuds. To start, Lyonnaise sausage served on a bed of waxy new potatoes was tender and well-spiced, while a blue cheese salad helped us work up an appetite for the mammoth mains that followed. A sturdy cassoulet was, as it should be, a delicious stew of sausages and meat in a creamy white bean sauce. More impressive still was the Provençal roast lamb – the tender meat enriched by the tomato, garlic and sweet peppers of the dish. Against all odds we even managed to squeeze in a slice of the home-made apple tart and ice cream. The owners were in no rush to clear us out once we had finished, so we lingered to enjoy the relaxed atmosphere.

4th Arrondissement

Café de la Poste

3 rue Castex, 4th (01.42.72.95.35). M° Bastille. **Open** Mon-Fri noon-2pm, 7-11.30pm; Sat 7-11.30pm. Closed Aug. **Average** €24. **Credit** MC, V. **Map** L7.

Keenly appreciative of the good things in life (especially chips) and looking for an authentic – but not stereotypical – good-value Parisian dining experience? This discreet and not noticeably massive café deserves your attention – it's in a different league from the tourist traps of the Bastille and rue de Rivoli. Just a word about the chips: orgasmic. We'd heard they rocked and so, emboldened by a quixotic set of paintings adorning the dining room walls, we requested a special pre-starter, a plate of house chips. Coming down from those, we had a robust chef's salad of cheese, ham (slightly uninspiring) and tomatoes and a mean rump steak in a winsome pepper sauce, which came with valiant (though not orgasmic) fried potato rounds. There are lots of trad plats du jour such as coq au vin, duck and roast salmon, all of which will confirm your faith in the superiority of standard French food. The fruit tarts for dessert will confirm your faith in a higher power; we chose a kiwi and a pear, both of which were delectable in terms of taste and texture. Saturday nights are especially good fun, with guest musicians including a Grapelli-style fiddler and his flamenco-guitarist sidekick – don't be surprised if your dining neighbours suddenly get up and sing.

La Canaille

4 rue Crillon, 4th (01.42.78.09.71). M° Quai de la Rapée or Sully Morland. **Open** Mon-Fri noon-2.30pm, 7.30pm-midnight; Sat 7.30-midnight. Closed three weeks in Aug. **Average** €25. **Prix fixe** €15, €18.50, €24 (dinner only). **Lunch menu** €11.50, €14. **Credit** MC, V. **Map** L7.

If you're shy about your French, the fact that the waiter gives you his pad and lets you write your own order is one of the several wacko aspects that enliven the dining at this refreshingly strange joint in a surprisingly drab part of the Marais. The noshing kicked off in fine style with a delicious feuilleté de légumes à la mozzarella in a cheeky parsley vinaigrette. The glistening pink côte de boeuf felt right on the tongue and was admirably partnered by a plate of cock-sure chips. Thai-style roast salmon was set atop a wonderfully crunchy peanut sauce that we'd happily have devoured by the bucket. Desserts of tiramisu and apple crumble were functional but not exciting enough to distract our attention from the mural of a lighthouse at the end of the dining room. 'Nice lighthouse,' we said to the leather-bereted waiter as he came to take our money. 'It's not a lighthouse', he said, 'it's the Colonne de Juillet'. Pinker than the beef, we dashed into the night.

Le Coupe Gorge

2 rue de la Coutellerie, 4th (01.48.04.79.24). M° Hôtel de Ville or Châtelet. **Open** daily noon-2pm, 7.30pm-midnight. Closed Aug. **Average** €20. **Prix fixe** €15 (dinner only). **Lunch menu** €10.50, €12.50. **Credit** MC, V. **Map** K6.

On a quiet street that runs from Hôtel de Ville to Châtelet, this convenient hideaway offers reasonably priced food in a central location. The red velvet curtains, original fireplaces and artwork almost compensate for the pong of vanilla-scented candles, and as you climb the stairs to the relaxed first-floor dining room you'll easily forget the hustle and bustle of the city outside. Our meal here began promisingly with a creamy and refreshing millefeuille of tomatoes and fromage frais, and baked tortellini covered in thick tomato sauce and satisfyingly gooey cheese. Mains were less exciting – magret de canard cooked with spices and honey wasn't as tender as it should have been; while perch in a buttery sauce with capers and green beans was fine if rather forgettable. Similarly average were the puddings which included lemon tart and crème brûlée. Once we'd added the cost of an unexceptional bottle of Bourgeuil (€15) to our bill, we didn't feel that we'd been ripped off, more that we hadn't quite got the bargain we had hoped for.

Galerie 88

88 quai de l'Hôtel de Ville, 4th (01.42.72.17.58). M° Pont Marie or Hôtel de Ville. **Open** daily 11.30am-1am. **Average** €16. **No credit cards**. **Map** K6.

It's a distinctly soothing experience to move from the noisy and polluted speedway bordering the Seine into this most laid-back of restaurants. With its eclectic North African decor, low-lit relaxed ambience and simple, reasonably priced dishes, it has unsurprisingly become something of a Right Bank student colony. Food is light and uncomplicated, ranging from salads, plates of fish or assorted tapas to more warming concoctions of soups or pasta. Though it's touted as a vegetarian establishment, there is an unfortunate tendency for meat to crop up unannounced – the attractive assiette italienne was served not only with artichokes, sundried tomatoes and marinated peppers, but also with slices of salami. The chick pea and cumin soup was a little lacklustre – lacking in flavour generally and seasoning in particular – the smoked salmon plate a more heartening mixture of generous slices atop a green salad. The crowd (or the fumes) seemed to have overwhelmed the absent-minded but endearingly comic waitress who brought us a plate of salmon rather than mixed vegetables and a very different combination of drinks to what we had ordered. Confusion also cropped up in the bill – but as ever favouring the establishment, not the diner.

Le Temps des Cerises

31 rue de la Cerisaie, 4th (01.42.72.08.63). M° Sully Morland or Bastille. **Open** Mon-Fri 7.30am-8pm. Food served 11.30am-2.30pm. Closed Aug. **Average** €18.50. **Lunch menu** €12.50. **No credit cards. Map** L7.

If we were Bastille locals, this would be a favourite. Not for the good-value three-course lunch menu (consisting of salads, egg with mayonnaise, saucisson, chicken and chips, marinated fish, roasts, crème caramel and fruit tarts, of which nothing is spectacular), but rather for the cosy pleasure of a lunching-out experience on a human scale. A warm greeting is dispatched by the flamboyantly moustached Mr Vimard, who is at the bar serving up Stella Artois on tap or loading cups in the dishwasher while Madame might be chatting with the regulars or helping the waitress clear off the tables. At the peak of the lunch hour, service reaches Olympic speeds. Neighbourhood regulars, old and young, complete the well-worn flea market ambience along with motley posters, browning photographs and original paintings and cartoons. Seating is tight; we were in a booth sharing a common breadbasket and water carafe with two fellow diners. The bar, open until 8pm, is ideal for a convivial pre-dinner beer and plate of cheese or charcuterie.

Le Trumilou

84 quai de l'Hôtel de Ville, 4th (01.42.77.63.98). M° Pont Marie or Hôtel de Ville. **Open** daily noon-3pm, 7-11pm. Closed two weeks in July or Aug, 25 Dec. **Average** €25. **Prix fixe** €13.50, €16.50. **Credit** MC, V. **Wheelchair access. Map** K6.

Ducking into this oddly named bistro from the windswept quai behind the Hôtel de Ville, we were greeted by the expansive owner Alain Charven, Champagne glass in one hand, Gauloise in the other – a slightly louche image that captured the atmosphere here. The food is dependable and copious, and by sticking to the traditional and eschewing adventurous dishes, you'll be treated to well-executed French classics such as magret de canard, hearty stews, and generous steaks. From the starters, the cucumber salad was fresh but uninspiring, while the tarte au boudin noir turned out to be a more uplifting combination of slow-cooked apple segments with small slices of black pudding. The pot-au-feu, served in a steaming metal casserole, was clearly designed to provide natural protection from Parisian winters. Desserts, however, were below-par, and the apple tart grand-mère was anything but grandmotherly. Not ideal for a tête-à-tête, with its cloud of smoke and alcohol fumes, punctuated by raucous laughter from the owner as well as diners, the Trumilou is nonetheless deservedly popular.

5th Arrondissement

Les Degrés de Notre-Dame

10 rue des Grands-Degrés, 5th (01.55.42.88.88). M° Maubert-Mutualité. **Open** Mon-Sat noon-10.30pm. **Average** €25. **Lunch menu** €11.50. **Prix fixe** €21, €23. **Credit** MC, V. **Map** J7.

We first stumbled on Les Degrés de Notre-Dame on a search for a lunch spot for a hungry family of eight. Tables were put together by our amiable host and we enjoyed a meal that suited everyone, from the fussy six-year-old (farm chicken served with delicious sautéed potatoes with mushrooms) to the adventurous 18-year-old (couscous with merguez, lamb kebab and all the trimmings). There are two things going on here: a North African menu of couscous and tagines (€12.50-€20) and traditional French bistro favourites. The €21 and €23 prix fixes are good value, including filet and faux-filet served with pepper sauce in a separate dish for those who don't like their meat swamped, and tender veal kidney. Desserts – often a let-down in budget joints – were excellent. Ask for the pâtisseries maison; we loved the cheesecake-like coconut gâteau which came in a delicate crème anglaise drizzled with chocolate. The owner clearly takes his wine cellar seriously, and there are many good medium-range offerings. The setting is old Left Bank, a beamed restaurant filled with paintings – many of the establishment itself done by guests staying in the hotel above – and there is a fun terrace in summer.

L'Ecurie

2 rue Laplace, 5th (01.46.33.68.49). M° Maubert-Mutualité. **Open** Mon, Wed-Sat noon-3pm, 7pm-midnight; Tue, Sun 7pm-midnight. **Average** €20. **Prix fixe** €15. **Lunch menu** €11.50. **No credit cards. Map** J8.

This might not be the most sophisticated Latin Quarter bistro, but the 'stable' nonetheless draws hordes of carnivorous diners, with a popular formula of grilled meat and chips washed down with copious amounts of drinkable wine. Minie, supposedly a descendant of the original 17th-century stable owner, runs a tight ship, cajoling waiters and hesitant customers while dispensing complimentary drinks and teasing her favourite regulars. We followed her recommendation and opted for the €15 prix fixe. A selection of cold starters covers farmhouse pâté and a variety of salads, including 'salade au bleu' which turned out to be lettuce scattered with an unidentifiable grated blue cheese. The main courses are all slabs of red meat, flame-grilled in the makeshift kitchen behind the bar and accompanied by thick chips. This is followed – if you eat like a

Quality remains stable at **L'Ecurie.**

horse – with one of the traditional desserts, including a good crème caramel. The food here may be basic, the horsey theme overdone and service rushed, but – aided perhaps by our complimentary apéritif and Calvados digestif – we emerged from the restaurant feeling both satisfied and replenished.

L'Escapade

10 rue de la Montagne-Ste-Geneviève, 5th (01.46.33.23.85). M° Maubert-Mutualité. **Open** daily noon-3pm, 6pm-12.30am. **Prix fixe** €7-€17. **Credit** DC, MC, V. **Wheelchair access**. **Map** J7.

Anyone who thinks they miss being a student should go to this restaurant. It recreates an authentic element of higher education – the awful food. Anyone who is still a student, however, will be laughing. The deal is €17 for an all-you-can-eat starter buffet, pick of the mains and puddings. And, more importantly, wine is included and on tap – you drink as much as you can handle. Sadly, the deadly caterer's fridge chill had bitten into the crudités, pasta salads and couscous salad on offer at the buffet, taking away most of the taste. The converted cellar dining room could have done with a radiator or two, as well. Clearly coping with the terrible hardship better than we were, our neighbours – a coachload of physics scholars – were going back for second, perhaps even third helpings and bucketloads of wine. By the main course they had broken cheerfully into rugby songs. Fried chicken and faux-filet both came with giant portions of chips, but the lacklustre tastes cut us off from the will to be greedy. Apple tart, presented with a dollop of spray cream, was the overall highlight.

Le Jardin des Pâtes

4 rue Lacépède, 5th (01.43.31.50.71). M° Jussieu. **Open** daily noon-2.30pm, 7-11pm. **Average** €15. **Prix fixe** €8, €12. **Credit** MC, V. **Non-smoking room**. **Map** K8.

This tiny 'pasta garden' tucked away near the Jardin des Plantes offers a very Parisian take on fresh pasta. We opted for a spot on the pavement terrace, and dived into starters of fresh crudités and a crispy, fresh green salad soaked in a Dijon mustard vinaigrette, which was let down somewhat by an insipid yoghurt accompaniment. Main courses focus on pasta made on the premises from organic flour. The generous portions pleased everyone, and we sampled the hearty dish of buckwheat pasta accompanied by strips of warm poultry livers and prunes, the marine-themed barley pasta with fresh salmon and seaweed, as well as the vegetarian dish of rye pasta with a tasty soya sauce of stir-fried vegetables and tofu. Drinks range from wine by the glass to organic juices and, for the caffeine sensitive, a grain-based organic coffee substitute. The liquid highlight, however, was a few shots of the excellent thyme-based Provençal digestif, Farigoule.

Branch: 33 bd Arago, 13th (01.45.35.93.67).

Perraudin

157 rue St-Jacques, 5th (01.46.33.15.75). M° Cluny-La Sorbonne/RER Luxembourg. **Open** Mon-Fri noon-2.30pm, 7.30-10pm. Closed Aug, first week in Nov. **Average** €20 (lunch), €27 (dinner). **Prix fixe** €26 (dinner only). **Lunch menu** €18. **Credit** DC, MC, V. **Map** J8.

Even though Perraudin doesn't work at the week-

Filling stations

The jambon-beurre is taking a back seat to more worldly combinations.

Finding a good sandwich in Paris used to be tricky – that is, if your tastebuds call for something slightly more exciting than ham and butter. Search no longer; a number of hip (and relatively inexpensive) sandwich joints which have sprung up around the capital are quietly revolutionising the Parisian lunch.

Your sandwich quest could take off at **Airport** (1 rue St-Marc, 2nd/ 01.42.36.70.40), a modern, low-key spot whose cool-looking menu offers more than 20 sandwiches with names like Paris-Tel Aviv and Paris-Boston. The Paris-New Delhi, a mix of diced turkey, Indian spices, mango chutney, and veggies, hit the spot. With a long bar downstairs and big tables upstairs, you can fly solo or with a group.

Bypass the bland sandwich stands that line the streets of St-Germain and dip into **Cosi** (54 rue de Seine, 6th/01.46.33.35.36) for a freshly made panini. Working with oven-fresh flatbread, Cosi dishes out opera-themed sandwiches (the salmo has salmon, ricotta and chives; the perfide albion stars roast beef, tomato, coriander and onion), or you can create your own when you order. There's a non-smoking room upstairs.

Just off the beautiful Place des Vosges, the small Italian epicerie **Frascati** (14 rue de Turenne, 4th/01.42.77.27.42) works with the freshest ingredients – parmesan, olive oil, smoked ham – to serve up delicious sandwiches and salads. Be patient as all the fixings are gently sliced and picked apart before reaching the chewy Italian bread.

A last essential spot on the Italian circuit is **Mille Pâtes** (5 rue des Petits-Champs, 1st/01.42.96.03.04), an old-fashioned deli near the Palais-Royal. Local office workers know to show up early for an olive-oil-doused sandwich layered with bresaola and parmesan or mozzarella and sun-dried tomatoes.

Ever tried Danish fast food? Glogg, Scandinavian mulled wine, lingonberry jam, and other Danish products line the walls of **Nils** (36 rue Montorgueil, 1st/ 01.55.34.39.49 and 10 rue de Buci, 6th/01.46.34.82.82), while tasty pre-assembled sandwiches (most of them made with smoked fish or seafood) are packed into the deli case. With names like frikis and smyghuk, Nils' sandwiches offer pleasant surprises – go at lunchtime for the best, and freshest, selection.

Grab a tray and fill it with items from **La Ferme Opéra**'s (55-57 rue St-Roch, 1st/01.46.33.35.36) ultra-clean self-service section of sandwiches, mixed salads, fresh fruit and vegetable drinks. La Ferme is also equipped with a range of produce from the Ile de France. The friendly staff will ring up your choices before sending you off to the comfortable, barn-like dining room.

With branches all over Europe and America, **Le Pain Quotidien** (18 rue des Archives, 4th/01.44.54.03.07 and several other branches in Paris) offers an above-average bakery section with all-natural breads and a country-themed restaurant. The sandwiches are good and freshly made – the beef carpaccio with fresh basil, parmesan and olive oil was light and tasty, and the chocolate dessert was excellent. The branch in the Marais has a small, but pleasant terrace.

Bert's (4 av du Président Wilson, 8th/01.46.22.20.20) is a hip, deli-style joint which offers pre-made sandwiches, salads and other eats. Order at the counter, grab your tray and head for one of the wooden tables in the spacious dining room. It has a great terrace which fills up quickly at lunch. *Nicholas Katzenbach.*

end, it still seems a little tired. Our fellow clientele was on the Jurassic side of venerable, and they matched the decor. But, of course, all that can be filed under 'quaint', and it's preferable to eating alongside yuppies. Ah yes, eating: the tuna wore its salad like a bad wig, but was succulent; the rabbit pâté was salty and looked as if it had been glued. Our main events were pork sausages and a steak. Both were fine, neither was sensational and they seemed satisfied to be giving the crockery a raison d'être. For dessert, the custard, estranged as it was from the chocolate cake, was comforting. The apple tart seemed under pressure and prompted the witticism, 'Sedimentary, my dear Watson' from our merry band. But don't be misled by our quippery: Perraudin does good basic French grub and you're guaranteed never to find groovers doing coke in the lavs.

6th Arrondissement

Le Petit Saint-Benoît

4 rue St-Benoît, 6th (01.42.60.27.92). M° St-Germain-des-Prés. **Open** Mon-Sat noon-2.30pm, 7-10.30pm. Closed Aug. **Average** €16. **No credit cards**. **Map** H6.

Like archaeologists, we examined the trim boards and wainscoting, whose layers of paint applied over the ages have obscured the original detail work. Other evidence, like the tiny tiled sink in the loo, a brazen refusal to take credit cards or reservations, and a bent coat hanger holding open the door on a balmy night, proves Le Petit Saint-Benoît's venerable presence in this quartier that has given in to fashion. Tables share baskets of bread; a handbell rings when the unadorned food is ready to be unceremonously plopped before you. You'll find all the old-school French favourites: hard-boiled egg and mayonnaise, rabbit terrine and plain vegetable soup for starters. A cod, onion and potato casserole was surprisingly moist, as was the roast chicken, which came with mashed potatoes and a fine gravy. Crème brûlée, fruit clafoutis, crumble and compote are among the classic desserts. If this bistro keeps serving its no-fuss, 'what do you expect?' budget fare in St-Germain, there is hope for civilisation.

Le Polidor

41 rue Monsieur-le-Prince, 6th (01.43.26.95.34). M° Odéon. **Open** Mon-Sat noon-2.30pm, 7pm-12.30am; Sun noon-2.30pm, 7-11.30pm. **Prix fixe** €18. **Lunch menu** €9. **No credit cards**. **Map** H7.

Polidor may have become a Left Bank institution, and its prices may be pretty reasonable for the quartier, but it's hardly the pinnacle of excellent bistro cooking that it may once have been. Blame the guide books if you want, or the very uneven kitchen that has little to strive for since lines of tourists and, yes, some loyal locals, stream through the door each night, regardless of product. Since we'd chilled considerably standing outside waiting for a table (don't even bother reserving, it's useless), we stuck with warming soups for starters. The crème de lentilles with a touch of foie gras was satisfying. Rich and potent, it put the humble little lentil in a whole new culinary category. A big bowl of orange-hued pumpkin soup was far less remarkable; chunks of the too-stringy squash almost ruined it. Mains were equally mixed. The guinea fowl with bacon and cabbage was prepared exactly as it should be; no culinary somersaults here, just chunks of meat falling off the bone to the warm embrace of a rich broth. A simple steak with shallot sauce was, on the contrary, swimming in grease and full of gristle. Order wisely and don't expect too much. The jovial and relaxed mood is still hard to beat.

7th Arrondissement

L'Auberge du Champ de Mars

18 rue de l'Exposition, 7th (01.45.51.78.08). M° Ecole-Militaire. **Open** Mon, Sat 6-11pm; Tue-Fri noon-3pm, 6-11pm. Closed Aug. **Prix fixe** €17. **Credit** MC,V. **Map** D6.

Menus highlighted in fluorescent pink warned that this was not going to be a sophisticated evening. The interior, complete with red velvet benches, artificial flowers and over-loud background pop, confirmed the view. At €17 for a fixed menu, however, this small venue a short hop from the Eiffel tower is a pretty good find in a neighbourhood not know for its largesse to tourists. The choice is also far wider than in many budget eateries, with several dishes to choose from in both starters and mains. We started with the crunchy green salad with pine nuts, set off by a light vinaigrette, and the snails in garlic butter. That was followed by an over-ambitious sole in Champagne sauce – a very salty sauce drowning a rather rubbery piece of fish – and the confit de canard, a far better choice as it turned out. Desserts encompassed most standards including an average chocolate gâteau and a serviceable crème brûlée. Service was perfunctory bordering on the bored but, for the price, we didn't feel too short-changed.

Chez Germaine

30 rue Pierre-Leroux, 7th (01.42.73.28.34). M° Duroc. **Open** Mon-Fri noon-2.30pm, 7-9.30pm; Sat noon-2.30pm. Closed Aug. **Average** €15. **Prix fixe** €12. **Lunch menu** €9. **No credit cards**. **Non-smoking**. **Map** F8.

Run with a firm hand by two dinner-lady types, this old-style parlour restaurant expects nice manners from its customers – including not lighting up (it's one of the few non-smoking restaurants in Paris). One man was told sternly not to play with his food, and we received a rueful stare for not finishing the main course. The only snag in this otherwise enjoyably nostalgic experience is the fact that the food is quite school canteen-ish as well. Everything does what the menu says it's going to – no more, no less. Crudités and céleri rémoulade suffered from this lack of imagination, as did mains of salmon fillet and fricassée de volaille – a hotchpotch of overcooked rice and meat chunks. A moist chocolate cake with homemade custard went some way to fill in the taste gaps. Still, our American neighbour was a faithful regular and claimed never to have had a bad meal here. We'd feel ungrateful if we said otherwise.

9th Arrondissement

Chartier

7 rue du Fbg-Montmartre, 9th (01.47.70.86.29). M° Grands Boulevards. **Open** daily 11.30am-3pm, 6pm-10pm. **Average** €18. **Prix fixe** €15-€18. **Credit** DC, MC, V. **Non-smoking room. Map** J4.

Chartier is the one remaining 19th-century workers' canteen in Paris that has kept not only its gorgeous mirrored interior but also its unfussy menu. 'Bouillons' like this used to feed workers all over Paris with restorative soup. But soup is no longer the main feature here. For €15 (€18 at weekends), you get three courses (avoid the sausage, which matches the pink tablecloth), accompanied by a perfectly serviceable half-bottle of wine. Businessmen chomping their way through lamb chops and frites, teenagers ordering one starter each and tourists looking stunned by the noise – there's a seat for everyone at Chartier, and the waiters are miraculously unbothered by the glittering pandemonium around them. Cross the room to admire the decor, which still has the old napkin drawers for regular customers (today used for storing extra menus). The entire menu is reassuringly inexpensive, and our €12.50 bottle of Cahors was perfect to accompany the hearty meat and potato dishes on offer. Highlights included rollmops (pickled herring), generous green salads and the whole roasted fennel which accompanied good pork. Save room for that most traditional of French desserts: puréed chestnuts with cream.

La Nouvelle Galatée ★

3 rue Victor Massé, 9th (01.48.78.55.60). M° Saint-Georges or Pigalle. **Open** Mon-Fri noon-midnight. **Prix fixe** €17. **Credit** MC, V. **Map** H2.

La Nouvelle Galatée's bargain traditional fare with a few subtle twists attracts a happy throng of locals and tourists. We were quick to join them, ravenously tucking into starters of chicken liver and Armagnac pâté, and smoked herrings with warm potatoes. To follow, salmon cooked with fennel was enjoyable without being spectacular. However, magret de canard in a mulberry sauce was excellent – the sweet fruitiness combined deliciously with the tender duck meat, while tart acidity kept the richness in check. When we'd finished, the friendly staff were happy to let us enjoy our wine and make room for dessert. And a good thing it was too: a mound of profiteroles came smothered in thick dark chocolate sauce, and crème brûlée spiced with cardamom was another nice surprise that almost had us licking the plate clean. On top of the good food, the room itself is worth a visit – the walls are lined with mirrors from a 1930s cruise ship – and the magnanimous patron Charles seems keen to be on first-name terms with every guest.

10th Arrondissement

Chez Papa

206 rue Lafayette, 10th (01.42.09.53.87). M° Louis-Blanc. **Open** daily 11.30am-1am. **Average** €25. **Lunch menu** €9.15. **Credit** AmEx, DC, MC, V. **Map** L2.

It's called salade Boyarde, it costs €6.40 and it's probably the best meal deal in Paris. A deep (really deep) earthenware bowl comes filled (really filled) with warm sautéed potatoes, chunks of crisp lettuce and tomatoes, crumbly cantal and tangy blue cheese, all topped with a generous slice of cured ham. For 80 cents more, and if your appetite is up to it, Papa will add two fried eggs to make it a Boyarde complète. Even more substantial versions of this hearty salad are on offer – laden with chicken livers, bacon, goat's cheese on toast, or a hunk of confit de canard – and the most it'll set you back is €11.20. By the look of the lively crowd at lunch and dinner, the Boyarde is a neighbourhood institution. Other bargains include the four-egg omelettes (all around €5) and the daily lunch special: the last time we went it was a thick tournedos with a coffee for €8; there's also a long list of by-the-glass wines from €1.70. For dessert, you'll find it hard to choose between the warm, caramelised croustade de pommes à l'Armagnac and the decadent hot chocolate and pear tart.

Branches: 29 rue de l'Arcade, 8th (01.42.65.43.68); 6 rue Gassendi, 14th (01.43.22.41.19); 101 rue de la Croix-Nivert, 15th (01.48.28.31.88).

Rôtisserie Ste-Marthe ★

4 rue Ste-Marthe, 10th (01.40.03.08.30). M° Belleville or Colonel Fabien. **Open** daily noon-2pm, 8-11.30pm. Closed two weeks in Aug. **Average** €12. **Prix fixe** €10 (dinner only). **Lunch menu** €8. **No credit cards. Map** M3.

This small, friendly restaurant offers a solution for anybody who has ever worried about the lack of greater social good achieved through wolfing down platefuls of food. Run as a community restaurant at lunch, the kitchen is available in the evenings to fund-raising charitable groups. Each evening the incumbent cooks offer a basic three-course menu, at strictly low prices. On the evening that we visited, two women toiled in the tiny kitchen to raise money for a Brazilian crèche. Their menu was made up of a flavoursome pumpkin soup, followed by a choice of either hachis Parmentier (similar to shepherd's pie) or a vegetable ragout that came with rice and homemade bread. By the time we had found room for dessert (baked apple or chocolate cake with crème anglaise) and washed it all down with a bottle of wine, our total bill came to just €13 per head. Of course the standard of food will depend on whoever has taken over the kitchen for the evening, but this restaurant's homespun do-good feel and its location in a buzzing neighbourhood of north-east Paris make it well worth a visit.

There's room for everyone at the 19th-century bouillon **Chartier**.

11th Arrondissement

Bar à Soupes

33 rue de Charonne, 11th (01.43.57.53.79/ www.lebarasoupes.com). M° Ledru-Rollin or Bastille. **Open** Mon-Sat noon-3pm, 6.30-11pm. Closed last week in July, all Aug. **Average** €9. **Lunch menu** €8.80. **Credit** AmEx, MC, V. **Non-smoking room. Map** M7.

Weary of those mugs of semi-reconstituted anthrax with kryptonite croutons that pass for soup? Get ye down to the sunshine-coloured Bar à Soupes, where you can swill around such pukka potions as cream of garlic, carrot with pineapple and ginger, or cream of sorrel (to name but three choices from a constantly changing selection), all served up by staff with relentlessly chirpy attitudes. The broths are made fresh each day ('with fresh ingredients and love' coos the PR) and have a heavily vegetarian slant, but there's always at least one meat option that's far from being a mere gesture towards carnivores. If you decide to eat in, you get supplies of several kinds of excellent bread and the €8.80 formule includes a plate of cheese, charcuterie or dessert plus a glass of wine or coffee. You can, of course, opt for take-away and quaff deep while making the most of window shopping and über-groover spotting opportunies of the neighbourhood.

Branch: 5 rue Hérold, 1st (01.45.08.49.84).

Le Petit Keller

13bis rue Keller, 11th (01.47.00.12.97). M° Ledru-Rollin or Voltaire. **Open** Tue-Sat noon-2.15pm, 7.30-11pm. **Prix fixe** €15 (dinner only). **Lunch menu** €10. **Credit** MC, V. **Map** M7.

Maybe a quantum physicist could help. The question baffled us: how can a comparatively small place that's comparatively full still seem so comparatively spacious? Maybe our rods and cones had been thrown out of chop by staring at the dazzling red-and-white-checked floor, or by the huge, round fish tank that sits on the counter and houses underwater mobile phones. Très wacky – unlike the food, which is dependably filling and thoughtfully prepared. After a shared starter of so-so crudités, things looked up. A meek chunk of salmon lurked under a delicate sorrel sauce that lifted the dish to unexpected heights – we were on the verge of asking for a couple of straws to hoover up the last drops – and moist lamb brochette sprinkled with dried herbs prompted eyes closed in bliss and whinnies of delight. Then again, the girl at the table next to us was getting stuck into a great wodge of lettuce, lettuce and only lettuce and she looked happy enough, too. For dessert we chose a rhubarb tart that should have carried an acidic fruit alert but, lordy, was the pastry spot-on. Call us bland, but we also finished with a lemon ice cream that looked anaemic but tasted like sunshine.

Le Temps au Temps ★

13 rue Paul Bert, 11th (01.43.79.63.40/ www.ifrance.com/restaurant75). M° Faidherbe-Chaligny. **Open** Mon-Sat 8-11pm. Closed Aug. **Prix fixe** €16.77. **Credit** MC, V. **Map** N7.

This pocket-sized bistro, decorated with clocks and watches all telling a different time, is packed with a local crowd even on a Monday night. It doesn't take long to get the joke – the owner lives in a time zone all his own. If he tells you there'll be a table in ten minutes it probably means an hour, but you'll be offered a kir on the house and can spend the time looking at the satirical send-ups of *Libération* covers. The four-course menu for €16.77 is pretty good value and offers an unchanging choice of five starters, main courses and desserts with a cheese course. The warm foie gras on toast with salsify is a winner, the complementary flavours enhanced by a drizzling of walnut oil; from the main courses the magret de canard with a robust Port sauce was excellent both times we tried it and is further enhanced by crispy sautéed potatoes. Fillets of sole with beurre blanc are the only choice for non meat-eaters but got the thumbs-up – the sauce did not swamp the delicate flavour of the fish. A duo of quality cheeses followed but the jury is still out on the desserts: we enjoyed the chaud-froid of morello cherries but the tarte Tatin crust was a wee bit soggy. Wines are reasonable. Just one word of warning: towards midnight when you might be asking for the bill the owner gets obsessed with his CD collection (Bowie, Lou Reed, Iggy Pop) so don't expect to catch the last Métro.

Au Vieux Chêne

7 rue du Dahomey, 11th (01.43.71.67.69). M° Faidherbe-Chaligny. **Open** Mon noon-3pm; Tue-Sat noon-3pm, 7-11pm. Closed 10 June-15 Aug. **Average** €20. **Prix fixe** €18.30 (dinner only). **Lunch menu** €10.70. **Credit** MC, V. **Map** N7.

A couple of notes before you penetrate: don't be put off by the drab street, the fact that the Vieux Chêne is opposite a medical laboratory, or the foliage you have to negotiate before you find the door. Once you're in, you'll find kitsch rustic decor and attentive service that make you feel as if you're at your auntie's. The lunchtime three-course menu is good value, but do be warned that the food is only average. Our starters set the tone: the warm goat's cheese on toast wasn't quite warm or, indeed, goaty enough, and the herring fillets were bland, not to say a little too chewy. Mains – roast quail and roast chicken – were generous, but both meats were over-cooked. They did, however, feature the most impressive aspect of lunch Au Vieux Chêne: excellent gravy. The tarte aux pommes and crêpe au sucre struck us a being more of a filler than a satisfying third act. But let's not forget the value-for-money factor and the pleasant atmosphere created by the young clientele – not one titter was heard when we knocked our bread all over the floor. And it's very handy if you've got a blood test to fit into your schedule.

La Zygotissoire

101 rue de Charonne, 11th (01.40.09.93.05). M° Charonne. **Open** Mon-Fri noon-2pm, 7.30-

10.30pm; Sat 7.30-11pm. Closed Aug. **Prix fixe** €20, €25 (dinner only). **Lunch menu** €13. **Credit** MC, V. **Map** N7.

This rather modest-looking bistro is far enough up rue de Charonne from the Bastille masses to have found a corner of calm. Either the gold- and orange-hued decor or the quiet evening of our visit itself seemed to have lulled the waiters into a low-stress mood. We found the food accomplished and innovative without being pretentious. Harvest colours and flavours were on display this September night: oranges and golds, deep red beetroot, honey sauces and stewed mushrooms. The single langoustine ravioli, more like an Asian dumpling, was pleasingly delicate, while within a puff-pastry feuilleté tender escargots bathed in a garlic cream. A rather chewier breast of duckling was tempered by its sweet spiced honey sauce, and whiting fillet in a langoustine coulis was faultless. We especially liked the dollops of potato and cheese gratin, curried apple, tangy beetroot and courgette-mushroom sauté that decorated each plate. If you can't decide on dessert, take the assiette de la Zigo, a sampler platter of fruity rice pudding, banana sorbet, white chocolate mousse, apple compote and chocolate fondant, or whatever other sweets the chef has on hand.

12th Arrondissement

Comme Cochons ★

135 rue de Charenton, 12th (01.43.42.43.36).
M° Reuilly-Diderot. **Open** Mon-Sat noon-2.30pm, 8-11pm. **Average** €30. **Lunch menu** €13. **Credit** DC, MC, V. **Map** N8.

Tucked away in a quiet neighbourhood, this light, airy bistro has found a happy combination of high quality and low prices. In particular, the prix fixe lunch – three courses and two glasses of house wine – makes the trek to this otherwise plain neighbourhood worthwhile. The vegetable tartare, while not terribly exciting, was fresh and well accompanied by a subtle vinaigrette. More impressive was the warm chicken liver mousse, nicely paired with raisins. Mains change frequently, but we particularly enjoyed the salt pork with lentils. The salmon fillet, served with mashed potatoes and steamed broccoli, was overpowered by a slightly resinous teriyaki sauce. The best of the desserts was the overwhelmingly rich fondant au chocolat; those with high cholesterol would be wise to familiarise themselves with the location of one of the area's many hospitals before ordering. The crème café was a more pedestrian affair, but a better choice for the diet-conscious. Though somewhat hurried during the lunch rush, the service is friendly and forgiving of even the most atrocious French.

L'Encrier

55 rue Traversière, 12th (01.44.68.08.16).
M° Ledru-Rollin or Gare de Lyon. **Open** Mon-Fri noon-2pm, 7.30-11pm; Sat 7.30-11pm. Closed Aug. **Prix fixe** €15 (dinner only), €16, €19. **Lunch menu** €11. **Credit** DC, MC, V. **Wheelchair access. Map** M8.

You know that thrilling frisson you get from ignoring the doctor's warning about your profiterole habit? You'll never get that anywhere as acutely as at L'Encrier. We think these 'roles, defiantly, elephantinely testicular and drenched in a lustful chocolate sauce, are among the best in Paris. Upon opening the front door, you can tell that this is an establishment of dash and verve: you find yourself immediately confronted by a heavy velvet curtain, so you're forced to make an entrance. Our advice is to stand there like you own the place until the staff come and take care of you. You'll sit at plain wooden tables, and because L'Encrier is like a snug bar, you might have to share with strangers. It's especially popular at lunchtime, so arrive on the early side and do be prepared to project that voice – or hire a megaphone – in order to hold a conversation. L'Encrier's popularity is, of course, on account of its food, which is so confident that it knows it doesn't have to be fancy. We started with a breezy seafood salad consisting of plenty of al dente fishy bits, and a plate of zingy sausage. The mains, a delinquent boeuf bourguignon that hadn't quite assimilated its wine and a winsome liver with beetroot and mash were fine enough, but they knew what they were – mere warm-ups for the profiteroles. L'Encrier gives it to you straight, it gets fresh on a first date and you emerge weak but fulfilled.

La Liberté

196 rue du Fbg St-Antoine, 12th (01.43.72.11.18).
M° Faidherbe-Chaligny. **Open** daily 9am-1am. Hot dishes served noon-4pm. **Average** €10. **Credit** AmEx, DC, MC, V. **Wheelchair access. Map** N7.

The grungiest of Bastille bars on the upper reaches of the Faubourg St-Antoine, La Liberté, or 'La Lib' as it is affectionately known, is the local haunt of a group of friends who hang out here until the early hours of the morning, swaying to music that depends on the barman's flight of fancy. What is surprising is that, casting all thoughts of punch-induced hangover aside, the tiny bar gets its act together to produce a bargain lunchtime plat du jour (€7.60). On a recent visit we tucked into some top-quality fresh pasta with calamari, and a robust chocolate cake with crème anglaise. There is always a choice of two or three dishes, including a fresh salad. Providing you are not allergic to bustle, and don't mind sharing your life over a rocky table, you will enjoy the homely atmosphere and cooking. To accompany your lunch the boss has found a fine house Morgon and excellent Petit Chablis, served by the manic Christian, whose off-the-wall humour will do wonders for your spoken French.

Le Pays de Vannes

34bis rue Wattignies, 12th (01.43.07.87.42).
M° Michel Bizot. **Open** Mon-Sat 6.30am-8pm; food served 11.45am-3pm. Closed Aug. **Average** €15. **Lunch menu** €9.50, €12.50. **Credit** MC, V. **Non-smoking room. Map** Q10.

Just the kind of neighbourhood restaurant you would like to find on your doorstep, Le Pays de

Vannes delivers much more than its café-like exterior promises. At lunch we found a jovial crowd of office workers tucking into hearty fare. The only tables left empty were a few inches from the loo doors, so we were entertained throughout with a constant stream of visitors. This did not seem to bother anyone else at the other two tables near us and everyone got on with recounting the latest gossip while downing fair quantities of the so-so house wine. The crab cocktail was just the thing for a light lunch and featured a shower of shredded real crab, not the usual surimi, on a bed of crisp, freshly torn lettuce. The snowy-white flesh of our main course, melt-in-the-mouth sole meunière, came, at our request, with chunky, golden chips instead of the usual boiled or steamed spuds. We finished off this Breton-inspired meal with homemade far breton, a flan chock-a-block with plump, moist prunes, light-years from the often-profferred, dried-up version.

13th Arrondissement

Chez Gladines

30 rue des Cinq-Diamants, 13th (01.45.80.70.10). M° Corvisart. **Open** Mon-Fri noon-2.30pm, 7pm-midnight; Sat, Sun noon-2.30pm, 7pm-1am. Closed Aug. **Average** €15. **Lunch menu** €10. **No credit cards**.

Chez Gladines is in the Butte-aux-Cailles – a series of villagey streets hidden among the huge housing blocks south of Place d'Italie. In this little oasis, you could almost pretend to be somewhere in the Pays Basque as you're warmly welcomed at Chez Gladines, with its regional food, drinks and flag on the wall. Most diners go for the giant salads served in earthenware bowls with a choice of ingredients such as fried potatoes, jambon de Bayonne and just about any duck part you can imagine. Desserts such as the gâteau basque are reasonably priced although we suspected the tarte du jour of being the tarte de la semaine. This is a no-frills experience, but completely enjoyable: bare brick walls, paper-towel napkins, peeling menus, communal seating, and chaotic service (it was so busy during our visit that our friendly if slightly intense waiter went the whole evening with both his shoelaces untied).

Le Temps des Cerises

18 rue de la Butte-aux-Cailles, 13th (01.45.89.69.48). M° Corvisart. **Open** Mon-Fri 11.45am-2pm, 7.30-11.30pm; Sat 7.30pm-midnight. Closed 24, 25, 31 Dec, 1 Jan. **Average** €25. **Prix fixe** €12.50, €22 (dinner only). **Lunch menu** €10. **Credit** AmEx, MC, V. **Non-smoking room**.

'For God's sake turn your mobiles off!' This delightful message pinned to the door was our first greeting. The second was a 'Salut, tu vas bien?' from a waiter dressed in full-length denim dungarees. Fashion and formality are resolutely absent from this workers' cooperative restaurant – and no matter how hurried you are, the waiters won't be. It's worth spending time over a meal here, however, settled at one of the long tables (a great leveller), in the charming, old-fashioned dining room. A starter of légumes tièdes was, well, a plate of warm vegetables, cut into no-nonsense wedges. Amid the spuds and carrots, swedes and sweet potatoes did their best to liven things up a bit. You'll soon realise that the food is not going to be dazzling. A carafe of the incredibly cheap and surprisingly drinkable house red is probably a wise move. A chunky meat salad and ho-hum salmon with the same veg as in the starter made us envy our neighbour's guarantee of satisfaction – he had simply ordered creamy cheese and a basket of bread. Pudding was our last hope – dashed somewhat by the plastic-tasting Charlotte au chocolat. Plenty of bonhomie, but not really bonne bouffe.

14th Arrondissement

Au Rendez-Vous des Camionneurs

34 rue des Plantes, 14th (01.45.42.20.94). M° Alésia. **Open** Mon-Fri noon-2.30pm, 7-9pm. Closed Aug. **Average** €15. **Prix fixe** €12.50. **No credit cards**.

Au Rendez-Vous des Camionneurs is the kind of locals' restaurant where everyone seems to know one another. In one of the prettier parts of this arrondissement, the small dining room is decorated with French football posters, while two rickety tables constitute the terrace. The €12.50 set menu is limited, but served efficiently and generously by Monique as Claude toils in the kitchen (popping his head out occasionally to crack a joke). The starters were forgettable – red cabbage drenched in vinaigrette and a plate of sliced tomatoes. Mains (from a choice of three) were tastier – of note, the tender pork sauté cooked in a hearty sauce. An endless supply of fresh homemade bread and a good, cheap carafe of Côtes du Rhône accompanied our lunch, which ended in a friendly conversation between tables.

15th Arrondissement

Café du Commerce

51 rue du Commerce, 15th (01.45.75.03.27/ www.lecafedecommerce.com). M° Emile Zola. **Open** daily noon-midnight. **Average** €25. **Prix fixe** €22 (dinner only). **Lunch menu** €18. **Children's menu** €7. **Credit** AmEx, DC, MC, V. **Wheelchair access**. **Non-smoking room**. **Map** C8.

If we say that the decor's more memorable than the food, we should explain that this three-level art deco former workman's cafe has a tree growing through the middle of it and balconies lined with flower boxes that burst with colour. Tradition rules here, and a recent change of ownership has made no dramatic difference; Monique, head waitress and auntie to the world, told us she had seen to that. Thus the pat of butter you get with your smoked salmon starter arrives still wearing its wrapper, and the pale yellow roquefort sauce that accompanies the grilled steak is still disappointingly restrained. And you still can't rave about the food as much as the glorious warmth of Monique and her colleagues makes you wish you could, because of little niggles like the empereur fillet being overcooked and the consituent parts of the poire belle Hélène never quite getting on well enough together to do their job and make you feel glad you abandoned your diet. That said, you'll never regret a visit, and the up-side of the preservation of the status quo is that the chips, the chubby slabs of golden-beige allure that they are, still hit peaks of Paris frite perfection.

Au Métro

18 bd Pasteur, 15th (01.47.34.21.24). M° Pasteur. **Open** Mon-Sat noon-3pm, 6pm-1am. Closed Aug. **Average** €15. **Prix fixe** €14, €21. **Credit** MC, V. **Map** E9.

This little bar/bistro proudly wears its south-west colours on its sleeve, from the hearty cassoulet to the wall-to-wall rugby photos. With a tile floor reminiscent of the changing room of a public swimming pool, red paper tablecloths and a no-frills decor (paintings of sheep, basically), Au Métro is about good value in very simple surroundings: bring your own atmosphere. After-work drinkers gather around the bar quaffing cheap beer and going over the last Stade de France match while a dozen tables accommodate diners – just us on this occasion. Our salads were large and fresh, the magret de canard was juicy and the accompanying roast potatoes were a garlicky delight. The frites that accompanied the roast chicken had been undercooked in an oil that we suspected needed changing, but the bird itself was tender and, like everything else, huge. Basic desserts such as apple tarts and chocolate mousse are kept in the same display fridge as the Basque pâtés but this did not seem to affect their taste, for better or worse. The heavy portions are in sharp contrast with the featherweight bill.

16th Arrondissement

Restaurant GR5 ★

19 rue Gustave Courbet, 16th (01.47.27.09.84). M° Trocadéro. **Open** Mon-Sat noon-3pm, 7-11pm. **Average** €17. **Prix fixe** €20 (dinner only). **Lunch menu** €13.60, €16. **Credit** AmEx, MC, V. **Map** B4.

Savoyard food is meant for mountain folk and hikers, fuel for yet another stretch of the Grande Randonnée (the GR5 is the long-distance footpath that winds through the Jura to the Alps). Rather incongruously tucked away among the chic boutiques of the 16th is this mock refuge, with Chamonix posters, cowbells and old wooden skis crowding the walls. We walked in without a reservation on a busy night; instead of turning us away (there were clearly no tables left), staff warmly offered us two glasses of Crépy – a light, regional white wine – before a table opened up. Rib-sticking cheese and potatoes are the key ingredients here. We decided to test our strength on the massive queyrassienne (€35 for two people), a three-cheese fondue (emmental, comté and beaufort) with bacon and onions – one of those rare meals you keep eating even though you know you're full. If you're not the sharing type, try the raclette valaisienne (all you can eat for €17.60) or one of the tartiflettes, a cheese, potato, and bacon concoction (choose between reblochon, vacherin or chèvre de chavignol) that will give you the energy, if you can get up from the table, to climb Mont Blanc.

Scale a mountain of cheese at the Savoyard **Restaurant GR5**.

17th Arrondissement

Au Bon Coin

52 rue Lemercier, 17th (01.42.29.89.80).
M° La Fourche. **Open** Mon-Wed noon-3.30pm; Thur-Fri noon-3.30pm, 7.30-11pm. Closed Aug. **Average** €15. **Credit** MC, V. **Map** F1.
When the people who run the Tête de Goinfre and Cave du Cochon restaurants up the street took over this run-down corner café, local aesthetes winced. Here, after all, was a perfect example of a now-rare breed of Parisian café, complete with vintage floor tiles and a formica bar – even the word 'téléphone' stencilled on to the window (a service that really packed in the punters back in 1965). But the Cochon people didn't fill the Bon Coin with little plastic pigs (as they have their other joints), they made it usable for the hordes of design students from across the street and other young locals, while the very cheap prices mean the old regulars still pop in for a beer (€1.80) or a glass of Sauvignon (€1). If you feel like indulging in something stiffer – whisky, vermouth or a shot of rum – in most Parisian cafés you'd be in for a financial kick to the solar plexus. Not here. The lunches (plus dinner as the weekend approaches) are simple and cheap, sometimes good (mussels with cream, sautéed veal and 'mousseline' mashed potatoes) and rarely less than OK. This is a lively place to come with friends for even a very late lunch, or if you want to eat, unselfconsciously, alone.

18th Arrondissement

Chez Toinette

20 rue Germain-Pilon, 18th (01.42.54.44.36).
M° Abbesses. **Open** Tue-Sat 8-11pm. Closed Aug. **Average** €25. **Credit** MC, V. **Map** H2.
It's not easy to eat well inexpensively in Montmartre, so this is a valuable address tucked away in a side street behind the buzzing cafés of the rue des Abbesses. Even if prices have jumped over the past year, making Chez Toinette less of a bargain than it was, there are still plenty of good-looking locals and soft-spoken Anglos in the red-walled, low-ceilinged, candlelit dining room. Things start nicely with a rustic basket of amuse-gueules: radishes, olives and crisps. We ate very well on our last visit, enjoying a tangy starter of white anchovies, raw garlic and peppers and another of sweet grilled st-marcellin cheese on a bed of good, healthy mesclun. The deep, winey sauce of the daube provençale, a beef stew often served here, was as toothsome as always, while our little-seen 'quasi' cut of veal, cooked until rosé, was superbly tender and accompanied, in the best French tradition, by a simple cream sauce. Our strawberry tart and crème brûlée were good, if predictable. Service, though carried out by a single waiter, was efficient, pleasant and informative, while the choice of wines is strong and well-priced. Look out for the excellent Cabardès, Côtes de Thongues and Côtes de Thau reds from the Languedoc-Roussillon.

Le Relais Gascon ★

6 rue des Abbesses, 18th (01.42.58.58.22). M° Abbesses or Pigalle. **Open** daily 10am-2am. Closed 24 Dec evening. **Average** €25. **No credit cards. Map** H2.

We left Pigalle's tourist sauciness and walked 200 metres up the hill to this haven of cheery southern hospitality. The decor is rustic, of the oak-beamed, tiled-floor kind, and the service is attentive and speedy. A starter of 12 snails in garlic butter was fine if nothing special, but people come here for the speciality main course – the salades géantes. Though no-one will deny they are géante (they come in bowls the size of footballs), the claim to 'salad' status is more tenuous, a salade fraîcheur resembling nothing more than a delicious upmarket fry-up. A thick layer of smoky bacon was covered with eggs, lashings of Parma ham, walnuts and sweet tomatoes and the whole thing was topped with a golden heap of thinly sliced garlicky fried potatoes – the few lettuce leaves an afterthought. A chunky bavette steak was beautifully tender and draped in a delicate blue cheese sauce. A reasonably nice crème brûlée is probably the best dessert choice.

La Renaissance

112 rue Championnet, 18th (01.46.06.01.76). M° Jules Joffrin or Porte de Clignancourt. **Open** Mon-Fri 9.30am-midnight; Sat noon-3.30pm. Food served noon-3.30pm, 7-10.30pm. **Average** €22. **Credit** MC, V.

La Renaissance is buried deep in a residential neighbourhood, so before making the trip we called to make sure it was open for lunch, only to be rudely hung up on by a hurried waiter. We began the journey grumpy, but were pleasantly surprised by the good bistro fare served with a twist and traditional atmosphere. With no prix fixe, we skipped the expensive, meal-like starters and went straight for the main – a steak au poivre in a tasty, if crème-fraîche-heavy, pepper sauce served with small, fresh fried potatoes instead of the standard frites. Our neighbours dipped into a nice-looking poulet rôti served on a full cutting board with vegetables and a steaming baked potato. Portions are generous, but with a 25cl carafe of Bordeaux our bill was already more than it should be, so we skipped the uninteresting desserts. When it came time to pay, the overworked waiter forgot our change and we left feeling unfulfilled – a well-priced set menu and more attentive service might make the trip worthwhile.

Le Rendez-Vous des Chauffeurs

11 rue des Portes Blanches, 18th (01.42.64.04.17). M° Marcadet-Poissonniers. **Open** Mon, Tue, Thur-Sun noon-2.30pm, 7.30pm-11pm. **Average** €20. **Prix fixe** €13 (until 8.30pm). **Credit** MC, V.

Little here has changed over the past 80-odd years, and once you take your seat at one of the long tables, you'll understand why no-one is complaining. The inexpensive three-course prix fixe gives you a fair selection of dishes and even includes a pitcher of

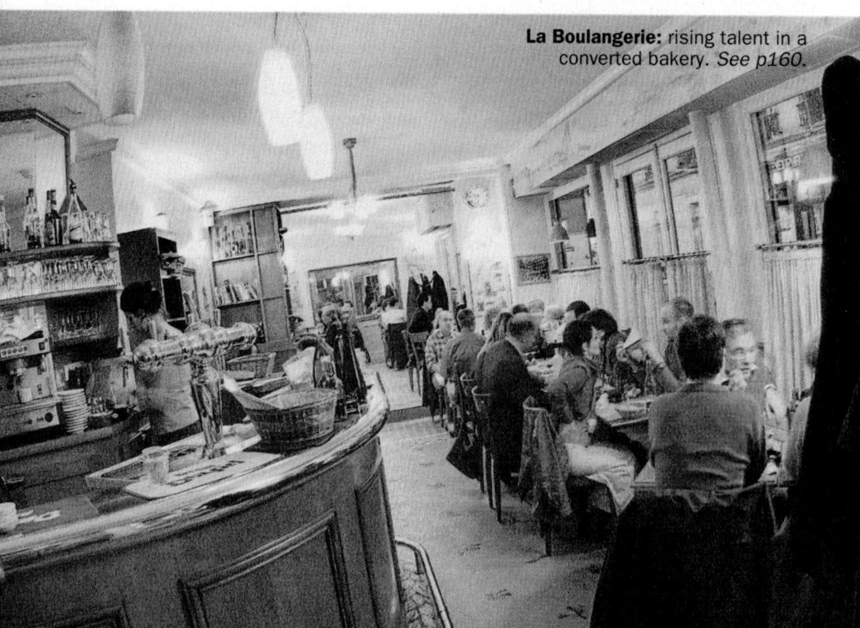

La Boulangerie: rising talent in a converted bakery. *See p160.*

house wine, which goes so well with the traditional fare that we ended up ordering a second. We started with a simple fisherman's salad, the mayonnaise of the potatoes a good foil for the firm white fish, along with a plate of saucisson sec. The waiter duly unhooked the sausage from its traditional hanging place behind the bar, and sliced it up before us. Try to order a main dish with frites, as they're made fresh with wide potato slices. If you're feeling particularly hungry, order one of the substantial à la carte dishes, such as the lamb. Be sure to accompany your meal with the well-priced bottle of the month (€15), which sits enticingly on every table.

Au Virage Lepic

61 rue Lepic, 18th (01.42.52.46.79). M° Abbesses or Blanche. **Open** Mon, Wed-Sun 7-11.30pm. Closed one week in Aug. **Prix fixe** €12, €18. **Credit** MC, V. **Map** H1.

A snug hideaway safely distanced from the tourist mayhem of Sacré Coeur, this restaurant is exactly what the neighbourhood's history demands. The walls are covered with music-hall posters and old film star stills and the red-checked tablecloths and traditional zinc bar provide the backdrop for a very satisfying two-course menu. We started with the feuilleté, a warm pastry filled with potatoes, cheese and bacon, and the onion soup, scalding hot with delicious slightly burned cheese. Though all the mains looked tasty, we went with the magret de canard – crisp, perfectly cooked and dressed with fried potatoes – and the equally good roast chicken. Desserts, riz au lait and parfait au chocolat, coupled with an inexpensive bill, sent us out the door smiling. Though the owner does his best to squeeze people in, showing up without a reservation will leave you stranded and envious.

20th Arrondissement

La Boulangerie

15 rue des Panoyaux, 20th (01.43.58.45.45/ www.restaulaboulangerie.com). M° Ménilmontant. **Open** Mon-Thur noon-2pm, 7.30-11pm; Fri noon-2pm, 7.30pm-midnight; Sat 7.30pm-midnight. No lunch in Aug. **Prix fixe** €15, €18. **Lunch menu** €10.50, €14. **Credit** MC, V. **Map** P4.

This neighbourhood bistro in a converted bakery feels immediately welcoming: waiters rush about but remain as pleasant as can be, and the happy crowd, aided by carafes of the house Chinon, creates a warm buzz. The quartier – part arty, part old-time immigrant Paris – is worth a visit too. We'd dined here before and had always been impressed by the quality and value, so our recent 50-50 experience somewhat surprised us. Our mushroom carpaccio with pesto and parmesan would have been more interesting cooked, though a starter of crab ravioli in lobster cream sauce was divine. A curried pollack steak didn't skimp on flavour, but the cut of braised duckling with spice-bread crumbs had obstacles of fat and bone to pick through to find the nevertheless succulent meat. Desserts were a huge success: an almond-apricot tart and chocolate cake with cinnamon and pistachio sauce. The menu changes every two months, so it's worth coming back to see what new twists on casual French food chef Laurent Lahaye has been brewing. Also a plus: they accept customers until midnight at weekends.

Chez Jean

38 rue Boyer, 20th (01.47.97.44.58). M° Gambetta or Ménilmontant. **Open** Mon-Sat 8-11pm. Closed Aug. **Average** €25. **Prix fixe** €15. **Credit** MC, V. **Map** P4.

This restaurant, with red-and-white checked tablecloths and mismatched crockery, offers a taste of time-warp Paris. The whiteboard brought to your table doesn't list a vast choice and the prix fixe allows no variants, but the menu is renewed every couple of months. Jean is happy to practice his English and draw pictures on the paper table covers to explain dishes, and larger-than-life Patricia can be almost overbearingly friendly. All bottled wines cost €13.50; Jean recommended the rare, prize-winning 1999 Côt. The sardine starter proved how delicious this humble fish can be – the extremely fresh fillets were marinated in oil with dill and served with salad. Vegetable soup, served with great bread, was also reminiscent of really good home cooking. Mains are rather basic, and expensive if you stray from the set menu. The faux-filet with shallots served with potato purée was a bit tough, but sauté de porc à la créole was better, cooked in tomato sauce and served with tasty brown lentils. Desserts rivalled the starters, particularly the firm chocolate mousse à la Patricia. There's live guitar music on Fridays and Saturdays, starting at 9pm. Book ahead.

Ma Pomme

107 rue de Ménilmontant, 20th (01.40.33.10.40). M° Ménilmontant or Gambetta. **Open** Mon-Fri and first Sat of the month 11am-2am; Sat 7.30pm-2am; food served noon-3pm, 7.30-11.30pm. Closed Aug. **Average** €26. **Prix fixe** €21. **Lunch menu** €10, €13. **Credit** MC, V. **Map** P4.

It's hard to see why this restaurant camouflages itself behind half-open blinds – except if you think a good thing should be kept secret. Possibly one of the best-value feeds you'll find along the Ménilmontant drag, it is also a bit of a looker inside. Yellow lamps give cheerful lighting, while pale wooden tables, plump red chairs and wooden floorboards add cosmo touches. The locals looked chuffed to be there, and well they might: the glutton-friendly three-course menu chalked on a giant blackboard is a bargain at €21. A starter of oeufs farcis aux cèpes – elegant scrambled egg – was modestly tasty if a little rubbery. Ostrich carpaccio was much better, coarse and full of flavour, enhanced by a delicious bottle of St-Pourçain. All that seemed irrelevant, however, with the arrival of the chef's special of spiced magret de canard, which tasted even better than it looked. Chocolate mousse offered no surprises, but left us contented.

Vegetarian

Paris is no paradise of veggie delights, but a few cooks have realised that meat-free cooking need not be a recipe for ennui.

In the wake of the mad cow crisis, Parisians remain remarkably resistant to vegetarian food. Some, though admittedly not many, bistros, contemporary and haute cuisine restaurants offer alternatives to meat, but the hard-core vegetarian restaurants are generally about as imaginative as they are fun-loving (read: strict minimum). A few exceptions are the creative **Le Potager du Marais** – the vegetarian dishes are imaginative and made with organic ingredients – the tiny Iranian restaurant **La Verte Tige** and the self-serve **Foody's**.

For inspiring sandwiches beyond the classic crudités (which contain tuna and egg) see **Filling Stations** *(p150)*. Vegetarians often fare well at ethnic restaurants, particularly Far Eastern *(p181)*, Italian *(p197)*, Indian *(p193)* and occasionally North African *(p210)* ones.

Foody's Brunch Café

26 rue Montorgueil, 1st (01.40.13.02.53). M° Châtelet or Les Halles. **Open** Mon-Sat 11.30am-5pm. Closed first three weeks of Aug. **Average** €9. **Prix fixe** €8-€12.50. **Credit** MC, V. **Wheelchair access**. **Map** J5.

An oasis of fresh, lovingly prepared food in a sea of panini stands, this is a pleasant place to grab a quick lunch at a good price. Salads are the house speciality. Help yourself to a tray and a bowl (small or big) and fill it up with whatever in the buffet catches your eye. Greek, pasta, red beans and artichoke heart are some of the ten or so salads you can choose from (there is even some ham, happily for the carnivores who were dragged along). There is also a soup and a plat du jour (the gazpacho is delicious). The interior, toeing the veggie party line, is somewhere between ski chalet and garden shed, and is spotlessly clean. The employees are friendly and helpful: we were sent back to the salad bar when our self-served portions were judged to be too modest (you are encouraged to pile as much into the bowls as possible, which makes even the small one a good feed). Accompaniments include fresh fruit and vegetable juices and smoothies, as well as fruit salads and fromage blanc puddings. Eat in or take away.

La Victoire Suprême du Coeur

41 rue des Bourdonnais, 1st (01.40.41.93.95/ www.vscoeur.com). M° Châtelet. **Open** Mon-Sat 11.45am-2.30pm, 7-10pm. Closed Aug. **Average** €19. **Prix fixe** €19 (dinner only). **Lunch menu** €10.80. **Credit** MC, V. **Wheelchair access**. **Non-smoking. Map** J6.

Opened in 1995 as a tribute to the Indo-American guru Sri Chinmoy– photos of whom adorn the bathroom-tiled south wall – this alcohol-free new age temple will meet all of your vegetarian and vegan needs. The coma-inducing synth music, kitsch indoor fountain, and pastel walls and tables may briefly give you the impression of dining in a psychiatric ward, but the friendly and completely sane staff soon have you feeling at home. We began our dinner menu with lightly fried pakora, which were some of the best we've had in Paris. The mushroom roast main dish, however, was disappointing. It was prepared like a terrine and resembled a meatloaf, without the charm. The blackberry sauce which covered it was a strange marriage and seemed incongruous with the austere accompaniments: a pile of onion confit, sautéed potatoes and sliced carrot. Fortunately our dessert, savoury stewed apples, saved the day. Though no alcohol is served, La Victoire Suprême du Coeur makes good use of its large bar, whipping up mango lassi and brewing spiced chai.

Le Potager du Marais ★

22 rue Rambuteau, 3rd (01.44.54.00.31). M° Rambuteau. **Open** Mon-Fri noon-4pm, 7pm-12.30am; Sat, Sun noon-12.30am. **Average** €20. **Prix fixe** €15 (dinner only). **Lunch menu** €10. **Credit** AmEx, DC, MC, V. **Map** K5.

It's rare for an organic vegetarian restaurant to feel just like a bistro – no stripped wood, incense or framed pictures of gurus. Le Potager du Marais achieves this with its long, narrow dining room, whose stone wall is brightened with contemporary paintings and sheaves of wheat. On a Tuesday lunch the room didn't fill up, but an obviously faithful crowd gave it a welcoming buzz. Choosing from the two-course €11 menu, we started with a tone-on-tone avocado filled with vinegared seaweed, and marinated herring with a waxy potato and strips of very fresh lettuce. Pseudo minced meat (some form of tofu, apparently) seemed an unecessary flourish in the vegetarian lasagne main – what's wrong with vegetables? – but the bright tomato sauce and accompaniment of sautéed fennel made this a lively dish nonetheless. One of a few fish options, the grilled sardines-on-steroids (not really, since only 'organic' fish is served here) were worth the effort required to extract the fillets from the tiny bones. The accompanying potato could have been cooked another minute, but this is carping. We splurged on dessert, a dense chocolate mousse and poached pear smothered in chocolate sauce, and with coffee and two glasses of (bottled) juice the bill climbed to more

than €20 a head – par for the course these days in Parisian restaurants. Organic pastas and fish dishes such as salmon with seaweed are also available à la carte.

La Verte Tige ★

13 rue Ste-Anastase, 3rd (01.42.77.22.15). M° St-Sébastien-Froissart or St-Paul. **Open** Tue-Sat noon-2.30pm, 7.30-10.30pm, Sun 12.30-4pm. Closed Aug. **Average** €20. **Prix fixe** €18 (evenings and weekends). **Credit** MC, V. **Map** L6.

The 'green twig' is a low-key but stylish restaurant run by an Iranian couple on the fringes of the Marais. Unusually for a vegetarian restaurant the menu is overflowing with alcoholic drinks, including cheap pichets of wine and, even better, a very fruity and drinkable organic cider. The chef conjures up original and appealing vegetarian dishes. The enduringly popular espinada is a simple but tasty starter of spinach, garlic, fried onions and yoghurt accompanied by a basket overflowing with breads and crackers. Viridis was a similarly uncomplicated dish consisting of avocado and garlic spread which, though tasty and well-presented, came on one measly slice of bread. The main courses were substantial, however. Vegetarian couscous substituted smoked vegetarian sausages for the traditional meat, but perhaps lacked the spiciness of the original. The Grenada dish, recommended by the owner, turned out to be an original combination of soy protein (which to a carnivore tasted uncannily like veal) sautéed with nuts and prunes in a pomegranate and prune sauce, served with a dome of saffron rice. To round off this pleasant, healthy and reasonably priced meal, we enjoyed the rose des vents, a pyramid of chocolate-coated cornflakes in a light crème anglaise; and the more traditional fromage blanc generously doused with maple syrup.

Piccolo Teatro

6 rue des Ecouffes, 4th (01.42.72.17.79/ www.piccoloteatro.com). M° St-Paul or Hôtel de Ville. **Open** daily noon-3pm, 7-11.30pm. **Average** €20. **Prix fixe** €15.10, €21.50 (dinner only). **Lunch menu** €8.90-€14.70. **Credit** AmEx, DC, MC, V. **Map** K6.

Tucked away on a pretty Marais street, Piccolo Teatro is a cosy hideaway for trendy Parisians and tuned-in tourists. Exposed stone walls, dark wooden beams and candlelight combine to produce an intimate and relaxed one-room restaurant. To start you can choose from a variety of salads or soups; this time we both opted for the soup of the day. The celery soup that arrived not long afterwards was deliciously thick and flavoursome, reminiscent of a home-cooked classic. Piccolo Teatro's house speciality is the filling gratin: a mix of vegetables cooked with cream and finished off with a layer of gruyère. Our experience was hit or miss: the potato, onion and mushroom version was hearty and satisfying, while spinach, carrot and mushroom proved watery and dull. There is a range of yoghurt-based desserts, but far more tempting was the rhubarb Charlotte – an inspired combination of fresh fruit, sponge and cream that comes in plate-dwarfing portions. A special mention should go to the waiter who

Pile your plate as high as you dare at **Foody's Brunch Café**. *See p161.*

managed to cover the whole restaurant in such a laid-back and polite style that he could single-handedly bury the myth of the snooty Parisian serveur.

Le Grenier de Notre-Dame

18 rue de la Bûcherie, 5th (01.43.29.98.29/ www.legrenierdenotredame.com). M° St-Michel or Maubert-Mutualité. **Open** Mon-Thur noon-2.30pm, 7.30-11pm; Fri, Sat noon-2.30pm, 7.30-11.30pm; Sun noon-3pm. Closed New Year. **Average** €22. **Prix fixe** €14.50 (dinner only). **Lunch menu** €12.50. **Credit** MC, V. **Non smoking. Map** J7.

Just over the river from the famous cathedral this quiet restaurant does indeed have an attic feel to it. The thriving plants intertwined around the spiral staircase and hanging from the ceiling give the place a welcoming feel. If you think vegetarian food is all lentils and chickpeas you'll be pleasantly surprised. We sampled dishes from the two good-value menus (three courses for €14.50) and drank a very reasonable pichet of rich organic Côtes du Rhône (€7.10 for 50cl). Our starters of tempura-style vegetable fritters were crisp and fresh but the miso soup bore little resemblance to true Japanese miso; the thick, dark broth with seaweed and tofu was more reminiscent of Bovril. Main dishes – ratatouille with wheat kebab, and seasonal vegetables fried with soya, tofu and white beans accompanied by brown rice and nutty bulgur – both highlighted the rich flavours of the vegetables. We finished this virtuous meal with a cold, wholesome compote of apples and cinnamon which would have been better warm, and a tasty combination of fromage blanc with grated coconut and raisins.

Les Quatre et Une Saveurs ★

72 rue du Cardinal-Lemoine, 5th. (01.43.26.88.80). M° Cardinal-Lemoine. **Open** Mon-Thur, Sun noon-2.30pm, 7-10.30pm; Fri noon-2.30pm; Sat 7-10.30pm. Closed Aug. **Average** €22. **Prix fixe** €25. **Credit** MC, V. **Non smoking. Map** K8.

Eating here is a treat. Hard to fathom when you realise the food is not only vegetarian, but organic, vegan and macrobiotic too – meaning no meat, eggs, milk, cheese, butter or sugar. This is healthy eating at its most serious; they don't use microwaves or freezers, they filter the table water and though they do serve fish, they steer clear of farmed fish – all very reassuring in these days of multiple food scares. Just behind the Panthéon, the restaurant feels cosy and elegant, with bright yellow walls, pine wood furniture, fresh flowers and candles on each table. The best seats are in the alcove at the back and all tables are non-smoking. We neutralised our tastebuds with fresh organic carrot juice and followed with soups, a slightly watery miso and a very smooth purée of rich pumpkin. Some courses can be slow to arrive but when they do you'll be impressed by the beautiful display of colours and textures. Each protein, be it fish, tofu, tempeh or seitan (vegetable meat substitute) comes with plenty of vegetables: cooked carrot, celery, swede and a delicious orange lentil purée with a floret of fresh broccoli, and/or raw chopped red and white cabbage with grated carrot and fresh tomato. You can also choose to add small domes of unrefined rice and couscous. Fish of the day, very fresh pollack flavoured with sage, was flaky and succulent; tofu stir-fried with spring onions was also delicious. For dessert we chose one of their many fruit tarts and apple crumble; being macrobiotic the pastry was rather thin and tasteless and the crumble was a crunchy mix of oats and grains, but the organic fruit was enough to satisfy any sweet tooth.

Guenmaï

6 rue Cardinale/2bis rue de l'Abbaye, 6th (01.43.26.03.24). M° St-Germain-des-Prés or Mabillon. **Open** Mon-Sat 11.45am-3.30pm. Closed Aug. **Average** €20. **Credit** DC, MC, V. **Map** H7.

Half restaurant, half health food shop, Guenmaï attracts a mainly local crowd with its Asian-influenced food. Although the restaurant serves only lunch, most dishes are also available for take-away and the shop stays open until 8.30pm. The green and white dining room is clean if slightly faded; tables jostle for position among racks of produce spilling over from the shop next door. The slight squeeze results in a friendly atmosphere whether you're with friends or on your own. The food is simple and healthy: on a cold winter's day two steaming pots of vegetable and miso soup were just right. The two lunch specials on our visit were a light tofu and vegetable soufflé, and delicately battered scorpion fish on a wooden skewer (the menu contains no dairy or wheat ingredients but usually has some fish). Each dish came surrounded by a colourful mix that included seaweed, leeks, bean sprouts and rice. The fruit tarts on display looked a little dry, so we chose instead to linger over another glass of carrot and apple fresh from the shop's busy juicer.

La Verte Tige: vertiginously good. *See p162.*

Aquarius

40 rue de Gergovie, 14th (01.45.41.36.88). M° Pernety or Plaisance. **Open** Mon-Sat noon-2.15pm, 7-10.30pm. Closed last two weeks in Aug. **Average** €15. **Prix fixe** €12 (dinner only). **Lunch menu** €11. **Credit** AmEx, DC, MC, V. **Wheelchair access. Non-smoking room. Map** F10.

If you need cheering up, this is the place for you. Apart from reasonably priced vegetarian food, Aquarius specialises in fun service. Master of ceremonies Richard Leigh (originally from Scotland) not only serves, but also maintains a steady stream of hilarious, off-the cuff commentary on his own personal beauty, the foibles of his clients and the state of world affairs. No-one keeps a straight face. From the lunch menu, we ordered a serving of crisp crudités and a big bowl of excellent watercress and potato velouté. This was followed by the ancient grain quinoa – roughly speaking, a slightly astringent cross between bulgur wheat and rice – served with celery, carrots and aubergines. The biryani is a broad assortment of curried vegetables, which comes with rice and the yoghurt-based cold sauce raïta. Though everything was acceptable, nothing was delicious – this is standard meatless cuisine, rather than a genuine attempt to capitalise on the possibilities of true vegetarian cooking. Sadly, a certain blandness seems inevitable. The desserts are another matter entirely. They have tarts, clafoutis, puddings, cakes and creams to defeat the most determined dieter, and the pavé au chocolat is exceptionally good. We left laughing, and will return.

Au Grain de Folie

24 rue de la Vieuville, 18th (01.42.58.15.57). M° Abbesses. **Open** Mon-Sat 12.30pm-2.30pm, 7.30-11.30pm, Sun noon-11pm. **Average** €15. **Prix fixe** €8, €12, €15. **No credit cards. Map** H1.

Seating just 14, Le Grain may not be the smallest restaurant in Paris, but there can't be too many other places where adult strangers can get this intimate without breaking the law. The menu, like the floor space, is limited but cleverly organised. For starters, the avocat au roquefort was nicely seasoned, the accompanying salad leaves crisp and fresh. The potage de légumes is a heart-warming mini-meal, the constituent vegetables changing with the season. If you want to sample the tzatzikis, houmous and guacamole, try sharing the €20 starter selection. Main courses are dominated by salads. Otherwise you can choose between vegetable tart, vegetable pâté or toasted goat's cheese. Everything comes with a generous dollop of lentils, plenty of bulgur wheat, and lashings of crudités. The food is produced to order in a kitchen about the size of a Japanese phone booth, but the ingredients are treated with respect and served with an almost Zen imperturbability. For dessert, don't miss the apple crumble with whole hazelnuts. Oh, and if you do need to visit the loo, don't close the outer door before you've opened the inner one. It's hard to remain dignified while reversing across somebody else's crottin de chèvre, especially with your knickers around your knees.

International

Africa & Indian Ocean

Set your tongue tingling with the tantalising tastes of the tropics: spice-infused fish curries, hearty maffé and soul-warming fruit flambées.

The traditional immigrant populations in Paris come from the Arabic-speaking former French colonies (*see p210*, **North African**), and Francophone West and Central Africa. Each country brings its own dishes to the table: from the ubiquitous yassa (citrus-soaked chicken) and maffé (meat in rich peanut sauce) to the fish stew thieb'oudjen and n'dolé (bitter leaf sauce with smoked fish or chicken). In a region that's not big on green vegetables, grains, plantains and root vegetables mashed into a paste (such as foufou, made from cassava flour) compensate. Desserts aren't the focus – usually ice cream or a pineapple flambée suffices. Instead, the meal might be sweetened with kora or balafon music, or sincere service.

Le Petit Dakar ★

6 rue Elzévir, 3rd (01.44.59.34.74). M° St-Paul.
Open Tue-Sun 11am-3pm, 7-11pm. **Average** €23.
Credit AmEx, DC, MC, V. **Map** L6.

C.S.A.O. (La Companie du Sénégal et de l'Afrique de l'Ouest), an association that runs a shop, gallery, cultural centre and charity, has practically transformed this narrow Marais street into a high-fashion version of La Goutte d'Or. Their restaurant's decor, like its cuisine, is impeccable and informal. West African prints adorn the tables and a string of blinking lights highlights the soft saffron interior, while hostess Katy Thiam, serving her fruity house cocktail from a huge glass punch bowl on the bar, makes you feel welcome. The menu is brief: four starters, four mains and four desserts, all predictable dishes from the region. But chef Daha Ly has a skilled hand and an eye for quality and detail, adding touches such as okra or manioc garnishes to dishes that usually go without. Save room for uncommon cakes such as a guava rouleau and the petit plaisir (a coconut-sprinkled angel food cake), both surrounded by a sublime mango sauce. The night of our visit, a Japanese fashion team photographed their plates of thieb'oudjen and veal maffé before sitting down to consume them – so expect Le Petit Dakar soon to appear on the to-do lists of international travellers.

Au Coco de Mer

34 bd St-Marcel, 5th (01.47.07.06.64). M° St-Marcel or Les Gobelins. **Open** Mon 7.30-10.30pm; Tue-Sat 11.30am-2.30pm, 7.30-10.30pm. Closed two weeks in Aug. **Average** €37. **Prix fixe** €30. **Credit** AmEx, MC, V. **Wheelchair access. Map** K9.

There aren't many Parisian restaurants that send you home with joy in your stomach and sand in your shoes. This small enclave of the Seychelles does both. Dried banana leaves, the huge, hanging sea coconut pods and pine furniture all conspire to convince you that a stroll along the beach after the meal would be entirely possible. The nearest you'll get is with the luxuriously soft sand that lines the wooden beach cabin room looking out onto the street – a fun-for-grown-ups touch that obviously appealed to the bourgeois dinner party being conducted in public by our neighbours. Rum cocktails set our tastebuds tingling as we studied the Indian-influenced offerings. Tuna tartare with grated ginger, fresh chives and lime juice was light, fresh and invigorating, while a swordfish carpaccio was rather heavily smoked. Filet de bourgeois (a Caribbean fish) was fleshy and meaty, but was rather overwhelmed by tomato sauce and curried cauliflower. Better was the octopus in a coconut milk curry, tantalisingly gentle on the spices. A St-André de Figuière rosé went down smoothly – and our coconut cake in caramel sauce made a stroll, beach or no beach, very necessary.

Le Dogon

30 rue René Boulanger, 10th (01.42.41.95.85). M° République. **Open** Mon-Sat noon-3pm, 7pm-1am. Closed one week in Aug. **Average** €23. **Lunch menu** €8.90. **Credit** MC, V. **Map** L4.

The ground floor isn't much – an empty bar – but the second floor feels like a West African hideaway with its rattan ceilings, snake and leopard skins, and singer strumming his kora. A bissap (hibiscus flower juice) or zingy ginger juice, spiked or not, is a fine way to start as you mull over the diverse menu which mixes and matches dishes from Mali, Senegal, the Congo and the Ivory Coast. We settled on a moist prawn mousse (with a heartbreaking flourish of ketchup and mayonnaise) and the assiette Dogon, an unusual plate of okra, black-eyed peas, raw cabbage and bean sprouts. Our neighbours went native – digging into their mains with their hands – while we used forks and spoons for our foutou, a mussel and prawn stew, with atieke, a mashed root vegetable. The spicy chicken (poulet spécial piment Dogon), with a fresh, tomato-based hot sauce, was exceptionally juicy. We were licking our spoons after ice cream and the mystère Congolais, whose secret is revealed only to patrons of Le Dogon.

Ile de Gorée

70 rue Jean-Pierre Timbaud, 11th (01.43.38.97.69). M° Parmentier. **Open** Mon-Sat 7pm-1am.
Average €23. **Credit** MC, V. **Map** M4.

Named after an island well-known as a refuge from

A vintage Paris bistro goes Senegalese at **Marie Louise**. *See p168.*

Dakar, the Senegalese capital, the Ile de Gorée has for the past 14 years also served as an urban escape. The snug, wicker-walled interior and soothing tones of Salif Keita (and, oddly, Marvin Gaye) should lull you into a West African dream state. We recommend starting with a ponch caïman, a stingingly-powerful ginger juice laced with rum, followed by starters such as féroce (an avocado and fish spread), accras (salt cod beignets) or aloko (fried plantains), then solidly Senegalese mains such as chicken or fish yassa (smothered in an onion-lemon sauce) and thieb'oudjen (a tomato-based fish stew with a dozen different spelling variations). Other options include dem farci (a fish 'loaf') or thiou boulettes de poisson (breaded and lightly fried fish balls). Chef Aziz Ndiaye makes an unusual rosewater-scented coconut flan, and his banane flambée with its blue flame is both eerie and delicious. Don't be surprised if the resident cat appears in the chair next to you, or a musician strumming his kora makes the rounds.

Restaurant Ethiopia

91 rue du Chemin-Vert, 11th (01.49.29.99.68). M° Voltaire or Père Lachaise. **Open** daily 7pm-midnight. **Average** €16. **Prix fixe** €15 (for at least four people). **Credit** AmEx, MC, V. **Map** N5.

If you're unfamiliar with Ethiopian food you might not expect big, TV-dinner-style trays, but if you go for the traditional prix fixe, like most people at this low-key, authentic restaurant, that's what your meal arrives on. The way you eat the food is supposed to be as informal as the presentation, with up to four people diving their mits into the sauces and meats spread on a traditional injera (or savoury pancake). The pancakes are made here with an Ethiopian grain that is difficult to find in Paris, and although it gives a fermented taste and a spongy texture that may seem a little odd compared to Indian breads, it is a good foil to a style of cooking that alternates between spicy and subtle. Richly marinated and fiery chicken wings sat in the middle of the platter like the molten core of the meal, with stewed beef, minced meat, spinach, boiled eggs, mashed lentils and chickpeas surrounding them, introduced little by little to work up the flavours. By the end of the meal you will have forgotten that you didn't know where to begin, and the best tastes come once everything has been mixed together. Herbal teas and soothing incense burners are needed to deflate stuffed stomachs – the ready supply of injera is filling, to say the least. In a neighbourhood that doesn't have much bad-a-bing to it, this refreshing, chilled-out way of eating would seem to have a lot of punter-pull power. Sure enough, the bare-brick dining room adorned with a few Equatorial accessories was full with chattering groups of friends by the end of the evening. Our neighbour ate alone, however, proving that while this food is great to share, it beats a TV dinner every time.

Waly Fay

6 rue Godefroy Cavaignac, 11th (01.40.24.17.79). M° Charonne or Faidherbe-Chaligny. **Open** Mon 8pm-midnight; Tue-Sat 8pm-12.30am. Closed one week in Aug. **Average** €23. **Credit** MC, V. **Map** N7.

With minimalist decor – artfully distressed walls,

subdued lighting, distant mood music, a few well-chosen objects – and utterly charming but unobtrusive staff, Waly Fay will lull everything but your palate into a total trance. From the first zap of ginger juice to the final bitter shot of fondant cocoa-café, this is food with a punch, borrowed from West Africa, the Caribbean and, occasionally, France. The accras de morue, freshly fried salt cod fritters with spicy tomato chutney, and boudin créole, a spiced black pudding, were equally fiery and absolutely delicious. Chicken yassa, a West African standard stewed with onions and lemon, had just the right tang and its accompanying mound of plain steamed rice couldn't have been better. We were less convinced by the n'dolé poisson fumé, strips of a hardish, smoked fish blended with ground peanuts and wild, bitter spinach. Like everything else it was packed with flavour, but the predominance of bitter-smoke was, in the end, overwhelming. We couldn't imagine this food with wine, so we stuck to refeshing juices, ginger and bright red bissap.

International

Entoto

143-145 rue Léon-Maurice-Nordmann, 13th (01.45.87.08.51). M° Glacière. **Open** Tue-Sat 7.30-11pm. Closed two weeks in Aug. **Average** €19. **Credit** MC, V. **Wheelchair access. Non-smoking room. Map** J10.

The Ethiopian food here challenges all but the heartiest appetites. You could order a three-course meal starting with azifa (a tangy lentil and lime mousse) or yechuibra (a heavy sauce smothering chickpea nuggets) but most likely a main alone will suffice. We ordered the doro wott (chicken cooked in its own fat, oregano and chillies) and the végétarien, served in little mounds on indjera, spongy bread used to scoop up the food. Salty spinach, sublime chickpeas, smooth yellow split peas, spicy chicken and hard-boiled egg, fresh aubergine, stewed courgettes and crumbled beef came prepared in spicy pastes. The tedj, a traditional honey wine, sweetly complemented all the flavours.

Marie Louise

52 rue Championnet, 18th (01.46.06.86.55). M° Simplon. **Open** Tue-Sat noon-4pm, 6pm-midnight. **Average** €17. **Credit** MC, V.

Malik (affectionately known as 'MGV', or 'Malik à grand vitesse') and Aïda (whose mother founded Chez Aïda, one of the first African restaurants in Paris) took over a cryogenically-preserved bistro in 2002 and transformed it into the humble Marie Louise, still a relative newcomer to the Senegalese food scene. In a rather bleak neighbourhood, this hole-in-the-wall just clings to the northern edge of the city. Within, you'll find overflowing West African hospitality, as well as generous portions of all the standard dishes – yassa, maffé, thieb'oudjen. A bland crabmeat and green salad starter was offset by a plate of little fried triangle pastries called pastels. More unusual dishes include kandia, a lamb, smoked fish and okra soup with a spicy, palm oil base (served Fridays only). Malik tells of a party of Australians wandering in expecting confit de canard, and instead being pleasantly surprised by this other 'French cuisine' of fish stews and peppery, lemony meat sauces. If you're lucky, a deft-fingered kora player, singing griot praise songs with an inspired voice, will stop in to serenade you.

Le Mono

40 rue Véron, 18th (01.46.06.99.20). M° Blanche or Abbesses. **Open** Mon, Tue, Thur-Sun 7-11.30pm. Closed Aug. **Average** €18. **Credit** AmEx, DC, MC, V. **Map** H1.

Named after a river that crosses the south of Togo, Le Mono offers a refreshing break from typical West African cuisine with its variety of grilled fish and uncommon side dishes, served single-handedly by the easy-going host. The five different punches may knock you flat before the food; beware the powerful house lemon, ginger and rum concoction. Begin with stuffed crab, prawn fritters or tasty bean cakes smothered in tomato sauce, then launch into generous mains such as akoboudessi, a tomato-based mackerel and okra stew with an island of pinon (manioc paste) in the centre, or expertly grilled chicken with a hardy semolina cake called akoume. There are two plates for vegetarians plus other side dishes; fish lovers should try the sea bream, mullet, grouper, capitaine or akpavi, an African carp, cooked whole with ablo rice, tomatoes and onions.

Rio dos Camarãos ★

55 rue Marceau, 93100 Montreuil-sous-bois (01.42.87.34.84/www.riodos.com). M° Robespierre. **Open** Mon-noon-2pm; Tue-Fri noon-2.30pm, 7.30-11.30pm; Sat 7.30-11.30pm. Closed Aug. **Average** €25. **Lunch menu** €10.50-€14. **Credit** AmEx, MC, V.

Unlike most African restaurants, Rio dos Camarãos doesn't focus on a single country. Its pan-African, multi-talented kitchen prepares an extensive menu from Senegal, Côte d'Ivoire and Cameroon, plus lesser-known destinations such as Benin and the Congo. Starters cleverly come under the category 'waiting for the bush taxi' while set lunch menus have tongue-in-cheek names such as 'sans papiers' (illegal immigrants) and 'Paris-Dakar' (featuring European food). With flashy paintings on the wall, the spacious dining room is playful and welcoming to children, as well as Champagne-sipping couples or parties sampling the selection of African beers. Dishes range from staples such as yassa and n'dole, to a high-test version of a peanut-based maffé kandja with prawns, beef, cod, carrots and okra. Try the two house favourites: attiéké, a braised whole capitaine fish with a spicy tomato-pepper sauce, and the Rio dos Camarãos, a gourd seed gumbo with cod and prawns. A warm cinnamon and banana Tatin makes a fine finisher. For the curious, chef Alexandre Bella teaches his secrets every Saturday (€50, call to reserve), and the first Tuesday night of the month listen to African folk tales over dinner. Expect a short hike from the Métro into the Montreuil hinterlands, unless you can find a bush taxi.

The Americas

Burgers, brownies, black bean stew, burritos and tostones, it's the united tastes of America – north, south and central – right here in la capitale.

They may not be the best in the west but the American legion in Paris does dish up some tasty spare ribs (**Planet Hollywood**) and burgers and fries (**Indiana Café**). If you're missing your eggs over easy, drop down to the aptly named diner **Breakfast in America**, or if it's Cajun you crave, there's always **Blue Bayou**. Don't expect culinary revelations, though – it's more about atmosphere and familarity than high art.

South of the border, **A la Mexicaine** and **Fajitas** wave the flag for authentic regional cuisine while **Anahi** puts beef all the way from Argentina on the table, and **Calle 24** suffers no crisis when it comes to Cuban food.

North America

Joe Allen Restaurant

30 rue Pierre Lescot, 1st (01.42.36.70.13/ www.joeallenrestaurant.com). M° Etienne-Marcel.
Open daily noon-midnight. Closed Aug. **Average** €28. **Prix fixe** €18, €22.25. **Lunch menu** €12.20. **Credit** AmEx, MC, V. **Wheelchair access. Map** J5

Although, with branches in New York, Miami and London, this is technically a chain restaurant, Joe Allen does without the busloads of tourist groups of the Hollywood burger bars. What it does have is a legitimate menu and, lo and behold, French customers! A good number of whom, while leaning on the wooden bar and examining the American iconography hanging on the brick walls, will no doubt be anticipating a happy meeting of high-quality French produce and big American portions. The menu gives a nod to almost every US region: Californian fusion, Tex-Mex, Cajun, and New York bagels and barbecue; with some steak tartare and salade niçoise thrown in for good measure. For the most part, it works. Our walnut-crusted goat's cheese salad with cranberry chutney looked and tasted fresh, while the Buffalo wings with blue cheese sauce were as messy as they were delicious. Louisiana fried chicken with honey and ginger sauce, spinach salad and ranch potatoes was tamely spiced, and if the barbecue spare ribs with corn on the cob and baked potato were pleasant, they were not quite up to the standard one would find in Joe Allen's New York cousin. Expats will find all of their dessert cravings catered to: brownies with whipped cream, pecan pie, cheesecake with red berry coulis.

Indiana Café

1 pl de la République, 3rd (01.48.87.82.35/ www.indiana-cafe.com). M° République.
Open daily 9.30am-2am. **Average** €24. **Credit** DC, MC, V. **Map** L4.

This American restaurant-cum-diner-cum-bar serves plentiful Tex-Mex and burger fare in standard 'you could be in the US but you're not' surroundings. There's MTV rocking in the corners and walls hung with revisionist portraits of dignified Native American persons. There is, of course, no shortage of these joints in the world, but only the Indiana is audacious enough to boast the American Burger, a concoction whose name suggests that it is the definitive version of its genre, the John Wayne of meat in a bap. Does the beast live up to its billing? It does exude a certain self-regarding machismo, arriving surrounded by adoring fries – but how does it taste? Let's put it this way – though the bun was nothing much, the meat rocked our homesick taste-buds. The same wild promise does not hold for the dégustation Indiana, a platter of Tex-Mex specialities. If these are specialities, God knows what ordinaries must be like. The guacamole was watery, the chicken enchilada soggy and fey, and the shredded taco beef had the apologetically processed aura of a cheap wig; it remained on the plate unmolested. Things cheered up with the desserts. The deep cheesecake with tangy raspberry coulis was as balm to the stomach and soul, and the selection of Ben and Jerry's ice cream was extensive and generously scooped. But the only compelling reason to come here is the American Burger, just as the only compelling reason to go to the Vatican is to see the Pope.
Branches include: 7 bd des Capucines, 2nd (01.42.68.02.22); 130 bd St-Germain, 6th (01.46.34.66.31); 72 bd du Montparnasse, 14th (01.43.35.36.28).

The Studio

41 rue du Temple, 4th (01.42.74.10.38/www.the-studio.com). M° Hôtel de Ville or Rambuteau.
Open Mon 7.30pm-1am, Tue-Sun 12.30pm-1am. **Average** €25. **Lunch menu** €12, €15. **Credit** AmEx, MC, V. **Map** K6.

With a sprawling terrace on a lovely, 17th-century cobbled courtyard that it shares with a dance school and the well-known Café de la Gare theatre, The Studio could rely on its location alone to attract business – and, unfortunately, it does. Your hopes will be high when you enter one of the two dining rooms, seating 200 in total. The walls, sponge-painted sand yellow, are covered with lizard murals, fake stone, and black-and-white photos of earnest looking Mex-

SUSAN´S PLACE

15th Anniversary

Europe's Finest Chili! • 'Spécialité d'or' for Texas Nachos • Vegetarian Mexican Dishes • Market produce • Home-made pastries

Susan will welcome you with Fajitas & a big Mexican starter for two with a **homemade Margarita.** Try the delicious vegetarian dishes. Don't miss Susan's excellent homemade desserts and the Mexican coffee...explosive!

51 rue des Ecoles, 5th (near bd St Michel). Tel: 01.43.54.23.22
Open Tue-Sat noon-2.15pm, 7-11.30pm. Sun dinner only. Closed Mondays

Craving a real American Breakfast...?

Open Mon-Sat 8.30am-10pm and Sun Brunch 9am-4pm
17 rue des Ecoles, 5th. Mº Cardinal Lemoine or Jussieu
Tel: 01.43.54.50.28
breakfast-in-america.com

ican farmers. Sipping a tequila cocktail, you can imagine these men in their white suits loading their fresh corn and chillies into a chartered plane bound for The Studio (judging from the prices, this must be the case). In truth, however, the Tex-Mex fare we sampled was below fast-food standard. We detected none of the promised sesame and basil in our salmon California wrap, which tasted of little other than salt. We considered sending it back but never got the chance as the four friendly yet distracted waiters were busy finishing their beers. Just as bad was a soggy enchilada. Any last glimmer of goodwill was flushed down the toilets, which were filthy by any country's standards. Visit the courtyard, have a cocktail while envying the dancing bods in the studios above, skip the meal.

Breakfast in America ★

17 rue des Ecoles, 5th (01.43.54.50.28/ www.breakfast-in-america.com). M° Cardinal Lemoine. **Open** Mon-Wed 8.30am-midnight, Thur-Sat 8am-2am, Sun 9am-5pm. **Average** €10. **Prix fixe** €11.50 (lunch only), €13.95 (weekend brunch only). **Credit** MC, V. **Map** J7.

Former American filmmaker Craig Carlson has transformed an old Paris café into a picture-perfect replica of an American diner, right down to the vintage furniture, hip movie posters and pale green bills. Clever touches include a genuine boomerang-shaped Formica-and-chrome counter salvaged from Pennsylvania, and individual toasters at each table. While some retro-themed restaurants can push the nostalgia envelope too far, any schmaltz is kept in checkhere with a low-key mood and Craig's personable style. The grub is straight-ahead, no-frills diner staples. For breakfast (available until 3pm), choose from bagels and cream cheese, eggs any style with bacon and hash browns, pancakes and a crispy French toast (both available with real maple syrup). 'Early bird' specials served until 10.30am are real breakfast bargains: big portions for €4.95. For lunch and dinner choose from compact club sandwiches; solid burgers garnished with grilled onion and pepper, lettuce, tomato, cheese, barbecue sauce and a side of fries; and tuna-cheddar melts. The hot chocolate is frothy, the OJ fresh-squeezed, the brownie supple and warm. Paul Simon and Chris Isaac croon, the perfume of frying fat infuses the air, and the waiter swings by with a pot(!) of coffee to ask if you'd like another fill-up: yep, aside from the Latin Quarter side-show passing by, this could almost be a truck stop somewhere off the Interstate.

Planet Hollywood

76-78 av des Champs-Elysées, 8th (01.53.83.78.27/www.planethollywood.com). M° Franklin D. Roosevelt. **Open** daily noon-1am. **Average** €25. **Credit** AmEx, DC, MC, V. **Wheelchair access**. **Map** D4

If only this really were Hollywood, then those of us who struggled to grind our way through the Chicken Crunch starters might have paid dental stunt artistes to do it for us. Crunch is the word. This dish is not for the faint of heart or plastic of teeth and those who are more Fay Wray than Schwarzenegger should start with the spinach dips: the dunking choice is extensive, and the vegetables seemed freshly-sliced. As we cut to the mains, the pressing question was: are the oversized BBQ ribs imported from Jurassic Park? But then ribs always polarise opinion; the Planet Hollywood variety are for those who like to have a bit of a wrestle to get the meat off. The meat, once separated from the bone, had a pleasant tang. So good were the fajitas that they required the coining of a new word – tonguetastic. Coming down from this high, we went for the brownies. They cast no dishonour on browniehood without elevating its status to any degree. The cheesecake didn't provide a happy ending. Its texture raised the spectre of having to scrape it off the roof of your mouth (never likely to impress your date), and it had a bland, almost downcast flavour. OK, it's not sophisticated, it's not suave, but Planet Hollywood provides a hearteningly populist option in a city that's too often up its own posterior when it comes to food (and, for that matter, cinema).

Hard Rock Café

14 bd Montmartre, 9th (01.53.24.60.00/ www.hardrockcafe.com). M° Grands Boulevards. **Open** daily 11.30am-2am. **Average** €17. **Children's menu** €6. **Credit** AmEx, DC, MC, V. **Wheelchair access**. **Map** H4.

You know the deal. The hanging, kerranging memorabilia (Lita Ford's guitar, anyone?) and the endless vids on ubiquitous screens should be enough of a clue even before you've been seated by a Queens of the Stone Age look-alike with piercings in places you don't have places. You're in the Paris branch of a franchise whose success depends on predictability – so let's have no disingenuous attacks of the vapours when you realise you can't get foie de veau here. A shared Ringo Combo starter (moist spring rolls and weary onion rings;, not much of a compliment we thought) paved the way for the Classic Bacon Cheese Burger. This was a fine compilation, though the burger meat was just too dry to merit the title 'classic' – 'basic' would be more like it. Our Caesar salad was really a Nero affair, chubby and prissily effete, but it conquered any residual hunger to such an extent that the desserts became a challenge. The explosion in the spray-cream factory that is the banana split was gargantuan, but, by Bon Jovi, was it tasty. The cheesecake was not unpleasant, but not remarkable. And that really sums up the Hard Rock experience; it's the same the whole world over, and if you like to collect the T-shirts, it's a dependable option. It's certainly the only place in Paris where sinking to your knees and grinding out the air guitar intro to 'Layla' won't attract old-fashioned looks from the waiter.

Blue Bayou ★

111-113 rue St-Maur, 11th (01.43.55.87.21/ www.bluebayou-bluebillard.com). M° Parmentier or St-Maur. **Open** restaurant 7.30pm-2am, bar

11am-2am. **Average** €26. **Prix fixe** €15-€24. **Credit** AmEx, MC, V. **Wheelchair access**. **Map** M5.
Someone has gone to a lot of trouble to create an authentic Cajun decor: with 13 tons of tree trunks and one giant stuffed alligator, eating here is like a trip to a hospitable log cabin on the Mississippi Delta. As you ascend the stairs from the pool hall you are immersed in the aromas of a light brown roux simmering with onions, celery, bell pepper and garlic, the signature redolence of Bayou country. Perhaps less refined than its close Creole cousin, Cajun cuisine is famous for its hearty one-pot meals and creative use of local ingredients. Full of crawfish – known alternatively as crayfish, écrevisses, crawdads, or mudbugs – our generous helping of jambalaya, scion of the paella, was a fiery mix of spiced sausage, chicken, peppers, rice and many more ingredients we could have also identified if we had not been so busy eating. Our other main course was that king of soups – if you can call a bowl of seafood and game a soup – gumbo. It was deliciously spiced with okra and ground sassafras leaf. It has been said before, but we will say it again: this is not an American restaurant; it is a Louisiana restaurant (don't expect to find any Coke on the menu). Visit on one of the monthly Cajun nights to experience the difference. Excellent service.

Latin America

Anahi

49 rue Volta, 3rd (01.48.87.88.24). M° Arts et Métiers. **Open** daily 8pm-midnight. Closed 25 Dec, 1 Jan, weekend of 15 Aug. **Average** €40. **Credit** MC, V. **Map** K4.
A rickety old building on a narrow and poorly lit street in the nether regions of the Marais houses Paris' trendiest Argentinian restaurant. That's if customers like Johnny Depp, Quentin Tarantino and Thierry Mugler are any sign of style. It's the slabs of grilled beef fresh (well, vacuum-packed) from the pampas that pull them in, and the cheery welcome from Carmina and Pilat, the sisters who started Anahi in this old charcuterie 18 years ago. The food is simple but standards seem to have picked up again after a disappointing meal last year. Surrounded by the original white tiled walls, stylish black and white photos of the sisters and an art deco ceiling painted by Albert Camus' brother, tuck into torta pascualina, a sweetish spinach tart with onions, or try the standout ceviche made with sea bass. Mains of skewered chicken breast marinated in lemon and served with apple and pineapple salsa and sweet potato purée, and cururù de camarào (grilled gambas with peanuts and okra) are satisfying and attractive but the bif angosto – a tender, juicy fillet served with a simple green salad – is the star. Try to sneak in a flan, immersed in sweet, thick caramel sauce, and wash it all down with a choice Spanish or Chilean red. Delicioso.

Breakfast in America: Diner might. *See p171.*

A la Mexicaine ★

68 rue Quincampoix, 3rd (01.48.87.99.34). M° Rambuteau or Les Halles. **Open** Mon 8-11pm; Wed-Sat noon-3pm, 8-11pm. **Average** €23. **Prix fixe** €23, €45. **Lunch menu** €15. **Children's menu** €12. **Credit** AmEx, DC, V. **Wheelchair access**. **Map** K5.
Festooned with a tasteful array of genuine Mexican pottery in all shapes and sizes, the long, sunny-yellow dining room extends down to the loos, which is predictably where the few non-smoking tables stand, but the waiters made no fuss when we asked to swap for one in a tobacco-free nook by the door. For anyone who has lived in Mexico the menu looks as promisingly authentic as they come and had us salivating in anticipation of a taste of the real thing. Unfortunately, from starters to dessert, every one of our first and second choices was unavailable, even though we had arrived reasonably early. Even the choice of three flavours of tamal was reduced to just one. However, the 'sold-out' factor was understandable given the quality of those savoury dishes actually available. Our tamales came as little packages of maize leaves encasing the most deliciously moist, salsa-spiked corn and pork we have tasted outside Mexico – they are made once a week by the waiter's Mexican wife. Other stars of the evening included the incredibly authentic corn tortillas which turned up to accompany the succulent lamb mixiote. As in Mexico, the desserts were nothing to write home about, as proved by our bland chocolate cake. We were disappointed to find that no Mexican wines were on offer and our Chilean red proved unexcit-

ing. The margarita was a sticky, syrupy affair despite claims that the restaurant is 'famed' for them; better to go for one of the selection of top-notch anejos or reposado tequilas.

Calle 24 ★

13 rue Beautreillis, 4th (01.42.72.38.34). M° Bastille.
Open Mon-Fri, Sun 6pm-11.30pm; Fri, Sat 6pm-midnight. **Average** €22. **Prix fixe** €18.
Credit MC, V. **Map** L3.

This tiny Cuban bar-restaurant on a side-street near Bastille exudes the sunny personality of its manager, Mechy, a Cuban dancer. Bare stone walls, Tiffany-style lights and posters on the ceiling make for clean and intimate surroundings; there are only five tables, and a bar where you can perch to drink some of the best mojitos in town. Inspired by the bar nibbles of fried plantain and black bean purée, we knew we'd be in for a treat when ordering dinner. We bypassed, wistfully, the Cuban lobster, and went for the excellent-value prix fixe. It starts with a selection of tapas, which came beautifully presented on a square plate: squid à la galicienne, salt cod fritters made with sweet potato, a black bean pâté with pork and a maize tortilla in tomato and basil sauce were all delicately delicious. We had also ordered the sea bass ceviche from the main tapas menu, which was surprisingly more carrot-and-orange than lime-flavoured but nice all the same. The tiny cod-stuffed squid in their ink were a delight to behold and tasted just as good, accompanied by an okra ratatouille, fluffy rice and a side dish of quimbombo, a kind of black bean stew. Spicy, marinated lamb chops were a tastebud-tingling surprise. Desserts are not terribly exciting – we found the touron de cacahuètes in honey a bit dry – but you probably won't need one. Push the boat out and have another mojito instead!

Anuhuacalli

30 rue des Bernadins, 5th (01.43.26.10.20).
M° Maubert-Mutualité. **Open** daily 7-11pm.
Closed last two weeks in Aug. **Average** €30.
Credit AmEx, V. **Map** K7.

Opinions are divided as to which is the best Mexican restaurant in Paris, this one or the more vivacious A la Mexicaine just across the river. Anuhuacalli is definitely more subdued in its approach – the decor is elegant and low-key, with no sombreros or fake cacti – and more bourgeois in its clientele and prices. Both prove that Mexican food is a far cry from rigid taco shells, runny beans and bullet-hard beef crowned with sour cream and guacamole. Start things off with a salad of cactus paddles, tomatoes and coriander or the summery, citrusy ceviche de pescado (it's firm because the acidity of the lime juice 'cooks' the fish) and bypass the dowdy prawn cocktail. Follow with a tender fillet of beef Moctezuma with cuitlacoche, a highly prized Mexican fungus that grows on the ears of maize, marinated pork cooked in banana leaves, or 'murky turkey' – actually mole poblano, turkey cooked in a seriously brown sauce seasoned with chocolate, chillies, cinnamon, cloves, nuts and more than a dozen other surprises. Finish off with slices of mango and a dollop of mango sorbet; lemon or pineapple sorbets; or quince paste with sharp cheese.

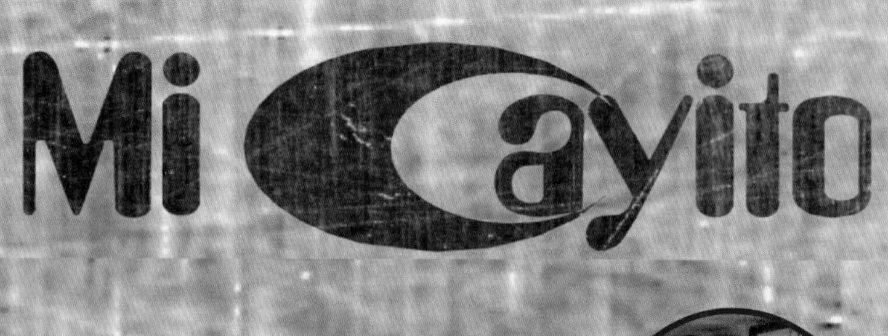

CUBAN RESTAURANT

A little corner of Havana in the heart of Paris

Open Daily 7pm-2am

10 rue Marie Stuart, 2nd
M° Etienne Marcel
Tel: 01.42.21.98.86 • Fax: 01.42.21.98.87

Botequim

1 rue Berthollet, 5th (01.43.37.98.46). M° Censier Daubenton. **Open** Mon-Sat noon-2pm, 8-11.30pm; Sun 8-11.30pm. **Average** €30. **Credit** AmEx, V. **Wheelchair access. Non-smoking room. Map** J9.

In the Carioca slang spoken with pride in Rio de Janeiro, botequim refers to a small, scruffy neighbourhood bar or restaurant. Import such a concept to Paris and it's bound to get dressed up a bit. The mood is lightened by jovial groups of French, leisurely enjoying the excellent food. Follow their lead and start your meal with a caipirinha, a potent cocktail made with fresh lime, lots of sugar and Brazil's liquid passion, cachaÿa. Mains are huge but if you want a starter, try the panaché, a sampling of well-prepared Brazilian snacks, or the fluffy aipo, a celery mousse topped with a tangy, prawn-flavoured dressing. As a main, there really is no avoiding the superb feijoada, Brazil's national dish made from several cuts of fresh and salted meats stewed with black beans and served up with rice, garlicky sautéed greens, orange slices and a grainy manioc flour called faraofa. Lighter, but just as good, the camarao en moqueca is a modified (possibly improved) traditional Bahian stew of succulent prawns, coconut milk and coriander. A varied selection of Brazilian confections made with coconuts and eggs promises to satisfy your sweet tooth.

El Palenque

5 rue de la Montagne-Ste-Geneviève, 5th (01.43.54.08.99). M° Maubert-Mutualité. **Open** Mon-Sat 12.30-2.30pm, 7.30-11pm. **Average** €30. **No credit cards. Map** J8.

El Palenque is an unpretentious eatery for the unconditional carnivore. For starters, try the grilled chorizo criollo, a mild cousin of the Spanish spiced sausage, simply served on a wooden platter with chunks of bread. After that, the options are all seriously high in protein. The parillada completa is a two-person challenge, a mountain of meat involving black pudding, sweetbreads, sausages, kidneys and ribs. Less stout hearts will find the steaks demanding in their own way, the standard cuts of Argentinian beef looming larger than their European equivalents. Our faux-filet was enormous, tender and perfectly cooked. Green salad and the thick corn pancakes called torrejas choclo are an unbeatable accompaniment. We washed it all down with a bottle of Trapiche pinot noir, light in colour but robustly fruity. The dessert list features quince and sweet potato in various guises, as well as a crème caramel doused in condensed milk. The milico membrill – sweet potato jelly with a slice of brie – was a surprising success. They serve dinner at 8pm and 10pm at El Palenque. Don't be late. There's generally a queue of hopefuls waiting to pounce – carnivores all.

Mexi & Co

10 rue Dante, 5th (01.46.34.14.12/ www.mexiandco.com). M° Cluny-La-Sorbonne. **Open** daily 10am-midnight. Closed 25 Dec, 1 Jan. **Average** €15. **No credit cards. Wheelchair access. Map** J7.

This small épicerie-cum-restaurant takes pseudo-Mexican food to an all-time low. Its ceiling, hung heavy with bric-a-brac including a dust-laden 'chandelier' of Sol beer bottles, old piñatas and ancient packets of spice provides the principal source of interest, while the 'restaurant' consists of a central bar and a few wonky, colour-worn tables. The lone waitress gave ours a perfunctory wipe with a grey rag as we sat down. Our order of quesadilla came as an undercooked, lukewarm flour tortilla filled with what appeared to be the contents of one of the huge tins of cheddar cheese sauce sitting on the fridge in the middle of the room and was accompanied by a stringy grey dollop of what should have been guacamole. We immediately regretted our main order of bandeja, a sample plate of several items on the menu – it consisted of a similar tortilla stuffed with a weird and off-putting mixture of black beans in tasteless cream and a watery mush of what tasted like boiled hen. This was surrounded in turn by a small, dried-out tamal, a bed of undercooked rice and a splodge of the dreaded avocado. We ordered a bottle of Los Reyes red to get us through the whole experience and turned our attention to the muted television in the corner. The bill arrived scribbled on the back of a concert flyer; getting the restaurant to officialise it required much insistence and a telephone call to the owner who eventually turned up with a rubber stamp. All in all Mexi & Co was an eminently missable experience; the épicerie, however, remains a useful source of Mexican and American staples.

Fajitas

15 rue Dauphine, 6th (01.46.34.44.69/www.fajitas-paris.com). M° Odéon or Pont Neuf. **Open** Tue-Sun noon-11pm. **Average** €24. **Prix fixe** €18.50. **Lunch menu** €10 (Tue-Fri). **Credit** AmEx, MC, V. **Map** H6.

This supremely pleasant little restaurant a few steps from the Seine has the bright, spick-and-span atmosphere of a Disney-style 'Mexican' eatery. Stone walls, wooden tables and large picture windows contribute to the feeling of what-you-see-is-what-you-get, namely simple, relatively authentic food prepared by Miguel and served with a smile by the friendly South American waitress. The ceviche looked as inviting as it tasted, featuring fat, fleshy chunks of white fish marinated in lime juice; the cocktail de camarones was a king's ration of coral prawns bright with fresh coriander leaves. We passed over the signature fajitas in favour of a tasty but unspicy chilli con carne and a parillada – mixed grill – whose focal point was a substantial rack of spare-ribs served with a sticky barbecue sauce and a golden, state-of-the-art empanada. Our only gripe was that everything was served not hot, but lukewarm. We washed all this down with a rich, berry-fruit Cabernet Sauvignon from Baja California. There's plenty of Mexican beer, including Tecate, and the margaritas are worth coming back for even though they come from a slush machine. Our sugar cravings were staved off for weeks after the 'bonita', an elaborate sundae with lashings of chantilly, ice cream and cajeta (a rich milk fudge).

Arriba Mexico

32 av de la République, 11th (01.49.29.95.40). M° Parmentier or République. **Open** daily 10.30am-2.30pm, 6.30pm-1am. **Average** €20. **Prix fixe** €21.34-€39.64. **Lunch menu** €8.99. **Credit** MC, V. **Non-smoking room. Map** M5.

Arriba Mexico makes no show of offering genuine Mexican food, but you can hardly expect more at these fiesta-provoking prices. Marcos, the friendly Argentinian waiter, burst out laughing when we asked if there was anything remotely Mexican on the menu. In fact, the only touch of local colour here is the joyful profusion of kitsch: plastic parrots, 'Aztec' hanging plates, huge murals of old, corn-grinding Indians and rainbow-bright serapes at each and every window. It all smacks of an Acapulco souvenir market. Yards and yards of fairy lights add to the over-the-top decor, which suits the young crowd that comes here for fun and quantity rather than quality. A massive plate of tortilla chips dripped with orange cheddar squares, its flavour coming courtesy of the bowl of jalapenos we had asked for as an extra. Our other first course of prawn cocktail was quite attractively presented, featuring a reasonable amount of firm shellfish nestling in a spicy tomato sauce crowned by hefty chunks of avocado and an inordinate amount of freshly cut lettuce. Having been forewarned about the copious portions, we had decided to share the chicken tostada. This arrived with yet another mountain of lettuce, underneath which snuggled enough tangy sauce-laden chicken to serve three. Unfortunately, the whole thing lay on the soggiest flour tortilla we have ever seen. Despite the hiccups, the overall impression is of an entertaining theme restaurant that doesn't take itself too seriously. If you know nothing about Mexican food and are out to have a good time, you won't be disappointed.

El Paladar

26bis rue de la Fontaine au Roi, 11th (01.43.57.42.70). M° République or Goncourt. **Open** Mon-Fri 11am-3pm, 8pm-2am; Sat 8pm-2am. Closed Aug. **Average** €27. **Prix fixe** €9. **Credit** MC, V. **Map** M4.

Grafitti-covered pink and aqua walls and wooden tables set the tone at this pleasantly understated, four-year-old Cuban outpost. Despite El Paladar being out of both Cuban beer and mineral water (the host offered us 'Château de Paris' tap water as consolation), the outgoing staff was happy to explain the regularly changing menu of Cuban food borrowing from the fried and stewed schools of cooking. Yuca con mojo (sautéed manioc with onions and garlic) proved oily but nonetheless delicious, and tostones (batter-fried plantains) were surprisingly light and crispy. Main dishes include pork, chicken, fish and the arroz a la cubana, an impressive load of tomatoes, eggs and rice. We sampled pavo saltiado – stewed turkey and potatoes seasoned with bay leaves – and a pollo pio-pio, chicken fried in citrus. The pescado guisado fish struck the only false note with its oddly muddy sauce of tomatoes, garlic, onions, potatoes and peppers. Overall the dishes had plenty of substance and character. The flan maison, a stupendous sugar-soaked coconut custard, ended the meal on a high note.

Fajitas: Wrap artist. *See p175.*

Caribbean

Tropical outposts don't make many waves on the Paris food scene, but their spicy food and island rhythm provide a great escape from the city of steak-frites.

Paris has a sizeable community of some 200,000 people from the French Caribbean, known as Les Antilles. Similar to African cooking, French Caribbean specialities show an Asian influence – as in colombo, the antillais take on curry. A meal generally starts with a rum-based ti'ponch and salt cod fritters (accras), continues with grilled fish or a hearty stew and ends with fresh fruit – often dramatically flambéed – or ice cream. Don't be dismayed at the often-relaxed pace of the service – Caribbean restaurants serve as an antidote to Parisian stress.

Chez Dom ★

34 rue de Sambre et Meuse, 10th (01.42.01.59.80). M° Colonel Fabien. **Open** Tue-Fri noon-2.30pm, 7pm-midnight; Sat, Sun 7pm-midnight. **Credit** MC, V. **Map** M3.

With its strawberry-print tablecloths, fruit-drop lights and group of trendy young things already installed on a red banquette, Chez Dom looked inviting – but where was the entrance? It's through the kitchen, where two luscious, big-haired ladies work behind an array of fruits preserved in rum. The cooking drifts somewhere between Senegal and the French Caribbean, and with Cuban music playing in the background, light falling on the faded school maps and the cracked shutters of the building opposite you can almost imagine you are in a beach hut somewhere tropical, despite the tower block looming in the distance. Planter's punch arrived immediately and, when one of us asked for a non-alcoholic alternative, it was replaced by refreshing ginger juice. The crabe farçi was more like stuffed scorpion with a hot sting in the tail under overtoasted breadcrumbs, while pastels de poisson were tasty little home-made fish pasties accompanied by a tomato salsa. They certainly whetted our appetites, and we ordered a carafe of merlot (a bargain at €5.30) with our main courses of gambas and lamb maffé. The gambas burst into colour on the plate and tasted just as fabulous once their crisp shells had been flaked off leaving spicy fingers too good not to lick, and the lamb, in its slow-cooked, African curry sauce, just fell of the bone. 'Sexy chocolate' more than lived up to its promise: a moist slab of rich, chunky chocolate fudge, chocolate mousse and a citrus-flavoured layer, while the lighter blancmange coco had a delicious raspberry coulis. A far cry from the glitterballs of many Caribbean places, this is a funky little joint – handy, too, for heading off to Café Chéri(e) afterwards (*see p264*).

La Créole

122 bd du Montparnasse, 14th (01.43.20.62.12). M° Vavin. **Open** daily noon-2pm, 7.30-11pm. **Average** €35. **Prix fixe** €22.50. **Credit** AmEx, DC, MC, V. **Map** G9.

White clapboards, tropical flowers, towering palm fronds: La Créole may be the city's most elegant colonial-themed Caribbean restaurant, with waitresses in colourful island plaid dresses, tables covered in white linen and a pretty stained glass island scene above the bar where a metre-high glass cylinder filled with cocktail maison awaits. The menu consists of lots of familiar dishes such as pork colombo, accras (salt cod fritters) and boudin (a rich black pudding). If you're in the mood for an exotic twist on standard potatoes, try the gratin of christophine, a squash-like starch staple topped with crispy cheese. The real standouts are the main dishes, which favour fresh seafood (a bit pricier than you'd expect; naturally, lobster tops the list). We tried blaff, a sea bream steak poached in lime juice and green onions, and the ouassou, three giant crayfish roasted in a hot pepper-tomato sauce (messy eating, so wear your napkin like a bib), both accompanied by rice and excellent stewed red beans. Desserts range from guava and passion fruit sorbet served in a pineapple half to coconut tart and a chocolate, hazelnut and orange cake.

L'Escale Caraïbe

46 rue Daguerre, 14th (01.43.20.45.75). M° Denfert-Rochereau. **Open** Tue-Sat 7.30-11.30pm. **Average** €22. **Prix fixe** (dinner only) €15. **Students' menu** €11. **Credit** MC, V. **Map** G10.

Unlike the real Caribbean, this dark and tiny outpost stashed in the depths of the 14th is a place where the sun doesn't shine. However, those in need of a getaway can enjoy a virtual trip courtesy of the huge selection of rums lining the wall. We began with a regulation syrupy ti'ponch but the waiter looked nonplussed when we then asked for the wine list, which he obviously considered surplus to requirements. Our acidic, watery sylvaner proved him right. From the short menu we chose the accras, which were much on a par with anywhere else. Tiny stuffed crab was tasty but overpriced at €7.47. For mains, forget the weird-tasting colombo of bony curried kid and go for the superlative ouassou which features giant, firm-fleshed crayfish flamed in rum and served in a tangy sauce with rice. In the mood for dessert, we selected a decent banane flambée and a deliciously creamy coconut 'suprême', allowing us to finish on a suitably tropical note.

Eastern Mediterranean

It's not all kebab news from the eastern front, though it helps if you speak a little Farsi. So yoghurt on down and you'll come back in good houmous.

The Ottoman empire seemed to spread kebabs, houmous and sticky honey sweets across half the Mediterranean seaboard. But beyond the grills and meze of the boisterous Latin Quarter taverna, **Mavrommatis** offers a creative interpretation of Greek cuisine. Paris also boasts more refined Iranian and Lebanese destinations, concentrated in the 15th arrondissement, which mainly serve the city's immigrant communities.

Les Délices d'Aphrodite

4 rue de Candolle, 5th (01.43.31.40.39/ www.mavrommatis.fr). M° Censier Daubenton. **Open** Mon-Sat noon-2.30pm, 7-11.30pm. **Average** €30. **Lunch menu** €15.80, €16.90. **Credit** AmEx, MC, V. **Map** J9.

Having Mavrommatis and this lower-priced offshoot in quick succession, we were surprised to find the quality of the cooking nearly as good here. Which is to say that Les Délices d'Aphrodite represents extremely good value. With its jolly Greek island decor, witty waiters (when not stressed by too many customers) and sunny soundtrack, Les Délices, however, offers a very different experience from Mavrommatis. Its aim is not to reinvent Greek cooking in a sophisticated, French-influenced style, but simply to do Greek peasant dishes well. You'll be amazed at the light texture and delicious herby notes in the aubergine fritters, and the freshness of the octopus salad. Cod cooked Lenten-style with tomatoes, onions and fennel reminded us of how noble this fish can be when accompanied by simple ingredients but timed so the flesh is perfectly firm and flakes off in large chunks. Our only disappointment was the too-solid pastitsio which was heavy on the cheese and very light on the pork. Delicious desserts of yoghurt and honey and mahalepi, a creamy pudding flavoured with rosewater and sprinkled with pistachios, ended the meal but there was no Greek coffee because the 'machine' had broken. Funny, we'd always thought it was made in a little pot held over a flame.

Mavrommatis ★

5 rue du Marché des Patriarches, 5th (01.43.31.17.17/ www.mavrommatis.fr). M° Censier Daubenton. **Open** Tue-Sun noon-2.15pm, 7-11pm. Closed Aug. **Average** €37. **Prix fixe** €28.50. **Lunch menu** €18.50. **Credit** AmEx, MC, V. **Wheelchair access. Map** J9.

If you've tasted the fabulous modern cooking you can now find in parts of Athens, you'll appreciate what the Mavrommatis brothers have been doing for some time now in the Latin Quarter. In the understated, grown-up dining room, barely audible Hadzidakis plays in the background and you'll have plenty of time to peruse the menu with its extensive descriptions of ingredients and cooking methods. The kaseri cheese that garnishes the aphelia comes from Metsovo, while kleftiko is cooked 'in the style of the 1821 Resistants'. If you know mainland Greece well this is terribly evocative, but does the food live up to its descriptions? Our starters certainly did, served as complete, garnished dishes in the French style. We chose dolmades to see if Mavrommatis could really justify charging €8.25 for this menu standard, but never had we tasted stuffed vine leaves like it. The crisp, chlorophyll-packed leaves were filled almost entirely with lamb and mint rather than soggy rice and sat in a perfect avgolemono sauce. The aghinares à la polita was a salad of artichoke hearts, fennel, red pepper and other crudités in lemon and aniseed sauce. Both our meat dishes were very slightly dry, but we adored the sweet fruity sauce and slice of salty kaseri that garnished the aphelia (pork knuckle) and the cumin-dusted sheftalia in its skin of pig's stomach. Mavrommatis also champions small Greek wine producers. The Hatzimichalis merlot complemented the salty cheese selection one of us chose in place of dessert. The crème de lait, meanwhile, was an ambrosial concoction flavoured with orange flower water; this dessert made a return visit a certainty.

La Voie Lactée

34 rue du Cardinal-Lemoine, 5th (01.46.34.02.35). M° Cardinal-Lemoine. **Open** Mon-Sat noon-2.30pm, 7-11pm. Closed Aug. **Average** €17. **Prix fixe** €14-€17. **Lunch menu** €9.50, €12. **Credit** MC, V. **Map** K8.

The French translation of Milky Way somehow has more culinary overtones than its English equivalent, and this Turkish restaurant makes for a relaxing evening out. The room is pleasantly decorated and refreshingly separate from the take-away offshoot around the corner in the rue des Ecoles. We began our meal with the hors d'oeuvres buffet,which can also be ordered as a main course for €8.40, or as part of the wide choice of prix fixe menus. The salads were remarkable not for their sophistication but for their freshness, and all the dishes were kept well topped-up. We were drawn to the various types of meatball mains: the pistachio and aubergine version and the thyme-flavoured boulettes à la nomade, served on a bed of vegetables, were particularly delicious. Ditto for an indigenous red wine, recommended by the ever-attentive waiter.

Al-Diwan

30 av George V, 8th (01.47.23.45.45). M° George V or Alma-Marceau. **Open** daily noon-1am. **Average** €32. **Credit** AmEx, DC, MC, V. **Non-smoking room. Map** D4.

We didn't think it was possible to eat cheaply, well and fast in this part of town. Al-Diwan, an upmarket Lebanese traiteur (two doors down from the restaurant of the same name), kitted out with a small stand-up counter, is justly popular with the diplomats and business types who work nearby. Two huge shawarma spits, juicy stacks of flavourful chicken and beef, dominate the sandwich bar, but that's just the beginning. You can choose from more than 20 inspiring pitta wraps, a mix of meat (€5) and vegetarian (€4), before moving on to the sombrero-sized platters of divine Middle Eastern sweets (€1 and €1.50 apiece). Everything is good, enlivened by the delicate herbs and spices that distinguish refined Lebanese food, so be adventurous. Try a kasbeh djaj (warm chicken livers with a twist of lemon) or the makanek (little cocktail sausages bursting with cumin and clove). Chankliche, a mix of tangy feta-like cheese with lots of chopped fresh herbs, is our favourite veggie option. You can help yourself to not-too-piquant chilli peppers for that extra zap.

Kibele

12 rue de l'Echiquier, 10th (01.48.24.57.74). M° Bonne Nouvelle or Strasbourg St-Denis. **Open** Mon-Sat noon-3pm, 7-11.30pm. Closed Aug. **Average** €20. **Prix fixe** €11.80, €14.90. **Lunch menu** €8.50. **Credit** AmEx, MC, V. **Wheelchair access. Map** K4.

On a Saturday night, Kibele was filled with families and students enthusiastically mopping up meze platters and, between bites, clapping and singing along with a trio of Turkish musicians. Following half their lead, we went for the meze, too: creamy houmous, stuffed vine leaves, feather-light, deep-fried calamari, baba ghanouj (aubergine dip) and a basket of puffy Turkish bread to wipe the plates clean. Kibele specialises in Turkish and Greek food so that means lots of grills, lamb and yoghurt. Grilled octopus, although not exuberant portion-wise, was tender and the chicken kebabs full of barbecued flavour. For something meatier, try eli nazek (garlicky yoghurt, lamb and aubergine) or sarapli kuzo (lamb and peppers fried in red wine). Desserts range from honey-drenched baklava to cinnamon-flavoured rice pudding. From Tuesday to Saturday, the cellar-bar is host to world music concerts.

Kazaphani

122 av Parmentier, 11th (01.48.07.20.19). M° Parmentier. **Open** Tue-Fri, Sun noon-3pm, 7.30pm-midnight; Sat 7.30pm-midnight. Closed last two weeks in Aug. **Average** €25. **Prix fixe** €14.50. **Credit** AmEx, DC, MC, V. **Map** M5.

On a chilly winter night, we entered Kazaphani's yellow-hued dining room and felt we'd been transported to the shores of Cyprus. Two big, affable parties had arrived just before us, so our starters took a while, but both the Cypriot salad (a scrumptious blend of feta, rocket and leafy herbs) and the pikilia chypriote meze assortment were well worth waiting for. We opted for comfort-food main courses: chunky pork brochettes, smouldering from the grill and encrusted with thyme and rosemary, and a

International

Oven bready at **Cheminée Royale**. *See p180.*

melting moussaka, thankfully not smothered in béchamel sauce. Each came with a small herby salad. By the time we got to dessert, the whole place was buzzing. Again we had to wait, but our délice d'Aphrodite was worth it: thick yoghurt with lashings of strong honey, both distinctively Greek, and a handful of walnuts. We washed it all down with a rough but palate-warming retsina and finished off with a shot of strong, sweet Greek coffee.

Zagros ★

21 rue de la Folie-Méricourt, 11th (01.48.07.09.56). M° Richard-Lenoir or St-Ambroise. **Open** Mon-Sat 12.30-2pm, 7.30-11.30pm. **Average** €18. **Prix fixe** €16, €22.50. **Lunch menu** €10.50. **Credit** MC, V. **Map** M5.

The jolly neighbourhood spirit is back at corner hangout Zagros, after a brief identity crisis when the popular owner Ali Ayverdi was spending more time down the street at kid-sister Auberge Seyran. Ali is now back, ladling out his trademark hospitality, while genial chef Neco Demir still turns out the brilliant Kurdish specialities that have always made Zagros worth crossing town for. Begin with delectable aubergine fritters, borek (pastry rolls filled with melted cheese), or the assiette Zagros, a generous assortment of cold starters including aubergine caviar, tsatziki, tarama and the more intriguing kanarya, mushrooms in a spicy yoghurt sauce. Regulars favour the Turkish classic kavurma, a spicy stir-fry of shredded beef, peppers and onions, but we prefer the expertly grilled brochettes, and in particular the eli nazik, beautifully spiced lamb kebabs served on a soothing bed of braised aubergine and yoghurt. While French punters gravitate to the Greek wines, it's cold beer and aniseflavoured raki that tend to fuel the animated exchanges between the artists, musicians and other Kurdish exiles who make Zagros their home away from home. For the rest of us, it's simply a holiday.

Cheminée Royale ★

22 bis rue de l'Ingénieur-Robert-Keller, 15th (01.45.79.44.22). M° Charles Michel. **Open** daily noon-3pm, 7.30pm-midnight. **Average** €30. **Lunch menu** €13 (Mon-Fri). **Credit** AmEx, MC, V. **Map** B8.

Do you have a hankering for fesenjan (poultry in pomegranate and walnut sauce), gormeh sabzi (meat stew packed with fresh herbs) or khoresht-e bademjan (beef with aubergine and split peas)? Do you read Farsi? A magnet for Iranian émigrés, the Cheminée Royale has two menus and mysteriously these classics of Persian cooking have been left off the French one. For the uninitiated, the hearty meat brochettes served with out-of-this-world fluffy Iranian rice (try chicken marinated in yoghurt and lemon, the lamby Caucasian or a koubideh, spiced, minced beef on a skewer) will satisfy even the most meat-weary palates. But, when we saw plates of our favourite stews whip by, we got curious. With characteristic Iranian hospitality, the waiter offered us a taste – actually, more like a generous bowl – of each: we'll certainly be back for more. Since we'd also tucked into a selection of starters (like mast moussir, thick yoghurt with wild garlic, and Caucasian salad, a misnomer for a delicious aubergine, onion and kidney bean soup) and polished off a jug of dough (a tangy mint and yoghurt drink), we didn't feel we had room for anything more than a cup of sweet black tea (you put the sugar cube in your mouth, not in the cup). Our ever-generous waiter thought otherwise and presented us with bite-sized Iranian pastries.

Mazeh

65 rue des Entrepreneurs, 15th (01.45.75.33.89/ www.mazeh.com). M° Charles-Michels or Commerce. **Open** Tue-Sat noon-10pm; Sun noon-9pm. Closed Aug. **Average** €18. **Prix fixe** €14.50, €17.50. **Credit** MC, V. **Non-smoking restaurant**. **Map** B8.

If your acquaintance with the most refined of Middle-Eastern cuisines – Iranian – comes from living in London, you may at first be disappointed by Mazeh. Where are the tinkling fountains, the mosaic-tiled bread oven, the pictures of the Shah and the melancholy music? Mazeh is the centre of a catering business and, though some effort has now been put into the decor, it's still utilitarian. Never mind, though, it's the food that attracts knowing locals and Iranian families. The parchment-like lavach bread was not as piping hot as it should be, but starter dips of luxuriant yoghurt with cucumber and mint and warm aubergine purée with its distinctive smoky flavour made up for it. Main courses are all variations on the kebab, served with the lightest, buttery, saffron-flavoured rice. Chargrilled skewers of minced or cubed lamb or coquelet (cockerel) draw flavours from exotic marinades, such as tarragon and green pepper, basil and white wine, or tandoori. We stuck with the traditional lemon and saffron, which was delicious. Our wine was an acceptable house red, but for authenticity try the zingy yoghurt drink 'dough' or – if it's in season (during winter) – fresh pomegranate juice.

Restaurant Al Wady

153-155 rue de Lourmel, 15th (01.45.58.57.18). M° Lourmel. **Open** daily noon-3pm, 7pm-midnight. Closed 1 Jan. **Average** €25. **Lunch menu** €9.91, €12.96. **Credit** AmEx, MC, V. **Map** B9.

After half an hour of concentrated menu study we settled on a meze lunch of five appetisers, vetoing the main course fish and grilled meats. Armed with a plateful of soft, warm pitta, we went straight for Al Wady's spécial moutabal, a delicately smoked aubergine caviar crowned with walnuts and juicy red pomegranate seeds. Like the chankaliche, chunks of mild goat's cheese and tomato tossed with tantalising spices, it was outstanding. A silky houmous made a tasty sauce for airy fatayer sabanich (spinach fritters). Last but not least was the fattouche salad: lettuce with chunks of cucumber, radish, red pepper and lightly fried pitta, laced with lip-puckering chilli and lemon, all guaranteed to cleanse the palate. The wines are Lebanese, the coffee is dark and thick, and for dessert there are stacks of honeyed pastries. A taste of Beirut in the 15th.

Far Eastern

From steamy affairs to spice blocks, Orient expression is rife in Paris. It's just a short table hop from Korea to Cambodia, Indonesia to Tibet.

While Paris' Chinatown, around Porte de Choisy in the 13th arrondissement, might seem *the* place to sate a craving for dim sum or bò bùn, there are other enticing neighbourhoods. Thai yourself out at **Khun Akorn** in the outer reaches of the 11th, or drop into funky Belleville and feast on piping hot Vietnamese ravioli at **Dong Huong**. Sample Khmer flavours at **La Mousson** near the Palais-Royal, barbecue slivers of beef at un-Korean-sounding **Restaurant Euro** in the 9th, or choose your own ingredients and watch the chefs flick and fry them at Bastille haunt, **Wok**.

Cambodian

La Mousson ★

9 rue Thérèse, 1st (01.42.60.59.46). M° Pyramides. **Open** Mon-Sat noon-2.30pm, 7.15-10.30pm. Closed 25 Dec, Aug. **Average** €25. **Prix fixe** €16.50, €21.10. **Lunch menu** €12.40, €16.80. **Credit** MC, V. **Map** H5.

The tiny cook here, known to her faithful customers as Lucile, moved to Paris in 1975 and has been recreating Khmer flavours ever since. Won ton soup, though originally a Chinese dish, is prepared in the Cambodian way with lettuce and prawns in a subtle broth. A chicken soup was bolder and spicier, with corn, bamboo shoots, kaffir lime leaf, fish sauce, ginger and zingy chilli. The waiter pointed us to the most authentically Cambodian main courses: amok, a soothing steamed fish dish made with coconut milk, galangal, lemongrass, lemon zest and kaffir lime leaf, and giant prawns in their shells with a mild tomato and chilli sauce. Feeling adventurous, we ordered the ta peir – fermented black rice – for dessert, an acquired alcoholic taste. Our waiter also urged us to try the steamed coconut cakes, which, though white and rather bland-looking, proved memorably squishy and sweet.

Le Cambodge

10 av Richerand, 10th (01.44.84.37.70). *M° Goncourt or République.* **Open** Mon-Sat noon-2.30pm, 8-11.30pm. Closed mid-July to end of Aug. **Average** €15. **Credit** AmEx, MC, V. **Map** L4.

This small restaurant doesn't take reservations, so it's best to go early. Upon opening, it filled immediately and those who had lost the race for seats were asked to wait at the neighbouring bar. We were given pen and paper with our menus to write our own orders and were served promptly. We started with a large prawn spring roll, tasty but cut into slices and difficult to handle – especially as the tiny, unsteady tables are set so close together that it's difficult to avoid poking your neighbour with your chopsticks. We followed with bò bùn, a fresh and nourishing bowl of bean sprouts, thin rice noodles, stir-fried beef and onions, mint, coriander and grated peanuts in a clear sweet sauce. The bò bùn special comes with their excellent nem. We also tried ban hoy, their 'Angkorian picnic', a variation on bò bùn. The same ingredients without the sweet sauce are served on a plate with stir-fried prawns, the beansprouts and salad on the side. The house specialty, natin, is a fabulous Cambodian curry – quality pork or prawns in a delicious, rich and creamy peanut sauce with coriander, served with rice or prawn crackers. We finished off with a soothing, typically Asian dessert of hot tapioca, bananas and coconut cream. Unusual and tasty as a meal here is, the modest surroundings allow the owners to keep the prices low.

La Coloniale

161 rue de Picpus, 12th (01.43.43.69.10). *M° Porte Dorée.* **Open** Mon 7.30-10.30pm; Tue-Sat noon-2.30pm, 7.30-10.30pm. Closed Aug. **Average** €22. **Lunch menu** €11, €14. **Credit** MC, V. **Non-smoking room**. **Map** Q9.

Chef Thaknol Moeur hails from Cambodia, while his French wife Dominique (who also speaks Khmer) flits about the dining room singing along to 20s jazz tunes that match the pleasing, Asian-themed bric-a-brac scattered about. We're neighbourhood regulars, drawn again and again by the very reasonable prices and the kitchen's exemplary skill with fresh basil, coriander and hot peppers in its tangy soups and creamy curries that are leagues above your corner Asian traiteur's pre-fab cuisine. Begin with a ginger-chicken soupe de l'Indo, an orange-bright, coconut-based curry, or the chicken beignets – actually baguette slices fused to breast meat and deep-fried. Then dive into the succulent chicken satay, the loc-lak (beef fried rice) or the seafood noodles sauté, a mix of mussels, squid, scallops and prawns seared in black pepper. The amok is a memorable little soufflé-like steamed salmon, coconut and lemongrass concoction served in a ramekin. Most dishes arrive with superb dipping sauces and cute pickle garnishes carved into sea creature shapes. Desserts can be fresh fruits, or try the bohbor kthi – jackfruit in squishy tapioca topped with toasted sesame seeds. Ask for one of the tiny non-smoking room's two tables for extra privacy (providing you don't smoke, of course).

Chinese

Chez Vong ★

10 rue de la Grande Truanderie, 1st (01.40.26.09.36/www.chez-vong.com). M° Etienne-Marcel or Les Halles. **Open** Mon-Sat noon-2.30pm, 7pm-midnight. **Average** €48. **Lunch menu** €23 (Mon-Fri). **Credit** AmEx, DC, MC, V. **Map** J5.

Just around the corner from the St-Denis porn shops lies this elegant Cantonese restaurant lined with green porcelain bamboo. The staff glide past in satin waistcoats and delicate music combines with the sound of falling water from a small fountain. While the trilingual menu holds no surprises, what makes the food special is the chef's commitment to authentic ingredients. There are no shortcuts: the seafood salad is generously heaped with real, freshly shredded crab; mushrooms and jellyfish strips have exactly the right consistency; and even simple dumplings contain firm, whole prawns. To contrast with the fine sizzling fish plates, choose at least one duck dish, such as the crispy-skinned five-spice duck. Order steamed rice wrapped in a lotus leaf as an accompaniment. With modest servings that invite sharing, this is an excellent place to sample traditional ingredients.

Noodle No. 1

54 rue Ste-Anne, 1st (01.49.26.01.51). M° Pyramides or Quatre Septembre. **Open** daily noon-3pm, 7pm-midnight. **Average** €15. **Credit** MC, V. **Non-smoking room**. **Map** H4.

Though the gardens of the Palais-Royal are one of the most beautiful places in Paris to sit outside for a drink, the better restaurants here are exorbitantly priced. So, for a perfect summer night on the town at budget prices, linger over a drink in the Palais-Royal, and then head for this simple, friendly little Chinese place. The only decor is a framed fibre-optics view of Niagara Falls, but the food is delicious and generously served, recalling Hong-Kong-style noodle shops. Start with the won-ton soup or, for something lighter, delicate grilled ravioli or nem (deep-fried spring rolls that you wrap in lettuce and mint), and then go for a large plate of sautéed noodles with different toppings, the best being the prawns, although the beef and pork are tasty, too.

Mirama

17 rue St-Jacques, 5th (01.43.54.71.77). M° Cluny-La Sorbonne or St-Michel. **Open** daily noon-10.45pm. **Average** €22. **Credit** MC, V. **Non-smoking room**. **Map** J7.

This is a popular haunt, well known to local student-types and budget-conscious tourists alike, and the Mirama's straightforward, well-priced cuisine attracts queues. Chinese ducks can be pretty scrawny creatures, involving hours of mucking around with bones, but our caramelised water-fowl was plump, well-proportioned and pleasantly crispy on the outside. We accompanied this with a big plate of Chinese greens and bottles of slightly sweet Tsing-Tao beer, the perfect match for this food.

Le Chinois

3 rue Monsieur le Prince, 6th (01.43.25.36.88). M° Odéon. **Open** Mon 7.30-10.30pm; Tue-Sat noon-2.30pm, 7.30-10.30pm. **Average** €24. **Lunch menu** €13.90. **Credit** MC, V. **Map** H7.

The Cultural Revolution has reached the 5th arrondissement in the shape of this excellent Chinese restaurant, with its striking decor of Mao-red walls, dark-wood tables and chairs, and shelves of revolutionary artefacts including *Little Red Book*s and figurines of heroic comrades. Although the cuisine is more orthodox, covering classics such as spring rolls, soups, noodles, Peking duck and spare ribs, the chef is as strong on presentation as his interior decorator, and the dishes are tasty, too. Marmite de boulettes was a sublime mixture of light pork dumplings in a delicious sauce of Chinese mushrooms, ginger, and chives; the canard à la Pékinoise consisted of tender slices of glazed duck in a thick soy sauce. For dessert, the grandly-named délices de l'Impératrice, a copious selection of Asian-style

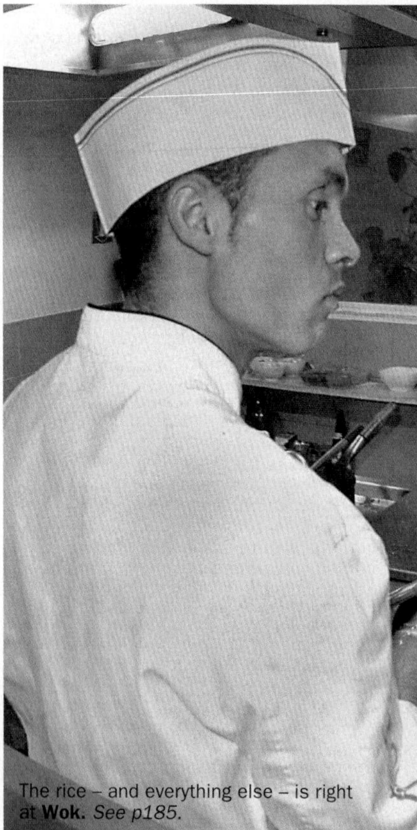

The rice – and everything else – is right at **Wok.** *See p185.*

sweets: crystallised ginger, cakes and lychees. A notch above the many Asian grills nearby, although this was inevitably reflected in the bill.

New Nioullaville

32 rue de l'Orillon, 11th. (01.40.21.96.18). M° Goncourt or Belleville. **Open** daily 11.45am-3pm, 6.45pm-1am. **Average** €17. **Lunch menu** €7.30-€12 (Mon-Fri). **Credit** AmEx, MC, V. **Wheelchair access**. **Map** M4.

Stick to the Sichuan/Cantonese portion of this overly generous menu, and you'll walk out as content as we did. The evening we visited, several dim sum carts were circulating through the vast restaurant, tempting diners with everything from shark to boiled ducks' feet. We browsed, looking under every bamboo cover as the carts passed by our table, and finally settled on a selection of prawn dumplings and shark roll, which was made in a tofu pancake and tasted wonderful, if a bit greasy. Then we moved on to main courses ordered from the menu, sharing sautéed green beans with minced pork, loaded with garlic, and spicy fried tofu that arrived sprinkled with ginger and chopped chilli pepper. As a lark, we ordered a half bottle of Chinese rosé, which was refreshing and worth drinking even if only for the name, Dragon Céleste.

Le Président

120-124 rue du Fbg-du-Temple, 11th (01.47.00.17.18). M° Belleville. **Open** daily noon-2.30pm, 6pm-2am. **Prix fixe** €121 (for 6 people). **Average** €18. **Lunch menu** €9 (Mon-Fri). **Credit** DC, MC, V. **Non-smoking room**. **Map** M4.

It's quite a trek through the lobby (porcelain, dried bits of shark, photos of visiting celebs – well, Serge Gainsbourg and Mitterrand – a 1989 award for Asian cuisine etc.) and up the imposing if un-hoovered staircase. But, if the place looks a bit tired, the food is fresh and bright, and there's a roaring trade in Big Fat Asian Weddings (always a good sign), hence the Imelda Marcos pavilion and sofa in the middle of the

Deliciously authentic Vietnamese food at an elegant Montmartre restaurant.

Salt & Pepper grilled Crayfish, Monkfish or Sole Saïgonaise, Vietnamese Fondue in Winter months...

Excellent wines at reasonable prices. Berthillon ice-creams.

Open daily 7.30pm-11pm

54 rue du Mont-Cenis, 18th. Tel: 01.42.23.31.16
Mº Jules Joffrin or Marcadet-Poissonniers

Open Mon-Sat
noon-2.30pm, 7.30-11pm

45 rue de Bourgogne, 7th • Mº Varenne • Tel: 01.45.55.18.89

dining room – perfect for those happy snaps. At Sunday lunch, we joined cheerful (Western) family parties pondering their orders over hot, fresh dim sum from the steam trolley. The kids devoured chicken noodles and ice cream, grimaced at the lobster tank and took turns on the sofa, while we tackled platters of tender pork with huge, firm, smoky-tasting mushrooms, stir-fried squid, and chicken with cashews, all colourfully garnished with broccoli, crunchy water chestnuts and neat little stars of carrot. Then came creamy, steamed coconut dumplings on bitter chocolate sauce. We didn't try (but will) the Peking duck, Thai dishes and chef's specials, including lobster with garlic, and stir-fried chicken with mango in a shredded potato basket. We were even treated (around 2.45pm) to a ravishing Chinese bride and much popping of corks. 'Whaddaya know', said our eight-year-old, 'dinner and a show!'

Wok

23 rue des Taillandiers, 11th (01.55.28.88.77). M° Bastille or Ledru-Rollin. **Open** daily 7.30-11pm, **Average** €19. **Prix fixe** €15.50-€19. **Credit** MC, V. **Map** M7.

If you like the Wagamama noodle chain in London, chances are you'll feel right at home in the cool, minimalist Wok. At this stir-fry restaurant, you choose rice or noodles, then take your lacquered bowl and wooden tray to the buffet to compile your own dish from the vast assortment of ingredients. This inevitably turns into a competition to see who can pile the most onto their bowl, knowing it will shrink in the cooking. Great for fussy eaters, the buffet is a real pick'n'mix of pork, beef, chicken – marinated or not – salmon, prawns, squid, and a wide choice of vegetables including bean sprouts, bamboo shoots and flower-shaped carrot slices. Next step is the open kitchen where you choose a combination of cooking oils and spices that you feel would complement your assortment. Expect the chefs to suggest alternative combinations before making a show of firing and tossing your chosen ingredients in their woks. Though the food is basic, the menu is good value and the novelty of compiling your own dish is a lot of fun. Watching it being cooked on the wok furnaces is quite spectacular too, but if you come much after 9.30pm you'll have to queue for the privilege.

Restaurant Lys d'Or

5 pl du Colonel Bourgoin, 12th (01.44.68.98.88). M° Reuilly-Diderot. **Open** daily noon-3pm, 7-11pm. **Average** €35. **Prix fixe** €21.50-€59 (for 2). **Lunch menu** €11.50-€14 (Mon-Sat). **Credit** AmEx, DC, MC, V. **Map** N8.

On the first page of its lengthy menu, we read that proprietor and chef Shin Ming Chen won two gold medals at a culinary competition in the northern Chinese city of Dalian. A leaflet stapled inside outlines his apprenticeship with one of China's master chefs. But, despite this pedigree, Chen's cooking caters better to European palates. This is Chinese food for the uninitiated, evident immediately in the menu, which introduces house specialities with colour photographs and lists of matching wines. Purists may balk, but the food is reassuringly palatable. Coquilles St-Jacques with green peppercorns and dried chillies may not deliver the promised zing, but the very tender scallops are cooked to perfection. The stir-fried duck in toban ya was somewhat tough, but saved by a zesty pepper, ginger and chilli bean sauce. Several other dishes tempt, but give yan ming a miss. The €18 combo platter included a curious 'salad' of rice, dried prawns, vegetables and raisins flavoured with a watery vinaigrette, and two 'spring rolls' containing lettuce, carrot shavings and the obligatory bean sprout – a concoction barely lifted above macrobiotic blandness by the spicy dip. But, at lunch, the dining room was packed with customers. Tellingly, not one was Chinese.

Tricotin

15 av de Choisy, 13th (01.45.84.74.44). M° Porte de Choisy. **Open** daily 9am-11pm. **Average** €15. **Credit** MC, DC, V. **Wheelchair access**.

Tucked away near a bustling Asian supermarket beneath a couple of the 13th's finest high-rise blocks, Tricotin's twin dining rooms – either side of a passageway – have an air of downtown Singapore. Windows lined with racks of whole unglazed and glazed ducks are a promising start, but Chinese staples served in the cheerful canteen-style eatery on the right were disappointing (gristly, greasy glazed duck and dry, unfragrant rice, among others). Better by far are the dim sum piled high in bamboo steamers, and the great-value meal-in-one soups and vermicelli salads, appealingly presented in big porcelain bowls and wolfed down with obvious relish by local Chinese, students, and a smattering of radical-chic media/fashion types. Across the way, the more intimate Malaysian/Thai half of the operation serves a fine choice of Thai curries, satays and thoughtfully seasoned fish dishes (monkfish accompaniments included coconut milk, fresh basil, blackbean sauce or 'young peppers'). Don't miss the oh-so-Asian drinks – sweet red beans mashed in milk, or fresh coconut milk with slivers of coconut.

Salon de Thé Wenzhou

24 rue de Belleville, 20th (01.46.36.56.33). M° Belleville. **Open** Mon-Wed, Fri-Sun 10.20am-9.30pm. **Average** €11. **No credit cards**. **Map** N3.

The most recent wave of Chinese immigration to France has been from the lesser-known Wenzhou province, yet the Paris restaurants still tend to focus on familiar Cantonese-style cooking. This popular address offers a taste of home cooking to neighbourhood residents. Easily the best thing on the menu are the unusual triangular dumplings stuffed with minced bamboo, carrots and pork, served in a simple broth with lots of bok choy. With only average noodle main dishes, stick to the filling soup and, if you're really hungry, add a side order of grilled herb ravioli, known to most English-speakers as 'pot-stickers'. (Cautionary note for vegetarians: the small, tasty herb gyoza are actually filled with a mixture of herbs and pork).

Sinostar

27-29 av de Fontainebleau, 94270 Le Kremlin-Bicêtre (01.49.60.88.88). M° Porte d'Italie. **Open** Tue-Fri, Sun noon-2.30pm, 7pm-1am; Sat 7pm-1am. Closed two weeks in Aug. **Average** €18. **Prix fixe** €21.50. **Lunch menu** €12. **Credit** MC, V. **Wheelchair access. Non-smoking room.**

Billed as 'the largest Chinese restaurant in Europe', Sinostar is deceptively small and unimpressive on the inside, with multiple private rooms ringing the plainly decorated central salon and small stage. The chef hails from Macau, a casino island off the coast of Hong Kong, which may explain the lacklustre, for-the-masses, not-quite-Cantonese cuisine. We enjoyed the crispy stuffed taro root appetiser, and the steamed dim sum pork and carrot dumplings weren't half bad, but the mains were dull: the Singapore vermicelli flavourless, the whole poached sea bass undercooked and the sickly-sweet sesame chicken (drenched in orange preserves) nearly inedible. Gloppy soups, like the overpriced shark fin (€12 a cup!), were equally mediocre. All in all, we'd expected a grander setting and more inventive food with fresher herbs and ingredients. But with expectations sufficiently lowered, Sinostar could be the backdrop for a tongue-in-cheek birthday party or kitschy night out. On weekends, a lounge cover band plays nearly note-for-note versions of American, Chinese and French pop classics. After plenty of cheap cocktails and Tsing Tao beers (both €4) you may find yourself sufficiently lubricated to strut your stuff on the dance floor.

International

Indochinese

Au Coin des Gourmets ★

5 rue Dante, 5th (01.43.26.12.92). M° Cluny-La Sorbonne. **Open** Mon 7-10.30pm; Tue-Sun noon-2.30pm, 7-10.30pm; . **Average** €22. **Prix fixe** €25 (Mon-Thur). **Lunch menu** €11.25 (Mon-Fri). **Credit** MC, V. **Non-smoking room. Map** J7.

This friendly Asian restaurant serves unusual food from Indochina (Cambodia, Vietnam and Laos). The menu offers a dazzling array including spicy soups, warm salads, rice dishes, Asian ravioli, savoury pancakes and curries. We started with soups and enjoyed two quite exquisite dishes: a sweet and tangy prawn and tomato soup flavoured with tamarind, and a thick, tasty soup of cod in a coconut and Thai red curry sauce with thin vermicelli and al dente courgettes. The small pomme d'amour ravioli offered a lighter starter of appropriately dainty prawns steamed in a sweet yellow egg yolk batter. For our main course we tried the house speciality, amok cambodgien, delicately cooked cod in a luxuriant coconut sauce lightly perfumed with lemongrass and baked in a giant banana leaf. The bành xeo, a Vietnamese pancake packed with soy beans, prawns and pork, and accompanied by sprigs of fresh mint, was original, though somewhat less flavourful than the other dishes.

Kambodgia

15 rue Bassano, 16th (01.47.23.08.19). M° George V or Charles de Gaulle-Etoile. **Open** Mon-Fri noon-2pm, 7.30-10.30pm; Sat 7.30-10.30pm. Closed three weeks in Aug. **Average** €50. **Lunch menu** €18, €23. **Credit** AmEx, MC, V. **Non-smoking room. Map** D4.

Kambodgia pretty much typifies its location, in the 16th but oh-so-close to the Champs Elysées – it's sophisticated and financially challenging. Nine euros for two weeny bowls of steamed rice illustrates its pricing policy. In a basement rendered Asiatic with low-lighting, teak flooring, Oriental artefacts and comfy wicker chairs, softly spoken, friendly staff dispense advice and freshly prepared dishes. Croustillant de crevettes, prawns wrapped in pastry and deep-fried, were excellent, so too the Laotian minced chicken wrapped in spinach leaves. The mains, however, lacked the spark and finesse of the starters. Grilled fish with chillies and lemongrass arrived as a slab of non-descript white fish with little flavour and even fewer spices, and a serving of cold vermicelli. Lightly battered prawns and calamari with onions, red peppers and basil (in microscopic amounts) seemed no more superior than a stir-fry you might find in one of Paris' many Asian takeaways. Desserts are better – try the flambéed banana pancakes or pear with ginger.

Indonesian

Djakarta Bali★

9 rue Vauvilliers, 1st (01.45.08.83.11/ www.djakartabali.com). M° Louvre-Rivoli. **Open** Tue-Sun 7-11pm. Closed ten days in Aug. **Average** €35. **Prix fixe** €16-€41. **Credit** MC, V. **Non-smoking room. Map** J5.

This superb Indonesian restaurant, with its pretty decor, gracious service and generously spaced tables, offers a splendid opportunity to discover the elegant, subtle and relatively little-known cuisine of the various islands that make up the Indonesian archipelago. If you think you know Indonesian cooking from having had a rijstaffel in Amsterdam, you will be surprised to find that this sincere and flavourful home cooking has nothing at all in common with the deracinated dishes that dominate most Dutch menus. The Hanafis, a brother and sister team, make dinner here seem like an invitation to their house. Start with the soto ayam, a delicious and delicate soup of chicken broth, rice noodles and vegetables, and then follow with several other starters to be shared: lumpia, handmade deep-fried spring rolls filled with chicken, noodles and prawns with a fresh peanut sauce; or saté daging, beef on skewers with peanut sauce. Outstanding main courses include rendang daging, tender slices of beef in coconut milk seasoned with Indonesian herbs, and ayam jahe, caramelised chicken in ginger sauce, accompanied by nasi goreng – Indonesian-style fried rice with shrimp and chicken. Finish with a coupe kolak, banana and jackfruit in coconut milk.

Korean

Han Lim

6 rue Blainville, 5th, (01.43.54.62.74). M° Place Monge or Cardinal Lemoine. **Open** Tue-Sun noon-2.30pm, 7-10.30pm. Closed Aug. **Average** €22. **Lunch menu** €14. **Credit** MC, V. **Map** J8.

The Han family's restaurant, a few steps from Place de la Contrescarpe, is especially popular with expat Koreans in need of a dose of fresh homestyle cooking. As in Korea, dishes arrive in the order that they're ready – a bonus if you're tired of French pre-set courses and menus. Consider sharing starters such as deep-fried pork and vegetable ravioli, the spring onion pancake, and even the bulot (sea snail) salad as portions are really quite generous. Bulgogi – thin slivers of beef, marinated in soy sauce, garlic, sesame oil and other seasonings which you barbecue at the table – accompanied by bowls of wilted spinach with sesame oil, steamed rice and kimchee (radish and cabbage versions), is also plentiful and tasty. Marinated squid sautéed with onions is at once sweet and salty, hot and sour, and garlicky. Vampires beware – garlic is central to Korean cooking.

Gin Go Gae

28 rue Lamartine, 9th (01.48.78.24.64). M° Cadet. **Open** Mon-Sat noon-2.30pm, 7-11pm; Sun 7-11pm. **Average** €20. **Lunch menu** €9, €10. **Credit** MC, V. **Map** J3.

Feeling peckish? Fancy some grilled cow intestines? How about non-spiced soup of cowhead meat? This is a restaurant that does not tone down Korean cooking for local palates. Fittingly, on an average day, half the diners are Korean. And when they say spicy they mean it. We sweated and nose-dribbled our way contentedly through a soup that was like a curried-up pot-au-feu before the plates started arriving for our bulgogi: wafer thin slices of tender beef grilled at the table. We had side-dishes of seaweed, soya shoots and transluscent bean thread noodles. To drink: a truly delicious ginseng tea. It gets busy at lunchtime so get here early or all the cowhead might be gone.

Korean Barbecue

22 rue de Delambre, 14th (01.43.35.44.32). M° Vavin. **Open** daily noon-2pm, 7-11pm. Closed 25 Dec, 1 Jan. **Average** €25. **Prix fixe** €19-€27. **Lunch menu** €11.50, €14. **Credit** MC, V. **Map** G9.

This stalwart trio of Left Bank Koreans doesn't seem as exotic as it did the first time we visited 15 years ago, and, in fact, it's a tough call to decide if their food is delicately seasoned or bland, especially when other outposts of Korean cooking make the point that the fire in this cuisine doesn't come uniquely from the gas burners, but from the kimchi, cabbage fermented with chili peppers. Still, you'll get a good feed with one of the set menus. The €19 menu leads off with grilled gyoza, delicate dumplings stuffed with vegetables and beef, while the €27 prix fixe debuts with five little appetisers, including deep-fried squid, gyoza and cucumber salad; then the meal continues with a bowl of hot broth, pleasantly lashed with sesame oil, and the waiter fires up your gas grill when a big plate of thinly sliced beef arrives. From here on, you'll be so busy grilling that conversation will likely stall, and this is surely another reason that these places are so popular – the DIY relieves everyone of responsability for too much social effort.

Branches: 1 rue du Dragon, 6th (01.42.22.26.63); 39 rue du Montparnasse, 14th (01.43.27.69.53).

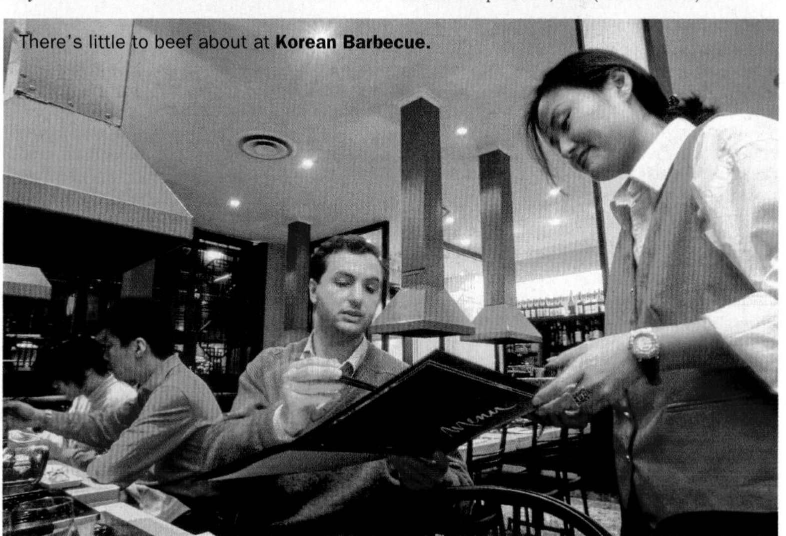
There's little to beef about at **Korean Barbecue.**

Fire and spice at **Khun Akorn**. *See p190.*

Restaurant Euro ★

65 rue du Fbg Montmartre, 9th (01.53.21.07.89). M° Nôtre-Dame de Lorette. **Open** Mon-Sat noon-3pm, 7-11pm. **Average** €28. **Lunch menu** €14, €15. **Prix fixe** €15, €20. **Credit** AmEx, MC, V. **Map** J3.

In one of Paris' more inconspicuous quarters, about midway between Opéra and Gare du Nord, is this equally modest Korean eatery. Traditional food, as cooked by Madame Oh at Restaurant Euro, rests on a foundation of garlic, ginger, soy sauce, rice vinegar and sesame oil, always accompanied by medium-grained white rice, in a steel bowl to match the metal chopsticks. Begin with a tasty binn dae teok, a type of fried bean pancake, or a kimchi version called kim tchi jeon. The vermicelli noodle starter, chapchae, is fried with tender carrots, mushrooms and pork. Dol sot bibimbap, or the veggie oh saek bibimbap, combines lettuce with seaweed, egg, bean sprouts, carrots and spinach, and if you look clueless enough your server will mush it all up for you in true local style. The most pleasing part may be discovering the panchan, various ceramic dishes filled with pickled ferns, dried fish, seasoned bean sprouts, cucumber salad, or any of the various kimchis (cabbage, but also radish or aubergine), automatically appearing with most dishes. The at-your-table charcoal barbecues are on the pricey side, but budget diners can fry their own gas wok versions of beef, chicken or seafood, especially excellent value when part of the €15 dinner menu. Diners should know that dishes can be laced with spicy changs or jangs, femented soybean and chili pastes, that add a distinctive zing.

Malaysian

Chez Foong ★

32 rue de Frémicourt, 15th (01.45.67.36.99). M° La Motte-Picquet-Grenelle or Cambronne. **Open** Mon-Sat noon-2.30pm, 7-11pm. Closed 21 July-26 Aug. **Average** €25. **Prix fixe** €14.50, €15 (Mon-Thur, Sat lunch). **Lunch menu** €9.90 (Mon-Fri). **Credit** MC, V. **Non-smoking room. Map** D8.

There aren't many Malaysian restaurants in Paris and this one is well worth the trek. There is a bewildering array of choices on the main menu, but the best bet is to go for the great-value prix fixe. We

started off with the potage chinois, a spicy chicken soup with slivers of tasty black Chinese mushrooms. This contrasted nicely with the beignets de légumes, crisply fried vegetables with the magical addition of a peanut sauce, both sweet and savoury. The main courses spanned a variety of seafood, meat and poultry dishes; we enjoyed the chicken cooked in soy sauce and lemongrass, served with sugary caramelised onions. Lamb, beef and chicken brochettes were accompanied by a rich satay sauce made with shallots, garlic, tamarind, lemongrass and ground peanuts. Small, cigar-shaped pancakes filled with coconut and drizzled with a honey sauce, and a crisp, amazingly light pineapple fritter rounded off the meal.

Thai and Laotian

Baan-Boran

43 rue Montpensier, 1st (01.40.15.90.45). M° Palais Royal. **Open** Mon-Fri noon-3pm, 6-11.30pm; Sat 6-11.30pm. **Average** €30. **Lunch menu** €12.50. **Credit** AmEx, DC, MC, V. **Map** H5.

When this restaurant run by two Thai women – one in the kitchen, the other in the dining room – opened three years ago, we hailed the authenticity of its regional, homestyle cuisine. Sadly, something has gone missing since; a recent meal was so bland it made us wonder if the kitchen had been raided by herb-and-spice robbers overnight. The €12.50 lunch menu sounds like a bargain, given the designer setting of body-enveloping plastic chairs, yellow walls and tropical flowers, but the Thai flavours in the supposedly spicy beef salad and the khoo phad kai, rice with chicken, were subtle to the point of invisibility. Far more expensive, the à la carte dishes were not much better. Krathong thong, tartlets filled with chicken, prawn and corn, seemed bereft of seasoning; tastier was the moo yang, pork with garlic, pepper, coriander, oyster sauce and soya, though we couldn't detect even a hint of coriander. The tropical sorbets and ginger ice cream were wonderful, but our tired and world-weary waitress was making us feel unwelcome by that point. Parisians might not be the most discriminating eaters of Asian food, but we think there is no excuse for taking all the excitement out of Thai cooking.

Far East side story at **Kim Ahn.** *See p192.*

Blue Elephant

43 rue de la Roquette, 11th, (01.47.00.42.00/ www.blueelephant.com). M° Bastille. **Open** Mon-Fri noon-2.30, 7pm-midnight; Sat 7pm-midnight; Sun noon-3pm (brunch), 7-11pm. **Average** €43. **Prix fixe** €44, €48. **Lunch menu** €20. **Credit** AmEx, DC, MC, V. **Non-smoking room. Map** M6.

At this Paris outpost of an international chain with a very good reputation you have to wander through a forest of tropical trees and tinkling fountains to find your table. It gives the impression of the Thai-village-style dining-room in an Oriental five-star hotel. The menu has lots of seductive choices, some of which have been framed into 'chef's suggestion' boxes, and elephant symbols denote the degree of spiciness. We were impressed by the seafood platter borne to our neighbour's table but plumped instead for the marché flottant for two (€23), a Thai-style bouillabaisse served in its own copper ring kept warm by candles. Having ladled the last morsels of this fantastic soup with its tasty chunks of black cod, prawns and mussels floating in a broth liberally flavoured with lemongrass and coriander, we could happily have left then and there, but we had already ordered a beef salad flavoured with mint, lemon and chillies, and pla neung mana (a steamed sea bass dish from north-east Thailand) for mains. Both were impressive, and huge – the two-elephant salad, be warned, however, is extremely hot, and the whole fish, deliciously seasoned with lime and served on a banana leaf, was just slightly over-cooked, but frankly nothing could have lived up to the starter. We finished with passion fruit and lemon sorbets – shiveringly zingy and citrusy.

Khun Akorn ★

8 av de Taillebourg, 11th (01.43.56.20.03). M° Nation. **Open** Tue-Sun noon-2pm, 7.30-11pm. **Average** €35. **Credit** AmEx, MC, V. **Map** Q7.

The first time we ate at Khun Akorn – a restaurant with branches in Bangkok and London – we loved the elegant surroundings and gracious service, but craved more spice. Now the kitchen appears to have let loose. Our waiter's eyes lit up when we told him that we liked our food spicy; we later realised that it might have been wise to order one or two milder dishes, for balance. Still, we had no complaints about the assertive cooking, fiery but not at the expense of other, more subtle flavours. A classic prawn soup, tom yum koong, was scented with lemongrass and kaffir lime leaves, while som tam, a salad of green papaya with dried prawns, carrot and peanuts, was refreshingly tangy. Both mains successfully combined sweet and spicy: a duck curry with grapes, pineapple, lychees and pea-sized aubergines, and seared scallops with Thai basil. By this time, a burning sensation was travelling from our throats down to our arms in a surprising but not entirely unpleasant way. Pineapple sorbet further cooled us off. And fear not: mild dishes are available 'for soft tongues'.

Sawadee

53 av Emile Zola, 15th (01.45.77.68.90/ www.sawadeeparis.com). M° Charles Michels. **Open** Mon-Sat noon-2.30pm, 7-10.30pm. Closed two weeks in Aug. **Average** €30. **Prix fixe** €20-€32. **Lunch menu** €13.50. **Credit** AmEx, MC, V. **Map** B8.

Try as we might, we just can't get everything right on the night at Sawadee. We're only half-convinced it's as good as people keep telling us. The fish cakes, full of red curry flavour, arrived still bubbling from the pan, while the chicken satay in a characterless peanut sauce slapped down at the same time was barely tepid. A nicer, spicier starter is the tom yam koong, prawn and lemongrass soup liberally sprinkled with the Thai mainstay, coriander. Mains followed the same unsilky road: prawns with basil good; three-flavour fish lacklustre; ped phad phed – duck fillets with basil and green pepper – fine if not startling. The lack of oomph in their green chicken curry, usually a Thai-tan dish in the right hands, has left us flat previously. The flavours are tame by Thai standards, obviously tempered to suit French palates – you can always ask them to up the heat factor, but getting through the staff's bored veneer is a challenge. Still, it's invariably busy and diners look happy enough; maybe it's the influence of the decorative golden Buddhas.

Lao Siam

49 rue de Belleville, 19th (01.40.40.09.68). M° Belleville. **Open** daily noon-3pm, 7-11.30pm **Average** €18. **Credit** MC, V. **Non-smoking room. Map** N3.

It can be hard to choose from the multitude of Asian restaurants around Métro Belleville, but you could do a lot worse than the plainly decorated and popular Lao Siam. It was full of regulars who had reserved tables for family gatherings – not a single Asian face among them, however. We started with the soupe spéciale de la maison, a large tin pot served on its own nightlight stand to keep it warm. This seafood soup was original and refreshing; lots of mussels, crab, squid, mushrooms, a touch of basil and a strong taste of lemongrass. Our other starter of salade crevette à la citronelle was surprisingly spicy with the freshest prawns, powerful mint and grated peanuts. We followed our starters with a chicken and ginger sauté, and duck with bamboo shoots and coconut milk. The chicken was disappointingly plain and gluey, with no vegetables at all. The duck was much better: thick slabs of tender meat, with basil and young bamboo shoots in a creamy coconut and chilli sauce. You'll need to order rice to soak up this curry-like dish, so try the sticky version which comes in traditional Laotian baskets. Sorbets were bland and served in ready-frozen scoops. The service can be frosty and it's hard to catch the waiter's eye if you're not a regular.

Tibetan

Pema Thang

13 rue de la Montagne Ste-Geneviève, 5th (01.43.54.34.34). M° Maubert-Mutualité. **Open** Mon 7-10.30pm; Tue-Sat noon-2.30pm, 7-10.30pm. **Average** €20. **Prix fixe** €13-€17. **Credit** MC, V. **Non-smoking room. Map** J8.

If you're looking for a subtly romantic meal with vegetarian options, this candle-lit restaurant filled with Tibetan photographs and fabrics should be on your list. By the time we had finished perusing the menu (which thoughtfully includes English explanations), we had been lulled by the chanting on the stereo and were in the mood to appreciate the subtle flavourings of little-known Tibetan food. We began with tsampthuk, a porridge soup of barley flour, very salty and buttery, two flavourings that seem to feature frequently (even the tea comes with salted butter). For less adventurous souls, there's pema thang, a comforting cream soup with roast tomatoes and coriander. We shared a perfectly-cooked shadré lamb curry and a sesame-flavoured tofu tseldremoug, which was a little rubbery. The relaxed crowd of locals and tourists all seem willing to try the buttery house tea, as we did. The tea might be an acquired taste, but we happily lingered over our warm rice pudding and apricot compote.

Vietnamese

Restaurant Pho

3 rue Volta, 3rd (01.42.78.31.70). M° Arts et Métiers. **Open** Mon-Sat 10am-4pm. Closed Aug. **Average** €7. **No credit cards. Map** K4.

This tiny canteen inside an ancient Marais building is a well-cherished neighbourhood lunch stop focusing on the Vietnamese classic soup, pho. With only rudimentary French at their command, the women here run an ideal soup joint – bowls are honestly prepared with fresh ingredients while you wait, either to eat at one of the long tables, or to grab in a take-away bag. The menu is simple: on Monday, there's a chicken special added to the selection, called bành canh; the rest of the time there are only three options, each of which involves a bowl filled with noodles, meat and mung beans, topped with a ladle of warming, fish-sauce-flavoured, broth. You can order one of three toppings for your noodles: meatballs, roast pork, or the three-mix special bò bùn (€6.60 and €7.40, depending on size), which includes chopped spring rolls (nem) and thin beef slices on top of the vermicelli noodles. Add some hot sauce and tuck into a nourishing, cold-beating lunch.

Thuy Long

111 rue de Vaugirard, 6th (01.45.49.26.01). M° St-Placide or Montparnasse. **Open** Mon-Thur 11am-8pm, Fri, Sat 11am-9pm. **Average** €12. **Prix fixe** €8.90-€12.90. **Lunch menu** €8.40. **No credit cards. Map** G8.

This minuscule Vietnamese canteen turns out copi-

International

ous and delicious house specialities to a mostly lunchtime and takeaway crowd, though you can stop by to have a bite at any time of the day. For just €8.40, you'll get three crispy nems or prawn ravioli, a wide choice of mains – such as a bowl of steaming, beefy pho, or a slow-cooked meat or fish dish – as well as a dessert. The carte offers some unusual northern and southern Vietnamese alternatives, including divine stuffed chicken with onions, coriander and lemongrass, which came served in thin, boneless slices atop shredded cabbage, carrots and cucumber. The bò bùn, prepared before your eyes in the tiny kitchen, is top-notch, covered in lemongrassy sautéed beef and slivers of carrot. Desserts such as banana-coconut cream and a tapioca pudding round things off nicely. The dirt-cheap prices and down-to-earth service make Thuy Long a welcome stop in the restaurant-chain wilderness of Montparnasse.

Le Lotus Blanc ★

45 rue de Bourgogne, 7th (01.45.55.18.89). M° Varenne. **Open** Mon-Sat noon-2.30pm, 7.30-11pm. Closed two weeks in Aug. **Average** €25. **Prix fixe** €15-€29. **Credit** AmEx, MC, V. **Non-smoking room**. **Map** F6.

For anyone who's actually been to Vietnam the kitchen here is surprisingly, wonderfully authentic. The bò bùn pho (noodle soup with deep-fried spring rolls and loads of fresh herbs) are every bit as fragrant and satisfying as what you'll find dished out by any of the numerous street-corner vendors in any Vietnamese city, and everything from skewered chicken to Vietnamese ravioli and beef rolls steamed with mulberry leaves brims with flavour and is remarkably light. The distinguished owner speaks impeccable French and English and oversees his compact dining room with delightful discretion – never for a minute will you find yourself wanting for anything, and yet he never lets on that he's overheard you. Main courses run to several excellent prawn dishes, plus unusual lamb and beef preparations, as well as a set menu of skewered fish, shellfish, meat and chicken, and a very good vegetarian menu. Finish up with fresh fruit, and stick with the inexpensive and harmless Côtes du Rhône if wine is a meal must.

Dong Huong

14 rue Louis-Bonnet, 11th (01.43.57.18.88). M° Belleville. **Open** Mon, Wed-Sun noon-11pm. Closed Aug. **Average** €14. **Credit** MC, V. **Non-smoking room**. **Map** M4.

The reason this place is always buzzing – they serve up to 2,000 customers a day – is because the food is so good. The preponderance of Asians testifies to the authenticity of the dishes served here. This is also one of few Parisian restaurants that understands that cigarette smoke can ruin your meal – smokers are banished to a completely separate room on the lower floor. Our dishes arrived promptly and in generous portions. The delicious bành cuôn, steamed Vietnamese ravioli, were served piping hot, stuffed with minced meat, mushrooms, bean sprouts, spring onions and deep-fried onion. Com ga lui, chicken kebabs with tasty lemongrass, though not as delicate, was served on particularly tasty rice. Bò bùn chà giò (noodles with beef and small nem topped with onion strips, spring onion and crushed peanuts) would have made a meal in itself. Be sure to try what everyone else is drinking: the dark, sickly-sweet iced lotus flower tea which comes with lotus seeds, lychees and seaweed jelly and is, our waiter insisted, 'very good for health'. Another good choice is the Vietnamese Saigon beer. For dessert, the mandarine, lychee and mango sorbets were so authentic they seemed to have been scooped directly from the very best fruit.

La Tonkinoise

20 rue Philibert Locut, 13th (01.45.85.98.98). M° Maison Blanche or Porte de Choisy.
Open Tue-Sun noon-3.30pm, 7-11pm (last orders 10pm). Closed in Aug. **Average** €20. **Lunch menu** €9.60. **No credit cards**.

Though the overlit Formica setting doesn't offer much to trill over, the food at this deservedly popular Vietnamese on a charmingly quiet and mostly Asian side street in the 13th is excellent. Come with friends so that you can share, and start with some of the best nems in Paris, lotus root salad (water lily stems garnished with fried onions, prawns, herbs and peanuts), rare beef salad in lemon (a ceviche-like dish, in which thin strips of beef are marinated in herbs and lemon juice), and wonderful Vietnamese ravioli. The main course not to miss is the catfish caramelised in palm sugar in a marmite (earthenware casserole); otherwise, try the skewered pork with shallots and minced prawns on sugar-cane sticks. Note, too, that you won't need extra vermicelli noodles or rice – as was suggested to us – since all dishes come appropriately endowed. After a trial run with the sour house rosé, the chilled Côtes du Rhône turned out to be the right quaff. Finally, if the service is professional – we appreciated our carefully annotated bill – it's also a bit slap-dash unless you assert yourself on the way to becoming a regular.

Kim Ahn

49 av Emile Zola, 15th (01.45.79.40.96). M° Charles Michels. **Open** Tue-Sun 7.30-11pm. Closed two weeks in Aug. **Average** €30. **Prix fixe** €34. **Credit** AmEx, MC, V. **Non-smoking room**. **Map** B8.

The upmarket decor – yellow, olive and imperial-red fabric panels and rich mahogany-coloured wood – gives fair warning of the slightly hefty prices. Caroline Kim Ahn's servings aren't copious – just two ravioli or spring rolls as a starter – instead, she emphasises quality and authenticity over quantity. The spring rolls bursting with chicken, prawns, vermicelli and Vietnamese mint were the standouts. Mains of lacquered, sliced duck with a sweet orange and soy sauce, and two giant, but pricey, langoustines caramelised in a sticky combo of onions and sugar showed refined, careful cooking. Fresh tropical fruits such as mangostan, a plum-brown fruit with a marshmallowy white centre and a taste akin to a sweet mini-banana, feature as desserts.

Indian

No doubt London wears the curry crown but Paris has some respectable, though less spicy, pretenders. So you can curry on across the channel.

If your first few minutes in an Indian restaurant include the appearance of a complementary kir or sugar-frosted cocktail, beware: you are probably in one of the many places where your tastebuds will be far from tickled by blandly Gallicised variations on the sub-Continent's finest. However, interesting and varied Indian cooking is to be found, if you know where to go. De luxe establishments such as **Gandhi-Opéra** and **Yugaraj** use quality ingredients and rich but subtle seasonings, and the availability of meats such as quail and duck mean that you might taste tandoori dishes that you haven't encountered elsewhere. At the other end of the price spectrum, the South Indian and Sri Lankan restaurants that cluster around the Gare du Nord and Faubourg St-Denis do less watering-down of their spicy cooking for a Paris audience. Try their giant dosai, potent meat and vegetable curries, and masala tea in no-frills surroundings, surrounded by the immigrants who live in the area.

Gandhi-Opéra ★

66 rue Ste-Anne, 2nd (01.47.03.41.00/ www.restaurant-gandhi.com). M° Quatre-Septembre. **Open** Mon-Sat noon-2.30pm, 7-11.30pm; Sun 7-11.30pm. **Average** €27. **Prix fixe** €23, €27.50 (dinner only). **Lunch menu** €11-€19.70. **Credit** AmEx, DC, MC, V. **Wheelchair access**. **Map** H4.

So frequently had we been disappointed by Indian meals in Paris that we had almost given up – when Gandhi-Opéra came to the rescue. The clientele is largely French but instead of pandering to the Gallic fear of spices the chef has taken one of the plusses of the French respect for tradition – excellent quality meat – and used it in authentic tasting dishes. The menu is wide-ranging but a speciality is the tandoori grill. We were thrilled by our hot, minty chicken starter of Gandhi mixt murg pudina, and not one but two tandoori quail. Then followed a delicious, sizzling Bombay-style chicken dish with spaghetti-thin strips of onion and wonderful spices. The lamb vindaloo, requested 'very hot', was nowhere near, but such were the quality and flavour that we

International

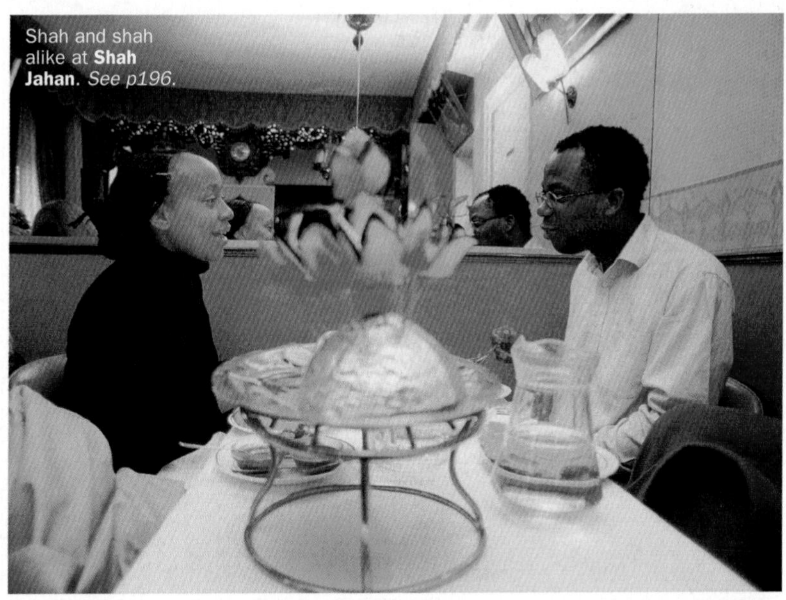

Shah and shah alike at **Shah Jahan**. *See p196.*

AUX COMPTOIRS DES INDES

Delicious selection of Biryanis, Massalas and much more. Large choice of vegetarian, fish and meat dishes. Excellent nan breads to accompany your main dish. Home-made ice-creams for dessert. Wash it down with one of our home-made Lassis or lemonade, or otherwise try an Indian red wine (Angoori) or beer.

Lunch set-menus: from €7-€15
Dinner set-menu: €15

Open daily noon-2.30pm, 7pm-11.30pm
Seating for large groups available.

50 rue de La Fontaine au Roi, 11th.
M° Goncourt.
Tel: 01.48.05.45.76.

Indian specialities
TANDOORI - CURRY

Take-away and
home-delivery available

Excellent Chef and owner of the restaurant for 25 years now, Arun Sachdeva puts all his know-how and his talent to work so that you can taste some exeptional cuisine. Let yourself be taken in by the slowly macerated and Char-grilled Tandooris, be sure not to miss the great variety and refinement of the curries on offer, and treat yourself to home-made Indian ice-creams.

"An untricked fireworks display" —*Le Figaro.*
Recommended by *Gault Millau, Pariscope, Routard Paris exotique, Le Point, Paris pas cher, guide Pudlo, Cuisines du monde à Paris.*

Open daily noon-2.30pm, 7pm-11.30pm
173 rue Lecourbe, 15th. M° Vaugirard. Tel: 01.48.28.66.68

weren't disappointed. The highlight, though, was the vegetable side dish of paneer sag, spinach in a creamy paneer cheese sauce – a chef's speciality. But, joy of joys, we were glad we plumped to have desserts, too. The kulfi was crunchy and tasted homemade, and the rose sorbet took us to heaven. With cooking this luxuriant, you should be sitting on cushions in a maharajah's palace.
Branch: Gandhi, 54 av Edouard Vaillant, 92100 Boulogne (01.47.61.05.04).

Yugaraj

14 rue Dauphine, 6th (01.43.26.44.91). M° Odéon or Pont-Neuf. **Open** Tue-Sun noon-2pm, 7-10.30pm. Closed Aug. **Average** €37. **Prix fixe** €28-€48. **Credit** AmEx, DC, MC, V. **Map** H6.
With its wonderful collection of Hindu statuettes and colonial teak furniture dating from as early as the 18th century, this luxurious restaurant clearly echoes the antique shops that cram the area. We were impressed by the wine list from which we chose what we consider to be one of France's best bottles – a lush Rosé des Riceys from Morel whose chocolate and spice bouquet provided the perfect foil to fiery food. It took some time to wade through the small-print encyclopaedic explanations of each dish but we finally settled on the sampler starter with various spiced (and unspiced) titbits: fried fish cubes, chicken kebabs and bhajis served with a selection of colourful sauces and chutneys. Our tandoori-baked cheese nan was delicious but the plain one was, well, rather plain. The highlight: two delectably plump, free-range Vosges quails, the legs fried and medium-spiced and the wings bathed in a creamy sauce of spice, herbs and raisins. We mopped up every last morsel. Our other main, the gosht rada, featured chunks of lean lamb prepared in a fragrant mixture of fenugreek, ginger and garlic.

Kastoori

4 pl Gustave Toudouze, 9th (01.44.53.06.10). M° St-Georges. **Open** Mon 6.30-11.30pm, Tue-Sun 11.30am-2.30pm, 6.30-11.30pm **Average** €16. **Prix fixe** €13 (dinner only). **Lunch menu** €8. **Credit** AmEx, MC,V. **Map** H2.
Kastoori offers the chance to enjoy tasty, inexpensive Indian cooking on a café terrace (decked with cotton lanterns) in a pretty, leafy corner of the 9th. At 2pm on a sunny, wintry Monday, two hardy souls sat outside, while the dining room was packed with earnest, arty, pale'n'interesting Parisians. White walls and a plate-glass shop window suggest a recently-converted launderette, compensated with taste and care by gold brocade cushions, candles, block-printed cotton cloths and menu covers. From the amazing-value lunch menu, starters included spicy beef and lamb sausage, and pan-fried lamb's liver in a perfect, savoury sauce swimming with fresh cardamoms. This was followed by the chicken Kastoori – huge chunks on the bone in a creamy green curry sauce – a moist, flavoursome vegetable biryani and huge, puffy cheese nans, all served in attractive copper and zinc dishes. Desserts included melting almond sweetmeats flavoured with orange flower water and other exotica, and a huge serving of delicious mango ice cream. Instead of alcohol, there is a tempting range of extra-large, freshly-whizzed fruit cocktails and lassis, and flavoured teas and coffees.

Ganesha Corner ★

16 rue Perdonnet, 10th (01.46.07.35.32). M° La Chapelle. **Open** daily 9am-11.30pm. **Average** €8. **Credit** MC, V. **Map** L2.
This corner institution in the Sri Lankan and south Indian neighbourhood just south of the Line 2 Métro tracks attracts probably four times as many customers as any of its rivals. Why? It's cheap, fast, delicious and has a hang-out vibe rather than a formal dining room. Indeed, Ganesha Corner serves as the cafeteria, pub and meeting place for dozens of locals, mostly single men and the occasional family, who constantly stream out of the tiny, yellow and pink dining room, or clog the entryway ordering breads and sweets from the to-go counter. The waiters may be hard to track down, but they are inevitably kind and laid-back (not blinking an eye when we knocked a glass of water onto a pile of menus) and happy to explain some of the more mysterious-seeming dishes. Begin with a fried vadai (made from lentils, chickpeas and veg) or a patis (a potato and fish dumpling) as you sip a lassi, but be careful to save room for the main dishes. Mounds of fried noodles, biryani or any of the dosai, such as masala dosai – Indian crêpes stuffed with yellow curry, potatoes and mustard seed – are unfinishably huge. For the more adventurous there's a deep-brown, strong and spicy fish curry. Idli is another southern favourite: saucer-like steamed rice and lentil cakes served with an assortment of cabbage and aubergine-based stews plus a yummy, fiery coconut, lime and chilli paste. A little rice pancake and sweet coconut sauce sandwich (appam) was perfect with masala tea made so fresh that green cardamom pods floated on the surface.

New Pondichery

189 rue du Fbg-St-Denis, 10th (01.40.34.30.70). M° Gare du Nord. **Open** daily noon-10.30pm. **Average** €10. **Prix fixe** €6.60, €8. **Credit** MC, V. **Map** K2.
New Pondichery's fading orange facade is a welcome contrast to the grit and grime of the Gare du Nord area. Inside, the plain yet pleasant-enough room has the spice smells and laid-back feel of a real south Indian restaurant. Excited to see idli, a spongy cake made with rice and white lentils, and ulundu vadai, a white lentil fritter, on a Paris menu, we ordered them both. The taste was right, but the texture wasn't – they seemed to have suffered from inexpert reheating. Infinitely better were the dosai, huge south Indian crêpes with spicy fillings. The brahmane came packed with vegetables spiced with mustard seed, chilli and curry leaves, while the samsara was an equally filling and flavourful lamb and potato version; we ladled sambar, a spicy vegetable stew, over both. Considering the hefty size of the dosai, it would be wisest to skip starters altogether

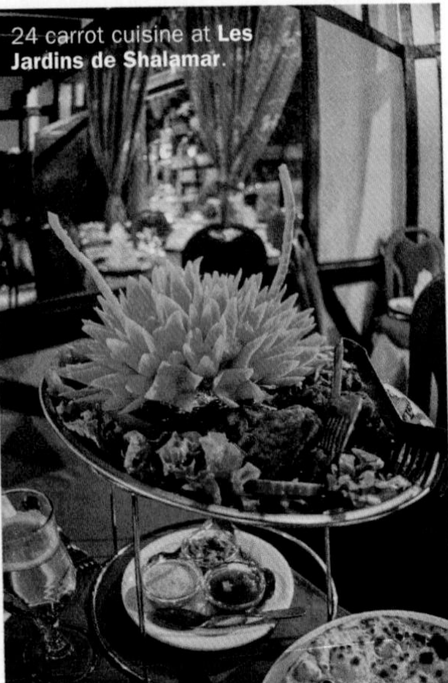
24 carrot cuisine at **Les Jardins de Shalamar**.

and beat the heat with a mango or rose lassi. Service was efficient on our visit, though we did wonder about the scratch marks around the serving hatch – do things get a little out-of-hand at peak times?

Shalimar

59 passage Brady, 10th (01.45.23.31.61) M° Strasbourg-St-Denis or Château d'Eau. **Open** daily noon-2.45pm, 7-11.45pm. Closed 1 May. **Average** €20. **Prix fixe** €13, €17. **Lunch menu** €9. **Credit** MC, V. **Wheelchair access**. **Map** K4.
Two details make this a solid address among the chaotic passage Brady options. First, there's the colour scheme of papaya-hued walls, embroidered hangings of elephants, and the complimentary pale-blue cocktails. Then there's the cheerful chef in the window, making fresh Indian breads. Be circumspect, though, and stick with meaty basics. We were impressed with the flavourful murgh tandoori, carefully spiced chicken, and the various breads did the chef proud. An excellent house special is the tandoori Shalimar, nan bread studded with pistachios and almonds. Though ample, the vegetarian curry was under-spiced. Service began to degenerate as the restaurant grew crowded and our polite but harassed waiter had a command of neither French nor English, which led to confusion over our orders.

Kirane's

85, av des Ternes, 17th (01.45.74.40.21). M° Porte Maillot. **Open** Tue-Sat noon-2.45pm, 7-11.15pm. **Average** €40. **Prix fixe** €29 (dinner only). **Lunch menu** €13, €15. **Credit** AmEx, DC, MC, V. **Map** B2.
It's worth the trip over here just for the starters: the tasty spinach and cheese palak panir, and the excellent aubergine bartha. The garlic nan was also a hit, appearing as it did with a tasty selection of seven chutneys and pickles, including good lime pickle and mango chutney. Things became less impressive with the main courses. Our vegetarian dish was a lame first cousin to the aubergine bartha: too little cooking of its spices left the mixture unpleasantly gritty. The house special lamb curry, however, was a generous serving accompanied by pilau rice, fragrant with nuts and raisins. We had a fine €18.50 bottle of the house Bordeaux, which we found surprisingly good with Indian food.

Shah Jahan

4 rue Gauthey, 17th (01.42.63.44.06). M° Brochant. **Open** daily noon-2.30pm, 7-11.30pm. **Average** €20. **Prix fixe** €18, €20. **Lunch menu** €8.50, €20. **Credit** AmEx, DC, MC, V. **Wheelchair access**.
Named after the ruler who built the Taj Mahal, this Indo-Pakistani restaurant may not be as architecturally glorious as its namesake might have liked, but the staff's courtesy coupled with our very tasty meal made us feel like royalty. We used the stuffed paratha loaded with morsels of curried potato and peas to lap up our dahl sag – dark green spinach dotted with whole green lentils. Chunks of flavourful lamb worked well with the mild aubergine purée and, if the chicken in our biryani was slightly dry, at least it had been grilled in the tandoor oven before being added to the saffron rice, almond and peas. We finished off sweetly with scoops of rose petal and pistachio ice cream.
Branch: Le Palais Shah Jahan, 14 rue Quatre Frères Peignot, 15th (01.45.78.21.07).

Les Jardins de Shalamar ★

174 rue Ordener, 18th (01.46.27.85.28). M° Guy Môquet. **Open** daily 11am-2.30pm, 6.30-11pm. **Average** €20. **Prix fixe** €17, €20. **Lunch menu** €9.15, €10.60. **Credit** MC, V.
On the dark side of Montmartre, not far from the edge of the 17th, lies this little gem of an Indo-Pakistani eatery, adorned with a big dark wood bar, beamed ceiling and red-clothed tables. The menu at first glance seems ordinary, divided into appetisers, tandoori, meat, seafood and poultry, biryani and the like, but even the humble vegetable fritters and handmade samosas at Les Jardins de Shalamar are exquisite. Our appetisers arrived on a platter festooned with a hedgehog-like carrot stick centrepiece (which we ate shamelessly). We were continually impressed by the freshness and vivid colours of every ingredient in our yoghurt raita, chewy garlic nan bread, cinnamony dahl, tangy green aubergine bagan bartha, and tender chicken jalfrezi stewed with tomatoes, green peppers and coriander. Puddings, too, impressed us – the rich slab of carrot and pistachio called gujrela, the badam halwa, a mild, bright-orange semolina cake, and the frozen cardamom kulfi. Shalamar tea, creamy and steeped with cardamom, wrapped up an ideal evening.

Italian

Savour the flavour of the Italian cucina in Paris; from topping-mad pizza to nettle risotto, there's something for every budget. Get ready to ciao down.

A crispy-crust pizza and an al dente bowl of pasta are simple pleasures that have too often been in short supply in Paris. Authentically good Italian food usually comes with a price tag that can knock the edge off your appetite, though there are exceptions if you know where to go. You can spend up big on pasta at the civilised **Il Cortile** or take the perfect pizza route at **Alfredo Positano**; tuck into razor-thin slices of carpaccio at **Lo Spuntino da Domenico** or plunder the antipasti table at **Da Mimmo**. And don't forget the organically inclined Italo booty of **Il Baccello**.

Il Cortile

Sofitel Demeure Hôtel Castille, 37 rue Cambon, 1st (01.44.58.45.67/www.alain-ducasse.com). M° Concorde. **Open** Mon-Fri noon-2.30pm, 7.30-10.30pm. **Average** €65. **Lunch menu** €45. **Credit** AmEx, DC, MC, V. **Wheelchair access. Non-smoking room. Map** G4.

Former sous-chef Tjaco Van Eikein is now in charge at this smart hotel restaurant (part of the Ducasse fold). A courtyard with fountain, trompe l'oeil stucco and outdoor tables under large parasols is the ideal place to enjoy the relative-bargain set lunch menu; otherwise, indoors there is a mock Villa d'Este dining room. Dinner begins with a small cube of warm focaccia, a couple of grissini and a mini baton of black olive bread, all made in-house, and an espresso cup of seasonal soup (fagioli, perhaps, in winter, or chilled fennel in summer). Ravioli with pumpkin and crushed amaretti comes with crisp Parma ham, while thickly sliced rabbit 'porchetta' (boned and rolled) is enlivened by a small dish of sweet and spicy mostarda di Cremona. Half the main course choices are fish – perfectly timed grilled John Dory for example, with salsa verde and confit vegetables, but game also gets a look-in (roast venison with Taggia olives and pale, creamy polenta). Desserts are particularly refined: three wobbly, mini panna cottas – one flavoured with lemon zest, another with a fig compote, and the most sublime caramel version. Service is particularly friendly and a female sommelier helps navigate the impressive, mostly Italian list.

La Bocca ★

59-61 rue Montmartre, 2nd (01.42.36.71.88). M° Sentier or Etienne Marcel. **Open** daily noon-2.30pm. Closed 25 Dec, 1 Jan. **Average** €30. **Credit cards** MC, V. **Map** J5.

Although the bistro-style La Bocca feels hip and easy-going, the kitchen is rigorously organised around day-fresh, seasonal produce. Sun seekers can sit on the terrace, if they don't mind teetering on the narrow kerb of rue Montmartre. We preferred to feast our eyes on the weathered mosaic-tile floor inside, and the pretty bar with its Victoria Arduino coffee machine. Further back is the non-smoking section, where you have the best view of La Bocca's spiral staircase leading up to the bright first-floor dining room. Our calamari e fagioli was a copious blend of tasty squid and moist white beans, while the caprese salad was made with good, if not great, mozzarella and avocado. The fat noodle-shaped cavatappi pasta is a vegetarian's delight, mixed with mushrooms, asparagus, crème fraîche, cherry tomatoes and big, heaven-scented basil leaves. The agnoloni (giant ravioli) were filled with market-fresh ricotta, sage, rosemary and basil, topped with cream and parmesan. We bravely finished with cantuccio, a gooey variation on tiramisu with crunchy nougat which went particularly well with the vanilla and blackberry bouquet of our Monica di Sardegna.

Gli Angeli

5 rue St-Gilles, 3rd (01.42.71.05.80). M° Chemin-Vert. **Open** daily noon-2.30pm, 8-10.30pm. Closed Aug. **Average** €35. **Credit** MC, V. **Wheelchair access. Map** L6.

Locals, business people and in-the-know tourists head to Gli Angeli, steps from place des Vosges, for traditional Italian cooking in a laid-back setting. Diners are greeted with a warm 'buon giorno' at this classic trattoria with stone walls, well-spaced tables and a menu of lovingly executed regional classics. One of our group waxed lyrical about the peppery garlic and tomato sauce ladled over a starter of slow-cooked mussels, and mopped it all up with crusty baguette. Our waiter warned him not to fill up on bread and when our mains arrived we understood why. As copious as it was delicious, the taglierini with shaved parmesan and rocket was creamy and intense. A massive, perfectly cooked steak with 'sweet and sour' sauce was swathed in a rich, meaty broth with a hint of balsamic vinegar and lots of cracked pepper, and the tuna steak elicited 'oohs' and 'ahhs' from our neighbours. Though stuffed, we licked up every last bit of tiramisu, with gooey mascarpone and espresso-doused biscuits, and a semi-freddo of homemade vanilla ice cream with candied fruit. The all-Italian wine list covers the main regions and starts at €4 for a carafe of house red; the €26 Rubesco our waiter recommended went down a treat. Gli Angeli's reasonable prices, friendly service and well-crafted cuisine are no secret, so book.

L'Osteria

10 rue de Sévigné, 4th (01.42.71.37.08) M° St-Paul. **Open** Mon 8-10.30pm; Tue-Fri noon-3pm, 8-10.30pm. **Closed** Aug, 25 Dec, 1 Jan, Easter Monday. **Average** €50. **Credit** DC, MC, V. **Map** L6.

Tony Vianello's tiny trattoria has become a magnet for all those who love the simplicity of northern Italian food. Tables are jammed close together, conditions are somewhat spartan and the chunky goblets do no favours for the wine – Italian, of course, featuring the very grand and a few mid-priced bottles of decent quality. But what marks this place is the real feel for seasonality. So in among the constant (but still beautifully executed) likes of a rocket and parmesan salad, tagliolini with veal ragù and spaghetti alle vongole, black truffles (with leeks, or with a scallop carpaccio), elvers (frighteningly expensive and probably from the Severn), morels (with gnocchi or tagliolini) and game (venison with port) crop up at their allotted time of year. Of course, this style of cooking relies on top-quality ingredients, precise timing and expert seasoning, and on all counts Vianello can't be faulted. If there is a downside (not counting the price – food this good doesn't come cheap), then the desserts (tiramisu, panna cotta with strawberries) are slightly less-than-exciting. We've also had reports of inaccuracies on the bill, so don't be afraid to check.

Alfredo Positano

9 rue Guisarde, 6th (01.43.26.90.52). M° Mabillon. **Open** Tue-Sat noon-2.30pm, 7-11.30pm. Closed Aug. **Average** €38. **Credit** MC, V. **Wheelchair access. Map** H7.

They don't take bookings on Saturday nights at this nondescript trattoria and, although tables turn over astonishingly fast, by 8pm the queue stretches out the door. And it's clear why. From a menu that features pizza, pasta and a small selection of meat and fish main courses (not their forte), we started with excellent antipasti di verdura – grilled courgettes, aubergines and mushrooms, glistening artichokes and plump butter beans. Although our neighbours and their children – this is an ideal family restaurant – were tucking into delicious looking pasta and risotto, we were here for the pizza. The Manou, named after the laconic pizzaiolo himself, stars tomato sauce, mushrooms, capers and mozzarella. But the napolitaine, the stripped-down quintessence of pizza, left us in awe: thin, crunchy dough – the kind with those big air pockets that look like volcanoes – straight out of the wood-fired oven, all charred base and yeasty aroma, smeared with tomato, oregano, garlic, fresh basil, anchovies and no cheese. Service is straightforward, tables are cramped, wine is decent and the tiramisu carries the endorsement of superchef Joël Robuchon. If you love pizza, join the queue.

Chez Bartolo

7 rue des Canettes, 6th (01.43.26.27.08). M° St-Germain-des-Prés or St-Sulpice. **Open** Tue-Sat noon-2.30pm, 7-11.30pm; Sun noon-3pm. **Average** €35. **No credit cards. Map** H7.

Accept the fact that your bill will be inappropriately high and the service inexplicably sullen (hello, these are supposed to be sunny Neapolitans) and you might enjoy eating here because at least the food is reliable. That's the reason, as opposed to the kitsch decor of Vesuvius in all her erupting glory, that it's always packed. Stick with starters such as chicory filled with warm gorgonzola and pistachio sauce and forget the individual servings such as marinated peppers. Our waiter refused to team them with anything else, insisting that the antipasto was too big for one person and the peppers were served alone, so there. They weren't worth their €10. Pizzas, including the ham-and-mushroom la reine, are good; they're prepared by an apron-wearing, dough-kneading Italian gent who deposits them in the wood-fired oven. The pasta is decent – try the classic spaghetti alle vongole (clams) – whereas our wood-fired prawns sailed too close to the volcano, arriving severely charred with a minuscule side of bruised young spinach leaves (the 'salad').

Il Vicolo ★

34 rue Mazarine, 6th (01.43.25.01.11). M° Mabillon or Odéon. **Open** Mon-Sat 12.30-2.30pm, 8-11pm. **Average** €40. **Lunch menu** €21. **Credit** AmEx, MC, V. **Map** H6-7.

Mercurial gastronomic showman Antonio Procopio may be gone (a waiter rather cryptically attributed his departure to a broken arm), replaced by his own Tuscan sous-chef, but the restaurant he left behind in St-Germain continues to attract a worldly, arty and international crowd that doesn't mind paying stiff prices for food that's very good, if not better. The attractive dining room is Milanese bold, with fibre optic lights in the parquet and an orange-piped brown banquette that recalls Man Ray's famous lips running the length of one wall. The salle, directed by a Gucci-glasses-wearing Italian (one wonders if she gets a break on these pricey frames from regular Tom Ford), feels a bit clubby, but service is prompt and polite. Procopio's menu hasn't changed – it would be nice if they added the odd seasonal special – and proposes light modern eating from all over the boot. The carpaccio of bresaolo (air-dried beef) and rocket salad is enlivened by a dab of delicious citrus-peel spiked ricotta. The homemade spaghetti with pesto sauce, green beans and potato slivers, a Genoan classic, is delicious, as is the tuna steak cooked in balsamic vinegar. All the pastas are freshly made and perfectly sauced, and the wine list offers a fine selection of unusual and affordable Italian bottles. Skip the dull desserts for cheese, or head directly to the good coffee and a grappa.

Le Perron

6 rue Perronet, 7th (01.45.44.71.51). M° St-Germain-des-Prés. **Open** Mon-Sat noon-2.30pm, 7.30-11pm. **Average** €35. **Credit** AmEx, MC, V. **Map** G6.

Anyone who laments the arrival of 'St-Germain d'après', now that fashion victims crowd the 'literary' cafés, will be reassured by this restaurant brimming with local intelligentsia. Not that anyone cares

Sunshine on a plate at **Sardegna a Tavola**. *See p202.*

UGGIANO'S FAMOUS SUPER-TUSCANS

FALCONERI CABERNET SAUVIGNON IGT

GRAPE VARIETY - Cabernet Sauvignon Toscano 85% Sangiovese 15%

COLOR - Intense ruby red

AGEING - In French oak barrels for 18 to 20 months

BOUQUET - Wild berries with hints of clove, violet and vanilla

PALATE - Full-bodied, slightly tannic with velvety finish

FOOD PAIRING - Flavorful pastas and wild game

SERVING TEMPERATURE - 18-20° C open bottle a least one hour before pouring

BOTTLE SIZE - Lt. 0,750

CHIANTI DOCG RISERVA

COLOR - Deep ruby red

AGEING - In French oak barrels for 18-24 months

BOUQUET - Ethereal with predominant violet and vanilla

PALATE - Full-bodied with velvety tannins that provide structure

FOOD PAIRING - Flavorful pastas, grilled meats and wild game

SERVING TEMPERATURE - 18-20° C open bottle at least one hour before pouring

BOTTLE SIZE - Lt. 0,750

50020 S.VINCENZO A. TORRI (FIRENZE) Via Empolese
Tel: +39 (0)55 769087 – Fax +39 (0)55 769211
www.uggiano.it – e-mail: info@uggiano.it

EX-VITIS INTERNATIONAL (Wholesale wine merchants) - Tel: 01.42.60.39.31
Fax: 01.40.15.03.90 (around the corner from the restaurant)

DELIZIE D'UGGIANO RESTAURANT Tel: 01.40.15.06.69. 18 Rue Duphot, 1st.
M° Madeleine. Open Mon-Sat 9.30am-11pm. Closes Sat lunch.
e-mail: losapiog@wanadoo.fr – www.delizieduggiano.com

This restaurant is owned by the illustrious son of Tuscany Guiseppe Losapio, for whom gracious hosting and fine dining are all-consuming passions. As it happens, Guiseppe also owns vineyards that produce some of the most highly acclaimed wines in all of Italy (for purchase in the boutique):

"The best of Italian cuisine is to be found at Delizie d'Uggiano…Bravissimo!"
—*Elle magazine*

"Guiseppe Losapio is one of the greatest specialists of Tuscan cuisine around"
—*Gault & Milaut (15 out of 20)*

As quoted from the Michelin Guide: "Italianissimo!"

who their neighbours are here; what attracts regulars is the serious cuisine, the delightful intimacy, and the relaxed hospitality of the Sardinian owner and his staff. Although the carte hardly changes, the dishes are consistently good and the seasonal plats du jour always imaginative. Enticing first courses include vongole in umido, a dish of lightly sautéed clams; salsicce abruzzese alla griglia, sausages marinated in wild fennel; and antipasto del Perron, sun-dried tomatoes, courgettes, aubergines, mushrooms and chicory baked to melting point in olive oil. Densely flavoured risottos are a feast, especially the devilish-looking risotto del scrivano, squid in its ink, and the chef has an assured touch with veal dishes. For afters, opt for cheese or homemade tiramisu, and stick to the constantly changing house wines, such as the Dolcetto d'Alba, which have an uncanny way of loosening writers' block.

Le Bistrot Napolitain

18 av Franklin D. Roosevelt, 8th (01.45.62.08.37). M° Franklin D. Roosevelt. **Open** Mon-Fri noon-2.30pm, 7-11pm; Sat noon-2.30pm. **Average** €28. **Credit** AmEx, MC, V. **Map** E4.

There is nothing new or overtly fashionable about Le Bistrot Napolitain – which, around the Champs-Elysées, makes it very refreshing indeed. A bastion of straightforward southern Italian fare for the past 15 years, this crowded and smoky bistro attracts a lively, unselfconscious set. Once you've been squeezed onto the banquette, sit back and enjoy the scenery – diners tucking into big plates of ham, fried red mullet or carpaccio, the pizzaiolo toiling before his oven, waiters dashing around bearing big plates of pasta. Though many people had come for a full Italian feast, we stuck to the pizzas, reputed to be among the best in town. Indeed, the crusts were thin and crisp with big air pockets, though the margarita topping was slightly bland – we preferred the rocket and fresh tomato version.

Le Stresa

7 rue Chambiges, 8th (01.47.23.51.62). M° Alma Marceau or Franklin D. Roosevelt. **Open** Mon-Fri noon-2.30, 7.15-10.30pm. Closed Aug, 25 Dec. **Average** €75. **Credit** AmEx, DC, MC, V. **Map** D5.

The Faiola brothers have run this perennially fashionable haunt for years and people just keep coming back for the impeccably fresh food and the welcome. The walls testify to the restaurant's link with le gratin de Paris: sculptures and photos by César, collages and personally signed pix by Peter Beard. On our visit the venerable Jean-Paul Belmondo and footballer Emmanuel Petit were à table. The menu, too, is full of classics: mozzarella and tomato pizza, sole with lemon, spinach ravioli and tiramisu. Mixed antipasti of fresh artichoke, roasted chilli, asparagus and aubergine salad and the spaghetti with small clams are excellent starters. Also good is the fiery spaghetti à la Jean-Paul Belmondo (yes, he ordered it, too) bathed in chilli, tomato, olives and garlic, as well as simple pan-fried veal with lemon and spinach. Finish with mixed berry gelato.

I Golosi

6 rue de la Grange-Batelière, 9th (01.48.24.18.63). M° Grands Boulevards or Richelieu-Drouot. **Open** Mon-Fri noon-2.30pm, 7.30-midnight; Sat noon-2.30pm. Closed Aug. **Average** €30. **Credit** MC, V. **Map** J3.

I Golosi is something of an Italian institution in the capital – a gourmet experience embracing wine and food, eat-in or take-away goodies (oil, wine, pasta and fresh stuff from the delicatessen). Owner Marco Tonazzo boasts over 500 different wines that he imports from his homeland and retails competitively as a flag-waving gesture. The modern restaurant over two floors is pretty and pink with a funky-shaped bar on the way in and a refreshingly original menu. We accompanied generous slices of exceptional two-year-old Parma ham and globe artichoke heart topped with poached egg and salsa verde with wines by the glass – Dolcetto d'Alba from Visadi and Pongelli Rossi Montepulciano. Main course macaroni with a slightly spicy rabbit sauce was comforting and delicious, as was baby squid pan-fried with chilli and chard. With these we sampled two stouter vintages by the glass: a young Barbera d'Asti Ca di Pian and a big Brunello di Montalcino 1997. The tiramisu looked winning but with no more room we were content to sit back and enjoy the jazz and grind of the coffee machine. Charming authentic staff sport 'slow wine' aprons and attitude.

Pizza Milano

30 bd des Italiens, 9th (01.47.70.33.33/ www.pizzamilano.com). M° Opéra. **Open** Mon-Thur, Sun 11.30am-12.30am; Fri, Sat 11.30am-1am. **Average** €20. **Prix fixe** €15.90 (Mon-Fri, Sun). **Credit** AmEx, MC, V. **Wheelchair access**. **Non-smoking room**. **Map** H4.

Among the area's chain restaurants, this place stands out – its low-key decor and low lighting contrast with the plastic Americana that prevails elsewhere and the food is decently priced and good. The continental branch of the successful UK-based Pizza Express chain, Pizza Milano is a fine eat-on-the-run or late-night option. We were pleased with the prompt, friendly service and the standard of our starters – a delicious insalata caprese (mozzarella and tomatoes with basil dressing) served with hot pizza-crust balls and a green salad. Pizzas were nicely topped, too – the siciliana is strewn with artichoke hearts, black olives, anchovies, ham and mozzarella and the calabrese is a tomato and mozzarella pizza that is sprinkled with parmesan shavings and fresh rocket when it comes out of the oven. Doubtless encouraged by the low lighting and proximity of the tables, people chat back and forth.

Lo Spuntino da Domenico ★

31 rue La Bruyère, 9th (01.42.82.01.84). M° St-Georges. **Open** Mon-Fri noon-3pm, 7pm-11pm; Sat 7-11pm. **Average** €25. **Credit** MC, V. **Map** H2.

Though you'll never see this tiny dining room with ochre-coloured stucco walls and polyester tablecloths in *Casa Vogue*, it has become very popular with a local crowd since opening in 2002, for the quality and generosity of the Neapolitan owner's cooking and hospitality. Portions are, in fact, large enough to share a starter such as the delicious beef carpaccio, cut in razor-thin strips and garnished with oregano, parmesan chunks and capers, or the bruschetta. You can continue with a pasta – the fettucine carbonara on a recent visit was excellent, as was the spinach-filled ravioli – or a pizza, also first-rate and made on the premises. The carafe wines are easy on the wallet, but go with the Montepulciano d'Abbruzzo, a good buy at €22, if you can. A complimentary limoncello (iced, sweet lemon liqueur as found in Sorrento) goes down a treat with coffee.

Da Mimmo

39 bd de Magenta, 10th (01.42.06.44.47). M° Jacques-Bonsergent. **Open** Tue-Sat noon-2.30pm, 7-30-11.30pm. Closed Aug. **Average** €34. **Lunch menu** €26. **Credit** MC, V. **Map** L4.

If it's not the regulation trattoria decor of red-checked tablecloths, matching tiled pizza oven, grappa bottle lamps and Napoli mural that pulls in the Italophiles, then it must be the puffy pizzas and freshly made pasta. You could quibble about the price (€19.50 for gnocchi ripieni or €16.50 for carpaccio) given the surroundings, but that would be ignoring the quality of the ingredients and the fact that, after all, you're in Paris. Antipasti – grilled octopus, prosciutto, marinated mushrooms, courgette, aubergine, calamari, frittata, sausage, broad beans, artichokes, carrots and sweet pickled onions – stretch over a central table. Don't resist; the plum-sized green olives are the best ever. Pizza roquette comes crowned with cheese and rocket leaves on a puffed, perfectly crisp crust while plump logs of gnocchi have a dusting of tomato sauce (ripieni) and grate-while-you-wait parmesan. A slice of boozy tiramisu and custardy, sugar-dusted lemon tart, the last drops of Valpolicella and a waiter calling 'arrivederci': la dolce vita in the 10th.

La Madonnina

10 rue Marie et Louise, 10th (01.42.01.25.26). M° République. **Open** Mon-Thur 12.30-2.30pm, 8-11pm; Fri, Sat 12.30-2.30pm, 8-11.30pm. **Average** €25. **Lunch menu** €10.50. **Credit** MC, V. **Map** L4.

The Vespa parked outside and posters of 1940s comedian Toto Fabrizi create a laid-back slice of Napoli a stone's throw from the Canal St-Martin. The setting is earthy; strings of garlic and peppers hang from the windows, and candlelit sturdy wooden tables are reflected in a big gilt-framed mirror. The antipasti were exquisite – fresh aubergine, courgette, mushrooms, sun-dried tomatoes and artichoke drenched in extra-virgin olive oil, served with good baguette so you don't miss a drop. Though the à la carte choice of mains is not vast – three meat dishes and three pasta dishes – each is well executed, genuine Italian fare. The linguine di frutta di mare, though not extravagant, was served with four juicy garlic prawns, and the scaloppine alla muscarolla, veal escalope served with mushroom and cream sauce, was tender with very fresh steamed spinach. The Italian wines range from inexpensive Valpolicella (€9 for a half-litre carafe) to more sophisticated Montepulciano (€15.50 for a half-litre). The tiramisu was deliciously soft and gooey while the panna cotta was artistically drizzled with chocolate sauce. On our visit everyone's meal was rounded off by a complimentary limoncello.

Sardegna a Tavola ★

1 rue de Cotte, 12th (01.44.75.03.28). M° Ledru-Rollin. **Open** Mon 7.30-11.30pm; Tue-Sat noon-2.30pm, 7.30-11.30pm. Closed Aug, 25 Dec, 1 Jan. **Average** €40. **Credit** AmEx, MC, V. **Map** N8.

Success has allowed the Sardinian couple who run this sunny restaurant to dress up the formerly sparse decor, making it more authentically Sardinian. Even without these efforts, though, Sardegna a Tavola would be worth a considerable detour for its beautifully prepared island specialities and hard-to-find wines. A meal might start with thinly sliced charcuterie and chunky vegetables – fat beans, aubergines cooked with wine, roasted peppers, courgette and cauliflower – unless you're feeling up to horse meat carpaccio. Then choose from perfectly prepared pastas such as hearty ravioli stuffed with ricotta and mushrooms in thick, tomato-mushroom sauce, farfalle pasta with a typically Sardinian combination of mint, crushed almonds, fresh (though mild) chilli pepper and plenty of olive oil, or linguine with a refreshing sauce of langoustines and orange. The house wine, served by the carafe, is delicious; the sweet Sardinian wines are also worth sipping with almond cakes for dessert.

Il Baccello

33 rue Cardinet, 17th (01.43.80.63.60/ www.ilbaccello.com). M° Wagram. **Open** Tue-Sat noon-2.30pm, 7.30-11pm. Closed three weeks in Aug. **Average** €40. **Prix fixe** €36 (dinner only). **Lunch menu** €15.50. **Credit** AmEx, DC, MC, V. **Map** D2.

Chef Raphaël Bembaron has an impressive culinary pedigree – Lucas Carton in Paris, Enoteca Pinchiorri in Florence, and Joia, the superb gourmet vegetarian restaurant, in Milan. It's the latter that the chef says has had the largest impact on him, and he cooks with as much organic produce as possible. Willow-green walls, spot-lit ceramics, industrial grey carpeting and polished mahogany give this snug dining room a Milan-meets-Tokyo-style, but the plump black olives and whole-wheat bread tell you that you're going to get the best of the boot. Starters of whole-wheat papardelle with wild mushrooms and chickpea soup garnished with pancetta-wrapped langoustines were superb, as were main courses of risotto cooked with Barolo wine and garnished with duck breast and aged mimolette cheese, and langoustines on toothpicks with almond-stuffed olives on spelt and broccoli in a pumpkin coulis. For dessert, go for the almond-flavoured panna cotta in plum sauce or the highly original gelée, two aspics of fruit brandy. The wine list, although small, is definitely interesting.

Japanese

If you knew sushi ... fans of the raw-fish diva and her pals sashimi, yakitori and teppanaki will find plenty to applaud in Paris. Stone cold soba or not.

Sushi (of variable quality) remains synonymous with Japanese food in Paris, but an increasing number of restaurants are offering lesser-known specialities, from refined kaiseki cooking at **Kinugawa** to elegantly prepared eel at **Nodaiwa**. Many of the best Japanese restaurants are clustered along rue Ste-Anne near the Opéra Garnier, but **Zen** near the Louvre has fabulous sashimi. In St-Germain, try **Yen** for soothing soba noodles and the recently opened **Abazu** for showy teppanaki.

Kinugawa ★

9 rue du Mont-Thabor, 1st (01.42.60.65.07). M° Tuileries. **Open** Mon-Sat noon-2.30pm, 7-10pm. Closed 24 Dec-7 Jan. **Average** €60. **Prix fixe** €86-€108 (dinner only). **Lunch menu** €26, €52. **Credit** AmEx, DC, MC, V. **Non-smoking room**. **Map** G5.

Everything at Kinugawa breathes excellence, from the decor to the the crockery and gentle, assiduous service. The food follows the highly refined kaiseki-ryori tradition, embodying the quintessential Japanese virtues of wabi (simplicity) and sabi (unstudied elegance) – meaning it's not (only) what you do, it's how you do it. We opted for the €86 menu: nine courses plus dessert. Describing the rapture could fill pages, suffice it to say that we were in heaven. From the classic, stunningly fresh sashimi to the original lime-scented fish consommé, via grilled fish, a vegetable pot-au-feu, salad, superbly light tempura, the fluffiest rice and wonderful miso soup, every fascinating combination of texture and flavour had us swooning. Even the house Bordeaux was a joy. **Branch**: 4 rue St-Philippe-du-Roule, 8th (01.45.63.08.07).

Laï Laï Ken

7 rue Ste-Anne, 1st (01.40.15.96.90). M° Pyramides. **Open** Mon-Sat noon-10pm; Sun 6-10pm. **Average** €14. **Prix fixe** (dinner only) €13.50, €21. **Credit** AmEx, MC, V. **Map** H5.

LLK certainly doesn't aim for the culinary stratosphere, yet it's pretty much unbeatable in the 'affordable, homely and flavourful' category: we've been coming regularly for five years now, and it hasn't disappointed once. The service is pleasant and atten-

Hubba-hubba shabu shabu at **Takara**. *See p205.*

International

After all that Eating & Drinking, get yourself an Eiffel!

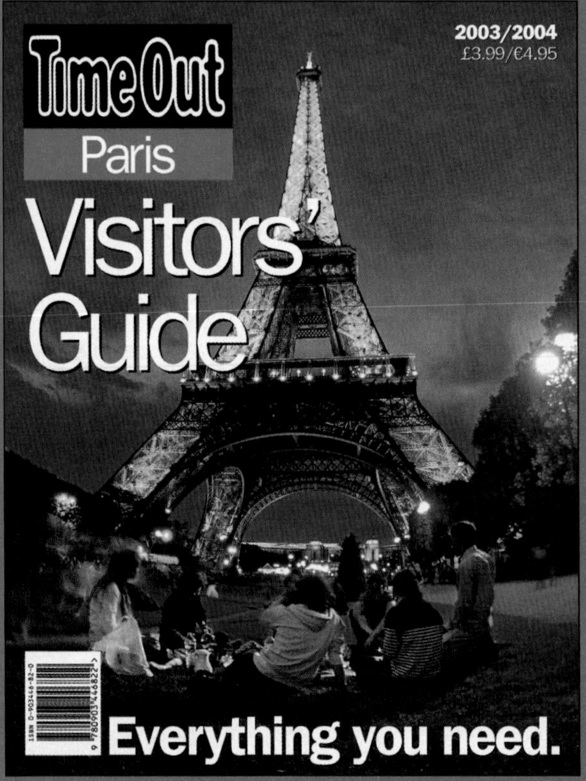

From the editors of this guide, 100 pages packed with the city's best sights, sounds, shopping and accommodation.

Just €4.95/£3.99 at good bookshops and newsagents.

Or send your address with VISA number + expiry date to:

Time Out, 15-17 rue des Martyrs, 75009 Paris.

Fax: +33 (0)1.44.73.90.60

E-mail: distribution@timeout.fr

tive and the surroundings clean and low-key. Ramen – noodle soup laden with bamboo shoots and pork slices – or well-made and generous dishes such as stir-fried beef with green peppers, fried rice or exotic jellyfish are the way to go. Above all, don't miss the sublime age gyoza, deep-fried pork and garlic dumplings in a crispy rice pastry wrapper, preferably accompanied by large cans of Asahi beer.

Nodaiwa ★

272 rue St-Honoré, 1st (01.42.86.03.42/ www.nodaiwa.com). M° Tuileries or Pyramides. **Open** Mon-Sat noon-2.30pm, 7-10pm. Closed 15 Aug-1 Sept. **Average** €30. **Prix fixe** €44-€55. **Lunch menu** €15-€23. **Credit** AmEx, DC, MC, V. **Map** G5.

This elegant modern branch of one of Tokyo's oldest and best 'unagi' restaurants is for eel lovers only. The grilled Japanese delicacy, prepared from a generations-old recipe, is without doubt the star attraction: the brief menu offers portions à la carte according to weight or as part of the reasonably priced set meals. The lunch menu served up a sublime slab of chopstick-tender eel in a large bowl of Japanese sticky rice, as well as a lightly seasoned crisp green salad and chawanmushi, a slippery, savoury custard steamed with flecks of eel, daikon radish and shitake mushrooms. The side dishes in the 'matsu' menu included generous cuts of fresh tuna sashimi, miso soup and a tiny bowl of pickled vegetables. For dessert, green tea bavarois, a subtle gelatine-based terrine, slipped down as easily as had the melt-in-the-mouth grilled eel.

Takara ★

14 rue Molière, 1st (01.42.96.08.38). M° Palais Royal. **Open** Tue-Fri 12.30-2.30pm, 7-10.30pm. Closed three weeks in Aug, two weeks in Dec. **Average** €60. **Prix fixe** €46-€59. **Lunch menu** €19-€42. **Credit** MC, V. **Map** H5.

In its choice of name at least, there's no sign of the famous Japanese modesty – takara means 'treasure'. Its owner, Ashibe-san, opened one of the capital's first Japanese restaurants over four decades ago, and this, his second venture, has been going since 1963. Ask for a delicious cold umeshu (prune wine) to start. They do first-class sushi and sashimi, as well as things that are harder to find in Paris: shabu-shabu, for instance, a hot pot served in autumn and winter. This set meal (€59 per person) comes with a sashimi course, but the centrepiece is a huge earthenware pot of boiling stock perched on a table-top gas burner, into which diners dip thinly-sliced beef, Chinese cabbage and konomono (edible chrysanthemum leaves). The summer equivalent, nabemono, comes with thick udon noodles and raw-egg dip. Delicious year-round desserts include the wonderful coconut ice cream with red bean jam.

Zen

18 rue du Louvre, 1st (01.42.86.95.05). M° Louvre-Rivoli. **Open** Tue-Sat noon-2.30pm, 7-10.30pm; Sun 7-10.30pm. **Average** €20 (lunch), €45 (dinner). **Prix fixe** €24-€55. **Credit** AmEx, MC, V. **Map** H5.

We walked into an eerily quiet room, populated mainly by Japanese customers who glanced up when we entered, but then swiftly returned their attention to their plates. We knew immediately the food would be authentic when we spied natto, a smelly, fermented soybean almost universally disliked by foreigners, on the menu. It came with a few petals of raw cuttlefish, a pinch of wasabi and shreds of dried seaweed. Absolutely divine. The tuna sashimi with igname (a Japanese yam that becomes glutinous when grated) was another unusual delight, for it is rarely found outside Japan. The tuna was smooth, meaty and fresh, made all the more sensual by the viscous texture of the yam. The superior sashimi selection, minimally presented on frosted glass plates, was everything we anticipated – thick tiles of the freshest salmon, tuna, and snapper, as well as scallops and sweet prawn. The tender grilled eel – the only hot dish we ordered – was also excellent, coated with a veneer of sweet, sticky marinade.

Aki

2bis rue Daunou, 2nd (01.42.61.48.38). M° Opéra. **Open** Mon-Fri noon-2.30pm, 7-11pm; Sat 7-11pm. Closed three weeks in Aug. **Average** €30 (lunch), €50 (dinner). **Prix fixe** €43-€68. **Lunch menu** €14.50-€27.50. **Credit** AmEx, MC, V. **Map** G4.

The two-level Aki is more moody than minimalist with its cushy red velvet chairs, gold walls, soft lighting and chunky dark wood tables. Chef Kazunari Kono's menu is equally modern – you'll find sushi, sashimi and a lunchtime bento box (popular with the Japanese business set), but the cooked

Well-eeled **Nodaiwa.**

Isami: heaven bento.

dishes are where his creativity shows. Ignoring the prix fixes, which in Parisian Japanese restaurants rarely go out on any kind of limb, we started with the confit aubergines, chunks of aubergine, prawns and gelatinous igname in a succulent peanut sauce. Next, the wafu beef fillet may not have been Kobe beef, but the thinly sliced rare meat couldn't have been more tender, with miso and soy-lemon sauces for dipping. We couldn't resist a sashimi platter, and were rewarded with something akin to Zen bouquet – there was fuschia, lavender, artful twigs, and fish sculpted into a rose with black roe in the centre. The salmon, tuna and sea bream were squeaky fresh; the octopus, however, defeated our jaws. We skipped dessert and relaxed over cups of smoked rice tea.

Isse

56 rue Ste-Anne, 2nd (01.42.96.67.76). M° Pyramides. **Open** Tue-Fri noon-2pm, 7-10pm; Sat 7-10pm. Closed three weeks in Aug. **Average** €75. **Lunch menu** €22.85, €30.50. **Credit** MC, V. **Map** H4.

In the heart of the Japanese district, discreetly signposted Isse has long been a favourite with the international fashion world as well as Japanese salary-men. An elegantly suited lady allocates your place at one of the few tables around the downstairs counter or upstairs in a calm cocoon of pale wood. A la carte offers sea bass, tuna, salmon, assorted fried fish dishes and rarer delights such as chrysanthemum leaves. The set lunch menu gets round the fiddle (and prices) of the carte and goes beyond the standard sushi or sashimi formula. A dark miso soup with ample flakes of seaweed was the prelude to a bento box containing an assortment of tasty nibbles, both hot and cold: a pleasant salad of pickled herring and cucumber, red tuna sashimi, tender if undistinguished, accompanied by chewy red pickle, fried mackerel plus a mixed salad with a European-style dressing, and two chunks of not-too-sweet Japanese omelette were all familiar elements. More unusual was a stew of onions, carrots and leeks in a slightly sweet dark sauce. The definite highlight, however, was the crunchy lotus sections deep-fried, tempura-style, in a light batter. The quality of the fish was fine, but prices seem high and the overall impression was rather bland. If you've got the budget, order à la carte and go for the rarer fish species.

Isami

4 quai d'Orléans, 4th (01.40.46.06.97). M° Pont Marie. **Open** Tue-Sat noon-2pm, 7-10pm; Sun 7-10pm. Closed three weeks in Aug. **Average** €42. **Credit** MC, V. **Map** K7.

An elegant French woman nestled at our elbow confided that she'd tried all the Japanese restaurants in Paris and Isami was simply the best in town. A quick glance at her and her pal downing their sushi like loose-jowled labradors, plus the tables of Japanese regulars and travellers, added some weight to her claim. It's a tiny place (seven tables plus half a dozen chairs at the bar) so book ahead. Sparkling fresh fish is the draw card: whelks and monkfish liver (complimentary appetisers), sushi of salmon or tuna, as well as sea urchin, eel and octopus served on trad wooden boards, and sashimi moriawase – slices of slinky tuna, swordfish, salmon, octopus and squid with wasabi and shredded white radish.

Abazu ★

3 rue Andre-Mazet, 6th (01.46.33.72.05).
M° Odéon. **Open** Tue-Sat noon-2.30pm,7.30-10.30pm; Sun 7.30-10.30pm. **Average** €35 (lunch), €50 (dinner). **Prix fixe** €33, €39. **Lunch menu** €15.50-€18.50. **Credit** AmEx, DC, MC, V. **Map** H7.

Just steps from the Odéon in a neighbourhood so touristy you might rightly despair of finding a decent meal, this compact new Japanese is a restaurant worth travelling for. The setting itself – a handful of tables and a few stools pulled up to the teppanaki (grilled fish, veg and meat) table where several chefs cook your meal under your hungry gaze – is so discreet and minimalist as to go almost unnoticed, but if you sit at the refrectory table downstairs, the bitter-almond painted walls and tiny trickling fountain in the corner will be a soothing background to some superb food. The menus are excellent value, beginning with soothing salted egg flan and tuna-and-ginger tartare with finely sliced white radish, and continuing with starters such as grilled lotus root topped with undulating ribbons of dried tuna, outstanding miso soup, rice, a choice of one of two main courses – the grilled fish or prawns are first-rate – and ending with a tomato salad. Dessert runs to green tea ice cream with sticky bean sauce, or cake, and there are six different sakes as well as wine.

Japotori

41 rue Monsieur-le-Prince, 6th (01.43.29.00.54).
M° Odéon. **Open** daily noon-3pm, 6-11.45pm. Closed 24, 25 Dec. **Average** €10. **Prix fixe** €5.49-€14.48. **Credit** MC, V. **Map** H7.

Low prices draw a young, lively crowd to this popular joint specialising in yakitori (Japanese-style kebabs), and at weekends it gets completely packed. Don't be surprised to see people queuing up outside; be prepared to do the same. The menus feature yakitori in varying styles and number – the top price brings eight. All menus include rice and soup with thin slices of onion and mushroom. The yakitori are delivered in batches of two or three – duck, chicken, molten cheese wrapped in a thin slice of beef, whole grilled mushrooms, meatballs and pork. A tiny cup of sake tops it all off at the end. Fun, filling and just about unbeatable value.

Yen

22 rue St-Benoît, 6th (01.45.44.11.18).
M° St-Germain-des-Prés. **Open** Mon, Sun 7.30-11.30pm; Tue-Sat 12.30-2.30pm, 7.30-11.30pm. Closed two weeks in Aug, 25 Dec, 1 May. **Average** €45. **Prix fixe** (dinner only) €60. **Lunch menu** €18.50, €30.50. **Credit** AmEx, MC, V. **Map** H7.

This ascetic but appealing duplex Japanese restaurant in the heart of St-Germain has a loyal following of stylish boutique owners, publishers and politicians thanks to its solicitious service, healthy but flavourful eating and a tranquil Zen setting. The house speciality is soba, buckwheat noodles, freshly made daily on the premises, and served cold in salad or hot in broth with a garnish of finely sliced leeks. At noon, there are two good-value menus – a bento box with tuna sashimi, smoked fish, Japanese omelette, and other tasty titbits, followed by the noodles of your choice, or a noodle-and-tempura menu that begins with sticky Japanese rice seasoned with peas and toasted sesame seeds and continues with noodles with a side of feather-light tempura. In the evening the carte is divided between starters – try the grilled buckwheat grains served with sweet miso – noodles, and side dishes. Portions are modest, but this food is so well-balanced that you leave the table completely satisfied, especially if you've mastered the simultaneous use of chopsticks and a wooden spoon, Japanese-style. Were it not for the rather hefty prices, we'd happily become regulars.

Jipangue

96 rue de La Boétie, 8th. (01.45.63.77.00).
M° St-Philippe-du-Roule. **Open** Mon-Fri noon-2pm, 7-11pm; Sat 7-11pm. **Average** €30. **Prix fixe** €17.50-€34.50. **Lunch menu** €13.70-€14.50. **Credit** AmEx, MC, V. **Map** E4.

This unatmospheric eatery labels itself a Japanese restaurant, yet most customers seem to come for the Korean barbecue on the second floor. At dinner, the sushi bar downstairs was practically empty, but not so upstairs, where multilingual chatter mingled with the sizzle of grilling meat. We decided to give both house specialities a try, starting with the 'superior' sashimi selection. The plate (not even a platter) dished up a paltry selection of salmon, scallops, tuna belly and snapper – although, happily, each cut was divinely fresh. To fill up, we ordered the California maki, stuffed with generous chunks of creamy avocado and cooked prawns (rather than the usual fake crabsticks) then rolled in toasted sesame. Barely sated, we moved on to the grilled meats, which again, were offered in small portions. Delicately thin raw beef fillet, marinated in sesame oil, melted in the mouth after a quick swirl on the grill. The beef cutlets, which required longer cooking, were thick with flavour, reminiscent of prime rib steak. Both were enhanced with light, mirin-based dipping sauces. On the side, we opted for the spicy cucumbers stuffed with shredded kimchi, a distinctly Korean staple.

Kifuné

44 rue St-Ferdinand, 17th (01.45.72.11.19).
M° Argentine. **Open** Mon 7-10pm; Tue-Sat noon-2pm, 7-10pm. Closed two weeks in Aug, two weeks in winter. **Average** €35. **Lunch menu** €23.50. **Credit** MC, V. **Map** C3.

The sleepy street is not very easy to find but that doesn't stop this small, understated restaurant from filling up with an entirely Japanese crowd – we were the only westerners. We started with a sublime crab and prawn salad – real crab claws with squeaky fresh prawns and ever-so-thin marinated cucumber slices – and richly flavoured miso soup with clams. Sushi and sashimi are expensive – a 'special' sushi assortment, presented on a wooden board, featured nine pieces, including raw prawn and tender squid. Still, we don't mind paying for quality fish and this was very respectable.

Jewish

If felafel is your fancy look no further than the Marais; otherwise take a culinary tour of the Jewish diaspora, from mittité to merguez.

Eating at one of the city's many Jewish tables is an intriguing way to become acquainted with a very particular slice of Parisian history. The first wave of Jewish cooking reached Paris as Ashkenazi (German and Alsatian) Jews drifted into the capital during the 19th century. Tumult in Eastern Europe and Russia greatly increased Paris' Jewish population at the beginning of the 20th century, and independence movements in French North African colonies brought an influx of Sephardic and North African Jews in the early 1960s and 70s. Head for Belleville to sample Algerian and Tunisian Jewish specialities and the Marais for central European and Middle Eastern eats – pastrami, chopped liver, chicken soup and felafel.

L'As du Fallafel

34 rue des Rosiers, 4th (01.48.87.63.60). M° St-Paul. **Open** Mon-Thur, Sun 11am-midnight; Fri noon-sunset. **Average** €7. **Credit** MC, V. **Wheelchair access. Map** L6.

We've always loved L'As du Fallafel for its felafel – surely the best in Paris, if not the world – and for its New-York-style energy. The felafel, thankfully, never changes – order the spécial and your pitta pocket will come loaded with crisp chickpea-and-herb balls, fried aubergine, crunchy cabbage and garlicky houmous, with spicy green (mild) and red (hot) sauces on the side. At lunch on a busy weekday, though, we found the experience rather intense. Both dining rooms were packed – we were handed menus and told to choose as we waited outside. Thirty seconds later we were seated and five seconds after that our felafel appeared on plastic plates. Given the quality of the food and the low prices, it's no surprise that L'As is so popular. It's all great entertainment, but not ideal for two friends who haven't seen each other in a while – we'd paid within 15 minutes of arriving and skulked around the corner to a café to begin our conversation.

Chez Marianne

2 rue des Hospitalières-St-Gervais, 4th (01.42.72.18.86). M° St-Paul. **Open** daily 11am-midnight. **Average** €16. **Credit** MC, V. **Map** K6.

Cheery and reliable, Marianne is a Marais institution that everyone loves, since it's not only a treat to put together your assiette composée – you select from a list of specialities, such as tzatziki, houmous, feta cheese, chopped liver, tabouleh, tahini, felafel and kefta (big herby meat balls) – but these savoury snack-like meals are perfect weekend eating if you're out shopping or have slept late. Bridging the culinary traditions of Jewish North Africa and Eastern Europe, Marianne is considerably better than most of the competition on rue des Rosiers, but would be considered middling in New York or London. Though we've always enjoyed this place, we couldn't help notice that prices are creeping up, even if portions are generous. The smoked salmon and salmon roe plate was mediocre for the price, and aside from the airy cheesecake, many of the desserts were rather dried-out.

Jo Goldenberg

7 rue des Rosiers, 4th (01.48.87.20.16/ www.restaurantgoldenberg.com). M° St-Paul. **Open** daily 8.30am-midnight. **Average** €28. **Credit** AmEx, DC, MC, V. **Map** L6.

There's been a Goldenberg establishment in the Marais since 1920. Sadly, all that remains of former glories are the name and a few fading photographs. Our lunch was truly dreadful, starting with watery, flavourless soups. While nearby tables were taking delivery of great-looking sandwiches and platters of charcuterie, we ordered 'Grandma's' meatballs and mittité à la Roumaine, but grandma was clearly having an off-day, and the mittité, grilled minced beef rolls, were simply inedible. The apple strudel was stodgy and bland; the puff pastry strudel better. The atmosphere in the narrow, crowded eating area is of the third class dining car on the Trans-Siberian Express. An American lady conspiratorily informed us that she had been trapped inside the upstairs loo. You have been warned!

Pitchi Poï ★

7 rue Caron, 9 pl Marché Ste-Catherine, 4th (01.42.77.46.15/www.pitchipoi.com). M° St-Paul. **Open** daily 10.30am-3pm, 6-10.30pm. Sunday brunch noon-4pm. **Average** €20.50. **Sunday brunch** €24. **Credit** AmEx, DC, MC, V. **Wheelchair access. Non-smoking room. Map** L6.

A terrace like this – on a charming cobbled square with a couple of trees and no traffic – is rare in Paris, and hopeful diners hover about waiting for the next available table. Much of the vast menu is Eastern European, accompanied by ice-cold vodkas. The popular Sunday brunch kicks off with smoked salmon and sour cream, served with fluffy blinis and a bowl of scrambled eggs sprinkled with paprika. An 'à volonté' (all-you-can-eat) buffet follows – help yourself to smoked herring, calf's liver or herring mousse, minced eggs, crudité salad, Pinkel ham and turkey slices, aubergine caviar, tarama and butter beans in oil, accompanied by speciality breads. At no time were we rushed by the busy waiters. Amazingly, we found room for dessert – a delicious pairing of fromage blanc with cinnamon and rich, stewed dried fruit sauce. Quite simply a feast.

Les Ailes

34 rue Richer, 9th (01.47.70.62.53/www.lesailes.fr). M° Cadet or Grands Boulevards. **Open** daily noon-2.30pm, 7-11.30pm. **Average** €34. **Credit** MC, V. **Map** J3.

The house speciality at this North African kosher establishment is char-grilled steak, with lamb, merguez, liver and chicken all sizzling away on the giant grill just inside the door. Forget the official starters – before you even get to glance at the menu, you'll be served with a dozen kamie, little dishes of olives, nuts, tabouleh, croutons, and marinated spiced vegetables. We tried two of the seafood specials – fish couscous and Moroccan-style grouper – which were tasty without being exceptional. The dessert list is dominated by fresh fruit, and they have the most exotic range, but avoid offerings that are obviously out of season. They also have North African pastries, super-sweet sabayon, and deadly sharp sorbets.

Patrick Goldenberg ★

69 av Wagram, 17th (01.42.27.34.79). M° Ternes. **Open** daily 9.30am-11pm. Hot food served noon-11pm. **Average** €23. **Prix fixe** €21.34. **Credit** AmEx, MC, V. **Map** D2.

Over the course of several generations, the Goldenberg family has made its way from Odessa to Paris via Bucharest, Sofia and Istanbul. Drawing upon a wealth of family recipes, Patrick Goldenberg offers five nation-specific menus. We paired the Russian harengs gras with the Romanian mittité, and strudel. The large herring fillet was perfectly marinated but it might have been better teamed with a crisp Russian vodka than with the pungent swica, a Romanian plum eau de vie, that we chose. The mittité were grilled to perfection – crispy on the outside and deep pink on the inside. A triumphant finish, the apple and nut strudel arrived steaming hot, fresh from the oven. Less elaborate, but equally traditional, the triple-decker pastrami sandwich is faultless.

Benittah

108 bd de Belleville, 20th (no phone). M° Belleville. **Open** Tue-Sun 9am-10pm. **Average** €15. **Credit** MC, V. **Map** N4.

Belleville is brilliant for good eating on the cheap, and Benisti, a sprawling cafeteria, is one of its better and more original places. Come here to sample the hearty, vigorously seasoned cooking of the Tunisian exile community, including couscous and sandwiches – a baguette generously stuffed with tuna, hard-boiled eggs, red pepper, tomatoes, and lettuce and lashed with fiery mayonnaise. The felafel plates are also good, and magenta-coloured links of locally made merguez are delicious, as are the crispy brik, deep-fried filo pastry filled with an egg or tuna. They often have chorba, a rich soup made from tomatoes, harissa (puréed chillies), broth, onions and tiny oval pasta, and grilled fish with salad, chips and pimento, served with a fried egg but not the deep-fried courgette flowers you'd find in the home country. Finish up with baklava or an assortment of Tunisian sweets, and mint tea or strong coffee.

Music and matzos on the terrace of **Pitchi Poï**.

North African

Maghreb restaurants offer a mosaic of princely pickings, from spicy soups and fruit-laced tagines to juicy grilled meats and feathery mounds of couscous.

International

If we're to believe the surveys, the French opt for a couscous almost as often as they do a bloody steak these days. Why the rise in popularity? No doubt the waves of immigration from Northern Africa over the years have played a major role in the proliferation of the cuisine. And, given France's former influence in the region, it's about time that the cultural exchange route was reversed.

A little vocabulary is a handy tool in Maghreb restaurants: couscous refers to steamed semolina but also to a complete dish, usually served with vegetables in broth and meat; tagines (Moroccan or Tunisian) are sweetened stews cooked in cone-shaped clay dishes; briouates or brik are fried triangles of crisp pastry, filled with egg and sometimes tuna; méchoui is spit-roasted lamb. Another Moroccan speciality is pastilla, meat (usually pigeon) wrapped in crisp pastry and sweetened with sugar and cinnamon. And the sugar-infused mint tea at the end is a must.

404 ★

69 rue des Gravilliers, 3rd (01.42.74.57.81). M° Arts et Métiers. **Open** Mon-Fri noon-2.30pm, 8pm-midnight; Sat, Sun noon-4pm (brunch), 8pm-midnight. Closed at lunch and Sun in Aug. **Average** €35. Lunch menu €17, €21 (brunch). **Credit** AmEx, DC, MC,V. **Map** K5.

Just in case you miss the crowd of trendies cluttering up the entrance to this North African gem, the huge 404 logo projected onto the street should help. It's a veritable Arabian Nights fantasy with a sexy red interior, lanterns and wrought iron everywhere, not to mention the beautiful waiters in their long-sleeved T-shirts with Arabic designs. Tables are tightly packed, but unusually for a place full of fashion puppies, portions are huge and the food seriously good. Don't come to 404 to pick over a salad and look glam; rather, come starving and dive into the signature dish loaded with tender meat and light, fluffy couscous. The tagines are a similarly good bet, the lamb and prune option providing a seductive combo of melt-in-the-mouth meat and succulent, plump fruit. The sticky sweets always look glorious but we've never managed to leave enough space for pudding. Brunch at the weekends is lower on stodge and higher on stars. Order plenty of mint tea to linger over and enjoy the Oscar-winning pouring spectacle before popping next door to 404's new bar, Andy Wahloo (*see p242*, **Bars**), for a hookah or two.

Chez Omar

47 rue de Bretagne, 3rd (01.42.72.36.26). M° Temple or Arts et Métiers. **Open** Mon-Sat noon-2.30pm, 7-11.30pm; Sun 7-11.30pm. **Average** €30. **No credit cards. Map** L5.

Gone are the days when dinner at Omar's meant you'd be rubbing shoulders with the likes of Naomi Campbell and Herb Ritts, and that means that you now stand a slightly better chance of snagging a table. Omar doesn't take reservations and by 9pm the queue stretches the length of the long zinc bar and out the door. And everyone is waiting for the same thing: couscous. Prices range from €11 (vegetarian) to €24 (royale); there are no tagines or other traditional Maghreb mains, so those who don't like couscous have to make do with a selection of French classics (duck, fish, steak). If it's your first visit keep your eye on neighbouring tables as the affable, overstretched waiters magically slip through the crowds with mounds of semolina, steaming vats of vegetable-laden broth, and steel platters heaving with meat and more meat. You won't be disappointed by the grilled slabs of lamb méchoui but what keeps us coming back is the merguez. These spicy lamb sausages are tangily top-notch with each bite surprisingly fresh. Really big appetites might find room for a starter but more alluring is the giant platter of Algerian pastries the waiter leaves at your table. Mint tea is de rigueur. Diners looking for Oriental atmosphere should go elsewhere (the converted bistro looks as French as it did 25 years ago when Omar moved in), but the hospitality is genuine: even on packed nights an offer of seconds – gratis of course – will encourage you to stay on. Non-smokers beware: the proximity of your neighbours means that you'll share more than just their conversation.
Branch: Café Moderne, 19 rue Keller, 11th (01.47.00.53.62).

L'Atlas

12 bd St-Germain, 5th (01.44.07.23.66). M° Maubert-Mutualité. **Open** Tue-Sun noon-2.30pm, 7.30-11pm. **Average** €45. **Credit** AmEx, DC, MC, V. **Non-smoking room. Map** K7.

Reading the huge menu it's immediately clear that Atlas is all about fusion takes on the Moroccan food routine, with inventive tagines (€20-€22) that feature grouper, saffron and mango; delicately seasoned sea bass and fennel; and even calf's brains. Starters include smoked fish with salad, and a memorable aubergine purée and artichoke salad. The soupe de son (bran and mint) may be the most unusual choice: it's blandish, but oddly soothing.

Meatless couscous is a refined version of the average standby, with a clear broth and plenty of veggies. Glazed pigeon with dates seemed too sweet, while the pigeon and wild mushroom tagine had been superbly roasted in its clay pot to bring out its spirited flavours. For dessert, the assiette gourmande mixes French faves such as ice cream with little Maghreb pastries. This is an over-the-top Moroccan wonderland, whose elaborate tiling and plasterwork trick you into thinking you're in a royal palace and not in the Latin Quarter. Almost.

Wally le Saharien

36 rue Rodier, 9th (01.42.85.51.90). M° Notre-Dame- de-Lorette or Anvers. **Open** Tue-Sat 11.30pm-2pm, 7.30-10.30pm. Closed July and Aug. **Average** €23 (lunch only). **Prix fixe** €40.40 (dinner only). **Credit** MC, V. **Map** J2.

At dinner time, don't ask for the menu – they hit you with everything they've got. Expect to start with a seriously spicy tomato soup, hints of coriander and mint sometimes overpowered by the pervasive peppers. That's followed by a mini-pastilla, a magnificent sugar-dusted pastry stuffed with pigeon, nuts, raisins and cinnamon. What comes next depends on availability. Wally's famous stuffed sardines had the night off when we visited, but were ably replaced by a lightly spiced ratatouille served with nutty brown bread. Then things get serious. On a bed of dreamlight couscous, Wally serves tender roast lamb and succulent merguez, both first-class. Forget the vegetable broth: when the grains are this good, you don't need it. We sampled a red wine, an undistinguished 1992 Coteaux de Zaccar – poor value at €28. Dessert is a platter of Berber pastries, light and unsticky, washed down with as much mint tea as you and your camel could store. The service is friendly, informed and well-paced. The only problem is the price. If Wally was prepared for some souk-style haggling over the bill, he'd have a queue around the block.

L'Homme Bleu ★

55bis rue Jean-Pierre Timbaud, 11th (01.48.07.05.63). M° Couronnes or Parmentier. **Open** Mon-Sat 7pm-12.45am. Closed Aug. **Average** €25. **Credit** MC, V. **Map** M5.

L'Homme Bleu makes do without the evocative decor – mosaics, brass, and coloured lanterns – that distinguishes so many other Maghreb spots; its authenticity is in the sizzle of tagines, nose-warming spices, and the bustle of the mammas-only open kitchen. At 8.15pm we got the last table on the small main floor (there is also seating in the stone cellar), watched smugly as the crowds gathered at the bar and on the pavement (no bookings are taken), and kept our eye on the giant platter of Algerian pastries that we promised ourselves for dessert. We weren't to know that, given the humongous portions, we'd never get to them. The pastilla starter, crisp sugar-and-cinnamon-dusted brik filled with slivers of chicken (rather than the traditional pigeon) and ground nuts, was generous and satisfying. But the

On the road to Morocco at **Le Souk**. *See p212.*

lamb tagines were too muttony for our taste. Lham lahlou had a refreshing blend of pears, prunes, and almonds, and s'lqarnoun d'oualmi came with artichokes, peas, preserved lemon and olives: they were packed with flavour but also much more meat (especially in proportion to the sauce) than we could manage. The seksu s'iftaten n'uralmi, a zingy couscous accompanied by two big beef brochettes and a pair of spicy merguez, was a better choice. We watched in amazement as couples around us devoured giant platters of seksu Homme Bleu replete with kebabs, merguez, lamb chops and meat balls. Smaller appetites should try the interesting amesfouf n'teslit, a meatless, brothless couscous that's laced with raisins and peas, cinnamon, orange flower water, almonds, honey and a dash of sugar; served with a glass of buttermilk, it is traditionally reserved for brides. While others found room for sweets, we were content to sip mint tea and soak up the atmosphere.

Le Mansouria

11 rue Faidherbe, 11th (01.43.71.00.16/ www.mansouria.com). M° Faidherbe-Chaligny. **Open** Mon, Tue 7.30-11pm; Wed-Sat noon-2pm, 7.30-11pm. Closed one week in Aug. **Average** €35. **Prix fixe** €29, €44. **Credit** MC,V. **Non-smoking room. Map** N7.

Fatema Hal continues to pack them in at this once ground-breaking Moroccan. Success, however, can have its downside and here it's in time-limited tables, surly telephone reservations staff and a somewhat harried meeter and greeter. Still, once you're in, service is friendly enough. Moroccans, Parisians, couples and families all take their places in one of three rooms (one in austere French bistro-style with chairs and starched tablecloths, the other two more lavishly decorated, with plush banquettes and rich colours). The food remains decent, if perhaps lacking its former finesse. Starters such as harira (a soup of lentils, chickpeas, meat, eggs, lemon, tomatoes and spices) or 'bride's fingers' (crisp, deep-fried rolls stuffed with spicy prawns) and meat briouates hit the spot, but mains failed to impress. La kmama, chicken stewed with tomato jam and rose petals and scattered with rosebuds, was tooth-achingly sweet; the couscous bidaoui (Casablanca style, with turnips, courgettes, sultanas, chickpeas and a large piece of lamb) simply dull. Only the tagine of farmer's chicken with olives and preserved lemons delivered any excitement. Still, with good pastries, mint tea and well-priced set menus, it remains a reasonable bet.

Le Souk

1 rue Keller, 11th (01.49.29.05.08). M° Ledru-Rollin or Bastille. **Open** Tue-Fri 7.30-midnight; Sat noon-2.30pm, 7.30pm-midnight; Sun noon-2.30pm, 7.30-11pm. Tea room 3-7pm. **Average** €27. **Prix fixe** €31, €35. **Credit** MC, V. **Wheelchair access. Map** N7.

The pungent aromas of cumin and coriander that assail you on lifting the kilim at the entrance to this colourful Moroccan restaurant are a quick fix for winter blues. The pistachio-coloured bars on the interior windows, offset against terracotta-painted walls, have a touch of the harem, but the djellaba-clad waiters are as sweet and soothing as a glass of mint tea. Once settled at one of the mosaic tables, choose a full-bodied Algerian wine (this will please the proprietor who is from Oran, even if the food is Moroccan) and nibble on the little dishes of spicy carrots and olives before ordering. From the small

Crowd-pleasing couscous at **Au P'tit Cahoua**.

choice of starters we chose brii m'tir, vine leaves stuffed with sardines dipped in a fresh tomato sauce, along with briouate, crisp goat's cheese wrapped in layers of crisp brik pastry. Both dishes were passable, more like a warm-up act. In fact the specialities here are sizzling hot, rich tagines and towering pots of couscous. We opted for the sumptuous-sounding tagine ouarzazate (lamb shank with preserved pears, almonds and raisins) and the tagine poulet (chicken stewed with dates and onions). The lamb was tender and tasty, but the sauce lacked punch despite the alluring ingredients. The chicken proved the better choice: moist and flavourful, with the contrast of sweet and sharp marrying impeccably with the tender flesh. Tagine alternatives include jebli (rabbit with sweet potatoes) and honey-lashed canette (duckling) with fresh figs. There are also big brochettes of lamb, along with all kinds of feathery couscous dishes. Although we had no room for dessert, the almond pastilla or crêpe berbère on nearby tables looked tempting . If you enjoy the frenetic, noisy atmosphere of a souk, you'll have fun at this popular play on North Africa. There are two sittings for dinner and you must book ahead.

Taninna

14 rue Abel, 12th (01.40.19.99.04/ www.taninna.com). M° Gare de Lyon or Ledru-Rollin. **Open** daily 5pm-2am (last orders 1am). Closed two weeks in Aug. **Average** €25. **Credit** MC, V. **Wheelchair access**. **Map** M8.

We'd arrived too early to eat but rather than pitching us back into the cold night, our welcoming host Youcef gave us the royal tour of Taninna. After seeing his upstairs art gallery/cultural space, with its own stage and bar, we sat together in a bar-side nook and chatted about blues music over mint tea and dates until the chef was ready to take our order. Admiring the star-lit ceiling and dreamy murals of rural Algeria, we were unprepared for Taninna's exceptional take on the tagine-couscous routine. Fresh-from-the-oven flatbread warmed our stomachs before the pastilla arrived, a crisp pastry-wrapped pie stuffed with chicken, egg, coriander, flower water and cinnamon and sprinkled with icing sugar. The adebsi n taninna sampler plate included aubergine purée and cakcuka, a stewed sweet pepper dish. Our chicken, dried fruit, almond and pear tagine was as exquisite as the barley couscous, which Youcef advised must be drizzled with his fragrant Algerian olive oil. Called ameqful n temzin, the fine barley came mixed with vegetables and accompanied by a selection of juicy grilled meats. The giant portions left little room for sweets, though we accepted a traditional pastry. No doubt, we were in the hands of a master, someone eager to share his unique world of food, music, and tradition.

Restaurant des Quatre Frères

127 bd de Ménilmontant, 11th (01.43.55.40.91). M° Ménilmontant. **Open** Mon-Thur, Sat noon-4pm, 6-11pm; Fri 3-11pm. **Average** €10. **Credit** MC, V. **Map** N5.

Have you ever wondered what 'family dining' might be like in Algiers? For less than €10 the four brothers who run this unassuming local hot-spot (paper cloths on Formica tables and help-yourself soft drinks) will give you a good introduction. A tiny blackboard menu lists the essentials but regulars know to ask for the extras (like bottles of olive oil for dousing the chickpea soup). For starters try the mhadjeb (a thickish crêpe stuffed with lightly spiced red peppers) or tangy chorba soup. Couscous, the most expensive main, boasts some of the lightest, fluffiest semolina in Paris at just €6.50 for carnivores and €4.50 for vegetarians, but the daily special is worth the adventure. On our visit it was a chicken chakchoukha: a thick crêpe covered in a saucy portion of potatoes and chickpeas and topped with a succulent, pan-grilled quarter chicken. The pot of harissa on the table lets you adjust the zing accordingly. What pulls in the locals, though, is the dazzling array of skewered meat (beef, lamb, turkey, liver, a liver-heart combo plus, of course, merguez), cutlets, chops and herb-filled patties, all laid out buffet-style. Pile your plate, don't be shy: the little sticks range from just 60 cents to €3. The waiter will whisk them off to the open grill (fanned inventively with a hairdryer) and before you know it you'll be chomping away like everyone else at an Algerian barbecue.

Au P'tit Cahoua ★

39 bd St-Marcel, 13th (01.47.07.24.42). M° St-Marcel. **Open** daily noon-2pm, 7.30-11pm. Closed 25 Dec. **Average** €27. **Prix fixe** €25, €28.50. **Lunch menu** €11. **Credit** AmEx, MC, V. **Map** K9.

Tented ceiling, broken-tile tables and pretty, glazed earthenware dishes conjure up Morocco with aplomb, but it's the food that keeps this place busy every night. After some tasty chopped raw vegetables in a cumin dressing, we by-passed starters such as briouates and harira soup, to get straight down to business; we reckon the couscous here is possibly the best in town. Even so, you'd need a gargantuan appetite to do justice to the couscous P'tit Cahoua — a bowl of excellent, light, fluffy semolina, sultanas, chickpeas, vegetables in broth, harissa, and a platter sizzling with two merguez, a lamb kebab and the méchoui, a chunk of baked lamb knuckle, gleaming in its fat and waiting for you to pull the tender meat from the bone. Other aficionados go for the tagines, which run from traditional chicken with preserved lemons to lamb with artichokes and peas. Lamb with pears and honey came piping hot under its conical hat: a pyramid of thick pear slices and roast almonds encasing the lamb in a spice-and honey-drenched sauce, that we mopped up with flat bread. Au P'tit Cahoua describes itself as 'nostalgic cooking from Morocco', but with the friendly young waitresses, noisy, convivial atmosphere and background music that leaps from Arab singers to Zebda to the strains of Le Temps des Cerises, it is perhaps not so much nostalgia as joie de vivre.

Branch: 24 rue des Taillandiers, 11th (01.47.00.20.42).

Spanish

Forget the siesta and fiesta, Spain's greatest gift has been culinary: addictive tapas, inky rice paella, acorn-flavoured ham and robust grills. Costa bravo!

There's a clutch of restaurants hoisting high the Iberian flag and Parisians are gradually gathering round to salute it, embracing the easy-going Spanish way of eating. **Bellota-Bellota** offers slices of ruby-red ham from black porkers, **Fogón Saint-Julien** dishes out sensational paellas while **Caves Saint Gilles** is more your trad tapas territory.

International

Caves Saint Gilles

4 rue St-Gilles, 3rd (01.48.87.22.62). M° Chemin Vert. **Open** daily noon-2pm, 8-11.30pm. **Average** €23. **Credit** MC, V. **Map** L6.

You've got to love this place, if only for the staff with their gorgeous Spanish-accented French (and sometimes English) and their enthusiastic welcome. You can't book so if it's packed (as it usually is) sidle up to the bar, grab some olives and a beer and watch the footie on the telly, or the restaurant frenzy. Prices might be higher than you'd pay in Spain but that doesn't bother the Spanish ex-pats and with-it Parisians, of all ages, who troop in for the trad tapas and the lively atmosphere. And who can blame them? Tortilla, patatas brava (spicy fried potatoes), chipirones (small squid) straight from the grill, and gambas pil pil (big prawns grilled and doused in garlic and chilli) are first-rate. Also good is the jamón pata negra – other ham seems pedestrian after this one – and red peppers stuffed with salt cod. Forget the ice creams and go straight for the crema catalana, the wonderful Spanish take on crème brûlée. Wines are pricey but the red Rioja Paternina is well worth the investment.

Fogón Saint-Julien ★

10 rue St-Julien-le-Pauvre, 5th (01.43.54.31.33). M° St-Michel or Maubert-Mutualité. **Open** Tue-Fri 7pm-midnight; Sat, Sun noon-2.30pm, 7pm-midnight. Closed last week in Aug, first week in Sept and first two weeks in Jan. **Average** €35. **Prix fixe** €35. **Credit** MC, V. **Map** J7.

Considered by many Iberian peninsula ex-pats to be the best Spanish restaurant in Paris, Fogón Saint-Julien serves up superb paella and creative tapas in a tiny but cheery yellow dining room in one of Paris' oldest streets. Owner-chef Alberto Herraiz, a Castilian, is serious about quality; thus the paella is made with genuine Spanish rice (from Calasparra for meat versions, and the Ebro delta for seafood versions) while the tapas are market-driven (an oyster on a bed of cool cucumber, a salad of warm wild mushrooms with little spinach leaves, a cup of frothy brandade de morue with a pear square). Also excellent are the cured meats and sausages, especially the lomo de cerdo. There are half a dozen paella renditions on the menu including the valenciana with snails, rabbit, saffron and vegetables, one blackened with squid ink and topped with prawns and fish, and a superb vegetable paella which, depending on the season, might feature tiny artichokes, broad beans, onions and broccoli. For dessert, tapas is the way to go: a droplet of strawberry sorbet, a square of rice pudding, foamy coffee cream with anise, chocolate with mint, and a shot of Tio Pepe sherry.

La Catalogne

4-8 cour du Commerce St-André, 6th (01.55.42.16.19/www.catalogne.infotourisme.com). M° Odéon. **Open** Tue-Fri noon-3pm, 7-11pm; Sat noon-3pm, 7-11pm. Closed Aug. **Average** €25. **Prix fixe** €14, €18. **Lunch menu** €11. **Credit** AmEx, DC, MC, V. **Map** H7.

Apart from the Dalí reproduction on the ceiling, the brightly lit bistro of the Maison de Catalunya (the Catalan tourist office) doesn't overdo the Spanish

effects, but brings you Spain in both plate and glass: one of the best bets for a meal in a street which contains some of Paris' most dubious eating and drinking experiences. The menu comes in Catalan, Castilian and, luckily, French, while a tempting wall of wines from the different Catalan appellations – mostly unknown to us more familiar with Rioja and the Navarre – is laid out by area. The waiter steered us to the supple yet oaky Clos de Torribas from the Penedès region south of Barcelona. There are tapas here, but with a selection weighted towards the potato that's not really the strong point. Instead it's more rewarding to explore the main menu, which feels authentic yet, with ingredients ranging from cod to ceps and cannelloni, takes you beyond the frontiers of ham and paella. We tried a warm starter of fresh spinach sautéed with raisins and a delicious if splashy salad of tiny broad beans, young salad leaves and slithers of serrano ham, cleverly set off by mint and a refreshing, finely minced purée of raw tomato. 'Land and sea', described in French as chicken with prawns, turned out to be a much more exciting combination of textures and flavours, with stewed, jointed chicken, tiny octopus, mussels and a giant prawn in a thick, orange fish sauce begging to be sopped up by the mashed potato. Similarly the bouillon with pasta and meat was an understatement for the satisfying bowl of broth, chickpeas, chunks of beef, ham, meatball and black pudding and a few pasta tubes. Helpings were vast, so after that, trying out what is probably Catalonia's greatest claim to world gastronomic heritage – crema catalana – had to be reserved for next time.

Bellota-Bellota

18 rue Jean-Nicot, 7th (01.53.59.96.96). M° Pont de l'Alma or La Tour Maubourg. **Open** Tue-Fri 10am-3.30pm, 5.30-11pm; Sat 10am-11pm. Closed two weeks in Aug. **Average** €40. **Credit** DC, MC, V. **Map** E6.

Though we were wary that it might be a bit too high-concept, this spot, attractively done up with blue-and-white Spanish tiles, wooden tables, a bar and soft lighting, is a very pleasant destination for a snack or a light supper. A bellota is an acorn in Spanish, a reference to the preferred food of the black, free-grazing Iberico race of pig, which produces this ham. The restaurant serves five different Bellota-Bellota (their trademark) hams from four different geographical regions of southern and western Spain, and each one is purported to have a slightly different flavour and consistency, which, with familiarity, you actually do come to recognise. The ham is served, along with manchego ewe's milk cheese from La Mancha province, anchovies, olives, pickled garlic and pimentos, and tuna, as part of various tasting platters, accompanied by excellent bread from Jean-Luc Poujaran, whose newly expanded bakery is just next door. A first-rate assortment of Spanish wines, by the bottle or glass, friendly and informative service and reasonable prices make this a very attractive new address.

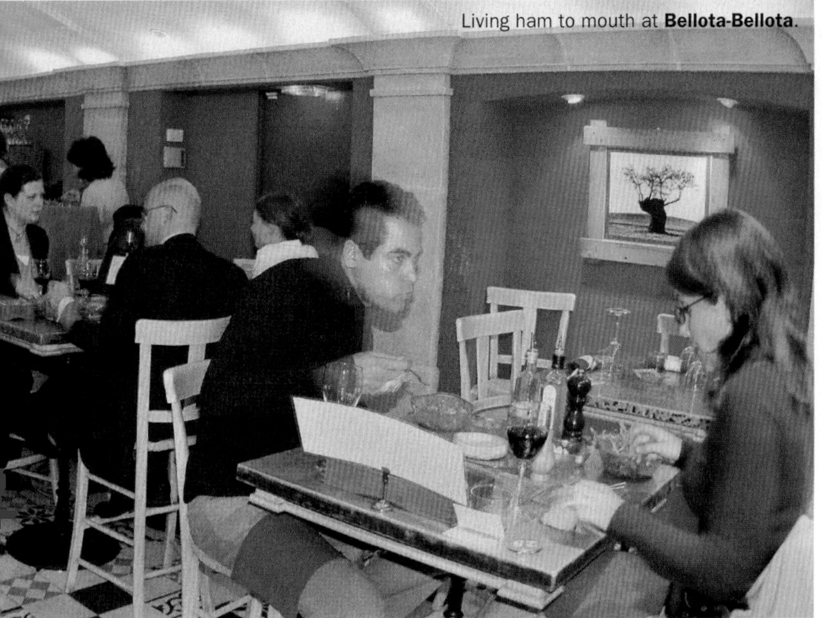
Living ham to mouth at **Bellota-Bellota**.

Other International

Pack your rucksack: from rib-sticking Afghan ashak to zakouski fit for a Czar, Paris can take you on a culinary world tour.

Parisians might not be the world's most adventurous eaters, but pockets of lesser-known ethnic cuisines exist, each with its own inimitable atmosphere and unusual eats.

Afghan

L'Afghani

16 rue Paul-Albert, 18th (01.42.51.08.72). M° Château-Rouge. **Open** Mon-Sat 8pm-midnight. Closed 25 Dec-1 Jan. **Average** €15. **Credit** MC, V. **Map** J1.

If you know nothing about Afghan food, this is an inexpensive introduction to a little-known, spicy cuisine. Start with dour, a cucumber, yoghurt and mint drink, then move on to mostly veggie-based starters, such as the irresistible gol-é-karam (cauliflower fritters in a piquant sauce). Bean-based mains include ashak (a plate of tender leek and lentil dumplings, red beans, chickpeas, garlic and yoghurt) and ashe (beans, noodles, mint and a drizzle of clarified butter) but there are also lamb and veal options. For dessert, try the halwa (toasted crumble and almonds) or firni (a cardamom flan). Although not nearly as daunting as the rugged Afghan peaks, a hike up the nearby steps to Sacré-Coeur is a fitting post-meal expedition.

Finnish

Au Soleil de Minuit ★

15 rue Desnouettes, 15th (01.48.28.15.15). M° Convention. **Open** Tue-Sat noon-2pm, 7.30-10.30pm; Sun noon-2pm. **Average** €35. **Credit** AmEx, MC, V. **Map** C10.

The sophisticated decor of Paris' only Finnish restaurant – sleek white with blue accents and stripped wood – matches the subtlety of a cuisine that bears the imprint of the Lapps (reindeer and wild tundra fruits), and the Russians (sturdy stews) as well as its fish-based Scandinavian heritage. We started with a plate of assorted fish à la finlandaise that gave new meaning to the lowly herring, and a trio of reindeer pâtés: tasty tongue teasers that whetted our appetite and hinted at chef Antti Tiempo's take on native classics. We had chosen our mains with difficulty; intrigued by the smoked hot salmon and puzzled by an innovative duck dish that pushed our waitress' French and English beyond the limit, we finally opted to splurge on a crepinette of elk and a divine fillet of reindeer. Deep pink and unbearably tender, at €29 the latter was the most expensive item on the menu, but (sorry Rudolf) worth every centime. We finished with a soupe froide de mûres jaunes: a tiny pot of chilled yellow berry purée came surrounded by a scoop of white chocolate mousse, strawberries, a sablé biscuit and a slice of roquefort that added a perfect, if surprising, salty tang. Apéritifs, many laced with berries, are imaginative and there is a decent wine list (we had 50cl of Cahors for €10). You'll leave wanting to know more about this undersung cuisine.

German

Le Stübli

11 rue Poncelet, 17th (01.42.27.81.86/ www.stubli.com). M° Ternes. **Open** Tue-Sat 9am-7.30pm; Sun 9am-1pm. Lunch served noon-3pm; tea room until 6.30pm. Closed three weeks in Aug. **Average** €16. **Prix fixe** €14.50. **Credit** MC, V.

Tucked half way along bustling rue Poncelet stands Hansel and Gretel's gingerbread house. On the ground floor, the rainbow of Austrian and German cakes and pâtisseries entices even the most determined dieter to cheat. Up the wooden staircase in the cosy Stübe-style room, ladies-who-shop, courting couples and families with little girls in embroidered frocks all abandon themselves to the host of goodies on offer. We ordered a generous plate of juniper-studded sauerkraut adorned with smoked sausage and pork from the Stübli delicatessen across the road. The other main of maultaschen (pockets of ravioli bulging with meat, spinach and herbs) was declared tasty and authentic by our Austrian friend. Then came the seriously challenging business of choosing a cake. The selection covers the whole gamut: classic Black Forest, linzertorte or sachertorte, rhubarb or apple streusel, and airy cheesecake with whipped cream and raspberries. We went for the cherry strudel: a mouth-watering pile of whole, sweetly-tart cherries wrapped in feather-light pastry. Unable to resist temptation, we went the whole hog with a heavenly chocolat viennois topped with fluffy whipped cream before we waddled out. Take advantage of the terrace tables to watch le tout 17th arrondissement go by.

Hungarian

Le Paprika

28 av Trudaine, 9th (01.44.63.02.91/www.le-paprika.com). M° Anvers or Pigalle. **Open** daily 9.30am-11pm. **Prix fixe** (dinner only) €20, €29.

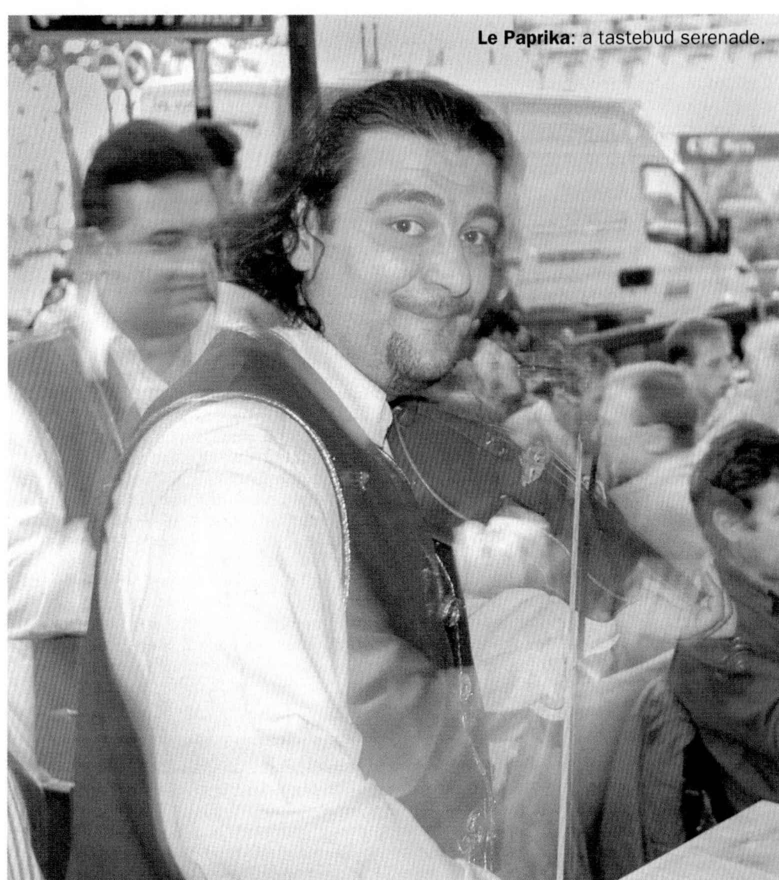

Le Paprika: a tastebud serenade.

Lunch menu €15, €29. **Credit** AmEx, MC, V. **Wheelchair access**. **Map** J2.

Whether you're sitting on this excellent restaurant's spacious terrace or in the old-fashioned dining room you're as likely to hear Polish, German and other Eastern European tongues as French: Le Paprika plays club-canteen for the city's not insubstantial Eastern European population. Young and old rub elbows; an appealing old-world bonhomie prevails. Ordering à la carte is a bit expensive so try the good-value menus, which include starters of paprika-spiked cheese, thin slices of the famous salami, crêpes filled with finely minced veal, or poached egg with crayfish. Savoury main courses include tender goulash served with spätzle (nubby egg noodles), duckling roasted in cabbage and sautéed foie gras. Desserts are delicious, too, including the crêpe Gundel filled with powdered walnuts and served with chocolate sauce and whipped cream, or an apple strudel. Finish off with one of Hungary's fine Tokaj dessert wines. French breakfast is served until noon, and you can drop by after lunch for tea.

Polish

Mazurka

3 rue André-del-Sarte, 18th (01.42.23.36.45). M° Anvers or Château Rouge. **Open** Mon, Tue, Thur 7pm-midnight; Fri-Sun noon-3pm, 7pm-midnight. **Average** €25. **Prix fixe** (dinner only) €18, €23. **Credit** AmEx, DC, MC, V. **Non-smoking room**. **Map** J1.

There are times when Polish folk ditties rendered live are just not sufficient accompaniment to one's smoked salmon blinis; sometimes one needs the meaning of the songs explained, maybe even acted out. If you're feeling that kind of need get yourself to Mazurka. No sooner had we burst into the red-velvet dining room and been greeted like friends than the waitress started plying us with ice-cold vodkas. Brits beware – it would be very easy to get very pissed before one morsel of food has been tasted. Inebriation would blunt your enjoyment of starters such as blinis and could degenerate into unconsciousness in the hour that it took for the main course to arrive. Sadly, the wait wasn't worth it. The pierogi (cheese, onion and potato dumplings) were unforgivably bland. Shredded cabbage and meatballs in tomatoes and wine seemed to be contractually obliged to turn up instead of aiming to give pleasure. We necked a quick poppy seed cake with coffee so thick it should come by the slice, bade farewell to an almost tearful staff and tottered off.

Portuguese

O Por do Sol ★

18 rue de la Fontaine-du-But, 18th (01.42.23.90.26). M° Lamarck-Caulaincourt. **Open** Mon, Tue, Thur, Fri, Sun noon-2pm, 7-10:30pm; Sat 7-10:30pm. Closed Aug. **Average** €25. **Prix fixe** €18.50. **Lunch menu** €10. **Credit** MC, V. **Map** H1.

Bacalhau, or salted cod, has been a staple of the Portuguese diet since the 16th century; they call it 'fiel amigo', faithful friend, and in José and Elesia's tiny dining room you'll find out why. We started by sharing a plate of beignets de morue – fluffy cod fritters that left us fighting for the last bite – and both took cod mains. Grilled cod, brushed with olive oil and pepper, was thick, moist and the perfect choice for those who like tasty, simple fish; but we were hard pressed to imagine anything better than the morue du chef: layered with roasted onion, pepper, tomato and potato in a heaving casserole. Portugal's favourite pasteis de nata, delicious custard tarts, finished the meal and left us swapping memories of remote villages with our convivial hosts. About the wine: vinho verde (young, green wine that has a distinctive fizz) is a perfect, refreshing match for the hearty cuisine. You'll find the white on the menu, but the red is kept secret: chilled, it is an excellent authentic accompaniment for the cod. Don't hesitate to ask Elesia to break open a bottle and give your tastebuds an adventure.

Romanian

Doïna

149 rue Saint-Dominique, 7th (01.45.50.49.57). M° Ecole-Militaire or RER Pont de L'Alma. **Open** Tue-Sun noon-3pm, 6pm-midnight. **Average** €25. **Prix fixe** €12. **Credit** AmEx, MC, V. **Map** D6.

Practically under the skirts of the Eiffel Tower, this Romanian restaurant attracts an expat crowd eager for home cooking. The host makes a point of greeting each table personally, and candles, scenes of Bucharest and blaring Romanian folk music add to the mood. Bowls of pickled cauliflower and peppers go well with the local wine Murfatlar, a sweet and fruity pinot noir. We passed on tripe salad to sample comforting corn polenta sprinkled with a tangy cheese, then dived into our mains. A moussaka made with aubergine and plenty of minced beef proved rib-stickingly satisfying. Fried sandre (pike-perch) came with capers and boiled potatoes but we found the batter greasy. Watch your head on the way down to the loo or you'll knock yourself out before you can sample the torte Bucharest which ended the meal with a chocolate-and-Chantilly flourish.

Russian

Dominique

19 rue Bréa, 6th (01.43.27.08.80). M° Vavin. **Open** Tue-Sat 7.30pm-1am (bar/boutique Tue-Sat 11am-12.30am). **Closed** late July-late Aug. **Average** €50. **Prix fixe** (dinner only) €40, €55. **Credit** AmEx, MC, V. **Map** G9.

Pass straight through the front bar and deli to the back dining room with its mix of 1920s decor, backlit wooden panels and folkloric carvings for typical fare like smoked fish, borscht and pirojok (beef-stuffed pastries). Zakouski is a good place to start: a salad plate which may include salmon or pork pâté, piquant aubergine or red beans. Frugal diners can opt for one of the €40 menus while à la carte options include honey-fried salmon, grilled lamb with dried fruit and onions, and nut-and-coriander marinated chicken. The spectacular apple strudel was hot and crisp, and the cheesecake modest but densely satisfying. Chilled vodka, first-rate caviar (at €69 a pop) and old-time Russian songs could make you believe you're a Russian expat holed up against the cold, in style.

Swedish

Gustavia

26-28 rue des Grands-Augustins, 6th (01.40.46.86.70). M° Odéon or St-Michel. **Open** Tue-Sat noon-2.30pm, 7-9.30pm. Closed 10 days in Aug. **Average** €22. **Prix fixe** €14.50 (dinner only). **Lunch menu** €12.50. **Credit cards** MC, V. **Map** J7.

Handily located for art-house cinemas and a quiet haven from St-Michel's tourist traps, Gustavia draws diners in search of gravlax, marinated herring and other classic foods from Sweden's chilly waters. The €16 assiette Gustavia (a tasty sampler of herring, salmon and shrimp with a helping of warm potato salad) is a good option for lunch: light, refreshing and, for this neighbourhood, not too overpriced; add a side order of blini if you want something a bit more filling. Less satisfactory are the hot (or rather, not-so-hot) daily specials. Paper-thin slices of smoked reindeer were given an Italian spin: paired with pesto and served on a bed of fusilli, the overall effect was singularly odd. Desserts are all safe Paris standards (chocolate cake, apple crumble) and wine is well-priced (a carafe of white cost €8.50). Fans of Swedish modern will like the spartan interior accented with muted yellow and blue and, if you remember the Moomintrolls, the loo is a treat.

On the Town

Cafés

The cafés in this town have been the scene of many crèmes (and misdemeanours), so pull up a brew and drink in the atmosphere.

While the stars of the Parisian café scene were once the dark dens of iniquity favoured by wine-guzzling novelists, many of today's hangouts are more designer-driven, catering to the tastes of the mojito generation. Tattered notebooks have been replaced by shiny laptops and Palm Pilots as portfolios are haggled and handed over and screenplays are finalised. Has the rise of these young pretenders signalled an end to smoky Parisian bohemia? Pas du tout – both species have learned to live side by side in the urban wilds.

It's worth remembering that prices can vary in cafés – it's usually cheapest to stand at the bar, and most expensive to sit on the terrace. Most places do light meals as well as more substantial lunches.

1st Arrondissement

Bar de l'Entr'acte

47 rue Montpensier, 1st (01.42.97.57.76). M° Palais Royal. **Open** Mon-Fri 10am-2am; Sat, Sun noon-midnight. Food served daily noon-3.30pm, 7-11pm. **Beer** 25cl €2.95-€3.75. **Credit** MC, V. **Map** H5.

Waiting in the wings behind the Théâtre du Palais Royal, the Bar de l'Entr'acte is a handy pit stop. Inside, the pokey bar area is scruffily comfortable either for a quick drink or several long ones, during which your mind will grow hazy with visions of thespian abandon. The tables outside make the most of the quiet street and stunning architecture. The satisfying burgers are always a popular choice.

On the Town

Le Café 221

221 rue St-Honoré, 1st (01.42.60.32.79/ www.hotel-royal-st-honore.com/rsh). M° Tuileries. **Open** daily noon-11pm. Food served all day. **Beer** 25cl €5. **Credit** AmEx, DC, MC, V. **Wheelchair access. Map** G5.

Nestled alongside the chic boutiques that line the rue St-Honoré, 221 serves up fuss-free food for shoppers, such as light fish dishes, salads, and pork with vegetables. The decor is very red except for the plush green seats and the service is warm and welcoming. Suprisingly, the prices aren't outrageous.

Le Café des Initiés ★

3 pl des Deux-Ecus, 1st (01.42.33.78.29). M° Louvre-Rivoli or Les Halles. **Open** Mon-Sat 7.30am-1am. Food served 12.30-3.30pm, 7-11pm. **Beer** 25cl €2.90-€4.50. **Credit** AmEx, MC, V. **Map** H5.

After a recent transformation from traditional Paris corner bistro to designer hangout, this café has retained only its long zinc bar. Now the room is lined with ergonomic red banquettes, and sleek black articulated lamps peer down from the ceiling. Dotted around the windowsills are tall, slender vases filled with fresh, scented lilies. The friendly staff and central location make this an excellent place to meet for a drink or a quick bite, either inside or out.

Café Marly ★

93 rue de Rivoli, cour Napoléon du Louvre, 1st (01.49.26.06.60). M° Palais Royal. **Open** daily 8am-2am. Food served daily noon-4pm, 7.30pm-1am. **Beer** 25cl €5. **Credit** AmEx, DC, MC, V. **Non-smoking room. Map** H5.

Opened in 1994 as part of the Grand Louvre project, Café Marly has become a Costes brothers' classic. The terrace is beautiful, ensconced in the stone balcony of the Louvre's Cour Napoléon with a privileged view of the glass pyramid. Snappily dressed waiters glide around delivering gaspacho, club sandwiches and €90 sevruga caviar to customers who sip cocktails and crane their necks to confirm celebrity spottings. The lush interior is also worth a visit. Lower-end wines – €4-€8 a glass – are hit-or-miss.

Café Ruc

159 rue St-Honoré, 1st (01.42.60.97.54). M° Palais Royal. **Open** daily 8am-1am. Food served daily 11.30am-1am. **Cocktails** €9. **Credit** AmEx, DC, MC, V. **Map** H5.

Another Costes brothers café; another exercise in coolly executed upmarket chic. Expect seductive red velvet banquettes, a flurry of cocktails and café snacks, jazz-tinged background muzak and (of course) waiters who are better dressed than anyone else in the room. The staff may be hip but they are efficient and friendly, too, and help to create a relaxed ambience far from the hustle and bustle of the street outside.

La Coquille

30 rue Coquillière, 1st (01.40.26.55.36). M° Les Halles. **Open** Mon-Sat 7am-10pm. Food served Mon-Sat noon-3.30pm. Closed three weeks in Aug. **Beer** 25cl €1.80. **Credit** MC, V. **Map** J5.

This down-to-earth, vintage 50s shoebox café is a local favourite. Its one-table 'terrace' is usually taken, so expect to end up inside. The budget food, served up fast and fresh, runs from entrecôtes to giant salads; the 'salade coquille' is particularly nice, especially with a glass of vinho verde (the owner is Portuguese) or dirt-cheap French wine.

shment

Papou Lounge

74 rue Jean-Jacques-Rousseau, 1st (01.44.76.00.03). M° Etienne-Marcel or Les Halles. **Open** Mon-Fri 10am-2am; Sat 11am-2am; Sun 5pm-1am. Food served Mon-Sat noon-4pm, 7pm-midnight; Sun 5pm-midnight. Closed at lunch in Aug. **Beer** 25cl €3.30. **Credit** MC, V. **Wheelchair access. Map** J5.

An eclectic menu, comfortable terrace and excellent €6.10 cocktails – the white Russians and whisky sours are expertly prepared – are all good reasons to stop here. Inside are masks, carvings, black-and-white tribal photographs, and all-year Christmas lights around the wood bar.

Taverne Henri IV

13 pl du Pont-Neuf, 1st (01.43.54.27.90). M° Pont-Neuf. **Open** Mon-Fri 9am-4pm, 6-9pm; Sat 9am-4pm. Food served all day. Closed three weeks in Aug. **Beer** €2.60-€3.40. **No credit cards. Map** H6.

This ever-so-trad haunt of the legal profession is an institution, and though the decor is rather spartan, you can hardly go wrong with its fabulous location on the tip of the Ile de la Cité. Expect grumpy moustachioed waiters, a varied selection of reasonably priced regional wines and food (good tartines, or garlicky snails), and great people-watching.

2nd Arrondissement

Le Café

62 rue Tiquetonne, 2nd (01.40.39.08.00). M° Etienne-Marcel. **Open** Mon-Sat 10am-2am; Sun noon-midnight. Food served daily noon-midnight. Closed weekend of 15 Aug. **Beer** 25cl €3. **Credit** MC, V. **Map** J5.

A young and hip crowd is drawn to this café which buzzes with loud and funky music, matching its customers' attitude. The interior looks like a fusion between Ali Baba's cavern and an explorer's attic, filled with African statuettes, antique globes, a bust of Lenin, and browning maps of exotic locations. The food is somewhat less adventurous, consisting of generous salads, plates of smoked fish and plats du jour such as salmon tagliatelle or quiche lorraine. Drinks are reasonably priced and standard; the only concession to exotica is a bottle of 'Famosa' Guatemalan beer. The chronically overworked waiter is amazingly polite and efficient.

Le Dénicheur ★

4 rue Tiquetonne, 2nd (01.42.21.31.01). M° Etienne-Marcel. **Open** Tue-Sat 12.30-3.30pm, 7pm-midnight; Sun brunch 12.30-3.30pm. Food served all day. **Beer** bottle €2.80. **Map** J5.

The row of garden gnomes standing to attention in the window give the game away: Le Dénicheur doesn't take itself too seriously. Even better, a few steps from the tourist-fleecing joints of Les Halles, it's a place where you can pick up a very affordable light lunch or supper, such as a huge plate of very fresh salad followed by a crunchy homemade apple crumble. There's also a Sunday brunch worth catching. The decor – bright blue paint, jumble on the walls, a chalk-scrawled tribute to (who else?) Kylie – creates a kitsch charm that the cheek-by-jowl seating arrangement in this tiny café only enhances.

Sun loungers at **Les Arts et Métiers**.

Au Vide Gousset

1 rue Vide-Gousset, 2nd (01.42.60.02.78). M° Bourse. **Open** Mon-Fri 7.30am-8pm; Sat 9am-7.30pm. Food served 11.30am-5pm. Closed three weeks in July/Aug. **Beer** 25cl €3.10. **Credit** MC, V. **Map** H5.

A stone's throw from the elegant place des Victoires, this café-tabac is the archetypal smoke-filled Parisian café, complete with battered tables, shiny crimson banquettes and hideous 70s lights. Nonetheless, it attracts a diverse clientele of expensively perfumed professional shoppers, stockbrokers, caffeine addicts and Gitane-smoking barflies. Simple but pricey food is served at lunch.

3rd Arrondissement

L'Apparemment Café

18 rue des Coutures-St-Gervais, 3rd (01.48.87.12.22). M° Filles du Calvaire or St-Paul. **Open** Mon-Fri noon-2am; Sat 4pm-2am; Sun noon-midnight. Food served Mon-Sat 12.30-3pm, 7pm-midnight; Sun 12.30-4pm, 6pm-11.30pm. **Beer** 25cl €3-€4. **Credit** DC, MC, V. **Non-smoking room. Map** L5.

This café is decorated like the front room of an eccentric friend with a drinking problem. Board games, comfy leather and velvet armchairs, and a heaving pile of books and magazines – all the comforts of home, plus a bill.

Les Arts et Métiers

51 rue de Turbigo, 3rd (01.48.87.83.25). M° Arts-et-Métiers. **Open** daily 7am-midnight. Food served all day. **Beer** 25cl €3-€4.50. **Credit** MC, V. **Map** K5.

Across the road from the museum with which it shares its name, this café offers one of the quartier's rare sunshine spots at which to munch on a salad. Inside, funky faux-art deco stylings bring a trendy air to the traditional-shaped bar, while waistcoated waiters rush between tables. As well as the main dishes and salads (€10-€13), there's a good range of toasted sandwiches (€7).

4th Arrondissement

Baz'Art Café

36 bd Henri IV, 4th (01.42.78.62.23). M° Sully Morland or Bastille. **Open** daily 8am-midnight. Food served all day. **Beer** 25cl €3.70-€4. **Credit** AmEx, MC, V. **Map** L7.

Baz'Art offers good-quality café fare and a relaxed, stylish atmosphere in which to linger. The sandy yellow walls, red velvet chairs, heavy iron chandeliers and jazzy soundtrack make a pleasant backdrop and the service couldn't be friendlier. There are plenty of market-fresh salads and great-value Sunday brunches from €17 to €19.90.

Bricolo Café

Basement of BHV department store, 52 rue de Rivoli, 4th (01.42.74.90.00/www.bhv.fr). M° Hôtel de Ville. **Open** Mon, Tue, Thur, Sat 9am-7.30pm; Wed, Fri 9am-9pm. Food served all day. **Beer** 33cl €2.25. **Credit** AmEx, MC, V. **Non-smoking room. Map** K6.

In the bowels of the legendary DIY-lovers' store, this basement hangout strewn with dusty, rusty, greasy tools and fix-it ephemera offers a nostalgic setting for refuelling during a shopathon. Too bad the self-serve salads, sandwiches, quiches and tarts are so ordinary. At least the breakfast and lunch set menus are reasonably priced. Almost daily, free 'master-classes' demonstrate skills such as glass cutting, garden irrigation and lamp hanging, while a small library of do-it-yourself books lets you fantasise about home improvement projects.

Café Beaubourg

43 rue St-Merri, 4th (01.48.87.63.96). M° Hôtel de Ville or RER Châtelet-Les Halles. **Open** Mon-Wed, Sun 8am-1am; Thur-Sat 8am-2am. Food served all day. **Beer** 25cl €5. **Credit** AmEx, DC, MC, V. **Non-smoking room. Map** K6.

Christian de Portzamparc's design for this beacon of fashionable Parisian café culture opposite the Centre Pompidou dates back to 1985 and it's starting to show its age. The red velvet curtains over the downstairs entrance seem wearily heavy, while the minimalist sheen of the walls is broken up by cracks in the peeling paint. Yet somehow this absent-minded grubbiness only enhances its charm, providing the ideal setting for rich kids in ripped denim to sip on expensive cocktails while poring over their laptops.

Café des Phares

7 pl de la Bastille, 4th (01.42.72.04.70). M° Bastille. **Open** daily 7am-3am. Food served all day. **Beer** 25cl €3.50. **No credit cards. Map** M7.

The late Sorbonne lecturer Marc Sautet established the continuing tradition of Sunday morning philosophy talks (11am) here. You can ponder the very essence of the menu on the terrace slap-bang on place de la Bastille. And, if freedom is having infinite choice, as the Existentialists believed, then the menu is liberating.

L'Escale

1 rue des Deux-Ponts, 4th (01.43.54.94.23). M° Pont-Marie. **Open** Tue-Sun 7.30am-9pm. Food served noon-3pm. **Beer** €2. **Credit** MC, V. **Map** K7.

With an idyllic Ile St-Louis location and grumpy regulars reading *L'Equipe* at the counter, L'Escale remains a real neighbourhood café/wine bar. Its decor of wall-mirrors and check tablecloths includes a blackboard menu displaying the day's specials. Expect all the veg to be cooked in olive oil and garlic, and the small portions of meat to be tender. The service is unrushed and good humoured. Well-chosen vins du mois are reasonably priced.

L'Etoile Manquante

34 rue Vieille du Temple, 4th (01.42.72.48.34/www.cafeine.com). M° Hôtel de Ville or St-Paul. **Open** daily 9am-2am. Food served noon-1.30pm; hot food noon-5pm. **Beer** 25cl €3. **Credit** MC, V. **Map** K6.

One of five venues that Xavier Denamur owns on

the same street, L'Etoile Manquante shows that he is fully in tune with local café culture. The salads are delicious and filling, the cocktails punchy and the decor both trendy and comfortable. As ever with Denamur's places, no visit is complete without a trip to the loos. An electric train runs between cubicles, starlight beams down from the ceiling and a hidden camera films you washing your hands. Don't worry, though, the images aren't bound straight for TF1 – just the small screen on the wall behind you.

Le Flore en l'Isle

42 quai d'Orléans, 4th (01.43.29.88.27).
M° Hôtel de Ville or Pont-Marie. **Open** daily 8am-2am. Food served daily 11am-midnight. **Beer** 33cl €5.50. **Credit** MC, V. **Map** K7.
Le Flore en l'Isle is particularly popular on hot summer afternoons as the dessert menu includes ice creams and sorbets from the famous glacier Berthillon. The rest of the rather expensive menu consists of dressed-up, mostly meaty traditional fare. Dark wood panelling and obscure classical music create a sombre atmosphere inside, but most customers come to enjoy the terrace and the view.

Grizzli Café ★

7 rue St-Martin, 4th (01.48.87.77.56). M° Châtelet.
Open daily 9am-2am. Food served noon-2.30pm, 8-11pm. Closed 1 Jan, 1 May, 25 Dec. **Beer** €3.60. **Credit** AmEx, MC, V. **Map** K6.
The pedestrian streets around the Centre Pompidou are sometimes too crowded for comfortable people-watching. So snag yourself a table at this modish café/bistro off rue de Rivoli. Order the Grizzli, a huge salad topped with duck and sliced apples, or the equally good antipasti salad, and watch the pretty people stroll by. The sun hits the terrace at just the right angle, even in the cooler months, so order another glass of wine and linger. In winter, sit inside and tuck into one of the heartier main courses.

L'Imprévu Café

7-9 rue Quincampoix, 4th (01.42.78.23.50/ www.imprevu.com). M° Hôtel de Ville/RER Châtelet-Les Halles. **Open** Mon-Sat noon-2am; Sun 1pm-2am. **Beer** 25cl €3. **Credit** MC, V. **Map** J6.
Cluttered with battered but super-comfy sofas and faux leopardskin easy chairs, this café exudes a relaxed and stylish charm and offers friendly, laid-back service. There's a wide choice of exotic cocktails, ranging in strength from those earmarked for 'les chérubins' to those reserved for 'les machos'. The back, with its tented ceiling and fluorescent Arabian Nights mural, feels like the living room of a schizophrenic Moroccan – actually a lot of fun.

Au Petit Fer à Cheval ★

30 rue Vieille du Temple, 4th (01.42.72.47.47/ www.cafeine.com). M° Hôtel de Ville or St-Paul.
Open daily 9am-2am. Food served noon-1.15am. **Beer** 25cl €2.50. **Credit** MC, V. **Map** K6.
Despite being inundated by the throngs wandering this street, the Little Horseshoe manages its clientele with grace (Christophe is especially kind). Seeing those freshly fried potatoes alongside succulent confit de canard and the imaginative veggie platter is enough to draw you in. The space is cramped, and the five little round tables facing the street are barely large enough for two – but it's hard to imagine a better place for people-watching. The smoky back room comes into its own in winter – while you're there, check out the loo, clad in stainless steel like an impregnable fortress or submarine, a strange departure from an otherwise picture-perfect old Paris café setting.

Le Petit Marcel

65 rue Rambuteau, 4th (01.48.87.10.20).
M° Rambuteau/RER Châtelet-Les Halles.
Open Mon-Sat 7am-midnight. Food served all day. Closed first three weeks in Aug. **Beer** €3.60. **No credit cards. Map** K5.
This little bar comes from the Parisian school of authentic faded charm. You sit on old wooden chests beneath a cracked painted ceiling and gaze through decorated window panes as the lunches sizzle in the corner kitchen. The waiter will run through the day's blackboard menu and suggest a suitable wine. Three plats du jour (€8.50-€10) are marked next to the good range of steak dishes, omelettes, pastas and salads, all prepared by an impossibly French chef.

Les Philosophes

28 rue Vieille du Temple, 4th (01.48.87.49.64).
M° Hôtel de Ville. **Open** daily 9am-2am. Food served noon-1am. **Beer** 25cl €3. **Cocktails** €8. **Credit** MC, V. **Map** K6.
Smack in the centre of the Marais, Les Philosophes does a booming business morning, noon and night. It's part bistro (turning out succulent honey-pepper confit de canard and heaving slices of the deepest amber tarte Tatin, though the salads can be uneven) and part philosophical pretension. Each of the two all-steel loos has a one-way window (at least we hoped it was one-way) looking onto a book-shelf filled with posey titles, while judiciously placed inspirational slogans encourage you to linger longer.

5th Arrondissement

Café Delmas

2-4 pl de la Contrescarpe, 5th (01.43.26.51.26).
M° Place Monge. **Open** Mon-Thur, Sun 8am-2am; Fri, Sat 8am-4am. Food served daily 11.30am-11.30pm. **Beer** 25cl €4.20. **Credit** DC, MC, V. **Wheelchair access. Map** J8.
Place de la Contrescarpe was one of Hemingway's numerous stomping grounds and, despite the incursion of pizzerias and ice cream parlours, it still retains an alcoholic theme with two prominent cafés dominating either side of the square. One, Café Delmas, has gone decidedly upmarket, and is now shoulder-to-shoulder perma-tanned style gurus and Gucci-clad fashionistas. When darkness descends, things become a little less civilised as students and tourists stumble out of nearby kebab joints and Vespa buffs gather around the Contrescarpe fountain.

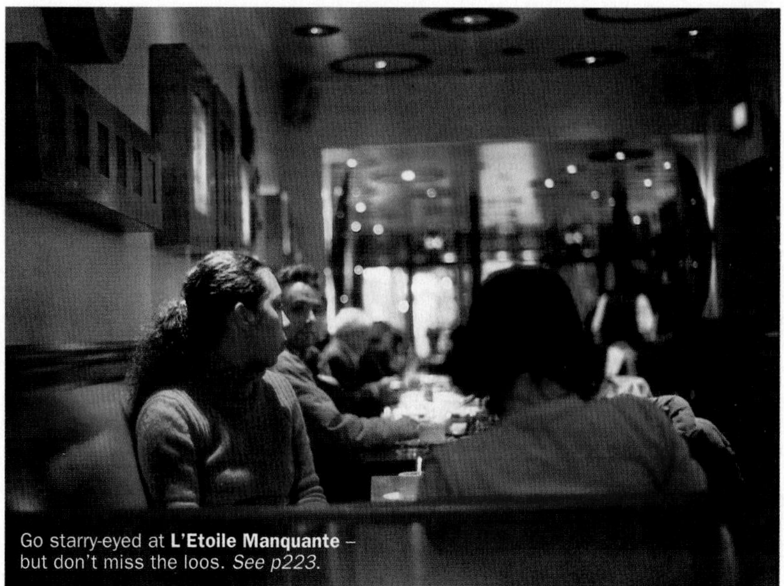

Go starry-eyed at **L'Etoile Manquante** – but don't miss the loos. *See p223.*

Le Comptoir du Panthéon

5 rue Soufflot, 5th (01.43.54.75.36/ www.comptoirdupantheon.com). RER Luxembourg. **Open** Mon-Sat 7am-2am; Sun 9am-7pm. Food served 11am-11pm. **Beer** 25cl €3.20. **Credit** MC, V. **Wheelchair access. Map** J8.

With a modish dark wood and crimson velvet interior, abstract art and funky sound track, this café provides a caffeine and nicotine refuelling point for hordes of students. Inevitably the atmosphere is thick with strident opinions, though the 1968 student-demo types do seem to have given way to a more affluent breed. The real draw is the fabulous terrace with a view of the Panthéon on one side and the law faculty on the other; sit here and enjoy one of the lunchtime snacks, particularly the salads.

Les Pipos ★

2 rue de l'Ecole-Polytechnique, 5th (01.43.54.11.40/ www.lespipos.com). M° Maubert-Mutualité. **Open** Mon-Sat 8am-midnight. Food served noon-11pm. Closed three weeks in Aug. **Beer** 25cl €3.10-€4.60. **No credit cards. Map** J8.

Our first evening visit to the ancient, atmospheric Les Pipos was smoky and uncomfortable with all the tables taken and very little room to manoeuvre at the tiny bar. But, on a warm afternoon in early spring, it was another vibe completely: the door wide open and all quiet except for a few solitary literary types, scribbling away. A clique of eccentric regulars provide excellent entertainment and there's a surprisingly modern selection of wines available as well as simple, cheap cheese and charcuterie plates (€5-€9.90) and hearty plats du jour, all under €15.

Le Rallye

11 quai de la Tournelle, 5th (01.43.54.29.65). M° Jussieu or Maubert-Mutualité. **Open** Mon-Fri daily 7am-2am; Sat, Sun 9.30am-2am. Food served daily noon-3pm. **Beer** 25cl €2. **No credit cards. Wheelchair access. Map** K7.

The Tour d'Argent may be next door, but this bric-a-brac bar-tabac is for those in a very different frame of mind. Inside is a Tintin fetishist's paradise, with crumpled Hergé posters and a huge red rocket from the cosmic adventures of the be-quiffed cartoon character, while a menagerie of poodles plays with the debris on the dirty floor. Outside, moustachioed locals sip expressos under the sign 'pastis is served here by the metre'. Oblivious to the surreal backdrop, a group of habitués gathers around the bar and indulges in high-volume conversation oiled by very early apéritifs. With most tourists frightened off by the circus surroundings, this is an ideal place to enjoy cheap drinks with an authentic and diverse Parisian group of workers, expensively perfumed ladies, taxi drivers and idle Parisian shoppers.

Le Reflet

6 rue Champollion, 5th (01.43.29.97.27). M° Cluny-La Sorbonne. **Open** daily 10am-2am. Hot food served noon-midnight. **Beer** 25cl €2-€2.80. **Credit** AmEx, DC, MC, V. **Map** J7.

Across from the arthouse cinema of the same name, Le Reflet is a temple to film. Black-and-white photos of stars past and present litter the walls and lights hang from a tubular steel rigging. The service can be hazy, but is always friendly. Cheap beer and food and good music make a visit worthwhile.

Tabac de la Sorbonne

7 pl de la Sorbonne, 5th (01.43.54.52.04). M° Cluny-La Sorbonne/RER Luxembourg.
Open *Apr-Oct* daily 6.30am-2am; *Nov-Mar* 6.30am-11pm. Food served all day. Closed 25 Dec, 1 Jan. **Beer** 25cl €3.60. **No credit cards. Wheelchair access. Map** H7.

The Tabac de la Sorbonne is the cigarette supplier to most Sorbonne students, as well as a pleasant terrace meeting spot. Reasonably priced omelettes, croques and plats are doled out by moustachioed waiters. The interior becomes obsolete in the summer, when the terrace reigns supreme.

Le Verre à Pied

118bis rue Mouffetard, 5th (01.43.31.15.72). M° Censier-Daubenton. **Open** Tue-Sat 9am-9pm; Sun 9am-3pm. Food served Tue-Sun noon-2.30pm. Closed two weeks in Aug. **Beer** 25cl €2.80. **No credit cards. Map** J9.

Open since 1870, this gritty, typically Parisian café (it featured in the film *Amélie*) defies the laws of economics and relentless competition from neighbouring trendy coffee shops, providing espressos and sustenance to a crowd of habitués. Essentially made up of one long corridor, it nonetheless manages to cram in a tobacconist (well-stocked with exotic rolling tobacco), an exhibition space, a dining room, and the dominating marble and dark wood bar. Interlopers, initially greeted with suspicion, are soon drawn into lively comptoir discussions, while market stallholders crowd in for cheap lunches thrown together in the back room and washed down with glasses of rouge.

6th Arrondissement

Bar de la Croix-Rouge

2 carrefour de la Croix-Rouge, 6th (01.45.48.06.45). M° Sèvres-Babylone or St-Sulpice. **Open** daily 6am-9pm. Food served all day. **Beer** 25cl €4.50. **No credit cards. Map** G7.

The Bar de la Croix-Rouge is an ideal place to stop mid-shop for a quick espresso or kir. On a sunny afternoon, though, you'd be hard-pushed to bag one of the pavement tables on the compact terrace. The dark brown interior is fairly cramped but buzzing, and the simple food is good value. Choose from a range of cheese or cold meat platters, or one of the deservedly famous Poilâne tartines.

Bar du Marché★

75 rue de Seine, 6th (01.43.26.55.15). M° Odéon. **Open** daily 8am-2am. Food served 9am-6pm. **Beer** 25cl €2-€3.50. **Credit** MC, V. **Map** H7.

You'll find all the ingredients you need for dinner on nearby rue de Buci but once you get a table here hang on to it, as the high standards of food and service keep the Bar du Marché perennially popular with both locals and visitors. Order an excellent omelette from one of the flat-capped, overalled waiters, then sit back and enjoy.

Café de Flore

172 bd St-Germain, 6th (01.45.48.55.26). M° St-Germain-des-Prés. **Open** daily 7.30am-1.30am. Food served all day. **Beer** 40cl €6.90. **Credit** AmEx, DC, MC, V. **Map** H7.

Bourgeois locals crowd the terrace tables at lunch,

eating club sandwiches with knives and forks, while anxious waiters frown upon couples with pushchairs or single diners occupying tables for four. This historic café, once the HQ of the Lost Generation intelligentsia, also attracts plenty of tourists who eye passers-by hopefully. And, yes, celebs have been known to alight here from time to time (recent sighting: Jude Law). But a café crème is €4.60, a Perrier will set you back €5, and the omelettes and croque monsieurs are shockingly poor (the better dishes on the menu range from €15-€25). Play readings are held every Monday night and philosophy discussions on the first Wednesday of the month, both at 8pm, upstairs, in English.

Café de la Mairie

8 pl St-Sulpice, 6th (01.43.26.67.82). M° St-Sulpice. **Open** Mon-Sat 7am-2am. Food served all day. **Beer** 25cl €2.10-€3.60. **No credit cards. Map** G7.

This very ordinary-looking little cafe has the perfect pavement terrace bathed in dappled sunshine, and most of the fashionable crowd is busy reading newspapers or gazing at the mighty St-Sulpice church and its lion-guarded fountain. A traditional range of food and snacks is served all day by the polite staff, so you can re-fuel before a stroll in the Luxembourg – but avoid the grotty loo.

Les Deux Magots

6 pl St-Germain-des-Prés, 6th (01.45.48.55.25/ www.lesdeuxmagots.com). M° St-Germain-des-Prés. **Open** daily 7.30am-1.30am. Food served all day. Closed one week in Jan. **Beer** 25cl €5.20-€5.50. **Credit** AmEx, DC, MC, V. **Wheelchair access. Map** H7.

This is the epitome of the Paris literary haunt (since 1933, it has been awarding its own literary prize). Dishes include the usual suspects as well as more indulgent foie gras and sevruga caviar. This is one of the few cafés in Paris where wine by the glass is served from the bottle in front of you. With past regulars such as Sartre and de Beauvoir, Picasso, Verlaine and Hemingway, this was *the* place to have an Existential crisis; now, however, it's perhaps better suited for a financial one.

Cheap & kirful apéritifs

Once the drinks equivalent of the blue rinse, apéros are making a comeback.

Although the French penchant for apéritifs doesn't quite rival that of their Italian neighbours, most cafés provide unexpected alternatives to the obvious glass of Champagne or sweet wine. Different regions each have their own apéritifs and you should be able to find these in good regional restaurants. If you're after something traditional you could ask for a vin de liqueur such as Pineau des Charentes – a sweet mixture of Cognac and unfermented grape juice. Alternatively, why not whet your whistle with one of the below variations on some of the better known apéros?

The intoxicating swirls produced by mixing pastis with water don't have to be limited to the cloudy colour that delights grizzly old pétanque-players. Mixing the beloved 'pastaga' with flavoured syrup will turn it into a bright red tomate (grenadine flavour), a lurid green perroquet (mint flavour), or a golden mauresque (almond flavour). If blue's your colour you should seek out Pastis Bleu produced by Etablissements Germain. For a variation on pastis' potent cousin absinthe, try mixing it with Cognac to recreate Toulouse-Lautrec's tremblement de terre (earthquake).

Made from gentian roots that cling to the volcanic slopes of the Massif Central, Suze is a lip-puckeringly bitter apéritif. It can be sweetened with crème de cassis in a cocktail known as the fond de culotte ('the seat of your pants'), hence the punning saying: 'Ça ne s'use qu'assis!' ('it only wears out when you're sitting down').

The Queen Mother used to spice up the red vermouth of Dubonnet by drinking it with gin. Alternatively, it can be drunk with Campari and soda as an américano. Popular white vermouth Lillet Blanc is best enjoyed in traditional fashion – with ice and foie gras – although Hannibal Lecter fans looking to emulate their idol should sip theirs while slurping on human brains.

Kir or kir royal (crème de cassis with white Burgundy or Champagne) can be varied either by substituting the cassis with crème de mûre (blackberry), crème de framboise (raspberries) or crème de pêche de vigne (delicate vine peach), or by replacing the white wine with red to make a cardinal.

Even beer can be the basis of an interesting apéro. Aside from a panaché (the French word for shandy), you might also try a Monaco (beer with a shot of grenadine) or an amer bière (beer mixed with Picon, a bitter orange-flavoured liqueur).

Whatever you finally order, don't be disappointed if it doesn't come accompanied by an Italian-sized platter of dinky sandwiches, tarts and crisps. In Paris cafés, you'll be lucky to get even a tiny bowl of olives with your apéro; usually the best you can hope for is (quite literally) peanuts. *Tom Coveney*

4 et 1 SAVEURS

Unique in Paris
100% organic food

Vegetarian and macrobiotic specialities

Discover world specialties on our special Saturday theme-nights

open daily noon - 2.30pm, 7-10.30pm
(except Friday evening & Saturday)

72 rue du Cardinal Lemoine, 5th (near Panthéon)
M° Cardinal Lemoine • Reservation: 01.43.26.88.80

+++ 100% ORGANIC FOOD +++ 100% ORGANIC FOOD +++

LE STÜBLI

Breakfast - Lunch - Tea salon - Brunch

The best of Austrian-German tradition, applied with know-how and innovation!

The choice is yours:
Take away
Chocolates, Patisserie, and Deli specialities

And full catering service for parties and receptions

Patisserie
11 rue Poncelet, 17th
Tel: 01.42.27.81.86

Delicatessen
10 rue Poncelet, 17th
Tel: 01.48.88.98.07

Les Editeurs

4 carrefour de l'Odéon, 6th (01.43.26.67.76/ www.lesediteurs.fr). M° Odéon. **Open** daily 8am-2am. Food served daily noon-2am. **Beer** 25cl €4.20-€4.50. **Credit** AmEx, MC, V. **Map** H7.

Of the three café terraces on the carrefour Les Editeurs is the chicest, attracting low-key celebs such as chansonnier Benjamin Biolay to sip an apéritif and watch the world go by. You don't need to be feeling sociable; the shelves are stacked with books from nearby publishers, which customers are free to peruse. Should hunger strike, order choucroute or lighter dishes such as a club sandwich or roast cod.

Le Nemrod

51 rue du Cherche-Midi, 6th (01.45.48.17.05). M° Sèvres-Babylone. **Open** Mon-Sat 6am-11pm. Closed two weeks in Aug. Food served Mon-Fri noon-3pm, 7-11pm; Sat noon-4pm, 7-11pm. **Credit** MC, V. **Map** G7.

The Nemrod may have been revamped with burnt orange velvet and a lacquered ceiling, but at heart if remains your classic Auvergnat café, with a polished zinc, a long list of steaks and salads and a nostalgia for its roots, shown in Salers beef, pounti (minced pork with chard) and those rustic accompaniments of aligot and truffade. A salade oeuf mollet was a salad take on the great British breakfast – poached egg, lardons and chunks of fried bread. We also tried the saucisse d'Auvergne, accompanied by a massive portion of aligot, smooth potato purée rendered into a shiny, stringy mass with melted tomme cheese. Add the chic area, a busy lunchtime crowd and the constant to-ing and fro-ing of the stream of waiters and your entertainment is ready-made.

La Palette

43 rue de Seine, 6th (01.43.26.68.15). M° Mabillon or Odéon. **Open** Mon-Sat 8am-2am. Food served Mon-Sat noon-3pm. Closed Aug. **Beer** 25cl €4. **Credit** MC, V. **Map** H7.

Located behind the Ecole des Beaux-Arts and on a street lined with private galleries, La Palette, unsurprisingly, numbers quite a few gallery owners or frequenters among its clientele. The atmosphere on the large, popular terrace is slightly reserved during the day. At night, however, things can get downright wild. Service can be occasionally surly.

Au Petit Suisse ★

16 rue de Vaugirard, 6th (01.43.26.03.81). M° Odéon. **Open** Mon-Fri 7am-11pm; Sat, Sun 8am-1pm. Food served all day. **Beer** 25cl €2-€3.80. **Credit** MC, V. **Map** H7.

Named after Marie de Médicis' Swiss guards, the compact Au Petit Suisse has an enviable location next to the Jardins du Luxembourg. For those who don't live on coffee and cigarettes alone, the bilingual menu offers a range of predictable but generally decent food, served by old-school waiters. There is a wide selection of beers on tap, which draw in the students who make the most of the big tables. Be warned, it can get very smoky in winter.

Le Rostand ★

6 pl Edmond-Rostand, 6th (01.43.54.61.58). RER Luxembourg. **Open** daily 8am-midnight. Food served all day. **Beer** 25cl €4.20. **Credit** MC, V. **Map** H8.

Le Rostand's terrace is best enjoyed with earplugs and a gas mask if its rush hour, but it has a superlative view of the Jardins du Luxembourg and the inside is classy and clean with Orientalist paintings, long mahogany bar and wall-length mirrors. The brasserie menu is pricey, but the café selection offers generous fluffy omelettes and salads, great fruit tarts and there are lots of beers, whiskies and cocktails.

Le Select

99 bd du Montparnasse, 6th (01.42.22.65.27). M° Vavin. **Open** daily 7am-2.30am. Food served noon-1am. **Beer** 25cl €4.50. **Credit** MC, V. **Non-smoking room. Map** F9.

The introductory blurb on Le Select's menu is quick to remind you just how lucky you are to be sitting at its dark wooden tables which have been 'shined over time by so many celebrities'. Predictably the ghosts of Hemingway, Cocteau et al are long gone, and you are unlikely to run into any modern-day bohemians in such a pricey joint. However, you can have just as much fun spying on the efficiently sour-faced waiters, wealthy Parisian pensioners and cigar-chugging tourists, while tucking into an excellent, if expensive, croque-monsieur.

Au Vieux Colombier

65 rue de Rennes, 6th (01.45.48.53.81). M° St-Sulpice. **Open** Mon-Sat 8am-midnight; Sun 11am-8pm. Food served daily noon-10pm. **Beer** 25cl €2-€3.50. **Credit** MC, V. **Map** G7.

With a long, deeply varnished wood bar, teardrop chandeliers and other art nouveau touches, Aux Vieux Colombier attracts a cross-section of the area. Making colourful cocktails and serving cheapish beer and refreshing snacks with blinding speed, the young staff are friendly and efficient. Although it can get quite smoky, and you may find your elbows sticking to your table, these are small trade-offs for the vibrant atmosphere.

7th Arrondissement

Bar Basile

34 rue de Grenelle, 7th (01.42.22.59.46). M° Rue du Bac or Sèvres-Babylone. **Open** daily 7am-9pm. Food served noon-5pm. **Beer** 25cl €3. **Credit** MC, V. **Map** G7.

Bar Basile is a pleasant antidote to St-Germain style haunts with its lurid decor giving the impression of a 1960s diner-cum-school-canteen. A favourite hang-out of the student elite from Sciences-Po and local businessmen roughing it, this place gets jam-packed at lunch, when it serves a range of filling plats.

Café Le Dôme

149 rue St-Dominique, 7th (01.45.51.45.41). RER Pont de l'Alma. **Open** daily 7am-2am.

Peep into the real Parisian lifestyle at **Les Pipos**. *See p225*.

Food served all day. **Beer** 25cl €4.15-€4.40. **Credit** MC, V. **Map** D6.

The Eiffel Tower's upper half is just visible from the south section of this café's comfortable terrace, and the postcard rack and quadrilingual menus give away who makes up most of the clientele. Unpretentious with good plats, crêpes and view.

Café des Lettres

53 rue de Verneuil, 7th (01.42.22.52.17/ www.cafedeslettres.com). M° Rue du Bac. **Open** Mon-Sat 9am-midnight; Sun noon-4pm. Food served Mon-Sat noon-4pm, 7-10pm; Sun noon-4pm. Closed two weeks at Christmas. **Beer** 25cl €3.50-€4.80. **Credit** MC, V. **Map** G6.

Café des Lettres has a moody feel, with dark furniture, deep turquoise- and maroon-coloured walls, deeply meaningful abstract art and a heavy Gauloise-pervaded atmosphere. There may even be the odd brooding intellectual as the salon is used by the neighbouring Maison des Ecrivains for literary discussions and novel-reading sessions. Contrastingly airy, the courtyard is a good place to drop in on for an espresso on a summer's afternoon. Food can be of disappointing quality for the price, which reflects the swish location.

Le Café du Marché ★

38 rue Cler, 7th (01.47.05.51.27). M° Ecole-Militaire. **Open** Mon-Sat 7am-midnight; Sun 7am-5pm. Food served Mon-Sat 11.30am-11pm; Sun 11.30am-3.30pm. **Beer** 25cl €1.90-€3. **Credit** MC, V. **Map** D6.

For an in-the-action location amid the 7th's most lively market street, you can't do much better than Le Café du Marché, which serves as a hub of neighbourhood activity but is equally comfortable welcoming tourists and the curious. Dozens of tables are spread among interior dining rooms, a canopy and plastic-covered area plus an open-air terrace, so you have your choice of seating depending on the sun-cloud-rain continuum. Big salads at €9.50 and classic French main dishes at €10 (confit de canard, poulet rôti, entrecôte) are bargains, though quality varies depending on the dish (a fish special was fine, but pasta with a mix of both red and green pesto sauces was uneventful). Service had been friendly in the past, but was indifferent this time.

La Frégate

1 rue du Bac, 7th (01.42.61.23.77). M° Rue du Bac. **Open** daily 7am-midnight. Food served daily 11.30am-11.30pm. **Beer** 25cl €3.90-€4.30. **Credit** AmEx, MC, V. **Map** G6.

Next to the Musée d'Orsay, with a view over the Seine to the Louvre, there's plenty to look at from the orderly terrace here. The interior has been immaculately revamped with engraved metallic café tables and lovely curving bar at the front and a second room with larger restaurant tables, more accommodating for the fish-focused menu.

Café Le Varenne

36 rue de Varenne, 7th (01.45.48.62.72). M° Rue du Bac. **Open** Mon-Wed, Sat, Sun 7am-8pm; Thur 7am-11pm. Closed two weeks in Aug. **Beer** €4. **Credit** MC, V. **Map** G6.

Francis Tafanel has copped a supercool formula for revitalising the neighbourhood café. The key is

quality, since the blackboard menu changes daily and Tafanel shops at the best local suppliers, including fromager Barthélémy down the road. He has also shrewdly guessed that stylish locals would enjoy eating by candlelight in this homely setting when it's dressed with tablecloths, floral centrepieces and soft lighting once a week. This explains the amazingly good, if rather expensive, wine list, and excellent cooking, including starters such as white asparagus in mousseline sauce or spinach salad generously garnished with langoustines, and main courses of brandade de saumon, sole, and one of the best côtes de boeuf in Paris. Desserts run to tiramisu with raspberry, and sorbets, but most of the regulars opt for cheese and more wine.

8th Arrondissement

Atelier Renault ★

53 av des Champs-Elysées, 8th (01.49.53.70.00/ www.atelier-renault.com). M° Franklin D. Roosevelt. **Open** daily 8am-2am. Food served daily noon-12.30am. **Beer** 25cl €5. **Credit** AmEx, DC, MC, V. **Credit** MC, V. **Map** E4.

Upstairs, American elm, glass and steel provide surroundings that take their cue from a ship's cabin. There's a bar with armchairs and low tables, while five footbridges crossing the space give the 200-seat restaurant views over conceptual cars below and genuine traffic (jams) on the avenue. Food is modern/international (Moroccan-glazed roast lamb, spicy scampi with Chinese ravioli), or you can stop by anytime for snacks and ice cream sundaes.

Bar des Théâtres

6 av Montaigne, 8th (01.47.23.34.63). M° Alma-Marceau. **Open** daily 6am-2am. Food served all day. **Beer** 25cl €2.40-€5.40. **Credit** AmEx, MC, V. **Map** D5.

Nestling between Valentino and Emanuel Ungaro, bang opposite the Théâtre des Champs-Elysées, this popular bar/café is always buzzing in the evenings after the curtain falls, and attracts a steady daytime stream of trendy fashionistas. Yet Bar des Théâtres couldn't be less pretentious. Its cosy, informal atmosphere and service are reflected in the simple, though pricey, brasserie-style fare served in the café area or the slightly more formal restaurant section.

Granterroirs

30 rue de Miromesnil, 8th (01.47.42.18.18/ www.grandterroirs.com). M° Miromesnil. **Open** Mon-Fri 9am-8pm. Food served noon-3pm. Closed three weeks in Aug. **Credit** AmEx, MC, V. **Wheelchair access. Non-smoking room. Map** F3.

Welcome to snack-time, luxury-style. This gourmet delicatessen-cum-café is always packed out at lunch with gaggles of local office workers. It's possible to book before 12.30pm, but after that it's first come, first served. Don't be deterred – even if you have to be shoe-horned onto the benches alongside the two large picnic tables – because the huge assiette italienne and the tarte aux fraises are sensational.

Le Petit Bergson

10 pl Henri-Bergson, 8th (01.45.22.63.25). M° St-Augustin or St-Lazare. **Open** Mon-Fri

BAR RESTAURANT CLUB

OPEN ALL WEEK
9am-5am

Lunch and dinner served every day

DJ's and dancing into the night

49 rue du Faubourg Saint Antoine, 11th
Mº Bastille
33 (0)1.44.75.78.78
sanzsans@wanadoo.fr

11am-3pm. Food served all day. **Beer** €3. **Credit** MC, V. **Map** F3.
Le Petit Bergson's main selling point is its fabulous location – on the corner of one of the prettiest squares in Paris, with a view over a small park and the back of the St-Augustin church. At lunch the terrace is packed with local office workers enjoying a selection of set-price menus, which start at €11. A free fruit juice or kir is offered if you have wait for a table, and the service is friendly. The food is mainly salads, quiches and pies, plus a few hot dishes. The jovial owner bustles in and out but you may have to wait a while for your bill because he keeps stopping to have a drink with his mates at the bar.

9th Arrondissement

Café Gallery

16 rue Mogador, 9th (01.48.74.55.63). M° Chaussée d'Antin. **Open** Mon-Sat 7am-9pm (daily in Dec). Food served all day. **Beer** 25cl €3.70. **Credit** AmEx, MC, V. **Non-smoking room**. **Map** G3.
Nestled on a small street behind Galeries Lafayette, Café Gallery makes for a relaxing point from which to gather your thoughts before getting stuck into some serious shopping. Comfortable deep brown banquettes allow you to rest your feet while watching the dickey-bowed waiters scuttle back and forth across the room full of tourists and local workers. The appetising specials board had us licking our lips in anticipation, but we soon changed our minds about ordering when we saw the dry, unexciting dishes that arrived at a neighbouring table.

Café de la Paix

12 bd des Capucines, 9th (01.40.07.36.36). M° Opéra. **Open** daily noon to 12.30am. Food served noon-3pm, 6pm-midnight. Breakfast 7-11am (terrace only). **Beer** 25cl €6. **Credit** AmEx, DC, MC, V. **Wheelchair access**. **Non-smoking room**. **Map** G4.
Reopened after a 15-month restoration to resurrect its Napoléon III past, this café has a clientele list that reads like a veritable who's who – everyone from Maupassant to Zola, Oscar Wilde to Caruso, Josephine Baker to John Travolta. If you're on the way to or from the glittering Palais Garnier, treat yourself right and stop for a kir on the glassed-in terrace abutting the opulent celestial-ceiling dining room. You can dress up, or you can wander in from your Saturday shopping spree on rue La Fayette and rejuvenate with an incredible ice cream sundae, such as the house 'coupe' made with vanilla, hazelnuts, coconut, chocolate mousse, meringue, and whipped cream. There's a separate bar scattered with red velvet couches under a huge glass atrium.

P'tit Creux du Faubourg

66 rue du Fbg-Montmartre, 9th (01.48.78.20.57). M° Notre-Dame-de-Lorette. **Open** Mon-Sat 8am-8pm. Food served all day. Closed mid-July to mid-Aug. **Beer** 25cl €1.90-€2.40. **Credit** MC, V. **Map** H3.
This modest little café is a great place to drop by if you're in the area and fancy a good-value, good-quality lunch. When we last visited our salade composée was just right – a hearty mix of crunchy fresh lettuce, waxy new potatoes, eggs, emmental and tender ham all sprinkled with a delicious mustard

Café Le Varenne: quality food and service on tap. *See p230.*

Men and women of **The World Bar** unite.

mayonnaise dressing. Ravioli stuffed with salmon and spinach and served in a rich creamy sauce was nothing short of a revelation – the meaty pink fish flesh bursting out of the large pasta squares. With a jovial, croaky-throated patron to match its homely setting, this café is an unbeatable pit stop for locals and passers-by alike.

Rose Bakery ★

46 rue des Martyrs, 9th (01.42.82.12.80). M° Notre-Dame-de-Lorette. **Open** Tue-Sat 10am-7pm, Sun 10am-5pm. **Beer** bottle €4.50. **Credit** AmEx, MC, V. **Wheelchair access. Non-smoking. Map** H3.

A little island of Covent Garden bio-chic in the heart of Paris, Rose Bakery is an Anglophone-staffed bakery-café good for breakfast, brunch or tea. The menu offers a mix of conventional bistro fare and comfort food for the homesick ex-pat with Vegimite, Marmite and sugar-free, crunchy peanut butter among the takeaway bonuses. The organic produce really makes a difference. The English breakfast (€11), for example, was no cholesterol-orgy but you could actually taste the mushrooms and bacon. To eat in or take away there is a good selection of English cheeses (Neal's Yard) and non-continental fare such as carrot cake, scones and marmalade. Whitewashed walls and the smell of fresh baking help brighten up the cave-like interior.

The World Bar

Level 5, Printemps de l'Homme, 64 bd Haussmann, 9th (01.42.82.78.02). M° Havre-Caumartin. **Open** Mon-Wed, Sat, Sun noon-10pm, Thur 9.30am-10pm. Food served noon-3pm. **Beer** 25cl €3.40, bottle €4.30. **Credit** AmEx, DC, MC, V. **Map** G3.

This Paul Smith-designed café provides a suitable setting for fashion-conscious shoppers to take stock of their latest acquisitions. Breezeblock walls are plastered with yellowing newspapers dating from Paul Smith's birth and a velvet Union Jack hangs decadently above the bar as house music pulses around the room. Food, provided by the ubiquitous Flo Group, is a continental version of modern pub grub that mixes French standards such as confit de canard with favourites from abroad that include spring rolls and nachos.

10th Arrondissement

Chez Prune

71 quai de Valmy, 10th (01.42.41.30.47). M° République. **Open** Mon-Sat 8am-2am; Sun 10am-2am. Food served daily noon-3pm; snacks 6.30-11pm. Closed between Christmas and New Year. **Beer** 25cl €2-€2.50. **Credit** MC, V. **Map** L4.

Should the producers of *Friends* ever decide to relocate shooting to Paris, Chez Prune would surely be the hangout chosen by Chandler et al to replace their beloved Central Perk. Unflaggingly popular with the trendy bourgeois who gravitate to the Canal St-Martin, Prune is the place both to catch up with old acquaintances and find a few new ones to bolster your contacts book. At lunch the dining room and terrace reverberate with the buzz of screenplays being pitched across the packed tables, while in the evenings a more laidback crowd suss each other out from behind their mojitos.

La Chope des Artistes

48 rue du Fbg-St-Martin, 10th (01.42.02.86.76). M° Château d'Eau. **Open** Tue-Sat 6pm-4am. Food served 6pm-midnight. **Beer** 25cl €3.50-€4. **Credit** MC, V. **Map** K3.

Arriving inside this candlelit café at 10.30pm we were disappointed that the only other customer was a dishevelled-looking gent nursing a solitary glass of red wine. Fifteen minutes later however, we were squeezing up to make space for the lively crowd flocking in from the neighbouring Théâtre Splendid. Discussion of the evening's performance buzzed around both the mirror-lined walls of the front bar and the cosy back dining room. But the biggest round of applause was saved for the much-maligned 'gent' who sprang into life at 11.30pm, knocking out a succession of big show numbers on the bar's upright piano.

Jemmapes ★

82 quai de Jemmapes, 10th (01.40.40.02.35). M° Jacques Bonsergent or République. **Open** summer daily 11am-2am; winter Mon 5pm-2am; Tue-Sun 11am-2am. Food served noon-3pm, 8-11pm. **Beer** 25cl €2-€3. **No credit cards. Map** L4.

The comfortably scruffy Jemmapes is a perennial highlight of the Canal St-Martin area. By day its lo-fi charm is ideal for relaxing over coffee or some tasty café grub. As evening draws in, the room buzzes with new arrivals and buskers turn the small bar into a stage. Best of all are summer evenings when the punters spill out on to the quayside to bask in the setting sun, although government killjoy Sarkozy has tried to spoil the fun by banning the sale of take-out drinks after 10pm.

Le Petit Château d'Eau

34 rue du Château d'Eau, 10th (01.42.08.72.81). M° Château-d'Eau or Jacques Bonsergent. **Open** Mon-Fri 9am-9pm. Food served Mon-Fri noon-3pm. Closed Aug. **Beer** 25cl €2-€2.50. **Credit** MC, V. **Map** L4.

A gem of a café on a grim street, this place oozes relaxed, classy charm. The high-ceilinged main room is stacked with flowers and dominated by a large circular bar around which regulars perch to knock back cheap glasses of Beaujolais and Bordeaux. It's the perfect spot for a lunchtime omelette or an early-evening demi, and a good place for meeting friendly locals.

Le Réveil du 10ème ★

35 rue du Château-d'Eau, 10th (01.42.41.77.59). M° Château-d'Eau or Jacques Bonsergent. **Open** Mon-Sat 7am-9.30pm. Food served noon-3pm, Tue only 7.30-9.30pm. **Beer** 25cl €1.80-€2.10. **Credit** MC, V. **Map** K4.

The perfect old-fashioned Parisian lunch? This snug corner bistro à vins decorated with faded photos

The finest electronic music played by the best DJ's

TUES-THURS 6pm-2am
FRI-SAT 6pm-5am

"the psychedelic WAX
invites house DJs to mix
in an orange swirly
environment to
cocktail-sipping
Bastille regulars"
—*Time Out*

15 rue Daval, 11 th
M° Bastille
33 (0)1.40.21.16.16
www.wax.fr
wax2@wanadoo.fr

chronicling the restaurant's history has tables packed with regulars, including the couple in the corner who've been coming once a week for the past 50 years. Mouth-watering portions of meaty food (chunky saucisse d'Auvergne, juicy rib steak, crispy confit de canard) are quickly delivered by the attentive staff and cheese and dessert boards are irresistible. It's all washed down with an extensive wine list that specialises in thirst-quenching Beaujolais. Yes, in a word, perfect.

11th Arrondissement

Ba'ta'clan Café

50 bd Voltaire, 11th (01.49.23.96.33/ www.bataclancafe.com). M° Oberkampf. **Open** daily 7am-2am. Food served daily 11am-1am. Closed Christmas and New Year. **Beer** 25cl €2.20-€3.80. **Credit** MC, V. **Wheelchair access. Map** M5.

Being annexed to the concert venue of the same name, this café often gets late consignments of excitable music fans cooling off after a gig. For the rest of the time, it looks and feels like a drowsy colonial hideout. Dominated by a gorgeous circular bar and pagoda-style columns (part of an old theatre), this is a good place for a chat amongst friends, settled on dog-eared leather sofas or wicker chairs. Food options are limited to mainly pasta and croques but it's useful as a late-night-hunger option. Weekly speed dating evenings are planned for the near future; in the meantime you can make do with the Soirée Mystique on Mondays and Fridays, or brunch with classical music on Sundays.The prices seem in proportion with the very high ceiling, but for a real rip-off try the ticket touts outside.

Le Bistrot du Peintre

116 av Ledru-Rollin, 11th (01.47.00.34.39). M° Ledru-Rollin. **Open** Mon-Sat 7am-2am; Sun 10am-2am. Food served daily noon-midnight. Closed 24, 25 Dec. **Beer** 25cl €2.80. **Credit** MC, V. **Map** N7.

If you've been disappointed by mediocre Paris café food, Le Bistrot du Peintre is the antidote. Beef carpaccio with parmesan curls, inventive salads with such toppings as seared scallops and marinated red mullet, or a plate of lovely lentils and salmon (the fillet cleverly cut into a fish shape) are highlights on the menu. Salad with ham and foie gras, escargots, confit de canard and steak are also there for traditionalists. Choose from a dreamily dark, 1907 art nouveau interior with fabulous zinc bar and wooden panelling, a brighter upstairs dining room or pavement seating, the al fresco experience marred somewhat by the busy street corner. Service is welcoming and usually efficient.

Café de l'Industrie

16/17 rue St-Sabin, 11th (01.47.00.13.53). M° Bastille. **Open** daily 10am-2am. Food served noon-1am. Brunch Sat, Sun €15. **Beer** 25cl €2-€3. **Credit** DC, MC, V. **Non-smoking room. Map** M6.

This popular hang-out of the turtleneck and thick-rimmed eyeglasses crowd has engulfed a former Moroccan restaurant across the street, bringing its total seating capacity to 350 and adding an occasional jazz programme. But the flea-market-chic decor remains the same in both locales, an exceptionally pleasing combination of vintage furniture and eclectic paintings. Food is reasonably priced (most mains €10-€12) and fast, but the quality is hit or miss: a salmon tartare with tagliatelli was tenderly divine, but a plate of dull and gloopy gorgonzola pasta disappointed. We love the industrial-themed steel saucers and holders for the clear glass coffee cups. Quiet in the off-hours between meals, at lunch and late nights the place is positively buzzing.

Extra Old Café ★

307 rue du Fbg-St-Antoine, 11th (01.43.71.73.45). M° Nation. **Open** daily 7am-2am. Food served daily noon-3pm, 7-11pm. **Beer** 25cl €2.30. **Credit** MC, V. **Map** P7.

The faded grandeur of a 19th-century salon provides the setting for a funky, glass-fronted spot patronised by the cream of Nation's café society. Cocktails don't feature on the menu, but the T-shirted staff will knock up a mean margarita or gin fizz if you twist their arms. Idiosyncratic little touches abound, like the rose-garden toilets and the wall-sized doll cabinet stuffed with toys and records. The music is rock 'n' roll, the terrace is heated, and bottles of wine start at €11.

Le Kitch

10 rue Oberkampf, 11th (01.40.21.94.14). M° Oberkampf. **Open** Mon-Fri 10am-4pm, 5pm-2am; Sat, Sun 5pm-2am. Food served Mon-Fri noon-3pm, 8pm-midnight; Sat, Sun 8pm-midnight. **Beer** 25cl €1.50-€2.30. **No credit cards. Map** M5.

Proof that the glory days of kitsch are pretty much over, this bar bedecked with colourful gewgaws has started to take on the feel of an abandoned Barbie mansion. Still, it's not all shell-encrusted mirrors: the barman does his best to get people to try his 'toxic' absinthe cocktails, although given the pink surroundings a blackberry kir is probably more appropriate. Snacking is good and cheap, and the place fills up steadily with regulars at night.

Pause Café ★

41 rue de Charonne, 11th (01.48.06.80.33). M° Ledru-Rollin. **Open** Mon-Sat 8am-2am; Sun 9am-8pm. Food served daily noon-5pm, 7pm-midnight; Sun noon-5pm. Closed 25 Dec. **Beer** 25cl €1.85-€2.80. **Credit** AmEx, MC, V. **Map** M7.

The jazzy Pause Café – made famous in its pre-expansion days by a role in the film *Chacun cherche son chat* – is a must on the Bastille circuit. At mealtimes, mime school graduates have the best chance of getting a waiter's attention. Still, the setting remains funky and bright thanks to the picture windows and the kitchen makes a real effort with hot specials, a selection of filling tourtes, and goat's cheese in brik pastry with sweet sautéed pears. Seats on the heated terrace are coveted even in winter.

Polichinelle Café ★

64-66 rue de Charonne, 11th (01.58.30.63.52).
Open daily 10am-1am. Food served noon-3.30pm, 7.30-11.30pm; Sun brunch noon-5pm. **Beer** €2.50. **Credit** MC, V. **Map** N7.

It's impossible to say quite what makes Polichinelle our favourite spot for a long lunch in Paris. Is it the charming Hélène who has taken us under her wing like a clucking mother hen, the 1950s mosaic floor, or the banquettes for winter and sunny terrace for summer? We'd probably still come here were the food not as good as it is, but fortunately it delivers every time. Go for the meaty options – succulent bavette d'alloyau with red onion jam or magret de canard with pain d'épices sauce – or, for those who prefer fish, salmon with a tapenade vinaigrette. The summer fruits in the crumble taste as if they had just been picked.

Le Sporting

3 rue des Recollets, 10th (01.46.07.02.00).
M° Gare de l'Est. **Open** daily noon-1am. Food served noon-3pm, 7.30-10.30pm. **Beer** €2.50. **Credit** MC, V. **Map** L3.

Le Sporting is a little bit more grown-up than most of the cafés along the Canal St-Martin, and not just for having wooden floorboards: the dining room carries its elegant trimmings of chandeliers, colonial-style plants and chocolate banquettes with real style. The best time to come here is Sunday afternoon, when lunch and brunch are served until 4pm and diners can boozily stretch out the length of their meals. Quality ingredients and cooking produce dishes such as a delicious melon and coppa salad, fried king prawns with Thai basil, and mushroom and scorpion fish risotto. The brunch looks tempting, too.

12th Arrondissement

Chez Gudule ★

58 bd de Picpus, 12th (01.43.40.08.28). M° Picpus.
Open Mon-Sat 7.30am-1.45am; Sun 3.30pm-midnight. Food served Mon-Sat noon-3pm. Closed 15 July-15 Aug. **Beer** 25cl €2-€2.80. **Credit** MC, V. **Map** Q8.

Once known for serving only snack plates and plenty of cheap beer, Chez Gudule now offers full meal service for lunch and dinner, and the food quality lives up to the smart digs and chatty staff (note that serving hours may be revised). A select group of young and middle-aged locals fills the quasi-industrial interior decorated with bicycles and upside-down tables hanging from the ceiling. Music ranges from Brazilian to old soul and funk. Earth Wind and Fire with your consommé de raviolis, anyone?

T pour 2 Café

23 cour St-Emilion, 12th (01.40.19.02.09). M° Cour St-Emilion. **Open** daily 11am-midnight. Snacks served all day. **Beer** 25cl €3. **Credit** AmEx, DC, MC, V. **Map** P10.

This fashionable modern café, restaurant and bar in the renovated Bercy wine district offers a vast selection of teas and coffees ranging from the traditional (lapsang souchong) to the exotic (Guadeloupe bonifieur) and the just plain amusing (grand jasmin monkey king). The atmosphere is relaxed – big comfy chairs, mugs of coffee and Fashion TV and M6 playing. There is a selection of light foods including desserts, sandwiches and salads (around €12).

Viaduc Café

43 av Daumesnil, 12th (01.44.74.70.70/www.viaduc-cafe.fr). M° Ledru-Rollin or Gare de Lyon. **Open** daily 9am-4am. Food served noon-3pm, 7pm-3am. **Beer** 25cl €4-4.50. **Credit** MC, V. **Map** M8.

At this spacious bar-restaurant-cafe you can eat a full meal up on the 50-seat mezzanine or in the dining room under the well-preserved stone arch of this 19th-century elevated rail line, but if you'd rather sit by the slinky New York-style bar and order drinks and vittles, that doesn't ruffle the staff. Food is eclectic and generally pretty fab; try the club sandwich with pan-fried red potatoes or chicken with peanuts served in a gleaming tagine dish. A terrace twinkles with candlelight until 4am every night and there's a jazz brunch on Sundays.

14th Arrondissement

Le Cadran

38 rue Raymond-Losserand, 14th (01.43.21.69.45). M° Pernéty. **Open** Mon-Sat 7am-9pm. Food served 11.30am-2.30pm. **Beer** 25cl €1.80-€2.10. **No credit cards. Map** F10.

Behind a sparkling green facade lies a beautifully prosaic slice of old Paris. Its mosaic floor and zinc bar emerge occasionally from the requisite cigarette fug as a gang of regulars downs apéros at the bar, and all ages head to the second room for lunchtime sustenance. He mans the bar; she waddles to and from the kitchen, bearing plates laden high with the plat du jour, perhaps rosy, roast lamb and green beans. The fruit tarts, fresh from the oven, are winners. Happily oblivious to trends.

Café de la Place

23 rue d'Odessa, 14th (01.42.18.01.55). M° Edgar-Quinet. **Open** Mon-Sat 7.30am-2am; Sun 10am-11pm. Food served Mon-Sat noon-1am; Sun noon-10pm. **Beer** 25cl €3.70. **Credit** MC, V. **Map** G9.

At Café de la Place, you can choose between the homely, dark-wood-panelled interior, the glassed-in terrace or, during warmer weather, the pavement under a canopy of green trees. We went for the giant Poilâne-bread croques: the vegetarian tomato and cheese version was served atop a huge pile of salad. At the edge of the famous cemetery, you'll feel miles away from Montparnasse mania.

La Chope Daguerre

17 rue Daguerre, 14th (01.43.22.76.59). M° Denfert-Rochereau. **Open** Mon, Sun 7am-8pm; Tue-Sat 7am-midnight. Food served noon-3pm, 6.30-11pm. **Beer** 25cl €2-€3.70. **Credit** MC, V. **Map** G10.

Rue Daguerre positively drips with cafés, from the humblest plastic tabac to nouveau design velour. La Chope falls somewhere between the two, but is the

Don’t miss out on your just desserts at **Polichinelle Café.**

Just call me **Dada**-cool.

rendezvous of choice for locals. Spruced up with dark wood, new chairs and glowing red lamps, this is a place to skulk inside over an apéro, or bask on the terrace absorbing the sights, sounds and smells of the market. Food is fresh and generous, with big salads and blackboard suggestions such as chicken with morels or five-pepper steak.

15th Arrondissement

Au Dernier Métro ★

70 bd de Grenelle, 15th (01.45.75.01.23/ www.audernieremetro.com). M° Dupleix. **Open** daily 6am-2am. Food served noon-1am. Closed 25 Dec, 1 Jan. **Beer** 25cl €1.90-€2.60. **Credit** AmEx, MC, V. **Map** C7.

This adorable café makes you feel at home. The walls are covered with colourful memorabilia and a football game plays on the small TV behind the bar. Lots of the Basque-influenced dishes tempt – we tried the juicy fish brochettes served with saffron rice and one of the big salads, both made with care. There's a bit of pavement seating and the big windows open right up. Beer is a bargain for the neighbourhood. Service could not have been friendlier or more attentive – where else might the waiter address two diners as 'my angels'?

Au Roi du Café

59 rue Lecourbe, 15th (01.47.34.48.50). M° Sèvres-Lecourbe. **Open** daily 7am-midnight. Food served until 11pm. **Beer** 25cl €2-€3.40. **Credit** MC, V. **Map** D8.

If you happen to be in this corner of the 15th, this scruffy art deco gem makes a pleasant stop for a cheap carafe of wine; it's one of the only bits of retro Paris on an architecturally challenged street. You'll find the basics – croque monsieurs and madames on Poilâne bread, typical café salads, omelettes and soupe à l'oignon. The decor is the real reason to spend an hour or three here, soaking up a slice of Paris gone by. Shame about the charmless service.

16th Arrondissement

Café Antoine

17 rue La Fontaine, 16th (01.40.50.14.30). RER Kennedy-Radio France. **Open** Mon-Sat 7.30am-11pm. Closed two weeks in Aug. Food served Mon-Sat noon-3pm, 7-10.30pm. **Beer** 25cl €2-€3. **Credit** AmEx, DC, MC, V. **Map** A7.

Hector Guimard slipped this tiny café into one of his famous art nouveau buildings, with a view over a small but classy food market on Tuesdays and Fridays. Inside is a strawberries-and-cream idyll of days gone by: roses on the tiles, a painted-glass ceiling and blowsy scenes of horseracing and rowing. An excellent Italian espresso comes on a tiny tray with a chocolate coin; they also do hot chocolate and mulled wine, while tiny blackboards announce tempting, if pricey, foie gras, poulet à la normande, steaks and charcuterie. Adorable.

Le Totem

Musée de l'Homme, 17 pl du Trocadéro, 16th (01.47.27.28.29/www.letotem.fr). M° Trocadéro.

Open daily noon-2am. Food served noon-2.30pm, 7.30-11.30pm. **Beer** 25cl €4.30. **Credit** AmEx, DC, MC, V. **Wheelchair access. Map** B5.
Two giant totems from British Columbia give the café-restaurant its name, while a panorama of the Eiffel Tower provides a spectacular view. A chic mix of branché bourgeoisie, tourists, businessmen and celebrities meets at the well-stocked bar. Contemporary French food is served at lunch, while at night it's best to reserve for adventurous dinner fare. As the museum is closing in 2004 to move its collection to the new Quai Branly site, do call to check before venturing here.

17th Arrondissement

Le Dada ★

12 av des Ternes, 17th (01.43.80.60.12/ www.dada-bar.com). M° Ternes. **Open** Mon-Sat 6am-2am; Sun 6am-midnight. Food served noon-11pm. **Beer** 25cl €3.50. **Cocktails** €7.50. **Credit** AmEx, MC, V. **Map** C3.
Perhaps the hippest café on this classy avenue, Le Dada is best known for its well-placed, sunny terrace, but the kookily dada-influenced two-floor interior is ideal for lunch. Standard brasserie dishes, brought out by efficient but obviously overworked waiters, are placed on wood-block carved tables, and the red walls provide a warm atmosphere for the Parisian crowd. If terracing is your thing, you could probably spend a whole summer afternoon here.

18th Arrondissement

Chez Camille

8 rue Ravignan, 18th (01.46.06.05.78). M° Abbesses. **Open** Tue-Sat 9am-1am. Food served all day. **Beer** 25cl €2.30. **No credit cards. Map** H1.
Proof that Montmartre isn't just about ripping off busloads of tourists, Chez Camille attracts branché locals. On sunny days regulars pack out the tiny wooden terrace, the bar staff in their midst taking on all comers at backgammon. Inside the snug bar, colourful blackboards list the cocktails on offer, stacks of board games fill the shelves, and a clubby soundtrack pumps from the wall-mounted speakers. Food is available, but choice is limited.

Le Chinon

49 rue des Abbesses, 18th (01.42.62.07.17). M° Abbesses. **Open** daily 7am-2am. Food served daily 7am-1am. **Beer** 25cl €1.80-€4. **No credit cards. Map** H1.
Many of the bars and restaurants in Montmartre are filled entirely with tourists, but in this stretch of the road the atmosphere is more Parisian. With trendy tables and chairs worthy of a collector, this café can almost be forgiven for serving watery-tasting wine, such as our vieilles vignes Chinon. As long as you stick to coffee or beer, like the mostly French clientele, you should be fine.
Branch: Le Troisième Chinon, 56 rue des Archives, 4th (01.48.87.94.68).

Francis Labutte ★

122 rue Caulaincourt, 18th (01.42.23.58.26). M° Lamarck-Caulaincourt. **Open** Mon-Sat 8.30am-2am; Sun 9am-2am. Food served noon-4pm, 6.30-11pm. **Beer** 25cl €2.30. **Credit** MC, V. **Map** H1.
Bypass the tourist-flooded cafes near the Sacré-Cœur and take a stroll down the backside of the butte to marvel at the Montmartrois architecture and this convivial café. The interior vibrates with colours but the heated terrace (covered in winter) is where it's at – a funky crowd of all ages convenes here in any season for drinks or salads. Good croques monsieurs and vegetarian tarts fill the menu, plus a range of mojito-family cocktails (€6.50) for when things turn bar-like.

19th Arrondissement

La Kaskad'

2 pl Armand-Carrel, 19th (01.40.40.08.10). M° Laumière. **Open** daily 9am-1am. Food served daily 11am-midnight. Closed 25 Dec. **Beer** 25cl €2.70-€3.90. **Credit** MC, V. **Wheelchair access. Map** N2.
Named after the impressive manmade waterfall in the Buttes-Chaumont park opposite, La Kaskad' has been a real hit with the local glitz (it's the *only* place worth donning your D&G shades for round here). Pose on the terrace and watch the limos roll up for wedding pictures in the park, or sit in the stylish taupe and mahogany interior and sip a cocktail to nu-jazz sounds. The food, while not cheap, is delicious, including mains such as luscious pork cheeks and steaks, and huge salads for €10.40; if you're feeling flush there are some serious wines on the list.

Le Rendez-vous des Quais

MK2 sur Seine, 10-14 quai de la Seine, 19th (01.40.37.02.81/www.mk2.com). M° Stalingrad or Jaurès. **Open** daily noon-midnight. Food served daily noon-11.15pm. **Beer** 25cl €3.50. **Credit** AmEx, DC, MC, V. **Wheelchair access. Map** M2.
You can easily while away hours watching the barges and tour boats from your table at this relaxed café on the esplanade of the Bassin de la Villette. Food-loving film buffs can't miss with the menu ciné, which includes a ticket to the adjoining MK2 cinema. The food is a cut above café fare, and desserts tend towards the rich and gooey.

20th Arrondissement

Le Soleil

136 bd de Ménilmontant, 20th (01.46.36.47.44). M° Ménilmontant. **Open** daily 9am-2am. **Beer** 25cl €1.70. **No credit cards.** Map N5.
Aptly named, as the terrace catches most of the afternoon sun, this brightly lit café is a standby for local artists, musicians and hipsters and always an interesting place to strike up a conversation. It's totally unexceptional inside, but you want to be outside anyway. No food, but plenty of beer.

Bars & Pubs

Slip into a dry martini or turn to jelly – vodka jelly, baby – in some intoxicating Parisian parlour. Licenced to swill ... oh, oh heaven.

It's hard to fathom what's going on in the Paris drinking world. The only rule seems to be 'thou shalt copy thy neighbour'. Yet for all the obvious plagiarism – not to mention countless theme bars – a more authentic scene exists off the beaten track. The 18th, 19th and 20th arrondissements spring to mind, as well as the delightful Butte aux Cailles (13th) and even the odd cheeky surprise in the Latin Quarter or off the Champs-Elysées. Perhaps the most important tip is that things are different here; swanky prices don't guarantee a garnish and a smile. Parisian bars are a reflection of the city: attitude-prone, sexy and, above all, great spots to pout.

1st Arrondissement

Cabaret

2 pl du Palais-Royal, 1st (01.58.62.56.25). M° Palais Royal. **Open** Mon, Tue 7pm-3am, Wed-Sat 7pm-6am. Food served Tue-Sat 8-11.30pm. **Beer** 25cl €10-€13. **Cocktails** €13. **Credit** AmEx, MC, V. **Wheelchair access**. **Non-smoking room**. **Map** H5.

This über-design phenomenon has recently enlarged and revamped. Hence it has moved on to cocky monosyllables, tagging the new club area 'Cab'. Jacques Garcia's luminescent dining room remains, while Ora Ïto has killed off the wildlife theme and replaced it with stark, dark retro. Leather padding lines the walls, and doughnut-shaped table pods accompany deep banquettes – the bed-sized versions in the 'tent' invite you to lounge back to the 70s amid swirly lights, Formica and expensive drinks. Donatella, Naomi and los Cruz/Cruise set the standard. So be beautiful and dress up, or the door police will most certainly eject you.

Carpe Diem

21 rue des Halles, 1st (01.42.21.02.01). M° Châtelet. **Open** Mon-Thur 9am-2am; Fri, Sat 9am-4am. Food served 11.30am-3.30pm, 6.30-11.30pm. **Beer** 25cl €3-€4. **Cocktails** €7. **Credit** DC, MC, V. **Map** J6.

Seize the day they have, and that is no easy feat given that the setting is the backside of Les Halles shopping centre, one of Paris' least savoury haunts. But Carpe Diem has successfully transformed a bustling street corner into an elegantbar-brasserie, with cappuccino-tone upholstery blending comfortably with the frosted glass windows and dark wood panelling of its former days as an Irish pub. Cosy in winter and breezy in the summer, when the sides are peeled open, it attracts both ageing barflies and the affluent. Grab a chessboard, and wander the contemporary art exhibitions downstairs in the vaults.

Le Comptoir

37 rue Berger, 1st (01.40.26.26.66). M° Les Halles or Louvre-Rivoli. **Open** Mon-Thur, Sun noon-2am; Fri, Sat noon-3am. Food served noon-3pm; 7pm-midnight. Closed 24, 25 Dec. **Beer** 25cl €4. **Cocktails** €10. **Happy hour** 5-8pm. **Credit** MC, V. **Map** J5.

Amid the hectic rush that is Les Halles, there is Le Comptoir: an oasis of calm overlooking the gardens beside St-Eustache. The decor is Moroccan to the last detail: deep-red rugs, coloured-glass chandeliers, low-slung, leather stools and banquettes piled high with cushions. A young, international crowd lounges around drinking mint tea – served as it should be with pine nuts bobbing on top. The service is friendly and the cocktails lethal.

Flann O'Brien's

6 rue Bailleul, 1st (01.42.60.13.58). M° Louvre-Rivoli. **Open** daily 4pm-5am. **Beer** 25cl €4. **Cocktails** €8. **Credit** MC, V. **Map** J6.

Apart from pouring one of the slowest pints of Guinness in town, this classic Irish Bar is well-known for its late licence allowing three hours of extra boozing time. From the outside it looks a bit cold but, once you're in, the pint-proud barmen and live folk bands will make you feel as if you are in the Emerald Isle. Before the playful masses pour in after midnight, punters and off-duty barmen slouch around the L-shaped bar, discussing politics and Roy Keane.

Le Fumoir ★

6 rue de l'Amiral-de-Coligny, 1st (01.42.92.00.24/ www.lefumoir.com). M° Louvre-Rivoli. **Open** daily 11am-2am. Food served noon-3pm, 7.30pm-midnight. **Beer** 25cl €4. **Cocktails** €10. **Happy hour** 6-8pm. **Credit** AmEx, MC, V. **Wheelchair access**. **Map** H6.

At this elegant bar directly opposite the Louvre, neo-colonial fans whirr lazily, oil paintings adorn the walls and even the bar staff seem to have been included in the interior decorator's sketches. A sleek crowd sipping martinis or browsing the papers at the long mahogany bar (originally from a Chicago speakeasy), gives way to young professionals in the restaurant and pretty young things in the library.

Hemingway Bar at the Ritz

Hôtel Ritz, 15 pl Vendôme, 1st (01.43.16.30.31/ www.ritzparis.com). M° Madeleine or Concorde. **Open** Tue-Sat 6.30pm-2am. Tapas served 6.30pm-2am. Closed 25 July-25 Aug. **Beer** 25cl €11. **Cocktails** €22-€23. **Credit** AmEx, DC, MC, V. **Map** F5.

This is simply one of the loveliest places in Paris to do cocktail hour. The dark wood, muffled laughter, black-and-white photos of the Old Man and the old-school charm of Colin the barman make the bar a cocoon from the horrors of the outside world. Pulling in its fair share of characters, honeymooners and expense-account nerds, it's also a wonderful place to people-watch. The cocktails are as near to alcoholic Nirvana as possible, in particular the raspberry martini, a divine blend of raspberries and vodka. Even the tap water comes full of iced berries and every drink for the ladies is presented with a flower.

Jip's

41 rue St-Denis, 1st (01.42.21.33.93). M° Châtelet or Les Halles. **Open** Mon-Sat 9am-2am; Sun noon-2am. Food served all day. **Beer** 25cl €3. **Cocktails** €8-€9. **Credit** MC, V. **Map** J5.

Jip's is a tiny oasis from the takeaways, second-hand clothes shops and prostitutes that loiter in the area. With a terrace protected by tarpaulin and warmed by heaters at night or in the depths of winter, Jip's facade is a festival of colours and action. Rum punches and Latino-inspired food fuel a multi-ethnic, multi-generational crowd. Music varies according to the night: Tuesday, for example, is tango.

2nd Arrondissement

Café Noir ★

65 rue Montmartre, 2nd (01.40.39.07.36). M° Sentier. **Open** Mon-Fri 8am-2am; Sat 3pm-2am. Food served Mon-Fri noon-3pm. **Beer** 25cl €3. **Cocktails** €7. **Credit** MC, V. **Map** J4.

Permanently packed with a rotating gaggle of bobo boys and girls, Café Noir is still the place to apéro around here. The cluttered bar, painted mirrors and neon striplights make it look like your local caff, if only your local caff were populated by such artfully messy, bright young things. Sip a Suze (retro chic, darling), and improve your French by taking advantage of the utterly glorious eavesdropping on offer.

Le Cardinal

1 bd des Italiens, 2nd (01.42.96.61.20). M° Richelieu-Drouot. **Open** daily 6am-5am. Food served noon-4am. **Beer** 25cl €5.50. **Cocktails** €8. **Happy hour** 5-8pm. **Credit** AmEx, DC, MC, V. **Wheelchair access**. **Non-smoking room**. **Map** H4.

Although Cardinal Richelieu's austere bust glares down on all those entering the café to which he lends his name, it can do little to dampen the spirits of those already ensconced inside. Corset-clad armchairs, bubbling green cocktail dispensers and beat-heavy music encourage tourists, office workers and trendy dragueurs towards positively un-holy behaviour. Due to its size, all-night opening and Grands Boulevards location Le Cardinal will always court the mainstream crowd that its unsurprising menu of hot food and salads plays up to, but its cheeky enthusiasm might well get you coming back for more.

Le Coeur Fou ★

55 rue Montmartre, 2nd (01.42.33.91.33). M° Sentier. **Open** Mon-Sat 4pm-2am. **Beer** 25cl €2.50. **Cocktails** €6.50. **No credit rds**. **Map** J4.

Colin Peter Field mixes a magic martini at the **Hemingway Bar**.

Be sure to arrive early for a chance of some air-kissing space at the bar, as the hipsters and chancers who pack this place out start their soirées while the rest of us are still staring into space at the office. The squishy sofas, eye-grabbing canvases and masses of mingling make a night at Le Coeur Fou feel like a particularly fun art opening. Some of the lines we heard were works of art in themselves, and the alcoholic slush puppies and generous measures make everyone feel a little like the next big thing.

Footsie

10-12 rue Daunou, 2nd, (01.42.60.07.20). M° Opéra. **Open** Mon-Thur noon-2.30pm, 6pm-2am; Fri, Sat noon-2.30pm, 6pm-4am. Food served noon-2.30pm, 6-11pm. **Beer** 25cl €3.60. **Cocktails** €10. **Credit** AmEx, MC, V. **Map** G4.

This is such a plummy idea it should be floated on the stock market: bar prices modelled on shares which rise and fall every four minutes depending on how many people buy them; popular brews go up, pensioners' tipples stay cheap. Footsie goads you into mixing your drinks and playing City whizzkids till dawn. A whisky can fluctuate between €5.80 and €10.50 in seconds. Yet among the throng, we were the only scabby ones looking up at the screens, scanning for bargains. Prices 'crash' occasionally, encouraging yet more windfall boozing.

The Frog & Rosbif

116 rue St-Denis, 2nd (01.42.36.34.73/ www.frogpubs.com). M° Etienne-Marcel. **Open** daily noon-2am. Food served noon-11pm. **Beer** 25cl €4.20. **Cocktails** €6.50. **Happy hour** 6-8pm. **Credit** MC, V. **Map** J5.

Paul Chantler and Thor Gudmundsson must be delighted with the success of their chain of English pubs that started with this one. Their ads call it 'a quintessential English pub', and it is, with thick wooden pews, autographed rugby shirts, traditional pub grub and five screens to broadcast the UK's top sporting events. The Frogpubs serve their own beers – bitters, lagers and stouts – all brewed on the premises and available on tap. We particularly enjoyed the strong bitter Parislytic and the full-bodied stout, Dark de Triomphe. Staff are well marshalled, the atmosphere friendly and there's even a good blend of testosterone and oestrogen.

Branches: The Frog & British Library, 113 avenue de France, 13th (01.45.84.34.26); The Frog & Princess, 9 rue Princess, 6th (01.40.51.77.38); The Frog at Bercy, 25 cour St Emilion, 12th (01.43.40.70.71).

Harry's New York Bar

5 rue Daunou, 2nd (01.42.61.71.14/ www.harrys-bar.fr). M° Opéra. **Open** daily 10.30am-4am. Food served Mon-Fri 11am-3pm. Closed 24, 25 Dec. **Beer** 25cl €5.40. **Cocktails** €10.10. **Credit** AmEx, DC, MC, V. **Map** G4.

Things will never be quite the same since the untimely demise of Harry's son Duncan a couple of years ago, but Paris' quintessential American bar is still the smoky, pennant-bedecked institution beloved of expats, visitors and hard-drinking Parisians. The white-coated bartenders mix some of the finest and most lethal cocktails in town, from the trademark bloody Mary (invented here, so they say) to the well-named pétrifiant, a paralysing elixir of half a dozen spirits splashed into a beer mug. They can also whip up a personalised creation: we remember (patchily) a string of unfailingly delicious vodka concoctions that had us swooning in the downstairs piano bar and outrageously overtipping the artiste.

La Jungle

56 rue d'Argout, 2nd (01.40.41.03.45). M° Sentier. **Open** Mon-Fri 10am-2am; Sat, Sun 4pm-2am. Food served Mon-Fri noon-2pm, 7pm-midnight; Sat, Sun 7pm-midnight. **Beer** 25cl €3. **Cocktails** €6. **Credit** AmEx, DC, MC, V. **Map** J5.

True to its name, this mini hotspot is the life and soul of the pedestrianised rue d'Argout. It was put together by charming George from Cameroon, who up-ends rum-based shots, dances, winks at the ladies and tries his utmost to make the loneliest of souls feel welcome. It's a little rough around the edges – tables dressed up as zebras, tawdry fairy-lights – but it is also refreshingly unpretentious.

Le Next

17 rue Tiquetonne, 2nd (01.42.36.18.93). M° Etienne-Marcel. **Open** Mon-Thur 6pm-2am; Fri, Sat 6pm-dawn. Closed one weekend mid-Aug. Snacks served daily 6-11pm. **Beer** 25cl €3. **Cocktails** €7. **Happy hour** 6-9pm. **Credit** MC, V. **Map** J5.

Tucked away on the rue Tiquetonne, velvet sofas, exposed stone walls, low lighting and African artefacts combine to give off a students' boudoir fantasy-feel which is surprisingly seductive. Grab a pair of plush purple thrones and make like Posh 'n' Becks. A few delicious caramel vodka shots later and you too will believe that you can sing.

3rd Arrondissement

Andy Wahloo ★

69 rue des Gravilliers, 3rd (01.42.71.20.38). M° Arts et Métiers. **Open** Mon-Sat noon-2am. Food served noon-midnight. **Beer** bottle €4. **Cocktails** €10. **Credit** AmEx, DC, MC, V. **Map** K5.

Andy Wahloo – created by the people behind its neighbour 404 (*see p210*) and London's Momo – is Arabic for 'I have nothing'. But it does, and bundles of it. From head to toe, it's a beautifully designed venue with a wide, swooping bar, Moroccan artefacts, and enough colours to fill a Picasso. Quiet early, the atmosphere heats up later on. The cocktails are good and the snacks fresh in from next door.

Le Connétable

55 rue des Archives, 3rd (01.42.77.41.40). M° Hôtel de Ville or Rambuteau. **Open** Mon-Sat 11am-3pm, 6pm-midnight. Food served 11am-3pm, 7pm-midnight. **Beer** 25cl €4. **Cocktails** €6. **Credit** AmEx, DC, MC, V. **Map** K6.

Look no further for the ultra-Parisian Piaf-and-pastis bar. While diners feast in the first-floor bistro, downstairs in the crowded bar, faded divas hold court in

Talking heads live at **Les Etages**. *See p247*.

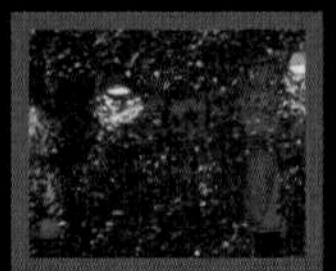

on en oublie d'aller ailleurs*

amnésia

café

42 rue vieille du temple, 4th Paris • 01 . 42 . 72 . 16 . 94

Open daily from 11am to 2am

* you'll forget to go somewhere else

the corner and struggling artists bash out chansons on the out-of-tune upright, accompanied (loudly) by messieurs with the types of moustaches normally seen only in Monty Python sketches.

4th Arrondissement

Le Bateau Ivre

19 rue des Deux-Ponts, 4th (01.43.26.92.15). M° Pont Marie. **Open** Mon 11am-4pm; Tue-Sun 11am-2am. Food served noon-3pm, 7-10.30pm. **Beer** 25cl €2.60. **Cocktails** €8. **Credit** AmEx, MC, V. **Map** K7.

This island hangout feels like a lurching pirate ship with its wooden interior complete with lifebuoy, hammock, ropes and a balustraded upper deck. Cocktails (including an appropriately named corsaire), wines by the glass, brasserie food and nibbles help punters find their sea legs.

Bubar ★

3 rue des Tournelles, 4th (01.40.29.97.72). M° Bastille. **Open** daily 7pm-2am. Closed 14 July. **Beer** 25cl €3. **Wine** glass €2.50-€6. **Credit** MC, V. **Map** L7.

A frequent customer at Bubar is a rotund shar-pei, who sits at the door watching the world go by. The wine list is a globe-trotting feast, with an unusually large selection of New World flavours (try delicious South African merlot Drostdy-Hof). Nibbles lining the bar in colourful plates form an edible decor.

Chez Richard

37 rue Vieille-du-Temple, 4th. (01.42.74.31.65). M° Hôtel de Ville or St-Paul. **Open** daily 6pm-2am. Food served 8pm-midnight. Closed two weeks in Aug. **Beer** 25cl €3.70. **Cocktails** €7-€10. **Happy hour** 6-8pm. **Credit** AmEx, MC, V. **Map** K6.

Chez Richard can be whatever you want it to be: a quiet cocktail spot, a pre-game fuelling station, or a surprisingly good restaurant. The long, squishy bar invites elbows in the dark front room while the tables over four coolly designed floors provide ample space for those travelling in a mob. Pick your spot and enjoy one of the Marais' most sublime bars.

Les Etages

35 rue Vieille-du-Temple, 4th (01.42.78.72.00). M° Hôtel de Ville or St-Paul. **Open** daily 3.30pm-2am. **Beer** 25cl €3.20-€4. **Cocktails** €6. **Happy hour** 3.30-9pm. **Credit** AmEx, DC, MC, V. **Map** K6.

If squalor is your thing and you don't mind picking bits of ceiling out of your hair, snagging your Wolfords on a sofa spring and contorting yourself into yoga positions to sit down, then this artfully distressed cocktail bar is the place for you. A weird caste system governs seating (apparently the top floors are the hippest places to squat).

The Lizard Lounge ★

18 rue du Bourg-Tibourg, 4th (01.42.72.81.34/ www.hipbars.com). M° Hôtel de Ville. **Open** daily noon-2am. Food served Mon-Fri 12.30-3pm, 7-10.30pm; Sat noon-4pm, 7-10.30pm; Sun noon-4pm. Closed one week in Aug, three days at Christmas. **Beer** 25cl €2.80. **Cocktails** €6-7.80. **Happy hour** beer from 8-10pm (cellar), cocktails 6-8pm (upstairs). **Credit** MC, V. **Map** K6.

There are two vibes at the Lizard Lounge – the dank downstairs cellar with chill-out music (DJs regularly) and the upstairs room equipped with a cool mezzanine. The downstairs, now legendary among American college students, is where you find the unbeatable happy hour and, when that runs out, the funky cocktail du soir (€4.40). Sunday brunch is an institution; arrive early for the Sunday papers, cheap bloody Marys and heart-stopping eggs Benedict.

Le Pick-Clops

16 rue Vieille-du-Temple, 4th (01.40.29.02.18). M° Hôtel de Ville or St-Paul. **Open** Mon-Sat 7.30am-2am; Sun 9am-3am. Food served noon-1.30am. Closed 25 Dec. **Beer** 25cl €3.30. **Cocktails** €7. **Credit** MC, V. **Map** K6.

The leitmotif here is resolutely kitsch, with top-to-toe pink neon and a wonderfully awful clock with bauble-adorned hands. Seventies retro chicks vie with trendy Marais locals in geometric specs for space at the bar. A place with as many mirrors as this is clearly designed for narcissists, and it does a roaring trade on a busy Parisian evening.

Stolly's

16 rue Cloche-Perce, 4th (01.42.76.06.76/ www.hip-bars.com). M° Hôtel de Ville or St-Paul. **Open** daily 4.30pm-2am. Closed 25 Dec. **Beer** 25cl €2.80. **Cocktails** €6. **Happy hour** 4.30-8pm. **Credit** MC, V. **Wheelchair access. Map** K6.

Some nights you'll laugh at the number of people this place packs in, while on others Stolly's becomes a nice place to quietly (and comfortably) sip a pint. You'll always find chatty expats getting hammered, and the music – think Credence and Cat – and friendly staff create a welcoming atmosphere. Also a good place to catch a footie game on TV.

Le Trésor

7 rue du Trésor, 4th (01.42.71.35.17). M° St-Paul. **Open** daily 11.30am-2am. Food served Mon-Fri noon-3pm, 7pm-12.30am; Sat, Sun 11.30am-12.30am. **Beer** 25cl €4. **Cocktails** €8. **Happy hour** Mon-Sat 5-8pm. **Credit** AmEx, MC, V. **Map** K6.

This modish bar/restaurant has come out of refurb with an eye-catching scheme of luminous pink, green, white and grey, and fairground-tastic concave mirrors. None of this, however, deters the mixed crowd of trendies. The food and wine have a distinct Franco-Italian twist, and the loos are definitely worth a gander with live goldfish swimming in the cisterns. Don't worry, you can't flush them away.

5th Arrondissement

The 5th Bar

62 rue Mouffetard, 5th (01.43.37.09.09). M° Place Monge. **Open** Mon-Thur, Sun 4pm-2am; Fri, Sat 4pm-3am. **Beer** 25cl €3.50 **Cocktails** €5-€6.50. **Happy hour** Mon, Wed, Fri-Sun 4-10pm; Tue, Thur all night. **Credit** MC, V. **Map** J8.

WHERE FRANCE MEETS THE REST OF THE WORLD

Panfoulia

Bar Cafe Expo

OPEN DAILY UNTIL 2AM

HAPPY HOUR 6PM-9PM

DJS AT THE WEEKEND

7 RUE STE CROIX DE LA BRETONNERIE, 4TH

Mº HÔTEL DE VILLE OR SAINT PAUL

TEL: 01.42.74.61.68

THE GREEN LINNET

new irish pub

Open 7 days a week
Noon-2am

Live Music & Food

Happy Hour
4pm-8pm

Pool Table

8, Avenue Victoria, 4th. • Mº Hôtel de Ville / Châtelet

Tel: 01.42.74.62.85

If you'd heard anything about this spot before, it would probably be linked to generous happy hours (on originally pricey drinks) and the friendly English-speaking bar staff. Yet there are several other major factors behind the success. One is the carefully assembled kitsch, which includes a leopardskin curtain, plastic fish and a Stars and Stripes flag. And the other is the impossible number of giggling American girls just dying for a chat. Nostalgic tunes and true Uncle Sam-style cocktails ensure the bar area is almost always packed. If it is, there's a downstairs chill-out lounge at the back.

The Bombardier ★

2 pl du Panthéon, 5th (01.43.54.79.22/ www.bombardier.com). M° Maubert-Mutualité/ RER Luxembourg. **Open** daily noon-2am. Food served Mon-Sat noon-3pm; Sun noon-4pm. **Beer** 25cl €3. **Cocktails** €5-€7.50. **Happy hour** 4-9pm. **Credit** MC, V. **Map** J8.

Snuck into a niche opposite the Panthéon, the Bombardier is a convincing recreation of a home counties pub (minus the retired colonels), with Bombardier beer on tap from Bedford brewery (and proprietor) Charles Wells. Despite the swirly glass and olde worlde tapestry, it's a lot less hardcore Anglo than most English pubs in Paris, managing to pull in healthy measures of pretty young French things. Great for a pint over the Sunday papers, the weekend footie or a raucous rugby session.

Connolly's Corner

12 rue de Mirbel, 5th (01.43.31.94.22). M° Censier-Daubenton. **Open** daily 4pm-2am. **Beer** 25cl €3. **Cocktails** €6.50-€7.20. **Happy hour** 4-8pm. **No credit cards. Map** K9.

This cosy pub is unabashedly Irish. Revellers from the nearby rue Mouffetard join staunch regulars to knock back stout and generous measures of Paddy or Breton beer Coreff at beer-barrel tables. The live music on Tuesday, Thursday and Sunday at 7.30pm, while charming, takes up half the main bar.

Le Crocodile

6 rue Royer-Collard, 5th. (01.43.54.32.37). RER Luxembourg. **Open** Mon-Sat 10.30pm-6am (closing varies). Closed in Aug. **Cocktails** €6. **Happy hour** Mon-Thur 10.30pm-12.30am. **Credit** MC, V. **Map** J8.

It's worth ignoring the apparently boarded-up windows for a cocktail at Le Crocodile. Young, friendly regulars line the sides of this small, narrow bar and try to decide on a drink – we were assured that there are 267 choices, most of them marginally less potent than meths. Pen and paper are provided to note your decision; the pen comes in handy for point-and-choose decisions when everything gets hazy. We think we can recommend an accroche-coeur, a supremely 70s mix of Champagne and Goldschläger, served with extra gold leaf.

Finnegan's Wake

9 rue des Boulangers, 5th (01.46.34.23.65). M° Jussieu. **Open** Mon-Fri 11am-2am; Sat 6pm-2am. Sandwiches served noon-2pm. **Beer** 25cl €2-€3. **Cocktails** €7. **Happy hour** 6-8pm. **No credit cards. Map** K8.

Beams, bonhomie and beer are all on offer at Finnegan's Wake, which steers clear of the piss-up-and-pulling atmosphere of many faux-Irish pubs. As it's popular with French students from nearby Jussieu, you're more likely to come across black-clad thinkers discussing their dissertations than twinkly-eyed charmers with firsts in sweet-talk. Exactly the kind of place you always thought you'd find in the Latin Quarter. Bone up on your Yeats and ponder all things philosophical over a pint.

La Gueuze

19 rue Soufflot, 5th (01.43.54.63.00). RER Luxembourg. **Open** daily 11am-2am. Food served Mon-Sat 11.30am-12.45am; Sun 11.30am-10.45pm. **Beer** 25cl €4. **Cocktails** €7.90. **Happy hour** 4-7pm. **Credit** AmEx, MC, V. **Non-smoking room. Map** J8.

La Gueuze may not be the most stylish Latin Quarter hang-out, but its raison-d'être is drinking and not posing. The vast array of beers ranges from the eccentric raspberry-flavoured Bécasse to the potent, and aptly named, Mort Subite. The Belgian theme is evident in the Trappist classics available, as well as in the ghastly mock-abbey interior, which most drinkers eschew in favour of a pavement seat in the sun. Liver relief is on hand with hearty moules marinières, choucroute and assorted salads.

The Hideout

11 rue du Pot-de-Fer, 5th (01.45.35.13.17). M° Place Monge. **Open** Mon-Thur, Sun 4pm-2am; Fri, Sat 4pm-5am. Closed 25 Dec. **Beer** pint €5. **Cocktails** €5-€8. **Happy hour** 4-10pm. **Credit** AmEx, MC, V. **Map** J8.

The end of many a big night out and the beginning of many morning-after nightmares, the Hideout remains a top spot on any serious pub crawl. Dingy, dark and frequently rather damp (it gets very hot in here), it's definitely not a place to arrive at sober. Friendly staff, massive measures, cheap beer and music so loud that body language is the easiest means of communication all add to the fun. Full of language students, Americans on their grand tour, Brits on the piss and stag parties on the lookout.

Le Pantalon ★

7 rue Royer-Collard, 5th (no phone). RER Luxembourg. **Open** Mon-Sat 11am-2am. **Beer** 25cl €1.80-€2.40. **Happy hour** 5.30-7.30pm. **No credit cards. Map** J8.

The neighbourhood bar you always wished was your local, Le Pantalon is at once deeply familiar and utterly weird. The strange vacuum-cleaner sculpture and disco-light loos give a clue to the madcap nature of the place, but it's the regulars and staff who tip the balance firmly into eccentricity. Friendly and seriously funny French grown-ups and international students chat away in a mish-mash of accents and languages. Happy hours are fantastic, but drinks here are always cheap enough to get happily tipsy without worrying about a cash hangover.

Le Piano Vache

8 rue Laplace, 5th (01.46.33.75.03). M° Maubert-Mutualité. **Open** daily noon-2am. Food served noon-

Ale-fellow-well-met attitude at **The Bombardier.** *See p249.*

2.30pm. **Beer** 25cl €2.50-€3.50. **Cocktails** €5.50-€6.50. **Happy hour** noon-9pm. **Credit** MC, V. **Map** J8.
For those who think Parisians don't drink, this is the place to be proved wrong. Perfect for 80s revivalists dying to get into goth, Le Piano Vache is the place to relive previous experiments with manic-depressive music, spookily dripped candles and far too much cheap black lace. Old posters are plastered all over the walls, lights are low and a dense cloud of smoke shrouds the bar. Indie nights look like a Robert Smith tribute evening staged on the set of *The Lost Boys*. Steer clear on Wednesday nights (soirée gothique) and go in when people wearing colour are welcome.

Aux Trois Mailletz

56 rue Galande, 5th (01.43.25.96.86/ www.lestroismailletz.fr). M° St-Michel. **Open** daily 6.30pm-4am/5am. Food served 7.30pm-3am. **Beer** bottle €5-€10. **Cocktails** €10-€15. **Credit** AmEx, DC, MC, V. **Map** J7.
Life is a cabaret in the bowels of Aux Trois Mailletz on weekends from 11pm until the small hours. For a €15-€20 entry fee you'll be tunefully entertained with everything from Latin to rock 'n' roll and discover how sophisticated, image-conscious Parisians let their hair down. Upstairs, a more civilised set lines up numbers for a pianist and enjoys a sing-along. Dine on typical French cuisine, or guzzle the odd cocktail, including the house special, coco punch.

Le Violon Dingue

46 rue de la Montagne-Ste-Geneviève, 5th (01.43.25.79.93) M° Maubert-Mutualité. **Open** Tue-Sat 8pm-4.30am. **Beer** pint €3. **Cocktails** €6.50. **Happy hour** 8-10pm. **Credit** MC, V. **Map** J8.
The haunt of many a dodgy dragueur, this stalwart of the American collegian run is perhaps the best bar to go to alone, if you intend to leave accompanied. Alcoholic slush puppies, lethal Long Island ice teas and a generous happy hour help to move things along. If you spend more than half an hour without a chat-up line, it's definitely a very slow night. It's buzziest at the back of the bar; only the very bravest (or most desperate) should venture downstairs.

6th Arrondissement

AZ Bar (Mezzanine) ★

Alcazar, 62 rue Mazarine, 6th (01.53.10.19.99/www.alcazar.fr). M° Odéon. **Open** daily noon-3pm, 7pm-midnight/2am. Food served 7-10.30pm. **Beer** 25cl €6. **Cocktails** €10. **Credit** AmEx, DC, MC, V. **Wheelchair access. Map** H7.
Slick, swanky and super-fun, Conran's AZ bar is one of the few destination drinking haunts in Paris worth the cab fare. Swan up the impressive staircase to the long aluminium bar, squished-together tables and great view of the brasserie below. DJs play varying sets, while slinky girls sip Champagne and toss their hair around. Popular with people moving on to the WAGG club next door, AZ is the only posh Paris bar where we've seen several people crammed into one loo cubicle. Don't bother with the bar menu – it might get you a table, but this isn't the place to be seen ruining your lip-gloss with fish and chips.

Le Bar Dix

10 rue de l'Odéon, 6th (01.43.26.66.83). M° Odéon. **Open** daily 5.30pm-2am. **Beer** bottle €2.90-€3.70. **Cocktails** (sangria) €2.40-€3. **Happy hour** 6-9pm. **No credit cards. Map** H7.

Sangria is the key ingredient here as students and oldies merge to produce a convivial, chatty atmosphere. The decor is cool (think faded Toulouse Lautrec posters) and the jukebox just begs to be played. Despite the daunting vertical decline, the stairs actually lead to an equally packed, equally smoky cellar.

Le Comptoir des Canettes

11 rue des Canettes, 6th (01.43.26.79.15). M° Mabillon. **Open** Tue-Sat noon-2am. Closed Aug, 25 Dec. **Beer** bottle €3.50-€4. **Credit** MC, V. **Map** H7.

Le Comptoir des Canettes (aka Chez Georges) provides an appropriate mix of young and old in the heart of St-Germain. The upstairs fills with locals sipping a beer or a glass of regional wine; the basement plays host to a talkative young beer-drinking crowd hoping to catch an occasional live band. On warm summer nights, both young and old spill out the front door, turning the street into one big party.

Coolín

15 rue Clément, 6th (01.44.07.00.92). M° Mabillon. **Open** Mon-Sat 10.30am-2am; Sun 1pm-2am. Closed 25 Dec. **Beer** 25cl €2.90-€3.80. **Happy hour** 5-8pm. **Credit** MC, V. **Wheelchair access. Map** H7.

No shamrocks and shillelaghs here; the Irish theme extends only to trendy Guinness posters, adverts for hurling competitions and conspicuous consumption of vast amounts of alcohol. Friendly staff and just the right amount of good natured flirting for a Friday night complete the picture.

Fu Bar ★

5 rue St-Sulpice, 6th (01.40.51.82.00). M° Odéon. **Open** daily 5pm-2am. **Beer** 25cl €3.50. **Cocktails** €6.50-€7. **Happy hour** 5-9pm (Tue 5pm-2am). **Credit** MC, V. **Map** H7.

Beautifully bijou, the Fu Bar proves that size really doesn't matter. It looks tiny, but there's plenty of extra seating upstairs and anyone who's ever tasted one of the apple martinis would happily cram in at the bar anyway. The cosmopolitan is glorious and the 'suite tart' would make the *Sex and the City* girls squirm. A buzzy Anglo crowd and plenty of punter interaction are perfect for a big night out.

The Highlander ★

8 rue de Nevers, 6th (01.43.26.54.20/www.thehighlander.fr). M° Pont-Neuf. **Open** Mon-Fri 5pm-5am; Sat, Sun 1pm-5am. **Beer** 25cl €3. **Cocktails** €8. **Happy hour** 5-9pm. **Credit** MC, V. **Map** H6.

The Highlander always feels a bit like a house party, and if you don't already know everyone in there, you will by the end of your pint. Reinforcing the chez soi feel are sing-along sessions which only occasionally degenerate into ear-splitting karaoke, quiz nights and a cellar bar used for anything from poetry readings to private piss-ups. Barmen Michael and Jimmy serve generous measures and banter in equal parts.

Hôtel Lutétia

45 bd Raspail, 6th (01.49.54.46.46/www.lutetia.com). M° Sèvres-Babylone. **Open** daily 10.30am-1am. **Beer** bottle €7.50. **Cocktails** €12-€14. **Credit** AmEx, DC, MC, V. **Map** G7.

The decor is a colourblind interior designer's folly, the over-dressed waiters are uptight, and fatigued cigar-smoking businessmen are perhaps not the funkiest company, but the Lutétia's trio of bars is as popular as ever, thanks to its range of potent cocktails. The main attraction is the fabulous low-lit and louche Ernest bar, where ladies-who-shop become ladies-who-down-vodkas.

Extra terracetrial beings at **Le Trésor**. *See p247.*

On the Town

La Marine

59 bd du Montparnasse, 6th (01.45.48.27.70). M° Montparnasse-Bienvenüe. **Open** Mon-Thur 6am-3am; Fri, Sat 6am-5am; Sun 6am-2am. Food served all day. Closed 24 Dec. **Happy hour** Mon-Fri 5.30-7.30pm. **Beer** 25cl €3.10. **Cocktails** €8. **Credit** MC, V. **Map** F8.

Looking every bit the standard northern French tavern and with all the requisite moules-frites on the menu, La Marine distinguishes itself with a liver-threatening selection of quality beers. Fifteen brews on tap (including the excellent Kwak in its bulb-bottomed glass in a wooden holder) are supplemented by some 250 bottles from around the world.

Le Mazet

61 rue St-André-des-Arts, 6th (01.46.33.62.17). M° St-Michel or Odéon. **Open** Mon-Wed, Sun 5pm-2am; Thur-Sat 5pm-5am. **Beer** 25cl €3. **Cocktails** €7. **Credit** AmEx, MC, V. **Map** J7.

Despite the Guinness sign outside, this American pub (now part of the Mayday Inn chain) doesn't actually serve it, although it does have Beamish. Most nights are either themed or have live music from 10pm (Tue-Thur), with a DJ at weekends. On Sunday you can catch up on American TV (episodes of *The Simpsons* alternate with NFL football). The atmosphere is cross-cultural, as French rub shoulders with American expats and Japanese tourists.

The Moose

16 rue des Quatre-Vents, 6th (01.46.33.77.00/ www.mooseheadparis.com). M° Odéon. **Open** Mon-Fri 4pm-2am; Sat, Sun 11am-2am. Food served until 11pm. **Beer** 25cl €3.50. **Cocktails** €7.50. **Happy hour** 4-9pm. **Credit** MC, V. **Map** H7.

This friendly Canadian bar is always packed with an international crowd getting smashed on bottled beer and old-fashioned Canuck hospitality. The extra-long bar provides loads of elbow room, but there are very few seats so get there early if standing in stilettos is an issue. Lots of drinks promotions help things along and the Long Island ice teas are legendary (and lethal). Bar food is excellent.

La Taverne de Nesle ★

32 rue Dauphine, 6th (01.43.26.38.36). M° Odéon. **Open** Mon-Thur, Sun 6pm-4am; Fri, Sat 6pm-6am. Closed 1 May. **Beer** 25cl €2.40-€3.20. **Cocktails** €8. **Happy hour** daily 6-11pm. **Credit** MC, V. **Map** H6.

Not as olde-worldly as its name might suggest, La Taverne has three distinct drinking areas: a zinc bar at the front, a sort of Napoléonic campaign tent in the middle and a trendily-lit ambient area at the back, encouraging a gradual progression to the horizontal state. Among the hundred or so brews you'll find the best of Belgian (all the Trappists, de Koninck on tap, great Gueuze...), but it's the choice of French beers that really sets it apart. Don't miss the house special L'Epi, brewed in three different versions: Blond (100% barley), Blanc (oats) and Noir (buckwheat), or Corsican Pietra on tap.

Zéro de Conduite

14 rue Jacob, 6th (01.46.34.26.35/ wwwzerodeconduite.fr). M° Mabillon or St-Germain-des-Prés. **Open** Tue-Thur 8.30pm-1.30am; Fri, Sat 6pm-2am; Sun 9pm-1am. **Cocktails** €8. **Credit** MC, V. **Map** H6.

Everything about this place is a little strange: the layout, the staff and, most importantly of all, the concept. However, it's definitely worth going once just

Swizzle your cocktail schtik at **Fu Bar**. *See p251.*

to have been there, done that. In a move that would make Freud breakdance in delight, the drinkers here reject triangular glasses, umbrellas, swizzle sticks and all manner of naff yet trad cocktail paraphenalia in favour of sipping their sickly sweet drinks from a baby's bottle. Cartoons are screened and the only nibbles are sweets. We were rather disturbed by the sight of so many big boys being soothed by Mothercare's finest, but it's cheaper than therapy.

7th Arrondissement

Café Thoumieux

4 rue de la Comète, 7th (01.45.51.50.40/ www.thoumieux.com). M° La Tour-Maubourg. **Open** Mon-Fri noon-2am; Sat 5pm-2am. Snacks served until 3am. Closed 24 Dec-2 Jan, Aug. **Beer** bottle €4. **Cocktails** €9. **Happy hour** Mon-Sat 5-9pm. **Credit** AmEx, MC, V. **Map** E6.

A long, suck-me-in comptoir and a score of Absolut bottles stuffed with fruit make this an attractive meeting spot for the affluent Americans studying in the area.This is a world of thick banquettes, spiky Aztec lamps, classy drinks and a burly bouncer to ensure that the high spirits don't get out of control.

8th Arrondissement

Bindi

63 av Franklin-Roosevelt, 8th (01.53.89.66.66). M° Franklin D Roosevelt. **Open** Mon, Sat 8-11pm; Tue-Fri noon-3pm, 8pm-2am. Food served noon-2.30pm, 8-11pm. **Beer** bottle €8. **Cocktails** €11. **Credit** AmEx, DC, MC, V. **Map** E4.

Rumour has it that Bindi's decor was modelled on the Buddha Bar, and you can see why. This likeable underdog has all the trappings of its more illustrious peer though, thankfully, none of the gold-chained punters to tarnish the furniture. It's essentially a classy Indian restaurant with a bar at the back – a hybrid of Oriental bric-a-brac and neo-kitsch – which plays host to relaxed trendsetters, smitten couples and simpler folk who believe that bars are basically about decent drinks and genuine service. Perched above the lounge, DJs spin a cocktail-sipping blend of ambient and downtempo sounds.

The Bowler

13 rue d'Artois, 8th (01.45.61.16.60/ www.thebowlerpub.com). M° St-Philippe du Roule or Franklin D. Roosevelt. **Open** Mon-Fri 11am-2am; Sat, Sun 1pm-2am. Food served Mon-Fri noon-3pm, 7-10.30pm. Curry & quiz Sun night. Closed 25 Dec, 1 Jan. **Beer** 25cl €3.50-€4. **Cocktails** €7. **Happy hour** Sat, Sun 8-11pm. **Credit** AmEx, DC, MC, V. **Map** E3.

Formerly beloved of the girls-in-pearls set, the Bowler has lost a little of its Chelsea-on-the-Champs feel and is considerably more fun for it. A bright, airy pub with plenty of tables, it's now a great place to go for a gossip with colleagues after work or a noisy Saturday night session. Jugs of beer are reasonably priced and the large selection of alcopops on offer are enough to transport you back to the student union. The home-flavoured vodkas are best avoided, though, particularly if they seem like a really, really good idea at the time. Sunday night's curry and pub quiz is a blast.

Le V ★

Hotel Four Seasons George V, 31 av George V, 8th (01.49.52.70.00). M° George V. **Open** daily 9am-2am. Food served 11am-midnight. **Beer** bottle €11. **Cocktails** €20. **Credit** AmEx, DC, MC, V. **Wheelchair access. Map** D4.

The swanky V bar (read 'cinq') is the place to indulge any oil magnate fantasies. Dark wood, a roaring fire, amazing floral displays and utterly loaded punters combine to make it a must for bling-bling beverages, although we weren't quite brave enough to go for the mysterious 'monkey's gland'. The martini list is superb, the purple being the best. A barman appears at your table to make like Tom Cruise and shake it just for you, the parma-violet-flavoured drink is then poured into a stemless crystal triangle, resting in a bowl of crushed ice, all lovingly cocooned on a posh silver tray. Looks and tastes divine but more than two and the stemless glass becomes tricky.

Freedom

8 rue de Berri, 8th (01.53.75.25.50). M° George V. **Open** Mon-Thur, Sun noon-2am; Fri, Sat noon-5am. Food served Mon-Fri noon-3pm, 7-10pm. **Beer** 25cl €3-€4. **Cocktails** €7.50. **Happy hour** Mon-Fri 5.30-7.30pm. **Credit** AmEx, DC, MC, V. **Map** D4.

As we approached the bar, a buxom, puppy-faced American was twiddling her straw as a pin-striped nine-to-fiver listed over her drink – that's the sort of place Freedom is. Despite the excessive number of English pubs in Paris, even this unremarkable tavern has little trouble pulling in the punters. Most come for a few pints and a chance to exorcise the demons of the day; others are unashamedly on the pull. The barmen are dog-friendly, a bit dizzy but always keen to cheer on the good-time bands and DJs.

Hôtel Plaza Athénée

25 av Montaigne, 8th (01.53.67.66.65). M° Franklin D. Roosevelt. **Open** daily 6pm-2am. Snacks served all day. **Cocktails** €20. **Credit** AmEx, DC, MC, V. **Wheelchair access. Map** D5.

Decked out by Patrick Jouin, the bar is all luminosity, glass (the icy blue bar), metal and a tall Louis XV-ish stool or 30. The famed vodka jellies, favoured by the ladies who lunch then lurch, are on the table; so too the elegant rose royale – Champagne and raspberry coulis. Just dahvine dahling.

Impala Lounge ★

2 rue de Berri, 8th (01.43.59.12.66). M° George V. **Open** Mon, Tue 9.30am-2.30am; Wed, Thur 9.30am-3am; Fri, Sat 9.30am-5am. Food served noon-midnight. **Beer** 25cl €6.50. **Cocktails** €10. **Credit** AmEx, DC, MC, V. **Map** D4.

Dubbed the 'African Bar' by regulars, this trendy escapade hams up the colonial with zebra skins, tribal masks and a throne hewn out of a tree trunk. Beer, wine, tea and coffee can all be found here, but

The Auld Alliance

The first & best Scottish Pub in Paris

The only pub
with real
Scottish cuisine!
Over 300
whisky's too!

Lunch: Tue to Fri
Brunch: Sat & Sun

Whisky tastings
Haggis a speciality

Showing
regularly:
Football
Rugby
Golf
Formula One
Super Bowl
Athletics

80 rue Francois Miron,
75004, Paris, Metro St. Paul
Tel: 01.48.04.30.40
www.theauldalliance.com

best beverages are the cocktails, one of which claims to boost a waning libido with its mystery mix of herbs and spices. DJs rock Sunday afternoon away.

Mathis

Hôtel Elysées-Matignon, 3 rue de Ponthieu, 8th (01.53.76.01.62). M° Champs-Elysées-Clemenceau. **Open** daily 11pm-dawn. **Cocktails** €15. **Credit** AmEx, MC, V. **Map** E4.

If you make it past the formidable hostess, expect to be pampered by the staff and exchange daring witticisms with your neighbours (if you can't be witty in at least four languages then you shouldn't be here). No one arrives until at least midnight and things hot up after 2am, when the pretty boys and girls start to party. Achingly hip.

Nirvana

4 av Matignon, 8th (01.53.89.18.91). M° Franklin D. Roosevelt. **Open** daily 8pm-dawn; lounge 11.30pm-dawn. Food served 8pm-midnight. **Beer** bottle €8. **Cocktails** €16. **Credit** AmEx, DC, MC, V. **Map** E4.

Championed as one of Paris' most happening venues, predictably the pseudo-Indian brainchild of lounge DJ Claude Challe attracts the type of folk ordinary folk might not want to meet. Nevertheless, it is fun and boasts some sparkling design touches, like the Mondrian-inspired glass bar with its exquisitely kitsch lighting. We'd recommend you press on to the downstairs bar area where a good-time mix of hip hop and 80s classics mean even the oafs can keep up. Cocktails are pricey, though you can grab a cheeky glass of rosé for €6.

Pershing Lounge

Pershing Hall, 49 rue Pierre-Charon, 8th (01.58.36.58.00/www.pershinghall.com). M° George V. **Open** daily 6pm-1.30am. Brunch Sun 11am-7pm. **Beer** €11. **Cocktails** €15. **Happy hour** 5-8pm. **Credit** AmEx, DC, MC, V. **Map** D4.

Expect lots of Ralph Lauren jumpers, few models but plenty to gawp at the Andrée Putman-designed Pershing Hall. With an eye for pleasing the rich, she has thrown in a plush blend of low-backed sofas and toe-toasting carpets with a shining metallic bar for contrast. But it's the candlelit balcony overlooking the Amazon-chic courtyard that really catches the imagination. Breezy sounds keep the ambience Zen, while square-jawed waiters offer diligent, low-key service, though we found the cocktails unfortunately watery and served without a garnish.

9th Arrondissement

Le Général Lafayette

52 rue Lafayette, 10th (01.47.70.59.08). M° Poissonière. **Open** daily 10am-4am. Food served all day. **Beer** 25cl €3.50. **Credit** AmEx, DC, MC, V. **Map** J3.

This attractive spot with a belle époque decor serves up nine different beers on tap, including several Belgian abbey brews and a variety of other quaffs by the bottle. The crowd runs from financial toffs to scruffy artists, giving the place a nice buzz. The food is good, too, including trout with bacon, cep omelettes and andouillette, making this ideal for a one-stop night out.

10th Arrondissement

L'Atmosphère

49 rue Lucien-Sampaix, 10th (01.40.38.09.21). M° Gare de l'Est or Jacques Bonsergent. **Open** Mon 6pm-midnight; Tue-Sat 10am-2am; Sun noon-9pm. Food served Tue-Sat noon-3pm, 8-11pm. **Beer** 25cl €2-€3. **Cocktails** €3.20. **No credit cards**. **Map** L3.

Despite having lost its evening live music permit after years of push and pull with neighbours and the mayor's office, L'Atmosphère remains at the centre of the Canal St-Martin renaissance. Parisians of all kinds chat, read and people-watch on the canal-side terrace while, within, the simple, tasteful interior, animated conversation and cheapish drinks provide spectacle enough for locals. Drop in for world and experimental music Sundays 5-7pm.

De La Ville Café ★

34 bd Bonne-Nouvelle, 10th (01.48.24.48.09). M° Bonne Nouvelle. **Open** daily 11am-2am. **Beer** 25cl €2.80-€3.40. **Cocktails** €6.40-€7. **Credit** MC, V. **Map** J4.

Grotty meets naughty in the remains of the old Marguerit brothel, with leftover crystal sconces and marble as proof. Pass under (uninvited) flying pigeons in the warehouse-like foyer, to oversized second-date wicker love seats facing the 'food and sex', mural, then to the summer cocktail terrace dotted with orange plastic chairs where flirty waiters weave between tables and the ripped tee-and-tattoo brigade on their way to Rex and Pulp. The virginal adjoining restaurant through the hole in the wall, complete with a romantic imported Italian mosaic ceiling and long bar, has two lounges and a 'butterfly room' for those more intimate moments.

Bar Le Panier

32 pl Ste-Marthe, 10th (01.42.01.38.18). M° Belleville. **Open** Tue-Sun 10am-2am. Food served all day. **Beer** 25cl €2.80. **Cocktails** €5.90. **No credit cards**. **Map** M3.

Just off rue St-Maur, place Ste-Marthe feels so down-to-earth: no rushing traffic, self-conscious posers or poncey decor, just a quiet cobbled square bordered by three cafés. Bar Le Panier is especially homely, with candles flickering against the orange walls. We were settled in minutes and lingering over mint tea, then wine, nibbles of popcorn sprinkled with cumin, and toasted baguette with anchovy paste.

La Patache

60 rue de Lancry, 10th (01.42.08.14.35). M° Jacques Bonsergent. **Open** daily 6pm-2am. Cold food served all day. **Beer** 25cl €2.50. **Cocktails** €5. **No credit cards**. **Wheelchair access**. **Map** L4.

Pleasantly seedy and small, this unlikely haunt of local lushes and slummers manages to keep its

Cassinus Café
PARIS
BAR DE L'ENTRACTE
CAFÉ-RESTAURANT
AU PALAIS ROYAL
47 RUE DE MONTPENSIER, 1ST
01 42 97 57 76
cassinus.cafe@wanadoo.fr

authentically alternative edge. The styling is humble with faded black-and-white photos, and you can add to – or read – the rantings, poems and polemics of drinkers past on the scraps of paper provided in old biscuit tins at the tables. Thesps put on live drama most Thursdays and Fridays (from 9pm); on other nights, the jukebox runs hot.

Le Sainte Marthe ★

32 rue Ste-Marthe, 10th (01.44.84.36.96). M° Belleville. **Open** daily 6pm-2am. Food served 8-11.30pm. **Beer** 25cl €2- €2.50. **Cocktails** €5. **Happy hour** 6-10pm. **No credit cards. Map** M3.

More in tune with provincial France than Paris, this apotheosis of a corner bar remains one of our favourites and the air of relaxed congeniality is confirmed by the beaming owner and his uncomplicated staff. Huddle around the metallic bar with friendly locals or sit outside at one of the neatly aligned tables on the square. What's more, it's not all booze and muse here; the boys in white churn out some fine fare. Be sure to reserve in summer.

Le Zorba

137 rue du Fbg-du-Temple, 10th (01.42.39.68.68). M° Belleville. **Open** daily 5am-2am. **Beer** 25cl €3. **No credit cards. Map** M4.

This is a drinker's institution and local classic, just off Belleville's human equivalent of Piccadilly Circus. Attracting everyone from red-nosed PMU gamblers to demi-swigging North Africans, Le Zorba buzzes from dawn till dusk, exploding on the weekends as punters drop in for an apéro before an Asian meal. It's cheap and working class, with red strip lighting, squat toilets, tobacco-stained walls and a noisy terrace that spills across the pavement. At times (especially late), exchanges can get overheated as local trade acts get fine-tuned to the background sounds of bar-pleasing oldies.

Put your money where your mask is at **Impala Lounge**. *See p253.*

11th Arrondissement

L'Ave Maria

1 rue Jacquard, 11th (01.47.00.61.73/ www.avemariacafe.com). M° Parmentier. **Open** daily 6pm-2am. Food served 8pm-midnight. **Beer** bottle €3. **Cocktails** €6.50. **No credit cards. Map** M5.

Caribbean steam cabin or Brazilian beach hut? It's a bonhomie-fusion thang here, the kind of place that likes to imagine there's a permanent but indistinct tropical rainstorm outside. A fuggy, orangey glow lights a cosy bar, dolled up with kitsch knick-knacks, making a mojito obligatory. There's more restaurant space at the back, where the world food comes courtesy of Favela Chic's former chef, who shoots from the hip to tasty effect with meat, fruit and spicy vegetables. Packed by mid-evening.

Bar des Ferailleurs

18 rue de Lappe, 11th (01.48.07.89.12). M° Bastille. **Open** daily 5pm-2am. **Beer** 25cl €2.50-€3.50. **Cocktails** €7. **Happy hour** 5-10pm. **Credit** MC, V. **Map** M7.

Decorated with the old junk worthy of a French grandad's garage (the name alludes to scrap metal merchants), this quirky little bar is one of the few places on the rue de Lappe where you're likely to find genuine Parisians hanging out with the hard-drinking out-of-towners. The staff is attentive and the thirsty clientele is grateful for the excellent happy hour prices on everything.

Boteco ★

131 rue Oberkampf, 11th (01.43.57.15.47). M° Parmentier. **Open** daily 9am-2am. Closed 25 Dec, 1 Jan. Food served noon-midnight. **Beer** 25cl €3.10. **Cocktails** €5.50. **No credit cards. Map** M5.

On the Oberkampf circuit, quirky Brazilian Boteco has that little bit extra. Throw yourself into the tiny, low-lit space, negotiate the wide bar and wooden tables, wedge yourself on one of the old benches, and get stuck in. The exquisite caipirinhas are sure to turn the dullest of souls into willing participants and the music, ranging from funk to salsa, melds the whole establishment into an atmospheric blur.

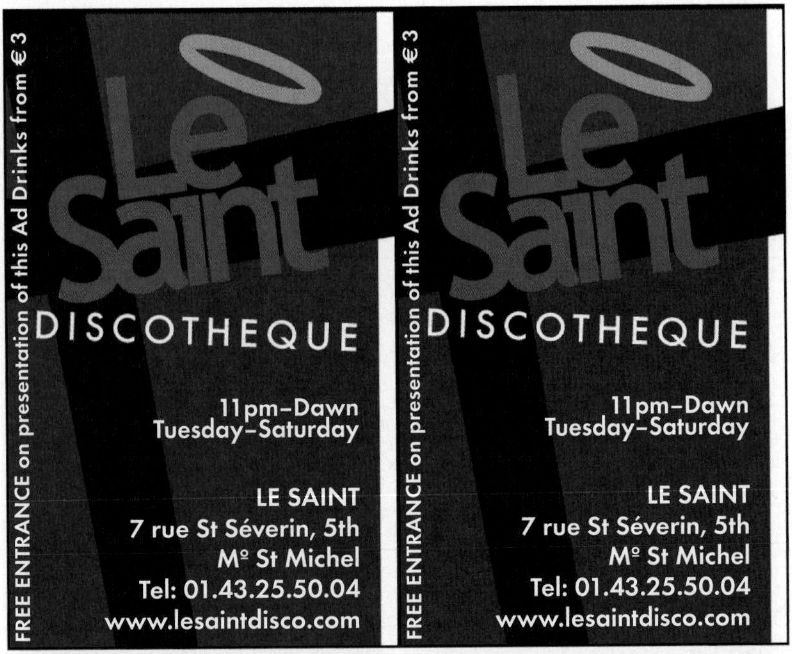

FREE ENTRANCE on presentation of this Ad Drinks from € 3
Le Saint
DISCOTHEQUE
11pm–Dawn
Tuesday–Saturday
LE SAINT
7 rue St Séverin, 5th
Mº St Michel
Tel: 01.43.25.50.04
www.lesaintdisco.com
FREE ENTRANCE on presentation of this Ad Drinks from € 3
Le Saint
DISCOTHEQUE
11pm–Dawn
Tuesday–Saturday
LE SAINT
7 rue St Séverin, 5th
Mº St Michel
Tel: 01.43.25.50.04
www.lesaintdisco.com

la fourmi
open daily 9am-2am
c a f é
74, rue des Martyrs • 18th • M° Pigalle • Tel: 01.42.64.70.35

Café Charbon

109 rue Oberkampf, 11th (01.43.57.55.13/ www.nouveaucasino.net). M° Parmentier. **Open** Mon-Thur, Sun 9am-2am; Fri, Sat 9am-4am. Food served 9am-midnight. Brunch Sat, Sun noon-5pm. **Beer** 25cl €2.30. **Cocktails** €7. **Happy hour** daily 5-7pm. **Credit** MC, V. **Wheelchair access**. **Map** M5.

It may no longer be the undisputed king of Oberkampf, but Café Charbon is still pulling the punters into its gorgeous belle époque interior. An over-enthusiastic crowd throngs the bar, while those smug enough to have got a table do their best to trip up the long-suffering waitresses fighting their way to the till as house music bouces off the ceiling. The café owns next-door club Nouveau Casino (*see p285*, **Clubs**).

Café de la Plage ★

59 rue de Charonne, 11th (01.47.00.48.01). M° Charonne or Ledru-Rollin. **Open** Mon-Sat 5pm-2am. Food served 8-11.30pm. **Beer** 25cl €3. **Cocktails** €7. **Credit** MC, V. **Map** N7.

There's a refreshingly simple air of socialising at the reborn beach café, which is just far enough away from the heave of Bastille. The Peruvian owner's pisco sour apéritifs (a nicely potent shake of pisco, lemon juice and cinnamon) may have something to do with it. In the cellar, DJs mix the usual electro-retro suspects in a white-stone alcove. Monday's Eazy offers chilled-out grooves and slam interludes.

Les Couleurs

117 rue St-Maur, 11th (01.43.57.95.61). M° Parmentier. **Open** daily 4pm-2am. Closed 1 May, two weeks in Aug. **Beer** €2.20-€2.70. **No credit cards**. **Map** N5.

Hypnotically red and hard to leave, Les Couleurs cocoons you in a womb-like world of the boho pale 'n' unshaven. The house punch, la Boulogne (€4.70), provides a potent, rum-based wake-up call before bar prices jump up at 10pm. The fairy lights and Steve Buscemi look-alike waiter provide distraction, along with the chirpy jazz and chanson, and the cerebral reading material slumped on shelves. This is a homely refuge, guaranteed to provide full immersion into the Ménilmontant mood.

F.B.I. Paris (Freestyle Bar)

45 rue de la Folie-Méricourt, 11th (01.43.14.26.36/ www.fbiparis.com). M° St-Ambroise. **Open** Mon-Sat 7pm-2am. Closed Aug. **Beer** bottle €6. **Cocktails** €8. **Happy hour** 7-10pm. **Credit** MC, V. **Map** M5.

Wander into this cringingly named but entertaining bar for a cocktail before heading to Oberkampf. The bartender will serve you a beer, but he'd rather juggle his bottles and mix up a concoction worthy of a legendary American bar. Why not experiment with the Japanese slipper (Midori, Cointreau and lime juice cordial) or stick to the tried and true gimlet (gin with lime), served in a bathtub-sized glass.

Le Lèche-Vin ★

13 rue Daval, 11th (01.43.55.98.91). M° Bastille. **Open** Mon-Sat 7pm-2am; Sun 7pm-midnight. **Beer** 25cl €2.15. **Credit** MC, V. **Map** M5.

The Lèche-Vin has raised idolatry to a new level with its bar-as-shrine-to-the-Virgin-Mary. Every available nook, cranny and wall offers up a kitsch, often irreverent tribute to the holiest of mothers. If the idea of knocking back pints under her tearful gaze doesn't make you fear for the safety of your soul, a trip to the toilets will surely be enough to make you abandon any hope of salvation. On the bright side, you'll be richly rewarded on earth with some of the cheapest and best drinks in the area.

Le Petit Garage

63 rue Jean-Pierre-Timbaud, 11th (01.48.07.08.12). M° Parmentier. **Open** daily 10am-2am. Cold food served all day. **Beer** 25cl €2-€2.50. **Cocktails** €6-€6.50. **Credit** MC, V. **Map** M4.

Forget Paris, and welcome to a 1950s parlour frequented by goths. Vintage ladies' periodicals and old-fashioned weighing machines can be spied from one eye and a greasy barman cloying over his vinyl collection from the other, as he spins some great garage-punk numbers. Friday night has an unusual head of steam for such a small place, as punters (skinned mostly in leather) stick closely to the bar and its everyman beers.

Pop In

105 rue Amelot, 11th (01.48.05.56.11). M° St-Sébastien-Froissart. **Open** Tue-Sun 6.30pm-1.30am. Closed Aug. **Beer** bottle €4. **Cocktails** €5.50. **Happy hour** 6.30-9pm (beer only). **Credit** MC, V. **Wheelchair access**. **Map** L5.

Any bar that hosts a Christian Dior after-show party has got to be cool, right? Wrong. At best, the Pop In reminds you of a London squat covered in a carcinogenic cloud – not the sort of place you'd expect to find Hugh Grant stammering over a G&T. But what this higgeldy-piggeldy bar lacks in finesse is more than made up for by the down-to-earth staff, cheap drinks, chilled punters and cellar that alternates between an open mike night and a club for DJs.

Le Pravda

49 rue Jean-Pierre-Timbaud, 11th (01.48.06.19.76/ www.lepravda.com). M° Oberkampf or Parmentier. **Open** Mon-Thur 11am-11pm; Fri, Sat 11am-midnight. Food served noon-3pm, 7-11pm. **Cocktails** €5.90. **Credit** AmEx, DC, MC, V. **Map** M4.

KGB-red windowpanes and matching bar shelves shine brightly against drab walls and wire-strung light bulbs, making for a slightly more convivial atmosphere than a Soviet interrogation chamber. Sit at the bar to meet neighbouring arty types, or bring friends and take over a corner table to sample the menu of flavoured vodkas, from house-concocted carambar to White Magic Crystal from India.

Les Triolets

33 rue de Montreuil, 11th (01.43.72.43.66). M° Faidherbe-Chaligny. **Open** Mon-Sat 10am-2am. **Beer** 25cl €1.80-€3.10. **Cocktails** €5. **Credit** MC, V. **Wheelchair access**. **Map** P7.

Les Triolets belongs to a less frenetic world than nearby Bastille bars. Green baize billiards tables

What's on this week in Paris?

Every week inside **Pariscope** (€0.40 at all Paris-area newsagents) you'll find the English-language supplement **Time Out *Paris***, six pages of essential arts and entertainment events, plus the hottest spots for going out.

Time Out *Paris*

15-17 rue des Martyrs, 75009 Paris

+33 (0)1.44.87.00.45

Fax +33 (0)1.44.73.90.60

editorial@timeout.fr

Now on sale from Wednesday morning at WHSmith Waterloo.

stretch out through the smoke-filled back room, there's an Internet space with eight terminals, while the main bar offers backgammon games and big-screen coverage of major sporting events. The place often looks a bit empty in the evening, but from time to time the atmosphere hots up with cues and dice cast aside in favour of more trivial pursuits.

Les Trois Têtards

46 rue Jean-Pierre-Timbaud, 11th (01.43.14.27.37). M° Oberkampf or Parmentier. **Open** Mon-Fri 8am-2am; Sat-Sun 5pm-2am. **Beer** 25cl €2. **Cocktails** €6. **Credit** AmEx, DC, MC, V. **Map** M5.

An interior of rickety chairs and murals is presided over by genial staff and a raucous crowd. Everyone seems to know everyone else, or maybe they're just very good with strangers. The eponymous house speciality is an intoxicating combination of vodka, grapefruit juice, mint and a 'secret' ingredient.

Le Trucmush

5 passage Thiére, 11th (01.48.07.11.91/ www.trucmush.free.fr). M° Bastille or Ledru Rollin. **Open** Tue-Sat 6pm-2am; Sun 4pm-midnight. Closed two weeks in Aug. Food served all day. **Beer** 25cl €3. **Cocktails** €5.50. **Happy hour** Tue-Sun 6-9pm. **Credit** MC, V. **Map** M7.

A half-Peugeot DJ booth, funky lighting, and a back section equipped with beach chairs and sand make up the random decor of this small Bastille bar. The energy is high as young punters file in before hitting the clubs, but the music is never overwhelming. Free theatre performances every Sunday at 4.30pm.

Le Zéro Zéro

89 rue Amelot, 11th (01.49.23.51.00). M° St-Sébastien-Froissart. **Open** daily 6pm-2am. **Beer** 25cl €2.60. **Cocktails** €6.10. **Happy hour** daily 6-8.30pm. **Credit** MC, V. **Map** L5.

This fine spot for a 'sesh' attracts a mixed crowd, from long-serving expats to spindly artists who cram their frisky butts into the tiny space. It's hard to know what to make of the bright wallpaper, mirrors on the roof, and mishmash of improvised furniture, but as the night wears on and the cocktails keep coming, you won't much care anyway.

12th Arrondissement

Barrio Latino

46-48 rue du Fbg-St-Antoine, 12th (01.55.78.84.75). M° Bastille. **Open** daily 11.30am-2am. Food served noon-3pm, 7.30pm-midnight. **Beer** 25cl €5.50. **Cocktails** €10.50. **Credit** AmEx, DC, MC, V. **Wheelchair access. Map** M7.

Like a Baz Luhrmann set kicking up 'ay caramba', Barrio Latino shudders with flamboyant excess in a blood-red rendition of a fantasy Havana hotel. Beware the after-8pm €8 entry fee. Young things come early to scan the talent before Rio-types dance manically on the tables and stairs, like a bunch of over-keen extras shaking their way to fame on a Christina Aguilera video. Effective antidepressant – take with mojito and weekend salsa classes.

Chai 33

33 cour St-Emilion, 12th (01.53.44.01.01/ www.chai33.com). M° Cour St-Emilion. **Open** Mon, Sun noon-midnight; Tue-Sat noon-2am. Lounge bar 7pm-2am. Closed 25 Dec. Food served noon-11.30pm. **Beer** 25cl €5. **Cocktails** €8.50. **Credit** AmEx, DC, MC, V. **Wheelchair access. Map** P10.

This recent offering from the team behind B*fly, Buddha Bar and Barrio Latino combines lounge bar, restaurant, terrace bistro and wine shop in a converted wine warehouse in Bercy. Wine comes first, but design has not been forgotten, from the stainless steel vats to pink-satin boudoir-style ladies. Upstairs sit along the bar or recline in Indonesian deckchairs over an unusual wine cocktail. If grands crus are your thing, venture into the 'Paradis' caves where you can purchase fine vintages to drink in for far less than a standard restaurant mark-up.

China Club ★

50 rue de Charenton, 12th (01.43.43.82.02/ www.chinaclub.cc). M° Ledru-Rollin or Bastille. **Open** Mon-Thur, Sun 7pm-2am; Fri, Sat 7pm-3am. Closed July-Aug. Food served 7pm-midnight. **Beer** €4.50. **Cocktails** €7-€9. **Happy hour** daily 7-9pm. **Credit** AmEx, MC, V. **Map** M7.

With huge Chesterfields, low lighting and a sexy long bar, it's impossible not to feel glamorous here. It's like an extremely relaxed gentleman's club with a distinctly colonial Cohibas-and-cocktails feel. They take their martinis seriously and you can't go wrong with a well-made Champagne cocktail. This is ideal seduction territory, but equally good for a gossip session, particularly during happy hour.

13th Arrondissement

Le Couvent

69 rue Broca, 13th (01.43.31.28.28). M° Les Gobelins. **Open** Mon-Fri 9am-2am; Sat 6pm-2am. Food served noon-3pm, 7-11pm. **Beer** €2.30. **Cocktails** €5. **Happy hour** Mon-Sat 6-8pm. **Credit** MC, V. **Map** J10.

For an address that might well read: 'middle of no-where', this heavily beamed bar creates a delightful hideaway. It first appeared in Pierre Gripari's novel *Contes de la rue Broca*, but has come a long way since those dingy days. Nowadays it's the chouchou of uni students and thirtysomething couples, especially at concert time when live chords get feet tapping. Always busy, always smoky.

Le Merle Moquer

11 rue de la Butte-aux-Cailles, 13th (01.45.65.12.43). M° Place d'Italie or Corvisart. **Open** daily 5pm-2am. **Beer** 25cl €2.30-€2.75. **Happy hour** Mon-Sat 5-8pm. **Credit** MC, V.

Le Merle Moquer fits perfectly into the bucolic Butte-aux-Cailles. It's basically a 'no' bar: no frills, no tables, no waiters, just get up there and order. The bamboo and kiddies' paintball attempts are intentionally tacky but no one cares, as most eyes are focused on the colourful lights refracted by the fruity punches or the barmaid's generous chest.

Pink noise at **Café Chéri(e)**. *See p264.*

14th Arrondissement

L'Entrepôt

7-9 rue Francis-de-Pressensé, 14th (01.45.40.60.70/ www.lentrepot.fr). M° Pernéty. **Open** daily 8am-1am. Food served noon-2.30pm, 7-11pm. **Beer** 25cl €3.50. **Cocktails** €8. **Credit** MC, V. **Wheelchair access.** **Map** F10.

This converted paper warehouse has something for every taste: a bar, a restaurant with leafy outdoor courtyard and an independent, three-screen arts cinema. Chill out and listen to music (jazz on Thursday, world music on Friday and Saturday) for a mere €5 or just drop past and see what's going down.

Le Rosebud ★

11bis rue Delambre, 14th (01.43.20.44.13). M° Vavin or Edgar-Quinet. **Open** daily 7pm-2am. Closed Aug. Food served 7-11pm. **Beer** bottle €6. **Cocktails** €11. **Credit** MC, V. **Map** G9.

Designed to satisfy the alcoholic needs of Montparnasse's mass of intellectuals, the Rosebud has been a social hub since 1962. Today, it pulls in a more varied clientele: cocktail lovers, the odd well-informed tourist and dishevelled eccentrics. The interior is classic aristo-chic but the real stars are the super-professional white-jacketed barmen. Down a daiquiri or a vodka and orange and enjoy the ethereal jazz before your senses are blurred.

Le Tournesol

9 rue de la Gaîté, 14th (01.43.27.65.72). M° Edgar-Quinet. **Open** daily 8.30am-1am. Food served Mon-Fri noon-3pm, 6-11pm; Sat, Sun noon-11pm. **Beer** 25cl €2.30. **Cocktails** €6.80. **Credit** AmEx, DC, MC, V. **Map** G9.

With theatres and sex shops for neighbours, this sibling of La Fourmi was always going to draw an unstuffy crowd – it's just a shame the staff don't have the same attitude. Apart from the eponymous sunflowers behind the bar, it's industrial chic all the way, with rope-wrapped ducts and raw concrete walls. Food runs to brasserie standards, salads and tartines. Cocktails are well-made classics, though the large drinking area is packed at most times, so chances are you'll be nursing that gin fizz at the bar.

15th Arrondissement

Le Bréguet

72 rue Falguière, 15th (01.42.79.97.00). M° Pasteur. **Open** Mon-Sat 5pm-4am. **Beer** 25cl €2. **Cocktails** €6.50. **Happy hour** Mon-Sat 5-8pm. **Credit** V. **Map** E9.

No prizes for the location (opposite a glaringly lit supermarket) nor the decor, but the vibe is relaxed and the drinks surprisingly eclectic. As well as the usual beers on tap, there are Strongbow cider, commendably smooth Guinness, flavoured vodkas and some exotic quaffs like limoncello. The speakers pump out anything from rock to jazz and world.

16th Arrondissement

Bar Panoramique

Hôtel Concorde La Fayette, 3 pl du Général-Koenig, 17th (01.40.68.51.31). M° Porte Maillot. **Open** daily

4pm-3am. **Beer** 25cl €8 (before 9.30pm). **Cocktails** €13.50 (before 9.30pm). **Credit** AmEx, DC, MC, V. **Map** B3.

Perfect for lovers or the alone and pensive, Bar Panaromique comes up tops with visual therapy, gazing from the 33rd floor over the Eiffel Tower, Arc de Triomphe and La Défense. At night, the mirrored 70s interior and city skyline create a soft-lens glamour, enjoyed by American business travellers, cupped in tiers of leather banquettes. Beware the 9pm watershed, when the piano bar hoicks all drinks up to €19.50, from Champagne to coffee.

Petit Défi de Passy ★

18 av du Président-Kennedy, 16th, (01.42.15.06.76/ www.defidepassy.com). M° Passy. **Open** Mon, Tue 10am-midnight; Wed-Sat 10am-2am; Sun 11am-midnight. Food served noon-2pm, 7.30-10pm. Brunch Sat-Sun noon-3pm. **Beer** 25cl €2. **Cocktails** €5. **Happy hour** 5-8pm. **Credit** AmEx, MC, V. **Non-smoking room**. **Map** B6.

Tucked into the viaduct below Passy station, this refreshingly no-fuss bar-restaurant challenges the local chichi rule, jollying along friendly students and English teachers through happy hour in a distinct whiff of late adolescence. For the occasional Thursday night live, DJs, Hooray Henris and pretty gals come out in force, pogoing and whooping on the makeshift dance floor to 80s French pop, sans irony.

Tsé

78 rue d'Auteuil, 16th (01.40.71.11.90/www.group-bertrand.com). M° Porte d'Auteuil. **Open** Mon, Sun 10am-2am; Tue-Thur 10am-3am; Fri, Sat 10am-4am. Food served Mon-Wed noon-3pm, 7-11.30pm; Thur-Sun noon-3pm, 7pm-midnight. **Beer** 25cl €5. **Cocktails** €9. **Credit** AmEx, MC, V. **Wheelchair access**.

The Asian fusion formula has even crept out as far as Auteuil, where Tsé has taken root in the old station, peddling Oriental style and alcoholic regeneration to a vogueish clientele wearing sharp specs and media manners. Although a bit far up its own concept, this is a relaxing and opulent addition, with enticing dark-red and gilt interior, attentive pretty-boy staff, live jazz and funk DJs, sushi nibbles and simply fantastic Asian-styled cocktails.

17th Arrondissement

3 Pièces Cuisine

25 rue de Chéroy/100 rue des Dames, 17th (01.44.90.85.10). M° Rome or Villiers. **Open** Mon-Fri 8am-2am; Sat, Sun 9.30am-2am. Food served noon-3pm, 7-11pm. **Beer** 25cl €2.40. **Credit** MC, V. **Map** G1.

This Batignolles bar looks like a scruffy old neighbourhood caff that's been taken in hand by a young *Elle Déco* reader. Red flock wallpaper and green study lamps create an intimate parlour at the back, with a few salvaged cinema seats thrown into the picture for boho credibility. Staff are cheery, but the clientele keep their voices pretty low – you get the impression that talk is more Serge Gainsbourg than Johnny Hallyday. Try the chocolate milkshake – it has far more ice cream in it than your mum would ever have allowed.

L'Endroit

67 pl du Dr-Félix-Lobligeois, 17th (01.42.29.50.00). M° Villiers or Rome. **Open** daily noon-2am. Food served noon-3pm, 7.30-11pm; Sun brunch noon-3.30pm. **Beer** bottle €4.50. **Cocktails** €8.50. **Credit** MC, V. **Wheelchair access**. **Map** F1.

Sharp but unassuming on its modish corner of a church square, this sleek mix of low-lit wood and wrought iron houses a set of thirtysomething professionals, rolling home to relieve le babysitter via some hefty whiskies from the revolving carousel.

Lush ★

16 rue des Dames, 17th (01.43.87.49.46/ www.lushbars.com). M° Place de Clichy. **Open** Mon-Fri 4pm-2am; Sat, Sun noon-2am. Closed 25-28 Dec. **Beer** 25cl €3. **Cocktails** €6.30-€7.50. **Happy hour** 4-7pm. **Credit** MC, V. **Map** G1.

At a prime address in upwardly mobile Batignolles, this recently opened bar is a sleek lair for chilled-out drinking. Soft grape purples and comfy banquettes provide a suitable setting for inexpensive pints, well-chosen New World wines and delicious cocktails. Premiership football and rugby on big-screen TV.

18th Arrondissement

Doudingue ★

24 rue Durantin, 18th (01.42.54.88.08). M° Abbesses. **Open** Mon-Fri 6pm-2am; Sat, Sun 11am-2am. Food served 7.30-1am. Brunch Sat, Sun 11am-4.30pm. **Beer** 25cl €3.50. **Cocktails** €7.50. **Credit** AmEx, DC, MC, V. **Map** H1.

This bar is just how one might imagine Anthony and Cleopatra's pad to have looked had things worked out, with lots of indulgent, palatial details (big plumplicious cushions, cherubs on the ceiling and dainty chandeliers). The food, such as tuna steak with wild rice, is generally delicious. And the atmosphere and music swing to the right side of the wannabe meridian. Would Tony and Cleo have waited an hour for their drinks to arrive, as we did? Not likely, but mere mortals could do a lot worse.

La Fourmi

74 rue des Martyrs, 18th (01.42.64.70.35). M° Pigalle. **Open** Mon-Thur 8am-2am; Fri, Sat 8am-4am; Sun 10am-2am. Food served noon-11pm. Closed noon 24 Dec-noon 25 Dec. **Beer** 25cl €1.50-€2.30. **Cocktails** €5.40. **Credit** MC, V. **Map** H2.

With a retro-industrial decor, long zinc bar and trademark Duchampian bottle-rack chandelier, this spacious bar in happening Pigalle buzzes all day and night with a young, arty crowd and even artier staff. A handy jumping-off point for nearby music venues.

Le Sancerre

35 rue des Abbesses, 18th (01.42.58.47.05). M° Abbesses. **Open** daily 7am-2am. Food served all day. **Beer** 25cl €1.70-€2.60. **Cocktails** €8. **Credit** MC, V. **Map** H1.

Bohemia is alive and well in this fashionably dishevelled café on the slopes of Montmartre. Don't let the scruffy appearance fool you. Service is efficient and the kitchen serves up appetising omelettes, salads and sandwiches. On busy evenings, bypass the terrace and join the throng inside. The people-watching is just as good and you're less likely to be jostled by sightseers. Music on Sundays 6-10pm.

19th Arrondissement

AbracadaBar

123 av Jean-Jaurès, 19th (01.42.03.18.04/ www.abracadabar.fr). M° Laumière. **Open** Mon-Wed, Sun 6pm-2am; Thur-Sat 6pm-5am. Closed Aug. **Beer** €2.50. **Cocktails** €8. **Happy hour** 6-7.30pm. **Credit** MC, V. **Map** M2.

Scruffy and camp, AbracadaBar ain't your normal Paris corner bar. Apart from the late licence, there's a huge concrete fountain in front of the bar. Then there's the shrine to trolls, menus on springs and, the night we went, a band thumping out cracking funk to a delighted twentysomething crowd. Our mojitos resembled an overgrown garden, but at twice the usual size, we weren't complaining.

Bar Ourcq ★

68 quai de la Loire, 19th (01.42.40.12.26). M° Ourcq. **Open** Wed, Thur 8.30am-midnight; Fri 8.30am-2am; Sat 2pm-2am; Sun 1pm-midnight. Food served Mon-Fri noon-2pm. **Beer** €2. **Cocktails** €4. **No credit cards. Map** N1.

After a flick at the nearby MK2, stroll past old groovers boule-ing it up, to this friendly bar. There's a lovely sofa'd section at the back, where you can enjoy a round of Scrabble, admire the photographic artwork or shield your head from the wacky lampshades. There are live DJs Thursday to Sunday.

Le Café Chéri(e)

44 bd de la Villette 19th (01.42.02.07.87). M° Belleville. **Open** daily 8am-2am. **Beer** 25cl €2.50. **Cocktails** €6. **Happy hour** 5-9pm. **Credit** AmEx, MC, V. **Map** M3.

This small clubby bar is packing in a colourful bunch of thrill-seeking grungies and vinyl diehards, as perfect proof that a bit of effort is sometimes rewarded. Live DJs are high on the agenda, with local talent during the week, a weekly lesbian night and an after-hours party at weekends. In summer, a large terrace doubles takings.

20th Arrondissement

La Flèche d'Or

102bis rue de Bagnolet, 20th (01.43.72.04.23/ www.flechedor.com). M° Alexandre Dumas. **Open** Tue-Fri 6pm-2am; Sat, Sun 10am-2am. Food served 8.30pm-1.30am; brunch Sun noon-4pm. **Beer** 25cl €2-€3.30. **Cocktail** €5-€7. **Credit** AmEx, DC, MC, V. **Wheelchair access. Map** Q6.

Music fans and a grungy young crowd cram into this funky former train station to catch local groups performing live (daily 9pm) or dig an alternative scene that runs from Télébocal community TV and salsa bals to impassioned debates. By day the enclosed terrace overlooking the abandoned tracks is a fantastic spot for brunch or a cocktail.

La Fontaine d'Henri IV

42 bis rue des Cascades, 20th (no phone). M° Jourdain. **Open** daily 6pm-2am. **Beer** 25cl €1.70. **No credit cards. Map** P4.

The poster outside says it all: 'Specialités: 1664 et Ricard'. La Fontaine d'Henri IV is possibly the city's oddest bar and its owner Zoubair one of the most affable. Just when you want to leave he locks you in, when it's a lovely day he's closed, and when you're not hungry, he's laying on a free barbecue. Payback comes when you are sitting outside, polishing off your third glass with the sun sinking over Paris.

Lou Pascalou

14 rue des Panoyaux, 20th (01.46.36.78.10). M° Ménilmontant. **Open** daily 9am-2am. **Beer** 25cl €2-€2.30. **Cocktails** €5.50. **Credit** AmEx, DC, MC, V. **Map** P5.

Dress down for a visit to this Ménilmontant mainstay, where a bohemian crowd spills on to the pavement on clement evenings. Chess matches roll on for hours as regulars settle scores over a pression or two (sets and a board are available from behind the bar). Guinness and Kilkenny (pint €5.80) are not much cop, but the selection of cocktails is remarkable.

Les Lucioles ★

102 bd de Ménilmontant, 20th (01.40.33.10.24). M° Ménilmontant. **Open** Mon-Fri 8am-2am; Sat, Sun 10am-2am. Food served noon-3pm, 8pm-midnight. **Beer** 25cl €2.70. **Cocktails** €5. **Credit** AmEx, MC, V. **Map** N5.

If you've got an interesting scarf and want to show it off, this is the place. You'll be competing for attention with dangling birdcages and old apothecary jars. It's boho a-go-go as animated chatter reaches ant-nest feverishness on slam poetry nights (Tue 10.30pm). The mike is open to all and sundry, allowing Paris' lowest-profile poets to declaim their latest and greatest, with a free drink proffered in return. There are also concerts on Sunday, occasional experimental cinema nights, and some nice-looking food.

Le Piston Pélican

15 rue de Bagnolet, 20th (01.43.70.35.00). M° Alexandre Dumas. **Open** Mon-Fri 8am-2am; Sat, Sun 10am-2am. Food served noon-3pm, 7-11.30pm. **Beer** 25cl €2.10-€2.90. **Cocktails** €6.50. **Credit** AmEx, MC, V. **Map** Q6.

Home to many hungover-looking zinc magnates lingering over papers and espressos, this authentic late-19th-century bar is in fabulously good nick. By night, the bar is occasionally worn as a vintage accessory by a trendier crowd, particularly when there are DJ sets or live jazz. The eponymous pelican has a packet of seed waiting for him at the bar.

Counter culture at **Lou Pascalou**.

Tea Rooms

In surroundings pastel-coloured to match their macaroons, Paris tea rooms offer a respite from the hustle and bustle of the city.

You might think they are just an excuse for a good old gossip over some gooey pastries, but Paris tea rooms actually take their brews seriously – especially the growing number of Chinese and Japanese salons. Sink into their squishy cushions and enjoy.

Angelina

226 rue de Rivoli, 1st (01.42.60.82.00).
M° Tuileries. **Open** Mon-Fri 9.45am-6.45pm; Sat, Sun 9am-7pm. **Tea** €5.65-€6. **Pâtisseries** €4.50-€6.20. **Credit** AmEx, MC, V. **Map** G5.
Between the two world wars, the smart set needed only to say 'meet you on the rue de Rivoli' when arranging a tea date, such was the fame of this neo-rococo tearoom. The salon was originally known as Rumpelmeyer's and the cakes still have an Austrian gooeyness; this also partly explains the excellence of the hot chocolate, made with African cocoa (€6.20). The speciality has always been the Mont Blanc: soft and chewy meringue with whipped cream and chestnut cream topping. Angelina's is currently in its element, with an excellent lunch menu. Seated in plump leather armchairs at solid green marble tables with flamboyant murals as a backdrop, the haute bourgeoisie and hoi polloi are equally content.

Jean-Paul Hévin

231 rue St-Honoré, 1st (01.55.35.35.96).
M° Tuileries. **Open** tea and shop Mon-Sat noon-6.30pm. Closed Aug. **Tea** €5.80-€6.20. **Pâtisseries** €3.90-€5.80. **Credit** AmEx, DC, MC, V (€20 minimum). **Map** G5.
If black minimalist à la Gucci is your cup of tea, and you have a cocoa habit, then Jean-Paul Hévin is your man. His dark chocolate desserts gleam like edible accessories against the silver and dark wood of his shop. Take the futuristic stairway to the unexpectedly warm first floor tea room with bare teak floorboards, dark wood panels and wicker chairs. Surprisingly, the quality of the cakes is slightly uneven. From the short but high-quality selection of teas we chose lapsang souchong and mango. The black-clad staff are friendly and courteous.

Technicolor tea time at **Antoine et Lili, La Cantine**. *See p270.*

A Priori Thé

35-37 galerie Vivienne, 2nd (01.42.97.48.75). M° Bourse. **Open** tea Mon-Fri 3-6pm; Sat-Sun 4-6.30pm; brunch Sat 9am-6.30pm; Sun noon-6.30pm. **Tea** €4.50. **Pâtisseries** €6.50. **Credit** V, MC. **Non-smoking room. Map** H4.

American Peggy Ancock knew exactly what the capital's creatures of comfort were lacking when she opened A Priori Thé in 1980. The tearoom inhabits one of Paris' glitziest covered passages, but the tea room's charm comes from its frumpy insouciance toward the gilded surroundings – and its comfort food. Alongside 25 staple brews such as orange pekoe and Darjeeling, Ancock serves up a blissfully fluffy cheesecake with raspberry coulis, intense chocolate brownies and deep-dish fruit crumbles, all in colossal portions. Though the tables under the arcade afford ample people-watching, regulars always fill up the wicker, cushioned chairs in the dining room first.

La Charlotte en l'Ile

24 rue St-Louis-en-Ile, 4th (01.43.54.25.83). M° Pont Marie. **Open** Thur-Sun noon-8pm. Wed tea and puppet show by reservation only; Fri 6-8pm piano tea. **Closed** July and Aug. **Tea** €4. **Pâtisseries** €2.50-€4.50. **Credit** V. **Map** K7.

This tiny tea shop has all the stuff of fairy tales – pictures of witches on broomsticks, lanterns, carnival masks – the only thing lacking is gingerbread. Poetess and chocolatier par excellence Sylvie Langlet has been spinning her sweet fantasies here for more than 25 years. In the minuscule front room she sells her superb dark chocolate and candied fruit sticks, while at six tightly packed round tables she offers 36 teas of a quality that would put some five-star hotels to shame. Our choice of violet and apricot were served in simple blue and yellow bowls from dinky cast-iron teapots; their aroma alone perked us up. The desserts are magic, and beware the potent hot chocolate.

Les Enfants Gâtés

43 rue des Francs-Bourgeois, 4th (01.42.77.07.63) M° St-Paul. **Open** Wed-Mon 11am-8pm. Closed Aug. **Tea** €4.20. **Pâtisserie** €4.90-€5.70. **Credit** MC, V. **Map** L6.

Smack in the middle of the modish Marais, Les Enfants Gâtés is, against all odds, the next best thing to home when the five o'clock yawn sets in. The tea room's cushioned wicker chairs form to every body shape and leave you feeling – hours later – like a permanent fixture in the otherwise undecorated tearoom (slow service compounds the sentiment). A short but complete list of Mariage Frères staples – Marco Polo, goût russe, jasmine and caramel – make up the tea selection, while a skinny set of pastries leaves sweet-tooths a little frustrated. The bright spots are Berthillon ice cream and a so-called brownie: a warm, oozing slab of chocolate dollopped with crème fraîche. The brownie can easily convert any non-chocolate-dessert-eating person to a new party line.

Glace houses

The inside scoop on the best boules.

Some daring tastes are emerging from Paris glaciers – but bear in mind that, illogically, many of them close in August.

The most famous Parisian glacier is **Berthillon** (31 rue St-Louis-en-l'Ile, 4th/ 01.43.54.31.61). Although its ices are available in almost every cafe on the island, people still queue up at all hours at the original outlet on the main drag. Seventy flavours are on offer, ranging from sweet wild strawberry to wickedly strong whisky. Berthillon no longer has the scoop on the island scene, however. Last year **Amorino** popped up (47 rue St-Louis-en-l'Ile, 4th/01.44.07.48.08), serving creamy Italian concoctions as well as refreshing fruity numbers such as limone and lampone (raspberry). Order a cone (3), and staff will present you with an ice cream rose.

Raimo (61 bd de Reuilly, 12th/ 01.43.43.70.17) has been in the business since 1947. Though the white-shirted waiters are not overly attentive, the ice cream more than makes up for it. At 2.70 for a small serving, it's not cheap, but the fleur de lait is heavenly as is the woody Vermont maple. Cheaper scoops are available at **La Tropicale** (180 bd Vincent-Auriol, 13th/01.42.16.87.27), which offers jazz music, friendly service, and fabulous curaçao and mango sorbets.

Paris' best value boules are at **Gelati d'Alberto** (45 rue Mouffetard, 5th/ 01.43.37.88.07) where 3 buys you a selection of Italy's finest, shaped into a rose, in flavours such as passion fruit and panna cotta. A stone's throw away is **Octave** (138 rue Mouffetard, 5th/01.45.35.20.56), whose beautiful sorbets and ices include fresh pineapple and blood orange.

La Butte Glacée (14 rue Norvins, 18th/ 01.42.23.91.58) is an unpretentious ice cream parlour near Sacré-Coeur. After the long climb reward yourself with stracciatella and banana yoghurt sorbet or a jaw-crunching crocante. At **Glacier Calabrese** (15 rue d'Odessa, 15th/ 01.43.20.31.63), a 70s-style glacier, Luigi Calabrese serves up ginger, liquorice and a brilliant basil sorbet. Finally, for taste thrill-seekers, there's **Le Bac à Glaces** (109 rue du Bac, 7th/01.45.48.87.65) and its creamy roquefort, camembert, carrot and avocado concoctions. *Rob Orchard.*

Le Loir dans la Théière ★

3 rue des Rosiers, 4th (01.42.72.90.61). M° St-Paul. **Open** Mon-Fri 11.30am-7pm; Sat, Sun 10am-7pm. Closed Mon in Aug. **Tea** €4. **Pâtisseries** €6. **Credit** MC, V. **Map** L6.

Alice in Wonderland would love this place, and not least because it's named after her old friend 'the dormouse in the teapot'. There is a charming disorder about the setting: vast, wrinkled armchairs and battered poufs crowd around square, rectangular and round tables, while ancient prams and cartoon-like teapots line deep shelves. Besides Darjeeling, Earl Grey, sencha and other staples, Le Loir has excellent perfumed teas, including the fabulously fragrant lotus. Desserts, including a sky-high lemon meringue pie, clafoutis packed with fat cherries and a divine rhubarb tart, are all equally uplifting.

Café Maure de la Mosquée de Paris

39 rue Geoffroy Saint-Hilaire, 5th (01.43.31.38.20). M° Place Monge. **Open** daily 9am-11pm. **Tea** €2. **Pâtisserie** €2. **Credit** AmEx, MC, V. **Map** K8.

When the sun streaks the capital there's perhaps no better spot to bask than on the blue-tiled terrace at the mosque. Speedy waiters serve tiny, super-sweet mint teas as soon as you take your seat, either here under the fig tree or beneath the tea room's stunning coffered ceiling, where a young, international crowd buzzes to Oriental pop music. Blue-gold banquettes and massive brass tables round out the splendid decor, while succulent pastries such as kidaif – a honey-hazelnut gooey base topped with fine threads of sizzled dough – complete the mint-tea experience. You can temper the sweetness with a mild, dense pistachio-almond cookie. For total relaxation, start off with a steam bath in the beautiful tiled hammam (men, women or mixed depending on the day) before retiring to the tea room.

La Fourmi Ailée

8 rue du Fouarre, 5th (01.43.29.40.99). M° Maubert-Mutualité. **Open** tea daily 3pm-7pm; July-Aug 5-7pm. **Tea** €3.50-€4.50. **Pâtisserie** €4.50-€5. **Credit** MC, V (over €16). **Map** J7.

The funky decor here can't really be called vintage, but it definitely aspires to an aged look, with its mustard-yellow vinyl banquettes, forest-green faux-marble tabletops, woven-straw laminated wallpaper and a quirky collection of books, Christmas garlands and framed butterflies draping the high-rising walls. La Fourmi Ailée is the quintessential Latin-Quarter tearoom – cultivating a stay-all-day ambience and lengthy intello head-bangs over its immense glass ashtrays. (Light-loving creatures should camp out in the bright, airy annex upstairs.) Among a tea selection of Chinese, Ceylon, Assam and interesting herbal blends such as caramel-orange, we have a soft spot for the green tea with jasmine and always pair it with the bourdaloue pear-walnut tart.

L'Artisan de Saveurs ★

72 rue du Cherche-Midi, 6th (01.42.22.46.64). M° St-Placide. **Open** tea Tue-Fri 2.30-6.30pm; Sat-Sun 3-6.30pm; brunch Sat-Sun 12-6.30pm. **Tea** €5.40-€6.40. **Pâtisserie** €6.50-€7.80. **Credit** MC, V. **Non smoking**. **Map** F8.

You can't blame L'Artisan for disallowing smoking in its butter-yellow tearoom, as the slightest speck of ash would stain the delightful provincial flavour here. Linen tablecloths, tasteful paper napkins and ivory-coloured tea sets stoke up country-home elegance; stacks of interior design magazines add to the ensemble. The selection of teas and pastries, meanwhile, surpasses urban sophistication. L'Artisan's menu eloquently explains 40 teas from the standard Darjeeling to the more exotic Marco Polo varieties, while a long list of innovative pastries, prepared to order, defies description. On a recent winter visit, we warmed up with a frothy pineapple gratin spiked with kumbawa, a succulent fruit reminiscent of lime.

Forêt Noire

9 rue de l'Eperon, 6th (01.44.41.00.09). M° Odéon. **Open** tea Mon-Sat noon-7pm; brunch Sun noon-3pm; tea Sat, Sun 3.30pm-7pm. **Tea** €4-€6. **Pâtisseries** €5-€6.70. **Credit** V. **Map** H7.

Curiously, nothing in the eclectic decor conjures up the tea room's title, the Black Forest. Still, fans of this famed cake needn't lose heart; owner Denise Siegal hails from this part of Germany, and the cake heads the short list of desserts. Connoisseurs won't be disappointed with her moist version, oozing with jam and fresh cream. The gâteau au fromage blanc, a creamy, less sweet version of a cheesecake, was equally wicked. Naturally, from an intriguing tea list we chose the fôret noire, a black tea with a bouquet of blackberries, bilberries and blackcurrants.

Mariage Frères

13 rue des Grands Augustins, 6th (01.40.51.82.50) M° Odéon. **Open** tea Mon-Fri noon-7pm; Sat-Sun 3-7pm. **Tea** €7-€11. **Pâtisserie** €10. **Credit** AmEx, MC, V. **Non smoking**. **Map** H7.

This tea room on a quiet street in St-Germain-des-Près is the legendary 149-year-old chain's most peaceful. After taking the stairs to the elevated seating area – a colonial backdrop with high-backed wooden chairs, hardwood floors, billowing flora and silver tea service – let the white-tailed waiters guide you through the labyrinthine menu cataloguing 500 teas from across the globe. Choosing a pastry requires only one eye on the dessert tray, the work of Philippe Langlois. Many of the selections, such as Langlois' Indes galantes, a saffron-flavoured sponge atop an Assam-tinged mousse decorated with poached pears and a pear coulis, use tea as an ingredient. A simple 'fantaisie' brew, such as cardamom, pairs nicely with the elaborate pastries. On a warm day, opt for the mousse de jade – cold milk beaten with matcha (green tea).

Branches: 30-32 rue du Bourg-Tibourg, 4th (01.42.72.28.11); 260 rue du Fbg-St-Honoré, 8th (01.46.22.18.54).

Le Bristol

112 rue du Fbg-St-Honoré, 8th (01.53.43.43.00). M° Miromesnil. **Open** daily 3-6.30pm. **Tea** €8.

On the Town

Drink to me only with thy nose

Tea is the new wine at Far Eastern salons where tasting is a high art.

Think you've passed a window of people burrowing their noses into empty teacups? You've witnessed the latest quirky trend in Paris. Across town, gourmets are inhaling the odours of infusions before tasting them, approaching tea like wine. As Madame Yu Hui Tseng, one of the world's ten leading tea experts and owner of Paris' La Maison des Trois Thés, says about tasting both drinks: 'It's all in the nose.'

The French still consume a lot less tea than the British – 200g versus 3.15kg per person per year, to be exact – but it's quality, not quantity that counts this side of the Channel. The city's range of Far East-influenced tea rooms is impressive, from the simple setting at **T'cha** (6 rue du Pont de Lodi, 6th/ 01.43.29.61.31) – a Chinese tea room with tasty but no-frills sweets such as apple loaf and ginger cookies – to the elaborate spread at **Toraya** (10 rue St-Florentin, 1st/ 01.42.60.13.48), a Japanese tea room with a groovy decor and modern, artistic revisions of classic Japanese desserts.

Paris is also strong on tea-related learning experiences. At **La Maison de la Culture du Japon**, two weekly tea ceremonies are constantly booked. The ritual, fundamental to Japanese notions of hospitality, takes place in a teahouse replica perched in a fifth-floor, glass-enclosed space overlooking the Seine. After a detailed demonstration, visitors sample a bowl of matcha, an intense, foamy green tea.

For an introduction to Chinese tea, **La Maison des Trois Thés** (33 rue Gracieuse, 5th/01.43.36.93.84) is the place to begin. With one of the largest tea cellars in the world, boasting more than 1,000 blends, the tea house is decorated with some 700 canisters of tea, suspended on the main wall of the unique brick-and-iron interior. Two menus list the likes of vintage (dating to 1890) and more humble brews, but a peek at the second-tier menu must be pre-approved by Madame Tseng. A soft-spoken waiter presents the menu before bringing boiling water to the chunky, high-rising tables carved from old Chinese doors, and then meticulously explains the infusion process. Before sipping, of course, comes the sniffing. Our blue-green si ji chun seduced with notes of coconut and acacia, and tasted subtly of honeysuckle. It's best to book, especially on weekends.

La Maison des Trois Thés: teeming with rare leaves.

L'Empire des Thés (101 av d'Ivry, 13th/ 01.45.85.66.33), another upmarket Chinese establishment, has drawn a predominantly French crowd to the heart of Chinatown since its opening two years ago. The shop serves 160 teas at four miniature tables in its earthy but elegant, butter-beige sitting area. You can also play chess while munching on a pastry provided by the Japanese pâtissier Sadaharu Aoki. His sesame macaroons and cool, green-tea éclairs with perfect choux pastry complement any of the multi-coloured brews. Green teas sell best, along with grand jasmin Impérial – rolled tea-leaves resembling miniature pearls. Though L'Empire has little trouble selling rare white teas at 60 for 100g to connoisseurs, the shop caters to beginners with tea initiations the final Sunday of every month.

Neophytes also frequent **La Maison de la Chine**'s teahouse (76 rue Bonaparte, 6th/ 01.40.51.95.00). The regularly changing menu includes intriguing names for house-created blends: felicity, prosperity and serenity, for instance. Our 'pledge of love', a semi-green with peony petals often shared by a couple on the verge of marriage, came with a tiny, dried rosebud floating in the teacup.

Nowhere is tea's newfound popularity more evident than at **Mademoiselle Li** in the Jardin d'Acclimatation, which attracts BCBG pilgrims. Nine blends are served in frumpy crockery alongside bowls of sunflower, pumpkin and watermelon seeds. Try to grab the cushions at the low-lying tables near the entrance. *Kristen Hinman.*

Pâtisseries €11. **Credit** AmEx, DC, MC, V. **Map** E4.
Cross the apricot marble foyer and trip down the steps to the right to a vast lounge complete with marble columns, magnificent bouquets and a view across the lawns. The hotel's teas appear to have been picked by a connoisseur, as confirmed by our choice of the excellent grand Foochow fumé pointes blanches and Assam doomou. The accompanying little sandwiches of tuna, smoked salmon and cheese were delicously buttery, although the absence of cucumber was a tad disappointing.

Hôtel Plaza Athénée ★

25 av Montaigne, 8th (01.53.67.66.65). M° Alma-Marceau. **Open** daily 8am-8pm. **Tea** €8. **Pâtisseries** €12. **Credit** AmEx, DC, MC, V. **Map** D5.
In the 18th-century-style Galerie des Gobelins, you can watch the wealthy mingle. On our visit, the Iranian royal family had gathered for tea, next to them a famous opera singer and further down an eminent statesman. People-gazing, however, is a very minor pleasure compared to the Plaza's superb teas and dessert trolley. Try the fraisier, a strawberry and pistachio cream cake that is close to perfection. As for the teas, don't miss the mélange Plaza, a masterly blend of fig, hazelnut, quince and grape. Listening to the harpist and pouring another cup from the armoury of silverware, we felt part of it all. Even the head waiter played the game, slipping us some juicy celebrity gossip.

Ladurée

16 rue Royale, 8th (01.42.60.21.79). M° Madeleine or Concorde. **Open** Mon-Sat 8.30am-7pm; Sun 10am-7pm. **Tea** €4.85-€7. **Pâtisseries** €4-€5.60. **Credit** AmEx, DC, MC, V. **Non-smoking room**. **Map** F4.
Avoiding someone's eye when they're desperately seeking yours is an art that French waiters have perfected, and Ladurée staff do it exceptionally well. Once you accept this, the effect on your temper will be neutralised and you can settle back and enjoy one of Paris' favourite institutions. The cake descriptions are Proustian, but it's the macaroons that regulars devour by the mound, whether coffee (arguably the best), coconut, chocolate, pistachio or mint. In terms of tea, we chose mint and verbena, a large pot filled with dozens of fresh leaves steeped to perfection, and yin hao jasmine, whose aroma conjured up acres of the flowers in full bloom.
Branches: 75 av des Champs-Elysées, 8th (01.40.75.08.75); Printemps, 64 bd Haussmann, 9th (01.42.82.40.10); Franck et Fils, 80 rue de Passy, 16th (01.44.14.38.80).

Les Cakes de Bertrand

7 rue Bourdaloue, 9th (01.40.16.16.28). M° Notre-dame-de-Lorette. **Open** Tue-Sun 2.30-7.30pm. **Tea** €4; tea with mini-cakes €7. **Pâtisserie** €3.25-€4. **Credit** MC, V. **Non smoking. Map** H3.
With its baby-blue cabinetry, tapestry-covered chaises and crystal chandeliers, Les Cakes de Bertrand feels like a collector's-item dollshouse. The dainty porcelain tea sets and fairytale placemats heighten the tea-taking experience here, a lovely (if prim) getaway from the gritty city streets. Alongside cheesecake, fondant au chocolat and fromage blanc with a fruit coulis, Bertrand's famous cakes – fruit and nut loaves – make a lighter complement for a South African red or Assam tea. With chai, a robust Indian blend spiked with cardamom, we enjoyed a plate of mini-cakes in a variety of flavours including pine-nut, chocolate, raisin, orange confit, walnut and almond. The tea room seats only 18, who are served, at tea time, by one.

Antoine et Lili, La Cantine

95 quai de Valmy, 10th (01.40.37.34.86). M° Jacques Bonsergent. **Open** Wed-Sat 11am-8pm; Sun-Tue 11am-7pm. **Tea** €3. **Pâtisserie** €3.50-€4.50. **Credit** AmEx, DC, MC, V (€15 minimum). **Non-smoking room**. **Map** L4.
Welcome to the temple of kitsch, cooked up by the women's fashion and home-decor designers Antoine and Lili. This whimsical duo won over Paris' deep-pocketed, bobo-chic hearts with faux-vintage, Eastern-inspired prints and patterns, and now it has tickled everyone pink by hosting a zanily-dressed tea loft near its flagship on the Canal St-Martin. Self-service is the principle here. Take your tray – with a white-chocolate tart with raspberries, and almond green tea – to a plastic-clothed table in the antique-red and pink-Technicolor smoking and non-smoking rooms. There is great seating for groups both on leopard-print stools and parrot-print benches. Our only gripe is the throwaway tableware.

Letting off some steam at the **Café Maure**. *See p268.*

On the Town

Wine Bars

Paris bars à vins range from the quirky to the quixotic; nowhere can you delve more deeply into the French obsession with fermentation.

Paris wine bars these days seem to fall roughly into three categories. First, there are the old-school places with a comptoir, where you often find a selection of simple, rustic and sometimes one-dimensional wines. The second category, the independents, offers a more eclectic selection – not necessarily French, and chosen individually on their merits, with the winemaker being championed more obviously. Thirdly, there are the new-school wine bars which offer strictly 'natural' wines from non-interventionist, organic or bio-dynamic producers. Whatever your taste, there's plenty to get you swirling and slurping.

Juveniles

47 rue de Richelieu, 1st (01.42.97.46.49). Mº Palais Royal or Pyramides. **Open** Mon-Sat noon-midnight. Food served Mon-Sat noon-11pm. **Glass** €3-€10. **Bottle** €14-€400. **Credit** AmEx, MC, V. **Map** H4.

Sometimes even the eternally youthful need a little facelift, and so here the doors have reopened after three weeks of rejuvenation. The bar has moved across the back of the room, creating more space, neat new frames surround the precocious artwork created by the owner's daughters, and there's a Rolls-Royce of a new loo. Foodwise, simple dishes and tapas continue as before. We munched our way through a pile of feather-light, crisp celeriac chips with a perfect apéritif glass of 1999 Pieropan Soave Classico at €4. With main courses of Duval sausages and mash with chutney, and nicely cooked salmon with lots of vegetables, we had excellent, surprisingly supple 1995 Rioja from Marques de Murrieta (€40). Tim Johnston remains an eccentric and genial host, a humorous Scot with attitude.

Le Père Fouettard

9 rue Pierre Lescot, 1st (01.42.33.74.17/ www.auperefouttard). Mº Etienne Marcel/RER Châtelet-Les Halles. **Open** daily 8am-2am. Closed 24, 25 Dec. Food served 11.30am-1am. **Glass** €2.80-€4. **Bottle** €12-€57. **Credit** MC, V. **Map** J5.

This is a useful address in the heart of Les Halles, decorated in traditional style with the obligatory shiny zinc bar, a small dining room and a large

La Robe et le Palais: taking the fear out of French wines. *See p273.*

Great Britain & Ireland on a plate

Over 1,200 eateries reviewed

Time Out

2004

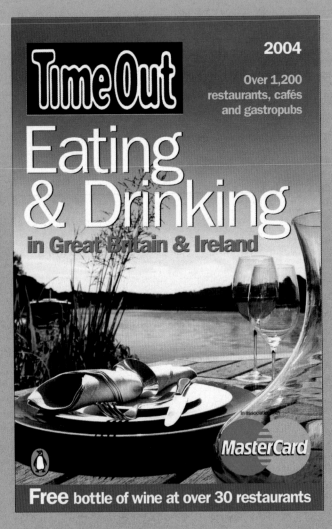

Over 1,200 restaurants, cafés and gastropubs

Eating & Drinking in Great Britain & Ireland

In association with MasterCard

Free bottle of wine at over 30 restaurants

Available from all good bookshops and at www.timeout.com/shop

terrace. The pumping soundtrack is slightly at odds with the junky decor, but it wasn't discouraging a steady flow of youngish customers on a freezing night. The selection of wines by the glass threw up a Rasteau 2000 from Trapidis; a good flinty Sancerre, Domaine Cherrier 1998; and a delicious, rich Vin de Pays des Bouches du Rhône from Château Roquefort 2001. A Brouilly 2000 from Descombes was disappointingly dusty, but swiftly replaced by the accommodating barman with a more interesting Morgon from Flache. We didn't have dinner, preferring just to nibble a little platter of saucisson sec served with cornichons, but reassuring signs such as Duval charcuterie and Berthillon ice cream suggest there was no reason not to. Meaty mains – steaks, duck confit, etc. – were on offer at around €15, plus a welcome 'coin végétarien' for herbivores.

La Robe et le Palais ★

13 rue des Lavandières-Ste-Opportune, 1st (01.45.08.07.41). M° Châtelet. **Open** Mon-Sat noon-2pm, 7.30-11pm. Food served noon-2pm, 7.30-11pm. **Glass** €3-€8. **Bottle** €17-€60. **Credit** MC, V **Map** J6.

An enthusiastic young sommelier went straight in, offering us blind tastes as apéritifs. While we contemplated our wines, an unusual dry savagnin distinctive of the Jura and a simple white from Abbaye de Valmagne, we pored over the vast selection of bottles which was presented by style (bubbly, dry, fruity, mineral, rich, tender, aromatic), so refreshing after endless lists by appellation. A kitsch-sounding vol-au-vent stuffed with creamy fat snails and button mushrooms was nonetheless heavenly, and the antithesis of a clean-tasting scallop tartare with lime to start. Next up, Bresse chicken with morels and chestnuts served in a mini casserole and an upmarket petit salé of lentils with duck, foie gras and sausage. Here our sommelier encouraged us to go for an interesting Minervois La Nine from J.B. Senat which wasn't on the list (which he suggested needed updating) and, with a gentle carafing, it opened up into something quite delicious. A noisy birthday party didn't interfere with the order of play and the atmosphere was bon vivant and infectious.

Wine and Bubbles

3 rue Française, 1st (01.44.76.99.84/ www.wineandbubbles.com). M° Etienne Marcel. **Open** Mon-Sat 6pm-2am. Food served 6-11pm. Closed Aug. **Glass** €3-€7. **Bottle** €7.50-€500. **Credit** AmEx, MC, V. **Non-smoking room**. **Map** J5.

This wildly successful wine-shop-cum-wine-bar is all clean lines and good lighting, with the wine beautifully displayed by region and country. The bar continues in the same vein – spindly modern tables and chairs, low lights and funky music. One of the secrets of its success seems to be a very reasonable corkage fee of €3 which is added to the shop price for bottles consumed on the premises. Arriving early we were a little alarmed to find them burning green tea oil which, they explained, was against the cigarette smoke. However as the space filled up with rake-thin, chain-smoking fashionistas, the essential oil began to make more sense. A helpful young caviste helped us select a delicious and original wine from South Africa (La Motte Millennium 1997) whose supple fruit we enjoyed with a selection of rather basic cured ham, garlic sausage and speck served with good bread and cornichons.

Au Sans Souci

183 rue St-Denis, 2nd (01.42.36.09.39). M° Réaumur-Sébastopol. **Open** Mon-Fri 7.30am-9pm. (Sat opening for major sports events). Food served noon-3pm. Closed three weeks in Aug. **Glass** €3-€4. **Bottle** €15-€35. **Credit** MC, V. **Map** K5.

Michel Godon, the charming, sparkly-eyed owner, has been holding the fort amidst the quartier's sex shops for 27 years, though it was only in 1998 that he revamped this former café and concentrated on the wine. Slightly incongruous for your average wine bar are the pinball, TV and a fantastic jukebox full of French hits of the 1970s. One lone regular was so moved he drained his glass, took out his air guitar and really went for it. Not so frivolous was the careful selection of the wines by the glass, with everything served in 7cl tasters at mad student prices (nothing over €2). We were suitably impressed by a very respectable gewurztraminer, crisp white Sancerre from Philip Raimbault, sound Vire Clesse and others. Then we were blown away by the superb raspberry fruit of a St-Chinian, Marquise des Mures. You can have tartines and charcuterie at the bar, and lunch is served upstairs.

Les Enfants Rouges ★

9 rue de Beauce, 3rd (01.48.87.80.61). M° Temple or Arts et Métiers. **Open** Tue-Sat noon-3pm; Thur, Fri 7pm-2am. Food served noon-2.30pm, 7pm-midnight. Closed three weeks in Aug. **Glass** €2.60-€5. **Bottle** €14-€100. **Credit** MC, V. **Map** L5.

This bar is a new venture from the couple who brought us the now-defunct Moulins à Vins (now Café Burq) in Montmartre. By a strange twist of fate we ate there, rather unfairly, on their very first night, the paint barely dry on the walls of the pretty little dining room. They were wisely keeping things simple as their first punters started piling in the door. Main courses included nice pink duck magret with lentils and faux-filet steak with exemplary home-made chips. From the small selection of wines by the glass, we tasted a 1999 Côtes du Rhône Viognier from Gaillard which made an aromatic and silky apéritif. We followed with a glass of Cairanne from Richaud which the patronne aptly described as 'charmeur comme lui', alluding to the charismatic Rhône winemaker. No surprises from a Cabernet de Touraine from Cadart, but the Vin de Pays de Vaucluse from Monardière was more solid stuff. With coffee we leafed through the impressive wine list, which includes some of France's top producers and some older vintages. Gentle rubbernecking revealed lots of familiar faces in the wine glitterati taking up their places at this wine bar to watch.

L'Estaminet

Marché des Enfants Rouges, 39 rue de Bretagne, 3rd (01.42.72.34.85/www.aromes-et-cepages.com). M° Temple. **Open** Tue-Fri 11.30am-3.30pm, 6-9pm; Sat 10.30am-9pm; Sun 10am-5pm. **Glass** €2-€5. **Bottle** €9-€30. **Credit** DC, MC, V. **Wheelchair access. Non-smoking room. Map** L5.

This bright and airy wine bar with wooden tables and a modern zinc bar has become the soul of the revamped Enfants Rouges market. We started with two Gaillac wines, a light and delicate still wine and a sparkling one. Brunch is served on Sundays but we were tempted by the seafood platter, which was traipsed in by the market's fishmonger in his wellies, coat and apron. We accompanied this breath of sea air with an interesting Touraine white, made from old vines of the obscure grape variety fie gris from producer Jacky Prey. Bliss.

La Belle Hortense

31 rue Vieille-du-Temple, 4th (01.48.04.71.60). M° St-Paul or Hôtel de Ville. **Open** Mon-Fri 5pm-2am; Sat, Sun 1pm-2am. **Glass** €3-€6. **Bottle** €14-€36. **Credit** MC, V. **Non-smoking room. Map** L6.

Bookshop, literary salon, wine bar and off-licence meet at this unusual Marais spot. Good wines by the glass include a strong contingent of from the Rhône by Guigal. It's standing room only at the bar, but the non-smoking reading room at the back is sure to enhance your intellectual credibility.

L'Enoteca ★

25 rue Charles V, 4th (01.42.78.91.44). M° St-Paul. **Open** daily noon-2.30pm, 7.30-11.30pm. Closed one week in Aug. **Glass** €3-€9. **Bottle** €15-€350. **Credit** MC, V. **Map** L7.

If you like Italian wine, then this classy Marais trattoria is a must. The list is astounding, with hard-to-find wines from all the best producers: Gaja, Aldo Conterno, Vajra, Felsina Berardenga and a stack of vintages. And what a pleasure to taste by the glass – we tried Moscato d'Asti and Barbera from Piedmont, and Sant'Agata dei Goti from Campania (the selection changes weekly). The food is delicious too, with antipasti such as porchetta alla romana, generous portions of pappardelle al ragu di salsiccie and a few meat and fish mains. Booking is recommended.

Le Rouge Gorge

8 rue St-Paul, 4th (01.48.04.75.89). M° St-Paul or Pont Marie. **Open** Mon-Sat noon-4pm, 6pm-2am. Food served noon-3pm, 7-11pm. Closed two weeks in Aug. **Glass** €3-€6. **Bottle** €19-€55. **Credit** MC, V. **Map** L7.

This charming little wine bar, with its wooden beams, exposed stone and excellent cellar, has undergone a change of focus recently. Owner François Briclot and passionate young sommelier Guillaume Dupré have introduced changing themes, rotating roughly every two or three weeks. On our visit, it was the Loire and we were treated to a terrific selection of artisan-produced, unfiltered wines such as Chinon Le Clos des Roches 1997 from Guy Lenoir, and the unclassified white, Les Bulles du Clos du Tue-Boeuf. The savoury dishes – goat's cheese and hazelnut terrine, paupiettes de veau, oignons farcis – are tasty and well-executed, if pricey. Wines are also available to take away.

The bookish **La Belle Hortense**.

Les Papilles ★

30 rue Gay-Lussac, 5th (01.43.25.20.79/ www.lespapilles.fr). RER Luxembourg.
Open Mon, Wed, Fri, Sat 10am-8pm; Tue, Thur 10am-10pm. Food served Mon-Sat 12.15-2.30pm; Tue, Thur 8-10pm. **Glass** €3-€6. **Bottle** €15-€200. **Credit** MC, V. **Wheelchair access. Map** J8.
Decorated in the style of a Provençal kitchen, Les Papilles ('tastebuds') is all about eating and drinking well. It's run by two couples dedicated to gastronomy – Brigitte and Julie look after the food while their husbands Gérard and Pierre trawl the countryside looking for new wines. The regularly changing menu emphasises seasonal cooking. There's a good selection of wines of the week and the regulars were lapping up an excellent red from Corsica. Jams, vinegars, olive oils, pasta, whiskies and vintage Ports are all there to take home, and shelves of wine await, like a fine library, to be perused.

Caves Miard

9 rue des Quatre-Vents, 6th (01.43.54.99.30). M° Odéon. **Open** Mon 2.30-8pm; Tue-Sat 10.30am-8.30pm. Food served noon-2.30pm; cold plates until 8pm. Closed two weeks in Aug. **Glass** €3.10-€6.50. **Bottle** €5-€316. **Credit** MC, V. **Non-smoking room. Map** H7.
The marble shelves and cupboards of this tiny vintage crèmerie are now stacked with wine bottles. At lunch the staff get out the tables and chairs and serve an array of savoury tarts, salads and charcuterie along with wines by the glass. But it's more than just a question of picturesque charm – our warm tart of girolles, duck gizzards and tangy reblochon cheese was crisp and appetising, the red from near Perpignan zingy and refreshing.

Fish

69 rue de Seine, 6th (01.43.54.34.69). M° Odéon or Mabillon. **Open** Mon 8pm-midnight; Tue-Sun noon-2pm, 7-10.45pm. Food served Tue-Sun noon-2pm, 7-10.45pm. Closed first two weeks in Aug. **Glass** €3-€12. **Bottle** €15-€500. **Credit** MC, V. **Map** H6.
Set up by a New Zealander who runs the panini shop Cosi across the road and an American with a wine shop around the corner, this friendly, informal place attracts well-heeled young French and slightly worse-heeled young Anglos in roughly equal numbers. The wine list is strong on the sunny, big-hitter wines of Languedoc-Roussillon (we chose a bottle of smooth, ample St-Chinian) and there's an interesting selection from the Rhône Valley. The food is Mediterranean (polenta, rocket salad, salt cod, tomatoes-a-gogo) and not bad at all.

La Tour de Pierre

53 rue Dauphine, 6th (01.43.26.08.93/ www.latouredepierre.com). M° Odéon.
Open Mon-Sat 8am-9pm. Food served noon-8.30pm. Closed two weeks in Aug, one week at Christmas. **Glass** €2.20-€3.70. **Bottle** €16-€38. **Credit** MC, V. **Wheelchair access. Map** H6.
Time stands still in this tiny, award-winning tabac/wine bar on the Left Bank. OK, so it might take an age to get served (particularly if you come in simply to buy a pack of cigarettes) but what atmosphere! Where else would you meet an Appeals Court judge dressed in tweeds and quoting Oscar Wilde, the elderly spouse of a newspaper war correspondent and a member of the jury for one of France's most notorious serial-killer trials? The wine is excellent – riesling late harvest, Médoc, Burgundy – and reasonably priced, and the food is decent.

L'Evasion

7 pl St-Augustin, 8th (01.45.22.66.20/ www.levasion.net). M° St-Augustin. **Open** Mon-Fri 8am-1am; Sat 11am-1am. Food served Mon-Wed noon-2.30pm, 7.30-10pm; Thur-Sat noon-2.30, 7.30-11pm. **Glass** €4.20-€8. **Bottle** €7-€150. **Credit** AmEx, DC, MC, V. **Map** F3.
Take one corner café, give it a lick of yellow paint and cover the walls with little blackboards listing the food and wines on offer. This seems all that was deemed necessary at L'Evasion, in terms of decoration, to turn the place around. The real changes are in your glass and on your plate. Consequently the clientele seems to be neatly divided between serious wine geeks and guys drinking beer at the bar and looking puzzled. For the wines we are talking natural, simply natural, bio-dynamic growers: Crozes Hermitage from Dard et Ribo, Morgon from Jean Foillard, Domaine Gramenon in Côtes du Rhône. By the glass a Costières de Nîmes from Domaine de la Perillière was full of fruit while Chablis from Laurent Tribut was crisp and good. To eat: top saucisson sec or thinly shaved Parma ham for incurable nibblers. More substantial appetites could choose from pan-fried guinea fowl, flank steak with marrow, cod, or veal kidneys, finishing with cheeses or ice cream from Berthillon.

Le Bar Rouge

Lafayette Gourmet, Galeries Lafayette, 40 bd Haussmann, 9th (01.42.82.34.56/ www.galerieslafayette.com). M° Havre-Caumartin.
Open Mon-Sat 11.30am-3.30pm. **Glass** €4.20-€8.32. **Bottle** €16.80-€41.60. **Credit** AmEx, MC, V. **Map** H3.
This showroom wine bar, designed to animate the souped-up wine emporium of Lafayette Gourmet, fails somewhat in its task. During a disappointing afternoon visit, the sterile atmosphere was heightened by a wide-screen telly playing a music channel uselessly to the near-empty room. A lone chef pottered around in the stainless steel open kitchen that was visible from the bar. The menu offers a main course for every day of the week, alongside slightly baffling 'round the world' tapas. A relatively interesting selection of ten or so wines was available by two sizes of glass (7.5cl or 15cl) or the bottle. There was something for everybody, with good winemakers from most of the major regions represented. We asked for small glasses and received large, no big deal. Mâcon-Grevilly from Domaine Guillot Broux had good fruit and balance and a young red from Corbières, Clos Combe Long, didn't disappoint. But the temptation to stay and taste different things quickly dissipated.

Le Coin de Verre ★

38 rue de Sambre-et-Meuse, 10th (01.42.45.31.82). M° Belleville. **Open** Mon-Sat 8pm-midnight. Food served 8pm-midnight. **Glass** €2.50-€3. **Bottle** €9-€15. **No credit cards**. **Map** M3.

A very special, rather secret destination, Le Coin de Verre is identifiable only by a single strip light over the door. It's all very cloak-and-dagger stuff – reservations are imperative and you ring the doorbell to be admitted. So we rang, then we rang again, and then we called by mobile phone to explain we were outside. Following this eccentric rigmarole we were greeted with extraordinary warmth by Michel, who led us past boxes and cases of wine, through to the rustic back room where a log fire was roaring. Here, Hugues (gorgeous red braces) set about us with paternal cordiality at a beautiful leisurely pace. The blackboard (everything seriously cheap, nothing over €11.50) offered simple charcuterie and cheese plates; we were advised to go for the daily specials (simple blanquette de veau or grilled andouillette) before they ran out. From a small selection of carefully chosen producers' wines with nothing over €13, he selected a Coteaux du Languedoc, Domaine de la Perrière 2000 which was fruity and smooth. Hugues smiled almost ruefully when challenged about their current success with a steady stream of bohemian insiders – not exactly what they'd set out for, but inevitable.

Le Verre Volé

67 rue de Lancry, 10th (01.48.03.17.34). M° République or Jacques Bonsergent. **Open** Mon-Sat 10am-11pm; Sun 11am-10pm. Food served Mon-Sat 12.30-2.30pm, 7.30-10.30pm; Sun noon-8pm. Closed Aug. **Glass** €3.30-€4.50. **Bottle** €7-€15 (plus €5 per table). **Credit** MC, V. **Map** L4.

A popular favourite of this newly cool quartier near Canal St-Martin, Le Verre Volé specialises in food and drink from the Ardèche region of France. Unsulphured, unfiltered wines join hearty black puddings, andouillette and pâté in a cheery atmosphere. Opened in 2000, it is run by two friends who clearly love their job and make every effort to ensure their customers have a good time. It's tiny, little more than a few very basic tables in a shop, but it's always full to bursting in the evening.

Le Clown Bar

114 rue Amelot, 11th (01.43.55.87.35). M° Filles du Calvaire. **Open** Mon-Sat noon-3.30pm, 7pm-1am; Sun 7pm-midnight. Food served Mon-Sat noon-2.30pm, 7pm-midnight; Sun 7pm-midnight. **Glass** €3-€5. **Bottle** €15-€48. **No credit cards**. **Map** L5.

Nestling next to the Cirque d'Hiver, a shortish walk from the Bastille or the Marais, the Clown Bar is decorated with comic-yet-sinister circus memorabilia. Much of the listed interior dates from 1919, but owner Jo Vitte, a former antique dealer, has added period bistro tables and a beautiful sculpted zinc bar. Open on Sunday evenings, Le Clown Bar serves excellent food for locals who'd rather not cook – petit salé aux lentilles or filet mignon de porc à l'ancienne, with mustard, cream and fried potatoes and a wonderfully moist pain d'épices dessert. There is a good selection of wines from the Rhône, Languedoc-Roussillon and the Loire.

Jacques Mélac

42 rue Léon-Frot, 11th (01.43.70.59.27). M° Charonne. **Open** Tue-Sat 9am-midnight. Food served noon-3pm, 7.30-10.30pm. Closed Aug. **Glass** €2.80-€3.66. **Bottle** €15-€32. **Credit** MC, V. **Wheelchair access. Non-smoking room. Map** N7.

Jacques Mélac, the owner of this crowded locals' bar, used to own a vineyard and his love of wine shows in every aspect of the place. The walls are draped with creeping vines and shelves bursting with bottles. Hams and cantal cheeses loom behind the bar, and Jacques hacks off generous chunks to accompany the good-value glasses of hardy young wines. The non-smoking room is on the other side of the bare-bones kitchen. Every September there is a little festival here where people with vines in Paris bring grapes to be pressed, having fun but producing mainly foul fermentations.

Le Vin de Zinc

25 rue Oberkampf, 11th (01.48.06.28.23). M° Oberkampf or Filles du Calvaire. **Open** Tue-Sat noon-2pm, 8-11pm. Food served noon-2pm, 8-11pm. Closed Aug. **Glass** €4-€5.40. **Bottle** €20-€56. **Credit** MC, V. **Map** M5.

This spacious bar is a welcome newcomer to the boho Oberkampf area, with simple red Formica tables and blackboards listing the day's specials. Winning starters – lovely, clean-tasting piquillo peppers stuffed with goat's cheese and little, fat snail ravioli with minced vegetables – were followed by less successful mains. A dryish tuna steak was cheered up by a herb salad and grilled veg, while creamy veal kidneys came with a delicate celery flan. The wine is all very new-school: lots of unsulphured and naturally produced bottles. A glass of Vire Clesse 1999 from Vergé had a delicate taste of star anise. The Morgon Côte de Py from Foillard was gorgeous and concentrated. An Anjou Villages from Rene Mossé was slightly on the woody side and a Vin de Bugey was a bit spritzy. The only real disappointment is the frostiness of the grim patronne.

Le Baron Bouge

1 rue Théophile-Roussel, 12th (01.43.43.14.32). M° Ledru-Rollin or Gare de Lyon. **Open** Tue-Thur 10am-2pm, 5-10pm; Fri, Sat 10am-10pm; Sun 10am-2pm. Cold food served all day. **Glass** €1.30-€4.50 **Bottle** €14-€30. **Credit** MC, V. **Map** N7.

Le Baron Bouge, next to the boisterous place d'Aligre market, may appear rather rough and ready, but the wines – including varied Loire selections, small châteaux from Bordeaux or Condrieu from the Rhône – are chosen with an eye for quality. There's a bit of bar food – charcuterie and some good goat's cheese – but few tables, so stand at one of the casks and try to act as insouciant as the habitués.

Belleville's hidden gem, **Le Baratin**.

Les Cailloux

58 rue des Cinq-Diamants, 13th (01.45.80.15.08). M° Corvisart or Place d'Italie. **Open** Tue-Sat 12.30-2.30pm, 7.30-11pm. Closed Aug, 25 Dec-3 Jan. **Glass** €2-€3. **Bottle** €17-€65. **Credit** AmEx, DC, MC, V.

Les Cailloux offers more than 40 wines, only six or so by the glass, and half the list is Italian, reflecting the first language of the staff and cooks. You can't really hang out by the bar, but expect a fine Italian meal with superb service and atmosphere. Mozzarella salad and grilled vegetables with gorgonzola, pastas such as linguine with crab or girolle mushrooms, and panna cotta, a wobbly baked cream, are some of the carefully prepared, satisfying dishes. With lights hanging over each table and plenty of distractions for the tastebuds, we could happily while away many a winter's evening here.

Caves Pétrissans ★

30bis av Niel, 17th (01.42.27.52.03). M° Ternes or Pereire. **Open** Mon-Fri 10am-10.30pm. Food served Mon-Fri noon-2.30pm, 8-10.30pm. **Glass** €4-€12. **Bottle** €16-€3,000. **Credit** AmEx, MC, V. **Non-smoking room. Map** C2.

A unique address, Caves Pétrissans is so authentically French as to be unmissable. A classic turn-of-the-20th-century wine-merchant-cum-restaurant, coyly shielded by dingy net curtains from the avenue Niel, it's split in three: the main dining room, slightly overlit but rich with cornicing, zinc bar and mosaic tiles; another smaller room which serves as the shop; and a tiny, booth-like corner room. Happily we were seated in the main room where we could best observe the bourgeois crowd of epicurean locals getting down to some serious eating and drinking. Tables are so tightly packed that conversation with the neighbours was inevitable, and enthusiastically taken up by the patronne. A three-course menu of robust classics was available at €31, but we chose à la carte. We shared a generous slab of foie gras to start, which permitted a rich oeuf en meurette to pass as a main. Steamed chicken with a creamy tarragon sauce came with perfect basmati rice. Weekly-changing wines by the glass were irreproachable: interesting Arbois chardonnay from Tissot; zingy Quincy 2001 from Jerôme de la Chaise; supple Côtes de Brouilly 2001 from Domaine Pavillon; nicely concentrated Bourgueil (Gauthier 2000). You can also choose from hundreds of bottles at shop price plus a hefty €16 corkage.

Le Petit Chavignol

78 rue de Tocqueville, 17th (01.42.27.95.97). M° Malesherbes or Villiers. **Open** Mon-Sat 8am-midnight/1am. Food served noon-3.30pm, 7-10.30pm. **Glass** €2.75-€7.50. **Bottle** €12-€91.50. **Credit** MC, V. **Map** E2.

There's a rustic feel to this popular little bistro with its copper bar and warm welcome from the woman behind it. We were soon chomping delicious saucisson sec from the Maison Conquet with a glass of rather banal Sancerre which had seemed the obvious apéritif in a bar of this name. It was all go: the bearded boss in his leather waistcoat was taking orders from a swelling crowd of locals, including a wonderful greying Jean-Paul Belmondo lookalike with a fluffy lapdog. The lure is simple: a good selection of artisanal charcuterie and hearty, generous hot dishes. We felt obliged to try the crottin de chavignol, which was suitably crumbly and served warm with salad. A hand-written wine list covering most regions included lesser-known small producers.

Le Baratin

3 rue Jouye-Rouve, 20th (01.43.49.39.70). M° Pyrénées or Belleville. **Open** Tue-Fri noon-2am; Sat 8pm-2am. Closed three weeks in Aug . Food served noon-2.30pm, 8pm-midnight. **Glass** €3-€5. **Bottle** €18-€100. **Wheelchair access. Credit** MC, V. **Map** N3.

A faint frostiness over the telephone quicky melted on arrival in this packed little bistro up in the farthest reaches of the 20th. We were offered little glasses of an unusual sweet Corsican wine from Antoine Arena as we waited at the bar for a table. The menu was a refreshing read. Mackerel and beetroot tartare was astonishingly good enhanced with a little lemongrass, while a generous hunk of cod was fresh, perfectly cooked and crowned with poached baby leeks. The wines are all from small artisan producers and prices stay under €30 or so. We drank famous Morgan Côtes de Py from Jean Foillard, reassuringly good at €26. Rammed with a lively bunch of thirtysomething locals and professional wine geeks, this is hardly the best-kept secret in the East, but it's well worth the hike.

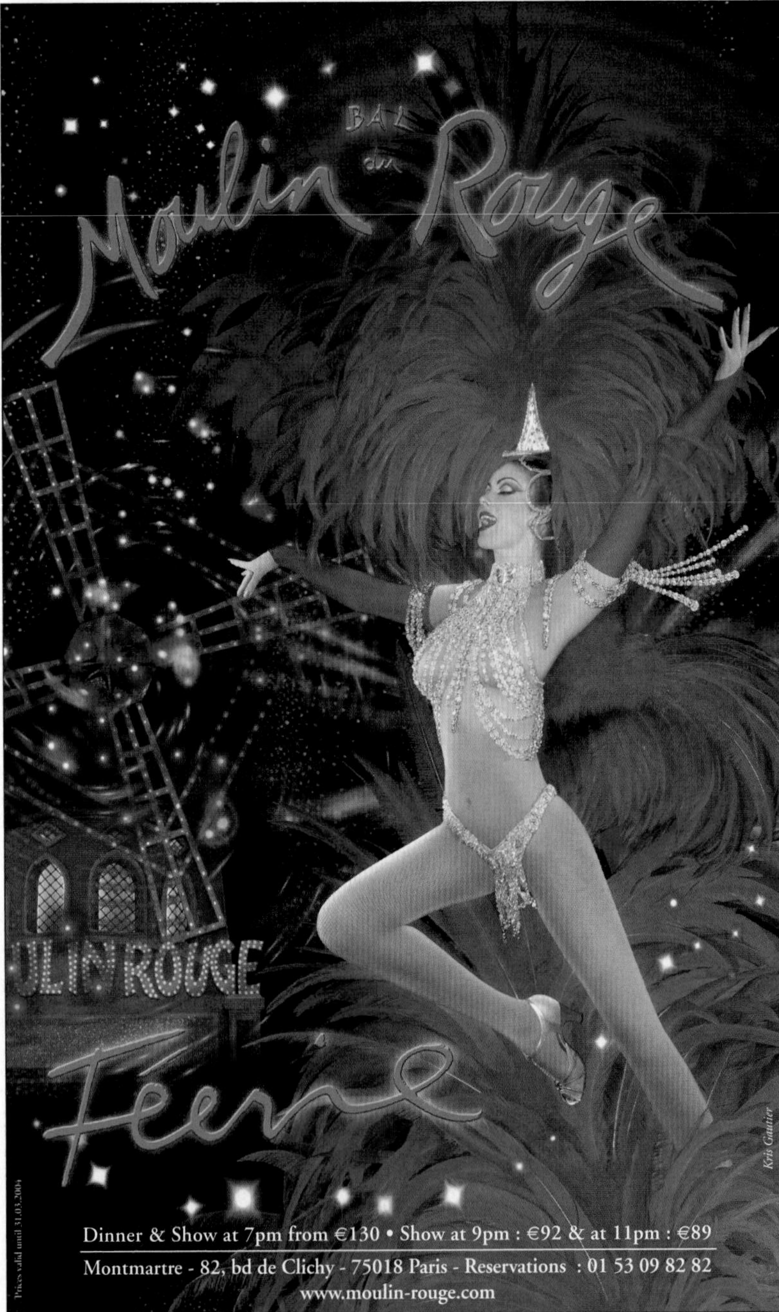

BAL du
Moulin Rouge
MOULIN ROUGE
Féerie
Kris Gautier
Prices valid until 31.03.2004
Dinner & Show at 7pm from €130 • Show at 9pm : €92 & at 11pm : €89
Montmartre - 82, bd de Clichy - 75018 Paris - Reservations : 01 53 09 82 82
www.moulin-rouge.com

Eating with Entertainment

After more than a rusty accordion or wilting roses to go with your meal? Seek out dinner cruises, cabaret, guinguettes and more.

Beyond this timeless selection, an increasing number of bars (*see p242*) also offer entertainment in unexpected forms.

Bawdy Songs

Aux Assassins

40 rue Jacob, 6th (no telephone). M° St-Germain-des-Prés. **Open** Mon-Sat 7pm-midnight. **Average** €30. **Prix fixe** €19.50. **No credit cards. Map** H6.

Maurice Dulac performs his smutty songs nightly at this antiquated restaurant. If you can't follow the lyrics then you'll have to make do with the dirty postcards lining the walls. Not a place to take the mother-in-law then, but a popular pre-nuptial hang-out as tablefuls of hen parties testify. The food is traditional French fare, and the wine list adequate.

Japanese jive at the **Troubador Coffee House.** *See p282.*

Boats

La Balle au Bond

(01.40.51.87.06/www.laballeaubond.fr). Oct-Mar: facing 55 quai de la Tournelle, 5th. M° Maubert-Mutualité. Apr-Sept: quai Malaquais, 6th. M° Pont-Neuf. **Bar** Mon-Sat 11am-2am; Sun 6-10pm. **Restaurant** May-October only. **Prix fixe** hot/cold buffets €38; dinner €49. **Concerts** 9pm. **Admission** €5-6. **Credit** AmEx, MC, V. **Map** K7.

From its prime mooring position, this concert-hall barge provides a good spot from which to soak up sunnier days on the Seine. Depending on when you visit, you will also be able to enjoy a range of concerts, plays and food. Ideal for a hot evening when you feel like sipping an exotic cocktail and watching the river go by.

Bateaux Parisiens

Port de La Bourdonnais, 7th (01.44.11.33.44/ meal reservations 01.44.11.33.55/ www.bateauxparisiens.com). M° Bir-Hakeim or RER Champ de Mars. **Departs** lunch cruise daily 12.15pm; dinner cruise daily 7.45pm. **Lunch** €49-€69. **Dinner** €90-€140. **Credit** DC, MC, V. **Map** C6.

A slick exercise in mass-market tourism, Bateaux Parisiens offer a range of lunch and dinner cruises along the banks of the Seine. Hurriedly delivered by panicky waiters, the food was abundant, overcooked and bland. Each table receives apéritifs and two bottles of wine; a sign that the cruise managers must have previously tried to sit through the onboard musical set while stone-cold sober. The boat ride itself is enjoyable enough, a relaxing option for those feeling too lazy to walk along the Seine.

Bateaux Mouches

Pont de L'Alma, rive droite, 8th (01.42.25.96.10/ recorded information 01.40.76.99.99/www.bateaux-mouches.fr). M° Alma-Marceau. **Departs** lunch cruise Tue-Sun 1pm; dinner cruise daily 8.30pm. **Lunch** €50. **Dinner** €85, €125. **Credit** AmEx, DC, MC, V. **Map** D5.

The best-known of the Seine's sightseeing cruises, the Bateaux Mouches have the formula down to a tee, doing a brisk trade in Japanese tourists and grey-suited businessmen. A well-drilled team of waiters works hard to make sure that the pace of the

A breath of French air...

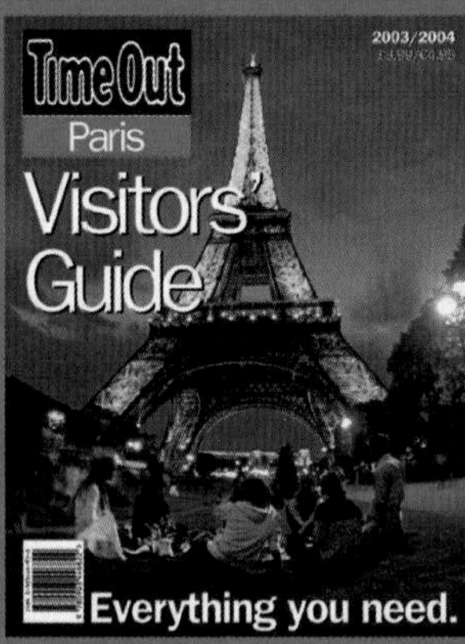

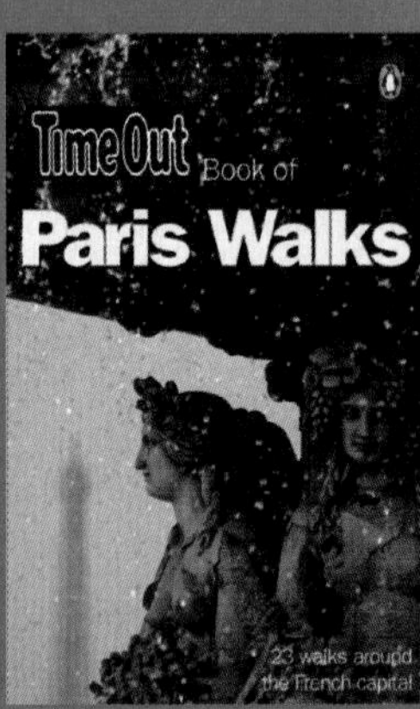

Available from all good bookshops and at www.timeout.com/shop

meal neither flags nor feels as if it's being rushed to keep up with the journey; the food maintains a reasonably high standard. At night, the boats' powerful searchlights illuminate the city's landmarks.

Cabaret & Jazz

Le Franc Pinot

1 quai de Bourbon, 4th (01.46.33.60.64). M° Pont Marie. **Open** Tues-Sat 7pm-midnight. Closed Aug. **Admission** €15 (free on Tuesdays). **Concerts** 9pm. **Prix fixe** €25. **Credit** MC,V. **Map** K7.
Housed in the medieval cellars of the Ile Saint-Louis this intimate jazz den serves up a warming mix of rhythm and food. Loved-up couples, old friends and jazz enthusiasts rub shoulders in the shadows of the exposed brick arches. The menu offers popular comfort food that can be enjoyed without taking too much attention away from the music (e.g. lobster bisque, steak and chips, chocolate cake and custard).

Un Piano dans la Cuisine

20 rue de la Verrerie, 4th (01.42.72.23.81). M° Hôtel de Ville. **Dinner and show daily** 8.30pm. **Prix fixe** €35 (Mon-Fri, Sun), €43 (Sat). **No credit cards. Map** K6.
Owner Serge Gilles greets guests at the door wearing sequins and his body weight in lipstick; later in the evening, he leads his troupe of middle-aged drag artists through a manic programme of chanson and cheese – Juliette Greco, Dalida, Mireille Mathieu, Barbra Streisand. Expect anything and be warned – the closer you sit to the stage, the greater your chances are of becoming a last-minute addition to the show. Food is passable, but clearly not the attraction. Small, packed and fun.

Le Lido

116bis av des Champs-Elysees, 8th (01.40.76.56.10/ www.lido.fr). M° Georges V. **Dinner** daily with show 8pm, 10pm, midnight. **Admission** with dinner €130, €145, €160; kids' menu (8pm show) €25; 10pm show €90. **Credit** AmEx, DC, MC, V. **Wheelchair access. Map** D4.
Operating since 1928, when it was known as La Plage de Paris, The Lido – renamed in 1946 after the Lido beach in Venice – still draws the tourists and the business revellers. Its galas have seen the likes of Elvis Presley, Sammy Davis Jr. and Richard Nixon. The current show is still (since 2000) C'est Magique: a series of hyper-choreographed stage numbers featuring ice-skating and flying beauties. Beware of ordering extortionately priced à la carte extras with the already pricey – and still disappointing – dinner menus crafted by Paul Bocuse.

La Nouvelle Eve

25 rue Fontaine, 9th (01.48.78.37.96). M° Blanche. **Dinner** daily 6.30pm, 10pm. **Show** 8pm, 10.15pm. Closed Nov-Apr. **Admission** with dinner €111; with Champagne €73. **Credit** AmEx, MC, V. **Map** H2.
Small fry compared to the big-name cabarets, La Nouvelle Eve offers a more intimate peek at

Le Franc Pinot: dinner, jazz, nice.

Pigalle traditions. With its flashy disco interior, you expect Travolta to strut his stuff at any moment. The garish, high-kick-littered show has audiences bellowing for more but the same cannot be said of the food: a chateaubriand steak, followed by ice cream fancies, was a feeble fanfare to the delights of the show that followed.

Restaurant le 8 ½

1 rue Maillard, 11th (01.44.64.11.92 /www.kiron-espace.com). M° Voltaire. **Lunch** Mon-Fri noon-3pm, **Dinner** Thur-Sat 7.30-11.30pm. Closed three weeks in Aug. **Show** alternate Fridays 8pm. **Admission** with dinner €32. **Prix fixe** €21-€24. **Lunch menu** €15-€24. **Credit** AmEx, MC, V. **Map** P6.
Named after Fellini's 1963 masterpiece, this unique restaurant serves tasty Italian cuisine in the basement of Kiron Espace's fully operational film studio. Every other Friday there is an After8 soirée – dinner accompanied by a variety of musical entertainment, often jazz or cabaret. From the €32 set menu we enjoyed a tasty vegetable gratin, cappelleti with pesto sauce and ribbons of parma ham, and a dessert of layered ricotta figs and maraschino-soaked biscuit. Both our wine – a well-rounded Valpolicella – and the live jazz were excellent. Book ahead.

Chez Michou

80 rue des Martyrs, 18th (01.46.06.16.04/ www.michou.fr). M° Pigalle. **Dinner** daily 8.30pm. **Show** 11pm. **Admission** with dinner €95; show and drink €31. **Credit** MC, V. **Map** H2.
Stylish traditional food (from duck breast to John Dory), lashings of Champagne and wall-to-wall mir-

rors combine to produce a mirthful Cage aux Folles atmosphere, where the false eyelashes have been defying gravity for over 40 years. Each night drag queens romp through a whirlwind of Charles Aznavour, Josephine Baker and Brigitte Bardot impersonations. Any initial disappointment that most of the songs are mimed will soon be tempered by the performers' infectious enthusiasm.

Moulin Rouge

82 bd de Clichy, 18th (01.53.09.82.82/ www.moulin-rouge.com). M° Blanche. **Dinner** daily 7pm. **Show** 9pm, 11pm. **Admission** with dinner €130-€160; show €92 (9pm), €82 (11pm). **Credit** AmEx, DC, MC, V. **Wheelchair access. Map** G2.

With new publicity courtesy of Nicole Kidman, you'll find more of her fans among the coach-loads of tourists than people interested in Toulouse-Lautrec's inspiration or Edith Piaf's concerts. Every year the Moulin Rouge boasts about a 'new show', but it's usually the same basic idea – prancing, flawless bods – with a little twist (they alter the 1000-plus costumes or chuck a few of the Doriss girls into a giant aquarium, etc.). With the dinner option you can expect to munch on posh nosh such as foie gras, veal and caviar.

Les Trois Châpeaux

48 rue des Cascades, 20th (01.46.36.90.06). M° Jourdain or Pyrénées. **Open** Tue-Sun 7pm-2am. **Average** €12. **Credit** AmEx, DC, MC, V. **Map** P4.

A real neighbourhood favourite, this laid-back Algerian restaurant doubles as a bar and music venue. There is no way of knowing what the entertainment's going to be – Afro-funk, Polish folk music or flamenco – but you can count on getting some of the best tagines in Paris. Especially good is the quail with figs and chestnuts one that comes sizzling in thick, sweet sauce. Portions are enormous – you will be discouraged from ordering the delicious, flaky brik starters by the waitresses. We've never got as far as even finding out if there are desserts because by that time we have been either dragged up to join the sweaty dancing throng by a Ukrainian who says he comes from 'heaven', or found ourselves deep in conversation with a gambling priest from Serbia.

Troubador Coffee House

70 bd de Ménilmontant, 20th (01.47.97.21.08). M° Père Lachaise. **Open** Tue-Fri noon-11pm, Sat-Sun 10.30am-11pm. Food served daily noon-3pm, 5-11pm. **Average** €25. **Lunch menu** €19. **Credit** MC, V. **Map** P5.

This moody 'medieval' café has big windows facing the tree-lined boulevard and tables outside to catch the sun. Gregorian chanting, wrought-iron chairs, chiseled antiques, antique books and dangling musical instruments fill up the cramped space, which doubles as a performance venue for everything from traditional Japanese dance to string quartets to poetry readings. Though the owner is eager to please and over-confident about how delicious you'll find his pricey dishes (such as tagliatelli with salmon and dill or a lamb and spinach sauté), you can't fault his dedication and enthusiasm. Brunch on weekends.

Guinguette & Dancing

Les Etoiles

61 rue du Château d'Eau, 10th (01.47.70.60.56). M° Château d'Eau. **Open** Thur 9pm-3.30am; Fri-Sat 9pm-4.30am. Closed Aug. **Admission** with dinner €18.30 (9pm); with drink from 11pm €10. **Drinks** €3-€6. **Credit** V. **Map** K4.

Up-for-it 30-somethings frequent this tatty music hall which holds friendly salsa nights with infectious Latino bands. Canteen-like tables encourage mingling, while a spicy Latin-American menu ensures that even those who aren't dancing get hot under the collar.

Chez Raymonde

119 av Parmentier, 11th (01.43.55.26.27). M° Parmentier or Goncourt. **Open** Tue-Fri 7pm-1am; Sat 8pm-1am. **Average** €22. **Prix fixe** €19 (Tue-Fri), €38 (Sat). **Credit** AmEx, DC, MC, V. **Map** M4.

Beware, ladies: the chef may ask you to tango (though only on Saturdays). Halfway through the dîner-dansant meal here – solidly French and scrumptious – the lights dim to rosy reds, the host sprinkles magic dust on the tiny dance floor, introduces a piano/accordion duo and invites the chef out of the kitchen and into his arms to inaugurate an evening of waltz, swing and other fancy steps. The meal is satisfying enough on its own; add in the dance, and the soirée delivers pure enchantment.

Chez Gégène

162bis quai de Polangis, allée des Guinguettes, 94345 Joinville-le-Pont (01.48.83.29.43/ www.chez-gegene.fr). RER Joinville-le-Pont. **Open** Tue-Sun noon-2.30pm, 7-10.30pm. Closed Jan-Mar. **Average** €25. **Admission** with dinner €38 (Fri, Sat); with drink €13.72, €15.24 (Fri, Sat); Sun lunch €45. **Credit** MC, V. **Wheelchair access.**

Typically French and thoroughly un-Parisian, Chez Gégène attracts dance addicts, grannies and urban hipsters. The band (Friday, Saturday nights, Sunday afternoons) sprinkles tangos, foxtrots and musette with disco hits, so those less sure of foot don't feel left out. Between dances, feast on steaks, moules-frites and wine.

Le Guinguette de l'Ile du Martin-Pêcheur

41 quai Victor-Hugo, 94500 Champigny-sur-Marne (01.49.83.03.02/www.guinguette.fr). RER Champigny-sur-Marne. **Open** *Apr-Sept* Thur-Sat 8pm-2am; Sun noon-7pm. *Oct-Nov* Sat 8pm-2am.. Closed Dec-March. **Average** €28. **Prix fixe** €24, €28. **Credit** V. **Wheelchair access.**

The Martin-Pêcheur (kingfisher), built on an island which is reached by raft, dates from the 1980s – but the bunting, gingham cloths, red plonk and gently lapping water are more real than real. Food is mildly inventive: red mullet with cinnamon butter, chicken breast with crayfish coulis.

Gay & Lesbian

Tout est fruity on the Paris gay scene, from bistros where the servers are as tasty as the nosh to bars where the cocktails are distinctly heady.

We've heard it said that gay Paris is getting old, packing up its platforms in favour of civilised dining-out. Nonsense! The restaurant scene is lively, cruisy bars and pumping clubs show no sign of letting up, and lesbian staff are the accessory that every bar-club now wants. The Marais is the gay heartland but there are rainbow pockets throughout the city.

Gay bars & cafés

Banana Café

13 rue de la Ferronnerie, 1st (01.42.33.35.31). M° Châtelet. **Open** daily 6pm-dawn. **Credit** AmEx, MC, V. **Wheelchair access. Map** J5.
Does the name give it away? Those who just have to sing can mangle show tunes in the cellar bar.

Don't bottle it up – let it all hang out at **Le Central.**

Le Tropic Café

66 rue des Lombards, 1st (01.40.13.92.62). M° Châtelet. **Open** daily noon-dawn. **Credit** AmEx, MC, V. **Wheelchair access. Map** G6.
This bright, upbeat bar hosts groovy bashes that draw a loyal band of party poppers.

Le Duplex

25 rue Michel-le-Comte, 3rd (01.42.72.80.86). M° Rambuteau. **Open** daily 8pm-2am. **Credit** MC, V. **Map** K5.
Smoky and atmospheric it may look, but it scores a conservative 11 on a one-to-ten cruisieness scale.

Amnesia

42 rue Vieille-du-Temple, 4th (01.42.72.16.94). M° Hôtel de Ville. **Open** daily 10am-2am. **Credit** DC, MC, V. **Map** K6.
A warm meeting place with friendly staff. It's not all about pulling here, but social intercourse instead.

Le Central

33 rue Vieille-du-Temple, 4th (01.48.87.99.33). M° Hôtel de Ville. **Open** Mon-Fri 4pm-2am; Sat, Sun 2pm-2am. **Credit** MC, V. **Map** K6.
One of the city's oldest gay hangouts, Le Central still passes muster against its sprightly neighbours.

Coffee Shop

3 rue Ste-Croix-de-la-Bretonnerie, 4th (01.42.74.24.21). M° Hôtel de Ville. **Open** daily 10am-2am. **No credit cards. Map** K6.
A laid-back café great for frothy coffee and gossip.

Le Cox

15 rue des Archives, 4th (01.42.72.08.00). M° Hôtel de Ville. **Open** daily 1pm-2am. **No credit cards. Map** K6.
With not an oarsman in sight, evenings here are a glitterball of promises often fulfilled.

Open Café

17 rue des Archives, 4th (01.42.72.26.18). M° Hôtel de Ville. **Open** Mon-Thur, Sun 11am-2am; Fri, Sat 11am-4am. **Credit** MC, V. **Map** K6.
An HQ for boys meeting up before heading off into the night. The management also runs the Open Bar Coffee Shop at 12 rue du Temple.

Le Thermik

7 rue de la Verrerie, 4th (01.44.78.08.18). M° Hôtel de Ville. **Open** daily 7pm-2am. **No credit cards. Map** K6.
This is a friendly, intimate place for those whose eardrums need a break from crowded cruising bars.

Gay restaurants

L'Amazonial

3 rue Ste-Opportune, 1st (01.42.33.53.13). M° Châtelet. **Open** Mon-Fri noon-3pm, 7pm-1am; Sat, Sun noon-5pm, 7pm-1am. **Average** €26. **Prix fixe** €14, €25. **Lunch menu** €11, €15 (Mon-Fri). **Credit** AmEx, DC, MC, V. **Wheelchair access. Map** K6.
Paris' largest gay restaurant features decent French cuisine and tight T-shirted waiters.

Aux Trois Petits Cochons

31 rue Tiquetonne, 2nd (01.42.33.39.69/ www.auxtroispetitscochons.com). M° Etienne-Marcel. **Open** daily 8.30pm-1am. Closed Aug, one week in Mar. **Average** €27. **Prix fixe** €23, €27. **Credit** AmEx, MC, V. **Wheelchair access. Map** J5.
Three Little Pigs eschews international boystown cuisine in favour of a tasty, daily-changing menu.

Le X Saint Merri

10 rue St-Merri, 4th (01.42.74.62.62). M° Hôtel de Ville. **Open** daily noon-3pm, 7.30-11.30pm. **Average** €25. **Prix fixe** €19.90. **Lunch menu** €13.50. **Credit** MC, V. **Map** K6.
The 6m-long mirrored mosaic bar leaves a lot to live up to, but the market-led menu is good value. The name's pronounced 'dix' – as naughtily as you like.

Maison Rouge

13 rue des Archives, 4th (01.42.71.69.69). M° Hôtel de Ville. **Open** daily noon-midnight. Food served noon-4pm, 8pm-midnight. **Average** €35. **Lunch menu** €20. **Credit** MC, V. **Map** K6.
This new Marais restaurant has been an instant hit with a fashiony crowd all dressed in black. Low-carb cuisine features tuna steaks, juicy entrecôtes and lots of balsamic vinegar. The basement lounge is the perfect setting for a raucous boys' or girls' night out.

Gay clubs & discos

Club 18

18 rue de Beaujolais, 1st (01.42.97.52.13). M° Palais Royal. **Open** Thur-Sat 11pm-dawn; Sun 5pm-dawn. **Admission** Thur, Sun free; Fri, Sat €11. **Credit** AmEx, MC, V. **Map** H5.
Classic discovations fill the dance floor.

L'Insolite

33 rue des Petits-Champs, 2nd (01.40.20.98.59). M° Pyramides. **Open** daily 11pm-5am. **Admission** Mon-Thur, Sun free; Fri, Sat €7.70. **Credit** MC, V. **Map** H4.
Bright and brassy with a distinctly disco vibe, this place pumps out dance classics.

Le Dépôt

10 rue aux Ours, 3rd (01.44.54.96.96). M° Rambuteau. **Open** daily noon-7am. **Admission** Mon-Thur, Sun €10; Fri, Sat €12. **Credit** MC, V. **Map** K5.
Amid the jungle netting decor, Sunday's Gay Tea Dance is not as restrained as its name suggests.

Le Tango

13 rue au Maire, 3rd (01.42.72.17.78). M° Arts et Métiers. **Open** Thur 8pm-2am; Fri, Sat 10.30pm-5am; Sun 6.30pm-2am. **Admission** Thur (with concert) €9, €5 after 10.30pm; Fri, Sat €6.50. **No credit cards. Map** K5.
Le Tango has returned to its roots with mixed dancing à deux and accordion concerts on Thursdays.

Folies Pigalle

11 pl Pigalle, 9th (01.48.78.25.26). M° Pigalle. **Open** Tue-Sat midnight-dawn; Sun 6am-noon, 6pm-midnight. **Admission** Tue-Sat €20; Sun (after) €17, (BBB) €7. **Credit** V. **Map** G2.
Come here for Paris' most popular gay tea dance, the Black Blanc Beur (BBB) (6pm-midnight Sun), and spectacular after-parties.

Red Light

34 rue du Départ, 14th (01.42.79.94.94). M° Montparnasse. **Open** Thur-Sun 11pm-6am. **Admission** €20. **Credit** AmEx, DC, MC, V. **Map** F9.
This huge club has become a must on the gay scene. Saturday house nights attract a crowd.

Lesbian bars & restaurants

Bliss Kfé

30 rue du Roi-de-Sicile, 4th (01.42.78.49.36/ www.bliss-kfe.com). M° St-Paul. **Open** daily 5pm-2am. **Credit** AmEx, MC, V. **Map** K6.
The shell of a former boulangerie houses a stylish bar, with intimate lighting and a trendy crowd.

Le Petit Picard

42 rue Ste-Croix-de-la-Bretonnerie, 4th (01.42.78.54.03). M° Hôtel de Ville. **Open** Tue-Sun noon-2pm, 7.30pm-11pm. **Credit** MC, V. **Map** K6.
This good-value bistro is always packed. A friendly atmosphere with plenty of inter-table chatter.

Au Feu Follet

5 rue Raymond-Losserand, 14th (01.43.22.65.72). M° Pernety. **Open** Mon-Sat noon-2pm, 7.30pm-11pm. **Credit** MC, V. **Map** E10.
This restaurant serves cuisine from the south-west of France. The crowd is mixed but mainly lesbian.

Lesbian clubs

Pulp

25 bd Poissonnière, 2nd (01.40.26.01.93). M° Bonne Nouvelle. **Open** Thur-Sat 11pm-dawn. **Admission** Thur free; Fri-Sat €7.50 with drink. **Credit** AmEx, MC, V. **Map** J4.
Thursday nights are the most mixed at this lesbian-centric club. The crowd is young and frisky.

Le Rive Gauche

1 rue du Sabot, 6th (01.42.22.51.70). M° St-Germain-des-Prés. **Open** Fri,-Sat 11pm-dawn. **Admission** €14 with drink. **Credit** MC, V. **Map** H7.
The women-only Rive Gauche attracts a crowd of all ages and styles with its fun, party atmosphere.

Clubs

Tango or trance, hip hop or house, salsa or chanson – whatever your (evening) suit, Paris clubs come up trumps. Just don't get there too early.

Paris does Latin well (**Les Etoiles**) while the **Rex Club** and **WAGG** pride themselves on quality DJs. Credit cards are usually accepted at the bar but not at the door, and while trainers are OK for dance clubs, slip on shoes for salsa or upmarket venues. For more of a bar-club atmosphere try Man Ray (*see p108*), the Mezzanine at Alcazar (*see p94*) and Café Chéri(e) (*see p264*).

Cool clubs

Rex Club

5 bd Poissonnière, 2nd (01.42.36.28.83). M° Bonne-Nouvelle. **Open** Wed-Sat 11pm-dawn. **Admission** Wed €10; Thur-Fri €11; Sat €12. **Drinks** €5-€8. **Credit** AmEx, MC, V. **Map** J4.

The Rex prides itself on its quality, up-to-date DJs. Arrive early when big names play. Friday's Automatik is one of Paris' few authentic techno nights.

WAGG

62 rue Mazarine, 6th (01.55.42.22.00). M° Odéon. **Open** Wed-Sun 11pm-5am. **Admission** €5-€12. **Drinks** €9-€15. **Credit** AmEx, DC, MC, V. **Map** H7.

The Terence Conran/Fabric partnership has created a London-style club, with imported staff and DJs spinning UK house. Personality-'physionomist' Valéry B and a flow of local DJs add Gallic flavour.

Le Queen

102 av des Champs-Elysées, 8th (01.53.89.08.90). M° George V. **Open** daily midnight-dawn. **Admission** Sun-Thur €9 with drink; Fri-Sat €18 with drink. **Drinks** from €9. **Credit** AmEx, DC, MC, V. **Map** D4.

Wednesday night's Break is open to all, Saturday is especially gay and Friday is the night for big names. Mondays, Thursdays and Sundays it's kitsch disco.

Bus Palladium

6 rue Fontaine, 9th (01.53.21.07.33). M° Pigalle. **Open** Tue-Sat 11.30pm-dawn. **Admission** €20 with drink; Tue women free. **Drinks** €10. **Credit** AmEx, MC, V. **Wheelchair access. Map** H2.

This venerable bourgeois haunt now has a house music policy. Wednesday night is run by the Respect team, recalling the glory days of French Touch.

Le Gibus

18 rue du Fbg-du-Temple, 11th (01.47.00.78.88/ www.gibus.fr). M° République. **Open** Wed-Sat midnight-dawn. **Admission** free-€18. **Drinks** €9-€11. **Credit** AmEx, DC, MC, V. **Map** L4.

Still Paris' major venue for trance on Wednesdays and Fridays, Le Gibus has widened its net. Tuesdays and Thursdays have faster hardcore BPMs and Saturday soirées feature house and disco.

Nouveau Casino

109 rue Oberkampf, 11th (01.43.57.57.40/ www.nouveaucasino.net). M° Parmentier or St-Maur. **Open** Wed, Sun 7.30pm-midnight; Thur-Sat 7.30pm-6am (depending on concert). **Admission** €8-€14. **Drinks** €3.50-€7. **Credit** AmEx, MC, V. **Wheelchair access. Map** N5.

While the space-age decor is a little cold and the early closing a tad restrictive in this club at the back of the historic Café Charbon, the eclectic policy of live music and DJs makes it a place to watch.

Batofar

in front of 11 quai François-Mauriac, 13th (01.56.29.10.33/www.batofar.net). M° Bibliothèque or Quai de la Gare. **Open** Mon 9pm-midnight; Tue-Sat 9/10pm-midnight/6am depending on programme; two Suns per month 6am-3pm. **Admission** €7-€12. **Drinks** €3-€8. **Credit** MC, V. **Map** N10.

The new team on the lighthouse boat has put on a full and eclectic programme ranging from jazz (Mondays) though electronic music, techno, drum'n'bass and Latin. Concerts are followed by quality DJs.

Le Divan du Monde

75 rue des Martyrs, 18th (01.55.79.09.52). M° Pigalle. **Open** concerts daily 7.30-10.30pm. Club Thur-Sat 11.30pm-dawn. **Admission** €10-€15. **Drinks** €4-€8. **Credit** MC, V. **Map** H2.

Le Divan sees an eclectic mix of alternative club nights at weekends, plus regular jungle, raï, ragga, R'n'B, Brazilian and trance gigs. No strict dress code.

Elysée Montmartre

72 bd Rochechouart, 18th (01.44.92.45.36/ www.elyseemontmartre.com). M° Anvers. **Open** varies. Closed Aug. **Admission** €15-€30. **Drinks** €2.50-€9. **Credit** MC, V. **Map** J2.

This fine concert venue has a sprung dancefloor and a quality sound system. Regular nights include Scream, Club Europa and Panik. Every second and fourth Saturday in the month is the popular Le Bal.

La Loco

90 bd de Clichy, 18th (01.53.41.88.88/ www.laloco.com). M° Place de Clichy. **Open** Tue-Sun 11pm-5am. **Admission** €10-€16. **Drinks** €8-€16. **Credit** AmEx, MC, V. **Map** G2.

'La Loco' has turned into a mecca of pumping house with Radio FG's Club FG every Friday. Weekdays see gothic and metal concerts and R'n'B nights.

Posh & posey

Les Bains

7 rue du Bourg-l'Abbé, 3rd (01.48.87.01.80/ www.lesbains-club.com). M° Etienne-Marcel. **Open** Tue-Sun 11.30pm-5am. Restaurant 8.30pm-1am. **Admission** €20 with drink. **Drinks** €14. **Credit** AmEx, DC, MC, V. **Map** J5.

The concentration of beautiful people here is an eye opener but the door policy is draconian. Look for hip hop stars at 'Be-Fly' (Wed).

Club Castel

15 rue Princesse, 6th (01.40.51.52.80). M° Mabillon. **Open** Tue-Sat 9pm-dawn. **Admission** free (members and guests only). **Drinks** €16. **Credit** AmEx, DC, MC, V. **Map** H7.

The nearest Paris gets to St-Tropez. The strict door policy – members and friends only – ensures an elite clientele. Pretend you've just arrived from Cannes.

Duplex

2bis av Foch, 16th (01.45.00.45.00/ www.duplex.com). M° Charles de Gaulle-Etoile. **Open** Tue-Sun 11pm-dawn. **Admission** Tue-Thur, Sun €15 (girls free before midnight); Fri, Sat €19-€24 with drink (two with €24 admission). **Drinks** €10. **Credit** MC, V. **Wheelchair access**. **Map** C3.

The Duplex caters for young wannabes and privileged youths. The sultry upstairs restaurant turns chill-out room later on.

All hands on deck at the **Batofar**. *See p285.*

Latino, jazz & world

Caveau de la Huchette

5 rue de la Huchette, 5th (01.43.26.65.05/ www.caveaudelahuchette.fr). M° St-Michel. **Open** Mon-Thur, Sun 9.30pm-2.30am; Fri, Sat 9.30pm-3.30am. **Admission** Mon-Thur, Sun €10.50; €9 students; Fri, Sat €13. **Drinks** €4.50-€8.50. **Credit** MC, V. **Wheelchair Access**. **Map** J7

Enduringly popular with ageing divorcees and wannabe Stones during the week, the Caveau is best at weekends for boogying to live rock 'n' roll or jazz.

Les Etoiles

61 rue du Château d'Eau, 10th (01.47.70.60.56). M° Château d'Eau. **Open** Thur 9pm-3.30am; Fri, Sat 9pm-4.30am. Closed Aug. **Admission** €20 with meal; €11 with drink from 11pm. **Drinks** €3-€6. **Credit** MC,V. **Map** K3

Top-notch Latin musicians electrify a soulful crowd here. Women aren't likely to be left standing for more than a second.

La Java

105 rue du Fbg-du-Temple, 10th (01.42.02.20.52). M° Belleville. **Open** Thur-Sat 11pm-6am; Sun 2-7pm. **Admission** Thur €10; Fri, Sat €16; Sun €5 with drink. **Drinks** €5.50-€8. **Credit** AmEx, DC, MC, V. **Wheelchair access**. **Map** L4.

DJs and live bands play anything Latino and tropical to a fun-loving crowd. Unfortunately, serious Latin dancers are few and far between, while sweaty gropers are plentiful.

Le Balajo

9 rue de Lappe, 11th (01.47.00.07.87). M° Bastille. **Open** Tue-Thur 10.30pm-4.30am; Fri, Sat 11.30pm-5am; Sun 3-7pm. **Admission** Tue-Thur €16 with drink; Fri, Sat €17 with drink; Sun afternoon €8 with drink. **Drinks** €8. **Credit** MC, V. **Map** M7.

Wednesday's boogie and swing session attracts some colourful customers, some of whom are surprisingly young.

Cithéa

112 rue Oberkampf, 11th (01.40.21.70.95/ www.cithea.com). M° Parmentier. **Open** Tue-Sat 10pm-5.30am. **Admission** Tue, Wed, Thur free; Fri, Sat €4. **Drinks** €6-€10. **Credit** MC, V. **Wheelchair access**. **Map** N5.

The Cithéa is a prime concert venue for world music and jazz. At weekends, however, disco and funk nights pull everyone in at closing time – the result is a sweaty and (perhaps overly) friendly mêlée.

L'Atlantis

32 quai d'Austerlitz, 13th (01.44.23.24.00/ www.atlantis-club.com). M° Quai de la Gare. **Open** Fri-Sun, eve of public holidays 11pm-dawn. **Admission** €17 with drink. **Drinks** €11. **Credit** MC, V. **Wheelchair access**. **Map** M9.

At this French Caribbean club, the women wear painted-on dresses, the men wear suits and the dancing is always close contact.

Shops & Markets

Treat your senses to some culinary retail therapy. Discover palaces of chocolate and vanilla or temples to truffles and baguettes.

Forget generic supermarkets; Parisians still search out speciality shops and local markets for that certain something: orange-scented brioche, dreamy, creamy cheeses, fragant olive oils, plump hens and 100-year-old Armagnac.

Bakeries

Poilâne

8 rue du Cherche-Midi, 6th (01.45.48.42.59/ www.poilane.com). M° Sèvres Babylone or St-Sulpice. **Open** Mon-Sat 7.15am-8.15pm. **No credit cards. Map** F8.

The charismatic Lionel is no more after a helicopter crash in November 2002, but the Poîlane name lives on. Nowhere will you find a fresher version of his famous, dark-crusted miche than at this tiny, old-fashioned shop, where bakers toil around the clock before a wood-burning oven. The buttery apple tarts almost better the bread.

Branch: 49 bd de Grenelle, 15th (01.45.79.11.49).

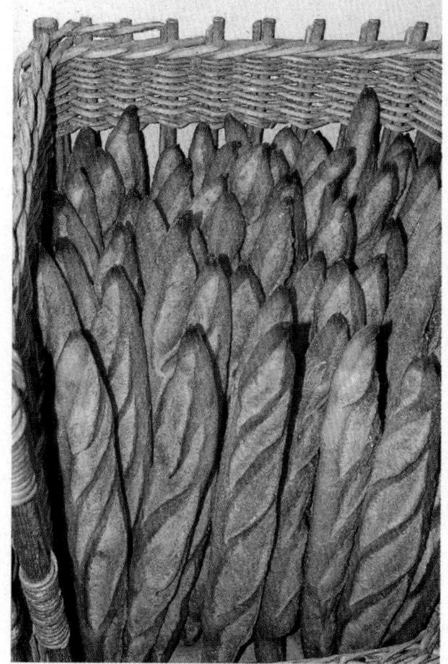

Bread-sitting room.

Moisan

5 pl d'Aligre, 12th (01.43.45.46.60). M° Ledru-Rollin. **Open** Tue-Sat 7am-1.30pm, 3-8pm; Sun 7am-2pm. **No credit cards. Map** N7.

An organic baking pioneer, Michel Moisan lovingly turns out crunchy boules de levain, fragrant petits pains, gorgeous orange-scented brioches and flaky apple tarts.

Branch: 4 av du Général Leclerc, 14th (01.43.22.34.13).

Max Poilâne

87 rue Brancion, 15th (01.48.28.45.90/ www.max-poilane.fr). M° Porte de Vanves. **Open** Tue-Sat 7.30am-8pm; Sun 10am-7pm. **No credit cards. Map** D10.

Using the venerable Poilâne family recipe, the lesser-known Max produces bread that easily rivals that of his more famous brother, the late Lionel.

Branches: 29 rue de l'Ouest, 14th (01.43.27.24.91); 42 pl du Marché-St-Honoré, 1st (01.42.61.10.53).

Moulin de la Vierge

166 av de Suffren, 15th (01.47.83.45.55). M° Sèvres-Lecourbe. **Open** Mon-Sat 7am-8pm. **No credit cards. Map** C6.

Basile Kamir learned breadmaking after falling in love with an old abandoned bakery. His naturally leavened country loaf is dense and fragrant.

Branches include: 82 rue Daguerre, 14th (01.43.22.50.55); 105 rue Vercingétorix, 14th (01.45.43.09.84); 77 rue Cambronne, 15th (01.44.49.05.05); 15 rue Violet, 15th (01.45.75.85.85).

Boulangerie au 140

140 rue de Belleville, 20th (01.46.36.92.47/ www.au140.com). M° Jourdain. **Open** Wed-Sat 7.30am-8pm; Sun 7.30am-1.30pm, 4-8pm. **Credit** MC, V. **Map** P3.

A great baguette is an all-too-rare thing in Paris – so head up the hill to this bakery, where Pierre Demoncy handles levain (natural yeast) with an artist's touch that has earned him the city's 'best baguette' award and made him the supplier to the Elysées Palace.

Pâtisseries

Finkelsztajn

27 rue des Rosiers, 4th (01.42.72.78.91). M° St-Paul. **Open** Mon 11am-7pm; Wed-Sun 10am-7pm. Closed Aug. **No credit cards. Map** L6.

Filled with poppy seeds, apples or cream cheese, the dense Jewish cakes in this motherly shop pad the bones for the Parisian winter.

BRÛLERIE DES GOBELINS

Our coffee is roasted daily on the premises. Choose coffee from 14 different pure origins or one of our wide range of delicious blends.

We aslo have a rotating selection of quality fresh teas. Many authentic jams from the Savoie and natural honeys as well as delicious treats to accompany your coffee.

2 avenue des Gobelins, 5th.
M° Censier-Daubenton
Tel: 01.43.31.90.13 • Fax: 01.45.35.83.00

La Maison du Miel

founded in 1898

40 flavours of honey from different regions and plants, and a wide range of honey-related and hive produce on offer

Taste before you buy...

Open Mon-Sat, from 10am-7pm

24 RUE VIGNON, 9TH.
Mº MADELEINE, HAVRE-CAUMARTIN
RER AUBER.
Tel & Fax: 01.47.42.26.70
www.maisondumiel.com
email: maisondumiel@wanadoo.fr

Gastronomy is a feast

Spices, herbs, vanillas, teas, coffees, truffles, edible oils, vinaigres and mustards, wines & alcohols, cooking tools, cooking books, all kinds of quality professional products from Jm Thiercelin, since 1809, to cook, to entertain, to offer...

GOUMANYAT
& SON ROYAUME

New shop in the Haut Marais of Paris • Open Mon-Sat 2pm-7pm
3 rue Dupuis, 3rd • Mº Temple, République • Tel: 33 (0)1.44.78.96.74 • Fax: 33 (0)1.44.78.96.75
contact@goumanyat.com • www.goumanyat.com

Gérard Mulot

76 rue de Seine, 6th (01.43.26.85.77/www.gerard-mulot.com). M° Odéon. **Open** Tue, Thur-Sun 6.45am-8pm. Closed Aug. **No credit cards. Map** H7.
Picture-perfect cakes – bitter chocolate tart and the mabillon, caramel mousse with apricot marmalade – attract local celebrities.

Pierre Hermé

72 rue Bonaparte, 6th (01.53.67.66.65). M° St-Sulpice. **Open** Tue-Sun 10am-7pm. Closed Aug. **Credit** AmEx, DC, MC, V. **Map** G7.
Pastry superstar Pierre Hermé attracts the crème de la crème of St-Germain; the sumptuous '2000 feuilles' and carrément chocolaté, the ultimate chocolate cake, are among the reasons.

Sadaharu Aoki

35 rue de Vaugirard, 6th (01.45.44.48.90/ www.interq.or.jp/gold/sada/). M° St-Placide. **Open** Tue-Sun 11am-1.30pm, 2.30-7pm. **Credit** DC, MC, V. **Map** G8.
This discreet Japanese pastry chef, who opened his minimalist boutique in 2001, has achieved perfection with his green tea éclairs and the astounding vanilla and chocolate millefeuille.

Peltier

66 rue de Sèvres, 7th (01.47.34.06.62). M° Duroc or Vaneau. **Open** Mon-Sat 9am-7.30pm; Sun 9am-6.30pm. **Credit** AmEx, MC, V. **Map** F7.
Philippe Conticini was hired in 2002 to whisk this historic pastry shop into the 21st century. Alongside conventional cakes are sultry mousses filled with pear chutney or dried-apricot jam.
Branch: 6 rue St Dominique, 7th (01.47.05.50.02).

Cheese

Marie-Anne Cantin

12 rue du Champ-de-Mars, 7th (01.45.50.43.94/ www.cantin.fr). M° Ecole Militaire. **Open** Mon-Sat 8.30am-7.30pm. **Credit** MC, V. **Map** D6.
Cantin, a vigorous defender of unpasteurised cheese, is justifiably proud of her dreamily creamy st-marcellins, aged chèvres and nutty beauforts. The cheeses are ripened in her cellars.

Alain Dubois

80 rue de Tocqueville, 17th (01.42.27.11.38). M° Malesherbes or Villiers. **Open** Tue-Fri 9am-1pm, 4-8pm; Sat 8.30am-7.30pm; Sun 9am-1pm. Closed first three weeks in Aug. **Credit** MC, V. **Map** E2.
Dubois, who stocks some 70 varieties of goat's cheese plus prized, aged st-marcellin and st-félicien, is a darling of the superchefs.

Alléosse

13 rue Poncelet, 17th (01.46.22.50.45). M° Ternes. **Open** Tue-Thur 9am-1pm, 4-7pm; Fri, Sat 9am-1pm, 3.30-7pm; Sun 9am-1pm. **Credit** MC, V. **Map** C2.
People cross town for these cheeses – wonderful farmhouse camemberts, delicate st-marcellins, a choice of chèvres and several rarities.

Chocolate

Christian Constant

37 rue d'Assas, 6th (01.53.63.15.15). M° St-Placide. **Open** Mon-Fri 8.30am-9pm; Sat 8am-8.30pm; Sun 8.30am-7pm. **Credit** MC, V. **Map** G8.
A true master chocolate maker and traiteur, Constant is revered by le tout Paris. Trained in the arts of pâtisserie and chocolate, he scours the globe for new and delectable ideas. Ganaches are subtly flavoured with verbena, jasmine or cardamom.

Jean-Paul Hévin

3 rue Vavin, 6th (01.43.54.09.85). M° Vavin. **Open** Mon-Sat 10am-7.30pm. Closed three weeks in Aug. **Credit** MC, V. **Map** G8.
Chocolatier Jean-Paul Hévin dares to fill his chocolates with potent cheeses, to be served with wine as an apéritif. Even more risqué are his aphrodisiac chocolates.
Branches: 231 rue St-Honoré, 1st (01.55.35.35.96); 16 and 23bis av de La Motte-Picquet, 7th (01.45.51.77.48).

Debauve & Gallais

30 rue des Saints-Pères, 7th (01.45.48.54.67/ www.debauve-et-gallais.com). M° St-Germain-des-Prés. **Open** Mon-Sat 9am-7pm. **Credit** DC, MC, V. **Map** G7.
This former pharmacy, with a facade dating from 1800, once sold chocolate for medicinal purposes. Its intense chocolates filled with tea, honey or praline do, indeed, heal the soul.
Branch: 33 rue Vivienne, 2nd (01.40.39.05.50).

Richart

258 bd St-Germain, 7th (01.45.55.66.00/ www.richart.com). M° Solférino. **Open** Mon-Sat 10am-7pm. **Credit** AmEx, MC, V. **Map** F6.
Each chocolate ganache has an intricate design, packages look like jewel boxes and every purchase comes with a tract on how best to savour chocolate.

La Maison du Chocolat

89 av Raymond-Poincaré, 16th (01.40.67.77.83/ www.lamaisonduchocolat.com). M° Victor-Hugo. **Open** Mon-Sat 10am-7pm. **Credit** AmEx, MC, V. **Map** B4.
Robert Linxe opened his first Paris shop in 1977 and has been inventing new chocolates ever since. Using Asian spices, fresh fruits and herbal infusions he has won over the most demanding chocolate-lovers.
Branches: 19 rue de Sèvres, 6th (01.45.44.20.40); 225 rue du Fbg-St-Honoré, 8th (01.42.27.39.44); 52 rue François 1er, 8th (01.47.23.38.25); 8 bd de la Madeleine, 9th (01.47.42.86.52).

Treats & traiteurs

Torréfacteur Verlet

256 rue St-Honoré, 1st (01.42.60.67.39). M° Palais Royal. **Open** shop Mon-Sat 9.30am-7pm; tea room daily 9.30am-6.30pm. Closed Aug. **Credit** MC, V. **Map** G5.

Sweet-talking **La Maison de la Vanille**.

The freshly roasted coffee in this gem of a shop smells as heavenly as the priciest perfume. Eric Duchaussoy roasts rare beans to perfection – sip a petit noir at a wooden table, or treat yourself to the city's best coffee at home.

Goumanyat

3 rue Dupuis, 3rd (01.44.78.96.74). M° Temple or République. **Open** Mon-Sat 2-8pm. Closed one week in Aug. **Credit** AmEx, DC, MC, V. **Map** L5.
Jean-Marie Thiercelin's family has been in the spice business since 1809. Star chefs come for Indonesian cubebe pepper, gleaming fresh nutmeg, long pepper (an Indian variety) and Spanish and Iranian saffron.

L'Epicerie

51 rue St-Louis-en-l'Ile, 4th (01.43.25.20.14). M° Pont Marie. **Open** daily 11am-8pm. Closed 25 Dec, 1 Jan. **Credit** MC, V. **Map** K7.
A perfect delicatessen gift shop crammed with pretty bottles of blackcurrant vinegar, five-spice mustard, orange sauce, tiny pots of jam, honey with figs and indulgent boxes of chocolate snails.

Jean-Paul Gardil

44 rue St-Louis en l'Ile, 4th (01.43.54.97.15). M° Pont Marie. **Open** Tue-Sat 9am-12.45pm, 4-5.45pm; Sun 9am-12.30pm. **Credit** MC, V. **Map** K7.
Rarely has meat looked so beautiful as in this fairytale shop, where geese hang in the window and a multitude of plaques confirm the butcher's skill in selecting the finest meats, such as milk-fed veal and lamb, coucou de Rennes chickens, free-range Barbary ducklings, and Bresse poulard and geese.

La Maison de la Vanille

18 rue du Cardinal Lemoine, 5th (01.43.25.50.95). M° Cardinal Lemoine. **Open** Wed-Sat 11.30am-7pm; Sun 2.30-7pm. **Credit** AmEx, DC, MC, V. **Map** K8.
All the vanilla in this soothingly scented shop and tea room comes from Réunion Island – buy it powdered for baking, liquid for milkshakes or whole to flavour a crème anglaise (aka custard).

Huilerie Artisanale Leblanc

6 rue Jacob, 6th (01.46.34.61.55). M° St-Germain-des-Prés. **Open** Mon 2.30-7.30pm; Tue-Sat 11am-7.30pm. Closed two weeks in Aug. **No credit cards.** **Map** H6.
The Leblanc family started out making walnut oil from its family tree in Burgundy and selling to its neighbours before branching out skilfully to press pure oils from hazelnuts, almonds, pine nuts, grilled peanuts, pistachios and olives.

Fauchon

26-30 pl de la Madeleine, 8th (01.47.42.60.11). M° Madeleine. **Open** Mon-Sat 9.30am-7pm. **Credit** AmEx, DC, MC, V. **Map** F4.
Paris' most famous food store is like every specialist deli rolled into one. There's a prepared-food section, cheese, fish and exotic fruit counters, an Italian deli, fine wines in the cellar, chocolates and a plush tea room for refreshment.

Hédiard

21 pl de la Madeleine, 8th (01.43.12.88.88/ www.hediard.fr). M° Madeleine. **Open** Mon-Sat 8.30am-9pm. **Credit** AmEx, DC, MC, V. **Map** F4.
The first to introduce exotic foods to the Parisians, Hédiard specialises in rare teas and coffees, unusual spices, imported produce, jams and candied fruits. The original shop, dating from 1880, has a posh tea room upstairs.
Branches include: 126 rue du Bac, 7th (01.45.44.01.98); 31 ave George V, 8th (01.47.20.44.44); 70 av Paul-Doumer, 16th (01.45.04.51.92); 106 bd des Courcelles, 17th (01.47.63.32.14).

La Maison de la Truffe

19 pl de la Madeleine, 8th (01.42.65.53.22/ www.maison-de-la-truffe.fr). M° Madeleine. **Open** Mon-Sat 9am-9pm. **Credit** AmEx, DC, MC, V. **Map** F4.
Come here for truffles priced like precious jewels – Piedmontese white truffles from Alba cost a cool €4,573 a kilo – or for the more affordable truffle oils, sauces and vinegars.

Allicante

26 bd Beaumarchais, 11th (01.43.55.13.02/ www.allicante.com). M° Bastille. **Open** daily 10am-7.30pm **Credit** AmEx, DC, MC, V. **Map** M6.
A paradise of oily delights, including rare olive oils from Liguria, Sicily and Greece, fragrant pine nut, pistachio and almond varieties, and oils extracted from apricot, peach and avocado pits. Wow your guests with pricey argania oil, pounded by hand by Berber women in Morocco.

Poissonerie du Dôme

4 rue Delambre, 14th (01.43.35.23.95). M° Vavin. **Open** Tue-Sat 8am-1pm, 4-7pm; Sun 8am-1pm. Closed Aug. **Credit** MC, V. **Map** G9.
Jean-Pierre Lopez' tiny shop is probably the best fishmonger in Paris. His fish are individually selected, many coming straight from small boats off the Breton coast. Each one is bright of eye and sound of gill. Try the drool-inducing (but bank-breaking) turbot, the giant crabs or the scallops, when in season.

International

Kioko

46 rue des Petits-Champs, 2nd (01.42.61.33.65). M° Pyramides. **Open** Tue-Sat 10am-8pm; Sun 11am-7pm. **Credit** V. **Map** H4.
Everything you need to make sushi (or good ready-made sushi for the lazy), plus sauces, snacks, sake, Japanese beer, tea and kitchen utensils. Staff will point you to the ingredient you're looking for.

Izraël

30 rue François-Miron, 4th (01.42.72.66.23). M° Hôtel-de-Ville. **Open** Tue-Fri 9.30am-1pm, 2.30-7pm; Sat 9am-7pm. Closed Aug. **Credit** MC, V. **Map** K6.
Spices and other delights from as far afield as

Mexico, Turkey and India – juicy dates, feta cheese, tapenades and lots of spirits.

Pasta Linea

9 rue de Turenne, 4th (01.42.77.62.54). M° St-Paul. **Open** Mon-Fri 11am-9pm; Sat, Sun 11am-8pm. **Credit** MC, V. **Map** L6.

Artichoke ravioli with truffle cream sauce or fresh linguine with tomato and rocket are among the heavenly hot pastas you might find here, or buy top-quality dried pastas and sauces to eat at home.

Mexi & Co

10 rue Dante, 5th (01.46.34.14.12). M° Maubert-Mutualité. **Open** daily noon-11pm. **Credit** MC, V. **Map** J7.

Everything you need for a fiesta, including marinades for fajitas, dried chillies, South American beers, cachaça and tequilas.

Jabugo Iberico & Co.

11 rue Clément Marot, 8th (01.47.20.03.13). M° Alma-Marceau or Franklin D. Roosevelt. **Open** Tue-Sat 10am-8pm. **Credit** MC, V. **Map** E4.

This shop specialises in Spanish hams with the Bellota-Bellota label, meaning the pigs have feasted on acorns. Manager Philippe Poulachon compares the complexity of his cured hams (at €95 a kilo) to the delicacy of truffles.

Sarl Velan Stores

87 passage Brady, 10th (01.42.46.06.06). M° Château d'Eau. **Open** Mon-Sat 8.30am-9.30pm. **Credit** AmEx, DC, MC, V. **Map** K4.

Nestled in a run-down arcade of Indian cafés and shops, plus restaurants whose waiters try to tempt you in, this is an emporium of spices, vegetables and saris shipped from Kenya and India.

Tang Frères

48 av d'Ivry, 13th (01.45.70.80.00/www.tang.fr). M° Porte d'Ivry. **Open** Tue-Sun 9am-7.30pm. **Credit** AmEx, MC, V.

Chinatown's biggest Asian supermarket is great for flat, wind-dried duck and all sorts of unidentifiable fruit and veg to put between your chopsticks.

Les Délices d'Orient

52 av Emile Zola, 15th (01.45.79.10.00). M° Charles-Michels. **Open** Tue-Sun 7.30am-9pm. **Credit** MC, V. **Map** B8.

Shelves here brim with houmous, stuffed aubergines, halva, Lebanese bread, felafel, olives and all manner of Middle Eastern delicacies.

Branch: 14 rue des Quatre-Frères Peignot, 15th.

Merry Monk

87 rue de la Convention, 15th (01.40.60.79.54). M° Boucicaut. **Open** Mon-Sat 10am-7pm. Closed Aug. **Credit** V. **Map** B9.

As tidy as your granny's larder, this shop stocks British expats' essentials and loose tea, along with a section dedicated to South Africa.

Wine, beer & spirits

Legrand Filles et Fils

1 rue de la Banque, 2nd (01.42.60.07.12). M° Bourse. **Open** Mon, Wed-Fri 11am-7pm; Thur

Get some pork for your fork from meat maestro **Jean-Paul Gardil**. *See p291.*

On the Town

10am-7.30pm; Sat 10am-7pm. **Credit** AmEx, MC, V. **Map** H4.
This old-fashioned shop offering fine wines and brandies, chocolates, teas, coffees and bonbons now has a showroom for its huge selection of tasting glasses and gadgets, housed within Galerie Vivienne. Free wine tastings on Thursday evenings.

Ryst Dupeyron

79 rue du Bac, 7th (01.45.48.80.93/ www.dupeyron.com). M° Rue du Bac. **Open** Mon 12.30-7.30pm; Tue-Sat 10.30am-7.30pm. Closed one week in Aug. **Credit** AmEx, MC, V. **Map** F7.
The Dupeyron family has sold Armagnac for four generations. You'll find bottles dating from 1868 (and nearly every year since) in this listed shop. Treasures include some 200 fine Bordeaux, vintage Port and rare whiskies.

Les Caves Augé

116 bd Haussmann, 8th (01.45.22.16.97). M° St-Augustin. **Open** Mon 1-7.30pm; Tue-Sat 9am-7.30pm. **Closed** Mon in Aug. **Credit** AmEx, MC, V. **Map** E3.
The oldest wine shop in Paris – Marcel Proust was a regular customer – is serious and professional, with sommelier Marc Sibard advising.

Les Caves Taillevent

199 rue du Fbg-St-Honoré, 8th (01.45.61.14.09/ www.taillevent.com). M° Charles-de-Gaulle-Etoile or Ternes. **Open** Mon 2-7.30pm; Tue-Fri 9am-7.30pm; Sat 9am-7.30pm. Closed first three weeks in Aug. **Credit** AmEx, DC, MC, V. **Map** D3.
Half a million bottles make up the Taillevent cellar. The three head sommeliers supervise the Saturday tastings. (10am-6pm).

La Maison du Whisky

20 rue d'Anjou, 8th (01.42.65.03.16/ www.whisky.fr). M° Madeleine. **Open** Mon 9.30am-7pm; Tue-Fri 9.15am-8pm; Sat 9.30am-7.30pm. **Credit** AmEx, V. **Map** F4.
Jean-Marc Bellier is fascinating as he explains which whisky matches which food, waxing lyrical about different flavours such as honey and tobacco. He also hosts a whisky club.

Bières Spéciales

77 rue St-Maur, 11th (01.48.07.18.71). M° St-Maur. **Open** Tue-Sat 10.30am-1pm, 4-9pm. **Credit** AmEx, DC, MC, V. **Map** M3.
Single bottles and cans from 16 nations (at last count) neatly cover the walls. Belgium might dominate but you'll also find Polish, Scottish, Corsican, Portuguese and Chinese brews.

Les Domaines qui Montent

136 bd Voltaire, 11th (01.43.56.89.15). M° Voltaire. **Open** Mon-Sat 10am-8pm. Lunch served noon-2.30pm. **Credit** MC, V. **Map** M5.
This is not only a wine shop but a convivial place to have breakfast, lunch or tea. Wines cost the same as they would at the producer's. Saturday tastings with up-and-coming winemakers are held in the shop.

Open-air orgy

Be fickle at Paris food markets.

In this city of fine food, luscious ingredients lurk provocatively in lively street markets. Not only are they fun places to buy food, but they also provide a good spot for people-watching and a chat with the locals. Today, the capital has 78 food markets – here are a few of special interest.

The recently re-opened **Marché des Enfants Rouges** (39 rue de Bretagne, 3rd), located on the site of a medieval orphanage where the children wore red uniforms, is Paris' oldest market, dating back to 1615. Come and find all sorts of treats from foreign soils (there is a good Italian stall) as well as French specialities.

In the heart of the Marais, **Marché Place Baudoyer** (Place Baudoyer, 4th) is the first roving market to open in the afternoons (Wed 3-8pm). A wonderful free-range egg stand (in front of the town hall of the 4th arrondissement) includes quail and goose eggs. Charcuterie and fish stand side by side across the square at Bob Hamon Salaisons, with homemade pastries, quiche, fresh paella and roast potatoes galore, plus great sausage sandwiches.

Don't miss the celebrated **Marché Mouffetard** (rue Mouffetard, 5th). A multi-coloured mass of a market at the southern end of this steep and narrow street, it's arguably the most beautiful of them all, with the marketeers trying to outdo each other in elaborate displays of fruit and vegetables.

The **avenue de Saxe** (7th) is packed on Thursdays and Saturdays with bourgeois Parisians parading their poodles. Pâtés, cheeses and olives are arranged as an art form here, but it's the stunning view of the Eiffel Tower that gives the Saxe-Breteuil market its unique touch. Watch your ankles as old ladies play at trolley rage.

Slap bang in the middle of the boulevard Raspail (6th) is the **Marché biologique** on Sundays. The enthusiastic crowd is a mix of intellectuals, new-agers and yuppies. Food scares have pumped up the popularity of organic foods, despite prices sometimes two or three times above the usual. This is definitely the cool dude of marchés.

Market streets and covered markets open Tue-Sat 8am-1pm, 4-7pm; Sun 8am-1pm. Roving markets set up at 8am and vanish in a flurry of green street-sweeping trucks at 2pm. *Sarah Barden.*

Home Delivery

Craving a croissant, couscous-merguez or a case of Champagne? Paris will bring it to your door with a smile.

After years of unremarkable home-eating options, Paris is catching on to the joys of cocooning. Be forewarned, however: deliveries are not always punctual, few places accept credit cards and most won't deliver after 11pm. Try to have exact change ready, as delivery people usually carry less than €15 cash. A tip of at least €2 is polite.

Asian

Le Lotus Bleu

17 rue de la Pierre-Levée, 11th (01.43.55.57.75/fax 01.43.14.02.72/www.lotus-bleu.fr). **Open** Mon-Fri 11.30am-2.30pm, 6.30-10.30pm; Sat, Sun 6.30-10.30pm. Closed Aug. **Minimum order** €12. **Delivery time** 30-40 mins. **No delivery charge. Area** 3rd, 10th, 11th (also 4th, 12th, 19th and 20th, but with a higher minimum order). **No credit cards. Map** M4.

The extensive Chinese and Thai menu at Le Lotus Bleu offers a quality alternative to the reheat masters that line Paris streets. The tame chicken in yellow curry sauce was cooked with fresh vegetables. while the nems, served with fresh mint, were still crispy – even after the hour-long wait. The €11.50 menu seems a safe and filling bet.

Branches: 26 rue Lakanal, 15th (01.45.32.24.20) – area 15th; 66 rue Anatole France, Levallois (01.47.58.05.55) – area Levallois.

French

Croissant Bon'Heur

12 rue de Rouen, 19th (tel/fax 01.40.34.03.33/ www.croissantbonheur.com). **Open** Mon-Fri 7-11am; Sat, Sun 7am-noon. Closed first three weeks in Aug. **Minimum order** €15. **Delivery time** one hour in the morning (best to order night before). **Delivery charge** included. **Area** Paris, suburbs (€4 to suburbs). **Credit** MC, V (by phone). **Map** M1.

Looking to spoil yourself? Paul Melay has been running this brilliant croissant delivery service for six years now, bringing baskets of fresh bread, croissants, homemade jams, butter, freshly squeezed orange juice, pastries, sandwiches and Champagne to your door. Delivery is impeccably timed.

Indian

Allô Indes

Vijaya, 22 rue Daubenton, 5th (01.47.07.56.78/fax 01.43.36.60.27/www.allo-indes.com). **Open** daily 7-11pm. **Minimum order** €12. **Delivery time** one hour. **Delivery charge** free in 4th-6th,13th,14th; €3.05-in 1st-3rd, 7th-12th, 15th-20th. **No credit cards.**

Allô Indes is the delivery wing of the Vijay, a charming Indian restaurant. We phoned from the pub and our order arrived at home as promised 45 minutes later. A huge bag of onion bhaji tasted fairly bland but perked up with dollops of hot pickle, while vegetable samosas were tasty. A chicken tikka masala was fine and aloo-palak (potatoes and spinach) good for vegetarians. Lamb Madras came with a devilishly hot sauce. Not a gourmet experience, but good if you need some comfort food for a lazy night.

Japanese

Sushi Company

22 rue des Pyramides, 1st (01.40.15.04.04/fax 01.40.15.97.97/www.holly-sushi.fr). **Open** daily 11am-2.30pm, 6-10.30pm. **Minimum order** €15 (in Paris), €23 (suburbs) **Delivery time** 45 mins-one hour. **Delivery charge** free-€3.80 in Paris, €5.35 in suburbs. **Credit** MC, V. **Map** H5.

As well as having a slick but laid-back restaurant, the Sushi Company provides a delivery service. The sushi and sashimi are of surprisingly good quality: well prepared, fresh and moist, with trimmings of thinly sliced pink ginger, wasabi and soy sauce. The choice goes well beyond the usual Westerner-friendly tuna and salmon.

Matsuri Sushi

26 rue Leopold Bellan, 2nd (01.40.26.11.13/fax 01.42.33.10.38/www.matsuri-sushi.com) **Open** daily 11am-3pm, 5.30-11pm. **Minimum order** €20-€40 (depending on area). **Delivery time** 45 mins. **Delivery charge** varies. **Area** Paris, suburbs. **Credit** AmEx, MC, V. **Map** J5.

Our pre-selected boxes arrived in a refrigerated container in precisely the time quoted to us on the phone – to the minute. The salmon sashimi was, like the ginger, tasty while the rice of the nigiri sushi was prepared with just the right amount of vinegar. Our only complaints were the slight over-saltiness of the rolled sushi's seaweed and the exorbitant cost of ordering à la carte from the vast menu.

Lebanese

Radis Olive

27 rue de Marignan, 8th (01.42.56.55.55/ fax 01.42.56.22.37). **Open** daily noon-3pm,

True American pizza? Maybe not, but **Speed Rabbit** is fast and filling.

7-11.30pm. **Minimum order** €23. **Delivery time** 45 mins. **Delivery charge** free in 8th, 15th-17th. Varies elsewhere. **Area** 8th, 15th-17th. Check for others. **No credit cards. Map** E4.
Getting food delivered from Radis Olive is a feel-good experience from start to finish. We ordered a chicken chawarma (€12.50) and a mezze platter (€18). Half an hour later, the delivery man climbed the stairs with a huge bag of delicacies; he was still smiling when he reached the fifth floor. The two dishes came in enormous portions, and contained pretty much the same stuff – slivers of chicken, tubs of creamy houmous topped with chickpeas, packs of fluffy pitta bread and Lebanese salad.

North African

Allô Couscous

70 rue Alexandre-Dumas, 11th (01.43.70.82.83). **Open** Mon 6-10pm; Tue-Sun 11am-2pm, 6-10pm. **Minimum order** €21. **Delivery charge** from €5. **Delivery time** 60-90 mins. **Area** Paris, suburbs. **No credit cards. Map** Q7.
Pack of wolves to feed on a shoe-string on short notice? Allô Couscous, run by the Halimi family, remains the easiest way to make heaps of hot food appear in your living room. Be sure to have some large containers ready to receive the chicken, mutton, beef and meatball stews; or request that they be delivered in disposable containers. Our couscous royal – all of the above plus merguez – arrived promptly and piping hot. Portions are enormous, so if there are four of you, order for three.

Pizza

Pizza Hut

(central phone 08.25.03.00.30/www.pizzahut.fr). **Open** Mon-Fri noon-2.30pm, 6-11pm; Sat, Sun, holidays 11.30am-11pm. **Minimum order** €10.90. **Delivery time** 30 mins. **No delivery charge. Area** Paris, suburbs. **No credit cards.**
From Manhattan to Moscow, Pizza Hut has seemingly global control over efficiently delivered American-style pizzas. Create your own pizza with a wide range of toppings or order a pre-determined mix of goodies (the suprême – a wild mix of veggies and meat – hit the spot). Beer, guacamole, chips, and wings can all be delivered as well.

Speed Rabbit Pizza

14 bd de Reuilly, 12th (01.43.44.80.80). **Open** Mon-Thurs 11am-2.30pm, 6.30pm-11pm; Fri 11am-2.30pm, 6-11pm; Sat, Sun 11am-3pm; 6-11pm. **Minimum order** €9.50. **Delivery time** 30 mins. **No delivery charge. Area** 12th and Charenton (see below for other branches). **No credit cards.**
Order the basic Harlem or the new Indiana from the place that boasts of its 'true American pizza', or build your own with a wide range of toppings including reblochon, egg, lardons, and crème fraîche... American? We tried the mega rabbit, topped with a sloppy yet tasty mix of meat and vegetables. Side orders include chips, chicken nuggets and barbecue wings.
Branches include: 47 bd du Montparnasse, 7th (01.45.44.28.81); 37 rue La Fayette, 9th (01.42.81.38.38); 167 av de Versailles, 16th (01.45.20.38.38); 205 rue Ordener, 18th (01.40.25.08.08).

Liquid Luxuries

Allô Apéro

9bis rue Labie, 17th (01.71.71.69.69/ www.chaud-devant-paris.com). **Open** daily 7pm-2am. **Minimum order** €20. **Delivery time** one hour. **Delivery charge** €6.90 in 1st-9th, 15th-17th, €8.40 in 10th-14th,18th-20th. **Area** Paris, Neuilly. **Credit** AmEx, MC, V.
Looking to get your booze on without putting your shoes on? This brilliant service can swiftly equip you with the spirits and mixers needed to slap smiles on faces in no time. Also: beer, chips, nuts and more keep the house party going strong.

Intermagnum

(08.00.80.20.20/fax 01.41.73.55.79/ www.nicolas-wines.com). **Open** Mon-Sat 9am-7pm. **No minimum order. Delivery time** 24-72 hours. **Delivery charge** €11 standard, €17 express; €16 anywhere in Europe. **Credit** AmEx, MC, V.
Say it with Champagne rather than flowers – this offshoot of off-licence chain Nicolas will deliver gift-boxed wine, with a message, all over France and even the world. The website includes tasting notes and offers discounts.

Learning & Tasting

Watch your culinary confidence rise like a perfect soufflé as expert teachers unleash the secrets of professional-tasting soups, sauces and sablés.

Cookery Courses

Ritz Escoffier Ecole de Gastronomie Française

38 rue Cambon, 1st (01.43.16.30.50). *M° Opéra.* **Courses** start each Mon; demonstrations Mon, Thur 3-5.30pm. **Fees** demonstration €45.75; half-day hands-on from €122. Professional training available. **Enrolment** in advance. **Credit** AmEx, DC, MC, V. **Map** G4.

Auguste Escoffier, the Ritz's inaugural chef, was the first to use an assembly line, now a restaurant standard. The cooking school, founded in 1988, offers a number of quality classes for enthusiasts of all levels. Across from the world-famous kitchen and deep in the hotel's bowels, students work with state-of-the-art equipment and experienced chefs who are willing to answer any inquiry. A recent four-hour shellfish and crustacean seasonal workshop (in French only) began with a lobstercide – the bare-handed dismembering of live lobsters – and ended with a perfectly simmered bisque, a genuine summer treat. Other short-term courses and demonstrations might focus on chocolate or jams, foie gras or fish sauces (often with English translations) and there's a number of half-day options for kids, with titles such as My First Terrine and Happy Mother's Day. For the more ambitious student, diploma courses are offered and could lead to an internship in the Ritz's kitchen. Book in advance, as the most intriguing offerings fill up quickly.

Françoise Meunier

7 rue Paul-Lelong, 2nd (01.45.87.11.37/ www.intiweb.com/fmeunier). M° Bourse. **Classes** Tue-Sat 10.30am-1.30pm; Wed 7.30-10.30pm. **Fees** €80 per class; five classes €320; classes and exam/diploma €1,200. **No credit cards. Map** J4.

Greeting her students warmly with a cup of coffee and an apron, Françoise Meunier plays host to a calm and convivial cooking school in her spacious kitchen. A well-travelled Ecole Hôtelière graduate, she covers everything from seasoning to silverware as a mix of international students prepares a balanced three-course meal. The highlight of our class was a juicy, perfectly cooked rôti de porc à la dijonaise, although menus can be designed according to students' preferences. The course provides lots of hands-on learning and easy-to-follow printed recipes. Be sure to schedule in advance as popular classes are limited to ten. English translations are available with advance notice.

Promenades Gourmandes

187 rue du Temple, 3rd (01.48.04.56.84/ www.promenadesgourmandes.com). M° Temple. **Classes** Tue-Sun 9am-3pm/6pm. Closed Aug. **Fees** €90-€290. **Enrolment** preferably at least one week in advance. **No credit cards. Map** L5.

In the intimate setting of her home's tailor-made kitchen, hosting six or fewer students, Paule Caillat makes sophisticated French cuisine seem attainable and enjoyable. 'All the necessary steps, and no unnecessary ones', is her philosophy. Students participate in planning the menu, which could include spinach or cheese soufflés, veal chops in citrus sauce or pheasant with tarragon, and apple or chocolate tart made with the Caillat family dough. All classes

Getting down to the serious business of cooking at **Promenades Gourmandes**.

– held in English (Paule is bilingual) – begin at the market, and the full-day offering includes an afternoon stroll to various places of culinary interest, such as Poilâne bakery, at which Paule and her guests benefit from a VIP welcome. A very personal – and personable – introduction to French cuisine.

L'Ecole du Thé

Le Palais des Thés, 64 rue Vieille-du-Temple, 3rd (01.43.56.96.38/www.le-palais-des-thes.fr). M° Hôtel de Ville. **Classes** daily. **Fees** connaissances €16; évasions €32. **Credit** AmEx, MC, V. **Map** L6.

L'Ecole du Thé offers courses for those looking to gain an understanding of the world's most humbly sophisticated beverage. The 90-minute 'connaissances' tastings for €16 have various themes that change monthly. Prepare yourself for the serious business of tea tasting: isolating essential flavours and fragrances, testing your skills on a worldwide selection of brews, and even studying complex graphs of the effects of aftertaste over time. The second course option, a 90-minute 'évasion', is often held at other locations: study the tea ceremony with a Japanese master, discuss the medical benefits of green tea at the Faculté de Pharmacie de Paris Sud, or savour thé à la menthe at La Mosquée de Paris. A free sample pack of teas with exact steeping and serving instructions is given when you leave.

Astuces et Tours de Mains

29 rue Censier, 5th (01.45.87.11.37/ www.astucesettoursdemains.com). M° Censier-Daubenton. **Classes** Tue-Fri 1-4pm; Sat 10am-2pm. **Fees** €80 each, Sat €95; €360 for five (weekdays only). **Enrolment** up to six months in advance. **No credit cards. Map** K9.

Laurence Guarneri's lovely little school is located in her custom-built kitchen in a renovated tannery with lots of natural light. Seated on comfortable stools at the counter, students can take notes on Laurence's tips while having a good view of the day's creation. The style is modern French, with recipes inspired by chefs such as Alain Ducasse, and workshops might include 'Italian vegetarian'. Most courses are booked up well in advance. The atmosphere is both professional and convivial as many of the students are regulars – an opportunity to meet people with similar interests and pick up valuable skills. Excellent, if your French is up to it or if you can convince a bilingual, food-loving friend to translate.

FERRANDI

ECOLE SUPERIEURE DE CUISINE FRANÇAISE

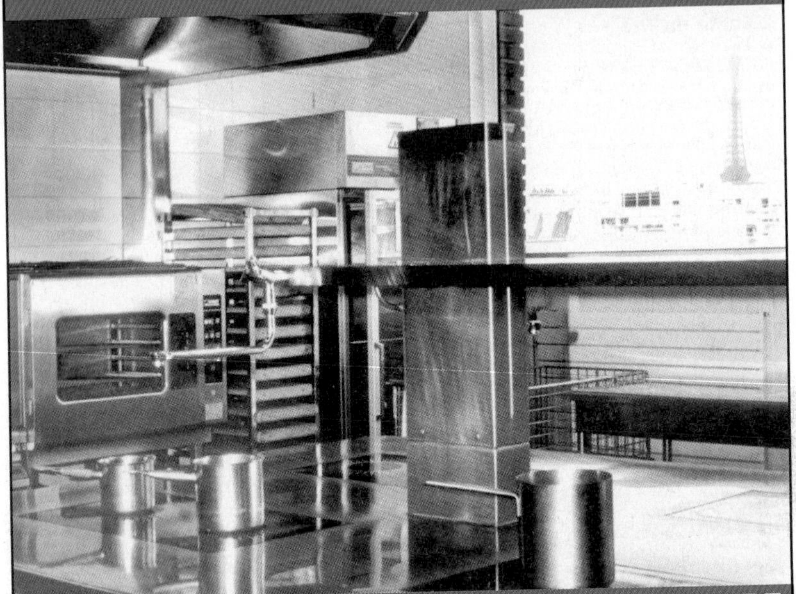

A PROUD TRADITION OF CULINARY SAVOIR-FAIRE

Two professional Bilingual Programs

Classic French Pastry and Bread Baking

The Art and Technique of French Cuisine

The highest level of Culinary Training in France
Awarded the title of Best Hotel School in Europe (1999)

Enroll now!
your contact: Stephanie Curtis 33 (0) 1.45.27.09.09

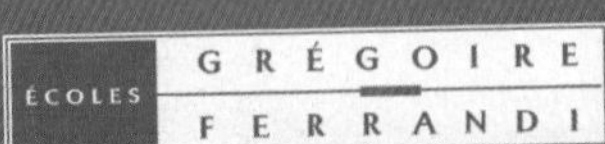

CHAMBRE DE COMMERCE ET D'INDUSTRIE DE PARIS

ESCF - 28 rue de l'Abbé Grégoire, 6th - Tel: 33 (0)1.49.54.28.17 - www. egf.ccip.fr

Ecoles Grégoire Ferrandi

28 rue de l'Abbé-Grégoire, 6th (01.49.54.28.03/www.egf.ccip.fr). M° St-Placide or Montparnasse-Bienvenüe. **Classes** cooking, pâtisserie and wine tasting courses Wed 6.30-10.30pm. **Fee** €60 per class. Professional training available. **Enrolment** three weeks in advance. **No credit cards. Map** G8.

This state-run cooking school offers evening cooking or pastry classes (maximum 12 people) for the general public. There are different seasonal themes to choose from – autumn's cassoulet or summer's 'festive dishes'. For dessert, this is a good place to learn the classics – crêpes, fondant au chocolat, and more. For the student committed to full-time professional training, Ferrandi also offers long, diploma programmes – a good deal at half the price of the Ritz or the Cordon Bleu.

La Cuisine de Marie-Blanche

18 av de la Motte-Picquet, 7th (01.45.51.36.34/www.cuisinemb.com). M° Ecole-Militaire. **Classes** Mon-Fri 10.30am-1.30pm, 2.30-4.30pm. Closed Aug. **Fees** 5-20 classes €550-€1,850; one week intensive €1,000. **Enrolment** ten days in advance. **Credit** MC, V. **Map** E6.

Cookbook author Marie-Blanche has welcomed students for over 25 years to a wide variety of courses ranging from dégustations to le grand diplôme. Fully bilingual and working from her beautiful apartment, she offers both a vast knowledge of French cuisine and idiosyncratic tips about the art of receiving guests. With just three people in our class (though typically six can be accommodated), we all prepared our own dishes and received as much individual attention as was necessary. The seasonal meal consisted of a tasty vegetable curry soup (served hot or cold depending on the weather), chicken in mushroom cream sauce, and lastly oranges surprises, Grand Marnier soufflés cooked to perfection inside hollowed-out oranges. On our way out the door, we felt confident with the recipes and ready to try them at home.

Le Cordon Bleu

8 rue Léon-Delhomme, 15th (01.53.68.22.50). M° Vaugirard. **Classes** Mon-Fri 8.30am-8.30pm; Sat 9am-3.30pm. **Fees** demonstrations €38; one-day workshop from €125. Professional training available. **Enrolment** three months ahead for long courses, two weeks for one-day courses. **Credit** MC, V. **Map** D9.

Although based in Paris for over a hundred years, Le Cordon Bleu has an international feel. With schools in 12 countries (from Mexico to Australia), the 80 staff chefs cater to a mix of students representing as many different nationalities. There is a wide offering of courses here ranging from three-hour demonstrations, market tours and full-day (hands-on) workshops to the more serious week-long gourmet sessions and, of course, the nine-month diploma. During the large, impersonal demonstrations, students take advantage of the modern technology – video screens and overhead mirrors – while watching the chef prepare his creation. Eager to snag the best seats, students (almost all English-speaking) were quick to correct the funny, wise-cracking French chef as he nearly forgot a key ingredient. The translation was very good, as were the sample tastings, but be sure to go on a full stomach – demonstations are by no means a meal. A selection of cookbooks, gourmet products and kitchen equipment is also available.

Ecole Lenôtre

Pavillon Elysée, 10 av des Champs-Elysées, 8th (01.45.02.21.19). M° Champs-Elysées Clemenceau. **Classes** Mon-Sat 9am-1pm, 2-6pm; Tue-Fri 7-10pm; Wed 2-4pm, 4.30-6.30pm (children's classes). Closed Aug; 20 Dec-5 Jan. **Fees** half-day €100-€200; one-day €185-€280; children €38. **Enrolment** three weeks in advance. **Credit** AmEx, DC, MC, V. **Map** F4.

With traîteur and chocolatier branches all over Paris, Lenôtre has become a temple for amateur cooks as well as a few sheepish professionals (this is where some private instructors come to hone their skills). At this new, central location, which also houses a restaurant, menus are carefully chosen at the beginning of each season. Ranging from the ever-elusive perfect soufflé to rôtisserie pigeon, Lenôtre's selection is vast; this is an especially good place to polish your French pastry technique. Classes are limited to seven so students have ample opportunity to have their questions answered by competent professionals – provided that you speak French, as no translations are offered.

Wine Courses

Le Jardin des Vignes

91 rue de Turenne, 3rd (01.42.77.05.00). M° St-Sébastien-Froissart. **Courses** on request, usually Tue, Wed or Thur 8-10pm. **Fees** evening session €85, three-session introductory course €250. **Credit** MC, V. **Map** L5.

Caviste Jean Radford is passionate about helping people understand the art of dégustation. His four starter classes cover the history of winemaking, different grapes and regions and the basics of tasting.

Grains Nobles

5 rue Laplace, 5th (01.43.54.93.54/ www.grainsnobles.fr). M° Cardinal-Lemoine. **Courses** introductory courses begin mid-Oct, details of evening courses on website. **Fees** classes from €69; courses from €130. **Enrolment** by post with cheque. **No credit cards. Map** J8.

Established in 1991, André Bessou's wine school offers courses and soirées to satisfy the most sophisticated tastebuds. More concerned with tasting than theory, Bessou cracks open some of France's most precious vintages during his regional étude du terroir and soirées prestige (wine lists a surprise), which are followed by a meal. The initation/perfectionnement session consists of three courses, each three hours long, and dissects 18 quality wines. Other regional soirées take to the revamped cellar to study the work of one particular château. A prior knowledge of wines is helpful and, if you don't speak French, tant pis (you're out of luck).

Centre de Dégustation Jacques Vivet

48 rue de Vaugirard, 6th (01.43.25.96.30/ www.ecoleduvin.info). RER Luxembourg. **Classes** Mon, Tue, Thur evening, times vary. **Fees** four introductory classes €195; four advanced classes €200. **Enrolment** a few weeks in advance. **No credit cards**. **Map** H7.

Jacques Vivet created his tasting centre 20 years ago. At the time, most of his clients were foreigners – French people apparently believing innate knowledge of wine to be a national birthright. However, the French have now wised up and humbly come to his introductory and perfectionnement courses. The introductory course covers the theoretical side of wine – the elements that make up its flavour – as well as lots of dedicated tasting practice. The perfectionnement course brings in more developed vocabulary and some very special wines. After his courses, Vivet hopes that 'you'll no longer just drink wine, as you did before, instead you'll taste it'.

Ecoles Grégoire Ferrandi

28 rue de l'Abbé-Grégoire, 6th (01.49.54.28.03). M° St-Placide or Montparnasse-Bienvenüe. **Classes** four Wed or Thur evenings, 6.30-9pm. **Fee** €229. **No credit cards**. **Map** G8.

Known mostly for its state-run cooking school (*see p299*), Ecoles Grégoire Ferrandi dabbles in wine as well. The initiation course covers all aspects of wine, beginning with soil and climate before moving towards tasting techniques, wine vocabulary and the significance of the grandes appellations. A whole session is dedicated to Champagne, and the last session is held over dinner, at which various wines are tasted with the dishes to which they are best suited.

Les Vins du Terroir

34 av Duquesne, 7th (01.40.61.91.87). M° St-François-Xavier. **Classes** Tue, Thur 8.30-10pm. **Fees** €60 per class. **Enrolment** 1 week in advance. **Credit** MC, V. **Map** E7.

Alexandre Gerbe opened this wine shop in 1998 and runs an evening class about once a month, each time tasting ten wines from a particular region. Classes run throughout the year except during the summer holidays, and accept a maximum of 12 people.

L'Ecole du Vin Ylan Schwartz

17 passage Foubert, 13th (01.45.89.77.39). M° Tolbiac. **Fees** €320-€600. **Enrolment** phone in advance. **No credit cards**.

Oenologist Ylan Schwartz brings an original approach to learning about wine. An advocate of 'the harmony between wine and music', Schwartz works with a Baroque ensemble and musicians from the Orchestre Philharmonique de Radio France in evenings (prices vary) that combine dinner, wine tasting and the music to suit it, matching a specific château to a particular piece or even movement of music. Other classes deal with matching wine and cheese, regional tastings, grands crus to go with grand food, and vineyard tours. Some classes are available in English or Spanish.

CIDD Découverte du Vin

30 rue de la Sablière, 14th (01.45.45.44.20). M° Pernety. **Open** Mon-Fri 10am-8pm. **Classes** days and times vary. **Fees** three-hour class €70; cycles of 3-14 classes €182-€738. **Enrolment** at least two weeks in advance. **No credit cards**. **Map** F10.

The CIDD (Centre d'Information, de Documentation et de Dégustation) was founded in 1982 by Alain Segelle, one-time winner of the best Paris sommelier of the year award. The centre covers just about every aspect of wine tasting, from organised regional vineyard trips and introductory soirées to high-level professional training. Segelle's personally trained trilingual staff (French, English and Japanese) will help you discover the art of wine-tasting. Also offered are portes-ouvertes, open tastings for the public, where you can learn more about the centre while tasting some good wines.

Institut du Vin du Savour Club

11-13 rue Gros, 16th (01.42.30.94.18/ lesavourclub.fr). RER Kennedy-Radio France. **Classes** Tue or Thur certain dates. **Fees** three classes (including a soirée gastronomique) €150. **Enrolment** at least one month in advance. **Credit** AmEx, DC, MC, V. **Map** A7.

Georges Lepré, former Ritz and Grand Véfour sommelier, heads these courses, taught in French, which focus on how to match wine to dishes. Courses on offer include 'an approach to wine' and 'a passion for wine'. The first involves three sessions, each covering six wines. Courses teach the basics of tasting, how best to stock a wine cellar and how to match wine with food. Classes are also available on specific subjects, such as dessert wines, late-harvest wines and vin jaune. Horizontal and vertical tastings and special wine-making processes are part of a second set of three classes.

Le Musée du Vin

rue des Eaux, 16th (01.45.25.63.26/ museeduvinparis.com). M° Passy. For information about courses, contact Monique Josse on 01.64.09.44.80. **Open** museum Tue-Sun 10-6pm; courses Sept-June Sat 10am-noon. **Fees** €39 per session; students €34. **Enrolment** at least one month in advance. **No credit cards. Map** B6.

This small museum is housed in 14th-century vaulted cellars that were once part of the Abbaye de Passy, which produced a wine enjoyed by Louis XIII himself. Discover the history and processes of wine-making (labels in French only) through displays of vats, corkscrews and cutouts of medieval peasants, followed by a short dégustation. Classes cover many different French regions, grape varieties and sensory analysis of wines.

Index & Maps

Alphabetical Index

Index & Maps

C

D

E

F

G

Q

R

V

W

X

Y

Z

Arrondissement Index

1st

2nd

Edited and designed by
Time Out Paris
15-17 rue des Martyrs
75009 Paris
Tel: +33 (0)1.44.87.00.45
Fax: +33 (0)1.44.73.90.60
Email: editors@timeout.fr
www.timeout.com/paris

For
Time Out Guides Ltd
Universal House
251 Tottenham Court Road
London W1T 7AB
Tel: +44 (0)20 7813 3000
Fax: +44 (0)20 7813 6001
Email: guides@timeout.com
www.timeout.com

Editorial

Editor Rosa Jackson
Consultant Editor Natasha Edwards
Consultant Restaurant Editor Alexander Lobrano
Production Editor Alison Culliford
Sub Editor Maryanne Blacker
Editorial Assistants Tom Coveney, Nicholas Katzenbach
Researchers Kristen Hinman, Emily Rueb

Managing Director Paris Karen Albrecht

Editorial/Managing Director Peter Fiennes
Series Editor Sarah Guy
Contributing Editor Ruth Jarvis
Guides Co-ordinator Anna Norman

Design

Art Director Paris Richard Joy
Design Assistant Oliver Knight
Ad Design Richard Randall, Philippe Thareaut

Group Art Director John Oakey
Art Director Mandy Martin
Art Editor Scott Moore
Picture Editor Kerri Littlefield

Advertising

Sales & Administration Manager Philippe Thareaut
Advertising Executives Olivier Baenninger, Christa Halby, Renaud Langlois

Sales Director Mark Phillips
International Sales Manager Ross Canadé

Distribution

Group Circulation Director Jim Heinemann
Circulation Executive Sue Carter
Distribution Manager Paris Colin Shaw

Group

Chairman Tony Elliott
Managing Director Mike Hardwick
Financial Director Richard Waterlow
Commercial Director Lesley Gill
Marketing Director Christine Cort
Marketing Manager Mandy Martinez
General Manager Nichola Coulthard
Guides Production Director Mark Lamond
Production Controller Samantha Furniss
Accountants Sarah Bostock, Abdus Sadique

Written and researched by

Karen Albrecht, Maryanne Blacker, Anna Brooke, Tom Coveney, Simon Cropper, Alison Culliford, Natasha Edwards, Duncan Fairgrieve, Michael Fitzpatrick, Ethan Gilsdorf, Neil Haidar, Paul Hines, Kristen Hinman, Rosa Jackson, Claire Kilvert, Nicholas Katzenbach, John Laurenson, Jennifer Joan Lee, Alexander Lobrano, Sophie Lyne, Nicola McDonald, Nicola Mitchell, Stephen Mudge, Lisa Pasold, Nicholas Petter, Isabel Pitman, Mark Rebindaine, Clothilde Redfern, Louise Rogers, Louise Rowland, Katherine Spenley, Sharon Sutcliffe, Natalie Whittle

Additional contributions by

Amy Brooke, Hannah Feldman, Joanna Hunter, Jonny Jacobsen, Toby Rose, Lucia Scazzoccio, Emily Rueb

Special thanks to: Philippe Landry, Sam Landry

Maps p332-341 by Mapworld, p343-347 Philippe Landry, p348 courtesy RATP.

Photography by Tom Craig
Additional photography Karl Blackwell
Cover photography Imagestate

© Copyright 2003 Time Out Group Ltd
All rights reserved

Contents

hotels.com

BEST PRICES, BEST PLACES. GUARANTEED.℠

Everything you want from a hotel in one visit

Paris'best hotels

Save up to 70%* on your hotel room

Rates start from
2 star hotel: 30 €
3 star hotel: 35 €
4 star hotel: 50 €

or choose from 8000 hotels in 350 destinations

From Europe, call toll free
00 800 1099 1099
From US
800 2-HOTELS

(*) inclusive price per person, based on 2 sharing a double room

About this guide

Time Out, an independent publisher, has published weekly magazines in London since 1968 and in New York since 1995; it also has a series of popular city guides. The Paris office, founded in 1992, produces weekly English-language listings inside *Pariscope*, the quarterly *Time Out Paris Free Guide*, and Time Out guides to Paris and the South of France.

How the Guide was produced

The contents of the Guide were entirely originated by journalists living in Paris, and based on real experiences in restaurants, cafés and bars. Restaurants are tested anonymously, with Time Out paying the bill.

For this sixth edition, as well as adding new restaurants, cafés and bars we have discovered over the past year, we have also retested most of the establishments listed in the fifth edition.

While every effort has been made to ensure the accuracy of the information contained in this guide, the publishers cannot accept responsibility for any errors it may contain.

How to use the listings

Restaurants are divided into sections denoting the type of establishment and style of food. Within each section, restaurants are listed in order of arrondissement, or area, then alphabetically. We also provide two indexes (*see p302*): one by arrondissement and type of restaurant, the other alphabetical.

Critics' picks

A star after the restaurant's name indicates that it is a critics' favourite, one of the best in its category. Stars are awarded not only for great food (or drinks, in **Bars & Pubs**), but also for a particularly fun atmosphere.

Telephones

Paris and Ile de France numbers begin with 01. From abroad, leave off the 0 at the start of the ten-digit number. The country code is 33.

Transport

The Métro or RER stop listed is the one nearest the restaurant. Two stops are listed if they are both very near the restaurant and on different Métro lines.

No payment of any kind has secured or influenced a review in this Guide. Time Out maintains a strict policy of editorial independence, and advertisers are never guaranteed special treatment of any kind.

On peut
APPORTER
SON MANGER

Opening hours

Times stated for restaurants apply to service hours, when you can order food, rather than opening and closing times. Those given for bars and cafés are opening and closing hours, with food service hours if relevant.

Credit cards & currency

The following abbreviations are used: AmEx: American Express; DC: Diners' Club; MC: Mastercard; V: Visa. A €15 minimum usually applies to credit card transactions. Most Paris restaurants will not accept travellers' cheques.

Prices and prix-fixe menus

Average means the average cost à la carte for a three-course meal without drinks. If no average price is listed, the only option is the prix fixe. In our listings, 'Prix fixe' indicates the price for the restaurant's set-price menu at lunch and dinner. If served only at lunch, the fixed-price menu is listed separately under 'Lunch menu'. Within reviews, we make a distinction between set menus and the 'carte', which allows you to order items individually. Set menus, or prix fixes, are the most popular way of eating in Paris restaurants and often represent the best value. A 'formule' is a type of prix fixe, but often with a more limited choice of dishes.

PIZZA MILANO

Pizza, pasta, vino e birra

Notre Dame

2, place Saint Michel - 75006 Paris - 01 44 07 32 27

Opera

30, boulevard des Italiens - 75009 Paris - 01 47 70 33 33

Montmartre

10 bis, place de Clichy - 75009 Paris - 01 40 16 52 30

• Exciting new menu • Al fresco dining

www.pizzamilano.fr

A PizzaExpress Restaurant

PIZZAEXPRESS

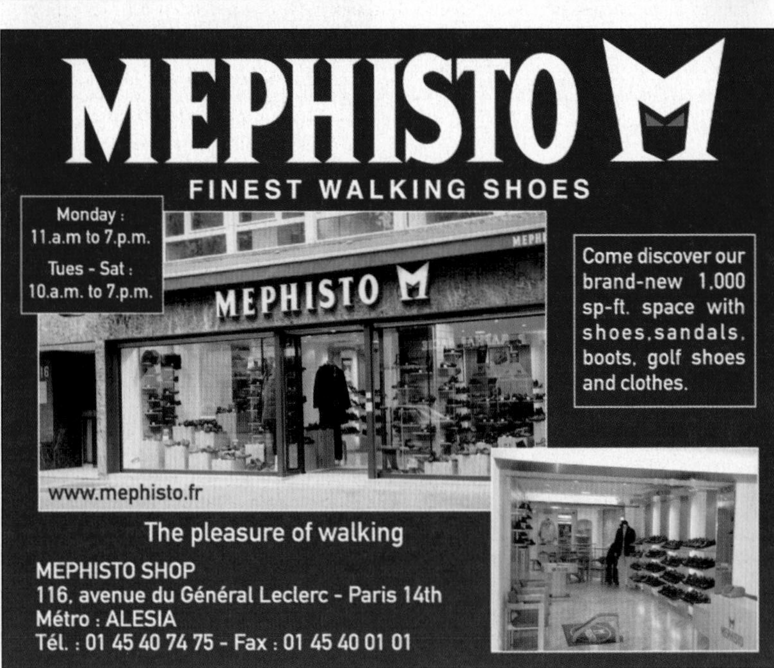

Service & tipping

Prices on restaurant menus (and listed in this guide) must by law include a 12-15 per cent service charge. A small tip of one to five euros (or small change in a café) is a nice, though entirely optional, gesture.

Wheelchair access

Where this is stated in the listing, the restaurant features full wheelchair access, including toilets. It's worth ringing ahead to check if an establishment can cater for you.

Smoking

Restaurants are required by French law to have a non-smoking section. However, most either allocate one or two tables near the loo to non-smokers or ignore the law altogether. In our listings, 'Non-smoking room' means that the restaurant has a separate room for non-smokers. 'Non smoking' means that the entire restaurant is smoke-free.

Maps

Each restaurant, café and bar in this guide has a map reference which corresponds to the maps starting on page 332. We also provide detailed area maps for five neighbourhoods: the Marais, the Champs-Elysées, St-Germain, Oberkampf and Bastille. Restaurants, cafés and bars are located on these maps by name. The same grid is used for all the maps.

Savoir faire

Learn to saunter into Paris restaurants with a certain insouciance.

Restaurants are busiest at lunch between 1pm and 2pm. In the evening, the French rarely venture into a restaurant before 8.30pm, much later in trendier places. Popular restaurants sometimes have two sittings, around 8pm and 10pm. For a meal in the middle of the afternoon, try brasseries, cafés and tea rooms.

Apéritifs, wine, water & digestifs In the more expensive restaurants, wine waiters might make it hard for you to refuse Champagne or other apéritifs, which can add significantly to your bill. However, it can be fun to indulge in old-fashioned French apéritifs such as Lillet or Pineau des Charentes (*see p227*).

As well as the standard 75cl bottles, wine comes in half-bottles (37.5cl) and in carafes or pichets, usually of 25cl (un quart), 46cl (un pot lyonnais) and 50cl (un demi-litre, or une fillette if served in a tall carafe).

You're entitled to ask for 'une carafe d'eau', which is tap water, though most waiters will try to sell you mineral water. Be warned that restaurants now commonly charge €4-€5 for a one-litre bottle of mineral water.

Digestifs offer the opportunity to discover potent drinks such as vintage Armagnac or a flaming prune eau-de-vie.

A matter of course French meals usually consist of three courses – entrée (starter), plat (main course) and dessert – although at more formal restaurants, there may be an additional amuse-bouche or amuse-gueule (appetiser or hors d'oeuvre), a fish course before the main course, cheese (before dessert), and petits fours served at the end with the coffee. This is invariably black (un expresso or un express) – if you ask for a café au lait after dinner, expect to receive a strange look.

Loafing Bread is served free with any café or restaurant meal and you're entitled to as much as you can eat – don't be afraid to ask for more, or to have it changed if it is stale.

Dress You are what you wear in Paris. Restaurant goers on the whole opt for the 'smart-casual' look, so while you won't need a tie, leave the bermuda shorts and tracksuits behind. Haute cuisine restaurants normally expect a jacket and tie.

Reservations It's always a good idea to book at popular restaurants. Famous haute cuisine establishments take bookings months ahead (they will ask you to call back to confirm the day before your meal) and the most currently fashionable bistros require booking up to a few weeks ahead. However, it's also worth trying at the last minute to see if there's room. Some hard-to-book tables are much more accessible at lunch.

Bar & café customs Drink prices often vary in a café: they're cheapest at the bar, more at a table and even more sitting outside. There will often be a further increase (majoration), generally about 50 cents, after 10pm. If you want a table, sit down and wait for the waiter to arrive.

Paying When you want your bill, ask for it – waiters don't like to give the impression they are rushing you out. Bills are paid at the table.

Eating in Paris

Whether you are after timeless Gallic charm or the latest fashion concept, food remains at the top of the menu in the French capital, writes Rosa Jackson.

As the city with the world's biggest culinary ego, Paris has an awful lot to live up to. It's no wonder, then, that restaurants recently confronted an identity crisis – one minute the Paris dining scene was being lauded as the most hip and happening in Europe, the next, wave-making designer haunts, such as Korova and Nobu, were going bust. Delirious restaurateurs had a rude shock: Paris putters down the avenue of change like a Citroën 4CV, and any restaurant with fashion pretentions must pry away customers from the smoky corner bistro with wry waiters and a bargain prix fixe. Happily, the dressed-up and the down-at-heel are learning to co-exist in a city that now offers more possibilities than ever in terms of food and mood.

Probably the most symbolic openings of the past year were Alain Ducasse's **Aux Lyonnais** and **L'Atelier de Joël Robuchon**. Ducasse, who is behind some of the most expensive restaurants in Paris (Alain Ducasse au Plaza Athénée) and New York, as well as the Spoon, Food & Wine fusion bistros worldwide, never fails to put his finger on a trend – this time the buzzword is terroir, a return to regional roots. He and business partner Thierry de la Brosse (of L'Ami Louis) barely needed to touch the decor of this museum-piece bistro, where a young chef now turns out updated renditions of Lyonnais classics. More experimental, but just as resolutely casual, is L'Atelier, where passers-by are treated to the bizarre sight of Left Bank publishers and lawyers queueing for exquisite food served in minuscule portions ('la grosse crevette', a single, actually quite modest prawn, costs €16). There are no tables and chairs in the red-and-black bento-box dining room, just 35 seats at the counter; it would all seem very democratic were it not for the prices.

The demise of some high-profile restaurants along the Champs-Elysées hasn't prevented the opening of flashy new spots off the beaten track: the oddly named **R** combines slick black-and-white decor with a stunning Eiffel Tower view and mod-Med food, while **L'Envue**'s tempting menu and tableware-for-sale prove that it isn't just for show. Outlandish designer Philippe Starck has dropped his austere health-food concept to dish up southwestern-inspired bistro fare at **Bon 2**, and the Costes brothers continue to reign over the café scene with the enduring **Café Marly**, ice-cool **Georges**, gloriously over-the-top **La Grande Armée** and several other temples of style.

For most Parisians, though, going out to eat means heading for an atmospheric bistro – and thankfully this category continues to thrive, from smoke-stained neighbourhood hang-outs to freshly painted dining rooms that showcase young chefs' talents (*see right*). **Chez René**, **Chardenoux**, **Allard** and the bargain **Astier** are classics, while chefs' bistros, such as **La Régalade**, **Chez Michel**, **L'Epi Dupin** and **L'Os à Moëlle**, continue to serve the best-value set menus in Paris.

The Paris dining scene might not be as cosmopolitan as that of New York or London, but this is still a great place to eat your way around the world. Start with North Africa – Moroccan tagines and Algerian couscous have made a real impact here – stop off in Japan, which has a number of worthy representatives, and then follow your tastebuds from Afghanistan to Ethiopia, Italy to Tibet. Just don't expect curry as fiery as you'd find in London.

One thing unites nearly every restaurant, café and bar in this edition, and that's inflation. Sadly, with the introduction of the euro in 2002 restaurateurs jumped on the chance to bump up their prices, often shamelessly: a bistro meal with an ordinary bottle of wine can now easily come to €100 for two, and haute cuisine prices have hit the stratosphere (expect to spend at least €400 for two, unless you go for the lunch prix fixe). This makes eating out more of a luxury than it once was, though figures on spending show that Parisians have sacrificed their clothing budgets in favour of food. Vive la France.

L'Envue: show and sell

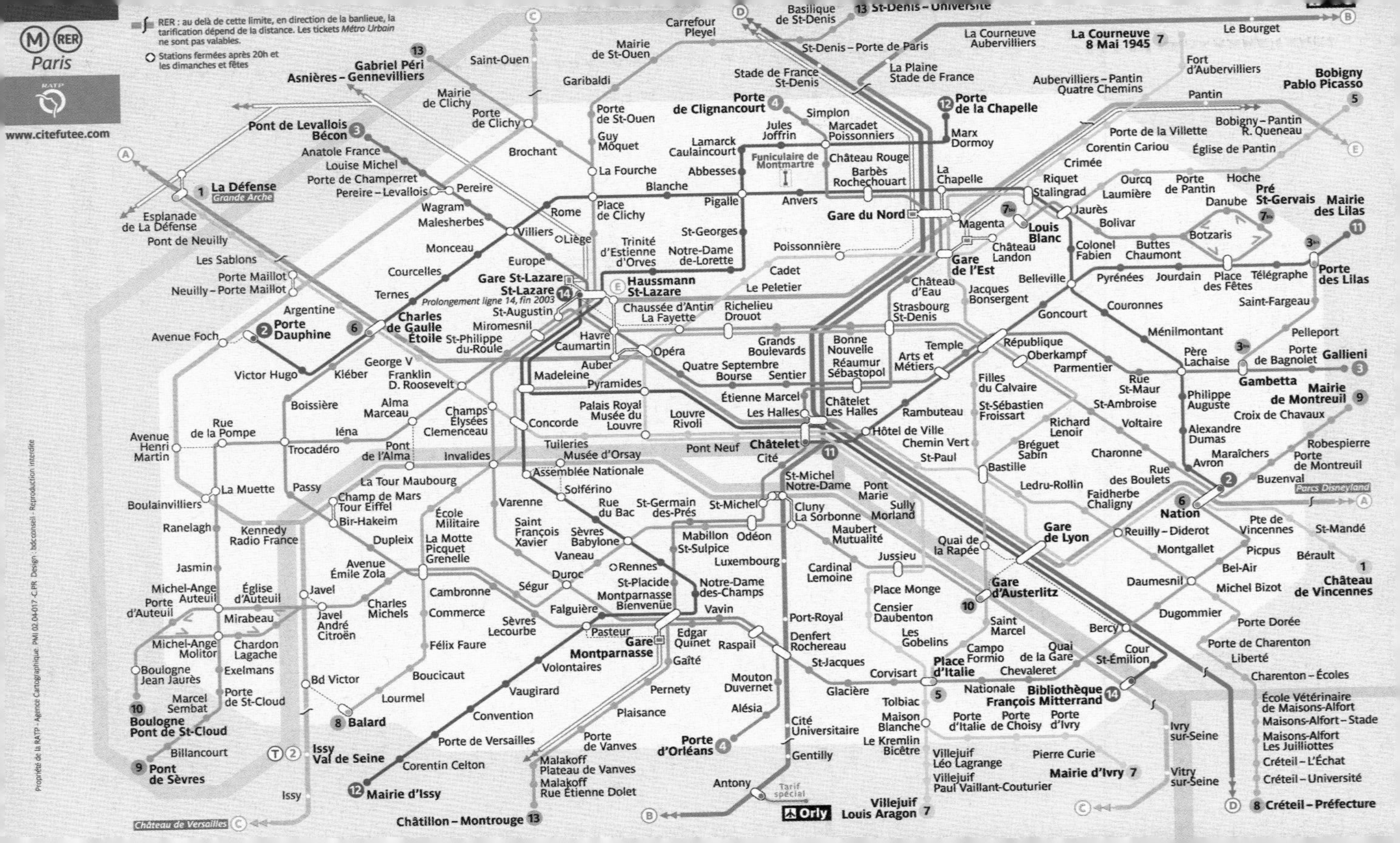

M RER
Paris
RATP
www.citefutee.com

RER : au delà de cette limite, en direction de la banlieue, la tarification dépend de la distance. Les tickets *Métro Urbain* ne sont pas valables.

Stations fermées après 20h et les dimanches et fêtes

La Défense Grande Arche 1
Esplanade de La Défense
Pont de Neuilly
Les Sablons
Porte Maillot
Neuilly – Porte Maillot
Argentine
Avenue Foch
2 Porte Dauphine
Victor Hugo
6 Charles de Gaulle Étoile
Pont de Levallois Bécon 3
Anatole France
Louise Michel
Porte de Champerret
Pereire – Levallois
Pereire
Wagram
Malesherbes
Villiers
Monceau
Courcelles
Ternes
Gabriel Péri Asnières – Gennevilliers 13
Mairie de Clichy
Porte de Clichy
Saint-Ouen
Brochant
Garibaldi
Mairie de St-Ouen
Carrefour Pleyel
Porte de St-Ouen
Guy Môquet
La Fourche
Place de Clichy
Rome
Liège
Europe
Gare St-Lazare
St-Lazare 14
Prolongement ligne 14, fin 2003
St-Augustin
Miromesnil
St-Philippe du-Roule
George V
Kléber
Franklin D. Roosevelt
Boissière
Alma Marceau
Champs Élysées Clemenceau
Avenue Henri Martin
Rue de la Pompe
Trocadéro
Iéna
Pont de l'Alma
Invalides
La Muette
Boulainvilliers
Ranelagh
Kennedy Radio France
Passy
Champ de Mars Tour Eiffel
Bir-Hakeim
La Tour Maubourg
École Militaire
La Motte Picquet Grenelle
Dupleix
Avenue Émile Zola
Jasmin
Michel-Ange Auteuil
Porte d'Auteuil
Église d'Auteuil
Mirabeau
Javel
Javel André Citroën
Charles Michels
Michel-Ange Molitor
Chardon Lagache
Exelmans
Boulogne Jean Jaurès
Porte de St-Cloud
Marcel Sembat
10 Boulogne Pont de St-Cloud
Billancourt
9 Pont de Sèvres
Bd Victor
T 2
Issy Val de Seine
Issy
Château de Versailles C
8 Balard
Lourmel
Boucicaut
Félix Faure
Commerce
Cambronne
Ségur
Sèvres Lecourbe
Falguière
Pasteur
Volontaires
Vaugirard
Convention
Porte de Versailles
Corentin Celton
12 Mairie d'Issy
Châtillon – Montrouge 13
Malakoff Plateau de Vanves
Malakoff Rue Étienne Dolet
Porte de Vanves
Plaisance
Pernety
Gaîté
Gare Montparnasse
Edgar Quinet
Raspail
Mouton Duvernet
Alésia
Porte d'Orléans 4
Antony
Tarif spécial
Orly
Cité Universitaire
Gentilly
Villejuif Louis Aragon 7
Varenne
Saint François Xavier
Duroc
Vaneau
Sèvres Babylone
Rennes
St-Placide
Montparnasse Bienvenüe
Notre-Dame des-Champs
Vavin
Rue du Bac
Solférino
Assemblée Nationale
Musée d'Orsay
Tuileries
Concorde
Madeleine
Havre Caumartin
Auber
Opéra
Pyramides
Palais Royal Musée du Louvre
Louvre Rivoli
Pont Neuf
St-Germain des-Prés
St-Sulpice
Mabillon
Odéon
St-Michel
Luxembourg
Port-Royal
Denfert Rochereau
St-Jacques
Glacière
Corvisart
Place d'Italie
Tolbiac
Maison Blanche
Le Kremlin Bicêtre
Villejuif Léo Lagrange
Villejuif Paul Vaillant-Couturier
Porte d'Italie
Porte de Choisy
Porte d'Ivry
Pierre Curie
Mairie d'Ivry 7
5
Nationale
Bibliothèque François Mitterrand 14
Chevaleret
Campo Formio
Quai de la Gare
Saint Marcel
Les Gobelins
Censier Daubenton
Place Monge
Cardinal Lemoine
Jussieu
Maubert Mutualité
Cluny La Sorbonne
St-Michel Notre-Dame
Cité
Châtelet
11
Pont Marie
Sully Morland
Quai de la Rapée
10 Gare d'Austerlitz
Gare de Lyon
Bercy
Cour St-Émilion
Ivry sur-Seine
Vitry sur-Seine
C
D
B
Haussmann St-Lazare
E
Chaussée d'Antin La Fayette
Trinité d'Estienne d'Orves
Notre-Dame de-Lorette
St-Georges
Pigalle
Blanche
Abbesses
Lamarck Caulaincourt
Funiculaire de Montmartre
Anvers
Porte de Clignancourt 4
Jules Joffrin
Simplon
Marcadet Poissonniers
Château Rouge
Barbès Rochechouart
Gare du Nord
Poissonnière
Cadet
Le Peletier
Richelieu Drouot
Grands Boulevards
Bonne Nouvelle
Quatre Septembre
Bourse
Sentier
Réaumur Sébastopol
Étienne Marcel
Les Halles
Châtelet Les Halles
Strasbourg St-Denis
Château d'Eau
Arts et Métiers
Temple
Rambuteau
Hôtel de Ville
Chemin Vert
St-Paul
Bastille
Filles du Calvaire
St-Sébastien Froissart
République
Oberkampf
Richard Lenoir
Bréguet Sabin
Ledru-Rollin
Faidherbe Chaligny
Charonne
Rue des Boulets
Voltaire
St-Ambroise
Rue St-Maur
Parmentier
Goncourt
Belleville
Jacques Bonsergent
Gare de l'Est
Château Landon
Magenta
La Chapelle
12 Porte de la Chapelle
Marx Dormoy
Basilique de St-Denis
13 St-Denis – Université
St-Denis – Porte de Paris
Stade de France St-Denis
La Plaine Stade de France
La Courneuve Aubervilliers
La Courneuve 8 Mai 1945 7
Le Bourget
Fort d'Aubervilliers
Aubervilliers – Pantin Quatre Chemins
Pantin
Bobigny Pablo Picasso 5
Bobigny – Pantin R. Queneau
Église de Pantin
Porte de la Villette
Corentin Cariou
Crimée
Riquet
Stalingrad
7bis Louis Blanc
Jaurès
Bolivar
Laumière
Ourcq
Porte de Pantin
Hoche
Danube
Pré St-Gervais 7bis
Mairie des Lilas
11
Botzaris
Buttes Chaumont
Colonel Fabien
Pyrénées
Jourdain
Place des Fêtes
Télégraphe
3bis Porte des Lilas
Saint-Fargeau
Couronnes
Ménilmontant
Pelleport
3bis Porte de Bagnolet
Gallieni 3
Père Lachaise
Gambetta
Mairie de Montreuil 9
Philippe Auguste
Croix de Chavaux
Alexandre Dumas
Robespierre
Maraîchers
Porte de Montreuil
Avron
2
Buzenval
Parcs Disneyland
A
6 Nation
Reuilly – Diderot
Pte de Vincennes
St-Mandé
Montgallet
Picpus
Bérault
Bel-Air
1 Château de Vincennes
Daumesnil
Michel Bizot
Dugommier
Porte Dorée
Porte de Charenton
Liberté
Charenton – Écoles
École Vétérinaire de Maisons-Alfort
Maisons-Alfort – Stade
Maisons-Alfort Les Juilliottes
Créteil – L'Échat
Créteil – Université
8 Créteil – Préfecture

Propriété de la RATP - Agence Cartographique. PMI 02.04-017 -C.PR Design : bdcconseil - Reproduction interdite

Bistros

Le Buisson Ardent p33
25 rue Jussieu, 5th
(01.43.54.93.02)

Chez René p34
14 bd St-Germain, 5th
(01.43.54.30.23)

L'Equitable p34
1 rue des Fossés-St-Marcel, 5th (01.43.31.69.20)

Les Fontaines p34
9 rue Soufflot, 5th
(01.43.26.42.80)

L'Intermède p34
4 bd du Port-Royal, 5th
(01.47.07.08.99)

Le Moulin à Vent p35
20 rue des Fossés-St-Bernard, 5th
(01.43.54.99.37)

Le Pré Verre p35
8 rue Thénard, 5th
(01.43.54.59.47)

Le Reminet p36
3 rue des Grands-Degrés, 5th (01.44.07.04.24)

La Rôtisserie de Beaujolais p37
19 quai de la Tournelle, 5th
(01.43.54.17.47)

La Table de Michel p37
13 quai de la Tournelle, 5th
(01.44.07.17.57)

Brasseries

Le Balzar p94
49 rue des Ecoles, 5th
(01.43.54.13.67)

Restaurant Marty p94
20 av des Gobelins, 5th
(01.43.31.39.51)

Budget

Les Degrés de Notre-Dame p148
10 rue des Grands-Degrés, 5th (01.55.42.88.88)

L'Ecurie p148
2 rue Laplace, 5th
(01.46.33.68.49)

L'Escapade p149
10 rue de la Montagne-Ste-Geneviève, 5th
(01.46.33.23.85)

Le Jardin des Pâtes p149
4 rue Lacépède, 5th
(01.43.31.50.71)

Perraudin p149
157 rue St-Jacques, 5th
(01.46.33.15.75)

Cafés

Café Delmas p224
2-4 pl de la Contrescarpe, 5th (01.43.26.51.26)

Le Comptoir du Panthéon p225
5 rue Soufflot, 5th
(01.43.54.75.36)

Les Pipos p225
2 rue de l'Ecole-Polytechnique, 5th
(01.43.54.11.40)

Le Rallye p225
1 quai de la Tournelle, 5th
(01.43.54.29.65)

Le Reflet p225
6 rue Champollion, 5th
(01.43.29.97.27)

Tabac de la Sorbonne p226
7 pl de la Sorbonne, 5th
(01.43.54.52.04)

Le Verre à Pied p226
118bis rue Mouffetard, 5th
(01.43.31.15.72)

Classics

La Truffière p112
4 rue Blainville, 5th
(01.46.33.29.82)

Clubs

Caveau de la Huchette p286
5 rue de la Huchette, 5th
(01.43.26.65.05)

Eastern Mediterranean

Les Délices d'Aphrodite p178
4 rue de Candolle, 5th
(01.43.31.40.39)

Mavrommatis p178
5 rue du Marché des Patriarches, 5th
(01.43.31.17.17)

La Voie Lactée p178
34 rue du Cardinal-Lemoine, 5th (01.46.34.02.35)

Eating with Entertainment

La Balle au Bond p279
(01.40.51.87.06)

Far Eastern

Au Coin des Gourmets p186
5 rue Dante, 5th
(01.43.26.12.92)

Han Lim p187
6 rue Blainville, 5th,
(01.43.54.62.74)

Mirama p182
17 rue St-Jacques, 5th
(01.43.54.71.77)

Pema Thang p191
13 rue de la Montagne Ste-Geneviève, 5th
(01.43.54.34.34)

Fish & Seafood

Le Bistrot Côté Mer p139
16 bd St-Germain, 5th
(01.43.54.59.10)

L'Huître et Demie p139
80 rue Mouffetard, 5th
(01.43.37.98.21)

Haute Cuisine

La Tour d'Argent p81
15-17 quai de la Tournelle, 5th (01.43.54.23.31)

Home Delivery

Allô Indes p294
Vijaya, 22 rue Daubenton, 5th (01.47.07.56.78)

Learning & Tasting

Astuces et Tours de Mains p297
29 rue Censier, 5th
(01.45.87.11.37)

Grains Nobles p299
5 rue Laplace, 5th
(01.43.54.93.54)

North African

L'Atlas p210
12 bd St-Germain, 5th
(01.44.07.23.66)

Regional

Alexandre p136
24 rue de la Parcheminerie, 5th (01.43.26.49.66)

Le Cosi p132
9 rue Cujas, 5th
(01.43.29.20.20)

Moissonnier p133
28 rue des Fossés-St-Bernard, 5th
(01.43.29.87.65)

Vivario p132
6 rue Cochin, 5th
(01.43.25.08.19)

Shops & Markets

La Maison de la Vanille p291
18 rue du Cardinal Lemoine, 5th (01.43.25.50.95)

Mexi & Co p292
10 rue Dante, 5th
(01.46.34.14.12)

Spanish

Fogón Saint-Julien p214
10 rue St-Julien-le-Pauvre, 5th (01.43.54.31.33)

Tea Rooms

Café Maure de la Mosquée de Paris p268
39 rue Geoffroy St-Hilaire, 5th (01.43.31.38.20)

La Fourmi Ailée p268
8 rue du Fouarre, 5th
(01.43.29.40.99)

Vegetarian

Le Grenier de Notre-Dame p163
18 rue de la Bûcherie, 5th
(01.43.29.98.29)

Les Quatre et Une Saveurs p163
72 rue du Cardinal-Lemoine, 5th. (01.43.26.88.80)

Wine Bars

Les Papilles p275
30 rue Gay-Lussac, 5th
(01.43.25.20.79)

6th

Bars & Pubs

AZ Bar (Mezzanine) p250
Alcazar, 62 rue Mazarine, 6th (01.53.10.19.99)

Le Bar Dix p250
10 rue de l'Odéon, 6th
(01.43.26.66.83)

Le Comptoir des Canettes p251
11 rue des Canettes, 6th
(01.43.26.79.15)

Coolín p251
15 rue Clément, 6th
(01.44.07.00.92)

Fu Bar p251
5 rue St-Sulpice, 6th
(01.40.51.82.00)

The Highlander p251
8 rue de Nevers, 6th
(01.43.26.54.20)

Hôtel Lutétia p251
45 bd Raspail, 6th
(01.49.54.46.46)

La Marine p252
59 bd du Montparnasse, 6th
(01.45.48.27.70)

Le Mazet p252
61 rue St-André-des-Arts, 6th
(01.46.33.62.17)

The Moose p252
16 rue des Quatre-Vents, 6th
(01.46.33.77.00)

La Taverne de Nesle p252
32 rue Dauphine, 6th
(01.43.26.38.36)

Zéro de Conduite p252
14 rue Jacob, 6th
(01.46.34.26.35)

Bistros

Au 35 p37
35 rue Jacob, 6th
(01.42.60.23.24)

Allard p39
41 rue St-André-des-Arts, 6th
(01.43.26.48.23)

Au Bon Saint-Pourçain p39
10bis rue Servandoni, 6th
(01.43.54.93.63)

Bouillon Racine p39
3 rue Racine, 6th
(01.44.32.15.60)

Les Bouquinistes p39
53 quai des Grands-Augustins, 6th
(01.43.25.45.94)

Brasserie Fernand p39
13 rue Guisarde, 6th
(01.43.54.61.47)

Aux Charpentiers p40
10 rue Mabillon, 6th
(01.43.26.30.05)

Chez Marcel p40
7 rue Stanislas, 6th
(01.45.48.29.94)

L'Epi Dupin p40
11 rue Dupin, 6th
(01.42.22.64.56)

Josephine 'Chez Dumonet' p41
117 rue du Cherche-Midi, 6th (01.45.48.52.40)

Le Mâchon d'Henri p41
8 rue Guisarde, 6th
(01.43.29.08.70)

Le Parc Aux Cerfs p43
50 rue Vavin, 6th
(01.43.54.87.83)

Restaurant Wadja p43
10 rue de la Grande-Chaumière, 6th
(01.46.33.02.02)

Aux Saveurs de Claude p43
12 rue Stanislas, 6th
(01.45.44.41.74)

Le Timbre p43
3 rue Ste-Beuve, 6th
(01.45.49.10.40)

Home Delivery

Croissant Bon'Heur p294
12 rue de Rouen, 19th
(01.40.34.03.33)

Regional

Pavillon Puebla p136
parc des Buttes-Chaumont,
19th (01.42.08.92.62)

20th

Bistros

Bistro des Capucins p78
27 av Gambetta, 20th
(01.46.36.74.75)

Café Noir p78
15 rue St-Blaise, 20th
(01.40.09.75.80)

Le Zéphyr p78
1 rue du Jourdain, 20th
(01.46.36.65.81)

Bars & Pubs

La Flèche d'Or p264
102bis rue de Bagnolet,
20th (01.43.72.04.23)

La Fontaine d'Henri IV p264
42 bis rue des Cascades,
20th (no phone)

Lou Pascalou p264
14 rue des Panoyaux, 20th
(01.46.36.78.10)

Les Lucioles p264
102 bd de Ménilmontant,
20th (01.40.33.10.24)

Le Piston Pélican p264
15 rue de Bagnolet, 20th
(01.43.70.35.00)

Budget

La Boulangerie p160
15 rue des Panoyaux, 20th
(01.43.58.45.45)

Chez Jean p160
38 rue Boyer, 20th
(01.47.97.44.58)

Ma Pomme p160
107 rue de Ménilmontant,
20th (01.40.33.10.40)

Cafés

Le Soleil p241
136 bd de Ménilmontant,
20th (01.46.36.47.44)

Eating with Entertainment

Les Trois Châpeaux p282
48 rue des Cascades, 20th
(01.46.36.90.06)

Troubador Coffee House p282
70 bd de Ménilmontant,
20th (01.47.97.21.08)

Far Eastern

Salon de Thé Wenzhou p185
24 rue de Belleville, 20th
(01.46.36.56.33)

Jewish

Benittah p209
108 bd de Belleville, 20th
(no phone)

Shops & Markets

Boulangerie au 140 p287
140 rue de Belleville, 20th
(01.46.36.92.47)

Wine Bars

Le Baratin p277
3 rue Jouye-Rouve, 20th
(01.43.49.39.70)

Outside Paris

Africa & Indian Ocean

Rio dos Camarãos p168
55 rue Marceau, 93100
Montreuil-sous-bois
(01.42.87.34.84)

Bistros

Le Soleil p78
109 av Michelet, 93400 St-Ouen (01.40.10.08.08)

Brasseries

Café la Jatte p105
60 bd Vital Bouhot,
Ile de la Jatte, 92200
Neuilly-sur-Seine
(01.47.45.04.20)

Eating with Entertainment

Chez Gégène p282
162bis quai de Polangis,
allée des Guinguettes,
94345 Joinville-le-Pont
(01.48.83.29.43)

Le Guinguette de l'Ile du Martin-Pêcheur p282
41 quai Victor-Hugo, 94500
Champigny-sur-Marne
(01.49.83.03.02)

Far Eastern

Sinostar p186
27-29 av de Fontainebleau,
94270 Le Kremlin-Bicêtre
(01.49.60.88.88)

Trendy

Quai Ouest p111
1200 quai Marcel Dassault,
92210 St-Cloud
(01.46.02.35.54)

eatdrink.timeout.com

Subscribe now for a taste of over 2,500 London bars & restaurants

eatdrink.timeout.com – Time Out's online bar and restaurant guide

Lexicon

Can't make head or tail of French menus? Our alphabet of taste will allow you to tell your tête de veau from your queue de boeuf.

Food

A point medium (for meat).
Abats offal.
Accra salt-cod fritter.
Agneau lamb.
Aiglefin haddock.
Aiguillettes thin slices.
Ail garlic.
Aile wing.
Aïoli ground garlic sauce.
Airelle cranberry.
Algues seaweed.
Aligot mashed potatoes with cheese and garlic.
Aloyau beef loin.
Amande almond; **– de mer** small clam.
Amer/amère bitter.
Ananas pineapple.
Anchoïade anchovy paste.
Anchois anchovy.
Andouille pig's offal sausage, served cold.
Andouillette grilled chitterling (offal) sausage.
Aneth dill.
Anguille eel.
Anis aniseed.
Araignée de mer spider crab.
Artichaut artichoke.
Asperge asparagus.
Assiette plate.
Aubergine aubergine (GB), eggplant (US).
Avocat avocado.

Baies roses pink peppercorns.
Ballotine stuffed, rolled-up piece of boned fish or meat.
Bar sea bass.
Barbue brill.
Basilic basil.
Bavarois moulded cream dessert.
Bavette beef flank steak.
Béarnaise hollandaise sauce with tarragon and shallots.
Belon flat, round oyster.
Betterave beetroot.
Beurre butter; **– blanc** butter sauce with white wine and shallots; **– noir** browned butter.
Beignet fritter or doughnut.
Biche deer, venison.
Bien cuit well done (for meat).
Bifteck steak.
Bigorneau periwinkle.
Biologique organic.
Blanc white; **– de poulet** chicken breast.
Blanquette a 'white' stew (with eggs and cream).
Blette Swiss chard.
Boeuf beef; **– bourguignon** beef stew with red wine; **– du charolais** charolais beef (a breed);**– gros sel** boiled beef with vegetables; **– miroton** sliced boiled beef in onion sauce;**– de salers** salers beef (a breed).
Bordelaise sauce with red wine, shallots and marrow.
Boudin blanc white veal, chicken or pork sausage.
Boudin noir black (blood) pudding.
Bouillabaisse Mediterranean fish and shellfish soup.
Bouillon stock.
Bourride fish stew.
Brandade de morue salt cod puréed with olive oil.
Brebis sheep's milk cheese.
Brik North African filo pastry package.
Brochet pike.
Brochette kebab.
Brouillé(s) scrambled (egg).
Brûlé(e) literally, burned, usually caramelised.
Bulot whelk.

Cabillaud fresh cod.
Cabri young goat.
Caille quail.
Calamar squid.
Campagne/campagnard country-style.
Canard duck.
Canette duckling.
Cannelle cinnamon.
Carbonnade beef stew with onions and beer.
Carré d'agneau rack or loin of lamb.
Carrelet plaice.
Cassis blackcurrants, also blackcurrant liqueur in kir.
Cassoulet stew of haricot beans, sausage and preserved duck.
Céleri celery.
Céleri rave celeriac.
Céleri rémoulade grated celariac in mustard mayonnaise.
Cèpe cep or porcini mushroom.
Cerfeuil chervil.
Cerise cherry.
Cervelas garlicky Alsatian pork sausage.
Cervelle brains.
Champignon mushroom; **– de Paris** cultivated button mushroom.
Chantilly whipped cream.
Chapon capon.
Charcuterie cured meat, such as saucisson or pâté.
Charlotte moulded cream dessert with a biscuit edge.
Chasseur sauce with white wine, mushrooms, shallots and tomato.
Châtaigne chestnut.
Chateaubriand fillet steak.
Chaud(e) hot.
Chaud-froid glazing sauce with gelatine or aspic.
Chausson pastry turnover.
Cheval horse.
A cheval with egg on top.
Chèvre goat's cheese.
Chevreuil young roe deer.
Chicorée frisée, or curly endive (GB), chicory (US).
Chiffonade shredded herbs and vegetables.
Chipiron squid.
Choron béarnaise sauce with tomato purée.
Chou cabbage; **– de Bruxelles** Brussels sprout; **– frisé** kale; **– rouge** red cabbage; **—fleur** cauliflower.
Choucroute sauerkraut (garnie if topped with cured ham and

sausages).
Ciboulette chive.
Citron lemon.
Citron vert lime.
Citronelle lemongrass.
Citrouille pumpkin.
Civet game stew in blood-thickened sauce.
Clafoutis thick batter baked with fruit.
Cochon pig; **– de lait** suckling pig.
Cochonnailles cured pig parts (ears, snout, cheeks...).
Coeur heart.
Coing quince.
Colin hake.
Concombre cucumber.
Confiture jam.
Congre conger eel.
Contre-filet sirloin.
Coq rooster.
à la Coque in its shell.
Coquelet baby rooster.
Coquillages shellfish.
Coquille shell; **– St-Jacques** scallop.
Cornichon pickled gherkin
Côte/côtelette rib or chop.
Côte de boeuf beef rib.
Cotriade Breton fish stew.
Coulis thick sauce or purée.
Courge vegetable marrow (GB), squash (US).
Courgette courgette (GB), zucchini (US).
Crème anglaise custard.
Crème brûlée caramelised custard dessert.
Crème fraîche thick, slightly soured cream.
Crêpe pancake.
Crépinette small, flattish sausage, often grilled.
Cresson watercress.
Creuse oyster with long, crinkly shell.
Crevette prawn (GB), shrimp (US); **– grise** grey shrimp.
Croque-madame croque monsieur topped with an egg.
Croque-monsieur toasted cheese and ham sandwich.
Crottin small, round goat cheese (literally, turd).
Croustade bread or pastry case, deep-fried.
en Croûte in a pastry case.
Crudités raw vegetables.
Crustacé shellfish.
Cuisse leg (poultry).
Curcuma turmeric.

Darne fish steak.
Datte date.
Daube meat braised slowly in red wine.
Daurade/dorade sea bream.
Demi-glace meat glaze.
Demi-sel slightly salted
Désossé(e) boned.
Diable demi-glace with cayenne and white wine.
Dinde turkey.
Duxelles chopped, sautéed mushrooms with shallots.

Echalote shallot.
Ecrémé skimmed (milk).
Ecrevisse crayfish.
Emincé fine slice.
Encornet squid.
Endive chicory (GB), Belgian endive (US).
Entrecôte beef rib steak.
Entremets cream or milk-based dessert.
Eperlan smelt; whitebait.
Epicé(e) spicy.
Epices spices.
Epinards spinach.
Escabèche fish fried, marinated and served cold.
Escalope cutlet.
Escarole slightly bitter, slightly curly salad leaves.
Espadon swordfish.
Espelette small, hot Basque pepper.
Estouffade meat stew.
Estragon tarragon.
Etrille small crab.

Faisan pheasant.
Farci(e) stuffed.
Faux-filet sirloin steak.
Fenouil fennel.
Feuille de chêne oak leaf lettuce.
Feuilleté puff pastry.
Fève broad bean.
Figue fig.
Filet mignon tenderloin.
Financier small rectangular cake.
Fines de claire crinkle-shelled oysters.
Fines herbes mixed herbs.
Flambé(e) sprinkled with alcohol, then set alight.
Flet flounder.
Flétan halibut.
Florentine with spinach.
Foie liver.
Foie gras fattened liver of goose or duck; **– cru** raw foie gras; **– entier** whole foie gras; **– mi-cuit** barely cooked (also called frais or nature); **pâté de –** liver pâté with a foie gras base.
Fondu(e) melted.
Fondue savoyarde bread dipped into melted cheese.
Fondue bourguignonne beef dipped in heated oil.
Forestière with mushrooms.
au four oven-baked.
Fourré(e) filled or stuffed.
Frais/fraîche fresh.
Fraise strawberry; **– des bois** wild strawberry; **– de veau** part of the calf's intestine.
Framboise raspberry.
Frappé(e) iced or chilled.
Fricadelle meatball.
Frisée curly endive (GB), chicory (US).
Frit(e) fried.
Frites chips (UK), French fries (US).
Friture tiny fried fish.
Froid(e) cold.
Fromage cheese; **– blanc** smooth cream cheese.
Fruits secs dried fruit and nuts.
Fruits de mer seafood, especially shellfish.
Fumé(e) smoked.
Fumet fish stock.

Galantine pressed meat or fish, usually stuffed.
Galette flat cake of savoury pastry, potato pancake or

buckwheat crêpe.
Garbure thick vegetable and meat soup.
Garni(e) garnished.
Gelée jelly or aspic.
Genièvre juniper berry.
Gésiers gizzards.
Gibier game.
Gigot d'agneau leg of lamb.
Gigue haunch of game, usually venison or boar.
Gingembre ginger.
Girofle clove.
Girolle wild mushroom.
Gîte shin of beef.
Gîte à la noix topside or silverside of beef.
Glace ice, also ice cream.
Glacé(e) frozen; ice-cold; iced (as in cake).
Glaçon ice cube.
Gombo okra.
Gougère choux pastry and cheese mixture in a ring.
Goujon breaded, fried strip of fish; also a small catfish.
Goût taste.
Goûter to taste, or snack.
Graisse fat, grease.
Granité water-ice.
Gras(se) fatty.
Gratin dauphinois sliced potatoes baked with milk, cheese and garlic.
Gratiné(e) browned with breadcrumbs or cheese.
Grattons pork crackling.
à la Grecque served cold in olive oil and lemon juice.
Grenade pomegranate.
Grenadier delicate, white-fleshed sea fish.
Grenoblois sauce with cream, capers and lemon.
Grenouille frog.
Gribiche sauce of vinegar, capers, gherkins and egg.
Grillade grilled food, often mixed grill.
Grillé(e) grilled.
Griotte morello cherry.
Gros(se) large.
Groseille redcurrant.
Groseille à maquereau gooseberry.
Gros sel rock salt.

Haché(e) chopped, minced (GB), ground (US).
Hachis minced meat (hash); **– Parmentier** minced meat with mashed potato topping.
Haddock smoked haddock.
Hareng herring.
Haricot bean.
Herbe herb; grass.
Hollandaise sauce of egg, butter, vinegar, and lemon.
Homard lobster.
Huile oil.
Huître oyster.
Hure cold sausage made from boar's or pig's head.

Ile flottante poached, whipped-egg white 'island' in vanilla custard.

Jambon ham; **– de Paris** cooked ham; **– cru** raw, cured ham; **– fumé** smoked ham; **– de pays** cured country ham.
Jambonneau ham hock; **– de canard** stuffed duck drumstick.
Jardinière with vegetables.
Jarret shin or knuckle.
Joue cheek or jowl.
Julienne finely cut vegetables; also ling (fish).
Jus juice.

Lait milk. **(agneau/cochon) de lait** milk-fed lamb/suckling pig.
Laitue lettuce.
Lamproie lamprey eel.
Landaise in goose fat with garlic, onion and ham.
Langue tongue.
Langouste spiny lobster or crawfish.
Langoustine Dublin Bay prawns or scampi.
Lapereau young rabbit.
Lapin rabbit.
Lard bacon.
Lardon cubed bacon bit.
Légume vegetable.
Lentille lentil.
Levraut young hare.
Lièvre hare.
Liégoise coffee or chocolate ice-cream sundae.
Lieu jaune pollack.
Limande lemon sole.
Lisette small mackerel.
Litchi lychee.
Lotte monkfish.
Loup sea bass.
Lyonnais served with onions or sautéed potatoes.

Mâche lamb's lettuce.
Madère Madeira.
Magret de canard duck breast.
Maïs maize, corn.
Maison homemade, or house special.
Mangue mango.
Maquereau mackerel.
Marcassin young wild boar.
Mariné(e) marinated.
Marjolaine marjoram.
Marmite small cooking pot, or a stew served in one; **– dieppoise** Normandy fish stew.
Marquise mousse-like cake.
Marron chestnut.
Matelote freshwater fish stew cooked in wine.
Mélange mixture.
Ménagère home-style.
Menthe mint.
Merguez spicy lamb or lamb and beef sausage.
Merlan whiting.
Mesclun mixed young salad leaves.
Meunière fish with browned butter and lemon.
Meurette red wine and stock used for poaching.
Mi-cuit(e) half/semi-cooked
Miel honey.
Mignon small meat fillet.
Millefeuille puff pastry with many layers.
Minute fried quickly.
Mirabelle tiny yellow plum.
Mirepoix chopped carrots, onion and celery.
Moelle bone marrow.
Morille morel mushroom.
Mornay béchamel sauce with

cheese.
Morue cod, usually salt cod.
Mou lights (lungs).
Moules mussels; **– marinières** cooked in white wine with shallots.
Moulu(e) ground, milled.
Mousseline hollandaise sauce with whipped cream.
Mousseron type of wild mushroom.
Moutarde mustard.
Mouton mutton.
Mulet grey mullet.
Mûre blackberry.
Muscade nutmeg.
Myrtille bilberry/blueberry.

Nage poaching liquid.
Nantua crayfish sauce.
Nature plain, ungarnished.
Navarin lamb stew.
Navet turnip.
Nid nest.
Noisette hazelnut, or small, round piece of meat, or coffee with a little milk.
Noix walnut.
Nouilles noodles.

Oeuf egg; **– à la coque** soft-boiled; **– cocotte** baked with cream; **– dur** hard-boiled; **– en meurette** poached in red wine; **– à la neige** see île flottante.
Oie goose.
Oignon onion.
Onglet similar to bavette.
Oreille ear, usually pig's.
Orge barley.
Ortie nettle, used in soup.
Os bone.
Oseille sorrel.
Oursin sea urchin.

Pain bread (see also p107); **– d'épices** honey gingerbread; **– grillé** toast; **– perdu** French toast.
Palombe wood pigeon.
Palourde a type of clam.
Pamplemousse grapefruit.
en Papillote steamed in foil or paper packet.
Panaché mixture.
Panais parsnip.
Pané(e) breaded.
Parfait sweet or savoury mousse-like mixture.
Parmentier with potato.
Pastèque watermelon.
Pâte pastry.
Pâté meat or fish pâté; **– en croûte** in a pastry case (similar to pork pie).
Pâtes pasta or noodles.
Paupiette meat or fish rolled up and tied, usually stuffed.
Pavé thick, square steak.
Pêcheur based on fish.
Perdreau young partridge.
Perdrix partridge.
Persil parsley.
Petit gris small snail.
Petit pois pea.
Petit salé salt pork.
Pétoncle queen scallop.
Pets de nonne ('nuns farts') light puffy fritters.
Pied foot (or trotter).
Pigeonneau young pigeon.
Pignon pine kernel.
Piment pepper or chilli.
Pimenté(e) spicy.
Pince claw.
Pintade/pintadeau guinea fowl.
Pipérade Basque egg, pepper, tomato, onion and ham mixture.
Pissaladière anchovy, tomato and onion tart.
Pistache pistachio nut.
Pistou Provençal basil and garlic pesto, without pine nuts.
Plat dish; main course.
Plate flat-shelled oyster.
Pleurotte oyster mushroom.
Poché(e) poached.
Pochetot skate.
Poêlé(e) pan-fried.
Poire pear.
Poireau leek.
Poisson fish.
Poitrine breast cut.
Poivrade peppery brown sauce served with meat.
Poivre pepper.
Poivron red or green pepper.
Pomme apple.
Pomme de terre potato (often referred to as pomme); **– à l'huile** cold, boiled potatoes in oil; **– au four** baked potato; **– dauphines** deep-fried croquettes of puréed potato; **– lyonnaises** sliced potatoes fried with onions; **– parisiennes** potatoes fried and tossed in a meat glaze; **– soufflées** puffed up, deep-fried potato skins; **– voisin** grated potato cake with cheese.
Porc pork.
Porcelet suckling pig.
Potage thick soup.
Pot-au-feu boiled beef with vegetables.
Potée meat and vegetable stew.
Potiron pumpkin.
Poudre powder or granules.
Poularde chicken or hen.
Poule hen; **– au pot** stewed with vegetables and broth.
Poulet chicken
Poulpe octopus.
Poussin small chicken.
Praire small clam.
Pressé(e) squeezed.
Primeur early or young, of fruit, vegetables or wine.
Printanière springtime; served with vegetables.
Profiterole ice-cream filled pastry puff, served with melted chocolate.
Provençal(e) with garlic and tomatoes, and often onions, anchovies or olives.
Prune plum.
Pruneau prune.

Quenelle poached dumplings, usually pike.
Quetsch damson plum.
Queue tail.
Queue de boeuf oxtail.

Râble saddle.
Racine root.
Raclette melted cheese served with boiled potatoes.
Radis radish.
Ragoût meat stew.
Raie skate.

Raifort horseradish.
Raisin grape.
Râpé(e) grated.
Rascasse scorpion fish.
Ratte small, firm potato.
Ravigote thick vinaigrette.
Ravioles de Royans tiny cheese ravioli.
Recette recipe.
Récolte harvest.
Régime diet.
Réglisse liquorice.
à la Reine with chicken.
Reine-claude greengage (plum).
Reinette dessert apple.
Rémoulade mayonnaise with mustard, chopped herbs, capers and gherkins.
Rillettes potted meat, usually pork and/or goose.
Rillons crispy chunks of pork belly.
Ris sweetbreads.
Riz rice; **– sauvage** wild rice.
Rognon kidney.
Romarin rosemary.
Roquette rocket.
Rosbif roast beef.
Rosette dry, salami-like pork sausage from Lyon.
Rôti roast.
Rouget red mullet.
Roulade rolled-up portion.
Rouille red, cayenne-seasoned mayonnaise.
Roussette rock salmon (dogfish).
Roux flour-and butter-based sauce.
Rumsteck rump steak.

Sabayon frothy sauce made with wine and egg yolks, sometimes a dessert.
Sablé shortbread biscuit.
Saignant rare (for meat)
Safran saffron.
St-Pierre John Dory.
Saisonnier seasonal.
Salé(e) salted.
Salmis game or poultry stew.
Sandre pike-perch.
Sang blood.
Sanglier wild boar.
Sarrasin buckwheat.
Sarriette savory (herb).
Saucisse fresh sausage.
Saucisson small sausage.
Saucisson sec dried sausage, eaten cold.
Sauge sage.
Saumon salmon.
Saumonette sea eel, or dog fish.
Sauvage wild.
gratin Savoyard potatoes baked in stock with cheese.
Scarole see escarole.
Sec/sèche dry.
Seiche squid.
Sel salt.
Selle saddle or back.
Sirop syrup.
Soisson white bean.
Soja soya.
Soubise béchamel sauce with rice and cream.
Souper supper.
Souris d'agneau lamb knuckle.
Speck Italian smoked ham.
Sucre sugar.
Sucré(e) sweet.
Supion small cuttlefish.
Suprême breast; **– de volaille** fowl in a white roux with cream and meat juice.
crêpe Suzette pancake flambéed in orange liqueur.

Tapenade Provençal black olive and caper paste, usually with anchovies.
Tartare raw minced steak (also tuna or salmon).
Tarte Tatin caramelised upside-down apple tart.
Tartine buttered baguette or open sandwich.
Tendron de veau veal rib.
Tête head.
Thon tuna.
Thym thyme.
Tian Provençal gratin cooked in an earthenware dish.
Tiède tepid or warm.
Timbale rounded mould, or food cooked in one.
Tisane herbal tea.
Tomate tomato; **– de mer** sea anemone.
Topinambour Jerusalem artichoke.
Toulouse large sausage.
Tournedos thick slices taken from a fillet of beef.
Tournesol sunflower.
Tourte covered tart or pie, usually savoury.
Tourteau large crab.
Tranche slice.
Travers de porc spare ribs.
Trénels lamb's tripe.
Tripes tripe.
Tripoux Auvergnat dish of sheep's tripe and feet.
Trompette de la mort horn of plenty mushroom.
Truffade fried potato cake or mashed potato with cheese.
Truffe truffle, the ultimate fungus, blanche (white) or noire (black); chocolate truffle.
Truffé(e) stuffed or garnished with truffles.
Truite trout; **– de mer/ – saumonée** salmon trout.

Vacherin a meringue, fruit and ice cream cake; or soft, cow's milk cheese.
Vapeur steam.
Veau veal; **– élevé sous la mère** milk-fed veal.
Velouté sauce made with white roux and bouillon; creamy soup.
Ventre belly, breast or stomach.
Vénus American clam.
Verdurette vinaigrette with herbs and and egg.
Viande meat.
Vichyssoise cold leek and potato soup.
Volaille poultry.

Yaourt yoghurt.

Zeste zest or peel.

Drinks

Appellation d'Origine Contrôlée (AOC) wine (or food) conforming to specific strict quality rules.
Bière beer.

What Londoners take when they go out.

Bock 12cl of beer.
Boire to drink.
Boisson a drink.
Blanche pale wheat beer.
Blonde lager (GB), beer (US).
Brune dark beer.
Café small espresso coffee; **– allongé** 'lengthened' (twice the water); **– au lait** milky coffee; **– crème** coffee with steamed milk; **– serré** strong espresso, (half the water); **grand –** double espresso.
Calvados apple brandy.
Cardinal kir with red wine.
Chope tankard.
Citron pressé freshly squeezed lemon juice.
Chocolat (chaud) (hot) chocolate.
Décaféiné/déca decaffeinated coffee.
Demi (demi-pression) 25cl of draught beer; **– ordinaire** 25cl of the least-expensive lager.
Demi-litre half a litre (50cl).
Express espresso; **double –** double espresso.
Gazeuse fizzy/carbonated.
Grand cru top-quality wine.
Infusion herbal or fruit tea.
Jus de fruits fruit juice.
Kir crème de cassis and dry white wine – **royal** crème de cassis and Champagne.
Lait milk.
Marc clear brandy made from grape residues.
Mauresque pastis with almond syrup.
Mirabelle plum brandy.
Noisette espresso with a drop of milk.
Orange pressée freshly squeezed orange juice.
Panaché beer and lemonade shandy.
Pastis anise apéritif.
Perroquet pastis with mint syrup.
Pichet jug or carafe.
Plat(e) still, non-carbonated.
Poire Williams pear brandy.
Porto port.
Pot lyonnais 46cl carafe.
Pression draught lager.
Quart quarter litre (25cl).
Rousse red, bitter-like beer.
Thé tea.
Tilleuil linden flower tea.
Tisane herbal tea.
Tomate pastis with grenadine syrup.
Verveine verbena tea.
Vieille Prune plum brandy.
Xerès sherry.

Saved by a phrase

Get out of sticky situations in Paris restaurants.

Is there any raw shellfish in this dish?
Y-a-t'il des fruits de mer crus dans ce plat?

I'm allergic to... peanuts/seafood.
Je suis allergique aux... arachides/fruits de mer.

I can't eat anything that contains...milk/wheat/fat.
Je ne peux rien manger qui contient... du lait/du blé/ de la graisse.

I'm a vegetarian – no white or red meat, no fish.
Je suis végétarien – je ne mange ni viande blanche, ni viande rouge, ni poisson.

Will you ask the chef not to put too much salt in it, please?
Pourriez-vous demander au chef de mettre très peu de sel, s'il vous plaît?

I'm on a diet, what do you recommend?
Je suis au régime. Pourriez-vous me conseiller un plat diététique?

Does the special include any pork/offal?
Est-ce que le plat du jour contient du porc/des abats?

What can you recommend for children?
Que pouvez-vous conseiller pour les enfants?

Do you have any less fragrant cheeses?
Avez-vous des fromages moins forts?

Which of the desserts is the lightest?
Quel est le plus léger des desserts?

Do you have any sandwiches without mayonnaise?
Avez-vous des sandwichs sans mayonnaise?

I liked it very much, but I have a small appetite.
C'était très bon, mais j'ai un petit appétit.

I'd love to eat something really spicy.
J'aimerais manger quelque chose de très épicé.

Savoir-faire

Addition bill.
Amuse-gueule (or amuse-bouche) appetiser or hors d'oeuvre.
Assiette plate.
A la carte ordered separately (i.e. not on the fixed-price menu or formule).
Carte des vins wine list.
Cendrier ashtray.
Commande order.
Commander to order.
Compris(e) included.
Comptoir counter.
Couvert cutlery, also used to express number of diners.
Couteau knife.
Cuillère spoon.
Dégustation tasting.
Eau du robinet tap water.
Entrée starter.
Espace non-fumeur non-smoking area.
Formule set-price menu.
Fourchette fork.
Majoration price increase.
Menu set-price selection, also called a formule or prix fixe.
Menu dégustation tasting menu, sampling several different dishes.
Monnaie change.
Plat main course.
Pourboire tip.
Serveur/serveuse waiter/waitress.
Rince-doigts finger bowl.
Verre glass.
Zinc bar counter.

Paris Arrondissements
N192
D909
SAINT
Marché a
PORTE DE
ST-OUEN
CLIGNAN
PÉRIPH
QUAI DU MARÉCHAL JOFFRE
Q. MICHELET
R.VICTOR HUGO
BD.JEAN JAURÈS
RUE MARTRE
BOULEVARD VICTOR HUGO
CLICHY
COURBEVOIE
AV.MARCEAU
AV.DE LA RÉPUBLIQUE
BD.DE VERDUN
RUE DE BEZONS
BD. DE BOURDON
RUE P. VAILLANT COUTURIER
PORTE DE
CLICHY
BD.BESSIÈRES
AV.DE ST-OUEN
BOULEVARD
La Grande
Arche
QUAI DU PRÉSIDENT
PAUL DOUMER
BD.DU GÉN.LECLERC
CHATEAU
LEVALLOIS-
PERRET
PORTE
D'ASNIÈRES
BERTHIER
MONTMA
N314
LA DÉFENSE
BOULEVARD DU
BOULEVARD
PORTE DE
CHAMPERRET
17
AVENUE DE CLICHY
CIRCULAIRE
BOULEVARD BINEAU
NEUILLY-
SUR-SEINE
WAGRAM
N13
RUE DE LA RÉPUBLIQUE
VICTOR
AV.DE VILLIERS
CLICHY
BD.DU GÉN.KŒNIG
AV.CHARLES DE GAULLE
BOULEVARD
BD. DES BATIGNOLLES
PUTEAUX
QUAI DE DION BOUTON
RUE DE LONGCHAMP
PORTE DES
TERNES
Palais des
Congrès
AV. DE WAGRAM
BD.DE COURCELLES
Parc
Monceau
MALESHERBES
Gare
St Lazare
RUE D'AMSTERDAM
PORTE
MAILLOT
TERNES
AV.DE LA
GR.ARMÉE
BOULEVARD
HAUSSMANN
BD.DU BORD DE L'EAU
RUE DE MAHATMA GANDHI
Arc de
Triomphe
8
RUE LA BOÉTIE
MADELEINE
ALLÉE DU BORD DE L'EAU
ROUTE DE SÈVRES À NEUILLY
MARGUERITE
PORTE
DAUPHINE
AVENUE FOCH
AV. MARCEAU
AV. DES CHAMPS ÉLYSÉES
Palais de
l'Élysée
Palais
Garni
ALLÉE DE LONGCHAMP
PÉRIPHÉRIQUE OEST
BOULEVARD LANNES
AVENUE VICTOR HUGO
AVENUE KLÉBER
AV.GEORGE V
Palais
Galliera
Madeleine
AV.DE L'OPÉRA
N185
PORTE DE
LA MUETTE
16
Grand
Palais
Petit
Palais
CONCORDE
ALLÉE DE LA REINE
Bois de
Boulogne
Palais de
Tokyo
See larger
QUAI D'ORSAY
Q.DES TUILERIES
AV. DE NEW YORK
Assemblée
Nationale
Pyramide
ROUTE DE L'HIPPODROME
PORTE DE
PASSY
PASSY
Palais de
Chaillot
QUAI BRANLY
AVENUE BOSQUET
INVALIDES
Musée
d'Orsay
SUCHET
Musée
Marmottan
RUE DE PASSY
Tour
Eiffel
Hôtel des
Invalides
St Germain
des Prés
R.DE VARENNE
RUE DU RANELAGH
AVENUE
AV.DE TOURVILLE
7
Hippodrome
d'Auteuil
BOULEVARD
Maison
de la Radio
BD.GRENELLE
École
Militaire
DE
R.DE BABYLONE
PORTE
D'AUTEUIL
AUTEUIL
UNESCO
A13
PORTE DE
BOULOGNE
VOIE G.POMPIDOU
Q.ANDRÉ CITROËN
RUE SAINT CHARLES
AV. ÉMILE ZOLA
SUFFREN
RUE DES SÈVRES
RUE DE RENNES
6
Palais
Luxemb
PORTE
MOLITOR
BOULEVARD MURAT
AVENUE DE VERSAILLES
RUE BALARD
RUE DE LA CONVENTION
GRENELLE
RUE
BD.DU MONTPARNASSE
N307
Parc des
Princes
RUE LECOURBE
RUE DE VAUGIRARD
Gare
Montparnasse
AVENUE DU MAINE
BD.RASPAIL
ROUTE DE LA REINE
Parc
André Citroën
RUE
CAMBRONNE
AV.A.MORIZET
BD.DE JEAN JAURÈS
BD. VICTOR
RUE DE VOUILLÉ
LOSSERAND
R.FROIDEVAUX
PORTE DE
ST CLOUD
QUAI
D'ISSY
Palais des
Sports
PORTE DE
VERSAILLES
15
See larger
scale maps
DENFERT-
ROCHEREAU
AV.DU GÉN.
LECLERC
Q.DU POINT DU JOUR
Héliport
de Paris
BD.
PORTE DE
SÈVRES
PÉRIPHÉRIQUE
R.E.
RENAN
Paris-Expo
R. RAYMOND
R D'ALÉSIA
AV.DU GÉN.LECLERC
BOULOGNE-
BILLANCOURT
ISSY-LES-
MOULINEAUX
GALLIENI
SUD
Marché aux Puces
de Vanves
BOULEVARD
BRUNE
AV. J
MOULIN
RUE D
N10
PORTE DE
LA PLAINE
PORTE
BRANÇION
14
QUAI DE STALINGRAD
Seine
AV. V. CRESSON
PORTE DE
VANVES
QUAI DE STALINGRAD
R.E.LAVAL
PORTE DE
CHÂTILLON
PORTE
D'ORLÉANS
AV.DE VERDUN
BD. RODIN
BD.G.PÉRI
AV. ARISTIDE BRIAND
AV.DE LA PAIX
VANVES
AV.PIERRE BROSSOLETTE
AVENUE JEAN JAURÈS
MEUDON
Fort d'Issy
MALAKOFF
BOULEVARD DE STALINGRAD
CLAMART
Fort de
Vanves
AV.J.JAUR
MONTROUGE
CHÂTILLON
D906
N20

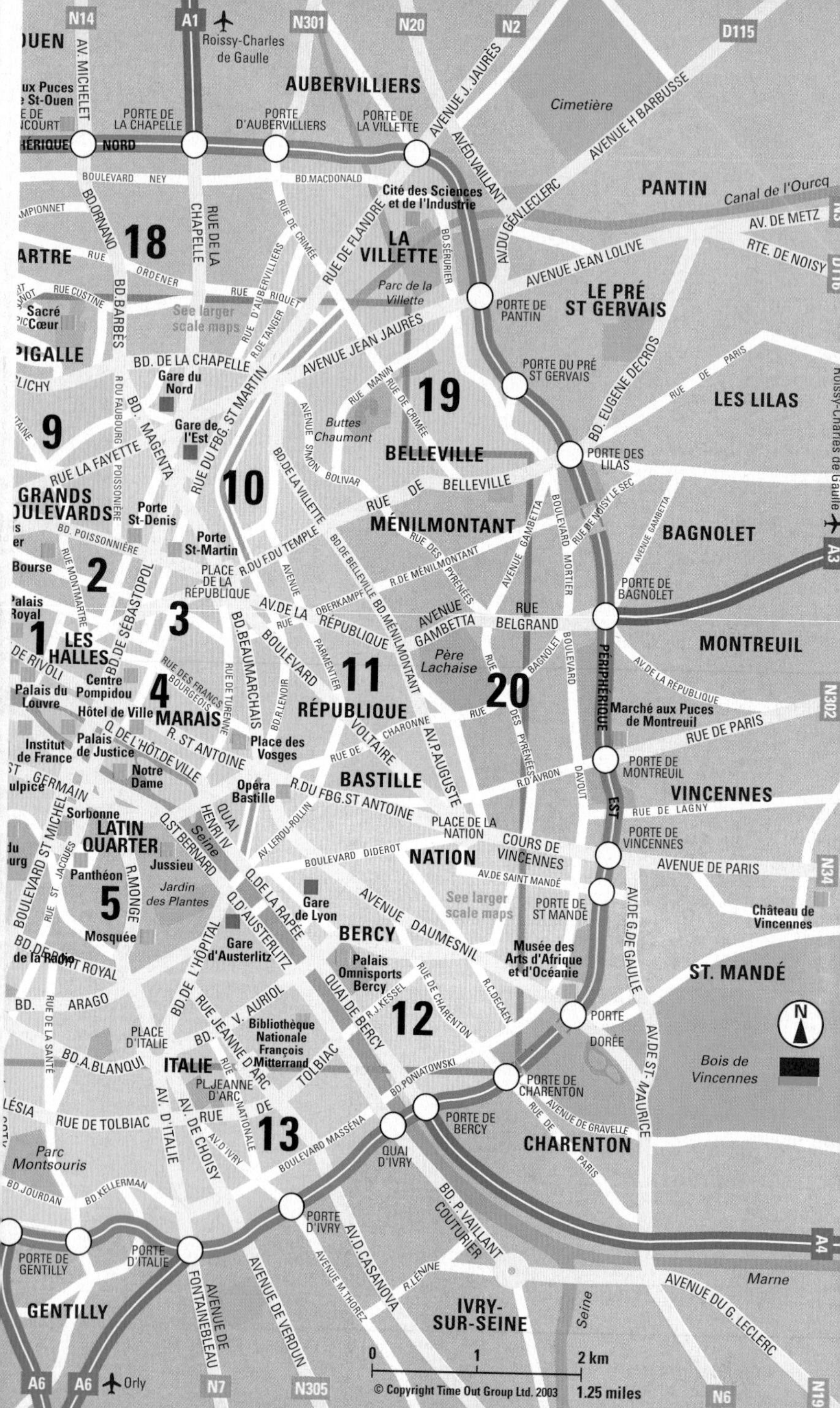

N14
A1
Roissy-Charles de Gaulle
N301
N20
N2
D115
AUBERVILLIERS
AV. MICHELET
Cimetière
AVENUE J. JAURÈS
AVENUE H BARBUSSE
PORTE DE LA CHAPELLE
PORTE D'AUBERVILLIERS
PORTE DE LA VILLETTE
NORD
AV.ÉD.VAILLANT
BOULEVARD NEY
BD.MACDONALD
Cité des Sciences et de l'Industrie
PANTIN
Canal de l'Ourcq
BD.ORNANO
RUE DE LA CHAPELLE
RUE DE CRIMÉE
RUE DE FLANDRE
AV.DU GÉN.LECLERC
AV. DE METZ
18
LA VILLETTE
BD.SERURIER
RTE. DE NOISY
RUE ORDENER
AVENUE JEAN LOLIVE
RUE RIQUET
RUE D'AUBERVILLIERS
Parc de la Villette
LE PRÉ ST GERVAIS
RUE CUSTINE
PORTE DE PANTIN
Sacré Cœur
BD. BARBÈS
See larger scale maps
R.DE TANGER
AVENUE JEAN JAURÈS
PIGALLE
BD. DE LA CHAPELLE
PORTE DU PRÉ ST GERVAIS
BD. EUGENE DECROS
RUE DE PARIS
Gare du Nord
RUE MANIN
RUE DE CRIMÉE
19
LES LILAS
RUE DU FAUBOURG POISSONNIÈRE
BD. MAGENTA
RUE DU FBG. ST MARTIN
9
Gare de l'Est
Buttes Chaumont
AVENUE SIMON BOLIVAR
BELLEVILLE
PORTE DES LILAS
RUE LA FAYETTE
BD.DE LA VILLETTE
10
RUE DE BELLEVILLE
Roissy-Charles de Gaulle
GRANDS
Porte St-Denis
MÉNILMONTANT
BOULEVARD MORTIER
RUE DE NOISY LE SEC
AVENUE GAMBETTA
BAGNOLET
BD. POISSONNIÈRE
Porte St-Martin
R.DU F.DU TEMPLE
BD.DE BELLEVILLE
RUE DES PYRÉNÉES
R.DE MÉNILMONTANT
A3
Bourse
RUE MONTMARTRE
2
PLACE DE LA RÉPUBLIQUE
AVENUE PARMENTIER
RUE OBERKAMPF
PORTE DE BAGNOLET
Palais Royal
BD. DE SÉBASTOPOL
3
AV.DE LA RÉPUBLIQUE
BD.MÉNILMONTANT
AVENUE GAMBETTA
RUE BELGRAND
1
LES HALLES
BD.BEAUMARCHAIS
BOULEVARD
Père Lachaise
RUE BAGNOLET
BOULEVARD DAVOUT
PÉRIPHÉRIQUE
MONTREUIL
RUE DE RIVOLI
RUE DES FRANCS BOURGEOIS
RUE DE TURENNE
11
Centre Pompidou
BD.R.LENOIR
20
AV.DE LA RÉPUBLIQUE
N302
Palais du Louvre
4
RÉPUBLIQUE
RUE DES PYRÉNÉES
Marché aux Puces de Montreuil
Hôtel de Ville
MARAIS
VOLTAIRE
RUE DE CHARONNE
AV.P.AUGUSTE
RUE DE PARIS
Institut de France
Palais de Justice
Q. DE L'HÔT.DE VILLE
R. ST ANTOINE
Place des Vosges
PORTE DE MONTREUIL
Notre Dame
BASTILLE
R.D'AVRON
GERMAIN
Opéra Bastille
R.DU FBG.ST ANTOINE
VINCENNES
Sorbonne
QUAI HENRI IV
AV. LEDRU-ROLLIN
RUE DE LAGNY
LATIN QUARTER
Seine
PLACE DE LA NATION
EST
BOULEVARD ST MICHEL
RUE ST JACQUES
Q.ST BERNARD
PORTE DE VINCENNES
COURS DE VINCENNES
BOULEVARD DIDEROT
NATION
AVENUE DE PARIS
Jussieu
AV.DE SAINT MANDÉ
N34
Panthéon
R.MONGE
Jardin des Plantes
Q.DE LA RAPÉE
Gare de Lyon
See larger scale maps
PORTE DE ST MANDÉ
AV.DE G.DE GAULLE
5
Q.D'AUSTERLITZ
AVENUE DAUMESNIL
Château de Vincennes
Mosquée
Gare d'Austerlitz
BERCY
Musée des Arts d'Afrique et d'Océanie
ST. MANDÉ
BD.DE L'HÔPITAL
Palais Omnisports Bercy
QUAI DE BERCY
RUE DE CHARENTON
R.C.DECAEN
BD. ARAGO
RUE DE LA SANTÉ
BD. V. AURIOL
R.J.KESSEL
12
PORTE DORÉE
N
PLACE D'ITALIE
RUE JEANNE D'ARC
Bibliothèque Nationale François Mitterrand
BD.A.BLANQUI
ITALIE
TOLBIAC
Bois de Vincennes
AV.DE ST. MAURICE
PL.JEANNE D'ARC
BD.PONIATOWSKI
PORTE DE CHARENTON
RUE DE TOLBIAC
AV. D'ITALIE
AV. DE CHOISY
RUE NATIONALE
13
PORTE DE BERCY
AVENUE DE GRAVELLE
RUE DE PARIS
CHARENTON
Parc Montsouris
AV.D'IVRY
BOULEVARD MASSÉNA
QUAI D'IVRY
BD.JOURDAN
BD.KELLERMAN
PORTE D'IVRY
BD. P. VAILLANT COUTURIER
AV.D.CASANOVA
PORTE DE GENTILLY
PORTE D'ITALIE
A4
AVENUE M.THOREZ
R.LÉNINE
Marne
AVENUE DU G. LECLERC
GENTILLY
AVENUE DE FONTAINEBLEAU
AVENUE DE VERDUN
IVRY-SUR-SEINE
Seine
0
1
2 km
1.25 miles
A6
A6
Orly
N7
N305
© Copyright Time Out Group Ltd. 2003
N6
N19

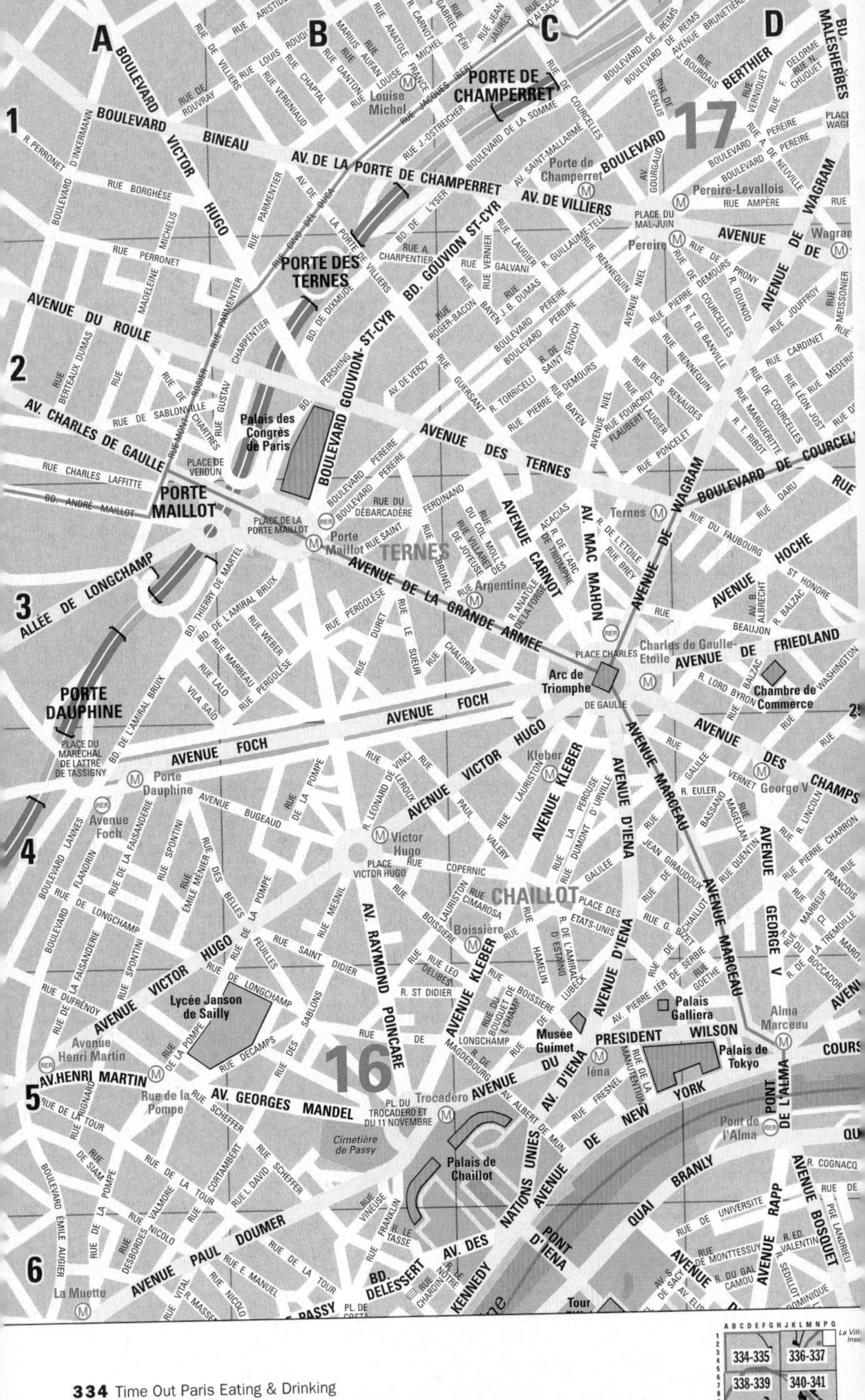
A
B
C
D
1
2
3
4
5
6
17
16
PORTE DE CHAMPERRET
Louise Michel
BOULEVARD BINEAU
BOULEVARD VICTOR HUGO
AV. DE LA PORTE DE CHAMPERRET
Porte de Champerret
BOULEVARD BERTHIER
AV. DE VILLIERS
Pereire-Levallois
PLACE DU MAL-JUIN
Pereire
AVENUE DE WAGRAM
Wagram
PORTE DES TERNES
AVENUE DU ROULE
BD. GOUVION ST-CYR
BOULEVARD GOUVION- ST-CYR
AV. CHARLES DE GAULLE
Palais des Congrès de Paris
PLACE DE VERDUN
AVENUE DES TERNES
BOULEVARD PEREIRE
BOULEVARD DE COURCELLES
RUE CHARLES LAFFITTE
BD. ANDRÉ MAILLOT
PORTE MAILLOT
PLACE DE LA PORTE MAILLOT
Porte Maillot
TERNES
Ternes
AV. MAC MAHON
AVENUE CARNOT
AVENUE HOCHE
ALLÉE DE LONGCHAMP
AVENUE DE LA GRANDE ARMEE
Argentine
PLACE CHARLES DE GAULLE
Arc de Triomphe
Charles de Gaulle-Etoile
AVENUE DE FRIEDLAND
Chambre de Commerce
PORTE DAUPHINE
PLACE DU MARECHAL DE LATTRE DE TASSIGNY
AVENUE FOCH
Porte Dauphine
Avenue Foch
AVENUE VICTOR HUGO
Kléber
AVENUE KLEBER
AVENUE D'IENA
AVENUE MARCEAU
AVENUE DES CHAMPS
George V
AVENUE GEORGE V
Victor Hugo
PLACE VICTOR HUGO
RUE COPERNIC
CHAILLOT
PLACE DES ETATS-UNIS
AV. RAYMOND POINCARE
Boissière
Lycée Janson de Sailly
Palais Galliera
Alma Marceau
Musée Guimet
Iéna
AVENUE DU PRESIDENT WILSON
Palais de Tokyo
AVENUE DE NEW YORK
PONT DE L'ALMA
Pont de l'Alma
Avenue Henri Martin
AV.HENRI MARTIN
Rue de la Pompe
AV. GEORGES MANDEL
PL. DU TROCADERO ET DU 11 NOVEMBRE
Trocadéro
Cimetière de Passy
Palais de Chaillot
AVENUE DES NATIONS UNIES
PONT D'IENA
QUAI BRANLY
AVENUE RAPP
AVENUE BOSQUET
AVENUE PAUL DOUMER
AV. DES
BD. DELESSERT
KENNEDY
La Muette
BOULEVARD EMILE AUGIER
Tour
334-335
336-337
338-339
340-341

© Copyright Time Out Group 2003

H
J
K
L
18
9
10
2
3
Musée de Montmartre
St Pierre
Sacré Coeur
Abbesses
Château Rouge
Barbès Rochechouart
Anvers
Pigalle
La Chapelle
Hôpital Lariboisière
Hôpital Fernand Widal
Gare du Nord
Gare de l'Est
Louis Blanc
St Vincent de Paul
Château Landon
Poissonnière
Hôpital St Lazare
Musée du Cristal
Notre-Dame de Lorette
Chateaudun
Cadet
Le Peletier
Hôpital St Louis
Château d'Eau
Richelieu Drouot
Grands Boulevards
Bonne Nouvelle
Strasbourg St Denis
Jacques Bonsergent
Palais des Glaces
Bourse des Valeurs
Bourse
Sentier
République
Bibliothèque Nationale
Conservatoire National des Arts et Métiers
Temple
Réaumur-Sébastopol
Arts et Métiers
Banque de France
Hôtel des Postes
Etienne Marcel
Palais Royal
Les Halles
Bourse du Commerce
Châtelet Les Halles
Filles du Calvaire
Cirque d'Hiver
Musée de la Chasse
St Sébastien Froissart
Rambuteau
Centre Pompidou
Forum des Halles
Palais Royal Musée du Louvre
Musée de Louvre
Louvre Rivoli
Archives Nationales
Musée Picasso
Pont Neuf
Châtelet
MARAIS
Musée Carnavalet
BOULEVARD DE LA CHAPELLE
BOULEVARD DE ROCHECHOUART
BOULEVARD BARBES
RUE LA FAYETTE
BOULEVARD DE MAGENTA
RUE DU FAUBOURG POISSONNIERE
RUE DU FAUBOURG SAINT DENIS
BOULEVARD DE STRASBOURG
RUE DU FAUBOURG ST MARTIN
BD. MONTMARTRE
BD. POISSONNIERE
BD. DE BON NOUVELLE
BD. ST DENIS
BOULEVARD ST MARTIN
RUE REAUMUR
BOULEVARD DE SEBASTOPOL
RUE ST MARTIN
RUE TURBIGO
R. DU TEMPLE
BD. DU TEMPLE
BOULEVARD VOLTAIRE
BD. BEAUMARCHAIS
RUE DU RENARD
RUE DE RIVOLI
RUE MARX DORMOY
334-335
336-337
338-339
340-341

0 250 500 750 m

273 547 820 yards

N

© Copyright Time Out Group 2003

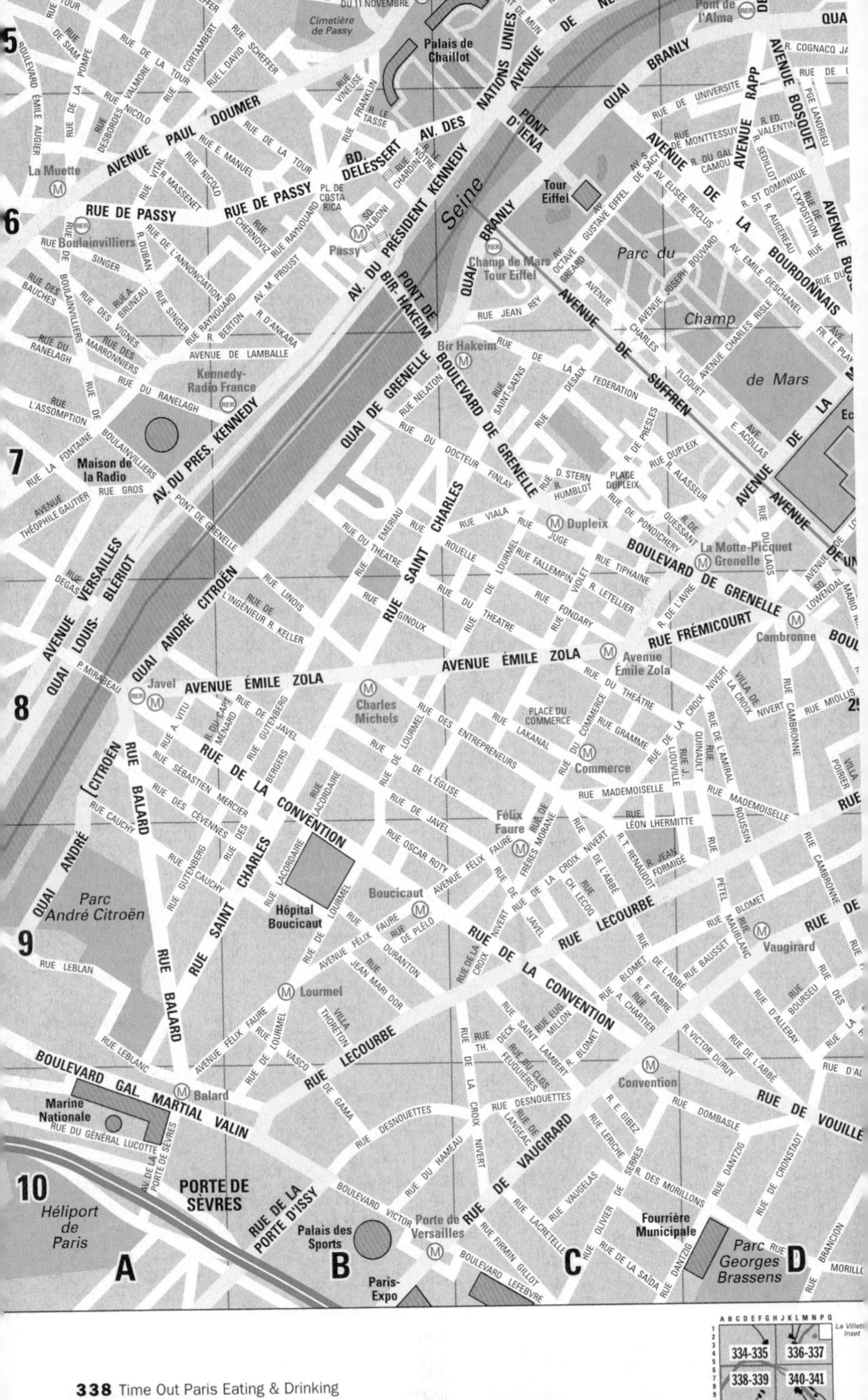

5
6
7
8
9
10
A
B
C
D
Palais de Chaillot
Cimetière de Passy
Trocadero et du 11 Novembre
Pont de l'Alma
Avenue Paul Doumer
Avenue de New York
Quai Branly
Avenue Rapp
Avenue Bosquet
Rue de Passy
La Muette
Boulainvilliers
Passy
Seine
Tour Eiffel
Champ de Mars Tour Eiffel
Parc du Champ de Mars
Avenue de Suffren
Avenue de la Bourdonnais
Av. du Président Kennedy
Pont d'Iéna
Pont de Bir-Hakeim
Bir Hakeim
Kennedy-Radio France
Maison de la Radio
Avenue de Lamballe
Rue du Ranelagh
Av. du Pres. Kennedy
Quai de Grenelle
Boulevard de Grenelle
Rue Saint Charles
Dupleix
La Motte-Picquet Grenelle
Cambronne
Rue Frémicourt
Avenue Émile Zola
Quai André Citroën
Quai Louis-Blériot
Avenue de Versailles
Javel
Charles Michels
Avenue Émile Zola
Rue de la Convention
Commerce
Félix Faure
Rue Balard
Hôpital Boucicaut
Boucicaut
Parc André Citroën
Rue Lecourbe
Vaugirard
Lourmel
Convention
Rue de Vaugirard
Rue de Vouillé
Boulevard Gal. Martial Valin
Balard
Marine Nationale
Porte de Sèvres
Héliport de Paris
Rue de la Porte d'Issy
Palais des Sports
Paris-Expo
Porte de Versailles
Boulevard Victor
Boulevard Lefebvre
Fourrière Municipale
Parc Georges Brassens
334-335
336-337
338-339
340-341

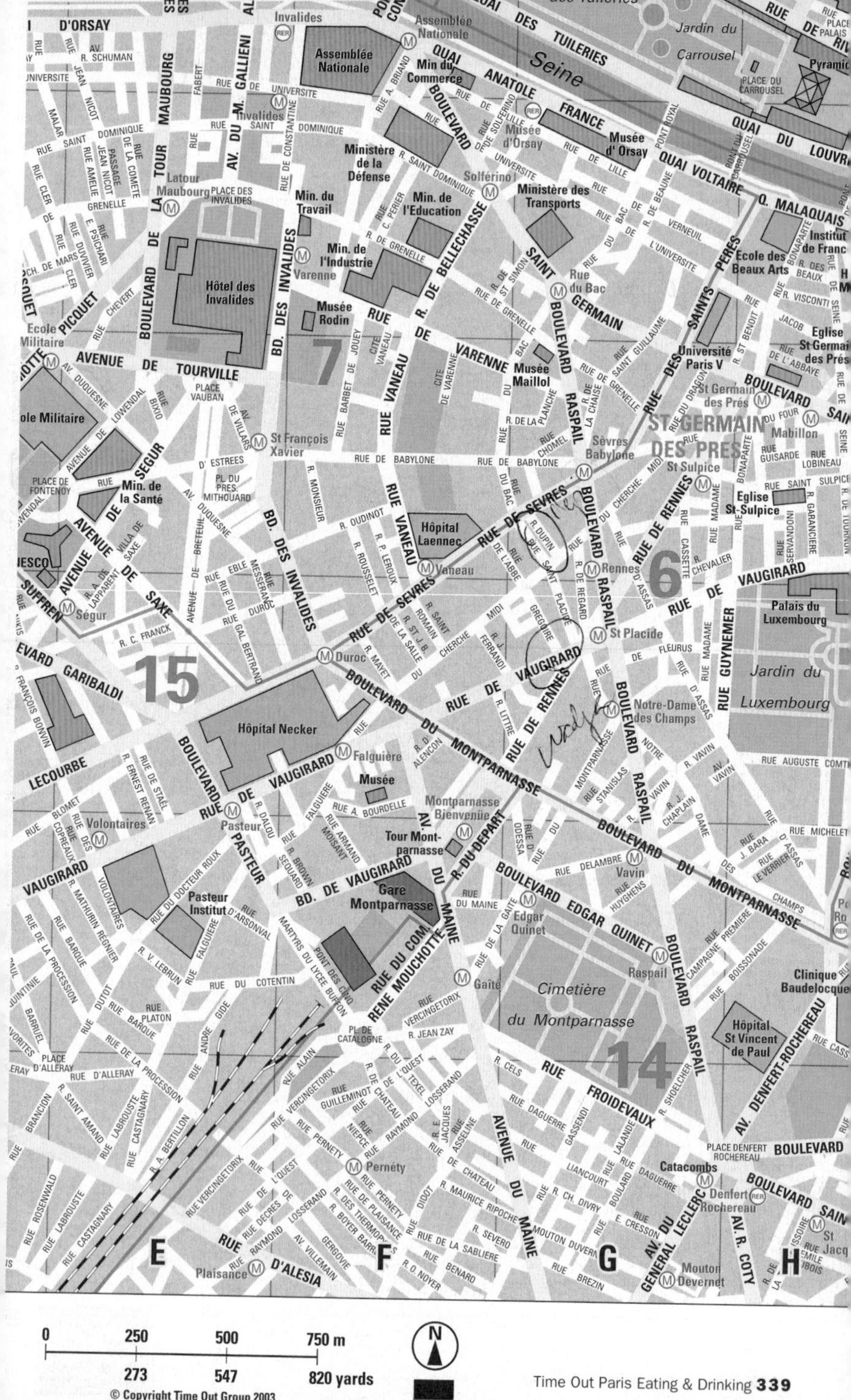

Seine
Quai des Tuileries
Jardin du Carrousel
Place du Carrousel
Pyramide
Quai Anatole France
Quai Voltaire
Quai du Louvre
Q. Malaquais
Institut de France
Ecole des Beaux Arts
Assemblée Nationale
Min du Commerce
Musée d'Orsay
Ministère de la Défense
Ministère des Transports
Min. du Travail
Min. de l'Education
Min. de l'Industrie
Invalides
Latour Maubourg
Place des Invalides
Hôtel des Invalides
Musée Rodin
Varenne
Solférino
Rue du Bac
Musée Maillol
Université Paris V
St Germain des Prés
ST GERMAIN DES PRES
Mabillon
Eglise St Germain des Prés
St Sulpice
Eglise St-Sulpice
Sèvres Babylone
Ecole Militaire
Place de Fontenoy
Min. de la Santé
UNESCO
St François Xavier
Place Vauban
Avenue de Tourville
Boulevard de la Tour Maubourg
Bd. des Invalides
Rue de Varenne
Rue de Babylone
Rue de Sèvres
Hôpital Laennec
Vaneau
Duroc
Rennes
St Placide
Palais du Luxembourg
Jardin du Luxembourg
Notre-Dame des Champs
Ségur
Avenue de Ségur
Avenue de Suffren
Avenue de Saxe
Boulevard Garibaldi
Hôpital Necker
Falguière
Musée
Montparnasse Bienvenüe
Tour Montparnasse
Gare Montparnasse
Boulevard du Montparnasse
Boulevard Raspail
Rue de Rennes
Rue de Vaugirard
Boulevard Pasteur
Pasteur
Volontaires
Pasteur Institut
Lecourbe
Vavin
Boulevard Edgar Quinet
Edgar Quinet
Raspail
Gaîté
Cimetière du Montparnasse
Hôpital St Vincent de Paul
Clinique Baudelocque
Av. Denfert-Rochereau
Pl. de Catalogne
Rue Froidevaux
Avenue du Maine
Pernéty
Plaisance
Rue d'Alésia
Place Denfert Rochereau
Catacombs
Denfert Rochereau
Mouton Duvernet
Av. du Général Leclerc
Av. R. Coty
7
6
15
14
E
F
G
H
0
250
500
750 m
273
547
820 yards
N
© Copyright Time Out Group 2003

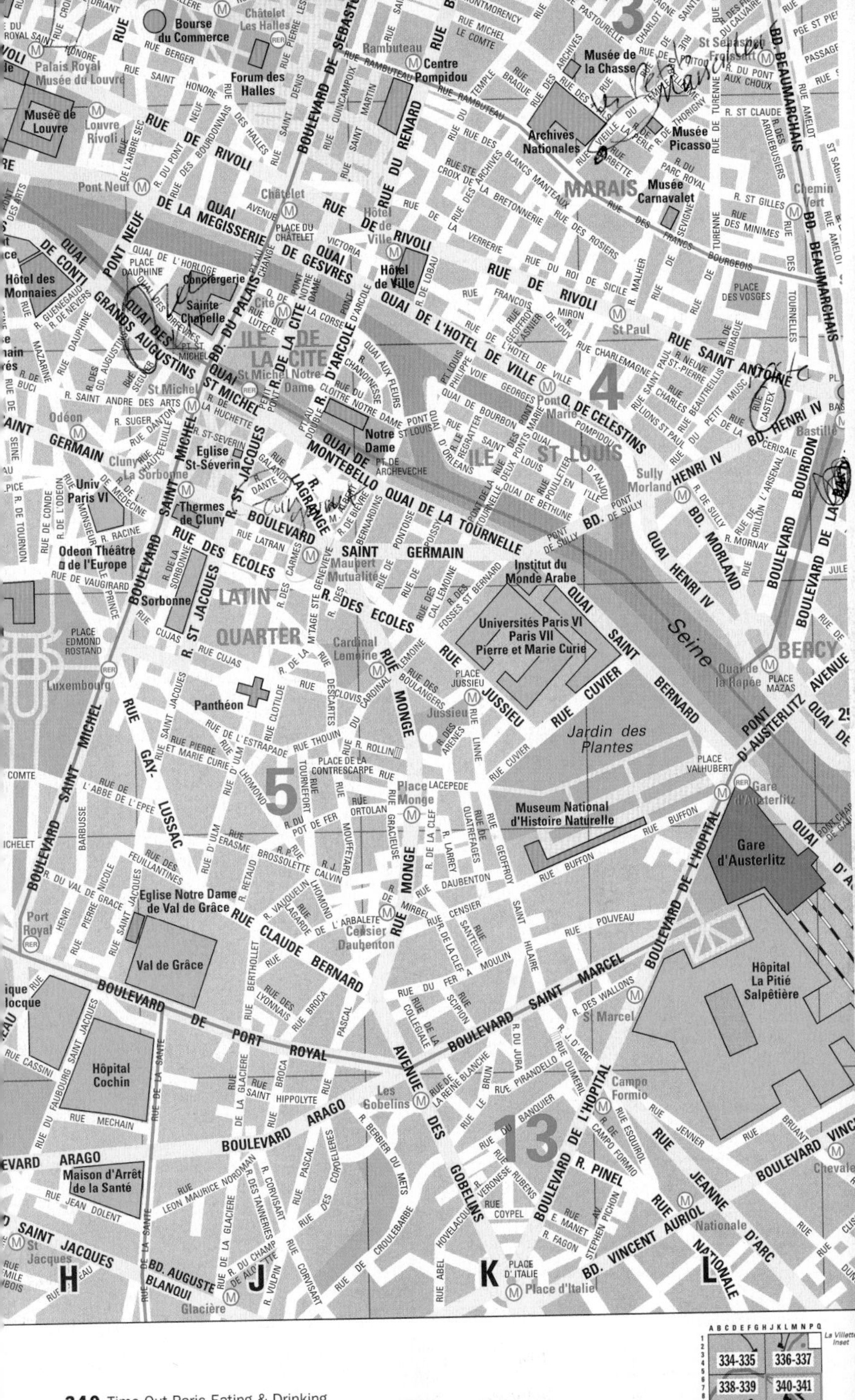

3
4
5
13
H
J
K
L
Bourse du Commerce
Châtelet Les Halles
Forum des Halles
Rambuteau
Centre Pompidou
Palais Royal Musée du Louvre
Musée de Louvre
Louvre Rivoli
Pont Neuf
Châtelet
Place du Châtelet
Hôtel de Ville
Musée de la Chasse
Archives Nationales
Musée Picasso
Marais
Musée Carnavalet
St Sébastien Froissart
Chemin Vert
Place des Vosges
St Paul
Pont Marie
Sully Morland
Bastille
Hôtel des Monnaies
Conciergerie
Sainte Chapelle
Place Dauphine
Cité
Ile de la Cité
St Michel Notre-Dame
Notre Dame
St Michel
Odéon
Cluny La Sorbonne
Eglise St-Séverin
Univ Paris VI
Thermes de Cluny
Odeon Théâtre de l'Europe
Sorbonne
Latin Quarter
Maubert Mutualité
Institut du Monde Arabe
Universités Paris VI Paris VII Pierre et Marie Curie
Ile St Louis
Seine
Bercy
Quai de la Rapée
Place Mazas
Place Edmond Rostand
Luxembourg
Panthéon
Cardinal Lemoine
Place Jussieu
Jussieu
Jardin des Plantes
Place Valhubert
Gare d'Austerlitz
Place de la Contrescarpe
Place Monge
Museum National d'Histoire Naturelle
Eglise Notre Dame de Val de Grâce
Val de Grâce
Port Royal
Censier Daubenton
Hôpital La Pitié Salpêtière
St Marcel
Hôpital Cochin
Les Gobelins
Campo Formio
Maison d'Arrêt de la Santé
Nationale
Chevaleret
St Jacques
Glacière
Place d'Italie
Rue de Rivoli
Boulevard de Sébastopol
Rue du Renard
Quai de la Mégisserie
Quai de Gesvres
Quai de l'Hotel de Ville
Q. de Célestins
Rue Saint Antoine
Bd. Beaumarchais
Bd. Henri IV
Boulevard Bourdon
Quai de Conti
Quai des Grands Augustins
Quai St Michel
Bd. du Palais
Quai de Montebello
Quai de la Tournelle
Boulevard Saint Germain
Rue des Ecoles
Boulevard Saint Michel
R. St Jacques
Quai Saint Bernard
Quai Henri IV
Bd. Morland
Rue Monge
Rue Cuvier
Rue Jussieu
Pont d'Austerlitz
Boulevard de l'Hôpital
Boulevard Saint Marcel
Rue Claude Bernard
Rue Gay-Lussac
Boulevard de Port Royal
Avenue des Gobelins
Boulevard Arago
Boulevard Saint Jacques
Bd. Auguste Blanqui
Bd. Vincent Auriol
Rue Jeanne d'Arc
Rue Nationale
R. Pinel
Boulevard Vincent

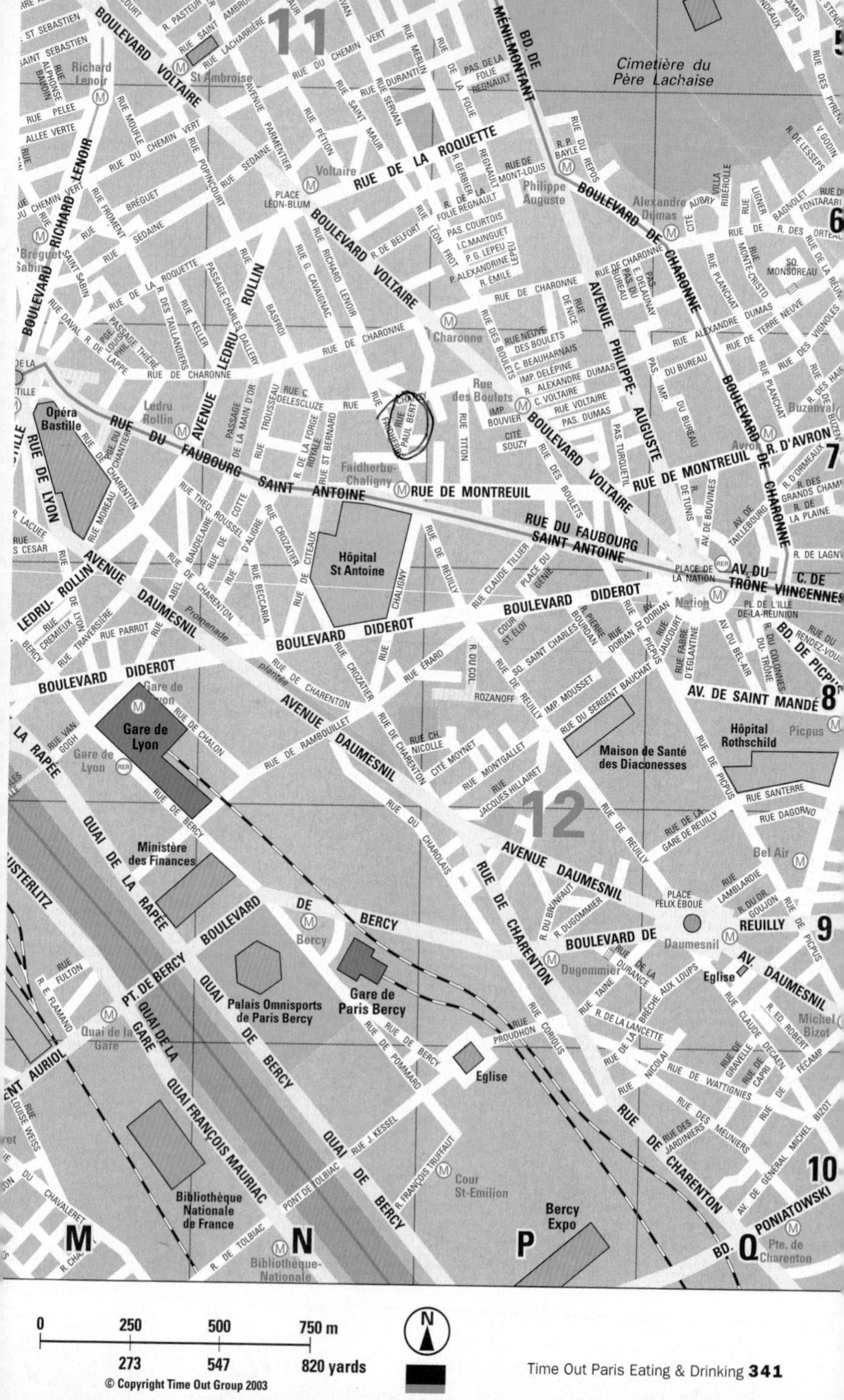

© Copyright Time Out Group 2003

Le Marais

J
5
6
7
2

404
Andy Wahloo
Les Bains
Auberge Nicolas Flamel
Taxi Jaune
A la Mexicaine
Le Petit Marcel
Le Hangar
Le Potager du Marais
Le Connétable
Georges
Café Beaubourg
L'Imprévu
The Studio
Le Dôme du Marais
Benoît
Un Piano dans La Cuisine
Chez Richard
Les Etages
La Belle Hortense
Lizard Lounge
L'Etoile Manquante
Le Petit Fer à Cheval
Le Trésor
Café des Phares
Pick-Clops
Le Coupe Gorge
Bricolo Café
L'Alivi
Stolly's
Galerie 88
Le Bourguignon du Marais

Centre Pompidou
Hôtel de Ville
Marcel
Rambuteau
Châtelet
et Métiers

Rue
R. de Turbigo
Turbigo
Rue au Maire
Rue des Gravilliers
Rue Chapon
Rue de Montmorency
R. Bg l'Abbé
Rue Saint Martin
Rue Beaubourg
Rue Michel le Comte
Rue du Temple
Rue Braque
Rue des Archives
Boulevard de Sebastopol
Rue Pierre Lescot
Rue Saint Denis
Rue Rambuteau
Rue Quincampoix
Rue St Martin
Rue du Renard
Rue Ste. Croix de Bretonnerie
Rue des Blancs Manteaux
Rue de la Verrerie
Rue de Rivoli
Place du Châtelet
Victoria
Quai de Gesvres
Pont Notre Dame
Pont d'Arcole
R. de Lobau
Quai de l'Hotel de Ville
Rue François Miron
Rue Geoffroy
Rue de l'Hotel de Ville
La Cite
La Corse

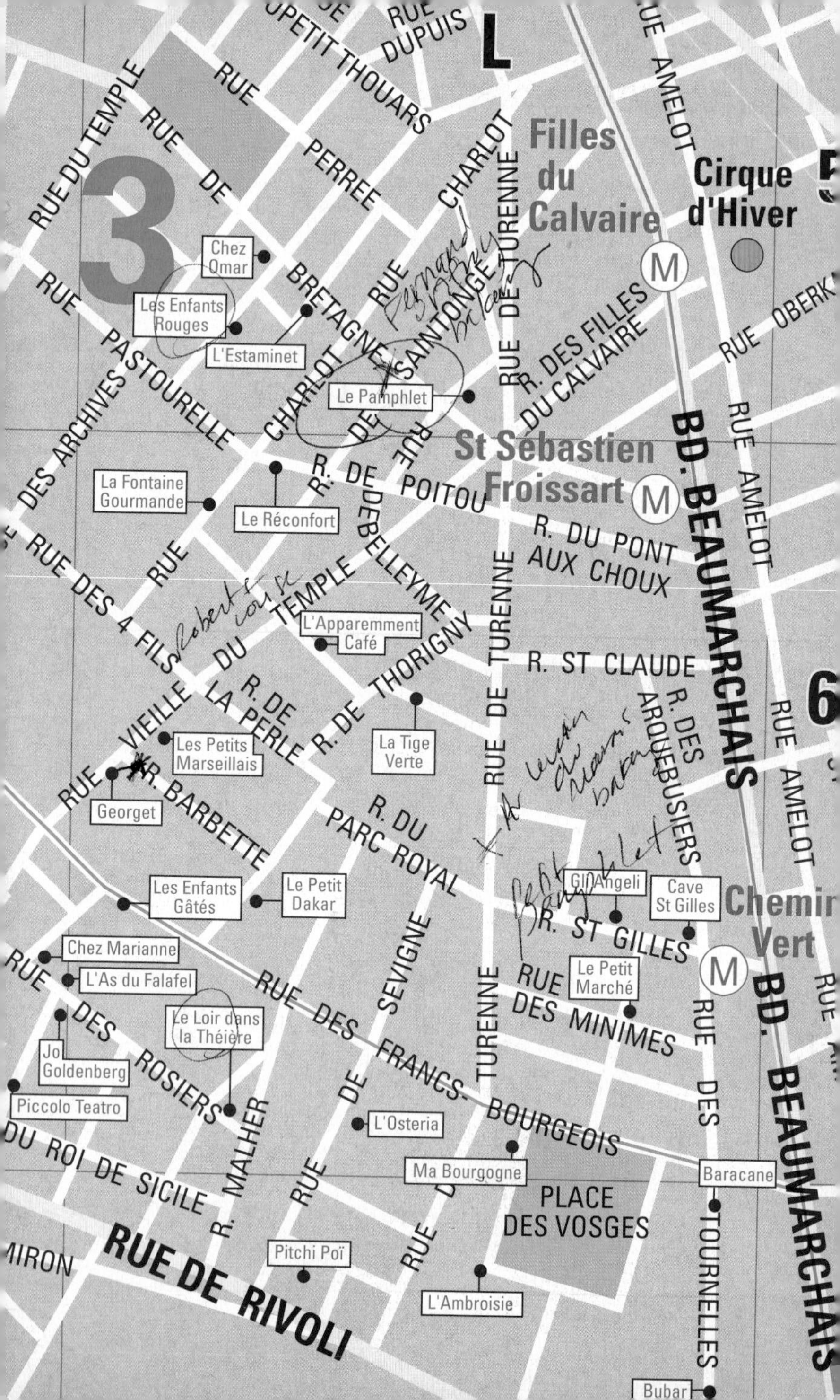

L
3
6
RUE DUPUIS
PETIT THOUARS
RUE DU TEMPLE
RUE DE PERREE
RUE DE BRETAGNE
RUE CHARLOT
Filles du Calvaire
Cirque d'Hiver
RUE AMELOT
RUE DE TURENNE
RUE DE SAINTONGE
R. DES FILLES DU CALVAIRE
Chez Omar
Les Enfants Rouges
L'Estaminet
RUE PASTOURELLE
RUE DES ARCHIVES
Le Pamphlet
St Sébastien Froissart
BD. BEAUMARCHAIS
La Fontaine Gourmande
Le Réconfort
R. DE POITOU
R. DE DEBELLEYME
R. DU PONT AUX CHOUX
RUE DES 4 FILS
RUE VIEILLE DU TEMPLE
L'Apparemment Café
R. DE THORIGNY
R. ST CLAUDE
R. DE LA PERLE
La Tige Verte
Les Petits Marseillais
R. DES ARQUEBUSIERS
Georget
R. BARBETTE
R. DU PARC ROYAL
Les Enfants Gâtés
Le Petit Dakar
Gli Angeli
Cave St Gilles
Chemin Vert
R. ST GILLES
Chez Marianne
L'As du Falafel
Le Loir dans la Théière
RUE DES ROSIERS
Jo Goldenberg
Piccolo Teatro
RUE DES FRANCS-BOURGEOIS
RUE DE SEVIGNE
RUE DES MINIMES
Le Petit Marché
RUE DES TOURNELLES
L'Osteria
Ma Bourgogne
Baracane
PLACE DES VOSGES
RUE DU ROI DE SICILE
R. MALHER
RUE DE RIVOLI
Pitchi Poï
L'Ambroisie
Bubar

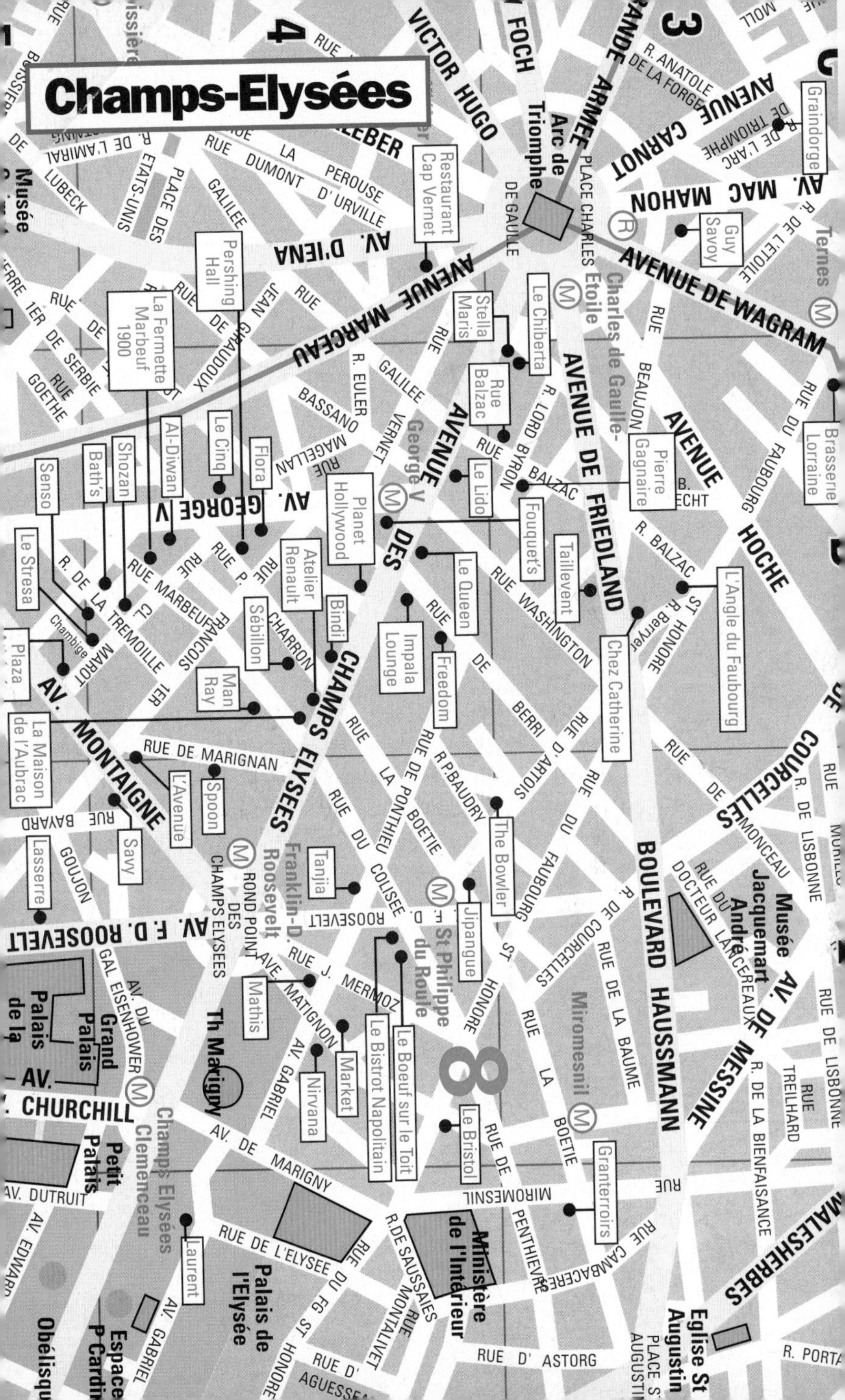

Champs-Elysées
4
3
8
Arc de Triomphe
Place Charles de Gaulle
Charles de Gaulle-Etoile
Victor Hugo
Foch
Avenue Carnot
Av. Mac Mahon
Avenue de Wagram
Avenue Marceau
Av. d'Iena
Avenue George V
George V
Avenue des Champs Elysées
Avenue de Friedland
Avenue Hoche
Boulevard Haussmann
Av. Montaigne
Av. F. D. Roosevelt
Franklin-D. Roosevelt
Rond Point des Champs Elysées
Champs Elysées Clemenceau
St Philippe du Roule
Miromesnil
Termes
Av. de Messine
Malesherbes
Rue de Courcelles
Rue du Faubourg St Honoré
Rue de Berri
Rue Washington
Rue Balzac
Rue Galilée
Rue de Marignan
Rue de la Boétie
Rue du Colisée
Rue de Ponthieu
Rue Marbeuf
Rue François 1er
Rue Pierre Charron
Rue Bassano
Rue Lord Byron
Rue Beaujon
Rue de Presbourg
Rue de Lübeck
Place des Etats-Unis
Rue Dumont d'Urville
Rue La Pérouse
Rue Jean Giraudoux
Rue Goethe
Rue de Tilsitt
Rue Quentin Bauchart
Rue Vernet
Rue Magellan
Rue Euler
Rue de Lisbonne
Rue de Monceau
Rue du Docteur Lancereaux
Rue de la Baume
Rue de Miromesnil
Rue de Penthièvre
Rue des Saussaies
Rue de l'Elysée
Rue Cambacérès
Rue d'Astorg
Rue de la Bienfaisance
Rue de Téhéran
Av. de Marigny
Av. Gabriel
Av. Matignon
Rue J. Mermoz
Rue Bayard
Rue Goujon
Av. Dutuit
Av. Churchill
Av. du Gal Eisenhower
Musée Jacquemart André
Grand Palais
Petit Palais
Palais de l'Elysée
Ministère de l'Intérieur
Th Marigny
Eglise St Augustin
Place St Augustin
Espace P Cardin
Obélisque
Restaurant Cap Vernet
Pershing Hall
La Fermette Marbeuf 1900
Stella Maris
Le Chiberta
Rue Balzac
Guy Savoy
Graindorge
Brasserie Lorraine
Pierre Gagnaire
Le Lido
Fouquet's
Taillevent
L'Angle du Faubourg
Chez Catherine
Le Cinq
Flora
Al-Diwan
Shozan
Bath's
Senso
Le Stresa
Plaza
Planet Hollywood
Atelier Renault
Bindi
Le Queen
Impala Lounge
Freedom
Sébillon
Man Ray
La Maison de l'Aubrac
L'Avenue
Spoon
Savy
Lasserre
Tanjia
The Bowler
Jipangue
Mathis
Market
Nirvana
Le Bistrot Napolitain
Le Boeuf sur le Toit
Le Bristol
Granterroirs
Laurent

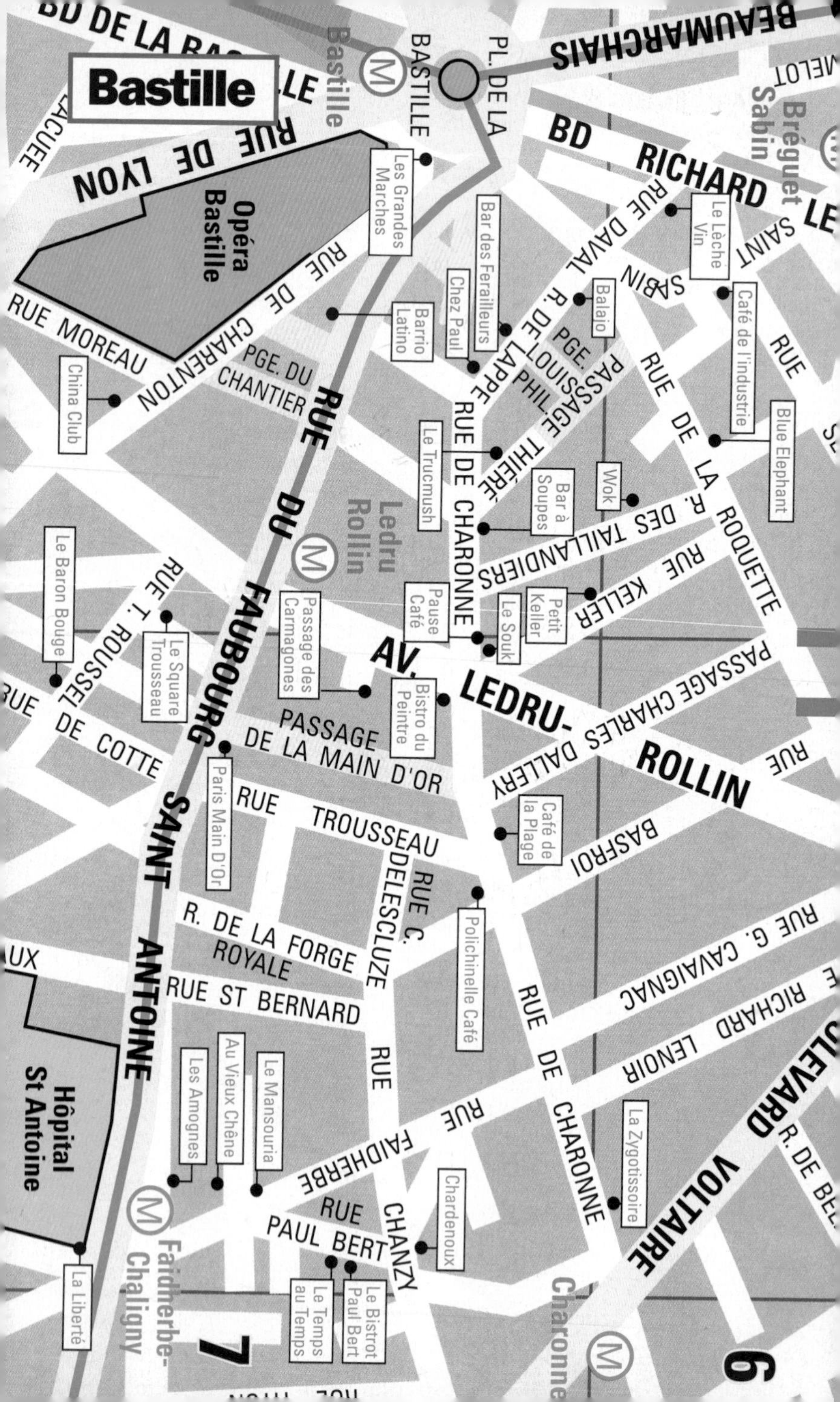

Bastille

BEAUMARCHAIS
BD RICHARD LE
PL. DE LA BASTILLE
Bastille
Bréguet Sabin
SAINT SABIN
RUE
BD DE LA BASTILLE
RUE DE LYON
Opéra Bastille
RUE DE CHARENTON
RUE MOREAU
PGE. DU CHANTIER
RUE DU FAUBOURG SAINT ANTOINE
RUE DAVAL
R. DE LAPPE
PGE. LOUIS PHIL.
PASSAGE THIÉRÉ
RUE DE CHARONNE
R. DES TAILLANDIERS
RUE KELLER
RUE DE LA ROQUETTE
AV. LEDRU-ROLLIN
PASSAGE CHARLES DALLERY
BASFROI
Ledru Rollin
PASSAGE DE LA MAIN D'OR
RUE TROUSSEAU
RUE C. DELESCLUZE
R. DE LA FORGE ROYALE
RUE ST BERNARD
RUE FAIDHERBE
RUE CHANZY
RUE PAUL BERT
RUE G. CAVAIGNAC
RICHARD LENOIR
BOULEVARD VOLTAIRE
R. DE BEL
Charonne
Faidherbe-Chaligny
Hôpital St Antoine
RUE T. ROUSSEL
RUE DE COTTE
6
7

Blue Elephant
Café de l'industrie
Le Lèche Vin
Balajo
Wok
Bar à Soupes
Petit Keller
Le Souk
Bar des Ferailleurs
Chez Paul
Le Trucmush
Pause Café
Les Grandes Marches
Barrio Latino
Bistro du Peintre
Café de la Plage
Polichinelle Café
La Zygotissoire
Chardenoux
Le Bistrot Paul Bert
Le Temps au Temps
Passage des Carmagones
Le Mansouria
Au Vieux Chêne
Les Amognes
Paris Main D'Or
Le Square Trousseau
China Club
Le Baron Bouge
La Liberté

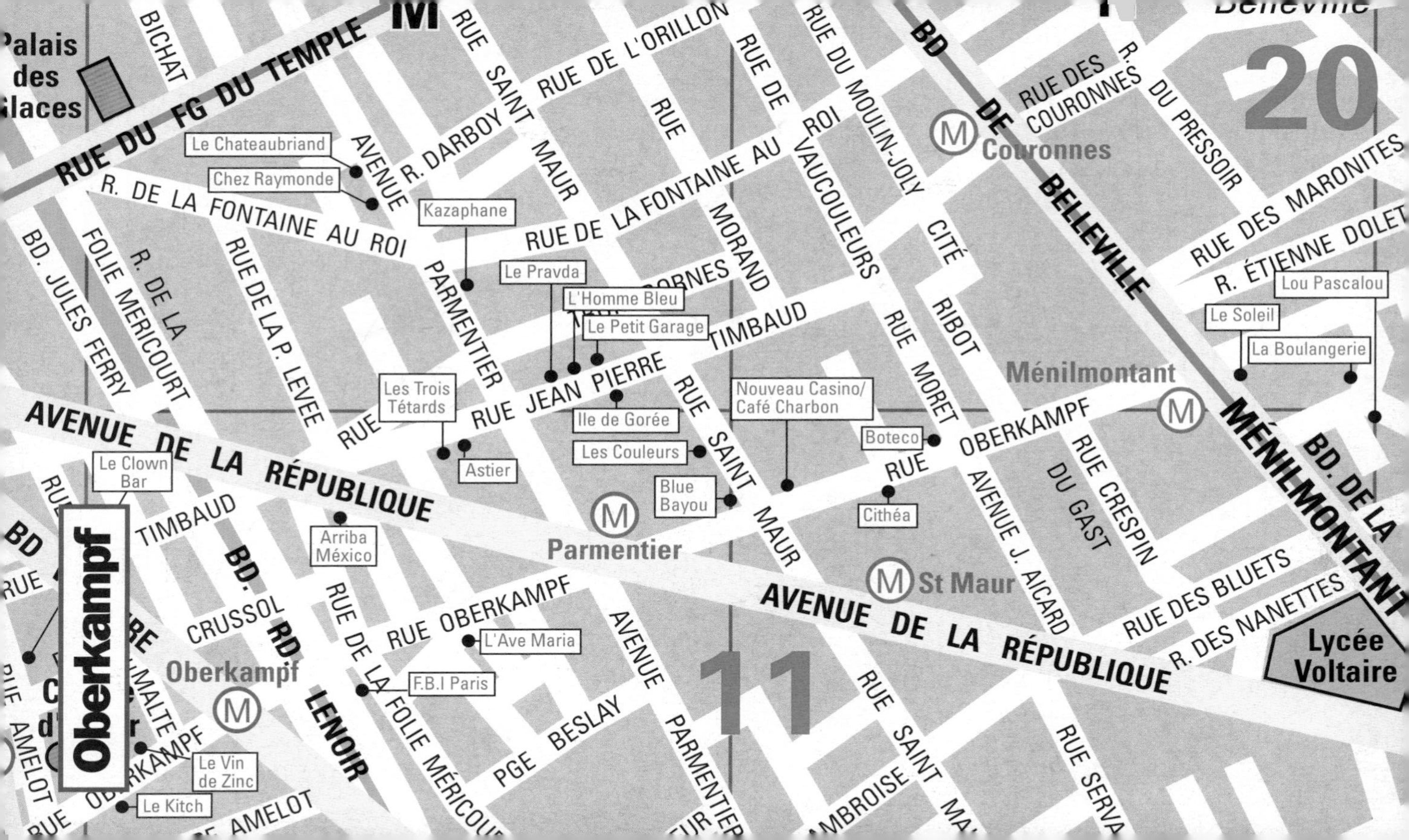

Oberkampf

Palais des Glaces
Bichat
Rue du Fg du Temple
Rue Saint Maur
Rue de l'Orillon
R. Darboy
Avenue
Le Chateaubriand
Chez Raymonde
R. de la Fontaine au Roi
Rue de la Fontaine au Roi
Kazaphane
Rue Morand
Rue de Vaucouleurs
Rue du Moulin-Joly
Couronnes
Bd de Belleville
Rue des Couronnes
R. du Pressoir
Rue des Maronites
R. Étienne Dolet
Lou Pascalou
Le Soleil
La Boulangerie
Ménilmontant
Bd. de Ménilmontant
Bd. Jules Ferry
Folie Mericourt
R. de la
Rue de la P. Levee
Parmentier
Le Pravda
L'Homme Bleu
Le Petit Garage
Timbaud
Cité
Ribot
Rue Moret
Rue Jean Pierre
Ile de Gorée
Les Couleurs
Rue Saint Maur
Nouveau Casino/ Café Charbon
Boteco
Rue Oberkampf
Les Trois Têtards
Astier
Rue
Avenue de la République
Le Clown Bar
Timbaud
Blue Bayou
Parmentier
Cithéa
St Maur
Avenue J. Aicard
Du Gast
Rue Crespin
Rue des Bluets
R. des Nanettes
Lycée Voltaire
Arriba México
Crussol
Bd. Rd Lenoir
Rue de la Folie Méricourt
F.B.I Paris
Rue Oberkampf
L'Ave Maria
Avenue Parmentier
Pge Beslay
11
Rue Saint Maur
Ambroise
Rue Serva
Oberkampf
Malte
Le Vin de Zinc
Le Kitch
Amelot
Rue Oberkampf
20

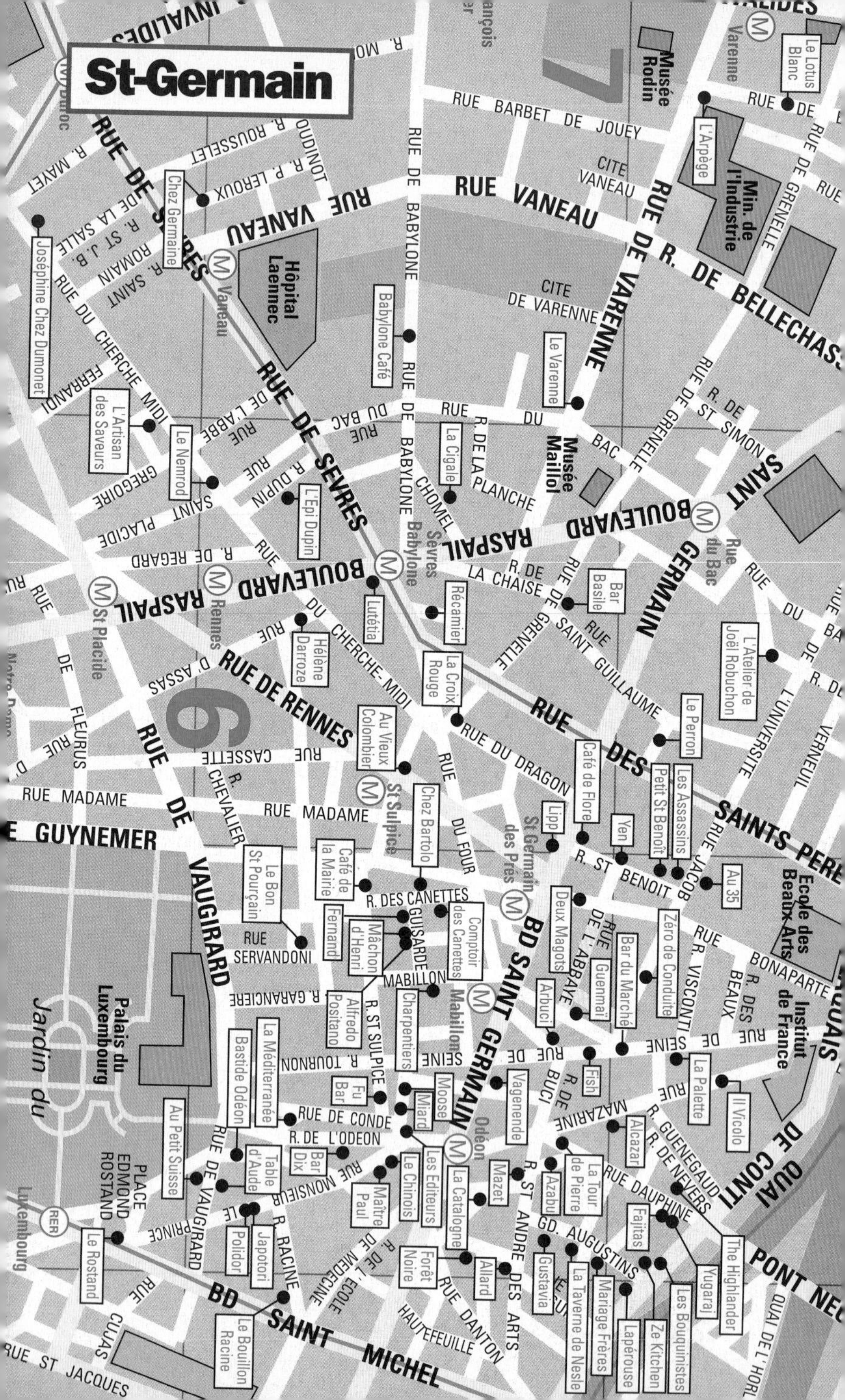
St-Germain
Invalides
Duroc
Varenne
Musée Rodin
Le Lotus Blanc
Rue Barbet de Jouey
L'Arpège
Min. de l'Industrie
Cité Vaneau
Rue Vaneau
R. Mayet
R. Rousselet
Oudinot
R. P. Leroux
Chez Germaine
Rue de Sèvres
R. de la Salle
R. St J. B.
Romain
R. Saint
Vaneau
Hôpital Laennec
Rue de Babylone
Rue de Varenne
R. de Bellechasse
Rue de Grenelle
Cité de Varenne
Babylone Café
Joséphine Chez Dumonet
Rue du Cherche Midi
Ferrandi
L'Artisan des Saveurs
Le Varenne
Rue du Bac
R. de la Planche
La Cigale
Chomel
Musée Maillol
R. de St Simon
Saint
Rue de l'Abbé
Grégoire
Le Nemrod
Saint Placide
R. Dupin
L'Epi Dupin
Boulevard Raspail
Sèvres Babylone
R. de Regard
Rue du Bac
R. de la Chaise
Rue de Grenelle
Bar Basile
Rue Saint Guillaume
Germain
Rennes
St Placide
Lutétia
Récamier
Hélène Darroze
Du Cherche-Midi
La Croix Rouge
L'Atelier de Joël Robuchon
Rue de Rennes
D'Assas
Rue de Fleurus
6
Au Vieux Colombier
Rue du Dragon
Rue des Saints Pères
Le Perron
Café de Flore
Les Assassins
Petit St Benoît
Rue de l'Université
Verneuil
Rue Cassette
R. Chevalier
Rue Madame
St Sulpice
Chez Bartolo
Du Four
Lipp
Yen
St Germain des Prés
R. St Benoit
Rue Jacob
Au 35
Ecole des Beaux Arts
Guynemer
Rue de Vaugirard
Le Bon St Pourçain
Café de la Mairie
R. des Canettes
Guisarde
Fernand
Mâchon d'Henri
Comptoir des Canettes
Deux Magots
Zéro de Conduite
Rue de l'Abbaye
Bar du Marché
Guenmaï
Rue Bonaparte
R. des Beaux Arts
R. Visconti
Institut de France
Quai de Conti
Rue Servandoni
Palais du Luxembourg
Jardin du Luxembourg
R. Garancière
Mabillon
Alfredo Positano
Charpentiers
Arbuci
Rue de Seine
La Méditerranée
Bastide Odéon
R. Tournon
R. St Sulpice
Fu Bar
Moose
Miard
Bd Saint Germain
Vagenende
Rue de Buci
Fish
La Palette
Il Vicolo
Rue Mazarine
Rue de Condé
R. de l'Odéon
Odéon
Alcazar
R. Guénégaud
R. de Nevers
Au Petit Suisse
Table d'Aude
Bar Dix
Rue Monsieur le Prince
Maître Paul
Le Chinois
Les Editeurs
La Catalogne
Mazet
R. St André des Arts
Azabu
La Tour de Pierre
Rue Dauphine
Place Edmond Rostand
RER
Le Rostand
Polidor
Japotori
R. Racine
R. de l'Ecole de Médecine
Forêt Noire
Allard
Gd. Augustins
Gustavia
La Taverne de Nesle
Mariage Frères
Lapérouse
Ze Kitchen
Les Bouquinistes
Fajitas
Yugaraj
The Highlander
Pont Neuf
Quai de l'Horloge
Bd Saint Michel
Rue Danton
Hautefeuille
Rue Cujas
Rue St Jacques